Conflicts and International Crimes
An Introduction to Research Methods

Conflicts and International Crimes

An Introduction to Research Methods

Catrien Bijleveld

eleven
international publishing

Published, sold and distributed by Eleven International Publishing
P.O. Box 85576
2508 CG The Hague
The Netherlands
Tel.: +31 70 33 070 33
Fax: +31 70 33 070 30
e-mail: sales@elevenpub.nl
www.elevenpub.com

Sold and distributed in USA and Canada
Independent Publishers Group
814 N. Franklin Street
Chicago, IL 60610, USA
Order Placement: +1 800 888 4741
Fax: +1 312 337 5985
orders@ipgbook.com
www.ipgbook.com

Eleven International Publishing is an imprint of Boom uitgevers Den Haag.

to EBB

Preface

International crimes are the gravest crimes we know. International crimes – under which are classified genocide, crimes against humanity and war crimes – entail murder, rape, looting, destruction, and in general the uprooting of families and entire societies. They also entail deep suffering. The destruction that such crimes generate is pervasive and long-lasting.

International crimes have mainly been studied within history, political science and psychology. Criminologists have only recently begun to discover these crimes, probably partly spurned by the rapid recent expansion of international criminal law and the establishment of international tribunals, truth commissions, and the international criminal court.

The empirical study of these crimes is not without its own peculiarities and obstacles. International crimes are often committed in conflict situations that are not particularly conducive to good quality data collection: situations are confused, the state is complicit and (attempts to) hide(s) the crimes, victims and witnesses are uprooted, many are killed, and the situation on the ground may be too dangerous to collect data. This generates particular methodological and statistical issues, that set the study of these offences out from ordinary (quantitative) social research or ordinary criminological research.

The purpose of this book is to discuss these methodological and statistical particularities from a non-technical, conceptual point of view. The book has been written as a textbook for a Master's course on research methods for the studies of conflicts and international crimes. The book first outlines – by necessity briefly – general statistical and methodological issues. Next, it zooms in on methodological and statistical particularities in the study of crime. In the last part of the book, the focus is on international crimes and the conflicts in which they occur. Using examples from various periods and conflicts (that do not necessarily entail the commission of international crimes), methodological and statistical points are introduced and illustrated. The examples stem from a limited number of countries and conflicts, as these are the conflicts have been particularly well studied or that drive home the points to be made. The book ends with broad, general recommendations. As it has been written for students with no to rudimentary knowledge of statistics and research methodology, the book hopes to cater as well for international lawyers and those involved in the investigation, prosecution and trying of perpetrators of international crimes.

Many colleagues and friends lent the author their insights, pointed out articles, books, and resource persons. She is grateful to all of them. They are, in alphabetical order: Diederik Aben, Xabier Agirre, Guilermo Bedoya-Jimenez, Lidewyde Berckmoes (whom the author thanks especially for her extensive input for the chapter on qualitative data analysis), Brigid O'Connor, Olivier DeGomme, Henk Elffers, Barbora Hola, Wim Huisman, Peter van Koppen, Rindert Leegsma, Marie Lindegaard, Hossein Mojtahedi, Marianne Nolte, Linda Polman, Elies van Sliedregt, Alette Smeulers, Ian Smillie, Ewa Tabeau, Joris van Wijk, Philp Verwimp. Many thanks to all. Any remaining errors are solely mine.

The author hopes that this book will contribute to the empirical study of conflicts and international crimes. She believes that unless much more is known about offences, perpetrators, victims, and the judicial as well as non-judicial response to these crimes, theorizing about, understanding, combating or even preventing international criminality will remain as hard as it has been. Some academicians have expressed opinions that given the extreme data paucity for these situations, (quantitative) empirical analysis is undoable. Agreeing on the gaps and biases in these data on international crimes, and agreeing on a pragmatic and careful, tailored methodology for studying them are a first step. The research community in this field is small, resources are few, the problems are complex and huge, but there is no valid reason not to make the effort. This book hopefully furthers more systematic and widespread study of the offences that, quantitatively and qualitatively, should be every criminologist's concern.

CB
Amsterdam, September 2019

Contents

II MEASUREMENT

III STATISTICS AND DATA ANALYSIS

V STATISTICS AND RESEARCH METHODOLOGY IN SUPRANATIONAL CRIMINOLOGY

List of Figures

List of Tables

Prologue

Bartolomé de las Casas was a Spanish priest, later Dominican, who departed for the Americas at the young age of 18, in the early 16th century. He lived and travelled in this New World for a long time, and at one point in his life became bishop of Chiapas. He is however best known for his 'Short account of the Destruction of the Indies', a small book in which he describes how the Spanish colonists in the New World abused, robbed and murdered the local Indian population. De las Casas' book was written in 1542 but first published in translation in 1552 in the Netherlands, the then Low Countries that were at that point embroiled in a lengthy religious war with the Spanish (De las Casas, 1552, reprinted in translation 1992).

Bartolomé de las Casas' book can be seen as a very early description of international crimes. While earlier treatises on wars and conquests (such as Flavius Josephus' recounting of the siege of Jerusalem) often recounted events as they had heard them from third parties, de las Casas presents himself as a witness to the destruction of the lands that the Spaniards conquered. His description is empirical: he relates what he has registered with his own eyes.

De las Casas describes how the *conquistadores* maimed and tortured the local population, the manner in which they terrorized the people in the new territories (in a sense their modus operandi) to force the population into submission. He gives estimates of the numbers that were killed, at times probably too high, but at times likely quite precise when entire villages were murdered but for a few women and children. In some instances he points out that the destruction is so complete that it is impossible to assess exactly what happened. De las Casas also recounts numerous examples of theft from the local population: foodstuffs to the extent that the local Indian population starved, and massive quantities of gold (in Castilian gold coins). On the underlying cause of all this De las Casas states in the preface to the book:

"The reason the Christians have murdered on such a vast scale is purely and simply greed. They have set out to line their pockets with gold and to amass private fortunes as quickly as possible so that they can then assume a status quite at odds with that into which they were born."

What is left of the Indian inhabitants of these lands is not only destitute, but mostly thrown into slavery, with the lands having lost their livelihood and cultures. Many who survived were transported as slaves, during which again many perished.

In De las Casas' book, we recognise the same topics that are today the object of study for scholars of conflict and international crimes. Such scholars aim to describe the acts and crimes committed, aim to shed light on the causes behind those crimes. De las Casas also describes, like current scholars, the consequences of the atrocities for the individual victims and afflicted societies.

The book is directed at king Philip of Spain, whom he heeds in the prologue to take action against the atrocities:

"It is my fervent hope that, once Your Highness perceives the extent of the injustices suffered by these innocent peoples and the way in which they are being destroyed and crushed underfoot, unjustly and for no other reason than to satisfy the greed and ambition of those whose purpose it is to commit such wicked atrocities, Your Highness will see fit to beg and entreat His Majesty to refuse all those who seek royal licence for such evil and detestable ventures, and to put a stop once and for all to their infernal clamour in such a way that nobody will henceforth dare to make such a request nor even to mention ventures of this kind. This, Your Royal Highness, is a matter on which action is both urgent and necessary if God is to continue to watch over the Crown of Castile and ensure its future well-being and prosperity, both spiritual and temporal. Amen."

Part I

INTRODUCTION

Chapter 1

International crimes

1.1 Introduction

International crimes are special crimes. Distinguished into the categories of genocide, crimes against humanity, war crimes and the crime of aggression, they in fact are comprised of what we will refer to as 'classical crimes', such as homicide, rape or pillage. In that sense, international crimes are nothing more than 'ordinary' crimes that are at the most serious side of the spectrum of crimes, where norms are violated such as the right to life or bodily integrity. But they are also different, in several ways. Firstly, they differ in a formal sense because the acts they entail have been criminalised not by a national government but through treaty (the Treaty of Rome). This means that they are in a sense universal. Secondly, and importantly for this book, they are crimes of large scale, committed under particular conditions, often during conflict.

The Rome statute[1] defines *genocide* as 'acts committed with intent to destroy, in whole or in part, a national, ethnical, racial or religious group' (article 6), entailing, amongst others, killing members of the group, causing serious bodily or mental harm to members of the group and deliberately inflicting on the group conditions of life calculated to bring about its physical destruction in whole or in part. Next, article 7 defines *crimes against humanity* as 'acts when committed as part of a widespread or systematic attack directed against any civilian population, with knowledge of the attack'. Crimes against humanity may entail a host of crime types amongst which murder, rape, enslavement, forced disappearance and other crimes. These crimes may be committed in peacetime or wartime. Article 8 next defines *war crimes*; the definition is long and we will not repeat it here, but summarise war crimes briefly as: grave breaches of the Geneva Conventions of 12 August 1949 as well as other serious violations of the laws and customs applicable in international armed conflict, as well as other serious violations of the laws and customs applicable in armed conflicts not of an international character, within the established framework of international law. The *crime of aggression*, last, is somewhat outside the scope of this book.

[1] www.icc-cpi.int/nr/rdonlyres/ea9aeff7-5752-4f84-be94-0a655eb30e16/0/rome_statute_english.pdf

For crimes against humanity (article 7) the widespread or systematic nature of the crimes is a so-called *element* of the crime. Even though the widespread or systematic nature is not an element of genocide or war crimes, international crimes – genocide, war crimes and crimes against humanity – are in practice large-scale crimes.

The widespread or systematic nature implies that international crimes are in practice committed in situations that are, to put it mildly, not particularly conducive to conducting fieldwork. International crimes are usually committed within a conflict situation, a war or civil war, or as part of a campaign against a particular ethnic, religious or political group. In such situations, parts of the population may have fled, be on the move, or may be held hostage in an area under conflict that is inaccessible. The police, usually the criminologist's 'helper' in the sense that they systematically collect data on crimes that come under their attention, may even be complicit and, instead of registering crimes, actively hiding or destroying evidence. In such a setting, there may be acute danger to data collectors, and field work will be difficult and costly – if not outright impossible.

As we will see in this book, in times of conflict or upheaval, vital registrations will often have broken down (or never functioned properly for quite some time) so that researchers have less, or no, recourse to statistical data that they in ordinary circumstances could employ for estimates or use as a baseline to gauge their findings against. With the advent of social media, a new source of data has become available, but how to use these data, how to judge reliability and quality of the data, are issues that researchers still need to gain much experience with.

These conditions in which crimes are committed (circumstances of societal upheaval, danger, complicity of authorities, and breakdown of governmental institutions) have massive and – unsurprisingly – negative implications for the extent to which empirical research can be conducted according to accepted standards. The particular circumstances make that at times special, non-standard methods are needed.

For criminologists, the prosecution and sentencing of perpetrators offers opportunities for studying international crime. Court files, transcripts of wire taps and forensic evidence, are gregariously used by researchers if they get access to such data. However, also the prosecutions of international crimes are different from prosecutions of 'classical' crimes such as homicide or rape, committed in ordinary circumstances. As Wald (2001) wrote about trials at the International Criminal Tribunal for the former Yugoslavia, '[such a trial, CB] is usually more akin to documenting an episode or even an era of national or ethnic conflicts rather than proving a single discrete incident' (p. 537). And, where 'classical' trials are largely conducted with mounds of forensic evidence, such as DNA traces, footsteps or witness testimonies for one single incident, by contrast international criminal trials, because of the large number of crimes committed and the difficulty in the collection of forensic evidence, deal with relatively little regular forensic evidence. International criminal trials rely heavily on witness evidence, although also witness statements are hard to collect because of the difficulties described above, compounded by language and cultural barriers, memory issues, and security issues for witnesses. Trials in general feature statements by a limited number of witnesses, sufficient (or not) to prove the guilt of the accused. Such witness statements generally cover only a (very) small part of the entirety of the criminal acts committed. For that matter, some have argued that such trials could rely more on findings from empirical social research (Bijleveld, Hola, & Poelhekke, 2014).

Until recently, criminologists hardly ever touched on the topic of international crimes. Studying genocide or war crimes was generally considered the arena of polemologists, and was conducted in topical institutes such as the Dutch NIOD (Nederlands Instituut voor Oorlogsdocumentatie – Netherlands Institute for War Documentation, founded 8 May 1945 to write the history of the Second World War in the Netherlands and in the former Dutch East Indies, see `niod.knaw.nl/`), or by groups focusing on particular aspects of wars and conflicts such as contained in the Norwegian PRIO database (that has information on armed conflicts, both internal and external, from 1946 to the present, see `prio.org/Data/Armed-Conflict/`, and see also section 13.2).

This situation changed rapidly in recent years. With the growth of international criminal law since the tribunals of the former Yugoslavia and Rwanda, since special and hybrid tribunals such as for Sierra Leone and Cambodia, and since the establishment of the International Criminal Court, criminology has finally embraced the study of these internationalised crimes. Collaboration with scholars from other disciplines who traditionally studied such atrocities is picking up. Mainstream criminological journals have started to publish articles on international crimes. The European Society of Criminology now has a European Criminology Group on Atrocity Crimes and Transitional Justice (see `http://www.esc-eurocrim.org/index.php/activities/working-groups/53-atrocity-crimes-and-transitional-justice`).

1.2 The *tesseras criminologica* of international crimes

This book has been written from the perspective of criminological research. Genocide, crimes against humanity and war crimes, are all crimes. As such they fall under the umbrella of criminology, the discipline that studies crime. Criminologists generally divide their field of study along four lines, a division or categorisation that we will in this book refer to as the *tesseras criminologica*, or the four pillars of criminology, and that we employ as an organising principle for the last part of the book. Below we detail these pillars.

1.2.1 Prevalence

Criminologists first want to know what crimes happened. They want, before attempting to explain crime, or study criminals, know their central variable: crime. They want to have measurements of the number of crimes that were committed, the types of crimes that were committed, the number of victims, the sex or ages of offenders, the spatial distribution of crimes, or the temporal ordering of crimes, the modus operandi of perpetrators. All these aspects of the occurrence of crime are captured under the label of 'prevalence'.

As such, prevalence measures could describe the development over time of killings in a certain region, or the spatial distribution of burglaries over a city in four quarters of a year. They could also describe the trend in police-registered sex offenses by juveniles from 1958 to 2018 in a country, or the development of the number of violent offenses per 100,000 population.

In all these examples, what is described is the occurrence of the criminologically central variable of interest: crime. It can be one type of crime, or all types combined, or a type committed by a certain group of offenders. Prevalence can refer to one crime occurring at one point in time, or over consecutive time periods. Prevalence can also describe the occurrence of crime in one area or region, or the spread over different regions. Prevalence measures are predominantly quantitative: they generally consist of numbers, or rates per a population size.

1.2.2 Etiology

The second main topic of interest in criminology is concerned with the causes of crime. After having described how many crimes occur, criminologists next want to find out why these crimes occurred.

Theories on the so-called ‘etiology’ (sometimes written as ‘aetiology’) of crime are numerous and vary in their focus. One group of theories seeks the causes of crime in the person of the offender. These (bio-/psychological) theories postulate that crime can be explained through the properties of the offenders: offenders differ from non-offenders in certain characteristics and if we know these characteristics then we can predict who will commit (what types of) crimes and who won’t. Such properties may be biological, in which case the theory attempts to explain crime from the biology of physiology of the offender, his or her physical properties. Person-based theories can also focus on the psychological correlates of offending, in which case they seek an explanation for crime from offenders’ personality characteristics or psychiatric disturbances.

A different group of theories attempts to explain crime from situational characteristics of the crime. Such theories postulate that crimes occur more often in certain areas (such as streets where bars or businesses are located), or occur at particular times (such as night-time) or in specific constellations (such as at times and places where few guardians are present). For the purpose of international crimes, such theories could also postulate that in countries with a certain socioeconomic, cultural or geophysical ‘make-up’ the occurrence of international crimes is more likely, or that it is areas with particular profiles within the conflict region that are more likely to witness international crimes.

(Many) more types of theories are distinguished, for an overview see Bernard, Snipes, Vold *et al.* (2015). Theorists have also assembled theories into combinations that contain for instance both person-based and situational factors. Such ‘integrated’ theories are presumed to have greater explanatory power. They are however harder to test, as they require data at numerous levels and – because of the multitude of explanatory variables – generally fairly large sample sizes. Explanations based on both so-called ‘macro-studies’ (studies where the properties of entire nations or conflicts are studied) as well as case studies (studies of just one offender or group of offenders) are not very prominent in regular criminology. As we will see, such studies are quite prominent in the study of international crimes.

Criminology is fairly unique in its abundance of theories. It is not surprising that so many theories congregate in criminological research, as criminology is a so-called *object science*. That is to say, while criminologists all want to explain one thing (crime), they may do so from widely different disciplinary backgrounds: a psychiatrist will likely seek a different kind of explanation than a sociologist, or than an anthropologist, a development economist or an expert in international relations.

1.2.3 (Non)-judicial responses to international crimes

A third area of interest is the responses to crime. Talking about traditional or 'classical' crimes, such responses are typically prosecution and sentencing, and punishment, such as imprisonment, a fine or a community service order. But responses may also be extra-legal, such as divorce from one's spouse or dismissal by one's employer, or even much less tangible such as disapproval, shaming or stigma. Ad hoc extra-judicial responses to international crimes are truth commissions or amnesties. 'Special courts' such as the *gacaca* courts in Rwanda, would also fall under this label.

Studies on prosecution and sentencing typically investigate procedural aspects such as witness participation or trial duration, measures on sentence length for particular crimes, or sentence disparities for ethnic minorities or men and women. But they may also investigate the execution of sentences, perceived procedural justice by perpetrators, or the perception of fairness by victims. Again, studies may focus on one point in time, or may investigate trends over time. Sentencing disparities over different jurisdictions may also be a point of interest.

1.2.4 Victims

Lastly, victims constitute one of the four pillars of criminological interest. Victim studies focus on issues such as victim characteristics, victims' well-being, the aftermath of crime victimisation, the extent to which victims' rights are respected, victims' needs, wishes for reparation. As international crimes are often so widespread, the societal impact of international crimes is also comprised under this 'victims'-label. Studies here may look for instance at the socio-economic burden of conflict, at the long-term health consequences of conflict-induced famine, or at the ecological impact of conflict.

1.3 Research methodology

This books discusses research methods and statistics for international crimes. Very few of the methods and statistical techniques we discuss are particular to international crimes. Instead, this book will present a conglomerate of general methodological tools used in a variety of (social) sciences. We will encounter research methods as employed in social science such as psychology, sociology and anthropology, but also methods from economics, and from epidemiology. A few methods we discuss have been specifically designed within criminology. Given that the study of international crimes brings together researchers from varied disciplines it is not surprising that the research methods employed to study these crimes are in a sense a motley crew.

This book regards research methods and statistical theory as necessary tools for the empirical researcher. Very simply phrased: if you want to build a cupboard you have to know what screws, wood, hammer, nails, glue, etc. to employ. You must know how to design the construction such that it does not sag. And you must know how to choose your materials such that you remain within the given budget. The same goes for research methods and statistics. They are the toolkit of the research effort. As such, this book offers the essential tools from the methodological toolkit that you need for studying conflicts and international crimes. Researchers of international crimes need to know about these tools, but so do policy makers who want to judge research reports on their merit, or those employed in the prosecution of these crimes who want to read up on empirical evidence.

Research methods is not among the most loved by students of social science. Part of this is because many students are uncomfortable with maths. As we will try to show, such unease is mostly not necessary. We will attempt to show that quantitative research methods and statistics are nothing more than a set of rules designed to make sense of empirical reality: to judge, gauge and understand what happened and why it happened. Nothing more and nothing less. Research methods and also statistics are not a set of esoteric rules understandable only for the enlightened few. Instead, they essentially are, as we will attempt to show, formalised common sense. They use decision rules that almost all of us employ in daily life. In research methodology, these rules have numbers and chances attached to them – but the reasoning follows the same logical steps and thought experiments that we all with ease employ in our daily goings.

Statistics and research methodology is not fool-proof. A well-known saying goes: 'lies, damn lies, and statistics'. Such a saying reflects the publicly-held notion that research methodology and statistics is a set of witchcraft-like rules, that can lead to ungraspable conclusions that ordinary people can be fooled with. While this author is convinced that it is not possible to lie with statistics, it is true that statistical and methodological particularities can be tweaked to throw a veil and obscure matters. For one research question, sometimes different methods are available to analyse the data, of which not one is a priori a preferred or evidently superior method. But different methodological choices may lead to different conclusions. This is exactly why research procedures should always be clearly described and choices made explicit, as these can have implications for the substantive conclusions.

A nice example of the variety of methods available to researchers and the impact of method choice, is given in a study by Silberzahn and Uhlmann, published in Nature. The authors compiled a dataset looking at sports statistics on football matches, with data on how often referees gave red cards to players with different demographics (including skin colour), team position, height and weight. They handed out the dataset to 29 teams of researchers and asked them to choose a data-analytic technique to investigate whether skin colour mattered for how often players were handed out a red card. Two findings emerged. First, the teams of researchers could not agree on one best method to analyse the data. Second, with teams choosing different methods, 20 teams found a significant association between skin colour and red cards, and nine did not. On average, the findings said that dark-skinned players were 1.3 times more likely than light-skinned players to receive red cards (and this 'meta'-finding the various teams agreed on), but by team the findings varied strongly: from insignificance to a strong and highly significant effect. Technique choice therefore matters, and this is where the 'lies and damn damn lies' saying resonates (Silberzahn & Uhlmann, 2015).

Not all research methods revolve around numbers. In fact, when research questions ask not after the quantity of a phenomenon under study, but when the aim is to explain why or how events occurred, quantitative methods may be highly unsuitable. In that case, qualitative methods are preferred, methods that generally use different data collection strategies, different analytical schemes. Statistical testing is only very rarely used in qualitative research.

Many students prefer qualitative methods to quantitive, assuming that qualitative research, without math and formulas, is easier. That is however generally not the case. Qualitative research requires strong theoretical skills, hard and good analysis, perseverance, and constitutes more often than not, a substantive investment (and may entail much more – tedious – work than quantitative research). A solid qualitative study is a feat accomplished only after extensive training, and is much harder to learn using textbook recipes.

Many researchers prefer in fact that not one approach is chosen (either qualitative or quantitative), but that both approaches are used concurrently. We will return to this in chapter 2.

1.4 Focus of this book

This book discusses methods used in the four pillars of criminological research described above, focusing on the most prominent methods in the study of prevalence, etiology, reaction and victims of international crimes. At times, new and particular methods are introduced, but often we discuss standard methodology that is simply applied in this novel empirical field.

The book will discuss a number of general methodological concepts and techniques that are employed in the examples in the later chapters. Such general social science methods and techniques would also be found – albeit with different examples – in a textbook on psychological or sociological research methods. First, in the following chapter, chapter 2, we will discuss general concepts such as reliability and validity, and delve deeper into the differences between qualitative and quantitative research methods. This concludes part I of the book.

Next we discuss sampling in chapter 3, measurement in chapter 4 and design issues in chapter 5. Together, these three chapters constitute part II of the book, focusing on measurement. In this part, qualitative and quantitative approaches are discussed alongside each other.

Next, Part III focuses on statistics and data analysis. In consecutive chapters, we discuss descriptive statistics (chapter 6), inferential statistics (chapter 7), model testing for quantitative data analysis (chapter 8) and qualitative data analysis (chapter 9). Part IV details a number of methodological issues particular to 'classical' criminological analysis, i.e. the study of classical crimes, in chapter 10 and chapter 11.

Part V outlines the methodological particularities of the study of international crimes. We first discuss in a fairly abstract sense, in chapter 12, the particularities of the criminological study of these widespread and extremely serious crimes. Next we outline methods for the study of prevalence in chapter 13, some of which are fairly standard criminological or social science methods, and some of which have found particular application in the study of international crimes. The chapters on etiology (chapter 14) and on (extra-)judicial reaction (chapter 15) employ mainly examples to illustrate the use of standard social science research methods. The chapter on victims and more generally speaking long-term societal consequences (chapter 16), contains examples of general social science research methods applied to the study of conflicts and international crimes, plus some tailored methods. We end with a general overview and conclusion.

This book devotes more space to quantitative methods than to qualitative methods. That is not because the writer believes that quantitative research is more important. Rather, this author is convinced that quantitative and qualitative research support and strengthen each other, and that better and more certain conclusions can be reached from studies that combine and integrate the two methodological perspectives. However, quantitative methods are easier to explain in textbook fashion while qualitative methods are harder to explain outside of a particular research context; these are described in more abstract terms in textbooks and perhaps best taught in real-life settings.

This book discusses a large number of issues in a fairly short space. This implies that most of the discussion is brief, dealing with conceptual issues, and that much detail and nitty-gritty practicalities are left out. Apart from the references given, readers who wish to read more on statistics are referred to standard textbooks such as Hinkle, Wiersma and Jurs (2003). For criminological research methods, we recommend the textbook by Maxfield and Babbie (2005) that is fairly quantitative, or either Ellis, Hartley and Walsh (2010) or Bachmann and Schutt (2017), that both have sections on qualitative research as well (particularly the Ellis *et al.* book). An often referenced textbook on qualitative research in general is Denzin and Lincoln (2011), and a fairly practical one on ethnography is Hammersley and Atkinson (2007). For international crimes, not many methodological books have been published. One edited book that gives some good further reading specifically on methodological issues in the adjacent field of human rights research is the book 'Statistical Methods for Human Rights' (Asher, Banks & Scheuren, 2008). An edited book that focuses mainly on methodological issues in the study of prevalence is Seybolt, Aronson and Fischhoff (2013).

Chapter 2

Social science research methodology: general issues

2.1 Introduction

This chapter discusses a number of issues that are at the basics of social science research methodology. This regards preliminary issues such as research question formulation, research ideas and hypothesis formulation. Next, extensive attention will be given in this chapter to quality aspects of measurement, such as validity and reliability of the measurement of constructs. We will pay attention to such issues for quantitative as well as qualitative research. We also discuss various levels at which explanations can be sought: the micro-, meso- and macro-level.

2.2 Empirical cycle

Researchers can come across a research idea at any time, in any place. No rules describe how researchers should pick a research idea. Some researchers come upon ideas when they are peeling potatoes, others while sitting in their study bent over thick books, others while jogging along a canal in the rain. No rules prescribe how you as a researcher should identify a new research idea. This phase is also referred to as the 'observational phase': you as a researcher observe phenomena, you walk around and take notion of things, out of which an idea bubbles up.

The empirical cycle starts with this *research idea*. As said, this can be a very rough notion of what you as a researcher want to zoom in upon. However, once you have identified a research idea (say: the relation between intelligence and criminal offending, or: the operations of organized crime businesses) there is a number of steps to follow for that idea to turn into a researchable question and to be able to find an answer. That sequence of steps is referred to as the 'empirical cycle'. Qualitative and quantitative research differ in how they progress through that cycle. We first outline the steps in the research cycle for *quantitative* studies.

After the research idea has taken hold, it should next be translated into a question. This phase is what is called the *inductive phase*. Here the rough notion is transformed into a question to which you want to find the answer. That question could be, for example: are offenders less intelligent than non-offenders? It could also be: are offenders more intelligent than non-offenders? or: is there a difference in intelligence between offenders and non-offenders? These three varieties may seem only superficially different but as we will see in chapter 7, the exact formulation of the research question does have implications for later analysis, in particular statistical testing. This phase is also referred to as the phase where hypotheses are formulated, or the 'hypothesis phase'.

Suppose that the research question we have chosen is: are offenders less intelligent than non-offenders? Then, before we can start carrying out our study to provide an answer to this question, we must become much more concrete. It is for instance unclear in this question what we mean by intelligence. Intelligence is namely what is often referred to as a 'construct' or 'hypothetical construct': something people have a common understanding of, but something we cannot observe directly like we could someone's height or weight or eye colour. We assume that it exists, but it is not observable, it is only hypothesized to exist. As the construct is not an immediately observable property, we have to define how we measure the construct. Do we intuitively infer it from someone's appearance when we talk to him or her? Or do we use their score on a validated IQ test?

Next, we also have to decide what we mean by a criminal offender. Do we mean by that anyone who has ever stolen something? Or during the past five years? Do we exclude juvenile transgressions and include only adults? Or people who have committed offenses with a certain minimum seriousness? And how do we measure this? Do we ask people themselves whether they ever committed a (certain) offense? Or do we use objective measures such as convictions? Or are police records fine too?

Subsequently, we also need to decide when we will answer our question in the affirmative. Suppose that offenders' average IQ equals 100.0000, and that that of non-offenders 100.0001, do we then say 'yes' to our question? Or do we only identify a difference as 'telling' from a certain magnitude onwards (say a 10-point difference, or a 5-point difference)?

In this phase, the research question or hypothesis becomes testable. It is specified to such an extent that we will actually be able to find the answer to the question through measurement. From the general question that was formulated in the inductive phase in which we wrapped the question in vague words, we have now in a sense come down to earth in this next phase, the *deductive phase*, and defined exactly how we are going to *measure* the concepts or constructs. It is sometimes jokingly said that after the deductive phase, after the questions have been turned into testable hypotheses, if the researcher would lamentably die in a road accident, the study could be carried out in exactly the same fashion as the researcher would have done had s/he not been killed. After his or her death another researcher could take over and would then be able to conduct the research in exactly the same way as the deceased researcher would have done. All decisions have been made, all steps have been outlined. The path or 'recipe' for the study has been laid down. This process of defining exactly what is meant by a construct and how it will be measured, is called *operationalization*. Operationalization is the process through which general ideas are turned into concrete to-do-lists, concrete operations. With operationalization, you lay down exactly through what steps you are going to measure the construct to be able to answer the research question.

After the deductive phase, the research proper can go ahead. According to the prescriptions laid down in the operationalization, measurements can be made, and we will be able to determine whether offenders are less intelligent than non-offenders, or whether no evidence for that is found. This phase is often referred to as the 'testing phase', that is, the phase where data are collected in the empirical world, to test the hypothesis.

Lastly, after the hypothesis that offenders are less intelligent than non-offenders has been accepted or rejected, the last phase encompasses the analysis of this result and its meaning for (criminological) theory. Suppose that it is found that offenders and non-offenders do not differ in terms of their intelligence, what are the implications for bio-psychological theories? Can this finding be true given that offending is in general not an act that pays off in terms of higher life-time earnings? How then can it be that those who do take the in principle not commendable decision to offend are seemingly just as bright as those who embark on likely more profitable life-paths? Or is it maybe so that there is *heterogeneity*: is it perhaps the case that certain kinds of offenders are in fact cleverer than non-offenders but that other offenders are on the contrary less intelligent than non-offenders – so that on average this evens out? Maybe we should design a new study in which we evaluate differences in intelligence for various kinds of offenders: separately for property, violent, public order offenders, etc? Here, in this so-called *evaluation phase* we are in fact describing the nascent of a new research idea: the idea that intelligence varies over types of offenders, evening out when taking the average. We have in fact described a new research idea.

In that sense, we have not come full circle after these five steps: at the end of the evaluation phase we have in fact identified future avenues of exploration. The empirical cycle is therefore not a cycle, but a spiral, with each answer generating new research ideas. Viewing the empirical cycle as a spiral rather than a cycle concurs with the idea that research is progressive and leads to knowledge in small steps, with each step and each subsequent study taking us further on the path to understanding the world around us.

This research cycle that we just outlined, is characteristic for quantitative research. It is not characteristic for qualitative research, where testing is generally not done, nor 'instruments' (such as an instrument to measure intelligence) commonly used. This is mainly due to the fact that the types of questions posed in qualitative research are generally different. In qualitative studies, we are generally not so much interested in the magnitude, frequency or scale of phenomena. Rather, we ask questions referring to the 'why' or the 'how' of phenomena. For instance, we may be asking why people decide to commit a crime, or to join gangs. Obviously, we could also answer that question using quantitative research. We could present gang members with a set of answers to this question (for instance: a. 'Because I needed money'; b. 'Because I needed protection'; c. 'Because I thought it would be cool to be a gang member'), but that is likely a fairly superficial approach. Qualitative studies delve deeper as they aim to study phenomena within context (why did this person who lives in this neighbourhood join that gang at that moment in time). Therefore, for this example, a researcher would not simply distribute questionnaires among a number of gang members, but would rather more or less join gang culture, or communicate often with people who joined gangs or may be about to do so, and as such *understand* through the research why, when and how decisions such as joining a gang are made. For that matter, qualitative research is also referred to as *interpretative* empirical, with quantitative research labelled *analytical* empirical.

Also, the way qualitative research operates is generally much less prescribed than quantitative research. Qualitative researchers often start by interacting with the people they aim to study, and draw up hypotheses as they go along, testing them while the research proceeds, modifying or rejecting them and drawing up new ones. As we will detail in chapter 9, in qualitative analyses researchers do not necessarily wait until the entire study is over to draw conclusions, but may do so after each data collection instance. They then draw interim conclusions that may be continuously adapted to new facts and insights as the research proceeds, developed into new hypotheses that are subsequently tested. In such studies, each interaction or interview or data collection instance may be seen as a separate 'mini' research cycle. As such, before an interview starts, the researcher has a preliminary explanation or answer to the research question, which may be adapted after the interview, which adaptation is then the prevailing explanation as the researcher enters a next interview, etc. After each data collection episode, new explanations or hypotheses (not often referred to as such, though) are formed, that are then tested again with every subsequent data collection activity. A qualitative study becomes then a spiral of small research cycles by itself. By the time the explanation or interpretation of the phenomenon under study converges in the sense that the explanation does not change anymore upon collection of new data, the research terminates. It is said that *saturation* has then been reached. This adaptable manner of data collection in fact makes qualitative research eminently suitable for research in unsettled or unexplored contexts, such as in the study of international crimes.

In fact, in qualitative research, the research cycle may even be inverted, with researchers starting with data collection, and formulating questions only after that, on the basis of what they observe, topsy-turvy in a sense, with some researchers even not starting literature study until after the study has been completed. This type of research is referred to as *grounded theory* and the data gathered in this fashion as *grounded data*; the term 'grounded' refers to the fact that the questions thus formulated are derived from empirical reality. As Strauss and Corbin stated (1990, p. 23), a theory is:

"(...) inductively derived from the study of the phenomenon it represents. That is, it is discovered, developed and provisionally verified through systematic data collection and analysis of data pertaining to that phenomenon. Therefore, data collection, analysis and theory stand in reciprocal relationship with each other."

In such grounded approaches one therefore does not design and operationalize a research question or hypothesis beforehand after which data collection starts, but the order is reversed. Grounded theory is an approach that is useful or even necessary in case one wants to study phenomena that are largely unknown terrain. As Stern 1995 said:

"(...) the strongest case for the use of grounded theory is in investigations of relatively uncharted water, or to gain a fresh perspective in a familiar situation (...)"

For more on grounded theory see Glaser and Strauss (1967) and Strauss and Corbin (1998).

2.3 Literature search and source evaluation

Often the research idea, the first phase of the empirical cycle, is not a lightning bolt (or light bulb) or epiphany. In fact, the idea phase often coincides with the period where reading of the literature is done. One may for instance be reading up on the scientific literature on offending, and find that researchers have postulated that offenders have lower intelligence than non-offenders. Such suggestions from previous research form a starting point for new research endeavours.

It is in fact highly inadvisable to start out on research without a thorough literature search. Once a vague idea or direction for the research has been formed (such as 'I want to know more about criminal offending and intelligence'), a first exploration should be done of the scientific literature. Reading recent work on the topic tells you what has already been found, what is still an enigma, what new directions are considered fruitful by the cognoscenti in the field. Reading up will also warn you against embarking upon topics that are very hard to study in practice, and reading about other researchers' struggles and dead alleys will save you time and money, and prevent you making the same mistakes. It will also enable you to improve and add upon earlier work, and as such contribute to the building of a knowledge base, to the idea that academic research is about accumulation of knowledge.

Literature searches can be done through the internet, or in literature databases. Not all academic literature is 'open access' (meaning it can be read without charge), and for many articles in scientific journals you need to search their content through a university e-mail account that grants you access. It is important to be critical when using information from the internet. For scientific purposes, it is in fact best to use only sources that have been published in academic, peer-reviewed journals. Even though that does not guarantee high-quality research (we will encounter a number studies below that were published in high-ranking journals that however did turn out to present findings that were terribly wrong), it does protect against some of the low quality work. Academic work published in academic peer-reviewed journals is ranked as more noteworthy and telling than work published in non-academic or non-peer-reviewed journals, or work published on researchers' own websites or wikipedia – which may offer excellent material but where have been few checks. Top ranking journals are journals such as *the Lancet* (for medical research), *Criminology* (for criminological research), *Nature* and *Science* – the latter two so highly ranked that they are in a sense in a separate universe. Journals have rankings that reflect the size of their readership and are a rough benchmark – within their discipline – of their standing and the quality of the articles published in them.

For very recent as yet unpublished work, it is possible to scan the websites of academic conferences: many publish conference abstracts online. These are abstracts of presentations that researchers gave at these conferences. Often, such work is in progress and as yet unpublished. While generally such abstracts do not contain sufficient material to go on, it is very well accepted to e-mail the presenters and ask them for their powerpoint slides or any unpublished papers they may have.

Relevant information may be around on non-academic websites as well. However, especially in the area of international crimes, where much is politicized and different combatant and interest groups vie for attention and may have an interest in painting a black picture of the enemy, one cannot be too cautious with using this information. It is important to always check and counter-check the source of the information, the medium where it was published, and to screen the publications themselves for information that helps determine whether the information meets your quality and independence criteria.

Searches are generally done using keywords, such as (for a study on sexual abuse of children) *sexual abuse* or *sex abuse* or *child sex abuse* or *sexual abuse minor*. In describing your work in a publication, it is common to list, apart from the keywords, the databases searched, the date the search was conducted and the number of hits. Your output is then *replicable* by others, by which we mean that other researchers should be able to carry out the search in exactly the same way as you did and arrive at the same list of references. Web references should give the day the information was retrieved from the website address. In searching for publications and information, many researchers 'snowball' in the sense that they scan the reference list of each of the publications found, retrieve those references, in turn scan the new reference lists, and so forth.

Some studies aim in fact to do no more than work from the findings of previous research: they do not aim to gather new information, but to synthesize and summarize what has already been uncovered in earlier studies. If such a summary aims to do no more than give an overview and summary of a number of relevant studies that have been published, this is referred to as a *narrative review*.

Such overviews can also be carried out in a systematic manner, whereby one aims to identify all relevant studies through a systematic search with keywords across multiple databases. The overview aims to be exhaustive, it aims to include everything that has been published, to scrutinize all the available evidence. Often, only studies meeting certain quality criteria are included. Next a synthesis of the findings is written. This is referred to as a *systematic review*. Some systematic reviews are reworked into a so-called *meta-analysis*, where not only a summary is given of all the available evidence on a certain question, but the data from all previous studies are combined into a new aggregated dataset, and re-analysed. The meta-analysis then gives a new, integrated result across all studies ever carried out on the topic. Meta-analyses and systematic reviews may comprise literally hundreds of studies.

Hensman Kettrey, Marx and Tanner-Smith (2019) carried out a systematic review of the available evidence on bystander programs for prevention of sexual assault among adolescents and college students. They identified 27 high-quality studies that met the inclusion criteria; almost all had been carried out in the USA. Review of the available evidence from these 27 studies revealed that bystander programs impact knowledge and attitudes, increase bystander intervention, but do not reduce sexual assault perpetration. For more on systematic reviews and meta-analysis, see `campbellcollaboration.org`.

2.4 Operationalisation, choice of variables

If we want to make statements about the explanatory power of theories, we need data. Empirical data are necessary to test whether a theory accurately predicts the phenomenon under study. For instance, if a particular theory states that offenses are committed in areas with little police presence, we could in a quantitative design gather data on police presence for a large number of small segments of a town, for a certain number of time intervals, and match these data with data on offenses committed in the same segments and time intervals. If the theory explains the occurrence of crime well, we would expect to find a strong correlation between police absence and offending incidence. If we find no such correlation, we have little empirical support for the theory. Similarly, if a theory says that people join gangs for status enhancement, then we should be able to observe that in a qualitative design, through repeated interactions with the research subjects. We would then attempt to elicit the meaning of gang membership from interviews and observation of gang members, carefully analysing in what manner status is affected by this membership, what meaning is attached to gang membership by the gang members themselves.

As noted previously, many theories employ so-called hypothetical constructs, that is, abstract notions that in (quantitative) research however need to be defined precisely before they can be measured, in qualitative research they are often defined during data collection and analysis. Gottfredson and Hirschi (1990) employed the construct self-control in their widely cited theory. Every reader will understand approximately what is meant by that – but how exactly should we measure self-control? The same goes for even vaguer constructs such as 'anomie'. Anomie has been defined as a general term for a condition of apathy, estrangement and in general un-well-being for the loss of goals. Martindale (1960) however defined anomie as the inverse of solidarity, or: "(...) *anomie is a state of confusion, insecurity, 'normlessness'* (...)". These examples show that different authors may use different so-called *conceptual definitions* for the same term.

Also, definitions of the same term may evolve over time. A good example is the hypothetical construct 'intelligence'. While the word intelligence is common usage in many languages, numerous definitions and measurement strategies have emerged over the years that it has featured in psychological research. In the early years, the Stanford Binet test was used to measure people's intelligence level. As the science of psychology evolved, more and more dimensions were added to the construct, such as visual-spatial processing and non-verbal abilities. Other tests are now around, such as the WISC or the Raven, that each operationalize intelligence (slightly) differently.

After a construct has been defined, after we have described what exactly we understand the construct to encompass through a conceptual definition, we next need to decide how the construct will be measured. This is done through a so-called *operational definition.* If for instance our conceptual definition of intelligence states that intelligence is the ability that individuals have for language, math, and logical reasoning, our operational definition should contain items to capture language skills, mathematical skills, and logical reasoning. If our conceptual definition also includes visual-spatial processing skills, then the operational definition should also contain items to capture visual-spatial processing. The definition of constructs in qualitative research is done much more inductively, generally working from the empirical data as they emerge, and taking into account the context and meaning of the phenomena under study, the interpretation respondents attach to these constructs, and perhaps even allowing for different definitions for different groups of respondents (for instance, status may be conceptualized differently for male respondents than for females).

2.5 Pilot study

In general, once the literature has been read and the variables operationalised, studies do not go ahead immediately full swing. It is in fact recommended to test all the study's elements before the study goes 'live'. The study's approach of respondents should be tested, any instruments should be tested: whether they are practicable, viable, acceptable to respondents. Questionnaires should be administered to a number of trial-respondents to see whether filling out the forms really does not take too long, whether all the questions are understandable to respondents, non-offensive, and the like. Even interviewers should be 'tested', research protocols, apps that are used, ICT settings. Particularly in qualitative research, we should investigate whether we are able to get access to our respondents. If the study focuses on crime and crime-related situations, we must scrutinize security issues. Such a general rehearsal for the study, is referred to as a 'pilot study'.

All studies should be piloted before they start. In spite of good intentions and years of experience of research staff, it turns out that, as the saying goes, also for academic research the proof of the pudding is in the eating. Only once the research is actually carried out in the field, can we find out whether it runs as we want it to. And often that research pudding turns out to need a few more tweaks before it is really up to standard. Thus, almost all researchers pre-test the crucial elements of their studies, and almost all find they need to adjust the study somewhat. Not piloting one's study is extremely risky.

2.6 Validity and reliability

But how can we be sure – staying with the example of intelligence – that our operational definition does give us good measurements of the construct we intend to measure? Perhaps the items have been chosen such that it is easy to guess them. Or perhaps the math skills items have been formulated so 'wordy' that they actually tap language skills so that only those with sufficient language skills are able to understand what is asked (in that case the test does not capture math skills but language skills). This issue – whether our operational definition enables us to measure the construct as we defined it – is generally expressed in two methodological properties: validity and reliability. Let us first turn to reliability.

Reliability refers to the *precision* with which we measure our construct. Suppose I would want to measure someone's height. I could do so using a measuring lint. If my measure of height is reliable, it is precise: each time I measure that person's height, I get exactly the same result. In the reverse case, namely if I get different results each time I take a measurement, the measure is unreliable. Using an elastic measuring lint would make for an unreliable measure: one time the result is 170 cm, the next it is 172, then it is 167, then 173 etc. If I repeat my measurements 100 times, I might on average arrive at the right result, but because of the variability in the measurements, we say that the measure is unreliable.

How can we know whether a measurement is reliable? The example above already gives already an indication. One way to do this is to test and then retest: if we get the same results upon retesting we call the measurement method reliable. If we do not, we call it unreliable. Testing and retesting is not always feasible, however: if we for instance interview respondents, it is generally not doable to return to respondents and re-interview them. Even if the objects we are investigating would lend themselves to retesting (for instance when we are conducting a dossier analysis), it still often does not make sense to retest: the coder would probably remember the value s/he entered previously. In such cases, we tend to have two coders investigate the material, independently, and each produce a measurement. If the results from these two raters concur, we say that we have *interrater reliability*. Other, less commonly used, methods exist for assessing (or estimating) the reliability of measures, that we will not go into here, but that can be found in general textbooks on research methodology.

Reliability is important, in quantitative and in qualitative research. However, while it is relatively easy to assess and achieve reliability in quantitative research, this is much less straightforward or easy in qualitative research. The qualitative method does not often rely on instruments, so interrater coding is then less obvious. Also, when qualitative researchers gather data in interaction with the research subjects, freely interviewing and observing them, it is not to be expected less that a different researcher would elicit exactly the same kind of information from the respondents. Respondents respond differently to different interviewers, different researchers pick up different cues. In a sense, in qualitative studies the researcher him- or herself may actually be the instrument with which data are collected. While not necessarily so, the same goes for the qualitative analysis of raw data, such as images or video material: different researchers may pick up different information. In that sense, reliability is more easily compromised in qualitative research and less easy to ascertain. The reliability of the coding of textified qualitative data can, however, quite well be assessed as we will see in a number of examples.

Next, validity refers to the extent to which our measures capture what we are after, whether they measure what we *intend* to measure. Where reliability refers to whether we measure our construct precisely, validity is much more fundamental in that it reflects to what extent an instrument to measure, say, criminogenic beliefs, actually captures those beliefs and not something else. Designing instruments such that they truly reflect the construct you are after, is a skill and requires extensive testing and probing before you can be confident that the instrument delivers what you want it to.

Focusing mainly on quantitative research, let us illustrate with an example some of the issues that complicate achieving valid measures. Suppose I would indeed want to measure criminogenic beliefs. Some of the questions I could pose respondents are whether they agree with statements such as, for instance: 'It is okay to steal', or 'If someone does not pay me respect, I am willing to use force'. Now some of your respondents who harbour criminogenic beliefs may answer 'yes' to the first question, and 'yes' to the second one. Most respondents with criminogenic beliefs will, however, realize that their beliefs are considered 'not done' by respectable citizens, perhaps even deviant. Anticipating disapproval, they may therefore choose to answer 'no' to your questions and present themselves like respectable citizens, just like the interviewer before them. If that happens, we say that the instrument is sensitive to 'social desirability bias'. The instrument then does not capture criminogenic beliefs, but rather what the interviewee believes the interviewer considers a 'correct' answer. Your instrument is then not valid. Tendencies like social desirability bias affect the validity of measures. We will not discuss them extensively here, but simply note that they exist; we return to them in chapter 4.

In social science research methodology, several kinds of validity are distinguished. The first one is the one that we just referred to: does the instrument measure what it is intended to measure? This is denoted more specifically as *construct validity*. For an instrument to have construct validity, it has to meet three criteria first.

To start with, the instrument must capture the construct across its entire 'spectrum'. For instance, an intelligence test that has math items only, does not capture intelligence as we understand it: it does not measure language skills or logical reasoning or non-verbal abilities or other relevant dimensions. It therefore assesses the construct only partially. It is said that the instrument then lacks *content validity*. Formulated conversely: only an instrument that assesses the construct across its entire breadth or spectrum is said to have content validity.

Second, the instrument must generate measures that correlate in the expected direction with other variables. This likely sounds fairly obscure, so we will try to clarify it with an example. Suppose that we have an instrument to measure driving skills. The scores on that instrument should be associated with the likelihood that people cause accidents. If the instrument tells us that someone has good driving skills, we would expect it to be unlikely that that person is regularly involved in traffic accidents. This is referred to as *criterion validity*: the scores obtained with the instrument should correlate with an external criterion that you would expect it to correlate with.

Third, we want our instrument to truly capture the underlying construct itself, and not something else. It is for instance possible that we design an instrument that has good content validity (say we are again measuring intelligence, and our instrument encompasses intelligence across all its dimensions), and also has good criterion validity (in the sense that people with high scores on the instrument do well in school). However, if my instrument is built using items written in formal Dutch, it does not capture intelligence but language skills. It would for instance be unable to measure intelligence for recent migrants who do not yet master Dutch well. Then this instrument still does not measure intelligence. This third criterion is referred to as *construct validity-in-the-narrow-sense*.

All in all, an instrument can only be said to have construct validity if it meets all of the three criteria of content validity, criterion validity and construct validity-in-the-narrow-sense. The operationalization of the construct is then valid. If all these three criteria are met, can we then say that the instrument has construct validity? Not yet, as for an instrument to have construct validity, we also require it to be reliable. Formulated in ordinary terms: we cannot say that our instrument measures what we are after if it produces imprecise measurements. So, summarising, we regard an instrument to have construct validity only when the instrument gives us precise measurements of the construct we are after, and meets all of the three above-described validity criteria. The instrument then has full construct validity. See the upper part of Figure 2.1.

But how then does one assess whether one's instrument has construct validity? This is a lot more complicated than assessing reliability. Researchers generally first inspect *face validity*, which may sound sophisticated but is not much more than judging whether, on the face of it, the instrument is likely to be content, criterion and construct (in the narrow sense) valid. More intricate methods are available to assess criterion validity; these investigate whether the scores generated by the construct correlate positively or negatively or do not correlate with other variables in the way they would be expected to if they were

Figure 2.1: Reliability and various kinds of validity

Construct validity

- Reliability -> *do we have precise measurements?*
- Validity of the operationalization
  - Content validity -> *do we measure the construct over its entire spectrum?*
  - Criterion validity -> *does the measurement predict an external criterion?*
  - Construct validity in the narrow sense -> *do we measure the intended construct?*

Statistical conclusion validity -> *is the association statistically significant?*

Internal validity -> *is the association non-spurious?*

External validity -> *does the result hold outside of the sample?*

a valid measure of the underlying construct. More about these can be found in general methodological textbooks.

Other kinds of validity are important as well. We discuss them briefly. First, *statistical conclusion validity* or *statistical validity* refers to whether a result is likely to be attributable to anything other than chance. Suppose that we have investigated 100 volunteers, young men aged 15-25 years old. We have administered our intelligence test and asked them whether they have ever been convicted. Now suppose that we find that our measurements of intelligence indeed correlate with our respondents' criminal convictions: the lower respondents' intelligence score, the more convictions they incurred. Statistical tests can tell us how likely it is that the observed association is a chance one. If our statistical test tells us that the observed correlation is a highly unlikely outcome were intelligence and criminal activity unrelated, we say that the correlation is significant. We then conclude that intelligence and criminal activity are related, and this finding then has 'statistical conclusion validity'. We discuss statistical testing in chapter 7.

Next, *internal validity* is distinguished. Continuing our example on intelligence and criminal activity, we might be tempted to believe that, given the statistically significant association between the two, intelligence and criminal activity are in fact causally related. We cannot be sure about this, however. It may for instance be so, that intelligence has nothing to do with criminal activities, but that those with lower intelligence are simply more likely to have been caught and convicted by the criminal justice authorities. Suppose then that we had asked respondents to themselves indicate how many offenses they committed over their lifetime. Would the association between intelligence and offenders measures then be more likely to be internally valid? Even then, we could not be sure that it is actually lower intelligence that makes people offend more. Perhaps those with lower and higher intelligence offend just as often, but those with lower intelligence are more honest? Or those with higher intelligence more sensitive to social desirability bias?

As there are several *alternative* explanations for our finding – other than that low intelligence causes criminal activity – we do not have internal validity. Even if we captured intelligence with a construct-valid measure and we therefore have valid measures of criminal activity, and even if the association is significant, we still cannot rule out other explanations than the causal one.

This happens very often in observational research: researchers find associations between an intervention and an outcome, but they cannot prove that the outcome has been *caused* by the intervention. If vegetarians live longer than meat eaters, this may also be due to the fact that vegetarians do more sports, or smoke less, or are generally more health conscious. If marathon runners live longer than non-runners, this may also be due to the fact that they are healthier in the first place (which enables them to do those gruelling runs). If ex-convicts taking part in a reintegration project reoffend less than ex-convicts who did not take part, this may also be due to the fact that those who self-selected into the reintegration project are simply more motivated, intelligent, less often addicted, etc. These properties (motivation, intelligence, addiction) are called *confounders*, they are 'third variables' generating an association between two properties that are not causally related.

Ensuring internal validity is extremely difficult in observational studies such as the examples given here. The only way to be absolutely certain that a causal relation exists between for instance participation in a reintegration project and the outcome reoffending, is when those who participate and those who do not are similar. The only way to be entirely sure about this is to administer the intervention at random. Just like for instance in pharmaceutical research, we would then randomly create two groups: those who do and those who do not get the intervention. If we have such a design, we will have ruled out any alternative explanations: as the two groups (those with and those without the intervention) have been formed by chance, there are no systematic differences between the two groups and they therefore also cannot differ anymore on any other characteristics. Then, no alternative explanations are left – only the causal one. We will return to this topic at length in chapter 5.

Lastly, suppose that we have a study conducted with a measure that has construct validity, and suppose our findings have statistical validity, and suppose as well that we have internal validity: we are certain that our, to introduce another example, training 'Stop Offending Now', randomly assigned among 1,000 Criminology student volunteers, achieves a significant reduction in criminogenic beliefs. A last question then is whether this result that we established in our research lab, would also be found in the outside world, outside of academia. If we went to schools and workplaces and prisons, and administered our training 'Stop Offending Now', would it also be effective? If that is the case, we have what is called *external validity*: the conclusion also holds in other situations than the research lab.

Note that the four kinds of validity we just discussed constitute in a sense steps or stages: each validity level has to be satisfied before it makes sense to check whether the next type of validity is present. If we do not measure what we are interested in, it does not make sense to test whether a result is statistically significant. If an association is not statistically significant (so that it is likely to be a chance result) it does not make sense to investigate whether the association is causal. Therefore, with each successive validity level ticked, we become more confident that our findings are meaningful. See Figure 2.1.

2.7 Qualitative and quantitative studies

An often used categorisation of studies, that we already briefly touched upon, is into qualitative and quantitative studies. While quantitative studies aim to measure the volume or *quantity* of some variable of interest, qualitative studies are geared to find out the 'why' or the 'how' of phenomena. Studies into the prevalence of crime are for that matter typically quantitative studies. Quantitative studies follow the standard empirical cycle, are studies where hypotheses are formulated and where statistical testing is often employed. But for understanding, for instance, why offenders desist, or how drugs dealers negotiate territories, or how corporate identity prevents organizational crime, so for questions on etiology, qualitative studies may be much better suited.

Qualitative studies differ in a number of respects from quantitative ones. Qualitative studies are generally much less strictly plannable beforehand, use lots of interviews and observation, have more room for adaptation as the research goes along, leave more room for respondents to put forward unexpected viewpoints. They may be ethnographic in which case the researcher spends time on a structural basis with his or her research subjects, to understand their world and reality and to be able to explain crime or any other phenomenon of interest 'from within'. Clearly, instruments are much less used, testing is hardly ever encountered.

While quantitative research gives a broad, generalisable, quantitative summary of a phenomenon (which is a plus point), its downside is that it is reductionist and can deal with only a small number of factors in relatively simple models (which are negative points). Qualitative research is richer, as it can describe complex situations, uncover intricate mechanisms and unexpected relations, and deal with multiple layers of interrelated causal factors (these are all plus points). But it often has limited generalizability and limited reliability (negative points).

In qualitative research, the aim is not to produce generalisable quantitative statements, but to unravel mechanisms, to *understand* what happened, or to understand the meaning that the research subjects give to phenomena that are being studied. This is why the inherent juxtaposition of qualitative and qualitative research can be portrayed as in Figure 2.2. The quantitative study as portrayed here gives a broadly generalisable result, but it is like a pancake: it is but one layer deep, it is shallow. A qualitative study, on the other hand, picks but a small part of the broad area, but it delves deep, it goes to the bottom of things and generates a deep and contextual understanding – but we cannot be sure whether the same result would have been found elsewhere, it applies only to the particular context studied. A qualitative study may even study just one respondent (a so-called N=1 study), a generally unthinkable design for a quantitative study. A quantitative study is generally exact and precise, and particularly strong on reliability, a qualitative study relatively stronger on

Figure 2.2: Abstract representation of quantitative and qualitative research

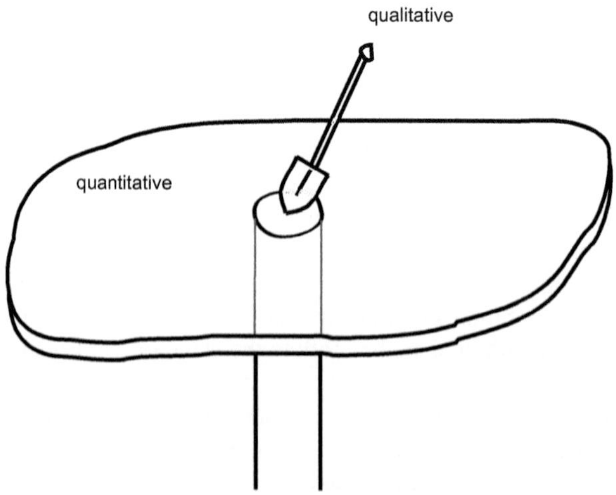

'validity' in the sense of capturing what you are after, unravelling mechanisms, capturing the intricacies of processes, observing beyond social desirability – all, obviously, given high-quality of the study design, measures and staff.

An eminently readable, extensive and thought-provoking discussion of quantitative and qualitative research traditions, their different values, beliefs, and norms, and how these unpack for the types of questions asked and type of answers given, can be found in Mahoney and Goertz (2006).

While the two types of research traditions are at times juxtaposed, and researchers from the two traditions tend to move in separate circles and cultures, this writer believes that qualitative and quantitative methods should whenever possible be combined. Through combination and integration, the simultaneous employment of the distinct methodologies, each approach in a sense buffers the weaknesses of the other type. Quantitative research may then give the broad, generalisable, replicable overview, with qualitative research shedding light on why the data have been observed as they are, what the processes were that generated the observed patterns. Such 'buffering' through combination of research methods is often referred to as 'triangulation'. Bolhuis and Van Wijk (2015) did this when they studied the exclusion from refugee protection of alleged war criminals in the Netherlands. They combined analysis of 358 case files with interviews among policy makers, representatives from the Netherlands National Prosecution Service and investigators.

Such a combination of qualitative and quantitative methods in one study is also often referred to as 'mixed methods', or as a mixed-methods study, or even a multi-method study. An excellent and concise introduction to both types of research, that compares their strengths and weaknesses and unique suitabilities for specific questions is Dixon, Singleton and Straits (2016, chapter 4). We also again refer to Mahoney and Goertz (2006).

2.8 Macro-, meso- and micro-level studies

The macro-meso-micro categorisation is often encountered in sociological research where processes and explanations may be envisioned to take place at different levels. The categorisation reflects the aggregation level at which studies attempt to draw conclusions.

The *micro*-level is the lowest or smallest possible analysis unit. Often this is the level of the individual, and micro-level studies generally focus on respondents: people, whether they are perpetrators or victims. They may be interviewed or observed, or data are collected about them from other sources. Explanations for the phenomenon under study are then also situated at this level, for example an explanation where it is postulated that personality disorders cause people to commit certain crimes. Studies may employ large samples in a quantitative analysis, or smaller samples in qualitative studies. As an example of the latter, McLoughlin and Weerdesteijn (2016) systematically compared the impact that strategies employed by two leaders (Kenneth Kaunda of Zambia and Robert Mugabe of Zimbabwe) had on the risk of mass atrocities. As the authors describe, while Zambia had generally been stable and peaceful, Zimbabwe experienced mass violence and repression. The authors conclude that, rather than the structural risk factors for mass atrocities, it was the behaviour and strategies of the two leaders that "*prompted patterns of violence or constraint that had a decisive influence on the perpetration of atrocities, or the effective mitigation of risk over time*".

The *macro*-level is found at the other end of the aggregation spectrum. As this is the highest level of aggregation, explanations focus on levels such as the nation or government. An example of such an explanation is one where it is said that unemployment rates and inflation cause higher crime rates. Harff (1987) searched for such macro-level explanations of international crimes when she investigated to what extent structural factors explain the occurrence of genocide, studying over a number of years countries where genocide had, and where genocide had not occurred. We return to this study in section 14.4. When studying international crimes, an even higher aggregation level may be that of the international community. Van Wijk and Smeulers (2017) argue that the American intervention in Iraq and the failure of the international community to address the situation in Syria may be regarded as an important breeding ground for the extremism and international crimes committed by Islamic State of Iraq and Syria (ISIS; often generically referred to as Islamic State or IS).

In between micro- and macro-level is situated the *meso*-level. At this level, there is some aggregation over individuals. Examples of this meso-level are neighbourhoods, criminal gangs, or rebel groups. Wood (2006) studied why sexual violence is committed by some rebel groups and armies during conflicts, but not by other groups. This is a typical example of a meso-level study, a study that we will discuss in more detail in section 14.3.

In part IV of this book, we will regularly discuss research methods along these lines: research methods may be geared to finding explanations at the societal level, meso-level or at the micro-level (which is mostly the perpetrator but may sometimes even be at the level of a single crime event).

2.9 Ethics

Whenever we conduct research in which we study humans, or even non-human entities, we have to observe ethical rules. Every discipline has its own – at times internationally agreed – ethical rules, that in general share a common core.

A first rule in research ethics is that research subjects or respondents have the right to be treated decently and respectfully. Appointments should be met, on time, and researchers should dress and behave according to the standards of the respondents. The same goes when we approach organisations whose data we might want to use. Attentive e-mails and swift responses are called for, rather than overly chummy or cursory responses. And, apart from common decency, experience teaches that treating respondents with respect, friendliness and flexibility is also much better for the research: respondents who feel they are not being treated correctly will sooner refuse to participate, or may give only brief or half-true answers, just to be rid of the researchers or to quickly cash any remuneration.

Second, respondents are entitled to be informed on what the research is about, who finances it, what will happen with the information they give, in short: they are entitled to be fully informed about all aspects of the research that may be relevant for them in deciding whether they want to participate or not. This is referred to as *informed consent*. We return to this topic in section 4.2.

Obviously, researchers should also ensure the safety of respondents. Especially in charged environments, such when studying inner city gang warfare, football hooliganism, or conflict and international crimes, participation in a study can by itself endanger respondents. In studying international crimes, governments and their security apparatus may keep an eye on who talks with the researchers, and respondents may be harassed afterwards. All these are matters to consider before a study goes ahead, and to consider when designing the study such that these kinds of risks are minimized and weighted.

A related, generally accepted standard is the 'Do No Harm-principle' or the principle of 'non-maleficence', entailing that as a researcher it is one's duty to minimize the risk that research participants suffer adverse consequences from participating in the research, and to ensure as much as possible that the research does good (beneficence). Many of the ethical rules discussed here and later on in section 4.2 serve this principle. All in all, the Do No Harm-principle entails: obtaining informed consent, minimising the risk of harm to respondents, guaranteeing anonymity and confidentiality to respondents, avoiding deception, and giving respondents the right to withdraw from the study at any point in time should they wish so.

In general, researchers promise respondents that they will treat the data that respondents give them confidentially, and that they will report their findings not only anonymously, but in such a manner that respondents are also unrecognisable and untraceable. Researchers should not only promise this, but also put measures in place that they can actually deliver on such promises.

Data should therefore be transported safely and stored securely. As of 25 May 2018, data privacy across the European Union (EU) is subject to the EU General Data Protection Regulation (GDPR), that aims to harmonize data privacy laws across Europe, to protect and empower all EU citizens' data privacy. The GDPR formulates very strict rules on the secure storage of privacy-sensitive data, and high fines can be incurred if researchers do not adhere to this regulation. It is likely that the GDPR will influence data privacy rules worldwide. See `eugdpr.org`.

Research ethics refers to respondents, but is equally important to consider for researchers. In studying possibly dangerous populations such as violent offenders, or when research takes place in dangerous settings, the safety of the researchers is an issue that needs consideration too. Insurance constraints may decide whether a research can go ahead (some universities simply do not dispatch research staff to regions that have negative travel advice). But even if insurance covers for the researchers, it is important to consider whether one needs or wants to expose interviewers to the risk of being mugged in shady neighbourhoods, and how to design procedures whereby such risks are minimised.

2.9.1 Ethical review boards

Many research institutes and universities call in the aid of independent or internal review boards for all research in which human subjects are involved. Such committees are hugely important. Not only do they give independent 'clearance' for studies to go ahead, something which is more and more often a general requirement for research funding to be released, they can also be extremely helpful in thinking about the mitigation of risks and the protection of respondents and staff.

Research and Ethical Boards (REBs) are necessary and invaluable steps in the design and preparation for studies. REBs screen study designs and protocols to see whether informed consent is guaranteed, whether respondents' safety is ensured, whether staff safety is secured, whether any breeches of principles are proportional.

Pager (2003) investigated whether having a criminal record affected African-American and Caucasian-American job applicants differently. In an experimental set-up, Pager asked matched pairs of college students to apply for real entry-level jobs. The students functioned as actors, they had been randomly 'assigned' a criminal record (as evidenced by having been in prison) or not, and were otherwise comparable on background profile and CV – apart from the fact that half were Caucasian-American students and half were African-American students. While these students were aware that they were not really applying for the entry-level positions, the employers were unaware of this. In that sense, the employers had not given informed consent for their participation in the study, which may be a considered a breach of research ethics (there was deception). Given that it would have been impossible to study the research topic validly while informing the employers, this breach of ethics had apparently been judged proportional to the importance of the study.

Pager found that while the impact of a criminal record was approximately a threefold decrease in call-back for African-Americans (5% call-back versus 14% call-back), this was two times so for Caucasian-Americans (17% call-back for former prisoners and 34% call-back for non-prisoners). The data show that Caucasian-Americans with a criminal record were in fact more likely to receive call-backs than African-Americans with a clean rap sheet. Similar patterns were found for the Netherlands for application letters where the ethnicity of the applicant was randomly varied: also here applicants with a foreign sounding family name without a criminal record were significantly less likely to be invited for a follow up than applicants with a Dutch family name who had a criminal record (Van den Berg, Blommaert, Ruiter *et al.*, 2017).

Part II

MEASUREMENT

Chapter 3

Measurement units

This chapter deals with important decisions to be taken when conducting a study: the choice of units that will be observed or measured. The chapter is also a building stone for subsequent chapters that will deal with qualitative analysis methods (chapter 9), and with descriptive and inferential statistics. Descriptive statistics (see chapter 6) are used to describe the general properties of our measurement units, such as their mean, or variability in the measures. Inferential statistics (see chapter 7) are used whenever we want to *infer* something from a sample and declare the findings from that sample applicable to a larger set of research or measurement units, a so-called *population*. In social science research, we very often work with samples as we generally do not have the time or resources to study an entire population. It is therefore important to ensure that, as far as possible, that sample resembles the population we are interested in.

In the following, we will first discuss the concepts of sampling and populations. We will discuss what constitutes a useful sample and what constitutes a less useful sample. We will also discuss practical constraints in drawing samples. Next, we detail concepts such as representativeness, bias and noise, sample size and issues of nonresponse. We end with a section that discusses statistical foundations of the practicalities of sampling decisions and more intricate diagnostics in assessing sample usefulness.

3.1 Populations and samples

The Netherlands has 17 million inhabitants. If I would want to know how tall Dutch people are, I could set out with a measuring lint to measure all Dutch, each and every one. This would take a very long time. By the time I am finished, quite a few will have died, new Dutch citizens will have been born, and perhaps I am ready for my pension by that time too, or even already dead. Assessing the whole population is clearly undoable.

The entire population of the Netherlands is what we also call in a statistical sense a *population*: a universe of units that we are interested to know something about. We could also be interested to know the height of all female Dutch citizens, in which case the population would consist of all female Dutch citizens. Or we might want to know the height of all adult Dutch, in which case the population of interest would be the population aged 18 and over.

In this example, 'population' is taken quite literally, in the sense that the statistical population is also literally a population: all inhabitants or citizens within a certain geographically defined unit or with a certain legally defined status. A population could however also be all offenders, or all cases registered at the International Criminal Tribunal for the former Yugoslavia (ICTY) in 2007, or all sex offences committed in a certain year. A population can even be household appliances or radio shows or burglaries or desserts. What matters is that there is a certain total reservoir of units of interest that we want to know something about. The people who together constitute the population, or the females or adults who do, court cases to light bulbs to desserts, are the *population members*.

Now in the example that we started with, it is clear that it would be an impossible task to measure all population members. It is clearly undoable. But even if a population would have 'only' 1,000 members, assessing each and every member of that population can be a hefty task. There is more.

Because what statistics teaches us, is that scrutinising each and every population member is actually not necessary. If we operate wisely and according to certain rules, we can with reasonable precision say something about the entire population while we investigate only a part of that population, a *sample*. Often, already a small part will do, like a 1% sample, or even less, depending on various issues that we will talk about later. So, basically, what statistical science teaches is that is not necessary to scrutinize each and every population member to infer something about that population. In fact, within limits we can get to know the population reasonably well through the study of only a selection of some of its members.

Sampling only a part of the population thus saves a lot of expenses. The flip side of the coin is that – obviously – we are not absolutely certain any more of what we say about the population, we have with our savings introduced uncertainty. Statistics is the science that teaches us how to deal with that uncertainty. It gives us the rules and procedures, and in a sense the language in which we communicate how we managed the uncertainty in a sensible way, how uncertain we exactly are – and therewith how confident we are about the conclusions we draw from the sample about the population. Much more about this in chapter 7.

3.2 Representativeness and generalizability

Let us start again with an example. We want to know what Dutch citizens of voting age will vote in the next general election in the Netherlands. In numerous countries, such questions are asked in polls right before elections, when politicians are bashed in TV shows and wise men and women air their views on why such and such party is losing and some other party has gained ground suddenly.

Now if we would want to conduct such a poll, we could not possibly interview all Dutch of voting age, there simply is no time. We therefore draw a sample. But how do we draw that sample? If I would conduct door-to-door interviews in my neighbourhood I would definitely not get a good prediction of the average Dutch person's voting behaviour.

My neighbourhood contains quite a few nice houses, no flats, to say it bluntly: it is a pretty, green, slightly upper-class area, with lots of academicians, some medical specialists and artists. I would predict perhaps, sampling only my fellow-neighbourhood inhabitants, that the Dutch social-liberal party D66 would win, or the Green Party, or the Party for Animals. That would not reflect the voting behaviour of the average Dutch citizen. My sample does not reflect the Dutch population, but only a specific segment – and while my conclusion about the voting behaviour in my neighbourhood might be right, I would draw the wrong conclusion about the entire population. Similarly, if I would interview only inhabitants of the Dutch multi-ethnic neighbourhood the 'Schilderswijk' in the Hague, or in the 'Bijlmer' in Amsterdam, I would probably also not get an accurate picture of Dutch voting behaviour, nor if I'd carry out my investigations in Wassenaar, the Beverly Hills of the Netherlands.

Clearly, what we would want, and what all the options above are lacking, is that my sample would resemble the population, would reflect the population. We would want the sample's properties to be like the properties of the population. In statistics-speak we call such a sample a *representative sample*. So, in this case we want the sample members to exhibit about the same voting behaviour as the population. We cannot check that, as we do not know the population's voting behaviour (that's what we're after!). Instead, we could check whether we have a sample with approximately the same age as the population, the same sex ratio, urban/rural and ethnic composition, the same geographical spread, income, housing situation, etc. as the Dutch population. The idea behind this is that, if sample members resemble population members on various pertinent characteristics, we expect the sample's voting behaviour to then also reflect voting behaviour in the larger population. See Figure 3.1 that gives a representation of that latter situation.

But how do we achieve this? What are the pertinent characteristics for which we must ensure that the sample is similar to the population? How many of such characteristics do we need? And how in practice could we achieve that similarity of sample to population? Luckily, these questions do not need to be answered nor do difficult procedures need to be followed. The best and easiest way namely to ensure that a sample's properties reflect those of the population is to draw that sample by *chance*, or: at random.

Suppose that we want to draw such a random sample from the Dutch population. All Dutch inhabitants are registered at their municipality, and all these registrations combined form a list of the population members. This list is referred to as the *sampling frame*. We can imagine random sampling from this sampling frame as follows: we could give every Dutch citizen of voting age a slip of paper with his or her name on it, we'd crumble all those slips, throw them in a big pan, stir them really well with a very big wooden spoon, and then we'd take out – blindly – as many as we need for our sample. Such a sample is called a *random sample*: it is formed only by chance as only chance determines whether someone ends up in the sample or not. For a random sample we may always assume that it is representative.

Once a sample is representative, it follows that we can *generalize* the sample properties to the population. So if we find that 36% of our sample members vote Labour, 14% Green, 35% Liberal, we conclude that 36% of Dutch voters would vote Labour, 14% Green and 35% Liberal.

Note that a sample is not just representative of any population, but is representative *for a certain population*. So a random sample of females of voting age is representative

Figure 3.1: Example of spread of sample members over the Netherlands

of female Dutch voters, but not representative of all Dutch voters. And a random sample of police suspects is representative of all police suspects, but not representative of all offenders.

Note also that from all of the above it follows that the sample by itself is wholly and totally uninteresting. No one is interested to know the properties of one or the other sample. The sample only begins to be of interest, once it is representative of a larger entity, once it tells us something about the population we are interested in. If I have interviewed a sample of sex offenders, then the properties of that sample are essentially unnoteworthy. If however, that sample was drawn such that it is representative of the larger population that I am interested in, then suddenly my sample findings become relevant. So, if my sample of sex offenders is representative of all sex offenders, then it is interesting to note (and declare that applicable to all sex offenders) that one in three were sexually abused as a child or that 40% report having trouble forming intimate relationships.

Note, thirdly, that for the sample there is no uncertainty. I can with certainty measure (and no one can refute my finding) that the average age of the sample sex offenders' victims is 12.3. This is a fact. I may generalize that finding to the population, so I infer that the average age of all Dutch sex offenders' victims is also 12.3. However, now I am not dead-sure. I have drawn a sample, so it might be that by chance I have a few too many offenders with younger victims, or by chance a few too many with older victims. This means that while the sample mean of 12.3 is a measurement, an irrefutable finding, the population mean of 12.3 is an *estimate*. We denote this by writing:

$$M_X \text{ for the sample mean,}$$

and by writing:

$$\hat{\mu}_X \text{ for the estimate of the population mean.}$$

We will return later to the issue whether and why the sample mean M is a good estimator for the population mean μ. Note that, by convention, we write sample characteristics with Latin literals (M, s, r_{XY}); whenever we refer to properties of the population it is the convention to use Greek literals (such as μ for the mean, σ for the standard deviation, ρ for the population correlation coefficient, etc.).

3.3 Types of samples

3.3.1 Probability samples

As we argued above, samples are useful only insofar as they tell us something about the population we are interested in. In technical terms: a sample is useful only if it is representative of the population of interest. We already said that random samples may always be considered representative. But how do we know whether a sample is representative?

The answer to this is fairly straightforward. A sample is representative if every population member had an equal chance of ending up in the sample. This is the litmus test of representativeness.

So, if I draw a sample from the province of zuid-Holland in the Netherlands to investigate voting behaviour, the sample cannot be taken as representative of the Netherlands – those not in zuid-Holland had a zero chance of ending up in the sample. Similarly, all Criminology students present at the Statistics class of Monday morning are not a random sample of all Criminology students at the university: those who have already passed will not sit in, nor will those who on a rainy Monday morning preferred their warm beds over a trip by bike through the rain to the university campus. That the latter is self-chosen and these students could have ended up being sampled, does not matter: what matters is that the students who dragged themselves from their warm beds differ systematically from those who napped on. The ones in class are probably more motivated, or more in need of the Statistics class than those who did not show up: the unmotivated or those unfearful of statistics therefore had a smaller chance to end up in the sample. The sample members differ in a structural, systematic way from those who did not end up in the sample.

To find out whether each population member really has an equal chance to end up in the sample sometimes requires a bit of brain jogging. As an example, imagine that we carry out a victim survey: we sample household addresses randomly, and at each address we interview that person older than 15 years of age who is the first to celebrate his or her birthday. Is this a random sample of all possible victims? Obviously no, as those under 15 years of age cannot participate. Is it then a random sample of all possible victims over 15 years of age? One might be tempted to say yes, as households have been sampled randomly, and as within each household again chance determines which household member is eligible. The sample is not random however, as members of larger households have a smaller chance to end up in the sample: someone living in a 6-person family has a chance of $\frac{1}{6}$ to be selected, whereas someone in a 2-person household has a chance of $\frac{1}{2}$ to end up in the sample. Constructing the sample this way we will end up with too many singles, and too few people from large families; persons living in large families are now as we say *underrepresented* in the sample, and persons living in smaller families are *overrepresented.*

So what kinds of samples are representative of a population, and what kinds of samples are not? In the literature two kinds of samples are distinguished: *probability samples* and *non-probability samples.* Drawing a probability sample, representativeness is guaranteed; drawing a non-probability sample, representativeness is not ensured. This does not mean that a non-probability sample is always a useless sample, or by definition non-representative. Non-probability samples may very well be representative, but there is simply no guarantee.

Four kinds of probability samples are distinguished, and four kinds of non-probability samples. We will briefly discuss them below.

(1) *Random sample*

The first kind of probability sample is the random sample, also known as the *simple random sample.* A random sample is a sample where sample members are drawn as if we would have a huge cooking pot, in which we toss a lot for each population member, stir very well, and next lots are drawn blindly, irrespective of any properties of the sample member. Such a sample one also encounters as a 'simple random sample', as an 'a-select sample' or as a 'flat' random sample.

The simple random sample is not used very often though. The reason for this is firstly that drawing such samples requires quite a bit of administrative infrastructure: if there is not such a thing as a pre-existing sampling frame it is an immense task to draw up a list of population members and then select a few of them randomly. Secondly, if we draw a random sample, we are left in fate's hands as regards the representation of certain segments of the population.

We will clarify the latter with two examples. Suppose that I draw a sample of 100 suspects from the police databases. I would then expect to end up in my sample with 85 male suspects and 15 female suspects as that is the distribution of male and female offenders in the population of suspects. However, it might very well be (as chance decides who ends up in the sample) that I end up with 25 females and 75 males. This is what we call *sampling error*: deviations that occur by chance, by chance I end up with relatively more females than I should have and relatively fewer males. And, even though these sampling 'errors' are due to chance, these deviations can be problematic: suppose for instance that I end up in the above example with 5 females and 95 males. In that case, I have really too little to go on if I wanted to say something about female offenders – 5 is a very small number to draw any conclusions from. So, in this case it might be wise not to let chance have its way entirely: it might be better to try to exert some control over the representation of the group of female suspects in the sample.

Similarly, suppose that I want to assess fear of burglary in a neighbourhood. If I would by chance select 25 houses in that neighbourhood, I could end up with all houses close to the shopping center, or relatively many on the edge of the neighbourhood (areas with typically a relatively high risk for burglaries). Or end up with disproportionately many apartments. Also here it might be desirable to enforce a certain spread over the various areas and types of houses in the neighbourhood.

Lastly, and most importantly, strictly random samples are expensive for data collection. If I would draw a simple random sample to interview 170 Dutch citizens out of all 17 million inhabitants, it would probably mean that I'd do seven interviews in Rotterdam, ten in Amsterdam, four in Utrecht or the Hague, and that I'd need to travel to another 100 or so municipalities to interview the remaining approximately 135 respondents. That is very time-consuming and costly. It is also unnecessary as we will see below. For all these reasons, researchers often use more efficient random samples than the simple random sample.

(2) *Systematic sample*

The first alternative to the simple random sample is the systematic sample. Suppose that we are interested in fear of being burglarized and we are investigating a newish neighbourhood in a big city. The neighbourhood has 250 standard family houses (in which we assume that each time 2 adults live). If we want to draw a 10% random sample of these adults, this means that we could visit 50 houses and in each house interview one adult. This would give us a sample of 50, which is 10% of all 500 adults living in this neighbourhood.

The systematic sample now works as follows. All houses are first numbered. We draw at random a starting number, say 137, meaning we start from house 137 on our map. Starting from house 137, we draw a track through the neighbourhood, following the outlay of houses, and we take every 5th house, ring the doorbell and ask to interview someone, for instance, the first adult to celebrate his or her birthday. We move up, stepwise at regular intervals, to house 250 and next finish sampling from house 1 up to house 137. As the first number has been drawn at random, and as after this number all other selected houses depend on this starting number, each house has the same chance to end up in the sample and so does every adult. This is a systematic sample, and it is an efficient one, and under some conditions a random sample.

Two conditions must namely be met for a systematic sample to be random and representative. Firstly, the starting number must be chosen randomly. Secondly, the physical layout of the neighbourhood, or in more general terms, the ordering of sampling units on the list, must not have the same *periodicity* as the sampling interval. To understand this, please inspect Figure 3.2, that gives a hypothetical example of a neighbourhood plan. In this neighbourhood, houses have been built in blocks of 5. Suppose that our random starting number is 15. There are 30 houses in this example, and if we want a sample of 6 houses, this means that we would have to sample each 5th house. However, if we start at number 15, and if we interview someone in every 5th house, this would mean that in our sample we would end up with houses at the corner end of a block only. And, obviously, the risk of a burglary is larger in a corner house than in a house in the middle of a block. This means that we end up

Figure 3.2: Example neighbourhood layout for systematic sample with inadequate periodicity

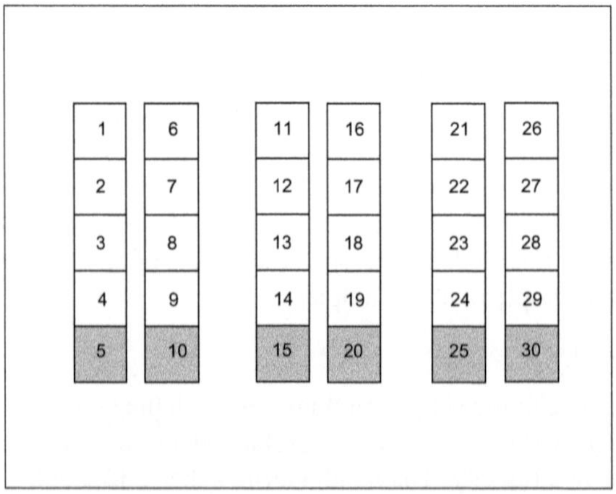

with a sample in which people who live in corner houses (that may be assumed to be special) are overrepresented and people who live in ordinary in-between houses are underrepresented. Because of this, the sample is not representative of the neighbourhood.

So, in this case it might be better to change the periodicity of the sample and for instance sample every 4th house (in which case you end up with a larger sample), or every 6th house (in which case you end up with a smaller sample), or sample every 4th house three times and next sample every 6th house three times (in which case you end up with a sample of 6 as planned). See Figure 3.3 that gives the last solution.

(3) *Stratified sample*

Let us return to an example that we gave above, the example of male and female police suspects. We said that if we drew a flat random sample of 100 respondents it might occur by chance that we ended up with only 5 female suspects. Five respondents is too small a number to draw meaningful inferences from: statements such as '40% of female suspects have committed a violent offence' are based on just two respondents – had it been not 2, but 3 females who had committed a violent offence the percentage would have shot up to 60%. So, if we want to make meaningful inferences about this smaller segment in the population, we have to ensure that we have sufficient numbers of females.

There are two ways to go about this. Sticking with the example, we could randomly draw 85 male respondents from the population of male suspects and similarly draw – at random – 15 female suspects from the population of female suspects. In this way, we have forced the sample to have the same proportional representation of males and females as we know is present in the population. The males and females are

Figure 3.3: Example neighbourhood layout for systematic sample

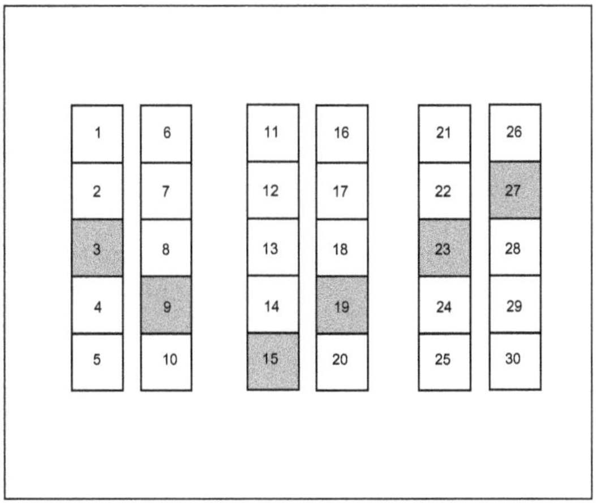

considered a 'layer' or *stratum*, and from each layer a sample is then drawn of the requested size. This kind of sampling is called stratified sampling.

Obviously, in this example, 15 female respondents is also not a lot to make stable inferences about. It might actually be best if we had 50 males and 50 females, so that we could investigate both groups of suspects with the same precision. So, what we could also do, is randomly draw 50 female suspects from the total population of female suspects, and another 50 males from the population of male suspects. This kind of stratified sampling is called *disproportionate stratified sampling* – as opposed to the previous kind that constituted proportionate stratified sampling. Obviously, now the ratio of males to females has been changed, which means that – while we can carry out computations within each layer – we cannot compute averages over the strata just like that. If we would for instance want to know how many offences suspects have committed on average, we cannot use the sample mean for that: there are too many female suspects in the sample, the sample is not representative of the population of suspects anymore. This can however be solved by *reweighting* the data. If for instance men have committed on average 2 previous offences, and women on average 1, we can compute the mean as $2\times85/100 + 1 \times 15/100 = 1.85$.

Stratified sampling is often used when the population under investigation is heterogeneous in the sense that it consists of several qualitatively different groups of unequal sizes. If we want to study each group with similar precision, the smallest groups are oversampled, and for generalising sample findings the results 'weighted back' afterwards.

(4) *Cluster sample*

Cluster samples (also referred to as two-stage sampling) are used very often, also in studies of victimisation of international crimes. The reason for that is that they save a lot in terms of time and money, and they can very well be carried out also when precise information about the population distribution is lacking – such as may often be the case in (post-)conflict situations.

To illustrate how a cluster sample works, suppose that we want to interview prisoners – we are for instance interested to know how well they adapt to prison life. In the Netherlands, on any given day, about 10,000 persons are detained. There are about 30 penitentiary institutions. Some are larger, some are smaller. A centralized list of detainees is maintained that keeps track of admissions, transferrals to other institutions, and discharge, so that there is a sampling frame. This means that in principle it would be very easy to draw a simple random sample. If we would want a random sample of 200 detainees, we could simply number the detainees on the central list and draw them using random numbers. However, if we would do that, it would mean that we probably would have to visit almost each and every penitentiary institution in the Netherlands. Even though the Netherlands is a tiny country, a lot of travel!

A much more efficient way is the following. We first randomly sample penitentiary institutions, and next draw random samples of detainees from those selected institutions. Assuming that each institution is of about equal size this generates a random sample: each institution has an equal chance of being selected for the sample, and within each institution again each detainee has an equal chance. Obviously, this is much more efficient. If we want to interview 200 detainees, we could simply randomly select 5 detention facilities, and from each interview 40 randomly selected detainees. That would save a lot in traveling time and costs. Of course in reality detention facilities are not of exactly equal size (so that detainees in smaller facilities have a bigger chance to end up in the sample), but that can be easily accommodated: we can simply give each detention facility a sampling chance proportional to its size.

Cluster samples thus have huge advantages, in terms of feasibility and cost. There is of course a price to pay, as in research methodology just as in daily life for every gain usually a price is to be paid. This has to do with the fact that every time we sample, we introduce sampling error.

Also in a flat random sample we may find – by chance – relatively tall Dutch, or suspects with a relatively high number of previous offences. Such sampling error is all in the game: we know that the price we pay for not investigating each and every population member is uncertainty. We know that when we generalize the findings in the sample to the population, there is always a margin of uncertainty because of sampling error.

However, if we sample twice (as we do in our example cluster sample: once over penitentiary institutions and again over detainees within those centers), we essentially accumulate sampling error. It might for instance be that by chance we have selected institutions with a lot of staff turnover and an unfavourable prison climate, and that in second instance that we have selected – by chance again – within those institutions, those individuals who have the biggest problems adapting to prison life. The fact that we sample in two steps, exposes us twice to sampling error. And sampling error in first instance is then in a sense 'multiplied' by sampling error in second instance. For that reason, results from cluster samples are more susceptible to sampling error, and estimates, one could say, more 'volatile'.

To illustrate this, think of the following example. If I draw 100 different flat random samples, each time from the same population, I will also get 100 different sample means and therefore 100 different estimates of the population mean. Given that the sample is of reasonable size, these 100 estimates are likely to cluster around the population mean. They fluctuate, but are likely to fluctuate just a bit around the population mean. If I however draw 100 cluster samples, I am likely to end up with 100 estimates that differ more: while I will also get 100 different sample means, these are likely to be more extreme. I may have interviewed 100 badly adapted prisoners in nasty prisons in one sample, who are obviously in a bad mood, but perhaps 100 well-adapted prisoners in model prisons in another cluster sample, who may be quite perky. The means from these cluster samples are therefore likely to fluctuate considerably around the population mean.

Such volatility or as it is called *noise* is especially likely to occur if members of clusters resemble each other. To understand what happens, imagine that we have a cluster sample existing of m clusters, with b respondents per cluster (so $b \times m$ sample members, generally written as N). Now, if we add one extra sample member, from one of our clusters, this gives us in principle more information on the population (we now observe more population members). However, suppose now that cluster members are very much alike. Then, adding a sample member from a cluster that is already present in the sample doesn't give that much extra information, as persons in a cluster are very much alike. Loosely speaking, adding one extra person from the same cluster gives us only a bit more on top of what we already knew.

Practice indeed shows that cluster members often share characteristics. Cluster members are more alike than population members from different clusters. This implies that if we draw a cluster sample of, say, 100 respondents from 5 clusters, we will have less information about the population than if we had drawn 100 respondents in a flat random sample from the population. Formulated differently, even though we may have 100 sample members in a cluster sample, the information contained in that sample is actually worth less, as with every additional cluster member we have sampled more of the same. This means that we will have more uncertainty in estimating for instance a population mean than if we had employed a flat random sample of the same size.

This fact – cluster members tend to be similar – leads to an unfortunate consequence, the so-called *design effect*. By this design effect we mean that estimates based on a cluster sample tend to be more volatile than estimates based on a flat random sample. This is due to the fact that cluster members resemble each other.

The design effect, usually abbreviated as DEFF, is expressed as a number that reflects the increase in variability of our estimates (and therefore our imprecision) due to the fact that a cluster sample has been chosen – relative to the variability that we would have had had we chosen a simple random sample. So, if DEFF = 3, this means that the variability is thrice that of a simple random sample of the same size. If DEFF is

1.40, this means that the variance is 40% increased – as DEFF is a ratio, a DEFF of 1 would indicate no difference. DEFF is computed as:

$$\text{DEFF} = 1 + \rho \times (b - 1),$$

with ρ the so-called intra-class correlation, a measure that reflects here the extent to which members from the same cluster resemble each other, and b the cluster size.

Note that if ρ is 0, in which case cluster membership does not make sample members more alike, then – as it should – DEFF becomes 1, i.e. there is no difference in variability between the cluster sample and a flat random sample. Note also that if $b = 1$, in which case the clusters have size 1 so that effectively we have a flat random sample, then also – as should be the case – DEFF becomes 1. As a rule of thumb, we find DEFF values higher than 3 problematic.

Now why exactly does this design effect lead to imprecision of our estimates, or differently said, to variability of our estimates? Let us make the previous example more specific and add numbers to it. We are as we said interested to measure prisoners' moods. We want to know whether they are depressed or not. If we would draw a simple random sample of, say, 200 prisoners, we might find that their average depression score is 5. If we would draw a new random sample of 200 prisoners, that outcome might differ a bit, it might be 4.9, or 5.1, or even 5.3 or 4.7. As we are drawing a sample, chance would give us a different sample each time, with slightly different results. That is the uncertainty we have to accept. That uncertainty is reflected in the variability of our estimates. Of course, in reality we will never draw several (or even 100) samples, but if we would, this is what would happen.

We now draw instead of a flat random sample (where we need to travel to perhaps 27 different penitentiary institutions, all over the country), a cluster sample. We draw by chance (proportional to their size) two penitentiary institutions, and we select 200 prisoners, 100 at random from each of those two institutions. It might be (chance is at work) that we drew two institutions with harsh regimes, large staff turnover, bad food, located far away from public transport. This affects the prisoners' mood. So we now find a mean of 8.3, the prisoners are on average quite depressed.

If we would redo the cluster sampling, and we again select just two institutions from which we then draw 200 prisoners to interview, we might, however, by chance end up with two glitzy new facilities: good food, closer to a metro station so good for visits, open regimes. Prisoners feel much better now, and we end up with a sample mean of 2.2. If we would redo the cluster sampling numerous times, we would all in all find a much broader band across which sample means vary: there is more variability.

What these examples show is that in a cluster sample, the selection of just a few clusters is in fact tricky business: we are vulnerable to ending up with one or two particularly nice or particularly nasty facilities. As a flat random sample generally makes us travel to many facilities, that risk is very much mitigated: we are likely to sample a bit from every kind of institution. If we would draw 100 simple random samples, the sample mean depression scores from those samples would vary much less than the mean depression scores of 100 cluster samples. We therefore say that cluster sampling gives more 'noisy' results.

Some researchers use instead of DEFF a measure called DEFT, which is nothing else than the square root of DEFF:

$$\text{DEFT} = \sqrt{\text{DEFF}}.$$

As DEFF relates to the variance in the sample, DEFT relates to the standard deviation (viz. chapter 6.3.2). DEFT can be interpreted as the increase in the standard deviation of the estimate relative to its standard deviation had a simple random sample been drawn. All in all, whether DEFF or DEFT is used, both are indicative of the precision-price you pay for the money you save in drawing a cluster sample. We elaborate on DEFF and DEFT in section 3.7.

Many surveys, especially in human rights monitoring and health surveillance, use cluster samples. This is mainly so for pragmatic reasons. Unfortunately, the key variables of interest generally tend to be fairly heavily clustered. Children in the same camp tend to have similar health status, either because the camp has just been settled, or because in this camp there is a fairly regular food supply, or there is a good water supply close by, etc. Neighbourhoods (that typically are used as clusters) can usually be ranked socio-economically: towns as well as IDP camps have nicer and less nice neighbourhoods as well as shanty towns, and people from one neighbourhood therefore will tend to be alike also in socio-economic status.

DEFF measures are computed *per variable*. So, separate DEFFs exist for income, for nutrition status, for physical handicap, for victimisation. Note that this implies that the DEFF may be high for one variable but need not be so for another: people living in the same area of an IDP camp will tend to be alike in socio-economic status but need not be alike in the type of physical disability they have.

As a general rule, many studies on victimisation in the course of violent conflicts employ at least 30 clusters, to keep the design effect within acceptable limits. Often, 7 units per cluster are assessed, resulting in a sample size of a little over 200 (30×7). Another internationally accepted scheme (Vogt, Heudtlass, & Guha-Sapir, 2011) is the '30×30' scheme, which implies that 30 clusters of 30 respondents each are selected, resulting in a sample size N of 900. Below (section 3.7) we will outline the statistical reasons for these rules.

We show some figures to illustrate simple random sampling, systematic sampling and cluster sampling for a situation where a camp with Internally Displaced Persons (IDPs) has to be surveyed. As can be seen, both the random sample (Figure 3.4) and the systematic sample (Figure 3.5) have an N of 19; the cluster sample (Figure 3.6) in this example simply selects two clusters and thus leads in this example to a much larger sample size (obviously we could have chosen to select 10 sample members from each). Note that for both the simple and the systematic sample the spread over the camp is pretty nice: for the systematic sample the area in the bottom left is perhaps a little less represented but such things

Figure 3.4: Fictional example of a random sample in IDP camp

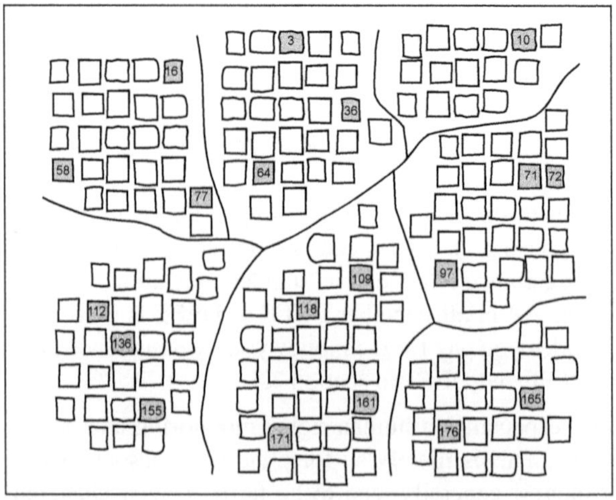

Figure 3.5: Fictional example of a systematic sample in IDP camp

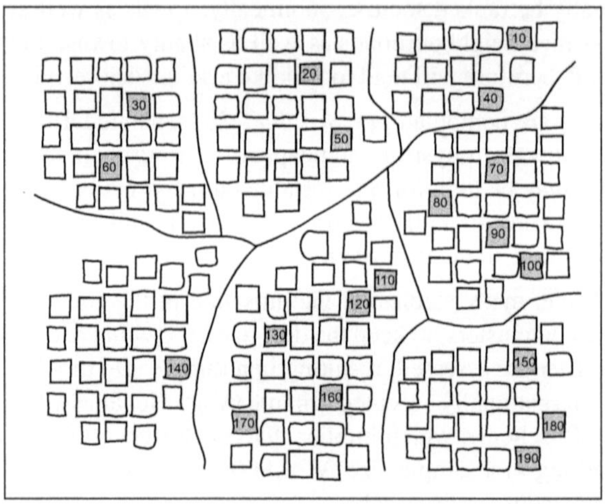

are bound to happen by chance. The cluster sample has a reasonable geographical spread as well (of course what could easily have happened is that we would have ended up with two adjacent neighbourhoods which may be less desirable as they may be alike in terms of relying on the same polluted water source etc.). There may be differences between neighbourhoods that we would want our sample to capture so that we would like the clusters to be wider apart geographically. However, as we need to sample randomly to ensure that our sample passes the litmus test, we cannot force this to be so.

Figure 3.6: Fictional example of a cluster sample in IDP camp

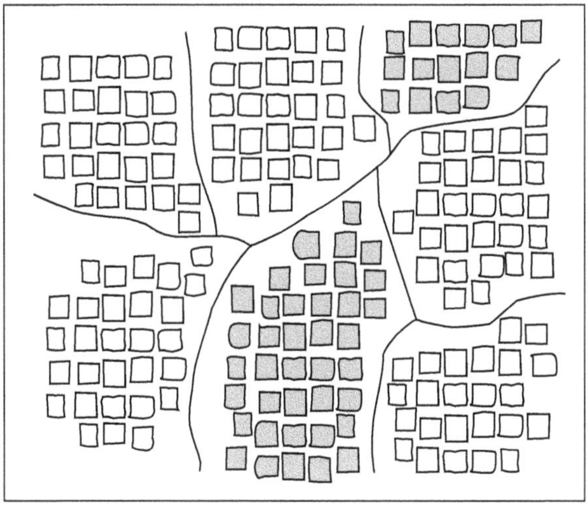

3.3.2 Non-probability sampling

If we cannot draw a random sample, we can always draw a non-random sample, and therewith likely a non-representative one. Reasons to draw a non-probability sample may be that there is no sampling frame. For instance, we may want to interview illegal migrants – persons who are typically not registered with official institutions. Other reasons for not drawing a representative sample may be that we do not have the time or resources to do so. Or the study may be just a first pilot study, or researchers may simply be lazy, sometimes combined with there being no need to generalize to a population: we may for instance be studying phenomena deemed universal in people, such as physiological reactions.

As said, it is not the case that non-probability samples are never representative. They may very well be, and some non-probability samples may in fact be quite adequate or almost representative. We however do not have the guarantee of representativeness that we would have if we would draw a probability sample, meaning that we also cannot rely on statistical sampling theory (see chapter 7).

We will now discuss four generally distinguished types of non-probability samples. There are clear quality differences. The least sophisticated is clearly the convenience sample. For some situations, the snowball sample approaches a probability sample and has good generalizability properties.

(5) *Convenience sample*

The first type of non-probability sample that we discuss is the *convenience sample*. It is also encountered under other names, namely as the *accidental sample*, *availability sample* or *haphazard sample*. These terms make clear that the convenience sample is not a very sophisticated type of sample. When one draws a convenience sample, one simply selects for the sample whomever is available, whomever is 'at hand'. The best example of a convenience sample is the sample that consists of university students: university researchers have such sample members at arms' length, in loads and on the cheap. In that sense, one could also say that the convenience sample is a lazy sample. For that matter, the term 'accidental sample' is perhaps less apt, as it seems to imply that some chance or random phenomenon is in operation to form the sample.

Convenience samples can be drawn in many contexts. We already mentioned the students who are very often used in smaller-scale experiments. Other examples are interviews with visitors of a shopping mall, or sending questionnaires to the readership of a journal. Samples in which respondents self-select, such as after a call, or by registering on a website, are also considered convenience samples. Self-selection is a clear marker of risk for non-randomness and likely unrepresentativeness.

Clearly, given the manner in which it is drawn, the convenience sample offers no perspective whatsoever of representativeness. If representativeness is important and a convenience sample has been drawn, it is very important to describe the manner in which the sample was drawn, and detail in what way the sample might be representative of (a part of) the population, as well as in what way biases might have occurred.

This does not mean that convenience samples are always a bad choice. Clearly, if a questionnaire needs to be tested, or a pilot study carried out, or an exploratory study is all that is asked for, a convenience sample may be a perfectly efficient choice. In such cases there is no need for representativeness – so why go to all the trouble? Also, it may be that we are testing universal human properties that are not affected by social class or intelligence, such as visual memory. Or, we may be investigating the association between a certain instruction A and B, and behaviour during an experiment, in which case we do not want to generalize to a population as such but are rather interested in comparing the group that had instruction A with the group that had instruction B, within the sample. Also, it may be the case that the easily available respondents, such as students or shoppers at a supermarket, are precisely the ones a researcher in interested in, for instance for studying student jobs, or sexual violence in fraternities and sororities, or for studying shoppers' awareness of discounts.

(6) *Quota sample*

The second type of non-probability sample we discuss is the quota sample. A quota sample is a non-probability sample that attempts to mitigate some of the drawbacks of the convenience sample by assuring that the distribution of relevant properties in the sample is similar to their distribution in the population. So, as an example, assume that we want to study 100 police suspects. We do not have a lot of time and/or money so we interview all suspects who have been held by the police and subsequently released: when they leave the police station we ask them whether we may interview them. Obviously, this is not a representative sample. Some suspects are transferred to jail after arrest or to psychiatric wards, and we miss out on those. However, given that we know that 15% of police suspects are female and 85% male, we can ensure that our 100 interviewed suspects have the same gender distribution, by interviewing 15 females and 85 males. Once we have interviewed 85 males, we then interview only females to arrive at a quota sample that has the same gender distribution as the population.

The quota sample is like a stratified sample in the sense that per stratum a desired number of sample members is drawn: the researcher attempts to guarantee that the relative representation of certain properties of sample members is as it is in the population. The manner in which that is achieved is however much less rigorous than in a regular probabilistic sampling procedure: there is no random sampling within strata. For that matter, the quota sample is also often referred to as the non-probabilistic cousin of the stratified sample.

(7) *Purposive sample*

In a purposive sample, sample members are selected because they have certain properties. For instance, they may be members of a notorious street gang, or they may be aid workers in a conflict zone. These categories of people have especially relevant, valid, in-depth, unique information that is of use to the researcher interested in street gangs, or aid workers in a particular conflict. In a sense, such sample members are selected as 'non-randomly' as possible – they are targeted as they are expected to have relevant information. Such respondents are also sometimes referred to as *key informants*, as they literally hold the key to the inaccessible topic or sphere. For that reasons, this sample is also sometimes referred to as a *targeted* sample.

Purposive samples are used often in qualitative research. De Jong (2007) carried out ethnographic research among a group of Moroccan young males who had become the police's and social workers' despair. He mingled and part-time 'lived' with this group of Amsterdam-based (male) youngsters of Moroccan descent: he drank with them in their neighbourhood-sheds, hung out with them on the streets, (almost) burglarized with them, did not betray them to the police, smoked with them, for four years. He concluded that it was not their Moroccan 'culture', but rather 'street culture' that was a contributing factor to their high levels of criminality. His sample was definitely not representative, but De Jong was not after broad generalizability. Rather, he wanted to investigate in-depth and *understand* the mechanisms behind the high crime rates of this particular group of young males. Obviously, the implicit assumption (or aspiration) is that the findings do have broader relevance than just the studied group. However, whereas in a probability sample the explicit aim is to arrive at a sample that is representative, in a purposive sample this is not at all the aim, either because it is unnecessary or because it is impossible.

Who should be selected for a purposive sample and when is the purposive sample 'ready' or of sufficient size? In general one seeks for a purposive sample persons who are willing to talk, who are accessible, who have a good overview of what one wants to study either themselves or who give that overview in complementarity with the other sample members. That raises the issue how one can be sure that the persons interviewed provide that overview. To decide on that, mainly qualitative criteria are available. Rubin and Rubin (1995) state that two criteria should be used. The first criterion is whether the set of interviews or observations give a complete overview of the phenomenon under study. As a researcher, obviously one can't be sure about that, so one has to use common sense, reasoning, and the face validity of the data to decide on this.

The second criterion is 'saturation', also referred to as 'theoretical saturation'. What is meant by that is probably best illustrated with the following. When conducting qualitative research using a purposive (or any) sample, there will usually come a point where new respondents don't really add new information. Each new informant tells you things you already got to know from others, reiterates what earlier interviewees told, and as such at most confirms what you already knew. This is what is meant by saturation: the picture becomes clear at a certain point, and adding new respondents does not add on to the collected information, does not change the picture or conclusion. This is also sometimes referred to as *theoretical validity*. This type of sampling is also referred to as *theoretical sampling*.

To enhance the significance of the findings, and to prevent 'cherry picking', some researchers advise to even purposely select cases that seem to deviate from the preliminary conclusions of the research, a practice that is called 'negative-case analysis' or 'deviant-case analysis'. This shows that sampling in qualitative designs is of a different nature than it is in quantitative designs: adding such a 'cherry-picked' negative case to the sample might even be considered as violating all rules of randomness! We return to this topic in chapter 9.

This shows that while in probabilistic samples a researcher can from the outset in a sense 'compute' the required sample size (for example 210, namely 30 clusters × 7 respondents), such advance planning is less or perhaps even entirely not doable when carrying out qualitative research with a purposive sample. It is harder to assess ahead how many interviews one needs: one simply does not know beforehand at what point addition of respondents will stop supplying you new information. As such, planning is also harder in qualitative research. This shows also how qualitative research is steered by the empirical reality one encounters on the ground: it may be that the picture is clear after 20 interviews, but it may as well take 30 or 40 interviews.

A purposive sample is in some cases the only solution. Bijleveld (2003) described the purposive sample that she used, in which respondents gave her as much information as they had on other respondents that were inaccessible to the researcher. Such sampling, i.e. interviewing knowledgeable informants who function as the window to an untreadable empirical realm, is also named *key informant sampling*. Key informant sampling can be very efficient: interviewing just a few gives an overview over many. However, one is also at the key informants' mercy: how can one be sure that they know about the phenomenon and about the inaccessible others, and don't simply feed the researcher juicy bits – that the researcher can never check anyway?

A purposive sample is not generalisable. That need not be a problem if one is interested in one particular group of persons, such as the troublesome youth group De Jong studied (2007). Another way of formulating this is by saying that if one uses a purposive one has actually studied the entire population of interest, i.e., the one particular youth group, or the particular conflict.

(8) *Snowball sample*

The snowball sample is an important type of non-probabilistic sample. It is often used for investigating inaccessible populations, or groups who are extremely shy or mistrusting. Examples are drug addicts, people who work in the illegal labour market, prostitutes or – indeed – criminals. Snowball sampling is also sometimes referred to as 'Respondent-Driven Sampling (RDS)', although respondent-driven sampling is actually a special kind of snowball sampling (see below).

When drawing a snowball sample, one starts with a certain number of accessible respondents (also sometimes called 'starting-respondents' or 'zero-stage respondents'). After interviewing each respondent, one asks the respondent whether he or she knows one or more other respondents who meet eligibility criteria and who might also be interested to be interviewed. The starting respondents are then asked to stimulate these respondents to get into contact with the interviewer, sometimes a small fee is offered. When these 'stage-one' respondents have been interviewed the same procedure is repeated up to a new layer of stage-two respondents, and so forth. When the respondents are extremely shy, the zero-stage respondents may be asked to conduct the interviews themselves with the stage-one respondents. The snowball sample indeed functions as a snowball, onto which more and more clings with each turn. Snowball sampling is a workable and relatively cheap way to study groups of persons who would be unsurveyable otherwise, that is, members of a so-called *hidden population*. It has a number of disadvantages, though.

First, the sampling process may be lengthy: it usually takes a while before respondents have traced new respondents, after which it takes a while before these contact the researcher etc. In addition, members of hidden populations may not lead the most mundane organized lives and for that reason not be the most punctual, so that appointments may have to be rescheduled several times.

A second disadvantage of snowball sampling is that the sample's quality is dependent on the choice of 'zero-stage respondent'. If this person has only a small circle of acquaintances, or does not instil a lot of trust, the trail will quickly run dead. For that reason Wright, Decker, Redfern *et al.* (2001) chose for their study of burglars as a zero-stage respondent someone who was a burglar himself, that is, someone absolutely unassociated with the criminal justice system who was most likely to generate trust in a next wave of respondents.

Third, persons with a large social network have a larger chance of ending up in the sample, and lonely or isolated persons a smaller chance. This means that snowball samples do have a certain bias towards 'more sociable' respondents. Also, respondents after the zero-stage are likely to resemble those who entered them into the sample, as friends and acquaintances tend to be alike too. This means that we will also have cluster effects in a snowball sample. In a statistical sense this implies that the estimates of the pertinent properties we are interested in may also be noisy.

Snowball sampling works from the assumption that all members of the population are sufficiently connected: this is necessary to be able to reach each population member eventually. If that is not the case, for instance when there are isolated 'islands' of subgroups, then respondents on one island will not be reached by snowball sampling starting on other islands. To minimize that risk, it is generally advised to use various zero-stage respondents, preferably from different segments of the population. As said, a precondition for any kind of snowball sampling is that respondents do know each other. For that matter, while much of the drug trade still took place on the street and in drugs dens, drug addicts were a good population for snowball sampling as they are likely to know each other from drugs dealers, methadone buses etc. Persons committing social security fraud on the other hand are less or not likely to know each other.

A variation of snowball sampling is so-called *respondent-driven sampling*, in which a respondent receives coupons that s/he can distribute among prospective new respondents. As soon as a successful interview with a new respondent has been completed, both the old and the new respondent receive some kind of bonus. The advantage is that both the old and the new respondent have an incentive for interviews to be completed: only then is the remuneration rewarded. The second advantage is that the identity of the new respondent remains hidden until the moment the actual interviewing takes place. It is also possible to have the recruiting respondent conduct the interview with the newly recruited respondent, so that extremely fearful respondents do not need to reveal their identity to the researchers. This has several advantages. A first is that it may be safer for the interviewers who now do not need to venture into dangerous parts of inner cities etc. Second, it is possible that some respondents are extremely wary to meet outsiders, but may be willing to be interviewed by recruiters whom they know. Obviously, the researchers must have a way to check the identities of these respondents to be sure that they belong to the target group, and to prevent double interviews or recruiters posing as new respondents.

A good overview of the potential and performance of respondent-driven sampling is given by Heckatorn (1997). Respondent-driven sampling is a flexible and eminently useful method for studying populations that are hard to reach (and with a few more reservations, that pertains to regular snowball sampling too). In simulation studies it has been shown that with a small number of waves – three to five waves appear to be generally sufficient – good coverage over the entire population may be attained.

Bøås and Bjørkhaug (2010) interviewed former youthful combatants from various warring factions in Liberia, in Monrovia (N = 491) and Voinjama (N = 275). The authors constructed their samples through respondent-driven sampling (without, it must be said, giving much information on the methods employed, remuneration given, possible saturation, etc). In Monrovia they conducted the fieldwork in two different sites to achieve a good spread over different warring factions and prevent 'islands' of respondents remaining inaccessible. The authors conclude, amongst others, that most youth led fairly normal lives before joining one of the factions, and that most appeared to be reunified now with their families and reintegrated.

3.3.3 Mixtures and practical issues

Silva and Price (2011) discuss a method that they call *indirect sampling*, in which one selects respondents via key informants (the method is also sometimes referred to as 'the informant method'). This indirect sampling is, one could say, a one-layered version of snowball sampling, or, one could also say, an amalgam of purposive and snowball sampling. Key informants may be community leaders, social workers, or members of a subgroup that it is hard to get access to. This may sound a bit abstract so we will attempt to illustrate it with an example.

Suppose one is interested to assess violent mortality in a certain village. Instead of interviewing door to door, one asks the village leaders the names and addresses of families who experienced a violent death due to the conflict, and one next corroborates with the particular families whether those violent deaths occurred, what the circumstances were, etc. This method is obviously efficient and cheap: instead of surveying a whole village, the village leaders point the researchers to those households where violent deaths occurred. One disadvantage is of course, that if one would want to check how much village leaders actually know, one can only find the false positives (families for whom it was said that a violent death occurred which turns out to be untrue), but not the false negatives. The method is contingent on the assumption that the key informants have complete information on the phenomena the researcher is interested in.

The method was employed in Uganda to estimate rape prevalence (Stark, Roberts, Wheaton *et al.*, 2010). Validation of the study showed that predominantly extramarital rape was well reported, and for instance rape inside marriage less well. Roberts, Morgan, Sultani *et al.* (2010) validated deaths reported by an informant method and found that 45% to 73% was accurately reported, depending on setting and recall period.

The WHO EPI (Expanded Programme on Immunization) program proposed a very simple method to arrive at a cluster sample. Suppose one is interested to assess the prevalence of a certain phenomenon in a certain region. To assess this using a cluster sample, one follows the following procedure. One draws up a list of settlements (villages, camps), and records their sizes. Next, one randomly selects a number of clusters (i.e. settlements), with selection probability proportional to size – referred to in epidemiological publications as 'PPS sampling'. At that stage one has a list of selected settlements, and next needs to select respondents from within each settlement. Subsequently, one draws up lists of population members per selected cluster, and draws sample members from those lists.

A pragmatic approach to sample respondents in this second stage – after the clusters have been selected in the first stage – is the so-called 'spin-the-pen'-method (also referred to as the 'EPI-method'). This method entails that the researcher stands in the center of each selected cluster, and spins a pen (or a bottle or any other item). Once the pen stops, it points in a certain direction. Next, the researcher numbers the houses along this direction or virtual line from the center of the settlement to its perimeter, and selects houses in systematic fashion (if 7 respondents are needed from the cluster, and 140 houses are counted from the center to the perimeter, every 20th house is selected, and a respondent selected from that house). Researchers have also chosen a random point along the line, and interviewed respondents in all adjacent houses. This method (selecting clusters proportional to size and then sampling along a random direction from the cluster centers) is highly efficient, as one does not need to know the names of all population members but only the sizes of the clusters, and as the procedure is easy to carry out. Even if census lists are dated, one can carry out the procedure – under the assumption of similar growth or shrinkage of settlements – as it is the relative size of clusters that counts in the proportionate sampling of clusters.

The EPI-sampling of respondents within the clusters does not, however, give a completely representative sample: houses close to the center of the cluster have a higher probability of being selected. It is for that reason that other sampling methods have been proposed for the second stage of this EPI-method, that do guarantee representativeness. One solution would be to draw up a complete list of households, randomly select one, and interview household members from this and all adjacent households. Other solutions are to draw a 'spiral' through the settlement and sample systematically along the coil.

While this method was proposed to be able to sample efficiently in less developed countries, Frerichs and Shaheen (2001) show that the method is also efficient and effective in developed countries. The entire cycle (drawing the clusters and drawing respondents from the clusters) amounts to a combination of cluster and systematic or random sampling, or cluster and cluster sampling depending on what one chooses for the second stage. Such combinations of cluster sampling with other types of sampling occur quite often in practice, even combinations of probability with non-probability sampling can be found.

3.4 Bias and noise

In the previous paragraphs we have at several places encountered the terms 'bias' and 'noise'. What is meant by these terms?

Roughly speaking, noise reflects variability. If we are trying to measure the height of Dutch citizens, and if there is a lot of variation around the population mean in the samples that we can hypothetically draw, then we have a *noisy* sample. The sample members' averages vary a lot around the true population score that we are interested in. On average, though, combined over all samples, they may provide a good estimate of the population mean.

Suppose however that sample means do not reflect the population mean: sample means are consistently lower than the population mean, or consistently higher. Then our sample means are *biased.* The sample averages then differ systematically from the population mean: they are most of the time lower, or most of the time higher. Even if we are not bothered by noise, a biased sample mean is not very useful: it does not give us a valid estimate of the population mean. This means that a biased sample is not a representative sample: it does not reflect the properties of the population.

Does that mean that a noisy sample is therefore always better than a biased sample? Yes and no. A biased sample is not very useful as it does not tell us the properties of the population. A sample that is only noisy gives at least (if we would draw a large number of samples) on average an unbiased estimate of the population mean. A noisy sample however gives problems: in practice we namely do not draw a large number of samples and repeat our analysis many times. We draw one sample. So if we have a noisy sample, our estimate may still be very far 'off', even if there is no bias. We will discuss these and related issues much more formally in chapter 7 below.

Figure 3.7: Visual representations of bias and noise

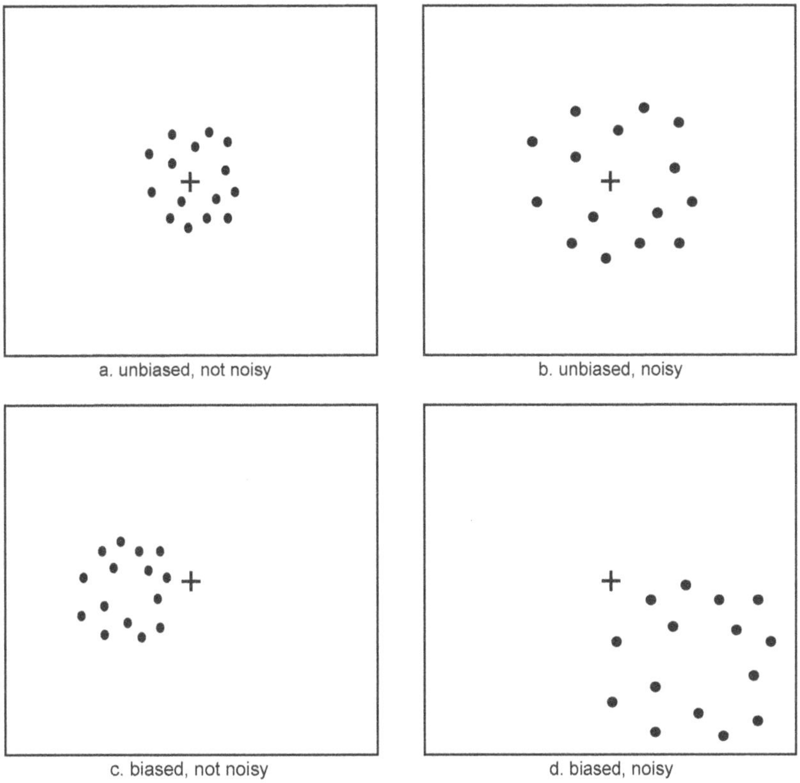

For now, it is important to remember that both noise as well as bias are a nuisance in samples. Samples can be noisy, samples can be biased and obviously samples can be noisy as well as biased. Ideally we would want samples to be both unbiased as well as not noisy.

Figure 3.7 is a visual aid to understand the concepts bias and noise; each picture should be viewed as a bull's eye that we try to hit with a pistol or with darts. The bull's eye represents the true population mean that we want to estimate, and the holes made by the bullets or darts represent the sample means that give us estimates of that population mean. In this figure, the upper left situation (a) is one where there is no bias and little noise: the cross '+' indicates where the bull's eye/population mean is, and we can see that the hits/sample means, indicated as '.', cluster closely around the population mean and would on average equal the population mean. In the upper right situation (b) there is more noise: the sample means spread much more around the population mean but, on average, the measurements would tell us what the population mean is. In the lower left situation (c), there is bias: the average of the sample means is off, and most individual sample means are off too: the sample means deviate systematically from the population value. In the lower right situation (d) finally, there is bias as well as noise: the sample means are systematically to the right of where they should be, and they also vary a lot.

3.5 Sample size

So far, we have spoken of samples and populations. As we said, in many cases the population is simply too large to investigate member by member, and we therefore have to make do with samples. We therefore 'draw' a sample, a group of members of the population, ideally at random, and what we find in the sample we declare to be generalisable to the population. Obviously, samples are smaller than the population. But how small may a sample be, or how large exactly should a sample be?

It is not so that sample size is always determined by strict, iron-fist rules. In practice, a lot depends on the amount of money and time available, and on the type of question asked. If we conduct qualitative research (see chapter 2 and chapter 9), sample size depends on 'saturation' and 'coverage'. In practice, researchers decide while their research is ongoing whether they do not need additional sample members to study. Qualitative samples vary in size between 1 and a few hundred (and seldom more). Because qualitative research is generally much more time-intensive, truly large sample sizes are extremely rare. Sample sizes of 20 to 30 are common.

Quantitative researchers often work with samples of between 100 to 300, to in some cases 500 or even more respondents. There are various statistical issues that may aid in determining the desired sample size for investigating a certain research question with a certain precision. We will return to these issues in section 3.7 below. Before delving into such statistical particularities, a few basic guidelines may help in understanding issues of sample size.

Firstly, very generally speaking, the larger the sample – assuming it was drawn randomly – the more the sample can tell us about the population. This is logical. Suppose that a sample constitutes about 1% of the population. Anything we measure about that sample, say its mean, may fluctuate quite a bit depending on the sample we accidentally happen to draw, and – although this is not very likely – it can theoretically even be quite far off the mark. Suppose now however that the sample size increases, to for instance 10% of the population. Again, theoretically speaking, it is still possible that the mean we find for the sample is quite different from the mean in the population, but as we are measuring so many more people, the sample mean can only be closer to the population mean. Suppose now that our sample is 50% (or even 60%, 70% – or say a whopping 90% of the population) now the sample mean approaches the population mean more and more as we are examining larger and larger chunks out of the population! It is with for instance 50% highly improbable that the sample mean would be very far off the real population mean, and it becomes impossible as we measure 80 or 90% of respondents. Thus: the larger the sample, the better that sample helps us to infer something about the population. The larger the sample, the more precisely we measure. Bigger is better. In terms of noise: larger samples are less noisy.

This is of course intuitively true: if we investigate more members of the population, we know more about the population, and then we are able to make more precise statements about that population. Adding more sample members adds more information and can thus only improve our analysis. This however, does not help us much in practical situations. Because – while larger is better – how large is then exactly large enough? We will return to this issue below, in section 3.7.

Even though we thus are not very precise as to sample size yet, a second general rule is that the number of so-called 'disaggregations' one would like to make, also determines the required size. What is meant by that?

Suppose that one is interested to know the number of offences that people have committed. One could investigate 100 persons, and find that on average they have committed 0.7 offences the past year. But now suppose that one would want to disaggregate this by men and women, and not only by men and women, but also by age – investigating young men and young women and older men and older women. Now, assuming age and gender are distributed evenly, this would mean that there would be 25 young men, 25 older men, 25 young women etc. Suppose now that I would also be interested to know the differences between persons with low and high educational level. Then, the groups would be divided up once more, into groups of about 12 to 13 persons – generally referred to as 'cells'. And suppose now that I also have reasons to believe that ethnicity plays a role: then my groups would dwindle down to about 6. Clearly any differences between the groups now become shaky: what if I find that 1 out of 6 young Dutch highly educated women committed an offence the past year, against 4 out of 6 young Dutch highly educated men? How confidently can I report that the chance to have committed an offence increases fourfold from one group to the other? Obviously, one more criminal young Dutch highly educated man would make the risk to be an offender actually five-fold – and reversely one criminal young Dutch highly educated man less would render the ratio to be three-fold. Because the groups that I compare have become so small, any statements depend heavily on small numbers: one man or one woman extra or less committing an offence can greatly affect the percentages, so that we may have sweepingly different conclusions, depending on just one or two sample members. The findings become *unstable*, so to say. In such cases, differences will also not likely turn up significant.

Clearly, the fact that one wants to compare so many groups, makes it necessary to start out with a larger sample: one would not want to make too strong statements based on just one or two sample members being criminal or not. In general, as a rough rule of thumb it is assumed that the number of respondents per cell, i.e. per group one wishes to compare, should not be less than 20 to 30. This means that if one wants to investigate just two cells, 40 to 60 respondents would be an absolute minimum, for comparing four groups 80 to 120 respondents would be needed, and if one wants to make so many subdivisions as in the example below that one would be comparing 16 different cells, 320 to 480 sample members would be needed. This is a very rough rule of thumb.

Summarising, we note that for qualitative studies, sample size is dictated by 'information gain' or saturation, meaning that sample size can generally only be decided as the research proceeds. For practical reasons, though, sample sizes tend to be smaller here than in quantitative research. For quantitative studies, larger samples are chosen to produce more precise estimates of the properties of the population. Also we note that if we want to investigate more in-depth and compare several subdivisions of the sample, for reasons of stability we need a larger sample. This applies to both qualitative and quantitative studies.

3.6 Sample nonresponse and representativeness

Above we said that samples are a part of a population. Instead of investigating all population members, we investigate only part of the population. If we choose that part, our sample, wisely, we make the sample resemble the population. Drawing random samples guarantees representativeness. Obviously, there is uncertainty, as we have not investigated each and every sample member, but statistics will help us deal with that uncertainty in a sensible and accepted way. Thus, the path to scientific research seems not too hard: we simply draw a random sample out of a population, interview or otherwise assess the sample members, do some statistical wizardry, and write it up to tell our captivated readers what's going on in the population!

Life is unfortunately not that uncomplicated. Suppose that in some quantitative study, we have been able to compile a list of sample members, drawn at random from the population. This means we have a random sample and may generalise the sample results to the population. We start approaching sample members, ringing their doorbells or telephoning them, asking them to participate. Two complications will quickly arise. First, we will be unable to contact all respondents: some will simply never be at home, or will never answer their phone. Secondly, not all those we establish contact with, will consent to participate. Some will say that they are too busy, are not interested, do not like the funding agency for the research. Some may simply be too ill to collaborate. These two mechanisms generate what is called *nonresponse* or *sample nonresponse*.

In almost all practical situations, sample nonresponse occurs. Depending on the topic of the study, the infrastructural possibilities, the persuasive skills of interviewers and the like, nonresponse rates in surveys generally hover between 20 and 50 to even 60% or 90%. This means that if we start out with an intended sample of 100 respondents, we may end up with just 40 (or fewer) completed and thus successful interviews, a so-called *retention rate* of 40%, and a so-called *attrition rate* of 60%. One might be tempted to think that this is not a real problem, as we could simply draw a larger initial sample, of say 250, and then end up with 100 interviewed respondents, reaching our planned sample size.

Unfortunately, this does not solve the problem that nonresponse generates. The problem is namely not just that we are left with fewer respondents, the problem is that nonresponse is generally not accidental. It is not a coincidence that certain respondents do not end up in our realised, interviewed sample. It is the weak and the elderly who are too ill to be interviewed, it is the distrustful, those who are afraid to talk to strangers or the busy bees with working weeks of 80 hours who refuse to talk to us. The final realised sample thus generally contains an overrepresentation of younger and middle-aged persons, of persons from less urbanised areas, and an underrepresentation of the elderly, of townspeople, of people employed in very busy management positions. In addition, those who refuse to be interviewed generally have more extreme perceptions of the topic under study. Thus it is probably the fervent religious opponents of abortion or those who believe that abortion is simply anyone's right, who will be underrepresented in our survey of citizens' views on abortion.

All in all, even if we start out with a randomly drawn list of sample members, the non-random attrition process will leave us with a non-random selection of the original random sample. Formulated more loosely: nonresponse messes up the representativeness of the sample. One might be tempted to think that this is a phenomenon particularly problematic when doing surveys with 'live' people to be interviewed, who can be ill and who may say 'no'. Attrition however also plays a role when studying for instance court files or treatment dossiers. Court files of defendants who have their case up for review are typically 'traveling' and therefore not to be found in the archive, the treatment files of recidivists may have been requested for inspection by the investigating psychiatrist or psychologist. Thus, also here, it is the particular, a-typical files that will be missed and a non-representative part of the original sample that will be left for inspection by us.

Nonresponse is essentially irreparable. One can inspect the resulting sample and see whether it resembles the population on background characteristics such as age, gender, geographical origin and the like. If there are no serious differences, that is, if the realised sample resembles the population on such background characteristics, then that is more comforting than if we had found there were differences. This 'background variables check' however does not tell you whether the non-responders differ from the responders on the key variables of interest, central to the main research question.

If there are differences between the realised sample and the population, another option would be to reweight the data. What is meant by that is best illustrated by an example. Suppose that it turns out that our realised sample has fewer females than there are in the population. We could then (assuming that the females who did respond are representative of all females – something which is unlikely) give the females' answers more weight than the males' answers, by counting their answers double or something else proportional to their underrepresentation. This solves the problem only if we have too few respondents of one kind. If we miss one kind of respondent altogether (for instance, we were unable to reach any pensioners), there is no way we could correct for this by reweighting, as we do not have pensioners at all! There is no way we can know what kind of answers to multiply and add to the existing ones, we miss such people altogether.

Reweighting has other disadvantages too. The easiest one to imagine is that findings become unstable, as they become heavily dependent on the few respondents of the underrepresented category who have been assessed. Suppose that females are underrepresented and that we have only one female respondent, and 50 males. In that case, we would in a sense have to 'multiply' this lone female's answers by 50 and add them to the dataset. The single female who is in our dataset now determines what all cloned females in our dataset report. Had we by chance interviewed another female, the 'female response' could have been wildly different.

It should be noted that in longitudinal studies where respondents are followed over time, any so-called *drop-out* that occurs, accumulates over waves. So, if we miss, say, 20% of our intended sample at wave 1, meaning we retain 80%, experiencing the same drop-out at wave 2 implies that we will then be left with 64% of our original respondents. Should such *attrition* occur similarly at wave 3, we would then be left with around 50% of our original sample.

By far the best is to prevent nonresponse and its resulting attrition. This is achieved by careful introduction of the study, good training of interviewers, re-visiting of respondents, offering respondents a monetary incentive, and more, which we will detail in chapter 4 below.

3.7 Technicalities: DEFF revisited and sample size

This section details some technicalities regarding the design effect and sample size. It is best read after studying chapter 7 and section 6.4.

In section 3.3.1 above, we discussed the design effect. We defined it as:

$$\text{DEFF} = 1 + \rho \times (b - 1),$$

with ρ the so-called intra-class correlation and b cluster size. We noted that if ρ is 0, in which case cluster membership does not make sample members have similar scores, then – as it should be – DEFF becomes 1, i.e. there is no difference in variability of the estimates between the cluster sample and an ordinary flat random sample. Note also that if b =1, in which case the clusters have size 1 so that effectively we have a flat random sample, then also – as should be the case – DEFF becomes 1.

We will in this last section become more specific. We will introduce a few more formulas and also show how we can, using an expected design effect and an expected value for the property we are interested in, pre-determine the sample size that is needed for achieving a certain precision.

First we introduce some more formulas. Remember that for each variable DEFF may differ. We therefore first write DEFF more specifically as :

$$\text{DEFF}(Y_k) = 1 + \rho_k \times (b - 1)$$

with Y_k the variable for which we want to compute the DEFF, ρ_k the intraclass correlation for the particular variable k, and b the size of the clusters. If we want to compute DEFF, we need a formula for ρ_k. This formula is:

$$\rho_{Y\,k} = \frac{b}{b-1} \times \frac{C^{-1}\sum_{c=1}^{C}(\bar{Y}_{kc} - \bar{Y}_k)^2}{s^2_{Y_k}} - \frac{1}{b-1},$$

with b the size of clusters, C the total number of clusters, $\bar{Y}_{kc}$ the mean value of Y_k in cluster c, $\bar{Y}_k$ the overall mean of the variable Y_k, and $s^2_{Y_k}$ the variance of Y_k.

Let us illustrate this with a small example. Suppose that we have 7 clusters of 30 respondents each, and that the means of Y_k for the clusters are: 2.7, 2.8, 2.9, 3.0, 3.1, 3.2, 3.3. The overall mean is therefore 3.0. Suppose for ease of computation that $s^2_{Y_k}$ equals 1. We can now compute $\rho_{Y\,k}$ as:

$$\frac{30}{30\text{ - }1} \times \frac{\frac{1}{7}(\text{-}.3^2) + (\text{-}.2^2) + (\text{-}.1^2) + (0^2) + (.1^2) + (.2^2) + (.3^2)}{1} - \frac{1}{30\text{ - }1},$$

that is,

$$\rho_{Y\,k} = \frac{30}{29} \times \frac{\frac{1}{7}\,0.28}{1} - \frac{1}{29} = \frac{30}{29} \times 0.04 - \frac{1}{29} =$$

$$(1.03448 \times 0.04) - .03448 = 0.04138 \text{ - } 0.03448 = 0.0069.$$

The intraclass correlation for this example is thus small, it is in fact almost zero. Suppose now, however, that – all else being equal – the cluster means are 2.5, 2.6, 2.7, 3.0, 3.3, 3.4, 3.5. The overall mean is then the same (3.0) but the cluster means are wider apart. This means that there are more differences between the clusters, and therefore there is stronger clustering. This means that ρ_{Yk} should become larger. Without computations we can see that the intraclass correlation will indeed become larger because the sum of $(\bar{Y}_{kc} - \bar{Y}_k)^2$ will become larger. Suppose now that the reverse is the case, that is – again with all else being equal – the cluster means are 2.8, 2.9, 2.9, 3.0, 3.1, 3.1, 3.2. The overall mean is again the same (3.0) but the cluster means are now more similar. Now cluster membership is less important for respondents' scores, which implies that cluster effects are less strong. It is easy to infer that the intraclass correlation will now become smaller because the sum of $(\bar{Y}_{kc} - \bar{Y}_k)^2$ is smaller.

With the intraclass correlation of 0.0069 that we just computed we can now determine DEFF. Putting all our data in the formula:

$$\text{DEFF}(Y_k) = 1 + \rho_k \times (b - 1)$$

we get:

$$\text{DEFF}(Y_k) = 1 + 0.0069 \times (30 - 1) = 1 + 0.20008 = 1.20008,$$

i.e. indeed a DEFF not dramatically different from 1. Remember that we noted in section 3.3.1 that DEFF should as a rule of thumb not exceed 3. We are, given this small intraclass correlation, even with our relatively small number of clusters (7) and relatively large number of respondents per cluster (30), still safely away from that 'critical' value.

As the formula for DEFF shows, DEFF tends to be higher when the clusters are larger (b), and it tends to be higher when the clusters are more dissimilar and therefore intraclass correlation (ρ_k) is larger. This is reflected in Table 3.1, that lists the value of DEFF for different values of ρ against different cluster sizes. Note that the value we just calculated, namely a DEFF of 1.20008 for a cluster size of 30 and an intraclass correlation of .0069 is indeed in between the values of 1.15 and 1.29 in columns 2 and 3.

The table shows that for remaining under the 'critical' value of 3 for the DEFF – even with these reasonably small intraclass correlations – cluster size should not exceed 30. The table shows that acceptable values for DEFF are found only when either cluster size is small or the intraclass correlation weak. When cluster size is 30, a reasonable DEFF is achieved only with a very weak intraclass correlation (less than 0.1). As we as researchers do not exert any influence over the intraclass correlation, this shows that for research practice, working with small clusters protects against the design effect.

It should be noted that in practice it may be unrealistic to assume such a small intraclass correlation. As Table 3.1 showed, if the intraclass correlation is stronger, a cluster size of 30 may imply that the DEFF will exceed 3. In practice, researchers therefore choose to be on the safe side by working with the reverse set up: relatively many clusters, each of small size. Instead of the '7$\times$ 30' example that we just detailed, an often encountered format is instead '30 $\times$ 7': 30 clusters of size 7 each.

The last thing we need to discuss is sample size. We announced at the beginning of this section that – using an expected value for DEFF and an expected rate for the property

Table 3.1: Cluster sample size, intra-class correlation and design effects

Cluster sample size (n_c)	Intraclass correlation (ρ)					
	0.005	0.01	0.05	0.10	0.20	0.30
1	1.00	1.00	1.00	1.00	1.00	1.00
10	1.05	1.09	1.45	1.90	2.80	3.70
15	1.07	1.14	1.70	2.40	3.80	5.20
20	1.10	1.19	1.95	2.90	4.80	6.70
30	1.15	1.29	2.45	3.90	6.80	9.70
50	1.25	1.49	3.45	5.90	10.80	15.70

Source: Yansaneh (2005), Table II.I

we are interested in – we can compute the sample size we need for measuring the property with a certain precision. This is done using the following formula:

$$N = \frac{(z^2 pq)}{d^2}$$

with z the critical z-value we are using (in many standard situations when we use a 5% type I-error z will be 1.96, see section 7.6.2 and section 7.2.1), p the estimated prevalence of the property we are investigating, q the proportion of observation units who do not have the property, and d the desired relative precision. So if we suppose that 50% of the people we will be interviewing have been victimised during the past year, and we want to estimate this victimisation prevalence within 10 percentage points, and we use an α of 5%, then the formula becomes:

$$N = \frac{(1.96^2 \times 0.5 \times (1 - 0.5))}{0.1^2} = \frac{1.96^2 \times 0.25}{0.1^2} = 96.04,$$

implying that – given these specifications – we need a sample size of 97 to achieve the required relative precision.

Suppose that we would wish to estimate prevalence more precisely, say with 5% relative precision. Intuitively speaking, we know that we would need a larger sample. If we feed these new data into our formula we get:

$$N = \frac{(1.96^2 \times 0.5 \times (1 - 0.5))}{0.05^2} = \frac{1.96^2 \times 0.25}{0.05^2} = 384.16.$$

This shows that if we want to double our relative precision, we need to quadruple our sample size.

These sample sizes are computed on the assumption that DEFF equals 1. What happens with the required sample size if DEFF were not 1, but larger? The required sample size is then simply N multiplied by DEFF:

$$N = \text{DEFF} \times \frac{(z^2pq)}{d^2}.$$

This means that if we, as in the above example, suppose that 50% of the people we will be interviewing have been victimised during the past year, and if we want to estimate this victimisation prevalence within 10 percentage points using an α of 5%, but now in a situation where DEFF equals 2, the formula becomes:

$$N = 2 \times \frac{(1.96^2 \times 0.5 \times (1 - 0.5))}{0.1^2} = \frac{1.96^2 \times 0.25}{0.1^2} = 192.08,$$

so simply twice as large.

Many studies assume that DEFF equals 2, and compute their necessary sample size on the basis of that assumption. Against this light, it is perhaps not unsurprising that the '30× 7' cluster design is so popular: it ensures a safe sample size that is well above 200, and can deal with moderate intraclass correlation. Assuming a design effect of 2 and $p = .5$, sampling 30 clusters of 7 respondents each will give an estimate that is not more than 10% away from the true value, which feels like a comfortable margin.

As the attentive reader will understand, if DEFF turns out to be larger than anticipated (and the researcher can check this only once the research has been completed for each of his variables of interest), the precision will be lower than aimed for. This means that it is generally better to be on the safe side, and to use a slightly larger sample size than strictly necessary. In general, larger clusters do not help much: it is in working with more clusters that safeguards are built in.

But what to do if it is unknown what the prevalence of the central property of interest is? If that prevalence is either very low, or very high (less than 10% or higher than 90%), intuitively speaking we already know that we need fairly large samples to be able to determine prevalence precisely. If the prevalence is unknown but expected to be within the 10%-90% range, it is safest to assume that it is 0.50: in that case the highest N will be prescribed and one can only end up with more precision if the prevalence is actually higher or lower than that 50%. See Figure 3.8 that gives a representation of the relation between prevalence and sample size needed to achieve a certain precision.

Summarising all these formulas in words, we arrive at the following. The design effect is a negative corollary of working with cluster samples. The value of the design effect tells us to what extent the estimates derived from our cluster sample are more variable than if we would have drawn a simple random sample. The design effect is larger when units in clusters are more similar, or, phrased differently, when clusters are more dissimilar. Working with many small clusters protects against the design effect.

The variability reflected in the design effect DEFF can be compensated for by increasing the sample size by the same degree: so, if the design effect in a cluster sample equals 2 for a sample of size N but one wants to achieve the same variability that would be achieved if the design effect equalled 1, one needs to double the sample size to $2N$.

Figure 3.8: Relation between prevalence and sample size

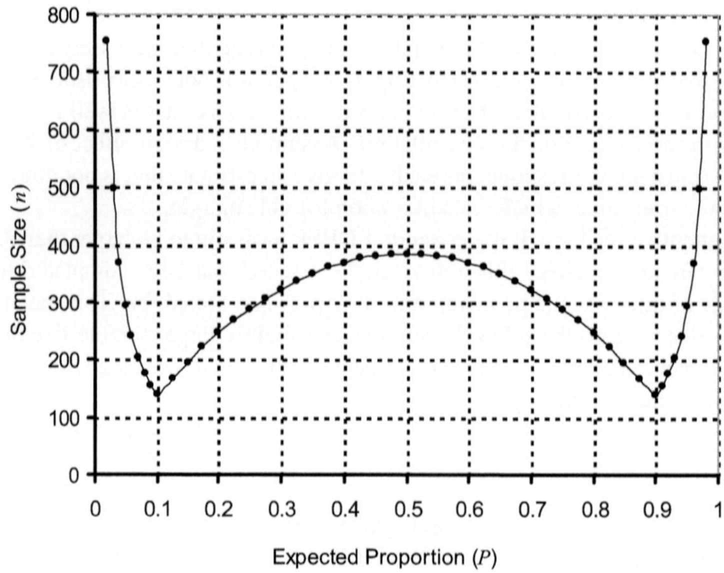

source: Naing, Wing and Rusli (2006)

Chapter 4

Data collection methods

4.1 Introduction

After it has been decided what the 'units of measurement' are to be – whether they are inhabitants of a certain region, court files, newspaper clippings, transcripts from radio shows, movies, verdicts or crimes – the researcher needs to determine how the required information is going to be 'extracted' from these units – even though 'extracted' may appear a slightly blunt, mechanical term if the units are living persons.

Humans can be interviewed, we can ask them to fill out questionnaires, or we could observe their behaviour. We can live with them for weeks or months, visit the pubs they frequent, join them in cooking meals, having fun. We can register their heart rate, make an archive of their tweets. We can also get information from paper or electronic files, or CCTV footage. Court files can be studied: in that case the data in those files need to be accessed in the sense that the generally written information is transferred into the format of variables, or that occurrences of for instance relevant statements is tallied, or transcribed to be coded into categories for later analysis. Analysable units need to be extracted from violent films, and sequences need to be identified in footage. Data rarely come in a format that is immediately ready for processing and analysis.

This chapter outlines a number of strategies for extracting such information. Information can be obtained from different sources, whether they be persons or records or audio-visual files. Particularly when researching respondents, there is a wide array of choices. Computer software and internet offer growing and still relatively underused and efficient possibilities. In the following, we will first discuss the various options for eliciting information from persons. The later parts of the chapter deal with data collection from other sources such as files, and with observation as a method of data collection.

4.2 Interviews and questionnaires

When we study a group of respondents, we generally want to obtain answers to a number of questions. The information we are after may be fairly factual such as age, sex, number of children. For other questions we may need some kind of operationalisation (see section 2.4), such as for questions after victimisation or attitudes. The information we are seeking may however also be such that it is hard to design beforehand as a researcher the exact questions you would want to pose. If I would for instance want to know why victims of violent crimes would choose not to enroll in mediation procedures with their attackers, a pre-designed pencil and paper questionnaire will likely not extract the information needed to understand victims' motivations. In all likelihood a lengthy interview, where the researcher him/herself can ask for clarifications, and where repeat sessions may be scheduled to clarify issues, may be needed. Thus, the type of question the researcher wants answers to in a sense dictates the method of interviewing. If one is after fairly factual, objectively determinable issues, a simple questionnaire may do. If one is after feelings, emotions, motivations, rationales, a more nuanced and less pre-set, more flexible approach may be warranted, more like a conversation than an interview, with possibly a lengthy phase for the interviewer and interviewee to get acquainted, so that the interviewee feels comfortable and at ease to share sensitive information or emotions.

Tracy (2013) distinguishes several types of interviews, depending amongst others on the goal of the research and the type of participant. The first type she distinguishes is the *ethnographic interview*, essentially a spontaneous conversation, instigated by the researcher. Questions may be factual, informative, and off the cuff. Questions are generally posed when there is respite from work or other business. The interview feels like a casual talk. Both researcher and interviewee are in their natural roles. By contrast, a *respondent interview* is a more formal setting, where the interviewer assumes an official role, and the interviewee does so as well. Here the interest is factual information as well as the respondent him/herself, his or her beliefs, motivations. *Informant interviews* on the other hand focus not on the interviewee him/herself but on a group of people, a set of situations that the informant has special knowledge of or can explain well.

The method or stance of interviewing can be ranked along a scale. This scale reflects the extent to which the questions and answers are pre-determined, and the degree to which the researcher and respondent are constrained by formats and instructions. This scale is best regarded as a 'structuredness'-scale. The freest format has the unstructured interview – the most strictly regulated and pre-determined is the CAWI-questionnaire (Computer Assisted Web Interview), where respondents fill out a questionnaire via internet and are guided through a set of questions to which only a pre-outlined number of answers is possible. This scale, along which interviews can be ranked, also corresponds with the intensity of contact between respondent and interviewer, with the CAWI interview basically a set of programmed operations that the interviewee follows with no personal interaction or even voice contact between respondent and researcher – and as such a cold and distant mode of data collection. The unstructured interview on the other hand is a vivid, sometimes intense and emotional interaction between two participants. We will discuss each, and intermittent interview formats below.

Two issues should be addressed before we do so. First, it should be noted that all data collection techniques in which one interviews or speaks with respondents, depart from three assumptions. To start with, it is assumed that interviewees understand the questions. This may seem like a trivial issue as in daily life if someone asks you a question you do not understand you will ask him or her to clarify that question. In interview situations things may not work that way: respondents may not admit that they do not understand the question, afraid that they are considered stupid. Some respondents are too polite or too eager to please the interviewer to let on that they did not get the question entirely – and may simply give that answer that they believe pleases the interviewer most or is what the interviewer is after. Then, it is assumed that respondents remember the facts you are asking after. Aids to remember events or to place them correctly in time may be warranted, such as a life history calendar (LHC), also referred to as the Life Event Calendar Method (Roberts & Horney, 2010). Lastly, an implicit assumption is that respondents speak the truth. Some researchers may however also be explicitly interested in the stories that interviewees weave and the half-truths or fabrications that they employ for various reasons. See section 14.2 and the article by Fujii (2010) discussed there.

Second, it should be noted that an interview, even if it appears to be unstructured, open, free-flowing and natural, is not a conversation. An interviewer is always respectful to the interviewee, and acknowledges the interviewee as someone insightful, who has information or knowledge that is important. Interviewers are non-judgmental. They are also sensitive in the sense that they pay attention to non-verbal cues that respondents give. In that sense they place the interviewee on a pedestal, the interviewee being the one who grants the interview to the researcher for which the interviewer should be kind and attentive. But besides being in that manner more accommodating than ordinary conversations, interviews are also more forceful. There is usually probing as interviewers have been trained not to take everything an interviewee says at face value, to point out (ever so friendly) inconsistencies and to interpret what the interviewee is saying ('Do you mean to say that you actually believe such-and-such to be untrue?'). See Tracy (2013, chapter 8) for more.

We will now discuss in more detail the range of interview options, from the open, free-format unstructured interview, to highly pre-structured programmed e-questionnaires.

(1) *Open-ended, unstructured interviews*

In an open-ended, unstructured interview, there is basically no format. The researcher wants to have the answers to a number of questions, or understand a number of issues, for instance how a respondent has rebuilt her life after experiencing sexual assault. The respondent has agreed to be interviewed, and the researcher asks along – as long as s/he deems necessary and as long as the respondent manages to sit in, until the interviewer is convinced that s/he 'has the picture'. This type of interview is also referred to as an *in-depth interview*.

This interview feels more like a conversation than a stylised, pre-determined questioning mode, it is free and naturally flowing, it may deviate here and there. This does not mean that there are no rules. Obviously, the researcher has to introduce him/herself, explain what the research is about, guarantee anonymity, describe the objective of the research, the funding agency, so that the interviewee can give *informed consent* (see section 4.2.1). It generally helps to establish trust and it increases openness from the part of the interviewee if the interviewer explains well why he or she is interested in the topic, what will be done with the results, when it will published, etc. After all, the researcher at times wants the interviewee to share private thoughts and feelings. A distant and reclusive, non-committal interviewer is not conducive to people venturing such information. A good introduction is highly important, perhaps especially for open-ended interviews.

As said, unstructured interviews generally proceed without a pre-set path. The interviewer can ask whatever questions he or she deems fit or important, as long as questions pertain to the central research question, or help in getting that question answered. Researchers may ask different questions from one interview to the next, in response to answers that also vary by interviewee. If one respondent voices concern over threats that her perpetrator has uttered, the interviewer will try to get more information on this and on how she has countered those threats or not, or why they instil such fear. If however another respondent stresses that she does not want to speak with her victimiser because she is afraid she will get nightmares or re-live the ordeal of the victimisation, a different set of follow-up questions will likely be posed.

For unstructured interviews it is hard to predict what questions will be asked and in what order, not only because there is no format but also because these interviews are supposed to be responsive to what the respondent says – which cannot be predicted. This means that it is also hard to predict how long in-depth interviews will take. Most take at least one and a half to two hours. Much longer stretches are unlikely as fatigue may set in. It is generally known that if interviews take too long (whether they be unstructured interviews or interviews with the aid of a questionnaire) the quality of answers decreases because respondents tire – and may even become fed up with the interview itself and in the worst case withdraw permission. For that reason, unstructured interviews may well stretch over several sessions.

Unstructured interviews where respondents are encouraged to relate their experiences or tell stories rather than respond to questions are referred to as *narrative interviews*. A special type that is relevant in the context of the study of conflict is the *oral history* interview, where eyewitnesses are asked to relate their experiences and witnessing of events during conflicts, in order to build an oral memory of past events. Portelli characterises oral history as follows:

"Oral history [...] is not only about the event. It is about the place and meaning of the event within the lives of the tellers" (Portelli, 2013).

Historian Scagliola (2011) was initiator and project leader of the Dutch Veterans Interview project (IPNV). In this project, 1,000 life history interviews were conducted and recorded digitally with a representative number of veterans deployed in all conflicts and military missions in which the Netherlands were involved (1940-2011). Because of the aim to document this collective memory, special attention was paid in the narrative interview to facts, such as times, locations, other people who were present. Part of the documentation is freely available, a restricted part is only accessible after a password. For more, see `www.eur.nl/sites/corporate/files/IPNVen_pres_04b_Pdf.pdf`. While the Dutch Veterans Interview Project is clearly qualitative in orientation, the representative sampling of veterans shows how the investigators attempted to achieve generalisability of their findings.

Similar oral history projects have been carried out in Bosnia, where 100 citizens of Bosnia and Herzegovina (BiH) from various social layers and regions were asked to relate their personal experiences during the Second World War and the recent war between 1991 and 1995, taped by a video camera. The taped interviews are publicly available; see `bosnianmemories.org/`.

A last type of unstructured interview distinguished by Tracy (2013) is the *biographical interview* or *life story interview*. Similar to the oral history interview, here the focus is on recounting events of the past, but the focus is now not historical events but the interviewee's own life.

While unstructured interviews are the least tied to rules and format, interviewers should of course at all times behave professionally and decently. This entails not only explaining the purpose of the research well so that the respondent can give informed consent, but also listening attentively, responding pleasantly, paraphrasing at times, reacting to verbal and non-verbal signs, creating a pleasant atmosphere. At times, behaving in a professional manner also implies, however, keeping a distance. Interviewees have been reported to ask the interviewer for help, or assistance in practical matters, sometimes extending well beyond what would be possible. In Hissel, Bijleveld and Kruttschnitt's (2011) study into incarcerated women, one of the interviewed women came to the interview bringing with her documents pertaining to her court case and demanded that the interviewer assist her with her court case. A good explanation beforehand of the study's aims and objectives and the role of interviewer and interviewee is necessary to help prevent (even though that did not prove effective in this case) such 'incidents' – incidents because obviously the interviewer has to say 'no' which may create tension or an unpleasant atmosphere so that subsequently the respondent may be less willing to divulge her feelings and thoughts. Sometimes interviewees ask for little things, such as help in reading a letter. Some researchers then do extend a helping hand. Those in ethnographic settings may do so more easily.

It may also occur – especially if interviews focus on high impact or traumatising events – that an interviewee becomes emotional. Also here the interviewer should remain professional although it may as well be important to show empathy or offer some consolation, and at least acknowledge what the respondent is experiencing. Being human, you may simply not be able to hold back your tears, and it would generate a distance if you would not allow your respondent to see that or to pretend that his or her story does not affect you. All in all, there is at times therefore a fine line to tread, between compassion and professional distance. That being said, most interviews generally proceed smoothly, and researchers proceed easily through the questions they want to ask, or issues they want to have covered.

Unstructured interviews are not always taped and transcribed. Audio- or videotaping may disturb the 'private' feeling of the interview setting, and some respondents dislike having every word recorded. Instead, interviewers may after conclusion of the interviews quickly make a summary of topics touched upon, of pertinent statements made. These are immensely important for later analysis of the findings over several interviews. Such short field notes are called *memos* or *field jottings*: they are quick summaries of what was said, quotes, specific words or marked expressions that respondents used, or other salient observations that one may forget, or words of which the specific meaning may be lost if one does not capture them verbatim. Zaitch (2003) describes how he during interviews and meetings with cocaine dealers quickly took notes (field jottings) when he went to the bathroom, as inconspicuously as possible and as close in time to statements made by his respondents so that he would lose as little detail as possible.

Researchers generally write more extensive summaries of what was said during interviews once they are away from the respondents or the setting where observations took place. These *field notes* are much more elaborate summaries of what was said, and the field jottings serve as memory aides to do so. Both memos or field jottings and the more elaborate field notes are, if interviews are unregistered, the rough data on which analysis must take place later. Such analysis generally starts immediately after interviews or observation has taken place; researchers then write so-called *analytic memos*, in which they describe – diary-like – everything that occurred, what patterns emerge in the data, what hypotheses are formed and rejected, what concepts best synthesise the findings. These analytic memos are an important resource for qualitative data analysis proper, to which we will return in chapter 9. See Dixon, Singleton and Straits (2016, chapter 9) for more.

One important reason, however, to have interviews taped and transcribed is that in unstructured, in-depth interviews, much more than in any other data collection method described below, it may be the *manner* in which respondents formulate things, the order in which or the context against which they bring up issues, the things they leave out, that turn out to be significant for the interpretation of the data and conclusions of the research. These aspects may very well emerge only after careful analysis, after prising apart and piecing together again the bits and pieces that were said, listening and re-listening to the interviewee's words and phrasings.

Such significance is usually not immediately clear at the data collection stage, but emerges only after (repeated) scrutiny of the material. If an interview is not transcribed (and also not literally – with all the 'erm. . . 's and 'ahhs' and 'weeeeelll. . . 's – as well as indications whether a respondent laughs, or sniffs, puts particular emphasis on certain words) one misses out on the possibility to uncover such issues. Tracy (2013, pp. 179-180) gives an overview of special characters and conventions to demarcate and transcribe such non-verbal meanings.

Transcription is an extremely time-consuming process. One hour of interviewing may easily cost three to four hours of transcribing. While software is available for automated transcribing which considerably speeds up the process, all transcriptions need to be checked for consistency and correctness. A disadvantage of such automated transcription is that it often is carried out through a web application, where one cannot be sure that the company that supplies the software does not store the audio material on its own servers as well – a practice that would conflict with confidentiality promises.

Obviously, for transcription, the interview must have been taped, to which respondents have to consent and which some respondents may not like. In the latter case, the only resort is to make notes quickly afterwards or during breaks, and compile extensive field notes and analytic memos after completion of the interview.

A classic about qualitative interviewing is Rubin and Rubin (1995, reprinted in 2004). A number of general books on qualitative research have good chapters on interviewing as well; recommended are Tracy (2013, chapter 7) and Dixon, Singleton and Straits (2016, chapter 9).

(2) *Topical interview*

Next, a so-called *topical interview*, or an interview with a *topic list* has some more structure. The researcher has a list of items that explicitly need to be covered, the 'topics', within the interview session. Contrary to the unstructured interview, the researcher has (generally) only one session with the respondent, during which the relevant topics need to be covered. The order in which this occurs, the particular questions that are asked to bring up the topics is however relatively unprescribed. Topical interviews are in that sense intermediate, in between the freest format (the unstructured interview) and the heavily structured varieties that will be discussed below. For that reason, topical interviews are categorised as *semi-structured*.

The free format of the topical interview also makes for a fairly natural and therefore pleasant atmosphere, in which the interview can proceed informally, just like a conversation, with maximum opportunity for the interviewer to respond flexibly and explore topics as they emerge. The list of topics that should be addressed assures that no gaps are left. The scope of issues discussed is generally narrower and more contained than in the unstructured interview.

Topical interviews, like in fact most interviews, should follow a certain 'intimacy-curve'. It would be rude (and unwise) to start the interview with very personal or intimate questions, and it would also be insensitive to end an interview right after sensitive or intimate issues have been brought up. Thus, it is recommended to start interviews with fairly basic questions, asking for instance after educational level, or marriage, or number of children. As the interview proceeds, and rapport is built between interviewer and interviewee and the interviewee has sketched some previous experiences, more personal or intimate topics may be delved into. Towards the end of the interview, it is wise to round off the interview by again moving away to a less personal level. Many interviews at the end ask the respondent how s/he experienced the interview, whether topics were left unaddressed that s/he feels would have needed dealing with, whether s/he has any recommendations. Many researchers – especially if the interview dealt with potentially emotional issues – leave a list of organisations the respondent can contact if s/he feels s/he would need assistance, or would like to go over issues again with a professional. In that end phase, distance is resumed, so that 'moving-away'-phase also serves to prepare ending the interview.

Topical interviews may also be held not with one, but with a set of respondents. One variety of such an interview is a *focus group* – although it must be said that some research methodologists would not agree with the hermeneutics to subsume the focus group under 'Interviews'. In a focus group a set of specialists (usually therefore a purposive sample, see section 3.3.2) is consulted regarding their knowledge and views on a particular topic, and in many cases also for a solution or recommendations. In a focus group, diverging views or opinions of the group members may be resolved or contrasted, and in that sense a focus group is a very efficient way to get an overview of viewpoints quickly. Often professionals, such as lawyers, youth workers, nurses, prison staff, are asked to participate in focus groups. Focus groups need analytical and strong chairpersons or moderators, who should ensure not only that all relevant topics are covered but also that shy respondents are not overwhelmed by more vocal and self-confident ones.

Topical interviews, like unstructured interviews, are often transcribed for the raw material to be used for analysis. Also for topical interviews, the researchers may after conclusion of the interviews quickly make a summary of the answers, as taking notes may disrupt the flow and naturalness of the conversation. Again, after transcription or conversion into summaries, the interview material can be analysed using any of the techniques for qualitative data analysis described in chapter 9. Just like for unstructured interviews, for an interview to be transcribed it should be taped, to which respondents have to consent and which some respondents may not like. In that case the only resort again is to make summaries quickly afterwards and/or take notes during breaks or write memos shortly afterwards.

Before we move on to more structured interviews, we mention two intermediate interview methods that are in a sense a combination of different kinds of interviewing. Both use an aid along which people are asked to respond. The first of these is the more qualitative 'Life as a Film' or LAAF procedure (Canter & Youngs, 2015). In the LAAF elicitation procedure, respondents are asked to describe their life as a movie, and to explain what happens in the film, who the main characters are, what the main events are, and how the film ends. Interviewees are probed by questions such as 'When does the film start?', 'What happens in the most exciting scene in the film'?, 'How do you change during the film?'. Transcriptions are next coded according to a pre-existing scheme, that has categories in four domains: descriptives (such as genre, victimisation, birth, happy ending/sad ending), explicit processes to organise content (such as empowerment, betrayal, unity, and the nature of changes occurring: redemption, contamination), psychological complexity, and agency.

Using data from interviews with 61 male incarcerated offenders, Cantor and Youngs report how these men described their own lives in the films, and how the dominant aspect of agency was 'self-mastery', i.e. struggling and overcoming their problems. Almost a third of the men described their lives as a tragic story. The films also revealed, after coding of the interviews, that many presented justifications and cognitive distortions for their criminal behaviour: denial of responsibility was most frequent in a third of offenders, one in six assumed the role of victim, and 4% condemned those who had disapproved of their behaviour. While clearly an aid for qualitative interviewing, the authors after coding the data presented frequencies of the categories in the domains, thereby giving also a quantitative overview of the findings – showing how qualitative data can also be analysed quantitatively.

The second is the Life History Calendar, mentioned briefly previously, and also referred to as the Life Event Calendar Method (see Roberts & Horney, 2010). In an interview with an LHC, respondents are asked to fill out their lives along a time line, for several domains such as housing, romantic relationships, offending, drugs use, parenthood, employment etc. The instrument, essentially a large carton sheet with coloured rows for the domains and columns for each age, facilitates recall of events, and enables crosschecking of the occurrence of events. As respondents are asked to fill in their first job, their graduation age, and the year when they had their first romantic relationship, their first child, were incarcerated, the simultaneous recall of these events with their mapping on the sheet makes it possible for interviewees to better place these events on the time line of their lives (they may for instance remember that they had their first child in a certain apartment, and will therefore know that they lived in that place until becoming a mother). An example of such a Life History Calendar is in Figure 4.1.

The idea is that during the filling out of the calendar, with a pencil and eraser for corrections as respondents generally move events as they proceed to fill out the calendar, respondents also discuss major events and why and how they occurred. Such comments can generally be added on the calendar, that should for that have sufficient space in the margins. Life History Calendars are often used in life-course criminological research. The Life History Calendar can be an aid to conduct an interview where more quantitative data are gathered.

(3) *Interview with questionnaire*

Many researchers – especially when they do quantitative research – prefer interviews along a questionnaire format to unstructured or topical interviews. Questionnaires have a fixed set of questions, that are asked in exactly the same order, whether or not a respondent at question 13 brings up an issue that is not addressed until question 36. The pre-set order must be followed. Obviously, if a respondent does not have children, the questions into those children's ages and gender etc. do not apply and may be skipped, but regardless such 'not applicable' questions, all questions are posed in exactly the same standardised order and format to all respondents, in exactly the same fashion. Where in unstructured and topical interviews the interviewer has much more freedom to adapt or rephrase questions and address issues in any order that appears apt, with questionnaires it is as if the researcher's role is erased, being standardised, made uniform and therewith in a sense minimised.

Such standardisation serves in fact to minimise distortion through interviewer behaviour or wording of the specific questions. By ensuring that each interviewer gives exactly the same introduction to the questionnaire, gives out informed consent forms in exactly the same order, poses each question in exactly the same manner and in identical order, one aims to minimise interviewer influence on the respondent's answers. Phrased differently, the aim of all this standardisation is to ensure that the interviewer is but the vessel through which the respondent's properties, experiences, attitudes or feelings are transmitted to the researcher. The interviewer functions as the medium through which the respondent's answers are passed on, and he or she should not influence the nature of those answers. Formulated differently again, if respondents' answers differ, we want those differences to be attributable to respondent

Figure 4.1: Example of a Life History Calendar

	Int: DOB:																
	Age	<11	11	12	13	14	15	16	17	18	19	20	21	22	23	24	25
Living situation	With parents (M/F/SM/SF)																
	With other family (see codes)																
	With partner (P1, P2, etc.)																
	Living with others (D/F, or use arrow)																
	Independent/alone																
	Institution (see codes)																
	Homeless																
	Home Type (WD/LR/PL/CB/BH)																
	Home Amenities (RW/EL)																
	Family violence																
	Parental substance use (A/D)																
	Parental CJS involvement (A/P)																
Relationships	Intimate relationship (AM/LM; also S)																
	Relationship satisfaction (1-10)																
	Gave husband money (I/R/A)																
	Partner substance use (A/D)																
	Partner crime (P/V/D)																
	Partner CJS involvement (A/P)																
Victim	Violence by **family** (see codes)																
	Type (E/P/S/N/O)																
	Frequency (1/O/R/D)																
	Violence by **partner** (P1, P2, etc.)																
	Type (E/P/S/N/O)																
	Frequency (1/O/R/D)																
	Violence by **others** (use codes/arrows)																
	Type (E/P/S/N/O)																
	Frequency (1/O/R/D)																
Child	Child birth (D/S)																
	Provision of daily childcare (S/F/O)																
Work	Formal employment (FT/PT)																
	Informal labor (see codes)																
	Not working																
Finances	Earnings (amount)																
	Income from crime (amount)																
	Financial hardship																
	Debts (amount)																
	Financial support from others																
Offend	Offending - type (P/K/D/V)																
	Arrest (P/SW/K/D/V)																
	Incarceration (P/SW/K/D/V)																
Health	Alcohol use (O/R/D/A)																
	Drug use (O/R/D/A)																
	Health Problems (H/P/M)																
Support	Institutional support (see codes)																
	Social support (see codes)																
	Religion & religious participation																
Other	Loss through death (see codes)																
	Important events (see code sheet)																

differences only, and not to interviewer particularities. Standardisation essentially serves to eliminate the interviewer.

Interviews with questionnaires or question schemes thus standardise the situation in which the questions are posed. Given such standardisation, it is possible to either allow respondents to answer the questions in any format they like (by providing so-called *open-ended questions*, see section 4.3), or to also standardise the answering options of the respondents (by supplying so-called *closed-end questions*, see also section 4.3), in which case a limited set of possible answers is provided by the researcher, that the respondent has to 'tick' or confirm. In the first case we could also label the interview as a *semi-structured interview*, the criterion being that the interview situation has been standardised, but the respondent is still free to answer any way s/he sees fit. If however only closed-end questions are provided, we label the interview as *structured*, also referred to in the literature as *completely structured*. When an interview situation is completely structured, not only is the setting constrained, but also the behavioural options of the respondent.

When the researcher or interviewer administers the questionnaire, and thus poses the questions, this is called *face-to-face* interviewing. It is also possible to have respondents fill out the questionnaires on paper, or on a laptop or via the internet. We discuss these interview modes below.

(4) *Self-administered questionnaire*

Obviously, respondents who can read or write may fill in questionnaires by themselves. This has a huge financial advantage (no interviewer need make an appointment, travel, sit in), but comes at the cost of no one being able to explain possibly unclear questions, or aid in filling out the questionnaire when needed. Another disadvantage is that – particularly for more lengthy questionnaires – it is more likely that respondents give up. Self-administration is possible only if respondents are sufficiently literate.

Self-administration of questionnaires puts heavy demands on questionnaires' clarity, lay-out and attractiveness. Questionnaires must be tested and piloted extensively before they can be used in a real-life setting, as no amendments can be made once the respondent has to do the job all by him/herself. If questionnaires are unclear, it is likely that respondents will not want to continue, generating missing data or in the worst case drop-out. It is then also more likely that respondents get confused and write down answers that are technically or practically impossible, such as having 33 children, or writing down that one has never been in contact with the criminal justice system, but later filling in that their last incarceration was from 2007 to 2009. Such impossible combinations of answers are sometimes jokingly referred to as 'pregnant grandfathers'.

Paper and pencil questionnaires have become increasingly replaced by e-versions, that we will discuss below.

(5) *Self-administered computerised questionnaire*

In recent years, ICT and the internet have grown tremendously in importance for research. While researchers not only write all their articles now on computers with word processing packages, computers (and the internet) are increasingly used for data collection too. The computer is important for several reasons.

A first reason is technical. Using special software (an example of user-friendly software is LimeSurvey) one can program questionnaires. This means that not only the text of all the questions is entered into the computer, but that the questionnaire itself is programmed in the sense that on the basis of the answers given, questions are skipped. This rids the respondent from tedious instructions such as *'If you filled in 'yes', please proceed to question 28'*. If someone has filled in that he is male, the questions on pregnancy are skipped automatically by the computer. This is much easier and pleasanter for respondents, speeds up the entry process, and if the questionnaire is programmed well, 'pregnant grandfathers' cannot occur any more. Obviously, such programming on the other hand makes correction of errors harder: if a respondent has filled in that he has never been in contact with the criminal justice system, the programmed questionnaire will not lead him to the questions on incarceration, and a previous mistake cannot be corrected in this fashion anymore. The respondent is also not triggered that s/he may have made an error in filling out a previous question.

Programming can be done in different ways. It is possible to demand that respondents fill in all previous questions before moving to a next screen with questions. The software will then refuse to proceed unless answers to all questions have been entered. While this in principle ensures that answers to all questions are obtained and no so-called *missing values* are accrued, one may doubt whether such a strict protocol is conducive to validity of the answers. If respondents do not want to answer a certain question but the software blocks progress, they might simply fill in a nonsensical answer, just to be done with it and get on with the questionnaire. In that case, one has *an* answer but what it signifies is hard to say – and it may be doubted whether it is useful at all. What may however also happen is that respondents who do not want to fill out certain questions just bin the whole questionnaire, dropping out altogether, which is perhaps even more problematic (see section 3.6). It is therefore perhaps preferable to give the respondent a gentle reminder that a question has not been answered yet, and ask whether s/he would be so kind as to do this after all. If a respondent tries proceeding without answering once more, one could allow respondents to do so. Some questionnaires provide special answering options *'would rather not answer'* which might be a solution to this, although some respondents also do not like to explicitly acknowledge that they do not want to answer a question.

A second reason why the use of software and computers is so important in social science research – and this is particularly so for criminological research – has to do with validity. If questionnaires are administered face-to-face with a laptop it is possible to let the respondent fill out questions after 'sensitive issues' by him- or herself. The interviewer then walks through the entire questionnaire until a set of questions arrives for instance about criminal offending, and asks the respondent to fill out those questions by him- or herself. The laptop is turned around and the respondent fills out the block of questions after the sensitive topics, after which the laptop is returned to the interviewer. It is generally assumed that this method yields better, more truthful answers and thus more valid and better quality data. Obviously, enhanced veracity of answers rests on the assumption that the respondent trusts that the interviewer cannot read back what s/he filled in. If one has designed the questionnaire such that it is impossible to page back to previous answers, respondents will likely more eagerly admit that they stole money than if they have noticed that everything can be read back. This would plead against a scroll-back-and-repair option. On the other hand, being able to scroll back and change previous answers is handy in case respondents realise that they filled out earlier questions wrongly. It is hard to say which option is to be preferred. We will discuss other options for eliciting answers to sensitive questions in section 11.7.1.

A third reason why computers are so useful in data collection is that, if answers are filled in on the computer, whether that be on a laptop or through internet, the so-called 'data entry' phase can be skipped. Data entry is the phase where handwritten questionnaires, or handwritten notes, are transformed into codes or variables on a computer, that can next be analysed. Obviously, doing so costs time, and builds in an extra layer in the data collection phase that is also an additional opportunity for mistakes to be made. Data entry by hand is fairly mind-numbing work, so mistakes in the transferral of the written material to the computer may occur. Some research firms have software to e-read filled-out questionnaires, but also that is an additional step in the process from answers to variables. Computers and web-based administration of questionnaires save much money and yield more reliable data.

A last reason is that computers generate a stronger sense of confidentiality and privacy. Computers are not judgmental, while interviewers may very well be feared by respondents to be so (even if they would not show it). Questionnaires filled in within the privacy of the own home, not in one's own handwriting, where shameful words need not be spoken aloud, may for that reason reduce the tendency that many respondents have to give answers that appear acceptable, normative, 'normal', the so-called *social desirability bias*. Thus, the use of computers or web-interviewing may also increase validity.

Experimental research has shown that web-assisted questionnaires yield data that are as good as data generated by paper and pencil questionnaires. Lucia, Hermann and Killias (2007) showed, in a study in which self-reported data on offending were obtained from secondary school students, that students were more motivated to respond through the internet, took less time for filling out the questionnaire, and were more confident of privacy. In addition, the school principals were less reluctant to allow classes to be interviewed through the internet. Baier (2017) concludes the same for prevalence of delinquency, prevalence rates of factors influencing delinquent behaviour, correlations between these factors and criminal behaviour, missing values and evaluations of the survey by adolescents. Given that web-based administration is so much more efficient, use of a computer and web-based administration of questionnaires appear to have clear advantages – with no disadvantages as yet emerging.

The computer and computer software can be used in a variety of ways. Most larger research departments and firms these days program their questionnaires, or use standard software to do so. The programmed questionnaire can then be administered through a telephone interview. The interviewer calls the prospective respondent, and asks whether s/he is willing to be interviewed, after which the interviewer, sitting behind a computer screen, reads out the questions over the telephone and fills in the answers. This is called Computer Assisted Telephone Interviewing or CATI. The situation where a face-to-face interview is conducted and a laptop is present on which answers are entered, possibly in part by the interviewee him/herself, is called Computer Assisted Personal Interviewing or CAPI. If the respondent fills in the questionnaire on a computer entirely by him- or herself, this is called Computer Assisted Self Interviewing or CASI. Such data collection methods are often used for self-report surveys (see section 11.5.3) in schools, where the computers in a computer classroom are equipped with the electronic questionnaire and students fill out the questionnaire in batches. If respondents fill out questionnaires at home (or elsewhere) via the internet, this is called Computer Assisted Web Interviewing or CAWI.

4.2.1 Informed consent

All interview modes that we discussed above, and in fact all studies in which human subjects participate, should start with so-called *informed consent*. But what is informed consent, and who gives it?

Informed consent is given by the person to be interviewed or surveyed, before the interview or survey starts. If a respondent gives informed consent, this entails an agreement ('consent') to partake in the study after full information ('informed') has been received on the purpose of the research and any possibly relevant background information to it (such as how long participation takes, whether any negative consequences are to be expected from it, who funds the study, whether the respondent may benefit from the study, why the study is important), what participation exactly entails, guarantees of confidentiality as well as of anonymity, unrecognisability and untraceability in any publications, the right to withdraw participation, and on incentives for participation (whether the respondent will receive some kind of remuneration or gift).

Researchers generally employ printed consent forms that they ask prospective research participants to date and sign. On these, respondents declare that they aware of all aspects enumerated above and that they agree to participate. Consent may also be given verbally.

Consent forms should be stored, whether they are on paper or electronic or are notes of verbal consent. For security reasons, consent information (that has identifying information) should be stored separate from respondents' answers. In exceptional cases, for instance in highly insecure settings, no names are entered on consent forms.

4.3 Design of interviews, questionnaires and questions

4.3.1 Interview design

As discussed in section 4.2, interviews generally follow a certain 'intimacy curve'. By that we mean that interviews generally start with easy questions, that build rapport, set the interviewee at ease, ask after simple unintrusive facts, such as age, profession, marital status and the like. Rapport-building questions should be inviting and pleasant, and should entice the interviewee to relate some facts, start talking about issues related to the interview. There could also be pleasant introductory remarks, such as: 'What a lovely green neighbourhood!', or: 'Beastly weather, isn't it?'. Introductory questions mainly function to get the interviewee speaking and to start conversation, to establish a pleasant atmosphere. After informed consent is given, generally factual issues are addressed first. The list of factual questions should not be too long, as rattling off many facts may be distancing and may undo the pleasant, conversational atmosphere in which the interview started.

To make it easier for respondents to talk, so-called *generative questions* may be asked. Examples are *tour questions*, such as 'Can you describe for me how a typical management team meeting looks?'. Respondents can be asked for elucidation, such as 'You just said that you never discuss incoming mail, why is that?', or for historical perspectives ('Since when is it that you only meet once every two weeks?'). Next hypothetical questions can be quite useful ('Suppose that you had only half an hour for your management team meeting, what would be the item you would definitely not skip?' or: 'Suppose you were in complete control of your job, what activities would you give prominence?').

Opposed to generative questions are directive questions, in which an answer to a specific question is sought. The most directive type of question is the closed-end question (see below in section 4.3.3), where a respondent can choose between a limited number of alternatives for an answer. Directive questions can also be posed to elicit reactions, for instance to pictures, or video fragments. Devil's advocate questions are useful to obtain additional insights in people views, for instance by saying 'You just said that you are overwhelmed by red tape, but if I were an outsider I could say that that is all in your own hands as you are the director.' Asking people to reflect about mistakes they made or actions they regret is also ranked as a directive question. Such questions (similar to devil's advocate questions) may be threatening for some respondents, and one should be cautious to pose them. One way not to offend a respondent is by posing a confronting question as something said by others ('Some people might say that your answer is self-serving because...').

At the wrap up, it is always wise to ask interviewees whether there is any topic that was not addressed but that should have been mentioned, or whether an important question was left unasked. Tracy (2013) suggests – for studies in which some of what respondents said will be quoted – to ask interviewees under what name they would like to appear in the report. This assures respondents once more of the anonymity promise, and also gives a gentle indication that the interview is drawing to a close. Tracy (2013) lists all these types of questions and has further suggestions.

4.3.2 Questionnaire design

Designing *questionnaires* is a science or perhaps even an art by itself. Most questionnaires start, like interviews, with relatively simple, 'getting-to-know' questions, such as questions after age, marital status, place of birth etc. *Screener questions* may follow in which it is for instance asked whether something was ever stolen from the respondent, whether the respondent was ever the victim of a burglary, a robbery, of assault, and so forth, after which more in-depth questions appear. After the in-depth phase, where the key issues are addressed, questionnaires again round off in the sense that they attempt not to end abruptly, but move back to a less emotional or intimate layer, for instance asking after the police reaction, or generally perceived fear of crime, perception of neighbourhood safety, etc. Most questionnaires end by asking the respondent whether he or she has anything to add to the interview, whether s/he has missed anything that should have been asked, remained unattended to, etc. If the questionnaire focused on possibly sensitive or emotional issues, such as victimisation, the end of the questionnaire should always have at the minimum a telephone number or e-mail address in case the respondent desires to talk about the study topic with someone else, or needs help, or a listening ear.

Before the questions proper of the study start, the questionnaire should introduce the study clearly, so that the prospective respondent can give informed consent. As stated in section 4.2.1, the respondent must know all relevant facts about the study: what the research question is, what the purpose of the study is, who finances the study. The introduction should also state that confidentiality, anonymity, untraceability and unrecognisability is promised, and guaranteed. All information divulged by the respondents will be treated confidentially, and remains with the researchers only; it may be discussed during intervision and feedback sessions, but must not be discussed at interviewers' home meals or in the pub to let off steam. When the report of the study is published, no names of respondents will appear, and the findings will be written up such that no outsider or insider can trace the findings back to individual respondents. For example, if a study would report on a 16 year-old red-haired sex offender with a drug-addicted one-legged father with a wart on his nose from a named small village, most of the inhabitants of that village would know who that sex offender is.

The introduction should also state that consent to participate can be withdrawn at any moment. The latter is not only part of the formal requirement that respondents must give informed consent, but will likely also make it easier for respondents to agree to participate: it shows that they have control and can withhold permission again when they want. Giving an average expected duration for the interview is also helpful, as the respondent then knows what time investment s/he is agreeing to. Specifying an expected duration also prevents respondents getting restless when the interview takes longer than they had really wanted.

Many introductions end by stressing that participation is very important for the research to get a full and complete picture; it is wise to also explain in what way society benefits or how people like the respondent benefit, to stimulate the respondent to agree to participate. In interviewing victims or detainees, it may be important to stress that neither the study nor the researcher or interviewer can do something for any individual participant. Often a sentence or two will be added to the effect that the research hopes to contribute to a better understanding of the topic under study, to better assistance to future victims of similar crimes, to offer information to help in improving the lives of family members of detainees, to give policy recommendations, or the like.

An interview is a gift, from respondent to researcher. To make respondents' task pleasant, to facilitate them to consent at all, questionnaires should be easy to fill in, as short as possible and attractive. Questionnaires should – whether they are administered as paper and pencil or are e-questionnaires – be designed such that respondents can easily see where they are in the layout, when the next question is coming, and – when the questionnaire is administered electronically – have an overview of how far a respondent is in filling it out; most questionnaire software enables to build in a bar that shows progress in percentage points. A printed questionnaire of 50 densely printed pages with font size 10 lettering is not going to generate valid answers – or only from a small masochistic subset of sample members. Designing your questionnaires badly results in nonresponse (and therefore bias in your sample) or sloppy answers (and therefore decreased validity). Not doing a good job here bites your study in the tail. The researcher proposes but the respondent disposes.

In research practice, telephone interviews should not be (although these are but rules of thumb) much longer than 10 to 15 minutes. Face-to-face interviews should not stretch beyond one and a half hours. If they do, respondents tend to tire, and their willingness to answer extensively decreases, thus also affecting validity. This is the reason that the central research question should be posited not at the very end of the questionnaire or interview, but somewhere midway to a little over: at that point in the interaction or the questionnaire maximum intensity or depth has been built, and respondents are not tiring yet.

Questions are best clustered by topic. It costs mental energy to flip from one topic to the other, and respondents prefer to see or hear announced what the next set of questions is going to be about. Clusters are therefore best introduced by small sentences like 'We would now like to ask you something about your school years', or 'The following set of questions refers to substance use'.

The context in which questions are asked may affect the manner in which respondents respond to those questions. If questions about the behaviour of respondents' children are framed as pedagogical issues, then the responses will likely differ from when they are asked against a backdrop of parenting 'styles'.

Similarly, the sequence in which questions are asked affects responses. This is another reason why there is so much focus on standardisation in interviewing, so that each and every respondent can be assumed to have undergone the same influence from the questioning sequence. Small changes in the order in which literally the same questions were asked, or the context in which these were posed, have been associated with differences in prevalence rates reported in victimisation studies.

Each newly designed questionnaire is best tested ('piloted') before the study proper starts. This means administering the questionnaire, assessing that respondents find the questionnaire clear, pleasant, not offensive, not too long and the like.

4.3.3 Types of questions and question design

Questions can be asked in any kind of interview, whether the interview is unstructured, topical or constrained in a very tight format such as for a web-based survey. Designing *questions* for questionnaires, that is, questions at the more rigid, prescribed end of the data collection-spectrum, is something not learned in half an hour. As every experienced researcher will tell you, even questions that appear at face value completely clear and unambiguous, may turn out to be multi-interpretable when administered to actual respondents. Just as questionnaires should be piloted in a real situation, so should questions be piloted, scrupulously, one by one. Researchers should sit down with volunteers who resemble the intended respondents and fill out the questionnaire with them, or have them fill it out, and check per question whether the respondent believes s/he understood the question, how s/he understood the question, whether the question was experienced as pleasant, not too intrusive, etc.

A number of general rules help in designing good questions. Questions should:

(1) *Be clear*

This may seem like a superfluous statement, but there should really be absolutely no ambiguity left in the question, no words that may have various meanings etc. Also, questions should ask after concrete phenomena. A question phrased like: 'Are you afraid of crime?' is not clear and pointed enough, as respondents may for instance be afraid to be burglarised but not afraid to have their bike stolen.

(2) *Not have (double) negations*

It is well known that double negations are confusing for most people and therefore also for respondents. Questions like: 'Do you disagree with the Christian party's standpoint that women should not be allowed to vote?' are therefore an absolute no-no. Some respondents have trouble as well dealing with (single) 'negatively' formulated statements, and it may therefore be best not to phrase questions in the negative – although this has the side-effect that all questions may become 'unidirectional' and therefore not stimulating respondents to think well about their answers.

(3) *Not be double-barrelled*

A double-barrelled question asks two questions in one. Respondents then obviously cannot know which question to answer to. Such a question would be: would you be in favour of more government spending on culture and infrastructure?

(4) *Not be suggestive*

Questions should always be formulated neutrally and not lead the respondent to believe that one answer or the other is the 'correct' one.

(5) *Have answering options that are mutually exclusive and exhaustive*

This rule applies only to questions that are closed-end. In a closed-end question the interviewee can select from a limited set of answers only. Open-ended questions on the other hand can be answered in any way by the respondent: after the question a blank is left in which the respondent can answer in whole sentences or a few words, as s/he pleases.

The first requirement (be mutually exclusive) above entails that respondents know which category to tick for their answer. If for instance boxes 1 and 2 that one can tick 'overlap' (1=before I went to secondary school, 2= before I turned 12), respondents may not know which one to choose. The second requirement (be exhaustive) has the desired effect that every respondent will be able to find a category for his or her answer. To ensure that this requirement is met, many questions have an 'other, namely . . . ' category, that ensures that if a respondent does not find his/her answer among the pre-printed categories, s/he can use this one. Obviously, literature study and pre-testing of the questionnaire should have ensured that only a small proportion of respondents fill out the 'other' category.

(6) *Minimise the risk for response styles to affect answers*

This rule is particularly relevant to questions that use rating scales for answers. Such questions usually have the format where respondents are confronted with a statement, and then are asked to tick on a scale ranging from 1 to 5 (or sometimes 1 to 7), whether they 1='strongly disagree' with the statement or, 2='disagree', 3='do not disagree, do not agree', 4='agree', 5='strongly agree'. Rating scales are very often used and efficient. In general, rating scales ranging from 5 to 7 categories are used, a finer grid such as with 9 or 11 categories does not generate substantively better answers as the labels then differ only marginally.

Rating scales however have the unfortunate side-effect that they may elicit *response styles*, such as the tendency to always give neutral answers (always ticking a '3'; referred to in the literature as the *error of central tendency* or as 'fence-sitting'), or the reverse (ticking '1's or '5's – referred to as *extreme response bias*). Other commonly occurring response styles are so-called *acquiescence bias*, or 'agreement response bias', with which is meant the tendency to agree with every statement. To counter this response style, it is advisable to phrase some questions in the negative, and some questions in the positive – which is as the attentive reader may note counter to the recommendation made above not to formulate questions negatively. Some respondents try to weed out any inconsistencies in their answers: they check their answers to make sure that their answers constitute an intrinsically logical set and are not inconsistent. This is called the *logical mistake*. A last fairly rebellious tendency is to fill out answers in visual patterns, such as page 1 incurring only '1's, page 2 a series of '2's, etc., or zigzaggingly, or Christmas tree-like.

Clearly, when response styles are present, answers may become almost useless: respondents then have not filled out what they really think or believe. One way to prevent such styles affecting the validity of the data, is to impress upon respondents not to think very long, and fill in the answers quickly, to state that it is the first impression that counts, that there is no 'wrong' answer, etc. Another option is to trigger respondents by formulating questions positively or negatively – as explained above. A third option is to choose the labels to the categories of the rating scale such, that ticking a visually neutral category ('5') amounts to a not at all neutral answer. For instance one could label '5' as 'I brush my teeth once a week' (with 7='never', 6='once a month', 4='once every 3 to 4 days', 3='every other day', 2='every day', 1='twice a day or more often'). Other researchers try to prevent the error of central tendency by offering not 5 or 7 categories (and thus a neutral category) but an even number of categories (4 or 6) – so that the respondent has to choose sides. This may force some respondents to reluctantly do so – others may simply not fill out the questionnaire anymore.

Because of the possibility of one or more response styles affecting the answers and validity, some researchers pose their crucial questions several times in a questionnaire, each time slightly differently, to be sure to obtain the information they are after, or at last to detect whether response styles are affecting respondents' answers.

(7) *Minimise the risk of socially desirable answers*

Many respondents have the tendency to give answers that are socially acceptable, afraid to be judged as deviant or weird, or unwilling to share attitudes they know would generally be regarded unfavourably. If one would ask respondents '*Are you a bigot?*', or '*Do you abuse your partner?*' it is not likely that many would say 'yes'. If one wants to know whether respondents have politically incorrect ideas, whether they use drugs, have particular sexual fantasies, it is therefore wise to ask so in a circumspect way, in which negative labels (such as 'bigot') are avoided and a number of different questions are drawn up to measure the various dimensions or aspects of for example bigotry, phrased as factually and neutrally as possible (such as: '*Do you agree with the standpoint of mr. Wilders that immigration to the Netherlands should be stopped?*'). Social desirability is believed to pose less of a risk when questionnaires are self-administered (CASI or CAWI). Social desirability scales have been developed that can be included in questionnaires to see to what extent the answers may have been distorted by a respondent's tendency to give socially desirable answers (an old and well-known example is the Marlowe-Crowne Social Desirability Scale; Crowne & Marlowe, 1960).

(8) *Operationalise the constructs for the respondent*

The two questions given as examples above ('*Are you a bigot?*' and '*Do you abuse your partner?*'), should for a second reason not be posed as such. What both of them namely fail to do is operationalise what is asked. One respondent may have quite a different idea what makes someone a bigot than another respondent. By using such generic terms, the researcher leaves it to the respondent to operationalise the construct. And the researcher essentially does not know how exactly the different respondents did this. Therefore, the researcher should specify what bigotry and abuse are, and not leave it to the respondent to operationalise these constructs. This is the reason that for instance in victim surveys (see section 11.5.2) a typical question about assault would be phrased something like '*Has anyone during the past year pushed you, shoved you, beaten you, such that you fell or fell against a wall?*'. Here, the question is posed very factually, and a respondent could in a sense tick whether one of these things happened to him or her.

Questions should all in all be as factual, clear and as precise as possible, be phrased neutrally, should not be double-barrelled, should never be leading. One can choose – as explained above – for closed-end questions where the interviewee can only select from a limited set of answers, or open-ended questions where the interviewee can answer freely. In general, open-ended questions are supposed to be beneficial for validity, as respondents can respond in a multitude of ways – at substantially increased cost to the researcher, however, as all the different answers must generally be coded afterwards into meaningful categories. Conversely, closed-end questions likely give better reliability, and save costs.

Not everyone can conduct each kind of interview. Interviewing is a skill that needs – for most – at least some training. In such a training, prospective interviewers acquire skills for probing, are trained in responding to different 'types' of interviewee, they practice paraphrasing, summarising, responding to questions about the research aims, procedure, etc.

For some studies, researchers have to pick their interviewers in the sense that interviewee and interviewer 'match'. In general, especially for sensitive topics, females are best interviewed by females. Many male interviewees also prefer to be interviewed by females. In some cultures, the age of the interviewer is also an issue to address. Especially traumatised respondents, such as victims of abuse, may not want to be interviewed by very young students. Sometimes respondents are best interviewed by someone from their own ethnic group, for language or cultural or other reasons. Examples exist however of studies where the opposite turned out to be true: in the Netherlands in a study on domestic violence, many interviewees stated that they preferred to be interviewed by someone who was *not* from their own ethnic group; the reason for this was that they were afraid – given the closely knit communities they moved in – that the 'dirty laundry' might be exposed.

When approaching respondents in person, the interviewer's dress and appearance are important. These should be tailored to the 'type' of respondents one is approaching. If drug addicts are to be studied, it is perhaps not wise to appear in suit and tie. If corporate managers are to be interviewed, it is not wise to appear in torn jeans. Interviewers should dress, speak and behave according to presumed interviewee expectations and according to the setting the interview will be conducted in. In general, overdressing (professional dress and behaviour) is better than underdressing (joviality, informality). After all, the interviewer conducts the interview in a professional, formal role.

The first few seconds in the approach of respondents are crucial. Even if respondents have been sent letters beforehand, many – and this is known from particularly criminological research – will not have read or taken note of those letters, and the research and its purposes must be explained at that first encounter during the first few instances when the respondent opens the door. This means that the timing of home approaches must be carefully chosen, during the daytime to start with, for those who are employed outside of the home perhaps very early evening, which however incurs the risk of ringing the doorbell when the family has just sat down to dinner – generating a first annoyance. Contact attempts late at night are not welcomed by respondents in general, increase the risk for non-contacts or refusal – and may be risky for interviewers.

Almost all that was written here for home approaches obviously goes as well for approach by telephone, where – while dress and smiles and general composure do not count – timing does, and voice and pleasantness of wording, and sensitivity to the respondent's answers and any hesitance do all the more.

The careful approach of potential respondents is so crucially important because insensitive behaviour will quickly generate refusal, and thus non-response, leaving us with a likely biased sample. Once a sample member has opened the door, contact has been established, the sample member is not anymore a 'non-contact' (see section 3.6). During the first few seconds that then follow, agreement to cooperate must be secured. Once a respondent has said 'no', experience teaches that it is very hard to turn that into a 'yes'. Therefore, if sample members hesitate, it may be best – and a lot depends on the interviewer's ability to correctly read verbal and non-verbal signs – to hand out the already sent letter, or a short introduction to the research once more and propose that the interviewer return at an agreed day and time so that the hesitant sample member can quietly think it over. It is advisable to leave a card with a name and telephone number and e-mail address so that the potential respondent can get more information, or call to cancel.

Obviously, instead of interviewing persons, a study can employ a survey of houses (instead of persons), assessing how many have latrines, running water and electricity, or of schools, investigating how many have books, chalk, blackboards etc. In that case, observation rather than interviewing is the data collection mode, although observations may be supplemented with interviews with officials, teachers, etc. It may also be the case that the research subjects are too young to be interviewed, or that the factors we are interested in are better observed than asked after, such as schoolyard play behaviour. Or we may want to extract information from documents, such as court files, or newspaper clippings.

We will discuss a number of such other data collection modes below.

4.4 Data collection from documents

Much of what was said for the design of questionnaires and questions, applies as well if we want to extract information not from human beings but from 'documents': files, radio programmes, newspaper clippings, song lyrics, CCTV footage, images, tweets, and the like.

This inanimate material is generally *raw*, meaning that it has to be transformed into analysable material. If a researcher has chosen to quantify the material, then a scoring list is often used – essentially the equivalent of a questionnaire except that it is not administered to a person but to a document in the broadest sense. The list contains not questions but variables, meaning that the scoring list basically has very brief indications of the variables such as 'IQ' or 'Number of children'. Again the same options of open-ended and closed-end entries exist. Scoring lists are generally a mixture of open-ended and closed-end entries. For instance, when analyzing court files, a large number of variables will be very short indications of the property that needs to be scored, like 'Does the defendant have an earlier criminal record' or 'Is the defendant married?'. But the scoring list may also have an open-ended entry that asks the scorer to describe briefly the nature of the offence, the facts that led to the offence, what happened during the offence, and how the offence came to be known by the police, in an open space of about half a page.

This 'patient' raw data material has the pleasant property that it is possible to perform the data collection operations several times, checking whether different scorers or raters generate the same scorings. To do so – and this is often done at the beginning of the data collection phase – two or more raters are handed out the same material, and they are asked to fill out – independently – the data collection forms. After scoring these, the data are compared. If they are exactly the same, we say that there is perfect *interrater reliability* (see also section 2.6). Often that is not entirely so, and we then at first inspect where differences emerged and discuss whether these can be prevented by a stricter, more precise *scoring protocol*. Next, a new test round of scoring is held, where again scores are compared between raters.

We may express the extent to which raters agree in various measures, such as the percentage agreement, the correlation coefficient or the so-called *Kappa-coefficient* or, where there are more than two raters, the intraclass correlation coefficient. As a rough indication, a percentage agreement of 80% and over is considered good, below 60% as unacceptable. Measures such as the Kappa coefficient are stricter as they correct for the fact that if we filled in random data on the data collection forms, we would also by chance get some agreement. The scoring protocol is an integral part of the data collection instrument.

Wijkman, Bijleveld and Hendriks (2014) analysed the court files, including psychiatric and psychological screenings, of all adolescent female sex offenders who had been prosecuted for at least one hands-on sex offence between 1996 and 2008. They screened all available court files for these young women, that virtually all contained psychological screenings. They used a scoring list that comprised a mixture of open-ended and closed-end entries. One of its pages is given as an example in Figure 4.2.

4.5 Observation

When we observe behaviour, we can do so either in a non-participatory or participatory fashion. When our observations are non-participatory, we are an outside observer to the behaviour we are interested in. We can only observe from the outside what (usually) people do. Examples are studies where researchers scrutinise children's behaviour at a school playground for the interaction between children, for instance to understand the manner in which hierarchy is built in small groups. The observers do not participate, and ideally speaking they should be as *unobtrusive* as possible. If the researchers are obtrusive (when the 'subjects' of the research are aware that they are being studied) this might alter the subjects' behaviour. They might show more socially acceptable behaviour, or might on the contrary become more bragging. When researchers are obtrusive, it is impossible to observe behaviour in its natural form. Therefore it is generally considered best if the objects of study are not at all aware of the fact that they are being studied. Obviously, this may conflict with the requirement of informed consent, see section 4.2.1.

Lindegaard, Bernasco and De Vries (2016) observed the unfolding of criminal events using CCTV footage. Lindegaard and her co-authors were interested to find out what kinds of victim and bystander behaviour prevented robberies unfolding successfully, and what kinds of victim and bystander behaviour prevented victims and bystander suffering physical violence. They coded CCTV footage from 21 robberies in Rotterdam and 37 robberies in Amsterdam. Using specific software developed for ethological research, Lindegaard and her co-authors coded all video material. In first instance they coded fairly simple properties of the robberies such as the number of victims and bystanders, location, outcome, use of violence and threats. In a second step they coded the body language of all present, in as neutral terms possible, such as 'moving arms backward and forward', 'direction of looking', 'orientation upper body'. In a third phase, they analysed behaviour and postures that are meaningful in dominance.

Figure 4.2: Scoring list court file

File number :
Year of birth :
Age at time commission:

	Describe crime briefly								
0	e.g.: Time Location Co-perpetrators Crime Bystanders								
	Variables	**1**	**2**	**3**	**4**	**5**	**6**	**7**	**8**
1	Ethnicity	Turkish	Moroccan	Surinamese	Antillean	Dutch	mixed	other	unknown
2	Intelligence	(<85)	below av. (85-90)	average (90-110)	above av. (110-115)	(>115)	verbal IQ:	perf. IQ:	unknown
3	Neuroticism	high	above average	average	low				unknown
4	Impulsivity	high	above average	average	low				unknown
5	Extraversion	high	above average	average	low				unknown
6	Thrill seeking	high	above average	average	low				unknown
7	Conscience formation	highly insuff.	insufficient	sufficient	good	denies			unknown
8	Self-image	very low	low	normal	positive				unknown
9	Gullible	not	lightly	considerably	strongly				unknown
10	Agression problems	no	yes, namely:						unknown
11	Authority problems	no	yes, namely:						unknown
12	Antisocial behaviour	before age 12	after age 12	yes, unknwn start	no				unknown
13	Depressive moods	somewhat	considerably	serious	no				unknown
14	School problems	yes	no						unknown
15	Previous counseling	yes, outpatient	yes, inpatient	no					unknown
16	Clinical syndr. (Axis I)								unknown
17	Persnlity disord. (Axis II)								unknown
18	Paraphilia	no	possible	yes, namely					unknown
19	Self-mutilation	no	yes, namely						unknown

The authors report that in 44 of 58 robberies no violence is used. Resistance is uncommon, and in most cases people try to hide, and there is some pushing and grabbing. In those robberies where violence was used, this occurred after a victim resisted, challenging the robbers' dominance. To transfer dominance, robbers use violence in an instrumental fashion, to ensure that the victim complies and the robbery is successful. Resistance by bystanders similarly leads to violence, directed at the bystanders. Remarkably, resistance by victims and bystanders immediately at the start of a robbery, does not incur violence. Congruent with what is known from interviews with robbers, such initial resistance is possibly a temporary shock effect. Analysis of the CCTV images indeed shows that it is resistance expressed later on in the course of a robbery that is responded to with violence. The authors report that robberies fail in two instances: when victims disregard the robbers and when victims seemingly cooperate but de facto resist as well. In both situations, robbers are unable to establish dominance, causing them to abandon their plan.

Some researchers argue that observation does not enable you as a researcher to *understand* why humans behave as they behave. Observation places you outside the context within which your research subjects are living, behaving, making decisions. Only observing their movements does not make you understand the constraints people live under, the pressures they experience. Observation as such, according to this reasoning, generates data that are limited in validity. For understanding what drives your research subjects, it would be necessary to *be* one of the group that is being studied, to undergo what they undergo and to experience from the inside what the research subjects experience. While this is never completely realisable (the researcher will be a researcher, will remain an outsider, will after the study return to his or her own realm) a number of researchers – also criminologists – therefore advocate the use of so-called *participant observation* for the study of deviant or subcultural groups.

This immediately generates a dilemma, as should not the researcher immediately tell the (unknowing until then) research subjects that s/he is not one of them, but is studying them? And if s/he does not do so, it is not unethical to study people undercover? And is it not dangerous? De Jong (2007) in his study of street youth told his study objects from the start that he was a researcher and wanted to understand their way of life. His subjects at first regarded him warily, but after a few tests of his toughness they accepted him in their midst. They shielded him from things he told them he had better not know. Zaitch (2003) also told his cocaine smuggling research participants that he was a researcher and asked them – after they had agreed that he frequently joined their social gatherings – not to ever let him know anything that would be relevant information for the criminal justice authorities. Other criminological researchers, however, have had to terminate research because respondents told them 'too much'.

4.6 Relative strengths and weaknesses

Summarising the above information, we can discern a few 'laws'. In general it applies that the more open and qualitative the data collection procedure is, the higher we may expect the validity of the data to be, and the deeper our understanding of the phenomenon under study. Unstructured and topical interviews give respondents the chance to venture all that is relevant in their eyes, also topics the researchers had not thought about and could thus never have provided as a question or an answering option in a questionnaire. Participant observation enables you as a researcher to see the world as it were through the eyes of your research subjects, and to understand from within why they act the way they act, to contextualise their behaviour and to infer the meaning of their surroundings to their lives. Participant observation – the observational parallel of the unstructured interview one could argue – gives a deeper understanding of the phenomena under study than observation, as it were, from the outside.

Structured interviews with closed-end questions on the other hand, or for that matter web-based apps, reduce the answering options of respondents, which makes the researcher's life easier, and reduces costs and effort. They make for greater reliability. The 'harnessed' nature of the data collection method, however, also makes that respondents cannot respond freely – and thus validity may suffer.

Open interviews and participant observation make high demands on the skills of field workers. They must have excellent social and verbal skills, be malleable, flexible, adaptable to unexpected situations. They must be able to let different kinds of people speak about sometimes touchy topics, express feelings and probe areas these people themselves perhaps had not ventured yet – and do that in such a way that it is a not unpleasant experience for the research participant. They must be able to interpret what respondents voice, to elicit meaning from respondents' words. Such interviews demand high-quality skills, and therefore extensive training. Researchers must also be able to compile field notes or memos that enable intricate qualitative analysis later on. Not everyone can be taught this trade.

The same goes for the analysis of the material gained from qualitative data collections. This contrasts with quantitative data analysis, that often follows a recipe-kind of format where, as in baking, simply following the recipe ensures a good cake. Quantitative data analysis is in that sense safe and – although especially the math-scary might not agree – a relatively predictable and straightforward process. For qualitative data analysis this is not the case. Coding the data, retrieving the bits that are relevant from the often masses of material is a much more 'winding road' – and therefore much more time-consuming and costly. This means that the more 'open', qualitative data collection methods are also much more costly in terms of data analysis than the quantitative 'closed' ones.

As said, the more 'open' and qualitative data collection methods may be expected to have in general higher validity, but to (generally) score lower on reliability. Miller (2013) illustrated that it can be difficult to achieve reliability in qualitative research. Presenting the same transcript of an interview to 31 qualitative scholars working in criminology, she asked each to retrieve the most important 'themes' (i.e. the topics that parts of the text refer to) from the transcript. To her surprise, the scholars varied greatly in the themes they derived from the one same text. While Miller acknowledges that analysis of qualitative material may vary across scholars and that such divergence is not worrisome per se, she states that when scholars disagree on what can be seen as the rough data, reliability is indeed at stake.

The Lindegaard, Bernasco and De Vries (2016) study discussed above shows however that this need not always be the case in qualitative research: as these authors describe, they coded and independently re-coded all CCTV fragments, showing how the reliability of their codings was well above commonly used thresholds. Of course, they were able to do this as they had in a sense archival material, that they could observe and re-observe as often as they liked. In the case of ethnographic field work, where one single researcher is immersed in the research setting, observing and talking and making notes and memo's now and then, such independent re-coding would be practically impossible. Also, in the Lindegaard *et al.* study, the coders all used the same previously developed deductive coding scheme, with pre-set categories, which likely enhanced reliability.

Qualitative data collections are almost always more costly, which means that in general smaller samples can be investigated. Qualitative data collection demands strong interviewer and researcher skills. The more quantitative data collection methods are generally cheaper, and generate data with higher reliability. Preliminary research and good piloting is necessary to achieve good validity here too, as once the study has gone ahead there is no possibility to modify instruments. Larger samples can generally be studied, and when samples have been adequately drawn generalisable statements can be made. The choice for one or the other method generally depends heavily on the research question, and the research setting and resources.

In many cases there may be good reason to combine the two. Lafree (2012) analysed 2,362 piracy events between 2005 – 2010, comprising boarding attempts, successful boardings and hijackings, from 91 countries. His database was built from the ASAM (Anti Shipping Act Messaging) database, the UN International Maritime Organization monthly reports, with all reports validated by an open media search ('open source data'). The texts were analysed to code, amongst others, for each event a number of opportunity characteristics (for instance whether the ship was berthed or anchored, or whether it was in the international recommended transit corridor (IRTC), a corridor where surveillance for ships is offered), and situational dynamics (for instance whether pirates had a mothership and were armed, whether the crew was vigilant and spotted the pirates, whether the crew used fire hoses to repel the pirates, sounded the alarm). After quantitative variables had been scored from the qualitative text material on these more than 2,000 events, analysis showed that the odds of a successful boarding were significantly lower when the ship was in an IRTC corridor, and that there was a big impact of a crew's watchfulness and response (firing hoses etc). The author however also concluded that additional qualitative analysis of the events is necessary to better understand the situational dynamics behind these outcomes.

Chapter 5

Measurement design

5.1 Introduction

In the literature, a research plan or research design is generally defined as the plan that details the steps that must be taken to be able to answer the research questions. A research plan in that sense is therefore a kind of 'road map', a protocol that describes how the various steps to be set for conducting the research will look and unfold. The plan cannot foresee what the findings will be, but it can outline that a pilot study (see section 2.5) should be conducted and that based on its findings, the questionnaire and strategy to approach the sample members may be adapted. It will specify whether it is necessary to have the plan itself reviewed by an *ethics committee* (see section 2.8) and will reserve time in the planning for approval by that ethics committee. The research plan will outline what sample shall be drawn, what data collection strategy or instruments employed, what 'design' will be used (for instance, whether a control group will be studied, whether respondents are to be studied repeatedly, etc.). A research plan generally also outlines the analysis methods: even though the data have not been collected yet, because of the research plan we will know what the data structure will be (we know the approximate sample size, we know the types of variables, we know whether respondents were interviewed repeatedly or not). This means that the research plan can – and should – also contain an analysis plan. Finally, it should contain a time plan and an itemised budget.

The part of research design that this chapter will be dealing with is the 'design'-part of the research plan, the design proper. Or: the research design 'in a narrow sense'. This part of research design is also often referred to as the 'measurement design', which is how we will in this book from now on call it, to distinguish it from the research design in a broader sense. The measurement design lays out the structure within which measurements are going to be evaluated. This will likely sound pretty vague, so let us give a few examples.

Suppose that we want to find out whether the number of registered cases of rape has increased because of a law change in the Netherlands in 1991. In that year, the criminalised behaviour in the legal description of rape was broadened. Amongst other changes that broadened the description, the relevant sexual behaviour was extended from 'sexual intercourse outside marriage' to 'the sexual penetration of the body'. The new law thus clearly entails a much wider range of sexual acts, so that it might be expected that the number of police-recorded cases of rape would be correspondingly higher. Rape before 1991 did not exist within marriage, men could not be raped, and rape could be carried out only with a male sexual organ. After 1991, penetration by fingers and objects and of other orifices could constitute rape too, resulting in the (in)famous 'Tongzoen'-case, where a man was convicted of rape for forcing a French kiss on another man. Now, for answering our research question we take the numbers of rape cases recorded by the police before and after the law change in 1991. And it might be so that we indeed see that numbers rose from 1991: let us say that 3,000 cases were registered in 1990 and 3,150 in 1991. Our problem now is that – while we have ascertained that an increase occurred – we do not know whether that increase occurred *because* of the law change. It could be that rape was on the rise anyway from a number of years hence, and that the increase from 1990 to 1991 is no deviation from this pre-existing trend and not a sudden rise due to the law change. Or the increase could be just some temporal fluctuation, with numbers of cases going up and down from year to year. Phrased differently, we observe a rise, but it is difficult to *attribute* the rise to the law change. Our design (where we observe the number one year before and one year after the law change) does not allow us to make such causal statements.

Let us discuss a second research question. Suppose that we want to know whether physical maltreatment of children by their parents increases the risk that these children will later themselves become violent as well. Suppose that we have designed our study such, that we investigate a group of adults who were maltreated when they were children by their parents, and a group of adults who were not maltreated as children. Now we have what is called a *comparison group* (the non-maltreated). Having a comparison group is a powerful feature of this design. It enables us to see whether we find more violence in the group of adults who were maltreated as children than in the group who were not exposed to such maltreatment. (Note that this is a measurement design we could not possibly have chosen for the first example: the law change took place for the whole of the Netherlands, and there is for that reason no way we could have found a comparison group.)

Suppose now, for the child physical maltreatment example, that we find that the adults who were maltreated as children by their parents are indeed more violent: they have for instance been more often convicted for violent offences (leaving aside whether this is a valid measure of violent behaviour). Do we now know they are more violent *because* they were physically abused as children? Even though we have a comparison group that was not abused and our evidence is therefore clearly stronger than in the first example, still we cannot be sure. There are several alternative explanations for the finding. It may be that the abused children inherited their violent temperament from their abusing parents. If that were the case, then it would not make a difference whether children were actually abused or not, as the temperament is passed on from generation to generation anyway. Or it could be that the children learnt a certain behavioural repertoire from their parents, by witnessing their parents solving conflicts or venting their anger through physical violence. Several so-called *confounding variables* or *confounders* – variables that co-vary with both the childhood physical maltreatment and the later violent behaviour – can also explain the association we find between having been physically abused and later violence. All in all, in this design we cannot be certain that it is the physical abuse to which later violent behaviour can be attributed.

Suppose as a last example that we want to know whether an intervention reduces antisocial behaviour. Now we can build an even stronger design. We can sample a group of antisocial persons, divide them in two, and give (administer) the intervention to one group, and some other likely non-effective intervention, such as watching a soap series, to the other group. How do we compose those two groups? If we let our antisocial respondents choose which group to belong to, we are actually opening the door to confounding. An obvious confounder is namely 'motivation to change': the respondents who are eager to change their antisocial behaviour will likely choose to belong to the group that receives the intervention, and the unmotivated respondents will watch the soap series. If the group with the intervention turns out to be less antisocial after completion of the intervention, then this could be due to the intervention itself. But it could also be due to their different mindset, their higher motivation to change.

What we should do to prevent this – and this 'trick' is likely known to most readers – is let *chance* dictate who belongs to which group. If we let chance determine who receives the intervention and who does not, it is not possible that there would be a third factor, a confounding variable, that could also explain the association between the intervention and antisocial behaviour. As only chance played a role in deciding who will undergo the intervention and who will not, there is simply no property that can be identified that is associated with receiving the intervention and that can also explain the findings: only chance determined group membership so there can only be chance differences between the two groups. Therefore, if we find that there is a difference between the group that underwent the intervention and the group that did not, it can only be explained by the intervention itself – and chance.

These three examples represent a spectrum along which designs can be ranked. The spectrum represents the strength with which statements can be made about causality, or the confidence with which we can attribute the outcome (the rise in rape cases, the prevalence of a violent temperament, a change in antisocial behaviour) to the factor we are studying. This spectrum will be discussed in more detail below.

Many of the designs we will discuss in this chapter are designs for quantitative studies, predominantly studies for assessing causality. Thus, in many of the examples we discuss we will speak about the effect of a certain factor X on an outcome Y. The designs we discuss will be assessed particularly for the strength with which they are able to make causal statements regarding the effect of X on Y. Measurement design issues play less of a role in qualitative studies, as causal inferences are generally not arrived at in the same manner as they are in quantitative studies. In qualitative research, causal inferences are generally derived within specific contexts, and are generally multifactorial. In quantitative research, we often conduct studies where we are interested in the effect, in isolation, of one or more factors X on one outcome variable Y. Qualitative studies would be employed once we want to unravel more intricate multifactorial mechanisms, that cannot be reduced to a bare $X \rightarrow Y$ scheme.

While we discussed the selection of research units in chapter 3, the choice of measurement instrument in chapter 4, and will discuss the choice of the measurement design in this chapter, it does not follow that decisions about the research plan are or should always be made in this order. In fact choices for sample, measurement instruments and measurement design are often made in an iterative process. This is so because the possibilities for sam-

Figure 5.1: Representation of relation between independent and dependent variable

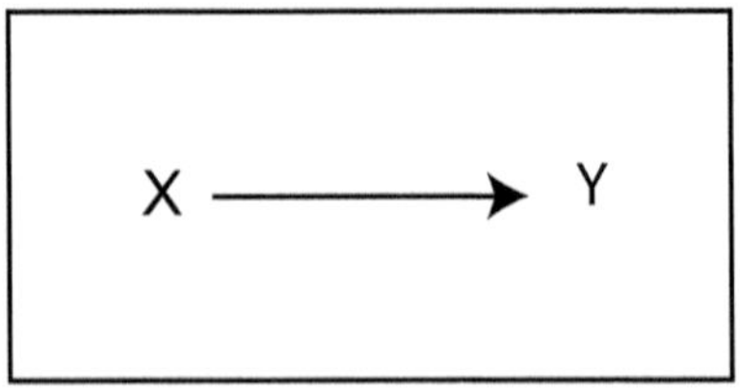

pling influence design choices, and the design that is desired given the research question also in a sense narrows the options for or dictates that certain instruments should be used. If we have decided that we want to know whether a demobilisation programme supported former child soldiers in reintegrating back to their communities, a quantitative design to investigate causality is not an obvious choice. The picture that explains the reintegration process would be complex, layered and contextualised. Therefore, we would want to study how demobilisation took shape, whether it differed for different child soldiers (boys, girls, of different ages, having stayed with fighting groups longer or shorter), why certain aspects fostered reintegration, as well as under what conditions such aspects could also be counterproductive.

Practically speaking, time and money greatly constrain the type of design that can be chosen. Also, it must be conceded that in choosing for a qualitative or quantitative design, researcher preference and skills play a role as well. Thus, the order in which issues are decided upon could very well differ from the sequence in which they are presented here, and the outcome may be decided by practical constraints and available expertise as much as by methodological desiderata.

5.2 Dependent and independent variables

All of the designs we discuss in this chapter are quantitative designs for causal inference. Using the cleverest possible design, we want to make as strong as possible statements about causality. This means that in our datasets we will have variables that we think of as 'causes' and variables that are considered 'effects'. For the purposes of this book, we will defy epistemological critique and equate variables that we consider causes with the term *independent variable*. The variables that we consider effects we denote as *dependent variables*. We represent the relations between these variables as in Figure 5.1. It is a convention that dependent variables are denoted as Y. Independent variables are often written as X (which we will do too in this book). When there are several independent variables, they are denoted as $X_1, X_2, X_3, \ldots$.

Obviously, dependent variables can be influenced by more than one independent variable, and independent variables (in the sense that they influence the Y variable) can themselves be influenced by other independent variables again. See Figure 5.2, where in the

Figure 5.2: Representation of more complex relations between independent variables and dependent variable

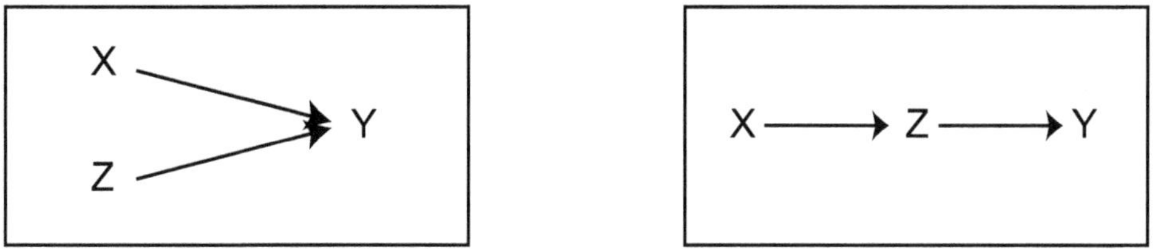

right-hand side the variable Z is both a dependent (predicted by X) as well as an independent variable (predicting Y).

5.3 Causality

As said, in this chapter we will be discussing measurement designs, focusing specifically on the strength with which they allow us to make statements about causality. Before doing so, we will therefore first briefly discuss conditions for causality, and complications in assessing causality.

For X to be the cause of Y, three conditions must be met:

(1) *X precedes Y*

(2) *X correlates with Y*

(3) *there is no alternative explanation for the correlation between X and Y*

Obviously, condition 1 is logical, as we generally do not believe that causes occur after their effects. Condition 2 implies that we require that X and Y are empirically associated before we accept X as a cause of Y. Condition 3 is crucial, as it requires that any empirical association cannot be explained by a third factor.

What is meant by this is the following. For instance, we may perceive that the number of firefighters at a fire is strongly associated with the ensuing damage. But do the firefighters *cause* that damage? The firefighters come before the eventual damage, the two are correlated, so the first two conditions for causality are met. However, and obviously, that damage is not caused by the firefighters, but both (firefighters and damage later on) are determined by the magnitude of the fire: when a large fire has erupted, many firefighters are dispatched and the damage will likely be large. We call this a situation of *spurious association* or spurious correlation: the number of firefighters and the damage are associated – not because they are themselves causally connected, but because they are each causally connected to the same *third factor*. See Figure 5.3.

Figure 5.3: Spurious association between number of firefighters and damage

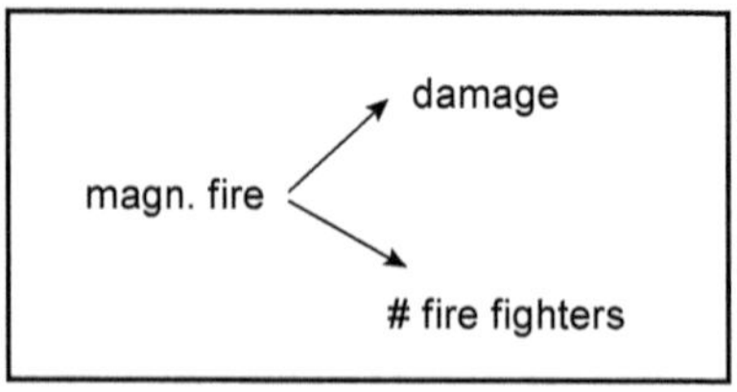

Figure 5.4: Model for the relation between alcohol consumption and fractures

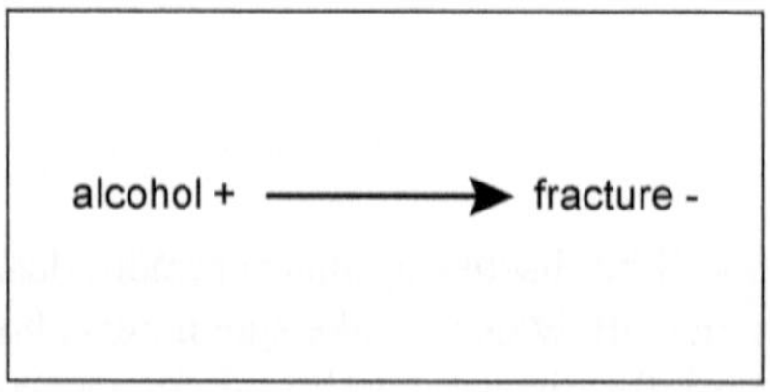

In this example, the magnitude of the fire is an alternative explanation for the association between the number of firefighters and the damage, a third factor or third variable, also called a *confounder*. Now in this example we would not be easily led to believe that firefighters damage fire scenes. But what of the association between (moderate) alcohol consumption and the risk of breaking your leg during skiing? A Dutch researcher a number of years ago published a study in which a clear negative association between these two variables was proven: people at skiing holidays who drank a number of alcoholic consumptions during the day, had a significantly reduced risk of fractures. The researcher stated that this finding confirmed his theory that alcohol relaxes people's muscles, and that those who drank some while skiing would be more relaxed skiers; if they fell, they would do so in a less cramped and more supple way thus reducing their risk to fall awkwardly and break something. See Figure 5.4.

After publication of the results, other researchers remarked that perhaps the association was due to the fact that people who drank more simply skied fewer hours per day, and thus were correspondingly less exposed to the risk of falling and breaking their bones. Re-analysis of the data (investigating the association between alcohol and bone fractures separately for those who skied 1 hour, 2 hours, 3 hours etc. per day) proved that this was indeed the case. See Figure 5.5.

Such painful mistakes are every researcher's nightmare. Hard thinking and the exploration of all thinkable alternative scenarios that may explain the association hopefully prevent the most blatant mistakes. However, clearly we can never be sure that we have

Figure 5.5: Real relation between alcohol consumption and fracture risk, including exposure time

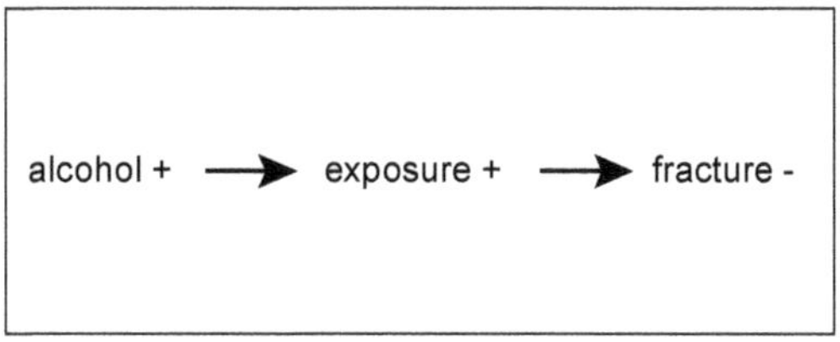

ruled out all the gazillion theoretically possible alternative explanations for the association between X and Y (condition 3). Therefore, whenever we observe an association between X and Y, and even after we have ruled out all alternative explanations we can think of, still we cannot be completely sure given a correlation and the right time order that the association between X and Y is causal. Formulated differently, correlation is a necessary, but not a sufficient condition for causality. Correlation is not causation.

5.4 Interventions and change

Suppose that we believe that therapy increases people's well-being. We have a variable X – reflecting whether or not someone underwent therapy – and a variable Y – measuring well-being. If therapy works as we believe it does, then people would before therapy score lower on well-being than after. See Figure 5.6, in which we sketch a hypothetical situation where the intervention (therapy X) was administered between month 4 and 5, and where it can be seen clearly that the scores for well-being (Y) are higher after therapy than before. This is consistent with our hypothesis. We might be tempted to think that therapy is effective.

As argued above, we know that we cannot be sure that the improvement we register is *attributable* to the therapy. The increase in well-being could simply be part of a general trend: see Figure 5.7(a) where it can be seen that a steady growth in well-being set in already before therapy was administered, and that this smooth increase proceeded seemingly unperturbed. It could also be that the change is not more than chance fluctuation, see Figure 5.7(b). Here it can be seen that the change from month 4 to month 5 is within the bandwidth of normally occurring fluctuation; in all likelihood, if the therapy had been administered between month 5 and 6 we would have witnessed a decrease in well-being!

The graph in Figure 5.7(c) appears to offer the most support for an effect of therapy X: the scores hover around 1.3 before the therapy is administered, and leap to a stable level of around 2.2 afterwards. The change cannot be explained by factors such as autonomous growth, or random fluctuation.

We are however still unsure, also for the situation in Figure 5.7(c), whether the change is actually attributable to the therapy. Suppose that we have our data from the Netherlands and that months 1, 2, 3 and 4 were very rainy, drizzly, dreary months, and that onwards

Figure 5.6: Well-being scores before and after therapy 'intervention'

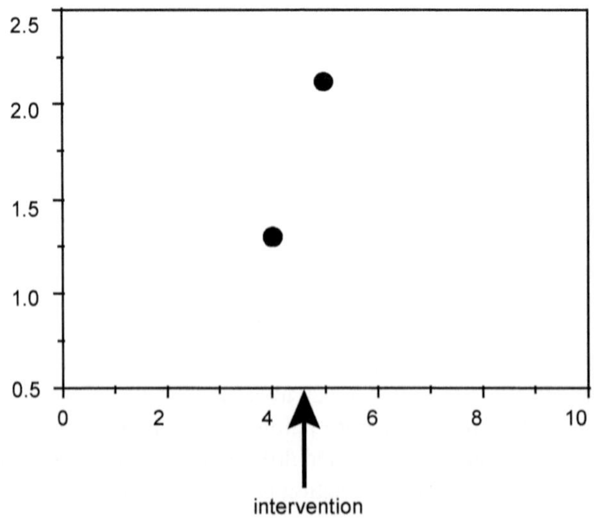

from month 5, the weather cleared, summer set in, so that everyone's well-being shot up? If we would want to know whether the increased well-being that we observe is due to the therapy or due to other factors, ideally we want to have comparison data from a group of people who are otherwise similar (a so-called *control group*) so that they were similarly under the influence of the weather or any other factors that impacted their well-being, and who differ from the group that received therapy (the *experimental group*) in that they did *not* get therapy, and in fact differed from the control group *only* in that respect.

Such a situation we have sketched in Figure 5.7(d). Here we see that the control group's scores (they were equal to those of the experimental group in months 1 to 4) after the therapy remain at around the same level. It thus appears as if we may be more confident here of the conclusion that therapy increases well-being: those who do undergo therapy have decidedly higher well-being scores afterwards than those who don't. For that conclusion to be defensible, however, what we would need to be sure of is that the scores of the control group may be regarded as the scores that the experimental group would have had had they not undergone the therapy. If that is so, the control group is then referred to as the *counterfactual* for the experimental group: the control group is 'the-experimental-group-without-the-intervention'. However, in the situation we just described we are not sure of that. It may be that the experimental group is composed of self-selectors, people who wanted to change, to improve their lives and who therefore elected to take therapy. In that case, the difference between experimental and control group may also be due (we do not know to what extent, but at least partially) to this difference in motivation, or to any other factors associated with the motivation to change.

Figure 5.7: Development of well-being scores from month 1 to 8

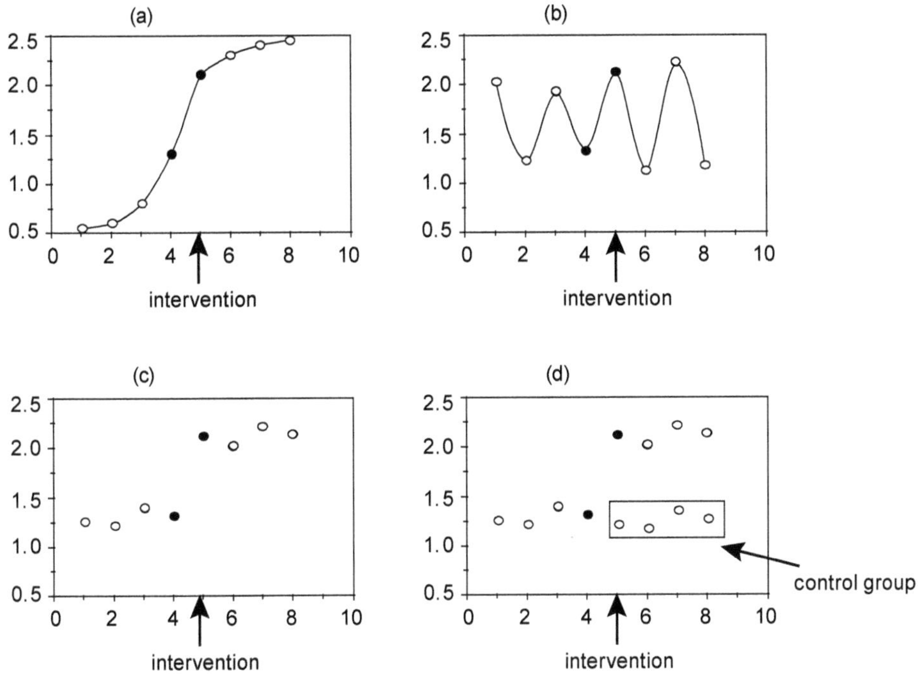

These stylised examples each illustrated alternative explanations for the beneficial effect of therapy that we appeared to be seeing. Each time the issue was not whether there was an effect, but whether there was not an alternative explanation for the occurrence of the effect other than the therapy. We went over several other explanations, such as an autonomous 'trend', and an effect of the changing of the seasons. Both these explanations jeopardised the *internal validity* (see also section 2.6) of our conclusion about the effect of therapy on well-being. We showed towards the end that we can only be confident that the effect is attributable to the therapy if an otherwise comparable group that did not undergo therapy performs markedly different.

In the sections below, we will first give an outline of the most important possible threats to internal validity. Their discussion will be brief and summary. After that, we will rank order designs by strength and discuss three main classes of designs, that correspond to the examples we started this chapter with. We will show how as designs become 'stronger' in the sense that they allow for more confident statements about causality, this is because threats to validity have been ruled out.

5.4.1 Threats to internal validity

(1) *History*

Suppose that I offer a training to combat fear of armed violence. I offer my training to a group of 100 volunteers, all with reasonable to serious fear of armed violence. I neatly measure their fear of armed violence before the training (my pre-measurement, also called *pre-test*) and after (my post-measurement, also called *post-test*). What I notice to my dismay, is that right during the week in which I offer my volunteers the training, a huge shootout occurs at a secondary school. Every citizen's fear of armed violence goes up, also that of my volunteers. This external event – that influences the scores on the dependent variable – is referred to as *history*. It is defined as a threat to internal validity because it jeopardises the conclusions that can be drawn about the effect of the intervention under investigation. As it is confounded with the intervention (it occurs around the same time and influences fear scores too) it affects my *internal validity*: I may not conclude that the change in fear scores ($Y_2 - Y_1$) is attributable to the intervention (X), as there is now a third factor (the shootout) that is an alternative explanation for the increase in fear levels.

I now, because of this external event, cannot judge anymore the effectiveness of my training. Maybe my volunteers' fear levels would have been much lower if that shootout had not occurred! If I only compare the pre- and post therapy scores of my volunteers, there is however no way I can find that out. Obviously, I would have had no problem if I had included a comparison or *control group* in my study. The control group would have to have been chosen to be comparable to the experimental group (the group undergoing the treatment). They should differ only in that these volunteers do not get the training. If we let chance decide who becomes a member of the experimental and control group, we are certain that there are no systematic differences between the two groups. Any differences between the two groups can then be attributed (and attributed *only*) to the training. There is (see section 5.3) no alternative explanation – but chance – for differences between the two groups.

See Figure 5.8, in which the solid dots represent the scores for the treated (experimental) group, the open dots those for the control group. The figure shows that the two groups are approximately equal at pre-test and that indeed the scores for the experimental group went up, from about 1.5 to about 1.75. The scores in the control group went up much more however, from about 1.5 to about 2.25.

Given that – if we have designed our study well and assigned respondents randomly to groups – the control group equals the experimental group without the treatment, i.e. the control group behaves how the experimental group had behaved had they not received the intervention, we may conclude that the gain in fear generated by the treatment is -0.5 (1.75 – 2.25), or: the reduction in fear due to the treatment is 0.5.

The conclusion we draw is that the use of a control group eliminates the risk of history acting as a confounder. Both groups, experimental and control, are influenced by the same historical events. Comparing changes in the two, we can simply subtract any changes in the control group from the changes in the experimental group, and we are left with the net change in the experimental group – net of any perturbances we

Figure 5.8: Control for threat *history* through use of control group

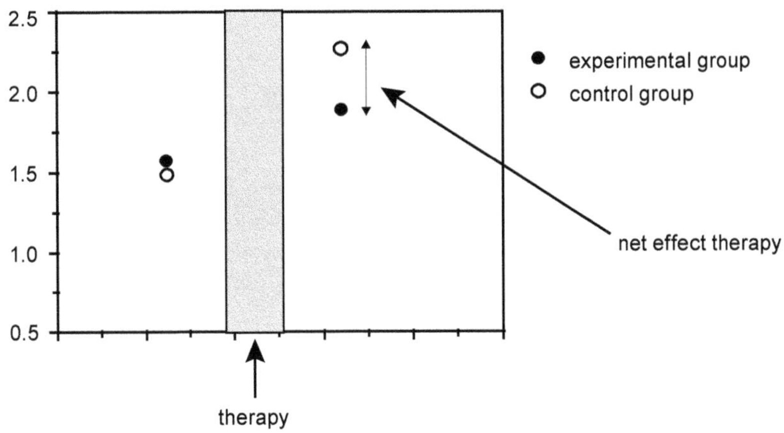

are not interested in – attributable to the intervention. Using a control group therefore makes that we may – if cause X precedes effect Y and if there is a correlation between X and Y – state that no alternative explanation exists for the association between X and Y and that therefore X causes Y. The use of a(n equivalent) control group is one of the most powerful aspects of experimental designs. It makes that experimental designs have good *internal validity*.

(2) *Maturation*

The threat we sketched previously in Figure 5.7(a), is referred to in the literature as *maturation*. Here it is not the intervention but an autonomous trend that generates a change from pre-to post-test. An often used example is that of maths training. If I would offer a new kind of maths training to school pupils, I would likely find that their math skills go up from pre-test to post-test. This may be due to the maths training. But it may also be due to the fact that students mature over the course of a school year. Part of the effect may be due to the training, part may be due to that ripening or maturation.

Only if I use a control group, can I determine what part of the improvement is due to the training, and what part of the improvement would have occurred anyway. Using a control group I can determine the change that the experimental group would have shown had it not received the new maths training:

$$\text{change}_{\text{control group}} = \text{autonomous trend}$$

The change in the experimental group is now due to that autonomous trend plus the effect of the maths training:

$$\text{change}_{\text{experimental group}} = \text{autonomous trend} + \text{effect maths training}$$

Comparing the two changes (for each group the difference between post-test and pre-test) gives:

$$\text{change}_{\text{experimental group}} - \text{change}_{\text{control group}} =$$

$$\text{(autonomous trend + effect maths training)} - \text{autonomous trend} =$$

$$\text{effect maths training}$$

We can write this more generally as follows. If E_1 is the average score at pre-test in the experimental group, and E_2 the average score at post-test, and if C_1 is the average score at pre-test in the control group, and C_2 the average score at post-test, then we can write the design for this study schematically as:

$$\begin{array}{lcl} E_1 & \ldots\ X\ \ldots & E_2 \\ C_1 & \ldots\ldots\ldots\ldots & C_2 \end{array}$$

with X the intervention. This design is officially referred to as the *untreated control group design with pre-test and post-test* or, more loosely in the criminological literature as the *randomised controlled trial* or RCT, and in other literatures often as 'classical experiment'. Given that the change in the control group is the counterfactual for the experimental group, so that $(C_2 - C_1)$ represents the change in the experimental group had the intervention not been administered, then the change in the experimental group $(E_2 - E_1)$ minus the change in the control group is the net effect of the intervention:

$$\text{net effect } X = (E_2 - E_1) - (C_2 - C_1).$$

Had we not used a control group, we would have been able to see only the gross effect of the intervention $E_2 - E_1$, being the combination of the effects of the maturation and the maths training, without being able to say which part was due to either.

(3) *Testing*

It is known from the literature that administering tests or questionnaires by itself changes people's ideas, skills, and thus possible scores on the next administration of that same questionnaire. A relative of the author once had to be operated and was asked, before the narcosis, to fill in a small test. After waking up she filled in the same test. To the surprise of the researcher, she had better scores – a few hours after narcosis – than before. She being a well-trained social scientist explained to him that this was due to *testing*, the phenomenon that people's scores are affected by the simple filling in of tests: she simply learned from filling out the test the first time.

As the attentive reader will have gathered, also this threat to validity can be countered by using a randomised control group. If testing affects the scores, then it will do so equally in control and experimental group, so we can again find the net effect of the intervention by comparing the changes in control and experimental group.

(4) *Instrumentation*

With *instrumentation* is meant that changes from pre- to post-test may also be generated by changes in the measurement instrument. Thus, one observes a change in respondents' scores from pre-test to post-test, but the different scores are not due to people changing, but due to the instrument changing from pre-test to post-test. If one could, one would therefore always keep one's instrument identical across multiple sweeps of the same study, across respondents, etc. See also section 4.2. But sometimes this is not possible: political parties have changed from one wave to the next, the meaning of church attendance for religiosity has changed from 1950 to the present, and the like. Again, this threat of instrumentation is countered by using a control group. If instrumentation affects scores, then it will do so equally in control and experimental group and comparing the changes between control and experimental group will again give us the net effect, net of any impact of instrumentation.

The first four threats that we just discussed are therefore all effectively countered if we use a control group. In each instance, any threat impacts both control and experimental group and is therefore eliminated by computing the net effect as $(E_2 - E_1) - (C_2 - C_1)$. It may even be that several threats occur simultaneously, or that other disturbances also affect the data. All that does not bother us, as the design is such that we will always be able to distill the net effect of the intervention:

$$\text{change}_{\text{experimental group}} - \text{change}_{\text{control group}} =$$

$$(\text{history} + \text{maturation} + \text{testing} + \text{instrumentation} + \text{any other} + \text{intervention}) -$$

$$(\text{history} + \text{maturation} + \text{testing} + \text{instrumentation} + \text{any other}) =$$

$$\text{effect intervention}$$

For the threats to internal validity that we will subsequently discuss, the use of a control group as such is not always sufficient. These threats either bear on issues that may affect the usefulness of a control group, the choice and retention of group members, or they deal with more practical issues such as whether control and experimental group members influence each other.

(5) *Selection*

We say that *selection* is a threat to internal validity when the experimental and control group have not been formed randomly. Whenever that is the case, we cannot rule out that a third factor (the factor that influenced who became member of which group) can also (partly) explain the difference between experimental and control group.

Selection definitely occurs if one lets sample members decide themselves whether they want to be a member of one group or the other. It may also occur if we work for instance with existing school classes. Even though it is hard to envisage how exactly conclusions would be affected, knowing that there are other systematic differences between the groups (for instance: different teachers), is sufficient to be aware that internal validity may be compromised.

If the control and experimental groups have not been formed by a random process, it may also happen that one or more of the threats discussed above occurs in one group but not in the other. If my fear of armed violence experimental group is based in Alkmaar, and my fear of armed violence control group in Alphen aan den Rijn, where a massive shooting incident took place in a shopping mall in 2011 just when I was offering my training, it is likely that this history-type of effect plays a larger role in the control group than in the experimental – this might make us overestimate the effect of the training to combat fear of armed violence.

(6) *Attrition*

As we discussed in section 3.6, attrition is generally non-random: those who drop out of the study generally have different characteristics than those who remain. In the context of experimental designs, attrition or drop-out (also called *experimental mortality*) may cause groups to become incomparable, as attrition may be different in one group from the other. This means that if we start out with two comparable groups, control and experimental, beautifully formed by chance, attrition will generally cause these groups to become non-random, and less comparable. It is likely that control groups (especially once they are aware that they are not receiving any special treatment) experience more attrition than experimental groups. Then, the same problems as outlined just above under 'Selection' emerge.

(7) *Insufficient separation between groups*

Suppose that we are conducting a study within a large firm. We are trying to train employees to work more efficiently. Now, we try to evaluate the training according to the state of the methodological art, that is, we have formed an experimental and control group out of employees within that same firm. However, having trained the experimental respondents, there is a risk that the training in a sense 'seeps through' to the control respondents: they meet each other afterwards at the coffee machine, in the elevator, over lunch. Control employees might even witness the experimental employees employ all these handy tricks, and decide that they want to become as efficient.

We call this situation one of *insufficient separation between groups*. Because the intervention also reaches the control group, 'leaks' to the control group members, we are likely to underestimate its effect.

A solution is hard to find in this case. Forming a control group out of employees from, say, a different branch will increase the separation and decrease the likelihood of seeping through, but will also make the control and experimental group less comparable, and thus generate selection problems.

(8) *Perceived differences between groups*

Continuing from the example we just discussed, it might also occur that a certain envy is generated in this study. Suppose that the experimental respondents are trained in a nice location, share fancy lunches together, while the control group respondents have to plough on in the same old dreary office. Examples have been reported where the control respondents gave up doing their job decently altogether (thus making that the effect of the training is overestimated) as well as the opposite where the control respondents worked exceptionally hard to demonstrate that the training they were deprived of was useless (thus making that its effect was underestimated).

(9) *Regression towards the mean*

To give an example for the last threat that we discuss, suppose that we want to investigate the effect of, again, a maths training. We have a group of children who have had consistently low scores on maths tests, and these are our experimental group. Of course, we know we must have a control group as well, so we administer a maths test to all other children in the school, and we take the children scoring lowest on that test as our control group. Regression to the mean is now likely to occur. But what do we mean by that? It is best understood as follows.

It is likely that in our lowest scorers who form the control group, a few scored low on the test just through some quirk. They had an off-day, a headache, they were madly in love. They were not consistently low scorers, otherwise they would have been members of the experimental group.

Now if we compute the scores of this control group on the post-test, it is likely that some of those accidentally low scorers, will at post-test not anymore have their off-day or their headache or bout of love sickness anymore. These will score higher at C_2 than at C_1. Their scores have regressed ('gone back') to the group mean. This means that we – in this example – will underestimate the effect of the maths training.

Regression towards the mean regularly occurs, also outside the context of experiments. It was first described by Francis Galton, an extremely broad and original scholar and half-cousin of Charles Darwin.

5.5 Types of (experimental) designs

The designs we discussed so far all have in common that they are structured such that we can make statements about the causal effect of an independent variable on a dependent variable. We have a pre-test and a post-test, which means that we measure at least twice, and always have a comparison group to gauge our results. Whenever we want to make causal statements, such as when we want to evaluate the effectiveness of an intervention, an experimental design is needed.

Experimental designs vary – as elaborated above – along the strength with which they allow to make causal statements. We saw that designs without a control group are vulnerable to threats of internal validity. Including a control group is a huge improvement. The strongest designs are those that have randomly formed experimental and control groups. In that case, it can be effectively ruled out that any systematic difference between the groups can explain differences between the groups: as the groups were formed randomly there simply are no systematic differences. The only systematic difference between the two groups is the intervention. A difference in scores can therefore be attributed to the intervention, and to the intervention only.

In criminology, the so-called *Maryland Scientific Methods Scale*, or MSMS (Sherman, Gottfredson, MacKenzie *et al.*, 1998), is often used as a reference to gauge the strength of particular designs. The MSMS defines five levels of increasing strength with which causal statements can be made. As Sherman and his co-authors are criminologists, the levels refer to crime. The levels are defined as follows:

(1) A correlation has been established between a crime prevention program and a measure of crime or crime risk factors at a single point in time.

(2) A temporal sequence between the program and the crime or risk outcome is clearly observed, or the presence of a comparison group without demonstrated comparability to the treatment group.

(3) A comparison between two or more comparable units of analysis, one with and one without the program.

(4) Comparison between multiple units with and without the program, controlling for other factors, or using comparison units that evidence only minor differences.

(5) Random assignment and analysis of comparable units to program and comparison groups.

While the first level is design-wise fairly vaguely described, level 2 describes a design where a control group is present, but it is incomparable. Level 3 describes a situation where a reasonably comparable control group is present. Level 4 describes the situation where the experimental and control group differ only slightly. At level 5, we have a truly randomised design, an RCT. Sherman, Gottfredson, MacKenzie *et al.* (1998) use as a rule of thumb that designs below level 3 are unfit for evaluation research. Any design that does not meet the criteria of level 3 or higher should therefore not be used for causal inference. Note that level 1 comprises not more than the existence of a correlation, and that this is the lowest level.

In a completely randomised design the researcher exerts control over all aspects of measurement: s/he assigns respondents to groups, (often although not always) administers the intervention, and conducts the measurements. Designs with non-randomised control groups (level 2, 3 and 4) are in the literature referred to as *quasi-experimental designs*. In a quasi-experimental setting, there is less control: while the researcher may still administer the intervention and conduct the measurements, s/he works with existing groups, such as classrooms, or companies.

Both the experimental and quasi-experimental designs look schematically as follows:

$$\begin{array}{ccccc} E_1 & \ldots & X & \ldots & E_2 \\ C_1 & & \ldots\ldots\ldots\ldots & & C_2 \end{array}$$

but differ in the nature of the control group (randomised or not). The MSMS disaggregates quasi-experimental designs into those with very well comparable control and experimental groups (level 4) and those with comparable control and experimental groups (level 3), and last those with actually fairly incomparable control groups (level 2).

Other types of designs than the randomised controlled trial are possible. The following is called the one group pre-test-post-test design:

$$E_1 \quad \ldots \quad X \quad \ldots \quad E_2$$

This is the design that we depicted in Figure 5.6. It is as we showed, and as the MSMS underscores, a weak design. A better design with just one group is the so-called *time series design* that we depicted in Figure 5.7(c), as with this design we will, even if we lack a control group, be able to detect maturation as well as testing. It does not, however, control for history occurring simultaneously with the intervention:

$$E_1 \quad E_2 \quad E_3 \quad \ldots \quad X \quad \ldots \quad E_4 \quad E_5 \quad E_6$$

If the intervention in such an 'experimental-group-only study' is not administered by the researcher, the study is denoted as an *observational* or *passive observational study*: the researcher does not administer the intervention, does not assign respondents to groups, all s/he can do is observe the data.

Luckily, some intermediate solutions are possible that improve upon the situation of having only observational data. One such possibility is to find, for every member of the 'experimental group' one or more observational units that are seemingly identical to the experimental group unit – but for the 'intervention'. Suppose that we are studying international crimes, and we want to investigate what structural or country-level factors play a role in the outbreak of genocide. Obviously, we are unable to randomly assign countries to the experimental condition 'genocide' or 'no genocide'. The genocide has occurred or has not, and we can only observe the countries and episodes where the genocide took place. We can however try to find similar countries to the genocide countries, in terms of GDP, type of manufacturing output, Gini coefficient, ethnic make-up, political system, etc., but that differ in the sense that no genocide occurred. Such a design is called a *case-control design*. The procedure that we apply is called 'matching'.

Matching is very broadly used when it is impossible to randomise the intervention we want to assess the effect of. It definitely improves upon the strength of our conclusions, but does not eliminate confounding. For instance, if we were able to match perfectly on a certain number of background variables, we would be sure that the experimental and control group are identical on those variables, and that any differences between the two are therefore not attributable to these matched factors anymore. However, we are still unsure whether there are not other factors that we have been unable to match on that are confounded with the 'intervention' we are studying. Matching does not solve our problem completely therefore. A second, more practical disadvantage of matching is that if we want to match on a large number of characteristics (which we would always want to do because then we eliminate the risk that these factors blur our conclusion on the relation between the intervention and the independent variables), it may quickly become impossible to do so. It may simply be impossible to find a matching country that is identical on political system as well as GDP as well as ethnic tensions as well as Gini coefficient, and so forth. Matching remains a second-best solution that one resorts to only when one has no better option. Recent methodological advancements in quantitative methodology have provided some routes to partially overcome these issues for quantitative research (see Bijleveld, Van de Weijer, Ruiter *et al.*, 2018).

This is often the case when we study international crimes, its etiology and aftermath. Matching is also often used in qualitative research, sometimes denoted as comparative analysis or negative-case analysis. McLoughlin and Weerdesteijn (2016) systematically compared the impact that strategies employed by two leaders (Kenneth Kaunda of Zambia and Robert Mugabe of Zimbabwe) had on the risk of mass atrocities. In their study, Zambia with its leader Kenneth Kaunda served as a matched control (where mass atrocities did not occur) for Zimbabwe with its leader Robert Mugabe (where mass atrocities occurred). The authors employed Mahoney and Goertz's (2004) so-called *possibility principle*, which states that two conditions have to be fulfilled for a case to be able to serve as a negative case. First, the positive and negative case must share at least one independent variable associated with the outcome, and second, the outcome must not be impossible in the negative case. These two conditions were met in this study.

5.6 Longitudinal and cross-sectional designs

Whenever measurement units are observed repeatedly, we call such a study *longitudinal* to denote that it stretches over time and that, crucially, we aim to investigate change. Longitudinal studies are often contrasted with cross-sectional studies, where measurements are made at one point in time, and the aim is not to observe or explain change.

Longitudinal designs can be classified into prospective and retrospective designs. Of the two, the prospective design is by far the strongest one. As an illustration, suppose that we study a sample of male child sex abusers. And suppose that we note that almost all of these sex offenders were themselves sexually abused as a child. We might then be tempted to hypothesise that child sexual abuse is a risk factor for sex offending. This statement is however based on *retrospective* data: because of our design, we only observe those who became a sex offender, but not those who were abused but did not become a sex offender. This is referred to in the literature as *selection on the dependent variable*: we miss out on the negatives, those who were abused but who did not become a sex offender.

If we want to be sure that sexual abuse victimisation is a risk factor in the etiology of sex offending we would have to investigate a sample of sexually abused children as well as a sample of not sexually abused children, following them up into adulthood. This is what is referred to as a *prospective* study, prospective because measurements are not obtained looking back, but looking 'forward' so to say. The big advantage of this prospective design is that we will now be able to see the negatives: the number of children who have been abused who do not become a sex offender. In a prospective design, we do not run the risk of selection on the dependent variable because at the start of the study it is still unknown how respondents will develop on the dependent variable.

While prospective studies are methodologically much stronger than retrospective studies, they are – not surprisingly – much more costly and may take a very long time to complete. Prospective research is so much more expensive mainly because it takes so long: it is extremely costly in terms of database maintenance, follow up of sample members, and staff costs. It often takes too long for policy purposes too.

The Cambridge Study in Delinquent Development (CSDD; Farrington, Gallagher, Morley *et al.*, 1990) has now followed up from the 1950s a cohort of inner city youth, from ages 11 to over 50; the world famous Pittsburgh study followed boys (and recently also girls) for an extended period (Stouthamer-Loeber, Loeber, Wei *et al.*, 2002). Both studies generated a wealth of data, and were important in testing and generating theories on life-course criminology. Both were however costly and lengthy, extending well into the pensioning ages of the principal investigators (and in fact of two subsequent principal investigators for the CSDD). Van der Geest, Bijleveld and Verbruggen (2013) tried to be more efficient by starting out with an archival sample. In 2005 they coded the treatment files of 540 men and women who had in the early 1990s at an average age of 15 been treated in a juvenile justice institution for, amongst others, conduct problems. In 2011, they interviewed the men and women still alive (they were able to reach and interview 50%). These men and women were by then on average 35. They thus, in six years, achieved a follow-up period of almost 20 years. In this manner they approached a prospective design without the associated cost however.

Longitudinal designs are also used to be able to investigate causality in situations where it is impossible to construct control groups, or where we may expect much confounding. Respondents (or often in the context of conflict: regions) are then followed-up over long periods, and periods within which certain events occurred are compared against time periods when these events did not occur, to assess what other factors co-vary with this. As an example, in recidivism research, many studies have investigated offenders over longer periods and investigated whether they offended more in periods when they were employed than in periods when they were unemployed, to find out whether employment has a reducing effect on offending. The respondents in such a design in a sense serve as their own controls: stable personal differences such as intelligence, previous criminal record, personality, cannot distort any conclusions anymore. Similar studies have been done on conflicts, comparing the characteristics of regions over time and investigating what distinguished periods of conflict from periods when peace prevailed. This is referred to as a *within-case analysis* or as a *fixed-effects analysis*. See also Bijleveld, Van de Weijer, Ruiter *et al.* (2018).

5.7 Pros and cons of (experimental) measurement designs

The experimental designs we discussed above, particularly the completely randomised design or RCT, are in a sense the golden standard of evaluation research. We reiterate – possibly to the boredom of the reader – that only this design gives us hard evidence of causality.

That being said, and being true, experimental designs have their drawbacks too. First, experimental designs score high on internal validity, but their so-called *external validity* – the extent to which these findings would be be generalisable to other settings – is disputed. A situation where a researcher divides two groups randomly in two is hardly a 'naturalistic setting' and examples have been reported in the literature where an effect of an intervention could be proven in a lab setting – but not outside in the 'real world'. This *external validity* is therefore a special kind of generalisability – not just from a sample to the population, but also from one setting to another setting. This weak point of experiments is also referred to as lack of *ecological validity*. Thus, even when conclusions are 'hard' as cast iron within the artificial research setting, they will be of little use if in real-life situations they would not emerge. This has led some scholars to propagate more naturalistic experiments in favour of more controlled ones.

The ecological validity of controlled experiments may be compromised by several factors. One such factor is the so-called *Hawthorne effect*. This effect is named after a factory in the US where the effect of lightning on worker performance was investigated. The (possibly apocryphal) story goes that whichever way the lightning in the factory was altered, work performance always improved. This finding was explained supposing that performance went up because the workers knew they were being investigated.

Another one of such threats to external validity is the *placebo effect*, also well known from pharmaceutical research. By this is meant that just from receiving some medicine (whether it has active ingredients or not) patients report feeling better. This effect can easily be countered by offering control respondents an intervention that has all the looks of the experimental intervention, but lacks the active ingredients. Thus, if we would want to investigate the effect of a training video on secondary school students' bullying behaviour, we would to counter the placebo effect have to offer the control group a video too, although on an unrelated topic.

The last threat to external validity we will discuss (a few more have been listed in the literature) is the so-called 'Biotex'-effect (Bijleveld, 2018). Now this may seem an odd name, as Biotex is a special kind of washing powder which Dutch housewives love because after soaking hopelessly dirty clothes in it for a while, these become sparkling clean being washed in the washing machine afterwards with regular soap. This Biotex-effect has also been observed in experiments, in the sense that an effect of the intervention could only be demonstrated after respondents had been 'sensitised' to the intervention by a pre-test. Of course, in the real world the intervention would generally not be administered after a pre-test, and then the effect would not emerge. This threat can be uncovered by adding a second control and experimental group to the experiment and not administering a pre-test to these additional groups.

Secondly, not all interventions can be – as it is sometimes phrased – manipulated by a researcher. It is impossible to randomly assign child maltreatment, or heroin use. The impact of such events can only be studied non-experimentally in naturalistic, observational settings. Science is sometimes aided by natural or manmade disasters that enable researchers to study the effects of the upheaval they cause. Bruinsma and Luykx (2003) studied the effect on crime of the disappearance of an entire neighbourhood after a fireworks disaster in Enschede in the Netherlands in 2000. Such occurrences are called *natural experiments*. Bruinsma and Luykx found, to their surprise, that the disappearance of this neighbourhood with all the ensuing confusion and disorder did not lead to marked changes in the number or nature of registered offences. Criminal enterprise in fact appeared relatively unperturbed.

Administrative changes often generate natural experiments. As an example, we discuss the following study. In the Netherlands, all men born in 1959 were exempted from military service. The Dutch government had introduced this one-year exemption as it could not handle the large numbers of men who were being drafted. If one would want to study the impact of military service on criminal behaviour, one could not do so by comparing the records of men who have served and who have not: medical and psychological checks for admission into service are likely confounded with characteristics that are associated with offending as well. However, as the men born in 1959 were exempted through a truly random mechanism, there is no reason to suppose that the cohort born in 1959 differs systematically on any of such characteristics from men born in 1960 or in 1958. Van de Weijer and Bijleveld (2016) compared the criminal records of men born in 1959 (of whom no one was drafted) with those born in 1960 and in 1958 (of whom part were drafted), and of other surrounding years (1961 and 1957, etc.). They found no differences between the groups in the percentage of men who had a criminal record. They did find, however, that men who had been drafted were less likely to follow in their father's criminal footsteps than men who had not been drafted, suggesting that military service may 'break' the intergenerational cycle of transmission of offending.

5.8 An example of a vignette study

A special type of RCT is the so-called *vignette study*. In a vignette study hypothetical cases (or 'vignettes') are offered to respondents. Properties of these cases have been altered purposely from case to case, with the relevant properties thus, as it is called, *manipulated*.

De Keijser and Van Koppen (2004) used such a vignette study. They investigated whether in the sentences that judges mete out in the Netherlands, there is evidence of so-called 'compensatory punishment'. Many lawyers state that judges tend to give more lenient punishment in cases where proof is not very strong: the idea is that judges 'compensate' the fact that the evidence is not overwhelming by giving shorter sentences. It would be very hard to investigate this assertion in real court cases as in judicial decision making so many factors play a role that could act as confounders.

The authors therefore constructed three types of court cases, a simple assault, a serious assault and a burglary case. They constructed the cases such that for each type of offence there was a description of the case ('vignette'), with one version where the proof was sufficient (otherwise judges would acquit) but not overwhelming, and one version where proof was very strong.

In this manner, the authors *isolated* the factor they were interested in: strength of proof. Each time, the case description was identical, the only aspect that varied was how strong the proof was. Any differences in sentence length could therefore be attributed only to strength of proof.

In total 36% of judges that were asked to participate consented. Each judge was randomly given one case with strong evidence, and one case (with another offence: otherwise judges would understand what the authors were after) with weaker evidence. The results of their study (with the properties of the fictional cases, and average sentence length in months) are in Table 5.1.

The authors concluded that their experiment did not show any evidence of compensatory punishment. They also note, however, that the cases they presented judges with are 'artificial' cases and lack the depth and complexity of real court files (De Keijser & Van Koppen, 2004). They therefore do not want to rule out that in reality compensatory punish-

Table 5.1: Results experiment compensatory punishment

crime	proof	sentence	t-value
serious assault	strong proof	28,7	1,85 (ns)
	weaker proof	32,9	
burglary	strong proof	5,4	0,66 (ns)
	weaker proof	5,7	
simple assault	strong proof	3,1	1,40 (ns)
	weaker proof	2,7	

ns = not significant

ment occurs (see also section 5.7 above). With these reservations, the authors concede that while the internal validity of their vignette study is high, the external or ecological validity may be less.

5.9 Further reading

The 'classic' read on experimental designs is Cook and Campbell (1979), with Shadish, Cook and Campbell (2002) its successor. Farrington (2003) is a lucid and much cited piece on standards for evaluation research.

Part III

STATISTICS AND DATA ANALYSIS

Chapter 6

Descriptive statistics

In this chapter we first introduce more formal notation for key concepts such as variables and respondents. Next, in section 6.2, measurement levels are discussed, that are important to consider before the properties of variables can be adequately described or simple computations be carried out. Subsequently, we discuss a number of descriptive measures. We continue with measures to describe the association between variables: for instance to investigate whether older people are more right-wing, or females more left-wing. We discuss two important classes of measures to investigate association: through correlation coefficients and through the analysis of crosstabulations.

6.1 Respondents and variables

When we carry out research, we usually – as stated on a number of occasions above – collect information on entities (people, villages, yoghurt desserts, light bulbs, crimes) and we generally do so with regard to a number of their properties (religious affiliation, population structure, creaminess of texture, lifetime, use of weapon). The entities are in methodology-speak called 'respondents', or 'research participants' or 'sample members'. In older texts one also often finds them referred to as 'subjects' but that is considered politically incorrect language these days. Although the term 'respondents' is thus the universally used term, respondents can also be non-people, such as files that contain information, or structures such as buildings, or conglomerates such as cities, occurrences such as crimes or therapy sessions, or even household-appliances. What makes all these observed units into sample members is that we have gathered information over a certain number of these entities of interest. In technical terms, we have 'replicated' our investigations over these entities.

Often, when we are not studying persons, we indicate the entities as the entities they are or simply as 'replications' - as 'respondent' then has an odd feel to it. Thus we say that we have studied villages with 200 replications over villages, or that we have studied the lifetimes of 500 light bulbs. In general, the number of replications over entities is indicated with the symbol 'N'. Thus in the villages example we just gave, N equals 200, and for the light bulbs $N = 500$.

What we are interested in, is the properties of these entities: respondents' political affiliations, profession, age, gender, income, intelligence, criminal record, listing in the half-marathon. When the entities are not people, we are still interested in their properties such as size for a village, percentage of migrant workers residing in a city, time to failure of light bulbs, rapport between therapist and patient in therapy sessions, creaminess for yoghurt desserts. These properties are called *variables.* Thus creaminess is a variable, as is lifetime for the light bulb and intelligence for a person. We may measure more than one variable per respondent. In general for the light bulb, we would not have a lot to measure other than lifetime as light bulbs are fabricated in identical fashion, although we might want to measure weight, and the period when the bulb was produced (it might be so that bulbs tend to be less solidly produced and to function for a shorter period as the machines start to need oiling or maintenance and repair). In general, whenever we are investigating 'richer' phenomena, such as people or crimes, we tend to register more than one variable.

We are therefore generally not only interested in one, but in several properties of our units of observation: this is so because generally we not only want to describe a variable, but also to describe its association with other variables, or even *explain* it. We might for instance want to know whether older people tend to be more right-wing or whether women's lower wages can be explained by the fact that they work fewer hours. The number of variables measured is generally referred to as 'k'. In some cases of social research, several hundreds of variables may be measured.

Variables are usually, if we write things more formally and mathematically, given symbols - such as X instead of 'age' or Y instead of 'political affiliation'. When we have many variables, variables may also be indicated with a subscript, such as X_1, X_2, X_3, etc., to indicate the first, second and third variable. As we have often at least several replications over respondents, the respondents can also be indicated with an index. The notation then becomes in purely abstract notation X_{ij}, with X_{ij} indicating the score of the i-th person on the j-th variable. See Table 6.1.

Table 6.1: Example of notation of variables and respondents

respondent (number)	age	gender
Johannes (1)	30	male
Gijs (2)	28	male
Kiki (3)	25	female
Boudewien (4)	22	female

In Table 6.1, X_{11} is 30 and X_{12} is 'male'. Kiki's score on 'age' is X_{31}, being the score of the third person on the first variable, and Boudewien's score 'female' is indicated as X_{42}, being the score of the fourth respondent on the second variable.

6.2 Measurement levels

6.2.1 Nominal to absolute measurement level

Variables can have varying information content. When a variable measures age, for instance, the values of that variable contain a lot of information. If one respondent is 50 years old, and another is 25 years old, we can safely say that the first respondent is twice as old as the second. And whether we measure age in weeks, or years, or minutes, that conclusion remains the same. If however, our variable measures religion, we can say no such thing. If a first respondent has category 'Buddhist' and the second has category 'Christian', the only inference we can draw is that the second person's religion is different from the first person's. We cannot say that the first person has more or less of the property 'religion' or that the second has twice as much, or half, the religion that the second one has. The only information content that the variable 'religion' has, is equality and inequality: we cannot order the categories, or say whether the properties are a multiple of each other.

The information content that categories of a variable have is commonly referred to as a variable's *measurement level*. In general, five measurement levels are distinguished, that can be rank ordered as to the information content of the categories. These measurement levels are: *nominal* measurement level, *ordinal*, *interval*, *ratio* and *absolute*. We will discuss each of them in turn.

(1) *Nominal measurement level*

Starting at the nominal measurement level ('nominal' from the Latin 'nomen' meaning 'name'), the categories of the variables are nothing more than distinct categories, that have no other relations than that they are different or identical. If we would have a variable that represented 'crime', its categories could be 'property offending', 'violent offending', and 'other offending'. These could be coded as 1='property offending', 2='violent offending', and 3='other offending'. But they could also have been coded as 100='property offending', -27='violent offending', and .00043='other offending'. The numbers have no meaning but to distinguish the different categories. As such, it would not make sense to compute a mean, or some such statistic.

As such, a nominal variable is a variable that classifies the respondents into distinct sets. Examples of nominal variables are: 'religion', 'hair colour', 'type of crime', 'profession', etc.

(2) *Ordinal measurement level*

When we move up to the ordinal measurement level, the categories of the variable reflect an *ordering* – the name 'ordinal' says it. This means that if John has score '1', Pete has score '2' and Mary has score '3', John has the least of the property that the variable measures, next comes Pete, and Mary has the most. If the property is for instance likeability, this means that John is the least likeable, next Pete, and that Mary is the most likeable of the three. As the variable is an ordinal variable, John, Pete and Mary could however have had scores -187, +2 and 236,000. As the scores of an ordinal variable reflect an ordering only, also from these values we would draw the same conclusion: John is least likeable and Pete follows him with Mary having the highest score and therefore being the most likeable.

An example of such a variable is the ordering of winners in a half-marathon. In that case we would know that Jeannette ended first and Bibi second and Marjan third, but we would not know their actual times. It can be that Jeannette ran in 1:59:03 and Bibi in 1:59:59, and Marjan in 2:11:04, in which case Jeannette and Bibi are very close and Marjan came in quite a bit later. However, it can also be that Jeannette ran in 1:52:45, Bibi in 2:13:33 and Marjan in 2:13:58, in which case Marjan and Bibi ended with only a small difference and Jeannette was way ahead of these two. That information is not contained in an ordinal variable, however.

Ordinal variables are encountered often in so-called 'preference judgements', e.g., when respondents are asked to say which of certain foodstuffs or smells they like best, which one comes next, which afterwards, or to compare such items pairwise (i.e., A against B, A against C, A against D, B against C, etc.).

When variables are ordinal, special techniques must be used to analyse them. Clearly, also for ordinal variables computing a mean score is not informative. What we could do, obviously, is compute a mean *rank* score, and carry out our computations on that, in a sense derived, variable. Such approaches will be briefly discussed below in section 6.3.1.

(3) *Interval measurement level*

Moving up the measurement level ladder, we arrive at the interval level. When a variable has been measured at interval level, we can compute a mean score, and get a meaningful summary of the scores on that variable. As such, the category values of an interval level variable contain more information than just equality and difference (that a nominal variable had) or ordering (that an ordinal variable had). Does this mean that if person A has scored '10' on the interval level variable and person B has scored '5', that we may conclude that person has twice as much of the property the variable is supposed to measure?

This can not be done because an interval level variable has no *fixed origin*. Let us explain this with an example. Temperature can be measured in degrees Celsius but also in degrees Fahrenheit. Suppose that at some day it is 24 degrees Celsius in Amsterdam, and 48 degrees Celsius in Khartoum. While 48 is twice 24, it does not make sense to say that it is twice as warm in Khartoum as in Amsterdam, because those temperatures could be equally well have been measured in degrees Fahrenheit (namely as 118 respectively 75) but would then have a very different ratio. That this is so, is because Celsius and Fahrenheit have a different point of origin.

In fact, the computation that we have to make when we want to express degrees from Celsius to Fahrenheit ($\text{temp}_{\text{Fahrenheit}} = 1.8 \times \text{temp}_{\text{Celsius}} + 32$) illustrates the freedom we still have to change scores when a variable has been measured at interval level. Formulated more abstractly, when a variable has been measured at interval level, we may change the scores as follows: $X' = a + bX$, and we would in the new variable X' preserve the information content of the original variable X. Formulated differently: whether I express my findings in Fahrenheit or Celsius (or Kelvin or Réaumur or Rankin...), I always measure temperature adequately. Other examples of interval level variables are rating scales, or psychological scales that do not have a natural origin. In an interval variable, we know that the intervals between the values of the variable are equidistant. So if Peter has a score 4, and Frank a score 6, and Stijn has scored 8, we know that the distance between Peter and Frank is equal to the distance between Frank and Stijn. We also know that the distance between Peter and Stijn is twice the distance between Frank and Stijn.

(4) *Ratio measurement level*

A ratio measurement level variable is a variable that does have a fixed origin. Examples are weight, or price. Prices for instance may be given in US dollars, Sudanese pounds or euros, so that the scale may vary. But if something is twice as expensive in dollars, it is also twice as expensive when the price is calculated in euros. And a product that is for free, is for free in whatever currency prices are expressed. This means that from a ratio variable onwards, we can make statements such as 'Product A is twice as expensive as product B'. The same goes for length which may be expressed in yards or meters or inches, but also here little John is half his father's height, regardless of the metric in which these heights were measured. This means that we may – formally speaking – change the scores in the following manner: $X' = aX$.

(5) *Absolute measurement level*

Once we have arrived at the highest measurement level, a variable's value contains all information there is. This subsequently implies that we cannot alter or transform the scores anymore without affecting the meaning of the score: the scores we have measured are the final, ultimate, only measurements. We cannot change the scores without affecting their meaning.

An example of an absolute variable is a variable that measure the frequency of occurrence of some phenomenon, for instance the number of children that respondents have. If someone reports that she has four children, we cannot transform this to eight children, or two. She simply has four children and that's it.

If we summarise the above, we note first that the various measurement levels are ordered in the sense that as we move up from nominal to absolute, variable values contain increasingly more information. At nominal interval level, a variable does no more than disaggregate the respondents into different categories. Once we are at ordinal level, these categories are ordered, we now know who has more and who has less of the property that the variable measures. At interval level the ordering becomes more structured, the distances between the categories have meaning, and we can do computations with the variable to summarise what we have found, and transform them linearly. Once at ratio level, the information content of the data is already so high that the only transformation that is allowed is multiplication or division. At absolute measurement level, the scores are exactly the information content of the variable and may therefore not be altered anymore.

The terminology employed here is the most often used. We may also encounter nominal variables as *categorical variables*; sometimes the same is said of ordinal variables. By contrast, interval and ratio level variables are often referred to as *continuous* variables. Interval, ratio and absolute level variables are also encountered under the label *numerical* variables.

6.2.2 Implications

Now why is it important at all to know what measurement level a variable has? This is important because the measurement level dictates the analysis method that can be used. To give a very simple example: if we have measured a variable at nominal level, it does not make sense to compute a mean score: there is for instance no such thing as a mean 'religion'. The best we could do is give a frequency tabulation or pie chart. Conversely, if we have measured a variable at ratio level (for instance 'age'), there are more efficient ways of describing the measurements than through a frequency tabulation that gives the number of cases with ages 18, 19, 20, . . . , 65. We could more efficiently compute a mean.

This applies to the choice of very simple descriptive statistics, as well as to the choice of more sophisticated methods. Knowing the measurement level is therefore important to be able to decide what methods can be used to summarise and analyse the data.

The interval measurement level constitutes in a sense a watershed, as from interval measurement level onwards, we can use standard quantitative statistical techniques. Ordinal variables need special methods and so do nominal variables. Dichotomous variables (variables with just two categories) are a special case, as technically speaking they are equivalent to interval variables, but in research practice they command special analysis techniques. Examples of such variables are 'gender', 'agree-disagree' judgements, 'guilty-not guilty' verdicts etc.

6.3 Describing the variables

Suppose that we have interviewed 100 secondary school students. We asked these students to tell us whether they committed during the past school year any of the three following offences: theft, assault, or vandalism. We noted the gender of these respondents, the type of secondary school they are in, and we asked them how much pocket money they receive.

If we want to report on our findings, we need to summarise them. What the reader would want to know is things like: how many students committed an offence last year? How many property or violent offences were committed on average? Did students differ a lot in how much pocket money they had?

If we want to provide the answer to such questions, we need simple summarising measures. Such summarising measures come in two classes. The first are *measures of central tendency*, that tell us what scores respondents tend to have, what the average of the students is. What a reader would want to know second, is whether all respondents tended to score on or around the average, or whether there is quite a bit of fluctuation in respondents' scores. In other words: the reader would want to have a measure of *variability* as well.

These measures, measures of central tendency and of variation, are labelled 'statistics', not because they incorporate complicated statistical reasoning, but because they in the etymological sense summarise a set of numerical values into one number: a statistic.

In the following we will discuss both groups of measures: measures of central tendency and measures of variability. Presenting such measures is called a *univariate analysis*: we present the results for just one variable.

6.3.1 Central tendency: the mean, median and mode

If we want to give the reader an overview of our findings, we generally start by giving mean values, or: measures of central tendency. The average or 'arithmetic mean' is the run-of-the-mill average that everyone employs automatically when we ask after his or her average grade, or mean daily alcohol consumption. In formula it is written as:

$$\sum_{i=1}^{N} \frac{X_i}{N},$$

which is nothing more than the sum of all observations X_i from the first to the N-th respondent, divided by the total number of respondents N – indeed our standard, run-of-the-mill mean. The average, or mean, is the most often used measure of central tendency. It is attractive because it is easily and intuitively understood by readers. The mean is written as $\bar{X}$, as M_X, or simply as M.

A disadvantage of the mean is, however, is that it is sensitive to so-called outliers, i.e., extreme scores. Suppose for instance that we have a list of observations 1-2-5-7-3-5-5, of which the average is 4. But imagine now that the highest score was not 7 but 27 – an extreme score. The average would then suddenly be 6.86! The number 6.86 is obviously not a good summary of the scores. In fact, all scores but the extreme 27 lie below that summary score. This means that the reader does not get the right impression, a good overview of the scores 1-2-3-5-5-5-27.

In such cases, the *median* is a good alternative. The median is that number below which 50% of the values lie (and above which therefore also 50%). It is that number that cuts the distribution of the scores in two. In the example we just gave, the median is equal to 5, with three values below, and three values above it. Note that the median is indeed insensitive to outliers: whether the highest score is 7, 27, or 27,000, the median remains 5. The median is therefore a good measure of central tendency whenever there are outliers, or whenever the data have a skewed distribution.

Lastly, for summarising the scores on a variable, the *mode* may be used. The mode is the score that occurs most often (as reflected in the word 'modal'). The mode is not often used as the only measure for central tendency, one reason for which may be that distributions may have more than one mode (they are then called bimodal as opposed to unimodal). Suppose for instance that in the example of the 100 students given above, an equal number would report vandalism and property offending, we would then have two modes. The mode in our example equals 5.

6.3.2 Measures of variability: variance and standard deviation

Central tendency is not the only relevant measure to summarise the distribution of scores. In practice, we do not only want to know what, for instance the mean

number of offences was, but we would also want to know whether all respondents scored the mean or close to the mean, or whether on the other hand there was a lot of variation in scores. In practice two measures are used to express such variability. The first is the *variance*, often used in computations but not aiding the reader so much in understanding what is going on. The second is the *standard deviation* which is more useful to grasp the extent to which respondents vary around the mean. We will detail them both.

The first measure is the *variance*; it is denoted with the symbol s^2, and computed as:

$$\sum_{i=1}^{N} \frac{(X_i - \bar{X})^2}{N - 1}.$$

In this formula the following happens. For each respondent i we take his or her score X_i and compute how much it deviates from the mean $\bar{X}$: $(X_i - \bar{X})$. We square all these deviations and then add them up (if we would not square them first, they would always add to zero). The sum of squared deviations, that is in the numerator, reflects how much people vary around the mean: if everybody had scores really close to the mean (so that there is little variability), the sum of the squared deviations would be small. As people's individual scores are further away from the mean, the deviations become larger, the squared deviations do so too, and so does their sum. So, the numerator is small when the scores cluster around the mean, it gets larger as they are further away from that mean which reflects that overall they vary more. Next, we divide that sum by the number of respondents minus 1: $(N - 1)$. This serves to standardise the measure: if we would not do so, the variability would be twice as high if I had a twice as large sample – which would be strange.

The statistic s^2 is therefore the mean of the squared deviations of the individual scores from the mean. If you don't understand this right away, that illustrates why the variance is of limited conceptual use. A problem with the variance as a measure of variability is namely that because of the squaring, the relation with (and our intuitive feel of) the original scaling of the variable is gone. It is hard to interpret the number that is generated by the formula.

For that reason, in most situations, the so-called standard deviation is used, which is simply the square root of the variance:

$$s = \sqrt{s^2}.$$

The main advantage of the standard deviation compared to the variance is that it is, because of the square root, expressed again in the original scale of the variable. This means that the standard deviation can easily be interpreted. If for instance the mean number of offences of secondary schoolers is 1.3 and the standard deviation is .7, this can be rephrased by saying that on average the secondary schoolers varied by .7 offences more or .7 offences less than average. We can also envisage this as the scores hovering – on average – between .6 and 2.0. The advantage of the standard deviation is that it gives you a 'feel' for how much fluctuation there was. The standard deviation is often abbreviated as 'sd' or 'SD'.

6.3.3 Descriptive graphs: pie chart, bar chart, histogram

As stated, the mean is meaningful only for variables from interval level up, and the same applies essentially to the median. The mode can be used for any kind of variable. If we want to give an indication of the variability in scores, the standard deviation is generally used, but again this is only for variables from interval level up. So what if we want to give an overview of variables of lower than interval level, such as a nominal level variable?

There are two approaches to describing the distribution of scores for such variables. The first is through simple *frequency tabulation*, such as produced in any computational software package. See Table 6.2 that gives an example of the distribution over the categories of the variable 'type of sexual abuse' from a study on juvenile sex offenders. The first column gives the meaning of the categories, the second gives the absolute numbers, the third gives the percentages. So we can deduct from Table 6.2 that a total of 236 sex offenders were investigated, of whom 96 were child abusers, 77 were peer abusers, meaning that they had abused someone from their own age group, and that 63 had committed sexual abuse in a group. The tabulation gives the absolute numbers, and lists in a last column the percentages, that may be easier to interpret.

Table 6.2: Frequency tabulation

type of sex offence	number	percentage
child abuse	96	40.7
peer abuse	77	32.6
group sexual abuse	63	26.7
total	236	100.0

A second approach to summarising nominal data is through the use of graphs. See Figure 6.1, that is an example of a so-called *pie chart* for the same data as in Table 6.2. In a pie chart the data are represented as a pie, and the chunks represent the proportion of cases scoring in each of the respective categories. Pie charts are very well understood by readers, also the non-academically trained, and informative at a glance. Pie charts are often used when the various categories to be represented graphically are categories of a nominal variable.

Graphics have the huge advantage that they are inspected quickly and in general also understood well by readers. Also readers who are numbers-anxious easily grasp the meaning of pie charts and similar graphics. In more lengthy, dry texts, they have the added advantage that they in a sense 'break' the text, making the look of the pages more lively, and thus adding to comprehension and retention of the material.

A second way to graphically display these data is by using a bar chart. See Figure 6.2, in which the categories of 'type of sexual abuse' have been ordered along the x-axis, and the y-axis gives the number of cases for each type of sexual abuse (obviously, the percentage

Figure 6.1: Example of pie chart for type of sexual abuse

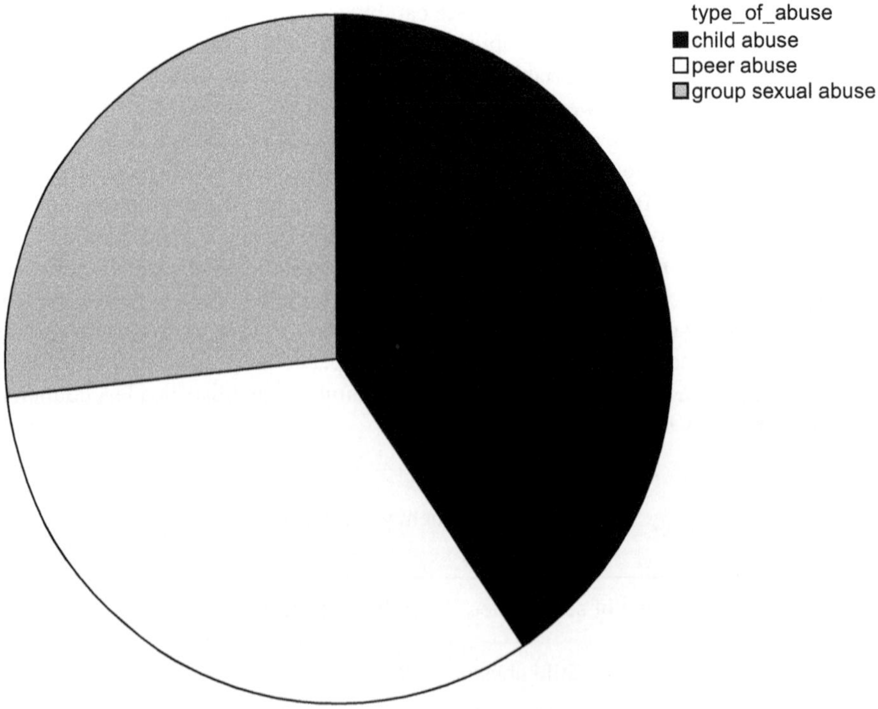

could have been taken just as well). Because the categories of the variable are unordered, the bars are not connected.

When a variable is at interval measurement level or higher, we generally use means and standard deviations to summarise the variable for the reader. However, also for ordered or continuous variables, graphs would have the advantage that they are easy to inspect and interpret. In addition, they can show how a variable may have a *skewed distribution*, something which means and variances do not show. See Figure 6.3, that gives an example of a so-called *histogram*. Note that, given that we are depicting a continuous variable, the various categories of age are now connected along the x-axis.

Figure 6.3 shows that the distribution of age is indeed skewed: we have a small number of juvenile sex offenders who are 10-12 years old, the distribution quickly peaks at 14 years of age, and tails off more gradually towards 16 and 17 years of age.

6.4 Describing the association between variables

So far, we discussed how to describe the variables. Descriptions generally entail properties such as the mean or variance, or distribution – either through frequency tabulations or using graphs. But often we want to go further and we want to investigate not only variables one

Figure 6.2: Example of bar chart for type of sexual abuse

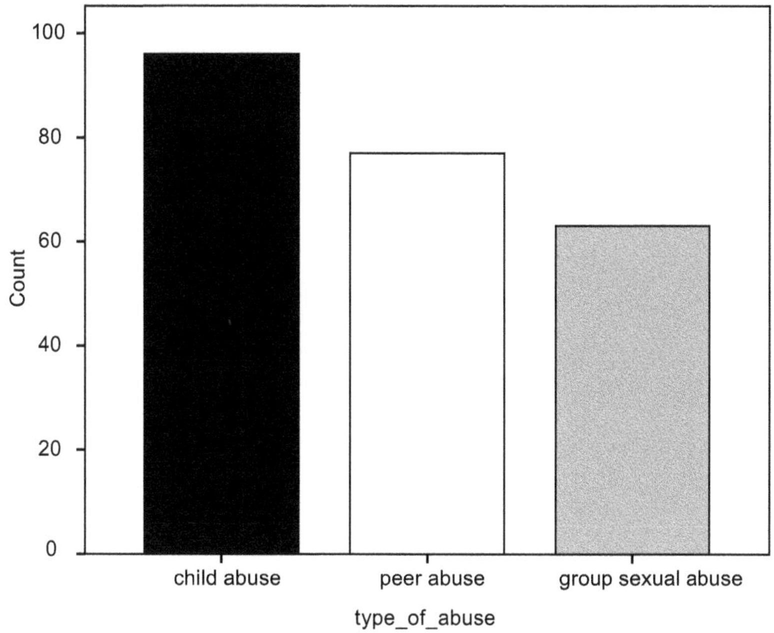

by one, but we want to look as well at how variables are interrelated. We might want to assess for instance whether male students commit more offences than females, or whether gender and type of offending are associated. Or we might want to investigate whether those reporting insufficient pocket money more often stole something.

In that case we also need tools to summarise such interrelations, just like the tools of mean (or median) and standard deviation for summarising central tendency and variability. Several of such tools (in fact numerous) are available. In general they are called coefficients of association, or coefficients of correlation. What tool is appropriate in a given situation depends on two criteria. Firstly it depends on the *measurement level* of the variables. If we want to report on the association between two continuous variables, a different measure must be employed than if we want to investigate the association between two nominal variables. Secondly, the choice of measure depends on the *distribution* of the variables. If this is very skewed, different association measures may be recommended.

While there is a host of different measures to represent association or correlation, measures are generally interpreted in a similar way. As such, not knowing each and every one of them in detail does not in practice hamper interpretation of their meaning. The class of coefficients for the association between two nominal variables stands a little apart however, so that we will treat those with some more detail below.

When investigating the association between two variables, it is often said that we are carrying out a *bivariate analysis*: we present the interrelation of two variables. This is dif-

Figure 6.3: Example of histogram for distribution of age for juvenile sex offenders

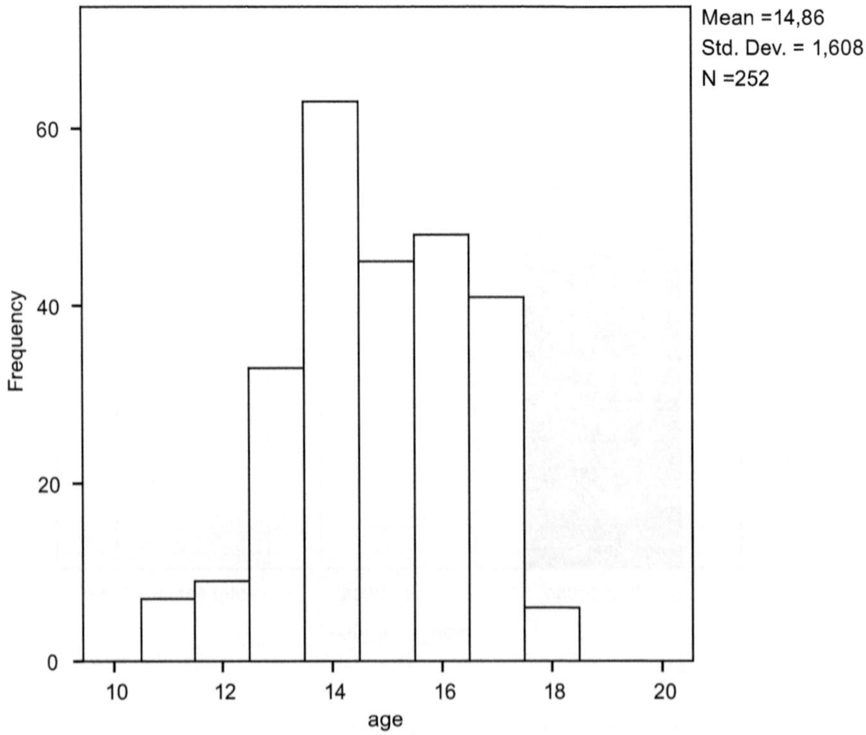

ferent from the univariate analyses we just discussed. In univariate analyses, we may also analyse more than one variable, and therefore analyse several variables. But then, in each case, we would be doing that for one variable by itself, it is a variable-by-variable analysis. In the following, however, we will each time investigate the variables in conjunction. As such, it is not variable A and variable B we are investigating, but it is the relation between variables A and B that is the object of interest.

6.4.1 Correlation coefficients for continuous data

The most often used measure for association is the Pearson product-moment correlation coefficient. Often, when speaking of 'the correlation', people refer to this correlation coefficient. In formula it is:

$$r_{XY} = \sum_{i=1}^{N} \frac{(X_i - \bar{X})\,(Y_i - \bar{Y})}{(N-1)s_X s_Y},$$

which is translated in words as: the correlation coefficient is the sum of the product of each respondent's score X_i in deviation from the mean of that variable X and each respondent's

Figure 6.4: Scatterplots for associations of various direction and strength

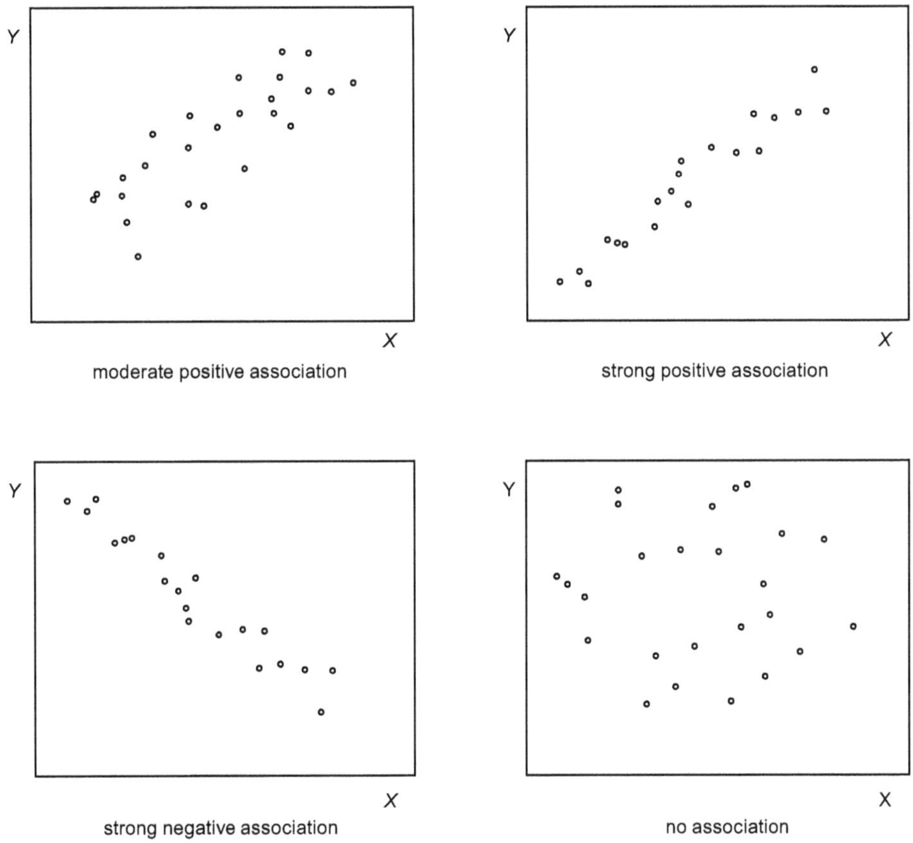

score Y_i deviation from variable Y's mean, divided by the product of the respective standard deviations of X and Y, divided by a correction factor for sample size. This may not all be immediately obvious to the reader, so we will now first look at the correlation in a more intuitive way, and then investigate whether this formula indeed gives us a quantity that corresponds with our intuitive idea of association.

For doing so, we use scatterplots, that is, plots of the scores of the respondents on the variables X and Y. For making these, we take the score on the X variable as an x-coordinate, and take the score on the Y variable as the y-coordinate. The scores on the variables X and Y then become points in a two-dimensional space. In Figure 6.4 we give four of such so-called *scatterplots*.

The first scatterplot in the top left corner depicts a situation of moderate to strong positive association. When X is high, Y tends to be high too; when X is low, also Y is generally low. The second (upper right) scatterplot depicts essentially the same situation but now the cloud of points has become much thinner. For this plot as well, if we know that the score X is high, we know that the score on Y will likely be high too, but we know that now with a much narrower margin: while in the upper left plot, there could still be quite a range in possible values for Y given a certain X, the picture has become much 'sharper' in the upper right one. Knowing X, I can gather within a fairly narrow band what Y will be. The thick Cuban cigar-shaped cloud in the first picture indicates therefore a weaker association between X and Y. As the cigar becomes slimmer and turns into a ladylike thin cigar, the association becomes stronger. If the cloud of points would form a straight line, the association is perfect. The third picture (bottom left) gives a situation of strong negative association – in fact it is the exact mirror of the upper right one. So the association is just as strong, it is only in the reverse direction: now high values for X are associated with low values for Y and vice versa. The last picture gives the situation of almost no association: knowing X does not tell us anything about Y.

Now let us return to the formula we gave above. If we employ this formula, the computed correlation coefficient r_{XY} will be high if X and Y vary in similar fashion. Suppose that a particular respondent i's score is much higher than the mean on X: $X_i - \bar{X}$ will then be high. And suppose that that respondent i's score on Y is also much higher than the mean on Y: $Y_i - \bar{Y}$ will then also be high. Simply said: this respondent scores higher than average on X and higher than average on Y. The product $(X_i - \bar{X})(Y_i - \bar{Y})$ – that is in the denominator of the formula above – will then for this respondent also be high. If this applies to all respondents, i.e. that those who score higher than average on X also score higher than average on Y (and vice versa: those who score lower than average on X also score lower than average on Y), we get for each respondent a large product term $(X_i - \bar{X})(Y_i - \bar{Y})$ and summing all these product terms, we get a large value in the denominator, and thus eventually – after the further divisions in the denominator – a large value for r_{XY}. If there is a positive association between two variables X and Y, the correlation coefficient r_{XY} will be high.

Thus, in a situation where people with higher than average scores on X also have higher than average scores on Y and vice versa (those with very low scores on X also have very low scores on Y), we would say that X and Y resemble each other, they are similar. In that case everyone would say, without needing to do any computations, that these two aspects are correlated. And we would expect r_{XY} to come out high. As we showed, that is exactly what r_{XY} does.

Now what if we have the opposite situation? That is, people with higher than average scores on X have lower than average scores on Y (and vice versa). In that case X and Y are not similar, they are each other's mirror in a way, X is the opposite of Y. In that case, in the formula, each case where X_i is higher than the average and $X_i - \bar{X}$ is positive will then couple with the situation that Y_i is lower than the average and $\bar{Y}$ and $Y_i - \bar{Y}$ is negative. Their product will then be negative. Then, the sum in the nominator does not become a large positive number, but a large negative number. In that case, we end up with a negative correlation coefficient. When a correlation coefficient is negative, say $r_{XY} =$ -0.7, the association is just as strong as when it is 0.7; the negative sign indicates that the variables now mirror each other.

So why are the terms $(N - 1)$, s_X and s_Y in the denominator? Couldn't we just add up the products of the variables' deviations from the mean for each i and have a good indicator of the extent to which two variables co-relate? The answer is no. First, we must correct for the number of cases. Otherwise, if we had exactly the same pattern in the data, but we had instead of 100 respondents, 200 respondents, our correlation would become twice as high. That is odd, and we would definitely want our correlation coefficient to be independent of the number of respondents: it would be undesirable if we could inflate it simply by using more respondents. This is why the correlation coefficient has a term $(N-1)$ in the denominator. (Why that term is $(N-1)$ and not simply N is discussed more in-depth in statistics textbooks.)

Secondly, the denominator contains terms for the standard deviation of X, s_X and the standard deviation of Y, s_Y. Why this is necessary is best understood as follows. Suppose that we are investigating whether shoe size X and height in meters Y are associated. Suppose that we have computed a correlation coefficient and that that coefficient equals 0.8, meaning that shoe size and height are correlated positively and strongly. Suppose now, that we decide to measure height not in meters, but in centimeters, or inches. Intuitively, this should not change the association between X and Y. However, if we change the scale for Y – moving from meters to centimeters they would be multiplied by a factor 100 – and the r_{XY} would also become 100 times as high! Dividing the denominator by the standard deviations solves for such undesirabilities.

In summary, the correlation coefficient is a scale- and sample size-independent measure for the association between two numerical variables X and Y. The correlation coefficient varies between -1 and +1. When r_{XY} equals 1, there is perfect correlation, when r_{XY} equals -1 there is also perfect correlation, but the association is negative, the variables are each other's opposite. When $r_{XY} = 0$, there is no association. Correlation coefficients between -0.3 and 0.3 we label 'weak'; if $.3 < |r_{XY}| <.7$ the correlation coefficient is judged as 'moderate'; correlation coefficients in absolute value larger than 0.7 are labelled 'strong'. So, the absolute value of the correlation coefficient tells us something about the strength of the association, the sign of the association tells us something about the direction (positive or negative).

We take this a little further in Figure 6.5. This graph depicts the situation of moderate association from Figure 6.4, and sketches the idea of prediction: if X and Y are correlated, then knowing X tells us something about Y.

Suppose that I do not have any information about a person's score on Y or on X. Then, if I were asked to predict a person's score on Y, all I could say is that it is between 2 and 18, the total range of the scores. I could also give one number: 11, which is the arithmetic mean of Y. Without any additional information, my best estimate would actually be the overall mean of Y (see Figure 6.5 along the y-axis). If, however, I knew that person's X score, I could make my estimate of Y much more precise! If I knew for instance that X equals 8, then the bandwidth for Y becomes 6 – 11, and a best estimate would now be 9 (see Figure 6.5). Thus, the fact that X and Y are associated helps me to make predictions about one variable, using information from the other.

Now we said above that a cigar-shaped cloud like we have in Figure 6.5, is indicative of moderate to strong association, and that as the cigar becomes slimmer the association becomes stronger. If that is the case, then we would expect our prediction to improve. Imagine therefore, in Figure 6.5 a similarly positioned, but slimmer cigar. Again, suppose that I know that X equals 8. Now, however, because the cigar is slimmer, the possible range for Y is narrower: it is possibly 8 – 10 instead of the wider 6 – 11 that we had. If

Figure 6.5: Relation between association and prediction

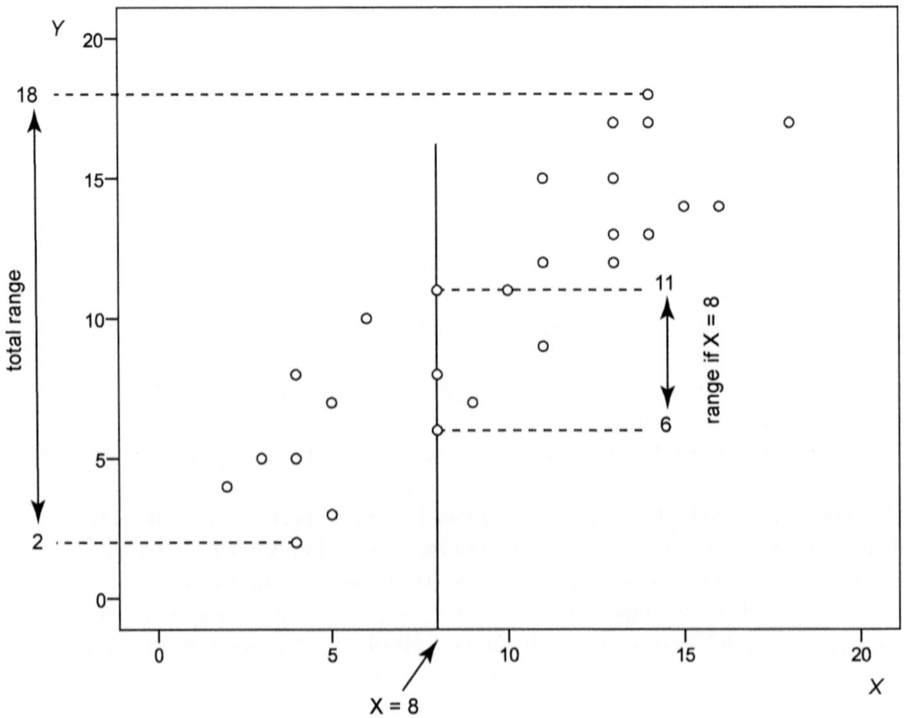

I would be required to give one number again for Y, again I would estimate Y at 9. So, a stronger correlation between X and Y does not lead to a different estimate for Y on the basis of X, but it leads to a *more certain* estimate, reflected in the smaller bandwidth of the possible values for Y. We will return to this in chapter 7.

The correlation coefficient is the most widely used measure for association, and many other measures are essentially variations on the structure of r_{XY}. There are two important issues to heed when using the Pearson product-moment correlation coefficient. The first is that the correlation coefficient is a measure for *linear* association. The Cuban and ladies' cigars we drew were all clouds around a *straight* line.

Suppose however that we have the situation as depicted in Figure 6.6. In this case there is a – strong – *non-linear* association: if we know X we can predict within a fairly narrow bandwidth what Y is. However, if we would compute the correlation coefficient for these data, it would turn out to be almost zero. That is not a wrong result as the Pearson product-moment correlation coefficient is a measure of linear association – and indeed there is no linear association here. However, from that we may not conclude that there is no association at all. Other measures would be needed to capture the non-linear association. Several of such measures (the best known is probably η) are discussed in standard statistics

Figure 6.6: Non-linear association between X and Y

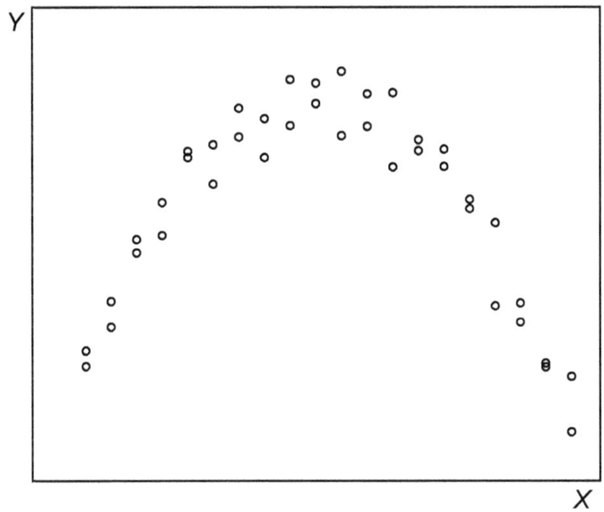

Figure 6.7: Outlier

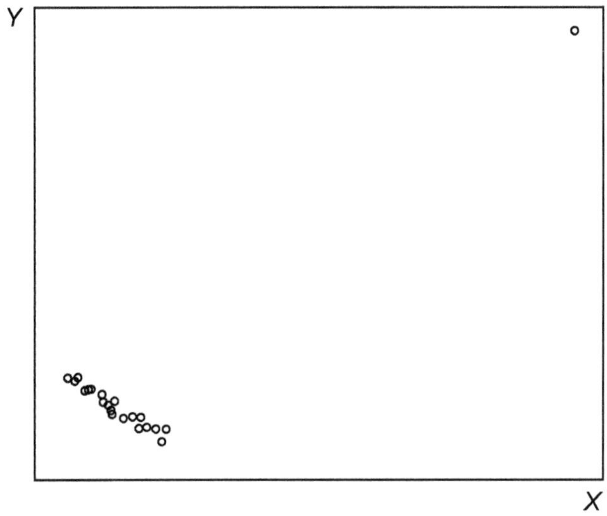

textbooks. For now, it is sufficient to know that the ordinary correlation coefficient is useful for assessing linear association between continuous variables only.

Eye-balling the graphs is important for the second issue too. The correlation coefficient is namely sensitive to so-called *outliers*. See Figure 6.7, in which an example is given of a sample in which the scores on X and Y are negatively associated: a cloud of points in the lower left corner forms a ladies' cigar, tilted to the left, indicative of a (fairly strong) negative correlation. However, because there is one person who combines a huge X with a huge Y, the correlation coefficient if we would simply compute it, would come up strongly positive. That correlation coefficient is however based on just one out of N sample members, so not a result one would like to report. Inspecting the scatterplots prevents mistakes one could make if one would simply – blindly – compute the correlation coefficient.

Most researchers compute their correlation coefficients with a software package or a calculator. Understanding the formula for the coefficient is noble, but not crucial. What is however crucial is to understand the scatterplots we discussed and to realise how much can be learned from them. Anyone – also the math-fearing – can read from a simple scatterplot whether there is a linear or a non-linear association between X and Y. Also, anyone can see whether the association is positive or negative. Lastly, anyone can get at least an idea of the strength of the association. It is only when we want to have an exact number, that we need to resort to computations. All the other much more relevant and much more interesting things we can do by simply eye-balling the graphs.

6.4.2 Other measures for association

As we said earlier, the ordinary Pearson product-moment correlation coefficient is but one measure for association: for the linear association between two continuous variables that – we hinted at this but did not make it explicit – are distributed pretty 'normally'. The moment one of the variables is not interval level or higher, or the association is perhaps not linear, or one of the two variables has a 'funny' distribution (like a skewed distribution) we must resort to other statistical measures. This is important to know.

We will not discuss all those measures: firstly it is all pretty tedious and not really necessary for our purposes, as most coefficients are interpreted along similar lines. The reader who needs to decide which coefficient to use can look up the various options in a textbook, for instance Hinkle, Wiersma and Jurs (2003). We will however briefly mention two fairly commonly used other correlation coefficients.

The first of these is Spearman's ρ (or 'rho') for variables X and Y both measured at ordinal level. Spearman's ρ varies – just like the ordinary correlation coefficient – between -1 and 1, and the interpretation given to these numbers is also identical to the interpretation for the ordinary correlation coefficient.

The second is Kendall's τ or 'tau', that is also a measure for the association between two ordinal variables. It is less commonly used for ordinal variables than Spearman's ρ. It is however also often used when the variables are interval level or higher, but their distribution is skewed. The value of 'tau' in that case tends to be somewhat lower than that of the ordinary correlation coefficient, because it takes along only ranking information of the scores.

6.4.3 Association measures for nominal variables

When we are interested in the association between two nominal or categorical variables, numerous measures are available. Each has weaknesses and strengths. In research practice,

Table 6.3: Crosstabulation of offending and gender

	offended	did not offend	
males	40	60	100
females	10	90	100
	50	150	200

however, two are most often used: the χ^2 (or chi-square) and the odds ratio. The first is not really a measure of association (although it is often interpreted as such); it is a statistical test, that does not actually tell us how strong the association between the two nominal variables is, but how likely our observed data is if the variables were unassociated. The second tells us something about the strength of the association between two dichotomous variables (i.e., variables with two categories each only). It expresses this association in terms of risk.

We will first discuss the chi-square (or χ^2), that is very often used. The examples that we use are, for ease of explaining, simple two-way tabulations; for the chi-square, all computations can be extended to higher-dimensional tabulations.

Suppose therefore that we have measured two nominal variables for a number of respondents, and that our findings are as given in Table 6.3. In this table we see that a total of 200 respondents have been investigated: the sample consisted of 100 males and 100 females. Of these 200 respondents, a fourth, or 50, admitted to having offended, and 150 said they had not committed an offence. Now the question is: are the two variables we are investigating here associated? Do sex and offending have something to do with each other? Phrased differently: if I would want to predict whether someone has offended, would it be useful to know whether that person is male or female? What we can see without any computational fuss that this does appear to be the case. Of the females, only one in ten has offended, while for the males this is 40%. Clearly: gender matters. But how strong is the association?

Most researchers would investigate the association between the two nominal variables as follows. They would compute the χ^2, which is written in formula as:

$$\chi^2 = \sum_{i=1}^{k} \frac{(\mathrm{O}_i - \mathrm{E}i)^2}{\mathrm{E}_i},$$

with k the total number of cells, O_i the observed frequency in the i-th cell of the crosstabulation, and E_i the frequency we would have expected in that cell if – in this example – gender and offending were unassociated.

How to compute this? Let us deal with the last term E_i first. We just said that E_i is the frequency we would have expected in a cell i if the two variables were unassociated. Going back to the example, we can determine what the E_i are as follows. Suppose that it does not make a difference for someone's likelihood of offending whether that person is male or female – which is the case when gender and offending are unassociated. Of all respondents, one in four offends. If being male or female would not make a difference, we would expect that in males as well as females also one in four offends. So, if gender

Table 6.4: Expected crosstabulation if offending and gender are unassociated

	offended	did not offend	
males	25	75	100
females	25	75	100
	50	150	200

and offending are unassociated, we would expect that of the males as well as the females one in four (or 25) offends and three in four does not offend (or 75). Thus, if gender and offending were unassociated we would find the results given in Table 6.4.

So, the values in the cells in Table 6.4 are the E_i. But what are the observed frequencies O_i? These are the frequencies we have measured as given in Table 6.3. We can now compute the chi-square value by comparing the frequencies that we would have expected to find if gender and offending were unassociated (the E_i) with the frequencies we did find (the O_i). The chi-square value then becomes:

$$\frac{(40-25)^2}{25} + \frac{(60-75)^2}{75} + \frac{(10-25)^2}{25} + \frac{(90-75)^2}{75} = 24.$$

Now this does not tell us a lot yet, and this is where statistical testing comes in – as we said at the beginning of this paragraph, the χ^2 is actually a statistical test – which we will elucidate later on. What can be seen is that if the observed frequencies had been identical to the ones we would have found had there been no association between gender and offending, the χ^2-value would have been 0. We could then have concluded that gender and offending have nothing to do with each other. The more the observed frequencies deviate from the expected frequencies, the more likely it is that the two variables are associated. In very general terms, the larger the χ^2, the stronger the association is; when χ^2 equals 0, we say the two nominal variables are unassociated.

As we noted, the χ^2-value does not actually measure association as such, although it clearly reflects association. Various measures are around that do give an indication of the strength of association between nominal variables – just like the correlation coefficient does for continuous variables. Probably the best of these, under some conditions, is the so-called *Cramer's V* that gives us a number between 0 and 1, with '0' reflecting no association, and '1' perfect association (meaning that from the score on one nominal variable, the score on the other nominal variable can be predicted perfectly). Other measures are around, such as the ϕ-coefficient for two-by-two tables, or λ.

However, whichever measure one uses, it is important to realise that we should always inspect the crosstabulation to understand what is going on. As the correlation coefficient deals with continuous variables only, it is easy to interpret: if the coefficient is high, high scores on X imply high scores on Y. For nominal variables, however, the interpretation is not immediately obvious. In our offending and gender example, the χ^2 tells us that the two are associated but it does not tell us whether that means that being a man increases the likelihood of offending, or whether it is being female that increases the likelihood of

Table 6.5: Crosstabulation of offending and gender

	offended	did not offend	
males	40	60	100
females	10	90	100
	50	150	200

offending! So, we always need to refer back to a crosstabulation to be able to interpret the association between the two nominal variables. For more, we refer the reader again to a statistics textbook such as Hinkle, Wiersma and Jurs (2003) for more information.

For dichotomous variables, another very often used measure to inspect association is the *odds ratio*. The odds ratio is not easy conceptually, but very easy in use and interpretation. It has gained ground in criminology and social science research. The reasoning behind it is best explained with an example. We suppose that we have the same data that we had before. See Table 6.5 which is repeated here for inspection purposes but is equal to Table 6.3.

The reasoning of the odds ratio is as follows. In the example we have data on gender and offending. For females the probability of offending is .10, and probability of not offending .9. This means that for females the probability not to offend is 9 times that of offending; these are called the *odds*. For males, we can do the same reasoning and then we find that the probability not to offend is 1.5 times that of offending. The odds ratio is then ratio of these two ratios or odds:

$$\text{OR} = \frac{\frac{\text{male offenders}}{\text{male non-offenders}}}{\frac{\text{female offenders}}{\text{female non-offenders}}} = \frac{\frac{40}{60}}{\frac{10}{90}} = \frac{\frac{1}{1.5}}{\frac{1}{9}} = 6.00$$

How can we interpret this? The literal interpretation is that for males the ratio of offenders to non-offenders is 6 times that of females. This is hard to master conceptually, and a mouthful of words. In practice the two terms in the nominator and denominator are perceived of and formulated as 'risk'. The odds ratio is thus conceptualised as a ratio of risks (or indeed 'odds'). In practice, the interpretation is formulated as: 'for males, offending risk is 6 times that of females'.

Note firstly that a risk is not a chance: risks can be larger than 1 while probabilities are always between 0 and 1. Secondly, it is important to note that if there were no difference in risk between males and females, the odds ratio would be 1 (not 0!). Compare the data in Table 6.4. This table reflects the situation where there is no relation between gender and offending, in other words: for the scores on offending it does not make any difference whether someone is male or female. Thus, we would also expect no difference in the odds. And, if we would want to compare the risk for men and women for this data set, we indeed get:

$$OR = \frac{\frac{\text{male offenders}}{\text{male non-offenders}}}{\frac{\text{female offenders}}{\text{female non-offenders}}} = \frac{\frac{25}{75}}{\frac{25}{75}} = 1.00,$$

which is exactly what we expected. Therefore, an odds ratio equal to 1 means no difference in risk, and an odds ratio larger than one means an increased risk. Obviously, if we had in our example in Table 6.5 reversed men and women in the equation, we would have ended up with:

$$OR = \frac{\frac{\text{female offenders}}{\text{female non-offenders}}}{\frac{\text{male offenders}}{\text{male non-offenders}}} = \frac{\frac{10}{90}}{\frac{40}{60}} = 0.166667,$$

and we would have reported that females have a six times *lower* risk. So, with the odds ratio, it is important to keep in mind how this risk is specified (i.e., what is in the nominator and what is in the denominator). Also, because of this, an odds ratio of 2 reflects just as large a difference in risk as an odds ratio of 0.5.

Now what is generally perceived as an increased risk, or as a not-so-strongly increased risk? Just like for the correlation coefficient, also here there are rules of thumb. In general, an odds ratio larger than 2 or smaller than 0.5 is judged to constitute a sizeable risk increase or decrease. This is a rule of thumb though, and for some research situations an odds ratio of 1.3 may already be judged to constitute a relevant increase in risk.

6.4.4 Graphs to visualise association

What we said in section 6.3.3 about the ease of visual representation for simple descriptives – such as the distribution of a variable – applies also when it comes to investigating the association between variables. Also here, graphs are an efficient tool to make the reader see and interpret association. Given however that association is investigated, graphs are bound to be more complicated.

A first way to graphically display association is by using a special kind of bar chart, a so-called *stacked bar chart*. See Figure 6.8, in which, just like we did in Figure 6.2, the categories of 'type of sexual abuse' have been ordered along the x-axis, and the y-axis gives the number of cases for each type of sexual abuse. Again, because the categories of the variable are unordered, the bars are disjunct, i.e., they are disconnected. The legend indicates that '0' means 'no recidivism', and '1' means 'recidivism'.

What is different in the stacked bar chart from the plain bar chart, is that we have divided up each bar into those who re-offended and those who did not (we are in this example looking at general recidivism). As can be inferred easily from Figure 6.8, a much smaller proportion of child abusers re-offended than of either peer abusers or group sexual abusers. The group sexual abusers in fact have the highest chance to re-offend: about two-thirds of this group were registered with a new offence.

When a variable is at interval measurement level or higher, we can also visualise association. Using a so-called *clustered histogram*, we can inspect whether the distribution of one variable differs by the categories of another variable. See Figure 6.9, in which, just like in Figure 6.3, the categories of age have been connected along the x-axis.

Figure 6.9 breaks up the distribution of age into three horizontal bars: one for child abusers, one for peer abusers and one for group sexual abusers. Note that, while in the previous plot the different chunks were stacked vertically, here the disaggregation is horizontal. Figure 6.9 shows that there is indeed an association between the nominal variable

Figure 6.8: Example of stacked bar chart for type of abuse and recidivism

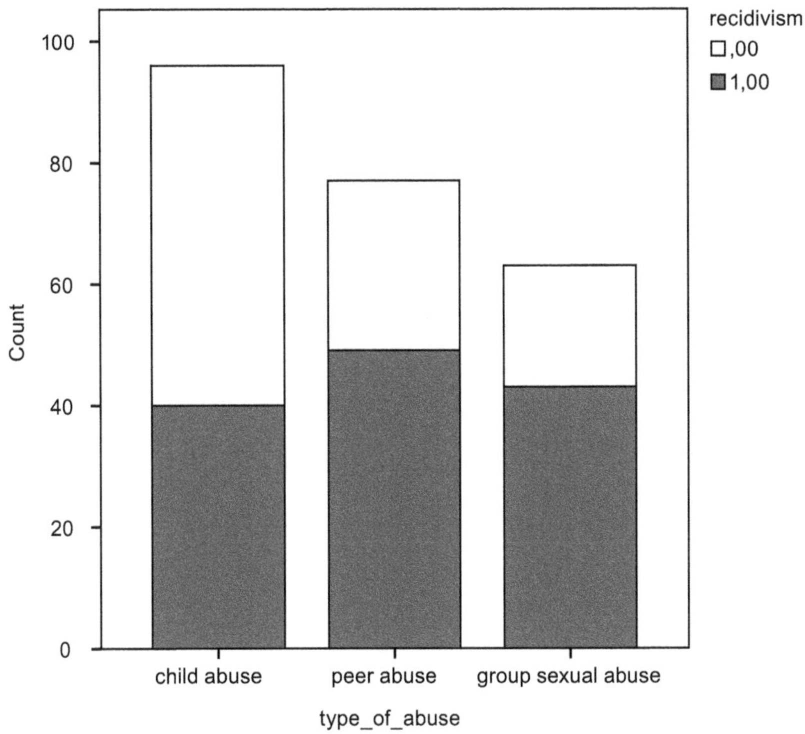

'type of sexual abuse' and the ratio variable 'age': child abusers are overrepresented in the youngest age brackets. A large proportion of group sex abusers are 14 years old, and as offenders get older, we find more and more peer abusers. Thus, child abusers appear the youngest, peer abusers appear the oldest, and group abusers appear pretty average as regards age; the plot shows however that there is quite a bit of variability as well, and that there is a remarkable peak around age 14 for group abusers.

6.5 Wrapping up

In this chapter, we introduced concepts such as respondents, variables and measurement levels. We gave a number of statistics to summarise variables, such as the mean and measures for variability. After such univariate statistics, we discussed bivariate measures, such as the correlation coefficient for numerical variables and the χ^2 for numerical variables and the odds ratio for dichotomous variables. We also illustrated how to use graphs to visualise the properties of variables and bivariate associations. Even though we each time gave the formulas for the measures we discussed, we also stressed that these formulas are not necessary to understand how the statistics should be interpreted. They are also not

Figure 6.9: Clustered histogram for distribution of age for different types of juvenile sexual abusers

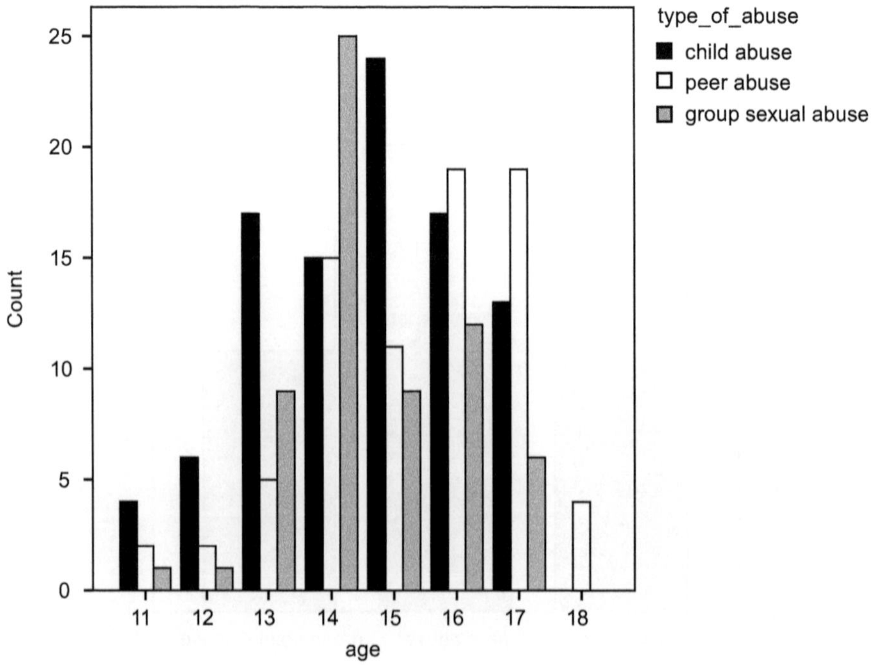

necessary for their use in practice, as statistical software packages will compute them – and even Excel can provide quite a few measures.

Chapter 7

Inferential statistics

This chapter takes statistics one step further, from descriptive – that we dealt with in the former chapter – to inferential statistics. Inferential statistics are necessary whenever we want to *infer* something from a sample, that is, declare the findings from that sample applicable to a larger set of units, a population. Whenever we use inferential statistics, we do this because there is uncertainty. We have studied a subset of the total universe we are interested in. We want to decide something about that total universe, but as we have sampled only a fraction of it, we cannot be sure that we know exactly what is going on in that larger universe. So our statements about the larger universe are always uncertain.

How to deal with that uncertainty, is what inferential statistics is about. In the following, we will introduce the basics of statistical testing. In doing so, we discuss hypotheses, testing, distributions and the power of tests, dealing with fairly abstract theoretical as well as practical issues. We end with a short paragraph that discusses some basic issues in estimation.

As we will hopefully transmit to the reader, the rationale behind statistical testing is not difficult or ungraspable for the mathematically insecure. In fact, statistical reasoning is quite logical and of the kind that we ourselves apply in day-to-day situations.

While we will try to keep the formulas and calculations to the minimum, we will employ formulas in order to show the reasoning that is formalised in the procedures and formulas, to illustrate why formulas were designed the way they were and to show that they indeed function as we would expect them to.

7.1 Statistical testing

Thus far, whenever we mentioned inferential statistics we did so pretty fuzzily and in an off-hand manner. It is now time to become more precise. In the following sections we will explain – again starting with logics and some fuzzy wording – how inferences are made in statistics, and how uncertainty is quantified using statistical techniques.

Let us assume that we have a representative sample. Given that the sample is representative, we may after calculating various properties of the sample, such as mean, median, variance, association between two variables and the like, declare those sample properties applicable to the population. We could find that burglars have higher IQs than robbers, or that juvenile child abusers are more socially isolated than juvenile peer abusers. However, even though we just stated that such inferences are well defensible, we obviously are not *certain* about such generalizations. We may conclude that burglars' IQ equals 110 on average and that of robbers 100, and that they therefore differ, but how can we be sure that this is not the consequence of a few bright burglars and a few stupid robbers who happen to have coincidentally ended up in our sample? Is our finding not simply attributable to chance, a random result, coincidence? Because our sample was drawn randomly, we may consider it to reflect the population, but even so, uncertainty does remain. After all, we have not observed each and every population member, and there is and remains always a chance that our findings, the differences between burglars and robbers, between child abusers and peer abusers, are maybe true for the sample but that patterns may be quite different in the population.

In order to deal with this uncertainty, we generally use statistical tests. There are very many different kinds of tests. The basic rationale of these tests is however always the same. And this rationale is not difficult, as it follows the kind of reasoning each of us applies in everyday life. We will give examples of that below.

7.1.1 Day-to-day statistical reasoning

Suppose you go out to dinner at a little new restaurant, around the corner from your house. The meal tastes wonderfully, you're having stuffed calamari. At night, however, you wake up feeling all queasy, and after a while, you have to throw up. The food clearly didn't become you. Now, there's tummy flu all around, so you simply assume that that must have been it, and you leave it there. A few months later, you invite a friend over to the same place. Again, the food is wonderful, you're having a salad and beef stew. That night, to your surprise the same thing happens as last time, and when you meet your friend the next day, you find out that also she has been hanging over the loo getting rid of the restaurant food. Now you draw your conclusion: this is a dirty restaurant. The first and the second time you went out to have dinner at the restaurant under the assumption that they would be serving good food. Now you cross out that assumption, you reject it. And you conclude that it is a dirty place. A very logical, intuitively reasonable conclusion.

Suppose, in a second example, that you walk one of the grotty shopping streets of Amsterdam, the Kalverstraat. About halfway, you spot a man, dressed in a suit, who tells you: 'I have ten dice. If I roll the dice and if for each of the ten dice, 6 pips come up, you pay me 100 euros. Anything else I roll, I pay you 100 euros'. You start calculating fast. The chance that this man will come up with ten times 6 pips, is really very small, actually it is $(\frac{1}{6})^{10}$ so that the chance that you will make 100 euros is actually almost 1, namely: $1 - (\frac{1}{6})^{10}$! You take the bet.

What happens? The man rolls ten times a 6 – and you have to pay him €100. What do you infer from this? Now most people respond here by saying that the man is a cheater, but that answer is incorrect. You would probably conclude that the dice are loaded, or 'iced', tampered with. In your calculations you did not work from the assumption that the man was honest, but that the dice had equal chances of 1, 2, 3 etc. pips coming face up.

However, the chances of the current outcome if the dice are fair are so incredibly extremely small, that you now conclude that you cannot reasonably stick to your initial assumptions and keep on believing that the dice are fair. Whether that is because the man has tampered with them, knew they were loaded, is irrelevant.

Are you *certain* of your conclusion, that the dice are loaded? 'No', is the right answer here, you are not 100% certain. You have not conducted a physical investigation of the dice, you have not inspected their weight per side on a weighing scale. You have only observed their behaviour, from which you infer something about their properties. Actually there *is* a theoretical possibility that someone would roll ten times 6 pips in one roll – but the chances of that happening are really so incredibly small. It is all really 'too coincidental'. And so you conclude: the chance that this roll is the result of chance is so terribly small if the dice were fair, that I dare conclude that the dice are loaded.

If we translate this example into statistics-speak, we would say that you accepted the man's bet working from the so-called *null hypothesis* or H_0:

$$H_0 : \text{the dice are fair.}$$

After the experiment, where the man threw 6 pips for each of the ten dice, you reject the null hypothesis and instead switch to the alternative hypothesis H_A, also referred to as H_1:

$$H_1 : \text{the dice are loaded.}$$

As said, you are not *certain* that the alternative hypothesis is true. However, given the null hypothesis, assuming the null hypothesis is true, the dice rolling results are so unlikely that you find the H_0 untenable, and you dare to switch to the alternative hypothesis.

If the null hypothesis is true, you draw the wrong conclusion – but the chance that you do so is however very small, namely:

$$(\frac{1}{6})^{10} = 0.00000001654,$$

or a little over one-and-half-millionth percent.

Statistical reasoning runs along exactly these lines – relatively common reasoning steps that all of us employ. In that sense, statistics is not difficult, and intuitively understandable. We will now discuss statistics more formally.

7.1.2 More formalised statistical reasoning

Above we discussed two examples. In each, we had first made an assumption about the state of the world: we assumed that a restaurant served good food, and we assumed that 10 dice were fair. Next we witnessed occurrences that were highly improbable if our assumption were true. We therefore each time concluded that the assumption must be untrue, and opted for the alternative scenario: the restaurant does not serve good food, the dice are loaded.

We note that in each instance we were not *entirely* certain of our conclusion. We had not subjected the cooking pots of the restaurant to bacterial tests, we had not fine-weighed the dice. We had a number of observations, a sample, and we drew a conclusion from what we saw. This means that there is a chance that we draw the wrong conclusion. We may conclude that the restaurant serves bad food, while it actually is a really clean place and we were simply both times unlucky to have been infected in some other manner right before we went there to eat. The same goes for the dice: it may all have been a coincidence.

We work from an assumption on the state of the world, our H_0 or null hypothesis. This null hypothesis is generally formulated as 'nothing out of the ordinary', such as 'there is no association between X and Y', or 'the IQ of Criminology students is not different from that of Psychology students', or 'the dice are fair'. Next, the researcher gathers some data. Then, it is calculated how likely it would be to observe these data if the null hypothesis were true. If finding such data is very unlikely under the null hypothesis, the researcher decides to abandon the null hypothesis and instead assumes that an alternative hypothesis about the state of the world is true.

Now, if the likelihood to find the results if the null hypothesis were true (in statistics-speak: *under* the null hypothesis) is very small, and if it is in fact smaller than a certain threshold value, we say that the finding is *significant*. In statistics-speak this likelihood to reject the H_0 when H_0 is true, is called α. This mistake is called the *Type I error*. This begs the question how high or low that threshold should be. For rejection, how unlikely under the null hypothesis should the results be? Is 1% enough, is one millionth of a percent enough? Would a chance of finding these results of 10% still be sufficient ground to switch from H_0 to H_1? In other words how small should α be?

In essence, this depends on the researcher. What this chance namely amounts to is the chance to reject H_0 while H_0 is true, and thus the chance to be wrong, to draw the wrong conclusion. It therefore depends on the researcher what risk s/he is willing to take, what α he or she deems an acceptable risk. As a rule of thumb, researchers generally set their α at 5% or 0.05. This rule of thumb means that we find it in general acceptable, as researchers in academia, to abandon our initial assumption 'nothing special is going on' and instead assume that 'something special is going on', for instance that there is an association between X and Y, or that Criminology students are indeed smarter than Psychology students, when that risk is below 5%. We generally accept a 5% or a one in 20 chance to be 'crying wolf' while in fact nothing is out of the ordinary. This 5% (the α) is called the *significance level*. And when the chance to observe our findings if H_0 were true is below this significance level, we say that the findings are significant.

This 5% is however a rule of thumb, and several criteria play a role in deciding what an appropriate significance level would be. Suppose for instance that we are not talking about restaurant food or about dice and 100 euros, but about the decision whether a sex offender in treatment for compulsive sex offending should be allowed to go on unsupervised weekend leave. Here the null hypothesis is:

$$H_0 : \text{the sex offender is still dangerous}$$

and the alternative hypothesis is:

$$H_1 : \text{the sex offender is not dangerous anymore.}$$

Suppose that some risk taxation instrument indicates that the sex offender is not dangerous anymore. However, obviously, such risk taxation instruments are not infallible. Would we

Figure 7.1: Overview of testing

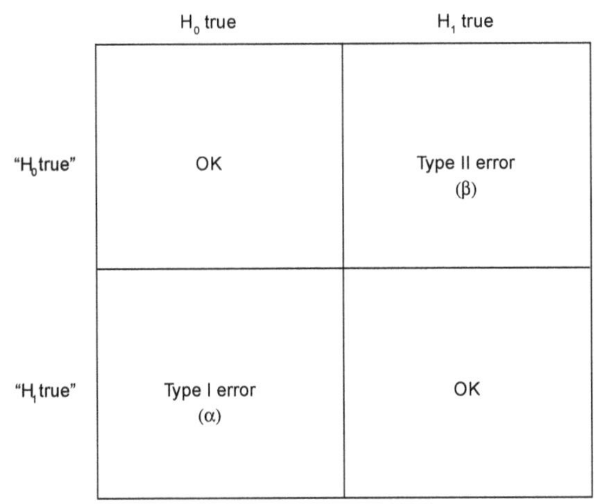

find 5% an acceptable risk now too? Would we find it acceptable that out of 20 sex offenders released on weekend leave, one would still be dangerous and thus perhaps commit a new sex offence? Given the seriousness of the consequences, we might decide here that we must scale down the chance to make a wrong decision, perhaps to 1% or even 0.1%.

Setting the significance level that low has it disadvantages too, however. If we set α smaller, this implies that the likelihood that H_0 is rejected becomes correspondingly smaller. Eventually, with decreasing α (meaning we tolerate increasingly smaller chances that we would wrongly reject H_0) we may in practice never reject H_0 anymore. This means that we will then never decide that H_1 is true. Obviously, if H_1 were true, our test with its very, very small α will hardly ever make us state that H_1 is true, and will not allow us to detect that H_1 is true. Formulated differently, if we are unwilling to make one kind of mistake (wrongly stating H_1 is true), we may in fact be increasing the chance that we make a different kind of mistake (wrongly stating H_0 is true).

Above, we said that α is also referred to as the 'Type I error'. This suggests that there might also be another type of error. This is exactly the kind of mistake we just discussed: the mistake of not stating that H_1 is true when it is true. This type of error is named *Type II error*. While the Type I error is the error of stating that something special is going on while everything is as it used to be, failing to note that something out of the ordinary is going on, is the Type II error. The probability to make this mistake is labelled β.

The possible outcomes of a statistical testing procedure are summarised in Figure 7.1. Two possible states can be the case: either H_0 is true, or H_1 is true. These are the columns of the matrix. There are two possible decisions we can take, that constitute the rows: either we decide that H_0 is true (indicated as "H_0 true"), or we decide that H_1 is true (indicated as "H_1 true"). This gives a matrix with four possible situations, that are sketched in Figure 7.1.

If H_0 is true, and we decide so, we are doing things right: we make the right decision. If however H_0 is true but we state that H_1 is true, we make a Type I error. Moving to the top right of the matrix we have the situation where we also make a mistake: here H_1 is true, but we fail to acknowledge this, this is a Type II error. In the bottom left of the matrix we are doing things right again: H_1 is true, and we acknowledge this.

Note that in all the text above, we have always made *conditional* statements. We have said that *if* such and such is the case, *then* the chances are ... Thus, we have never said that the chances to make the wrong decision are $x\%$ or $y\%$. We can in fact never say that, because we do not know whether H_1 or H_0 is true. Thus we only say that *if* H_0 is true, *then* ... Knowing that we are making conditional statements, we can not only specify the chances to make mistakes (α and β) but also the chances to make the right decision. If namely H_0 is true, and if the chance to make the wrong decision (Type I error) is α, it follows that the chance to make the right decision when H_0 is true is $1-\alpha$. Similarly, if H_1 is true, and the chance to make the wrong decision (Type II error) is β, it follows that the chance to make the right decision is $1-\beta$.

Because the hypothetical situations H_0 and H_1 are constructed so differently, with H_0 the 'normal situation' and H_1 the exceptional case where something really special is going on, the Type I and Type II errors are also fundamentally different mistakes, and of fundamentally different importance. While not a perfectly applicable analogue, the example of a fire alarm serves the purpose of explaining why.

Suppose that my house has a fire alarm. If that fire alarm rings also when someone bakes an omelette in my kitchen, it is set too lightly, it is too sensitive. Such false alarms (where I have to run upstairs and slam the alarm with a newspaper to silence it) are annoying – they are the analogue of the Type I error: much ado about nothing. Clearly this is something we do not want. To avoid this, I can set the alarm to lower sensitivity. The fire alarm may then, however, make a different kind of mistake. If its sensitivity is too low, there is the possibility that it will not detect a fire or detect it too late. This is the analogue of a Type II error: not detecting when something out of the ordinary is going on. Clearly this type of mistake is not just annoying, it may even be regarded as unacceptable as it constitutes a potentially deadly risk.

The example shows the different nature of the two types of errors. They are not simply each other's mirror image; they are of a qualitatively different nature. Ideally one would want the chance for Type I error as well as the chance for Type II error to be as small as possible, but that is difficult as they are linked. If I increase the sensitivity of the fire alarm, it will sooner detect a fire, but also more often give false alarms. If I screw the sensitivity down, I will have fewer false alarms, but the chance will be increased that a real fire is missed. The situation in testing is just like this: if I lower α, this increases the β, if I allow α to be bigger, this generally decreases β. We will return to this subject in section 7.4.

Before we move to the finale of this paragraph, we zoom in on a particular area of the matrix in Figure 7.1. The lower right corner denotes the situation where something out of the ordinary is going on (H_1 is true) and where the test is able to detect that. The chance that this happens if H_1 is true, is $1-\beta$. In terms of the fire alarm, this is the chance that the fire alarm starts screeching when there is a fire. In statistics this chance, $1-\beta$, is generally referred to as the *power* of a test. Ideally, we would want the power of any test, just like our fire alarm, to be really good. However, while we can ourselves decide how high we want to set the α, this is not generally possible for β and therefore also not for $1-\beta$. In general situations of hypothesis testing in social science research, where we have drawn a sample from a population, the power of a test is reduced as samples become smaller, and is increased as samples become larger. This is only intuitively logical, because when our samples become larger we inspect a larger part of the population and therefore must be able to better discern what is going on. We return to this topic below.

All this sounds – hopefully – pretty straightforward. But is testing always possible? Can things go wrong when we test? Yes, they can. Firstly, it may be the case that the sample we are working with is simply too small to generate meaningful results. When samples are too small, almost no difference or association will turn up *significant*, i.e. no test will decide that H_1 is true instead of H_0. Tests are then simply unable to detect what is going on, they have too few observations to confidently draw conclusions, will generally see any differences as likely chance results, and will thus always opt for: 'nothing out of the ordinary'. Small samples are therefore of little use statistically speaking, and samples of about 30 are generally regarded as at the absolute lower limit. From sample sizes of about 100 onwards, statistical tests can be carried out with more confidence and stronger conclusions drawn – for reasons to be detailed below.

Secondly, testing may be hampered if the data are very noisy. Any association or difference (see also above section 3.4) in a sense 'disappears' in the noise. Tests then cannot detect differences anymore, they are masked by the large variability in the data.

Third, it may be the case that the assumptions of the testing procedures have been violated. With the latter we mean for instance that a statistical test assumes that the data are distributed in a specific way, and generates significance levels based on that assumption – but the data are differently distributed, rendering the tests invalid.

While we will not go into this, we remark that there is currently much debate in academia on the 5% level for α, and in general on the statistical testing paradigm we introduce in this chapter. These issues are detailed in more particular statistical publications and are beyond the scope of this book.

7.2 Distributions and tests

In the above examples, we were mostly pretty vague. We spoke of 'unlikely' and 'too coincidental' mostly, and only in the example with the dice did we give exact chances for the occurrences under the null hypothesis. We did also announce that we would become more precise later on, and this is the paragraph where we will do so. Again we start with an example.

One crisp autumn morning, the sun barely risen and the air damp and foggy, I step out of my kitchen door to collect the windfall from my Armgard apple tree, when suddenly I spot in my back garden a huge dead heron. Yuk. It lies sprawled across the grass. Even though my garden is not large, this poor bird appears to almost stretch the entire breadth of the garden and that does look like quite some breadth for a heron's wings! I am convinced it is a huge beast, it must be one of the largest of its kind that has crashed in my garden.

I measure the dead heron's wing span. It is 2 meters and 3 centimeters. That really seems like a lot. This heron must belong to the top 1% largest of its kind! I look up *Ardea*

Figure 7.2: Normal distribution of wing span of *Ardea herodias*

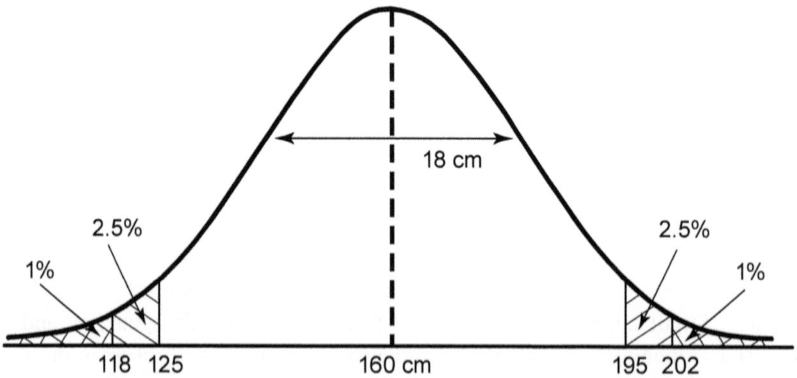

herodias (the Latin name of the blue heron, apparently a rare bird where I live): it appears that the wing span of this type of heron is according to biologists 'normally distributed' with an average wing span of 1.60 m and a standard deviation of 18 cm.

Figure 7.2 graphically depicts this information: it is a picture of a normal distribution with a mean of 160 cm and a standard deviation of 18 cm. The figure illustrates firstly that a wing span of 160 cm is the most frequent, the peak of the distribution is at 160 cm. This is so, because the y-axis reflects the number of herons for the various wing spans x. With most herons having a wing span of 1.60 meter, as we move to smaller and larger wing spans, we see that numbers tail off. Fewer and fewer herons are encountered as we move to more extreme values. In the picture, it is also shown that, on average, wing span deviates 18 cm from this mean of 160 cm (the standard deviation is 18 cm). We see also that the distribution of wing span is symmetrical: the distribution has exactly the same shape on the left and right-hand side of the average. We also said that wing span is normally distributed. But what does that mean? What additional information does that give me?

The normal distribution is a distribution that is often encountered in the natural world. Many properties of living beings are normally distributed: height, intelligence, whale teeth size, etc. All these properties have as a common property that they cluster around a mean, are symmetrical and that their distribution is 'normal'. This normal distribution is also referred to as the Gaussian distribution, or the bell curve. The normal distribution can be described by its *probability density function*:

$$p(x) = \frac{1}{\sigma\sqrt{2\pi}} exp^{\left(\frac{-(x-\mu)^2}{\sigma^2}\right)}.$$

This probability density function is bell-shaped (hence the 'bell curve'), being more or less attenuated depending on the standard deviation. The formula of the normal distribution's probability density function is not very interesting for our purposes. For us, it is enough to know that the height of the curve (the value on the y-axis) reflects the number of cases

Figure 7.3: Area under the curve

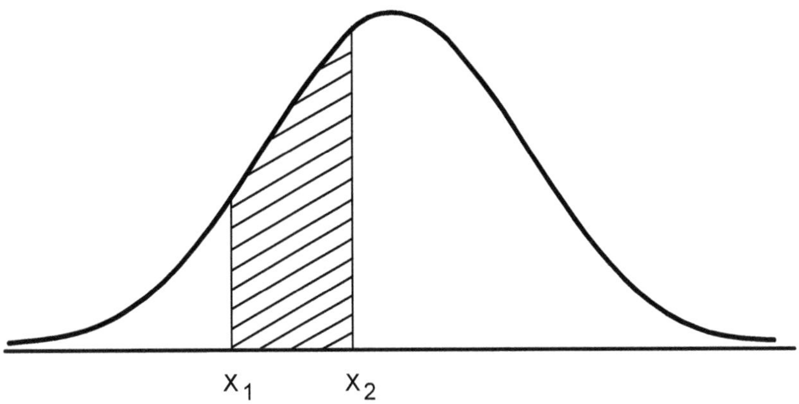

with a certain value X on the variable, the so-called *density*; the density is a mathematical concept best understood as – but not equal to – a frequency. The density has however nice properties that make it possible to translate the properties of the curve directly into statements on chances and probabilities. As an example: the probability for the normal distribution that a variable assumes values within a certain range, say from X_1 to X_2, is equal to the *area under the curve* of the probability density function between X_1 to X_2. See Figure 7.3.

This property is eminently useful as it enables us to make lots of inferences. Firstly, because the distribution is symmetrical, we know that the chance that a blue heron's wing span is more than 160 cm is equal to 0.5 (see Figure 7.2). For the same reason, the chance that a blue heron's wing span is less than 160 cm equals 0.5 as well. Because chances are always between 0 and 1, and the sum of all possible outcomes equals 1, the total area under the curve must be equal to 1, and the mean neatly chunks that area into two – because the distribution is symmetrical necessarily equal – parts. Note that the chance that a heron's wing span equals exactly 160 cm is not defined: chances are defined as areas under the curve, and the point 160 has no breadth and therefore no area defined under it. This means that we can only determine the likelihood of a *range* of outcomes, say a value being between values 160 and 180, or between $-\infty$ (minus infinity) and 140 cm.

The normal distribution has a number of useful properties. As said, firstly, it is symmetrical. This has the nice advantage that we know that the probability of a heron have a wing span larger than 160 cm is equal to the probability that a heron has a wing span smaller than 160 cm. Secondly and most importantly, because it is possible to compute the probability that a variable assumes values within a certain range A to B, we can also compute the chance that an observation from a normal distribution is higher than a certain value, or lower than a certain value. This is exactly what I wanted to do for my poor, magnificent, dead heron: I wanted to know what the chances are that a heron of this type has a wing span of 203 cm and over, or formulated more mathematically, between 203 cm and ∞ (infinity).

While it is possible to do these computations oneself, many statistical textbooks, online gadgets and statistical software packages do it for you. Using any statistical textbook or surfing the web, I can look up a table for the normal distribution and find that – for this normal distribution with mean 160 and standard deviation 18 – 95% of all herons have a wing span between approximately 125 and 195 cm, and 98% between 118 and 202 cm. As the distribution is symmetrical this means that only 1% of all herons have a wing span larger than 202 cm. My poor dead heron thus indeed belongs to the small fraction of 1% of herons with huge wingspans of 202 cm and above.

7.2.1 Standard scores

In working with the normal distribution, the values of the variables we are working with are often *standardised*. Standardization usually is done by subtracting from every score the mean, and then dividing the result by the standard deviation:

$$\frac{X_i - \bar{X}}{s_x}.$$

The resulting values are called standard scores, or standardised values, denoted by z, or z_x. Standard scores always have a mean of 0 and a standard deviation of 1. The resulting normal distribution of these scores is now called the *standard normal distribution*. The probability density function – given that μ equals 0 and σ equals 1 – simplifies to:

$$p(x) = \frac{1}{\sqrt{2\pi}} exp^{-x^2}.$$

Such *z-scores* have the advantage that they make comparisons over variables easier: we could state that respondent X has IQ scores in the top 15%, and extraversion scores in the lowest 30% range. If we had given the raw, unstandardised scores this comparison would have been less easily made: what does 120 and 43 tell me as a reader? A standard score of 2 tells me already much more: on this variable the respondent deviates twice as much as average (namely the standard deviation) from the mean. A standard score of -.5 tells me that for this variable the respondent is in fact much less ‘deviant’ as s/he deviates only half a standard deviation from the mean.

The standard normal distribution is depicted in Figure 7.4. Here, we see that the mean is 0, and as scores becomes lower or higher, they are more seldom. In the limiting case (when X approaches either ∞ or $-\infty$), the curve approaches the x-axis. The curve never actually reaches the x-axis, it creeps closer and closer. The area under the curve equals 1. The area higher than 0 equals .5, and the area lower than 0 equals .5 as well. Tables in any textbook will list the chances to find observations above certain values. Such tables will tell you for instance that the area beyond 1.99 equals .0233 or 2.33%. This tells you that the chance that a respondent has a standard score higher than 1.99 equals .0233. Because the distribution is symmetrical, the chance that a respondent has a standard score lower than -1.99 is then also 2.33%. The more extreme the score, the less likely it is to find respondents with such scores.

Figure 7.4: Standard normal distribution

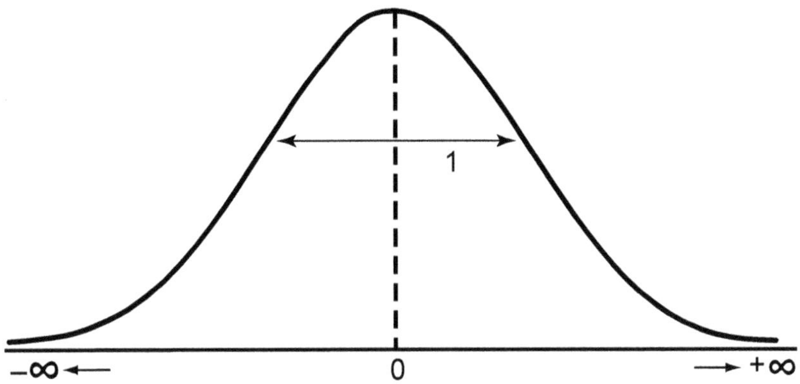

Now how does this translate to testing? Suppose that we have two hypotheses, of which H_0 is:

$$H_0 : \text{Criminology students are just as bright as they were 5 years ago,}$$

and the alternative hypothesis H_1 is:

$$H_1 : \text{Criminology students are not as bright as they were 5 years ago.}$$

Suppose further that I have measurements of the IQ of a random sample of all Criminology students, measured 5 years ago. On average, then, their IQs were 122. The standard deviation of their IQs was 2. Subsequently, for the current generation of Criminology students, I obtain measurements on IQ in exactly the same manner. I investigate the sample, and find that the sample's IQ is on average 127. Clearly, this is higher. But is this result so striking, so significant, that I dare to decide that current Criminology students have an IQ that differs from those who studied 5 years ago? That the current Criminology students stem from a different population than the old batch that has a mean of 122? Could this not simply be a chance result, coincidental?

We will now describe how we go about this, describing the process in a somewhat rudimentary way. We first formalise what we just enumerated by saying that we assume that under the old situation, 5 years ago, the population of students had an IQ of 122, so μ = 122. Also, we assume that in the population of students the standard deviation of IQ was 2, so σ=2. The hypotheses are now:

$$H_0 : \mu = 122,$$

and

$$H_1 : \mu \neq 122.$$

Figure 7.5: Standard normal distribution with critical scores

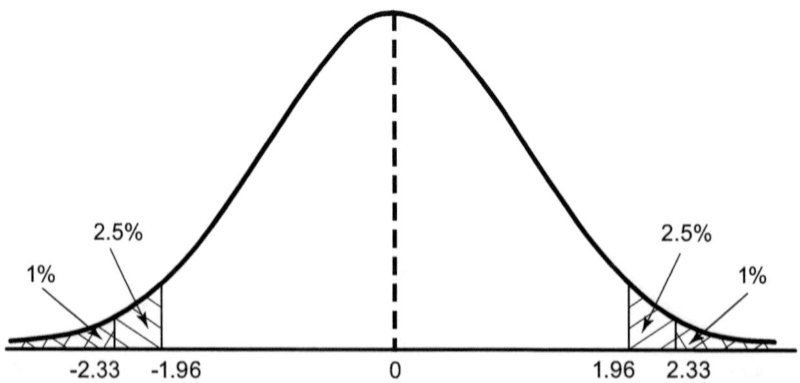

Note that in the hypotheses, that specify the properties of populations, we use Greek literals. Before we do the testing, first the raw scores are rewritten as standard scores:

$$\frac{X_i - \bar{X}}{s_x} = \frac{127 - 122}{2} = 2.5.$$

Now, this value of 2.5 is a z-value, a standard score. This means that we can – assuming that the data we are inspecting are normally distributed – look up what the chances are that a value is greater than 2.5. Tables with z-values are in the appendices of any statistical textbook, and can also be found on internet, see for an application `stattrek.com/online-calculator/normal.aspx`. Looking up the z-score, we find that if the z-score would have been 2.33, the area under the curve beyond it would have been 1%. With the value of z equalling 2.5, the area under the curve beyond 2.5 therefore is a little under 1%. This means that the chance that, if I draw this sample from a population with a mean of 122 and a standard deviation of 2, the chance that I find this result of 127 is a little under 1%. See Figure 7.5.

If we translate this into words, we say that *if* H_0 is true, that is, if current Criminology students are as bright as they were 5 years ago, the chance to find this result is pretty unlikely. Not as unlikely as the 0.00000001654 in the dice example, but even so a truly small chance to find this result if H_0 is true. So, we might decide that H_1 is true. Are we *sure* about this? No we are not. It *is* possible to find a mean IQ of 127 in our sample of Criminology students if they stem from a population with a mean of 122.

All in all, to reject the H_0 would be a logical thing to do. There is a small chance – if H_0 is true – that we make the wrong decision, but in general this probability is viewed as an acceptable risk. So, in this example, we would conclude that this year's Criminology students indeed have significantly different, and higher IQs than their forebears.

Above, we looked at the sample mean and investigated what the chances for this result were under the null hypothesis. However, we can also work the other way round. Then,

Figure 7.6: Normal distribution with critical raw values

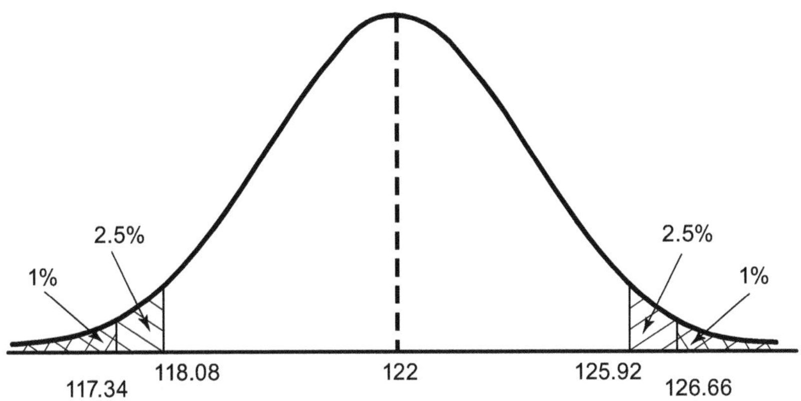

we decide first on the acceptable risk to make the wrong decision (α), draw the probability density function, and compute the so-called *critical value*: any sample mean in excess of this critical value leads to rejection of the H_0. See Figure 7.6, in which we have depicted the critical values for this example for α's of 5%, and 2%. So, if we are willing to accept a risk of making a Type I error of 5%, this means that we reject H_0 if the sample mean is above 125.92, or below 118.08 (we reject when the findings are either much lower or much higher than as specified in the H_0). If we feel that 5% is too high a risk, we set the critical value sharper, rejecting sample means only above 126.66 or below 117.34. These results are intuitively reasonable: if we want to reduce the risk for a Type I error, we reject only from values further away from the mean, we need sample results that differ more from the postulated population mean. See Figure 7.6.

This is a very cursory and rough description of the procedure of testing. We have discussed only the normal distribution. There are numerous other distributions, such as the t-distribution, the F-distribution, the χ^2- distribution. They generate different tabulations with probabilities for α's, but the principles for testing are identical. Each time we assume that the data follow a certain distribution (H_0). We look up what the probability is to observe the data we find in our sample if the data stemmed from that null-distribution. If that probability is very low, we say it is unlikely that the data stem from the H_0, and we conclude that H_1 must instead be true.

Having said so, we remark that testing can also be done using distribution-free tests (so-called non-parametric tests). We will leave such other parametric and non-parametric tests mostly undiscussed, as they are not essential for the purposes of this text. Suffice it to say that the rationale of testing, the choice of hypothesis, the procedure of rejection or acceptance are all identical: any differences are in the mathematics. For more information on testing, statistics textbooks such as Hinkle, Wiersma and Jurs (2003), chapter 14, 21 or 22.

7.3 Theoretical foundations for testing

In all our discussions so far, we have been a bit crude and sloppy. We talked about 'estimation' but never defined exactly what we meant by that. Also, in the example about the IQ of Criminology students we used the normal distribution to test whether the observed sample mean of 127 differed significantly from the null-value of 122, but we never explained why there was ground to employ the normal distribution. In this section, we will introduce the *central limit theorem*, a theorem that forms the basis for much statistical testing. The central limit theorem states that:

As the size N of a randomly drawn sample increases, the distribution of the sample mean, regardless of the original distribution (with mean μ and finite variance σ^2) from which the sample was drawn approximates a normal distribution.

This is a lot of abstract information to digest at once, so we will discuss it in parts. What the theorem firstly says is that, if I draw numerous samples from a population, that the means of these samples – if I draw large enough samples and draw them randomly – are distributed normally. This is so regardless of how the original variable was distributed. Let us try to visualise this.

Figure 7.7 gives a representation of four random samples (A, B, C, and D) of size 10 each, drawn from a population that has a certain distribution. For ease, we chose to use the normal distribution, but we could have used any other distribution for our figure. The samples are drawn randomly, so each time that a sample is drawn, the outcome will be slightly different. This is indicated in the figure, that contains four little graphs. Each graph sketches a normal distribution, in which the x-axis indicates the values that the variable of interest can assume, and the y-axis indicates how often a value occurs. In the examples, we each time drew a sample of 10, and the small arrows below the x-axis indicate the values of the respective sample members. And the average of those values, the sample mean, is for each different sample A, B, C or D, indicated by a large arrow above the x-axis.

Sample A, for instance, has a mean that is slightly below the population mean. Sample B's mean is on the face of it, a little closer to the population mean, just slightly above it. Sample C's mean is the most off: its sample mean is actually quite a bit higher than the population mean. And sample D has a mean that, although different from that of sample A, B or C, is again quite close to the population mean. The pictures show that, even though each sample is different, we may expect to draw sample members most often close to the distribution mean: it is very unlikely that sample members would all be drawn very much in the left or right tail of the distribution (although it is not impossible). As we draw most sample members close to the population mean, this implies that also the sample means (M or $\bar{X}$) will mostly be fairly close to the population mean (μ). In our four examples, we saw that one sample (C) had a mean that was notably different. But, taken together, our sample means would approximate the population mean quite nicely. In fact, if we would take the average of our sample means (the mean of the sample means), we would likely end up quite close to the population mean.

We just have sketched a situation where we had drawn just four samples. But now imagine that we would draw 100 different random samples. We would then get 100 pictures like the ones in Figure 7.7. The sample means would again mostly gravitate towards the

Figure 7.7: Example of four random samples drawn from a normal distribution

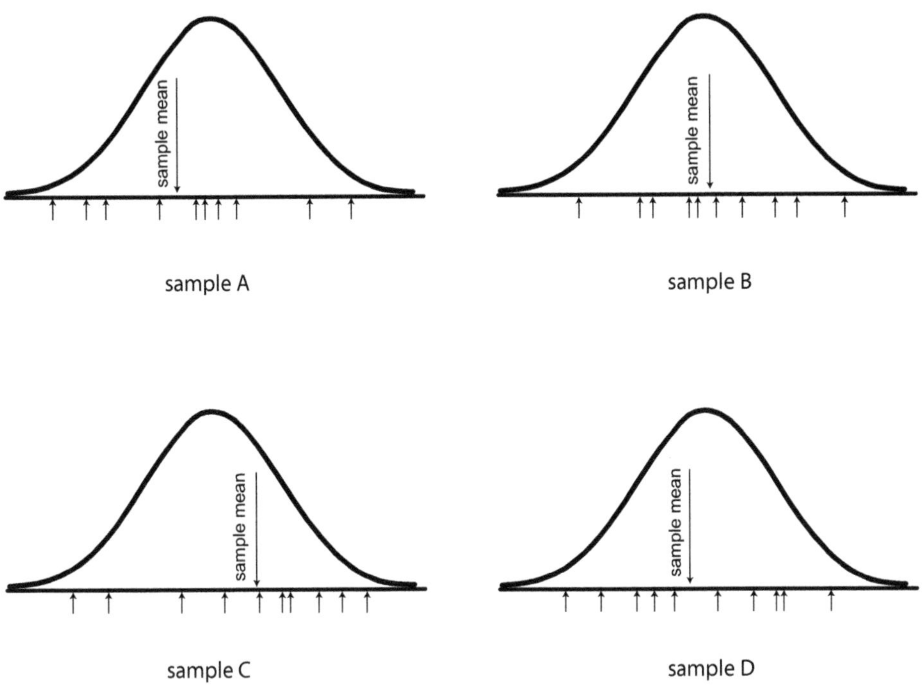

population mean, as we already saw in Figure 7.7, but we might also encounter – just by chance – a few rare situations where the sample mean is even further off than in example C. We could also draw 1,000 different samples, and then the 1,000 sample means would again mostly be quite close to the population mean, with again some exceptions further off, and maybe also a few that are quite far removed.

Those 100 or 1,000 sample means can be envisaged as themselves following a distribution: a distribution of means. These sample means are most often found around the population mean, and sample means are increasingly unlikely to be found as as we move further away – higher or lower – from the population mean.

This is exactly what follows from the central limit theorem. The theorem states namely, exactly, that the sample means are distributed such that they themselves follow a normal distribution. This becomes more and more the case as sample size increases. So while the sample means in our example in Figure 7.7 may not yet follow a normal distribution (sample size was only 10...), once we get to larger samples, the distribution of the sample means will more closely follow a normal distribution.

What the theorem also, interestingly, states that it is irrelevant whether the data from which the samples are drawn themselves follow a normal distribution: regardless the underlying distribution of the variable we are investigating, the sample means will be normally

Figure 7.8: 'Extreme' samples drawn from a normal distribution

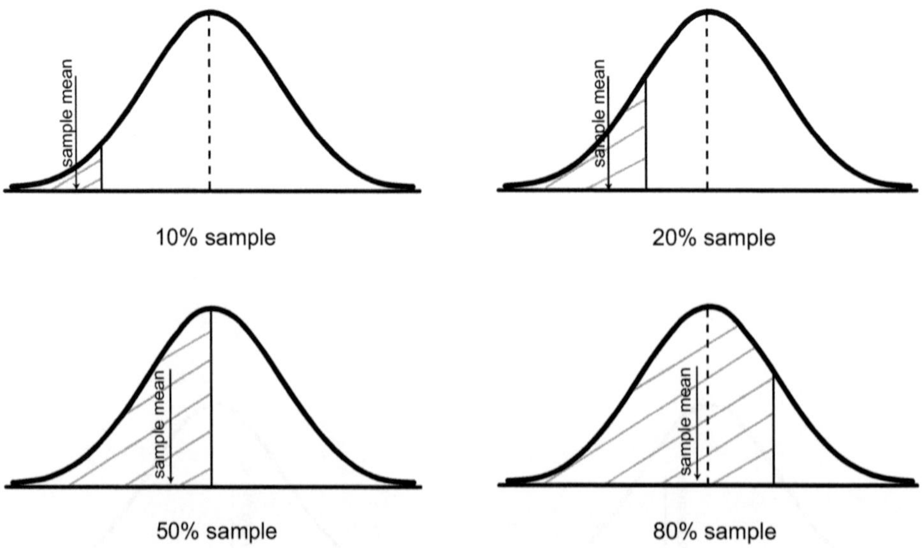

distributed. So we may draw samples from any kind of whichever way wildly erratically distributed variable: as long as we sample randomly and ensure that sample size is large enough, the sample means will be distributed normally.

Now why is this important? Because it forms the foundation for a large number of statistical tests that we carry out in research. In section 7.2.1 we investigated whether a new cohort of Criminology students had a higher IQ than an old cohort of Criminology students. We took the mean IQs of the cohorts and compared them, using a z-distribution and employing the IQ-measurements of the older cohort as our baseline, the H_0. Next we investigated how likely it was to find an average IQ of 127, for a sample drawn from a population with mean 122. To computed that likelihood, we used the normal distribution. We did not explain why we believed this was correct. The standard limit theorem gives us the justification for this assumption.

Secondly, the theorem tell us that sample size is important, and that larger samples are better. Obviously, drawing larger samples can only give better results: if we draw a larger sample out of a population, we have observed a larger proportion of that population and will be able to make more precise statements about that population. That is quite logical: it would be very strange indeed if by observing more and more of a population we would get a less precise image!

To first illustrate this, we have sketched four situations in Figure 7.8. In the left upper part, we sketch a situation where a 10% sample has been drawn from a population and where, by some quirk, all sample members turned out to stem from the left tail of the distribution. This is of course a highly unlikely outcome: as we showed in Figure 7.7, generally samples pan out pretty nicely, with sampled units mostly around, and some above and some below the population average. But: let us assume that this unlikely situation occurs and we are left in our 10% sample that has only those 10% population members with lowest scores. Our sample mean – estimate of the population mean – is then far below the true population mean (indicated by the dotted line). Of course, a similarly unlikely result could have occurred with the sample harbouring the only the top 10% from the population. The sample mean would then be equally far removed from the population mean, but then way too high.

Now if we move to the top right corner of the figure, we see sketched the situation where a 20% sample has been drawn, and again only those with lowest scores were included in the sample. Again, the sample mean is far from the population mean, but less strongly so now. Because we are now investigating 20% of the population, the sample mean cannot assume very extreme values anymore, but will inevitably be closer to the population mean. Again, we could also have ended up with the top 20% of the population in our sample, but the results would simply be mirrored.

In the bottom left of Figure 7.8 we see a sketch of the situation where the sample comprises half of the population and again only the 50% with lowest scores miraculously ended up in the sample. It is clear that the sample mean now can only approach the population average more: we are investigating such a large part of the entire population that our estimate cannot be very far off anymore. The bottom right illustrates a situation where an 80% sample has been drawn. Here it is easy to see that the sample mean is quite close to the population mean. Not illogical, given that such an immense part of the population is included in the sample.

All in all, we see from these pictures that the larger the sample size, the narrower the bandwidth of possible values for the sample mean and the more the sample mean creeps up to the population mean. While obviously in real life most samples will not be as extremely composed as the hypothetical cases sketched in Figure 7.8, and we will generally, also for 10% and smaller samples, arrive at estimates that quite nicely approximate the population mean, the examples do show that as sample size increases, the estimate of the population can only approximate the population average better, that is, become a better estimate.

This can also be shown in formula. Envisage again that we draw a number of random samples from the population, not one but several. Each sample has a sample mean. We said that the sample mean is a good estimate of the population average. But obviously, as sampling is random, samples differ and not each sample mean will be identical to the population average. As shown in Figure 7.7, sample means will fluctuate: one sample mean will be a bit higher, the other a bit lower. Now this variability of the sample mean can be written just like we express variability in a variable, namely as variance or standard deviation (see section 6.3.2). The standard deviation of the sample mean is written as: $\sigma_{\bar{X}}$.

The standard deviation of the sample mean, also called the *standard error of the mean*, is defined as:

$$\sigma_{\bar{X}} = \frac{\sigma}{\sqrt{N}}$$

with σ the standard deviation of the population. Given a value of σ, the standard deviation of the sample means, $\sigma_{\bar{X}}$, becomes smaller as N increases. Intuitively, this can only be so:

as I investigate more population members, I can only get a better and better picture of what is going on in the population, and the bandwidth of possible values for the my sample mean becomes smaller. The sample mean will generally approximate the population average better if I have drawn a larger sample. See once more Figure 7.8, that illustrates this.

The formulas show how fast this goes: increasing the sample size with a factor 4 decreases the variability of the sample mean with a factor 2. As samples become bigger, the sample means fluctuate less and less around the population mean. In the limiting case, as N approaches the population size and thus in the limiting case ∞, the variability becomes zero. This can be understood by imagining the following: if my sample size is as large as the population size (so the sample actually equals the population), then each time I draw a sample I will investigate the entire population and my sample mean will equate the population average. My sample mean is then each time exactly the same (namely the population mean). The variability of the sample mean is then 0.

So, summarising, the central limit theorem instructs us to do two important things. First, it tells us that it is vital to draw samples randomly, because then the sample means have the attractive property that enables us to use the normal distribution to test statements about these means. If we do not draw randomly, then the theorem does not hold, and we miss out on all the associated niceties. Second, the theorem gives us guidance on sample size. It states that as sample size becomes bigger, the distribution of the sample mean better approximates the normal distribution. Statistical research has shown that already from sample sizes of about 30, the distribution of the sample mean is pretty normal. From a sample size of a little over 120, it is in fact for practical purposes normal.

The central limit theorem is a crucial piece in the statistical puzzle as it gives us the basis for using the normal distribution in the testing of sample means: the theorem tells us that – like IQ, height and herons' wing spans – also sample means are normally distributed. We may therefore use, if we have random samples of reasonable size, the normal distribution in testing hypotheses about means.

The formula for the standard error of the mean assumes that the population variance σ^2 is known. While we assumed that as well in most of our examples above, the population variance is obviously more often unknown than known (we do not know the population, that is why we are trying to study it through a sample). We mostly use the sample variance as an estimate of the population variance. In that case, however, a sample size of 30 is not sufficient and we have to test using a different distribution, the so-called *Student's t-distribution*. From samples of 100 upwards, the t-distribution is practically equivalent to the normal distribution again, and we can use our standard testing procedure.

This section dealt with statistical theory. It was quite abstract as we described the behaviour of sample means under the condition that samples were drawn randomly and of sufficient size. What likely makes it so abstract is that of course in reality we generally draw just one sample. When we conduct research we identify the population of interest and devise a scheme to draw one sample that is representative of that population. We never draw 10 samples or let alone 1,000 samples... In that sense, the current section may seem to be far removed from the practicalities of research. The section, and the central limit theorem, is however explicitly included in this chapter because it gives the foundations for much statistical testing.

We summarise what was discussed as follows. If a sample has been drawn randomly and sample size is above 100, we use the normal distribution to test hypotheses on the population mean. If a sample has been drawn randomly and sample size is between 30 and 100, we use the normal distribution when the population variance is known, and we use the t-distribution when it is unknown (and where we must estimate the population variance from the sample variance). For sample sizes under 30, testing becomes harder even if samples have been drawn randomly: in practice the t-distribution is used, or researchers resort to non-parametric tests.

7.4 Sampling, significance, and power

So, if we summarise what we have described so far, the story goes as follows. In many research situations, we do not have the possibility to investigate all objects of interest. Instead, we investigate a small part of that entire collection, that population. We do that in a clever way. We make sure that the part that we investigate resembles the larger universe it comes from: we pick the sample members by chance. This ensures that any differences between the sample and the population are accidental differences, they are not systematic. Operating in this way, we construct a sample that is representative.

Obviously, we are not certain about the properties of the population: we have studied only a part. How do we deal with this uncertainty? We do that in a formalised way. This formalised manner of thinking is intuitively logical and reasonable. Because of the particular rules and calculations we follow, it becomes statistical reasoning. What we do, is calculate the chances of finding our observations, if a certain assumption about reality were true. If these chances are very small, we switch to an alternative assumption about reality. We then say that the finding is *significant*. Significant is a word we use in our daily lives as well, it means something like 'important' or 'meaningful'. In statistics, it has this particular meaning: the chances of opting for the alternative scenario if the regular one is true. In general, we work with significance levels of 5% or 1%, depending on sample size and other considerations. We then say that we 'set α at 5%' or that such-and-such is significant 'at the 5% level'.

We want our chances to make a wrong decision to be as small as possible. Deciding that the alternative scenario is true while the regular scenario holds, is one type of mistake. As we describe the regular scenario fairly precisely under H_0 (e.g.: $H_0 : \mu = 122$), we can make fairly exact calculations as well. If we assume that the data are distributed in a certain way (normally, or F-distributed, or χ^2), or if we know what the chances for a certain number of pips are when we roll the dice, we can therefore compute exactly what the chances are that a certain extreme result appears. This means that we can always ourselves determine α. It is for us to decide, and we can actually do so exactly, what risk we are willing to run to make a Type I error.

However, as described earlier, there is a second kind of mistake we could make. We could also on the basis of our sample results decide that there is no reason to reject H_0 while in fact H_1 is true. Then we would make a Type II error. The chance for that we call β. Now, while we can set the α, we can not beforehand design the test in such a way that we have an acceptable β. Why is that so?

Figure 7.9: Distribution of coping skills under H_0 and under H_1 with α=1%

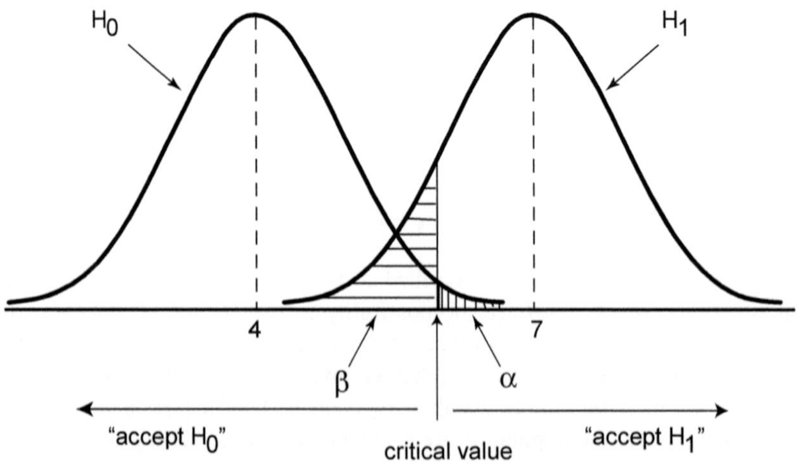

The reason that we cannot predetermine the β the way we can choose our α is because the alternative hypothesis actually comprises a range of options. In other words, while H_0 gives one and only one μ (such as 122 in the example above), under H_1 the μ can assume many different values: 121, 180, 85 ... So how are we then to compute what the risk is to make a Type II error? We cannot.

What we can do, however, is pick a certain alternative μ, and compute – for that alternative μ – what the chances are that we would actually miss that H_1 is true. Let us illustrate this with an example. Suppose that we are looking at the coping skills of ex-detainees. While they were detained their coping skills were 4 on average. We have trained all these detainees to increase their coping skills. A coping skills level of 7 is sufficient for normal societal functioning, 10 means excellent societal functioning. So, obviously, we would be really pleased if the training we gave our detainees had increased their skills to a level of 7: that would mean they would be equipped to return to society. This implies that we would be really unhappy if we would test the trained ex-detainees, but our test would be unable to pick up such a meaningful improvement. Figure 7.9 depicts the testing situation when α has been chosen to be 1% and where in reality – but we don't know this – μ equals 7.

Figure 7.9 shows the α as the area under the H_0-curve beyond the critical value, the area that has vertical dashes. The area under the H_0 curve to the left of that critical value is the chance that I accept the null hypothesis if H_0 is true. As the total area under the curve is 1, or 100%, and as α is 1%, this chance is therefore 99%. The second curve, on the right-hand side, is the situation when actually H_1 is true. We do not know whether this is the case but *if* this is the case then this is how the coping skills scores of our ex-detainees would be distributed, around 7, again normally distributed. Looking at the curve for H_1, we can see that the chance that we miss discovering that H_1 is true is equal to the area

Figure 7.10: Distribution of coping skills under H_0 and H_1 with larger α

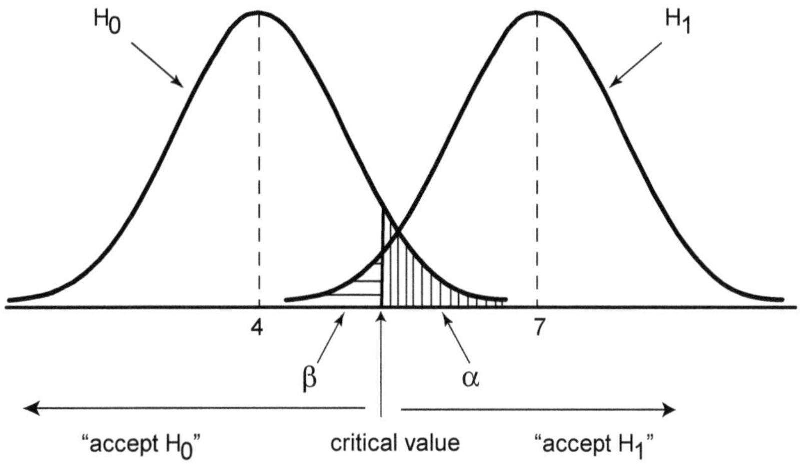

under the H_1 curve to the left of the critical value (the area with horizontal dashes). This is where we end up when we find a not very unlikely result in our sample and therefore see no ground to reject the H_0. If H_1 is true, then the chance that we make the right decision, that we decide in favour of H_1, is equal to the area under the H_1 curve to the right of the critical value: this is the chance that we decide for H_1 if H_1 is true. This is the power of the test.

The power in this example would be – eye-balling the graph – maybe around 80 to perhaps 85%, so a four in five chance if H_1 were true, that our test would pick that up, and would lead us to the right conclusion. In general, this is considered a reasonable power. If, however, we decide that that is not enough, that we want to have a higher chance of discovering that H_1 is true if it is, then – all else being equal – we can achieve this by relaxing α. If we decide that 5% or larger is also acceptable as a chance to make a Type I error, this reduces the Type II error, and increases the power. Compare Figure 7.10.

In this manner, α and β are connected, although not by some simple straightforward formula. In general when one decreases the chance for one type of error, the chance for the other type goes up, and vice versa.

While the chance for a Type I error is determined by the researcher, and generally set at a value between 5 and 1%, the chance for a Type II error, β, and therewith the power 1-β, cannot be pre-set. This is due, as we stated, to the fact that the alternative hypothesis covers many possible values for the property we are studying. What we can do, is deduce what the power would be for one particular value of the parameter of interest where the H_1 is true.

We showed how increasing the α decreases the β. So, for increasing the power, one has to accept paying the price of a higher chance for the other type of mistake. Obviously,

Figure 7.11: Decreased β with increased N

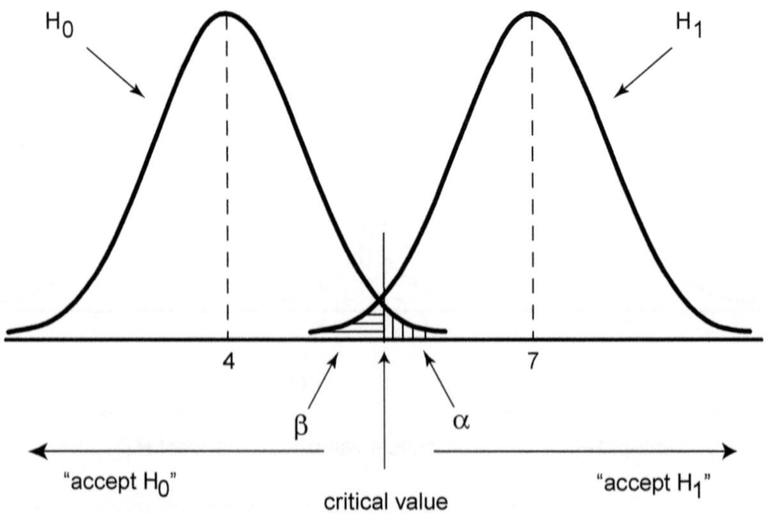

that is not very attractive. We gain in one area but we lose in the other. Is there then no other way to increase the power? For sure there is, and that manner is intuitively understandable. Obviously, if we would increase our sample size and investigate a larger part of the population, we have more information, so it can only be that we get better estimates, it can only be that we observe more sharply what is going on, what the properties of the population are. Inspecting a larger sample must therefore reduce the chance that we make mistakes. It would in fact be highly illogical if this were not the case.

We discussed above how the standard deviation of the sampling mean $\sigma_{\bar{X}}$, becomes smaller as N increases. To visually illustrate what implications that has for β, we refer to Figure 7.11, that repeats Figure 7.9 with the notable difference that now sample size has increased. What we see is that the two bell curves, one for H_0 and one for H_1, have become more attenuated compared to the earlier graph: they are slimmer, because the N is larger and therefore the standard deviation of the mean smaller, so that the 'spread' of the curve is correspondingly less. As we keep α at some pre-set level, we see that this affects the type II error β: it is now much smaller as there is simply less overlap between the two curves.

Figure 7.11 shows visually what the impact is of working with larger samples. Keeping a pre-set level of α, this will have the effect that β, the likelihood of the error where we stick to H_0 while H_1 is true, becomes smaller and the power of the test larger. Larger samples lead to more powerful tests.

Figure 7.12: Test situation for two-sided null hypothesis with critical raw values

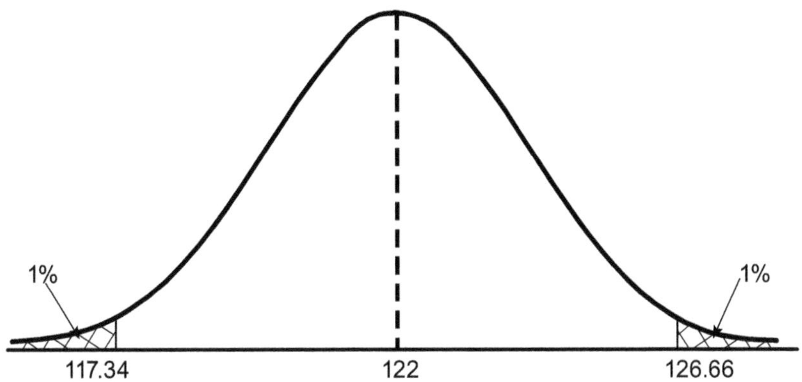

7.4.1 Hypotheses revisited

In the previous section, some readers may have been confused by the following. If we believe that the dead heron we found is extremely large, and if we believe that this year's Criminology students are brighter than those 5 years ago, why then do we have rejection regions both at the left hand and right-hand side of the graph as in Figures 7.5 and 7.6? Given that in both cases the result in the study is higher than expected under the null hypothesis, why would I need a critical value for the opposite result? The fact that in each of the examples we have areas under the curve both in the left and the right tail of the distribution is a consequence of the fact that we are investigating a so-called *two-sided hypothesis*, in the example of the Criminology students' IQs:

$$H_0 : \mu = 122,$$

and therefore

$$H_1 : \mu \neq 122.$$

If we design the null hypothesis this way, it means that we expect the mean to be 122, and that if it is either very much higher, or very much lower, we reject H_0. In both cases the result is so unlikely that we do not anymore believe the situation under the null hypothesis to have generated the data. Viz. Figure 7.12, that sketches the situation.

In this figure, it can be seen that the null hypothesis is rejected when $\bar{X}$, the mean value of X in our sample, is either larger than 126.66 or smaller than 117.34. If H_0 is true, and the observations have therefore actually been drawn from a population with mean 122, there is when I test in this way a chance of 1% that I find a sample mean higher than 126.66 and thus a 1% chance to take the wrong decision when I reject H_1. If I find a sample mean lower than 117.34, then I will also draw the wrong conclusion and the chances of that happening are also 1%. So, in total I accept, in this scheme, a 2% chance of making

Figure 7.13: Test situation for one-sided null hypothesis with critical raw value

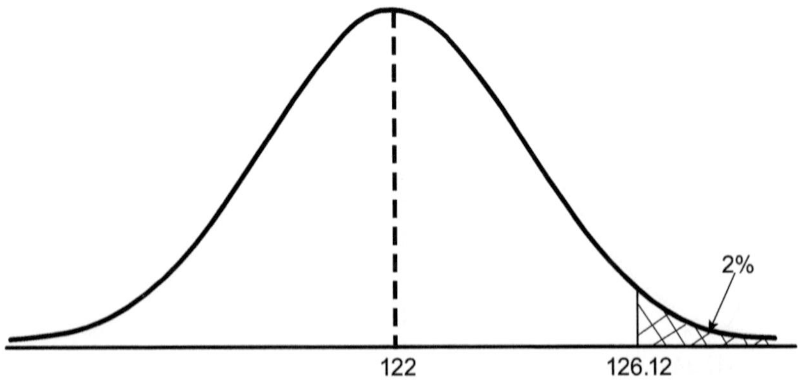

the wrong decision, 1% if the sample mean accidentally is very low, and another 1% if it happens to be very high. See again Figure 7.12.

Obviously, if I have strong reasons to suspect that the deviation from H_0 is in a certain direction, say that Criminology students if they have changed will for sure have become brighter, I do not really need the rejection area on the left hand side. If I am so sure that I will not find a sample mean in some other place, then I might as well skip that area. Then, if I stick to my α of 2%, the critical value from which point onwards I will reject the H_0 also changes, see Figure 7.13. The 2% area under the curve that was first divided over the left- and right-hand side of the curve, is now lumped on one side.

The corresponding null and alternative hypotheses are:

$$H_0 : \mu \leq 122$$

and

$$H_1 : \mu > 122.$$

This type of hypothesis is called a *one-sided hypothesis*. This means that by formulating the null hypothesis as a one-sided hypothesis, the critical value from which point onwards I reject, changes. Formulated differently, if I had used a two-sided null hypothesis and my sample mean had been 126.40, I would not have rejected this null hypothesis: 126.40 is outside the rejection area. If I however construct my null-hypothesis as a one-sided hypothesis and I find for the sample mean 126.40, I can reject the H_0! The α is the same, but in one case I reject and in the other I don't. This reeks of 'lies, damn lies and statistics', some would say, and clearly this offers possibilities for fiddling.

That is why there are clear rules for how hypotheses should be formulated. The first rule is that the hypotheses must be constructed before the data are investigated. They must be constructed beforehand, so that any such post-hoc fiddling is precluded. Secondly, there is a clear rule that one-sided hypotheses are formulated and tested only when there are strong theoretical reasons to suspect that any deviation will be in one direction only. Obviously, working with one-sided hypotheses has its risks too: if the sample mean suddenly does happen to be very low in the one-sided hypotheses formulated above, H_0 cannot be rejected even though the sample mean is obviously very different from what was expected.

The null and alternative hypothesis must always complement each other: together they encompass the entirety of what could possible be the state of affairs.

In the examples so far, we have always sketched the situation where one is interested in finding the mean μ of the population. It is however also possible that we would be interested to know whether two properties are associated in the population, in which case we would not be investigating μ but ρ. Tests can focus on other properties too. For instance, we may test whether the χ^2 is significantly larger than 0, or we may test whether the odds ratio (OR) is significantly different from 1. And, as we said, other distributions than the normal distribution may be used.

7.5 Practical limitations in sampling and testing

Clearly, all the above instructs us that the ideal situation in research is to draw random samples, to ensure that these are large and then we can do some regular standard normal distribution tests, and all will be well. Is that indeed the ideal situation? Yes and no.

Obviously, if one is able to draw a random sample, and thus achieve generalizability, this is better and more desirable than working with non-random samples. However, in many situations, samples simply are non-random, either because there is no sampling frame, or because non-response has affected the randomness of the sample, or for some other reason. In many practical situations, especially in criminological research, we have to make do with such samples. The research situation on the ground is simply not that clear cut and neatly organised.

Secondly, large samples, as discussed at length, have advantages but – seemingly paradoxical – have disadvantages too. If I draw a sample of 170,000 persons out of the Dutch population, a 1% sample, that sample size is so huge that any test I perform will turn up significant. Given that our test value z is defined as:

$$\frac{\bar{X} - \mu}{\sigma_{\bar{X}}},$$

but given that

$$\sigma_{\bar{X}} = \frac{\sigma}{\sqrt{N}}$$

the resulting test value z will be with the large N be divided by a very small $\sigma_{\bar{X}}$, and thus become huge, and therefore quickly significant. As can be seen from all the graphs shown before, more extreme values of the test statistic imply that the null hypothesis will be rejected. Thus, with such a large N, any test will turn up significant. This is logical, as with such a huge sample the likelihood that any results are attributable to chance is negligible. The flip side is however that testing becomes in a sense meaningless: tests will always be significant. Very tiny differences will be marked as 'significant': a correlation coefficient of 0.01 (that is: a situation where there is practically no association between two variables) will also be defined as not attributable to chance, i.e. significantly different from zero. In these situations, while there is statistical significance, there is no what is called 'practical significance'. It is also said that the *effect size*, that is the absolute magnitude of the effect we are investigating, is small. In that sense, samples can definitely become too large.

So also here there is a trade off. While a larger sample absolutely does give you a better idea of what is going on in the population, it makes judging how meaningful findings are harder. Small deviations from the situation under the H_0 are marked as 'significant' while they may be too tiny actually to warrant mentioning.

For that reason, the α is often set proportionate to the sample size. A regular α, for ordinary samples of say between 100 and 300, is generally set at 5%. Once sample sizes become larger or really big, researchers may revert to a smaller α, say 2.5%, or 1%. Conversely, if one has to work with very small samples of well under 100, researchers sometimes relax the α, and may accept 10% as a significance level. It is then the custom, however, not to speak of significance but to speak of a 'trend'.

A second instance when there is reason to use a stricter α, is when one wants or needs to perform many tests. If α is 5%, what this means is that out of 100 tests on the same phenomenon, one would expect 5% to turn up significant – just accidentally, that is what the reasoning says. So if one performs 100 tests, reporting a few of these as significant doesn't really prove a lot. This is referred to as *chance capitalization*. For that reason, if one performs a large number of tests on phenomena that may be not exactly identical but nevertheless capturing the same phenomenon, it is customary to balance this by also reducing the α. In some contexts, this is referred to as a *Bonferroni correction*.

7.6 Estimation and uncertainty

In the above, we have regularly spoken of estimation, of the mean of the population, of the variance of the population, and similarly we might want to estimate the association between variables. Each time when we estimate, we attempt to find the value of a so-called *parameter* in the population. The mean is a parameter, as are the variance and standard deviation. They are properties of the distribution of variables, that describe or characterise that distribution. The mean tells you around what value the values cluster, the standard deviation tells you how much the variable values fluctuate around that mean. So, the variable X has a mean μ, that is a parameter. For a certain population, it has one value, it does not vary. So, variables assume varying scores, parameters are stable.

7.6.1 Point estimates versus interval estimates

Above we said, that the sample mean is an estimator of the population mean. We write this as follows:

$$\hat{\mu} = \bar{X},$$

where the hat above the μ tells us that we have not actually measured μ and that we do not equate μ to the sample mean, but that we employ $\bar{X}$ as a mere estimate only.

Similarly the sample variance can be used to estimate the population variance:

$$\hat{\sigma}^2 = s^2,$$

where again the hat tells us that the sample variance is used as an estimator for the population variance.

Now all these estimates are what we call *point estimates*. They tell us what we infer from the sample about the population, what we believe μ in the population to be on the basis of the sample information. However, in some cases we may be more certain about this estimate than in other cases, for instance when we have investigated only a small sample we are obviously – even though we may present the same value as an estimate – less certain about our estimate than if we had drawn a large sample. A manner to give an indication of that certainty or uncertainty is to present an interval estimate. We will discuss interval estimates or confidence intervals in the next section.

7.6.2 Confidence intervals

A confidence interval for the mean is computed using the following formula:

$$CI_{95\%} = \bar{X} \pm z_{\text{critical value}} \times \sigma_{\bar{X}},$$

where '$CI_{95\%}$' stands for the 95% confidence interval. How does this work? Let us assume for our Criminology students' IQ example above, that we find that the sample mean is 122.8. The standard deviation in the population was 2, and let us assume that we have 100 students in our sample. Let us work with an α of 5%, use a two-sided null hypothesis, so that the testing situation looks exactly like it did in Figure 7.5: we have two areas of rejection, each good for an area of 2.5% under the curve. We have therefore two critical values: the critical values for the z-distribution beyond which we would reject are -1.96 and +1.96.

Filled in into the formula, the calculations then become:

$$z = \frac{\bar{X} - \mu}{\sigma_{\bar{X}}} = \frac{122.8 - 122}{\frac{2}{\sqrt{100}}} = \frac{0.8}{0.2} = 4.$$

Clearly, this is way beyond the critical value of 1.96. We therefore reject the null hypothesis that this year's Criminology students have the same IQ as the population of Criminology students 5 year's ago. The difference is not very big (only 0.8 on average), but given the relative small standard deviation and the large sample we investigated, it turns up significant.

Our estimate of this year's Criminology students' IQ is 122.8. We said that this is significantly different from what is to be expected under the null hypothesis. But how confident are we about this IQ? To answer that question, we compute the *confidence interval*. We plug our data into the formula we gave above, and we get:

$$CI_{95\%} = 122.8 \pm 1.96 \times \frac{2}{\sqrt{100}},$$

which is equal to

$$CI_{95\%} = 122.8 \pm 0.392,$$

so that the 95% confidence interval in this example is (122.408 – 123.192). How do we say in words what this means? A sloppy, intuitive way of describing the confidence interval is as your margin of uncertainty. A more precise way is to say that we are 95% confident that μ is in this interval.

Note that the μ under the null hypothesis, 122, is not contained in the interval we just computed. It would be very strange if it were, because we just rejected the H_0 so it should *not* be comprised in the interval we are 95% certain the true value lies.

As said, the confidence interval gives you a margin of uncertainty: wider confidence intervals mean more uncertainty, narrower confidence intervals mean less uncertainty. From that it follows that if we would investigate a larger sample, in which case we should be more certain of our estimate, the confidence interval must become correspondingly narrower. Is that the case? We can simply check this by recalculating the interval for a sample size of, say, 144 instead of 100. The calculations then become:

$$CI_{95\%} = 122.8 \pm 1.96 \times \frac{2}{\sqrt{144}},$$

so that

$$CI_{95\%} = 122.8 \pm 0.327,$$

so that the 95% confidence interval in this example is (122.473 – 123.127), which is indeed narrower than the 95% confidence interval when the sample size was 100. Similarly, it can be shown that as sample size decreases, the confidence interval widens.

These examples have given the 95% confidence interval. It is also possible to compute a 99% confidence interval. As we in that case are talking about broader 'coverage' it is logical that the interval would be wider. If we wanted to be 100% certain, the interval would span $-\infty$ to ∞!

We have given examples where samples of 100 and over were investigated, and where the population variance was known, so that regular z-scores could be used for the critical value. If however, the population variance is unknown, and smallish samples are used, the just like for the testing situation, also here for critical value a value from the t-distribution must be used.

Confidence intervals are widely used. The significance of odds ratios (that is, whether they differ significantly from 1) is often tested using confidence intervals. If the confidence interval of an odds ratio comprises 1, the ratio is said to be not significant.

Leaving aside the formulas and leaving aside all the nitty gritty tech specs of when to use z-and t- values, the important thing here to remember is that the confidence interval reflects statistical precision. Narrow confidence intervals tell you that we have a precise measurement, wider confidence intervals tell you the reverse. Confidence intervals narrow and widen with sample size, variability in the data, and the level of confidence we desire, all in a way that is intuitively logical.

Chapter 8

Model testing

In this chapter, we will slowly shift to the more applied side of statistics and research methodology, in the sense that we will discuss two models that are often used in applied research. These models, the *regression model* and the *analysis of variance model*, essentially try to do the same thing. They try to give us an answer to the question whether, in a certain set of measurements, the scores on a dependent variable can be predicted from the scores on one or more independent variables. While the models, and all their computational acrobatics, may seem quite different, they can in fact be rewritten such that they are conceptually identical. The difference between the regression and the analysis of variance model is that in the regression case the independent variables are of interval measurement level or higher, while in the analysis of variance model they are nominal. Note that in section 6.2 we said that it is important to know the measurement levels of your variables, as they determine what technique must be used. This is exactly such a situation: the measurement level of the independent variable(s) prescribes whether the regression or the analysis of variance model should be used.

In the following, we will first expand and philosophise a little on the term model. What are models and what do we use them for in research practice? Next, in section 8.2 we will introduce the regression model in its simple, bivariate form, as well as touch upon a number of more complicated varieties. Then, in section 8.3 we will introduce analysis of variance, again in its simple form with just one independent variable, as well as the more complicated variety, where more than one independent variable is allowed to play a role and where so-called interaction effects can be incorporated. For both models we will discuss tests, and the possibilities to assess model fit, i.e. to assess how well the model describes the data. We end with a short discussion of the similarities between the two techniques, illustrating their conceptual similarities.

8.1 Models

In daily life, we frequently use models. When we buy a new machine, usually there is a drawing of that machine, that tells you where essential buttons are, how to replace parts etc.

That drawing does not depict every detail, colour, or curve of the machine. The drawing serves to outline the basic properties of the machine or to point out the vital buttons. It is made such that you can find the essential elements for the operation of the machine, leaving out nonessentials. As such it is a summary of the machine's appearance. It is an abstraction, in which the essentials have been preserved and nonessentials left out. This has been done so that it is easier to understand the functionality of the machine, to focus on only the functions that you as a user are interested in.

For the same purpose we use models in daily life, we also use them in science. Models can be models of scale, to inspect what a still-to-be-built office would look like, what the layout of a Roman villa was. Other common models are computer simulation models. Models can also be simple drawings that outline the relations between variables; a number of examples of such conceptual models will be given below, and we already used some simple models in chapter 5, such as in Figure 5.3. All models have in common that they are an abstraction from reality, in which certain core elements have been retained. They also have a similar purpose: facilitate understanding of the functioning or structure of the object they represent.

From the above, we can deduce a number of properties of models. Firstly, models must have a similar structure as the object they are representing. Secondly, models should enable us to observe and possibly manipulate the object they represent, without interfering with the object itself however. Computer simulations of disease prevalence for instance enable us to model what happens to the spreading of the disease if half of the population is vaccinated, or 25% of the population is vaccinated, etc. We don't need to try this out ourselves: we would not want to! If we feed the right parameters into the model, the model will give us an estimate, a prediction of what will happen. Models can be physical (such as manikins) and virtual (computer models, or even mental representations).

Lastly, and that is exactly the reason that we work with them, it is much easier to observe the model than to observe reality. That is the crux, and makes models so eminently useful. Reality is often complex, and hard to oversee in its intricate entirety. Models are exactly the reverse: they are simple and you can look at them from all angles, roll them around in your hands, squeeze them, put them upside down, whatever you wish. Without needing to worry about that complex and multifaceted reality out there, where many things are interrelated and happen at the same time, with a model we can simply manipulate one aspect – and see what happens, and next manipulate another aspect – and see what happens next.

Summarising, a model of reality is a representation of that reality that is firstly *independent* of it, secondly *better observable* and, thirdly has a similar *structure*.

8.1.1 Models with dependent and independent variables

In scientific research we want to – in the end – find the causes of the phenomena we are studying. We try to discover with what factor our phenomenon of interest correlates, and – importantly – what it does not correlate with. We try to prevent our perception being muddled by any spurious associations. We try to get a grip on the phenomenon, we try to grasp what is going on and what is driving the trend we are seeing: the spread of the disease, the frequency of aggressive incidents, or whatever we are studying. All this builds up to the *why*-question: Why is it that ex-convicts recidivate? What factors support successful reintegration of ex-offenders? How can we better predict cell capacity needed by the criminal justice system to house detainees in future?

In these examples, there is each time one central property we are interested in: recidivism, reintegration, cell capacity. As discussed previously in section 5.2, we call such a central variable, that we in a sense want to find the causes of, the *dependent variable.* The dependent variable is the variable we are interested in, the variable we want to predict from other variables, the variable for which we want to know what the mechanisms are that generates it. Formulated differently, perhaps for meta-scientists not in the most exact way possible, the dependent variable is the result of some process that we want to find the driving forces of. We write the dependent variable as Y, similar to most statistics textbooks.

Given that the dependent variable is the variable we want to find the causes of, the independent variable is then – again formulated loosely – that cause. Defined more precisely, independent variables are variables that are not predicted by other variables, they are therefore also called exogenous variables, they are the external forces that exert some force on the dependent variable. Given that the independent variable may be named the exogenous variable, the dependent variable is called the endogenous variable, *output variable* or also, simply, *outcome*. Independent variables are also referred to as *predictors, input variables, explanatory variables* or even a bit confusingly as *covariates*.

If the independent variables are themselves also predicted by other independent variables, they may be called *mediating* variables when they explain the association between the exogenous and dependent variable. For instance, the bond between a pupil and a teacher (independent variable) is associated with a pupil's school marks (dependent variable). This effect is often presumed to be channelled through pupils' ties with school: good relations with the teacher will improve feelings of school bonding, which will stimulate pupils to work harder and thus improve marks. A mediating variable therefore in a sense 'channels' the impact of a variable X on Y, it is no more than a channel through which the impact is funneled. Such 'in-between' variables are called *moderating* variables when they affect the strength of the association between independent variable and outcome. Moderator variables are best thought of as interaction effects; we will return to these in section 8.3. More complex models can be built, with different kinds of relations between variables, that we will not go into here.

Unfortunately, not many of the phenomena we study are monocausal: often, more than one 'cause' or factor is relevant in explaining what is happening with a dependent variable. So, we may have more than one independent variable, generally denoted by X_1, X_2, X_3, and so forth.

Figure 8.1 gives an example of a model with a dependent and independent variable. In the model, variables have been indicated with a box, and the relations between them with an arrow, with the arrow pointing from cause to effect. In this – fictive – example, aggressive behaviour (A) in children is the dependent variable, temperament (T) is an independent variable and watching violent films (V) is in a sense independent as well as dependent variable. The figure attaches numbers – that for the time being are best viewed as correlation coefficients – to the arrows, with high correlation coefficients denoting a strong association, and low correlation coefficients denoting a weak association. The figure shows that there

Figure 8.1: Model for the effect of exposure to violent films on aggressive behaviour

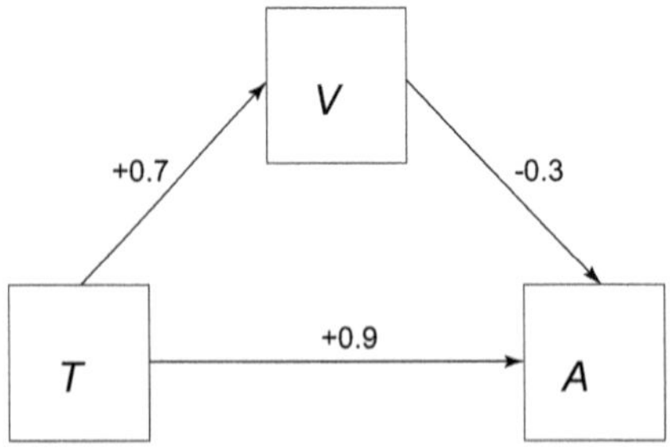

is a strong association between aggressive behaviour and having an aggressive temperament: the coefficient is 0.9. Having an aggressive temperament and viewing violent films is strongly associated as well: the coefficient is 0.7, meaning that those with aggressive temperaments often watch violent films. However, for viewing aggressive films and actual aggressive behaviour, the coefficient is much lower, it is with -0.3 actually even negative! It seems therefore that, if at all there is an association between watching violent films and aggressive behaviour, the viewing of such films 'regulates' aggressive behaviour rather than increasing it. The association between temperament and aggression is by far the strongest. Also, we see that temperament in a sense determines whether people watch violent films. If we had only regarded the association between watching violent films and aggression, our conclusion might have been quite different. Including the explanatory variable T makes our conclusion and understanding much more nuanced.

8.1.2 Model building

In practice, models have to be built. While a manikin can be a simplified replica of a physical entity, a model in social research practice is usually conceptual. Using data, and reasoning from theory, we try to explain some phenomenon by building a structure, just like in Figure 8.1. Then, we try to find out whether this model actually does describe our data well. Are we able to explain or predict all aggressive outbursts of the sample members under study? Or is that prediction often off the mark?

As models seldom explain all 'behaviour' of the dependent variable at once, models are generally built step by step, in an iterative process, to try to improve model performance. Researchers may do so themselves. Also, one researcher may start with a model, after which the next researcher adds on to it, specifying certain relations, adding new ones, inserting better measures of certain variables, or deleting or replacing old ones. In our example, for instance, it may be so that the model explains only pro-active aggression, and not reactive aggression. Or other personality traits (neuroticism, thrill seeking) may play a role. Or the context in which the films are viewed may be important: when they are viewed in an uncontrolled setting their effect may be larger than when they are viewed in a setting where parents or teachers comment on the action scenes, point out that some things are not funny at all or would be causing severe damage in real life.

Figure 8.2: More complicated model for the effect of violent films viewing on aggressive behaviour

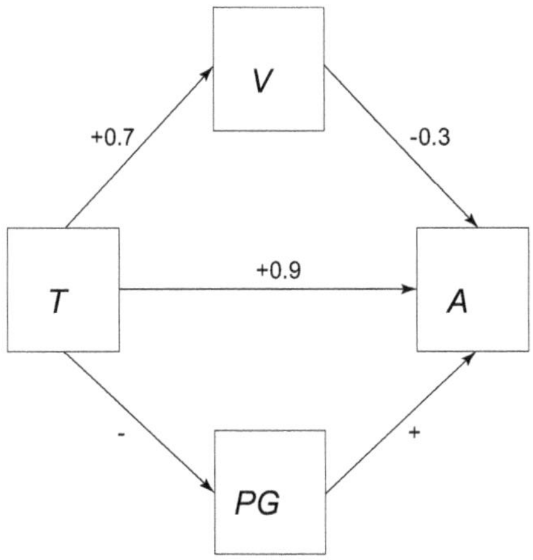

The simple model in Figure 8.1 as such gives us only the most salient factors, and the manner in which they relate to generate aggressive behaviour in children who view violent films. The simple model makes it possible to investigate the roles of these variables, and to test – regardless of numerous other intricacies – what impact certain predictors have on the dependent variable. Figure 8.2 gives an example of an extension to the model that attempts to incorporate the impact of parental guidance on the viewing of aggressive films. Suppose that we believe that parental guidance has an independent effect on the extent to which children can exhibit aggressive behaviour, then we can accommodate that by adding an arrow to our model. Once we add a new variable, the model becomes less simple.

Now suppose that we believe that temperament itself also exerts an influence on parental guidance (maybe parents who have a hot-tempered child tolerate less aggression from their kids), then an arrow could be added as well between temperament (T) and parental guidance (PG) – with a negative coefficient. See Figure 8.2, in which no numbers have been attached to the new arrows, only an indication of the direction of their effect: positive, indicated as a '+' ,or negative, indicated as a '-'. This renders the model more complicated again as we have added an extra relation, with an extra number to indicate the impact of the independent variable on the dependent one. Such coefficients in models are referred to as *parameters*.

In general, more complicated models better predict the scores on the dependent variable. As they are more complicated, we pay a price for that: our model is then less easy to understand, less easy to grasp conceptually, and to manipulate. Of course, we could choose to work with simple, easy to handle models, that describe reality in a few 'sound bites'. The price we pay then, is again that they will describe that reality not so well. The two are communicating vessels: improving on one generally affects the other negatively.

All in all, there is always a trade-off. We prefer our models to describe the data as well as possible. At the same time we want them to be as simple as possible – the latter is called the principle of *parsimony*. So, instead of adding parameters for improving the prediction of our models, we might want to delete elements from our models to make them simpler, more parsimonious. Suppose that we investigate whether our model describes the data well, and suppose that we find that a coefficient (the 'parameter'), say for the path between temperament (T) and watching violent films (V) is virtually equal to 0. In that case, we might as well remove the arrow between T and V. In doing so, we simplify the model – at little cost now, as the arrow that we remove did not really represent any relation at all. Such testing on real data, finding out whether postulated parts of the model actually aid in describing the data or might as well be removed, may contribute to simplify models. The analyses may show that some arrows can be left out altogether or whole variables actually do not add to the prediction of Y.

8.1.3 Model fit

In general, simpler models are easier to work with, easier to understand and conceptualise, easier to test. However, they have less explanatory power: they are simply less well able to describe the complicated world. How well a model describes reality, is often expressed in a number that represents how close the values of the dependent variable as predicted by the model are to the real, observed values. If the dependent variable as predicted by the model approaches the observed dependent variable very neatly, we say that the *model fit*, also termed the *goodness of fit*, is high. The model that we built is then able to predict what the scores on Y are. The model then, as we say, 'fits' the data. This is what we want. We have then a model that performs well.

Complex models generally describe reality better. If we include more factors that might play a role, i.e. more variables, it is logical that we can only become better able to capture what is happening and thus to describe reality better. We then have the possibility to model loads of causal relationships, the manner in which variables mutually influence each other, or influence the dependent variable through loops, mediate, moderate, etc., so that it is not surprising that we are then better equipped to describe all manners of behaviour of the dependent variable. Complex models have as a disadvantage, however, that they may become too complex to conceptualise, too complex to understand, too intricate to be of practical use. They may also become untestable. That is so, because for a very complex model, we would really need a lot of respondents (see also section 3.5) to be able to investigate whether the model 'holds'. If we need thousands of respondents while we only have 200, it is simply not possible to empirically test a model with 500 variables. Such extremely complex models may also become trivial in the sense that while they might predict the behaviour of the dependent variable very well, they do so by capitalising on small differences. Also, they may describe such complex relations that they are of little conceptual or practical use, the model is too complicated. As such, they do not offer a lot of insight in the mechanisms we are interested in, they distract from the core issues. Formulated differently, such very complex models are not really models any more: models are supposed to be an abstraction from reality, simplified for purposes of manipulation and easier understanding. Very complex models do not do that anymore.

So, as said, we prefer models to be simple, or 'parsimonious'. It is not difficult to attain a good model fit if you use a lot of variables. The art of model building is to arrive at a good fit using just a few variables, the crux of the mechanisms we are studying. This is why some techniques use a measure for model fit that takes into account not only how well the dependent variable is predicted by the model, but that also comprises a 'penalty' for the complexity of the model. If we have two models that fit equally well, the simplest one is then preferred.

The fact that a model fits the data well, does not mean that we have discovered the mechanism that drives the dependent variable. The ancient Greeks believed that malaria was caused by living at low altitudes – they had observed that in the mountains people never contracted malaria. Putting these variables in a model gives a good fit. But the real mechanism is not captured. One variable is omitted: the presence of mosquitos and more precisely the presence of mosquitos that carry the malaria parasite. This means that a crucial variable is missed. This we call *model misspecification.*

8.2 Regression model

In this section we will discuss the regression model. The regression model is a model just like the models we discussed above. It is a model in the sense that a mathematical formula is used in which one or more independent variables $X_1, X_2, \dots, X_k$ play a role, and that with these a dependent variable Y is predicted. Regression analysis can be carried out with just one predictor variable, or with several; the latter is the usual situation.

Regression models are used extremely often in applied social research. That is so, because many of the research questions we pose center around causality. The regression model, if specified adequately and under certain conditions, is suitable for investigating such causality. Regression analysis, or 'regression' for short, has been called the workhorse of social science.

The model is also very useful for pragmatic purposes. It will tell you what the best predictors are, out of a set $X_1, X_2, \dots, X_k$, of a given phenomenon Y. If the model fits well, then findings of the model – say that X_1, X_4 and X_5 contribute significantly to predicting Y – can be used to predict future Y's. Even though the models were not explicitly built for that purpose, regression analysis can therefore be used for forecasting as well. If for instance we have found in a group of ex-convicts whom we have followed for 10 years after their conviction, that recidivism rates in the subsequent 10 years are predicted by previous criminal career, gender, impulsiveness and addiction, then we can infer that it might be wise to organise for additional supervision for those out of the current group of convicts who have an extensive criminal career, who are male, who are impulsive and who are addicted.

8.2.1 When to do regression analysis

Regression analysis is a feasible technique if one wants to predict one variable Y from one or more variables X ($X_1, \dots, X_k$). The X_k are viewed as the causes or determinants in the process that the regression model attempts to capture, which means that they function as the independent variables. The Y is seen as the 'effect', which means that it functions as the dependent variable. See Figure 8.3.

Figure 8.3: Visual representation of regression model

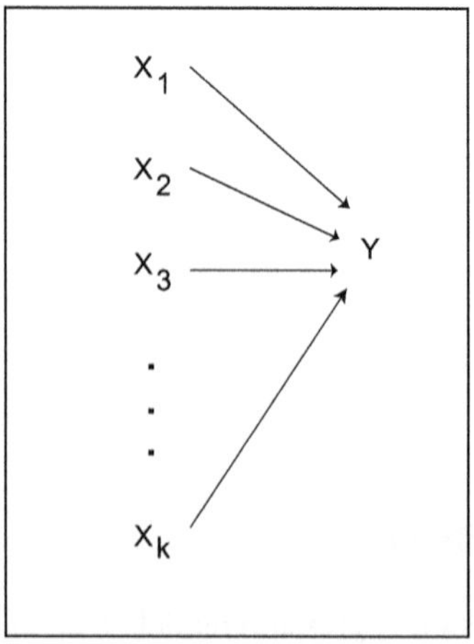

Regular linear regression analysis can be performed if all these variables meet some regularity requirements. This is meant to say that regression analysis is feasible if the dependent variable has at least interval measurement level and if it is not too quaintly distributed. If that is not the case, if Y is for instance very skewed, then regular regression analysis is not possible: the results from the analysis are then untrustworthy. The X are supposed to be interval-level variables too, even though some accommodations for this are possible in practice.

If the Y variable is not interval level, a different kind of regression analysis must be performed. If Y is a dichotomous variable (meaning it has values 0 and 1 only), a so-called logistic regression analysis should be performed. If Y is an ordinal variable, many researchers simply perform regular regression analysis on the rank ordered scores of the ordinal variable. If Y has yet other properties, other varieties are possible. We will discuss none of these in detail, for our purposes it is only important to know that it must always be checked whether Y has the properties it should have. See also section 8.2.6 below.

8.2.2 Simple regression analysis

When we speak of 'simple regression analysis' or 'simple linear regression', we are dealing with the prediction of one variable Y from one variable X. We are therefore carrying out a *bivariate analysis*. We investigate the association between X and Y: we are interested in the manner in which they have something in common. The model we employ for that is however different from the model we used for correlation analysis and other such bivariate analyses. See Figure 8.4. When we do correlational analyses, X and Y are interchangeable, the analysis is symmetric. When we do a regression-type of analysis, the two variables have different roles: one is modelled as the consequence of the other.

The analysis we are conducting is therefore directional. We want to predict Y, not X. We are not just interested in the strength of the association between X and Y or in the sign

Figure 8.4: Visual representation of association between X and Y, and of prediction of Y from X

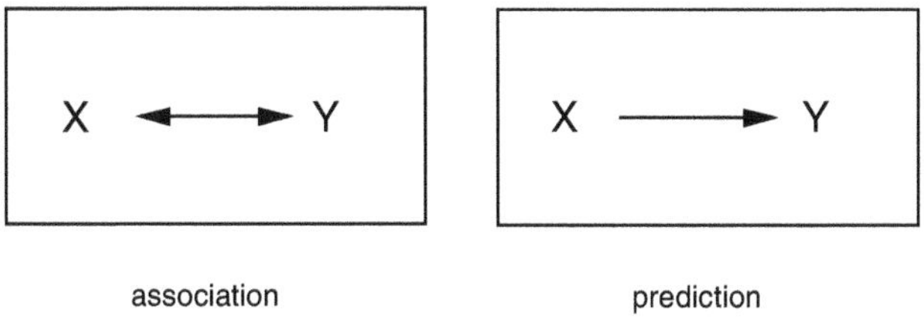

of that association (positive or negative), we want to know whether information on X helps us to conclude something about Y. If we denote the Y predicted by the regression model as $\hat{Y}$, then the art of regression analysis is to find a $\hat{Y}$, a predicted Y, on the basis of the regression model, that approaches the observed Y closely.

In order to predict Y from X, we construct the following linear equation:

$$Y_i = a + bX_i + e_i,$$

where Y_i is the score on the dependent variable for respondent i, a so-called *intercept* is denoted as a, added to which is the same respondent's score on the predictor variable, X_i, weighted with a so-called *regression weight* referred to as b. The $a + bX_i$ constitute what is predicted for Y, the $\hat{Y}$, on the basis of the model. As that prediction will generally not be perfect, a so-called *error term* written as e_i is defined.

This means that the regression model can be written as:

$$\hat{Y}_i = a + bX_i$$

The error term e_i is defined as the difference between the actual, observed Y, and the predicted Y, $\hat{Y}$:

$$Y_i - \hat{Y}_i = e_i,$$

so that the error term is actually best thought of not as an 'error' in the sense of a mistake, but as a prediction error. If we attempt to predict Y from X, that prediction will as said not be perfect: in some instances $\hat{Y}$ will be a little too low, in other instances it may be a little too high. The difference is each time our prediction error.

How do we find the regression parameters a and b? These can be computed as:

$$b = r_{XY}\frac{s_Y}{s_X}$$

and

$$a = \bar{Y} - b\bar{X},$$

with $\bar{Y}$ and $\bar{X}$ the means of the variables X and Y. As Figure 8.5 shows, the intercept is equal to the y-value where the regression line crosses the y-axis. The regression weight,

Figure 8.5: Visual illustration of regression analysis

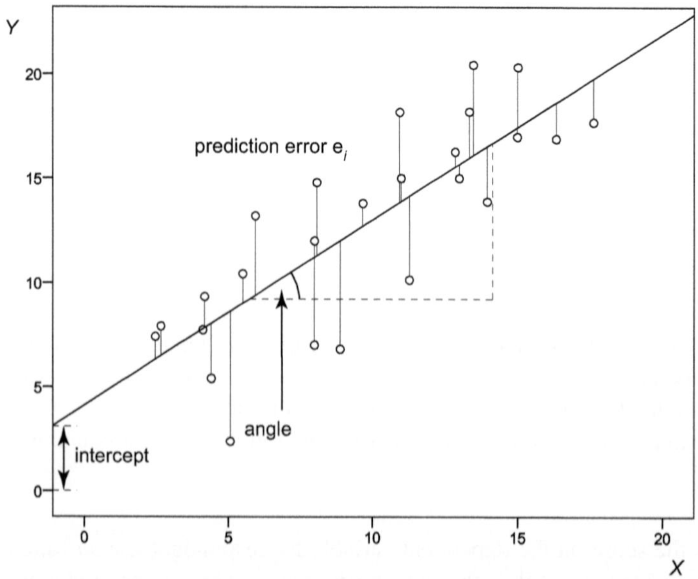

generally referred to as the *regression coefficient*, reflects the steepness of the regression line. It tells you how much is added to $\hat{Y}$ for every increase in X.

The regression coefficient b is constructed from the correlation coefficient r_{XY} times a fraction containing both the standard deviation of Y and of X. Note that if r_{XY} equals zero, i.e., if there is no association whatsoever between X and Y, then the regression coefficient b is also equal to zero. Then, knowing X does not tell you anything about Y. In that case a reduces to $\bar{Y}$, i.e., the best prediction you can make about Y is then simply the mean of Y. All this is logical.

Let us illustrate all these formulas with a simple example. Suppose that I want to predict someone's height from his or her shoe size. I myself am 170 centimeters tall and I wear a size 39. My daughter is 178 cm and she wears a size 40. My other daughter is 163 cm tall and has a size 37. The father of these girls has a size 45 and is 191 cm tall. Based on my own height and shoe size, the regression model could be written as:

$$\text{height} = 53 + 3 \times \text{shoe size}$$

which means nothing more than: if I would want to predict someone's height from his or her shoe size, I would have to start from 53 cm, and add 3 centimeters for every added unit of shoe size. For myself this would become $53 + 3 \times 39 = 170$, i.e. a perfect prediction (so that $e_{\text{Catrien}} = 0$). However, the model based on only my measurements is clearly not fitting for my two daughters and their father. For my taller daughter the formula would be $53 + 3 \times 40 = 173$, clearly a not-perfect prediction and an underestimate as it is 5 cm too low. For my shorter daughter, the formula would slightly overestimate her height: $53 + 3 \times 37$

= 164, while she is 163 cm long, so that $e_{\text{daughter 2}} = +1$. For the father, the formula would underestimate his height: 53 + 3 × 45 = 188, while he is 191 cm long, so that $e_{\text{father}} = -3$. In reality we would estimate a and b using the formulas for all four sample members at once; then the error terms always add up to zero. These examples show how the regression model works. For different data examples, the regression parameters a and b may differ. The principles are however the same.

Two issues remain that need to be touched upon. Firstly, as said, the model is not symmetrical. If we would switch Y and X, the a and b would change. Predicting X from Y gives different computations as now we do not multiply and add to go from shoe size to height, but the other way round. Secondly, it must be noted that a and b depend on the unit in which I am measuring my variables. If I had measured height in not in centimeters but in meters, the a and b would have come out different. The same goes for the shoe sizes, my size 39 could also be written as a 6 in UK sizes, in which case for sure the a and b would be different too. The prediction would be just as good, but the values needed for the computation would have to be modified accordingly.

The latter has one important implication. This is that the regression weight b is simply a weight that serves to predict a Y variable from an X variable. Its absolute value does not (unless it is 0) tell you anything about the strength of the association, or the usefulness of the independent variable for predicting the dependent variable. Note once more the formula for b, that we gave above. It contains also the values of s_X and s_Y. If these change, the regression weight changes correspondingly – without any difference in the strength of the association between X and Y. Only when X and Y have both been standardised, in which case their respective standard deviations are equal to 1, is the regression weight (then written as β instead of b, and referred to as the standardised regression weight) equal to the correlation coefficient between X and Y. So, if one regular regression weight b_1 is equal to 2.5 and another b_2 is 1.25, this does not say anything about their respective importance in predicting Y (it is not as if the first variable is twice as important for predicting Y). The '2.5' only tells you that for each increase on the X_1, you have to add 2.5 times that increase to the predicted Y, and that for each increase on the X_2, you have to add 1.25 times that increase to the predicted Y.

Now when is a regression analysis performing well? As said, we judge this by how close the predicted Y, the $\hat{Y}$, are to the observed Y. Ideally, we would like the differences between predicted and observed values of Y to be zero, a situation of perfect predictability that is in ordinary social research practice hardly ever achieved (and which if it occurs, is cause for suspicion and careful scrutiny of the data). So, if the error terms e_i are large, prediction is not going well, if they are small prediction is going well. In the latter case, the $\hat{Y}$ and Y will correlate strongly.

But how do we know whether we are getting the best possible prediction using these formulas? Are there not other formulas around that may for some cases predict Y better? This is not the case. It can be proven that by computing a and b in the manner we described, the sum of the squared error terms ($\sum_{i=1}^{N} e_i^2$) is minimal. Worded more freely: if we compute a and b using these formulas, we get $\hat{Y}_i$ that differ as little as possible from the observed Y_i and are therefore the best possible $\hat{Y}$. This manner in which a and b are computed is called 'least squares' or 'ordinary least squares' (OLS).

8.2.3 Multiple regression analysis

As we already announced, simple regression analysis is indeed a fairly 'simple' technique. If we would employ a simple regression model, we would assume that the variable Y is under just one external influence. For many practical situations, that is too simplistic. In criminology, we know almost for a fact that most processes are not monocausal. Mostly, various factors play a role in the processes we are interested in. So, it would seem wise to employ not one, but several independent variables in our models.

The model we then use becomes correspondingly more complicated:

$$\hat{Y}_i = a + b_1 X_{1i} + b_2 X_{2i} + b_3 X_{3i} + \cdots + b_k X_{ki}.$$

Note that, as we use k different independent variables to predict the dependent variable Y, we have also ever so many b-coefficients: one for each X-variable. Still, we have only one intercept, the in a sense 'starting value', to which multiples of the respective X-variables must be added to arrive at an estimated Y. Again, we arrive at a predicted Y-value, $\hat{Y}$, and again that $\hat{Y}$ hopefully deviates but a little from the observed Y:

$$Y_i - \hat{Y}_i = e_i.$$

While in the multiple regression case we still have one a to compute, we have to compute several b-coefficients, as many as there are independent variables. How are these computed? We give the example for the case when there are two independent variables, X_1 and X_2. We give for reasons of simplicity the standardised regression weights β_1 en β_2:

$$\beta_1 = \frac{r_{YX_1} - r_{YX_2} r_{X_1X_2}}{1 - r^2_{X_1X_2}},$$

and

$$\beta_2 = \frac{r_{YX_2} - r_{YX_1} r_{X_1X_2}}{1 - r^2_{X_1X_2}}.$$

As explained above, when a regression weight is standardised, this means that the regression weight has been adapted to the fact that the original variables have been standardised. The scale or unit in which they were measured therefore does not play a role anymore; they are the regression weights we would obtain if we worked with standardised variables only.

Now note, in the formulas just given, that the formula for β_1 includes r_{YX_2} as well as $r_{X_1X_2}$. And the formula for β_2 has r_{YX_1} as well as $r_{X_1X_2}$. Clearly, in computing the weight for estimating Y from one predictor X_1, the other variable X_2 plays a role as well, it is taken along in the formula. Why is this so?

This is so, because the regression weight does not so much tell you whether X_k and Y are associated, it tells you how much a variable X_k contributes to predicting Y. For illustrating that, let us imagine the following situation. We are predicting Y from X_1. As we have only one predictor, we are performing a simple linear regression. To this model, we now add a second predictor, X_2; this predictor is however identical to X_1. As X_2 is identical to X_1, adding X_2 to the model cannot improve our prediction of Y. All the information that X_2 adds, was namely already available in X_1. So, essentially, for improving the prediction of Y, adding the variable X_2 is of no use. One could say, given that X_1 is already there in the equation, X_2 might just as well receive a regression weight of 0, as it can not improve the prediction of Y because it does not add any new information. All that X_2 has, X_1 had already.

This may seem paradoxical, because, as X_2 is equal to X_1, it correlates just as strongly as X_1 with Y, so you would expect it to play a similar role in the regression equation! However, and this is what is really important here, the regression coefficients do not tell you how strongly variables are correlated with Y, but how much each variable adds to the prediction of Y, *given the other variables in the model.* Let us see what happens if we use an example with numbers for a situation like the one we sketched, but where X_1 and X_2 are very similar.

Suppose therefore that we have two predictor variables that are fairly similar. We suppose that they correlate really strongly so that for instance $r_{X_1X_2} = .9$. And, as both are equally strongly related to Y, we assume that $r_{YX_1} = .8$, $r_{YX_2} = .8$. If we would estimate a univariate model, once for X_1 and once for X_2, the standardised regression weights β would be r_{X_1Y} for X_1 and r_{X_2Y} for X_2, so in both cases equal to .8. Now, however, let us look at the regression weight for X_1 in the multivariate situation, i.e. after we have added X_2 to the regression equation. Then:

$$\beta_1 = \frac{r_{YX_1} - r_{YX_2}r_{X_1X_2}}{1 - r^2_{X_1X_2}} = \frac{.8 - .8 \times .9}{1 - .9^2} = .421.$$

The weight β_1 (and β_2 would be exactly similar) is now much lower than we would expect on the basis of the bivariate model. However, this is not strange if we realise that the weight tells us how important X_1 is *given the other variables in the model.* Given that X_2 is already present, X_1 adds only a bit, is less useful than it would be if it were on its own. In the univariate case, the regression coefficient is .8; in the multivariate case it becomes .42. This can be understood by realising that the *unique* contribution of X_1 to the prediction is less in the multivariate than in the univariate case.

Suppose now that the r_{X_1Y} and r_{X_2Y} are exactly the same, but that the correlation between X_1 en X_2 is not .9, but .3. Then β_1 becomes .615! The association between Y and X_1 is unchanged, but because there is less overlap between X_1 and X_2, the unique contribution of each variable to the prediction of Y is larger. Summarising, the regression weights must be interpreted net of the other variables in the model. That is why in reporting on regression weights the wording should always run like: 'Given the variables A and B, the variable C contributes so-and-so much to ...'.

Such 'overlap' between predictor variables is called *multicollinearity.* Multicollinearity is a nuisance. Multicollinearity makes it hard to interpret the regression coefficients. In extreme situations, it can make the model unstable. Researchers can prevent multicollinearity by first checking whether the predictors they want to include do not overlap too much (correlations above .8 are generally considered too high for variables to be combined in one regression equation).

8.2.4 Model fit

As in the bivariate case, also in the multivariate case the error terms give an indication of how successful the model has been in predicting the dependent variable Y from the set of predictor variables $X_1, \ldots, X_k$. It is standard practice to use as a measure of model fit the so-called *multiple correlation coefficient*. Given that

$$\hat{Y}_i = a + b_1 X_{1i} + b_2 X_{2i} + b_3 X_{3i} + \cdots + b_k X_{ki},$$

the multiple correlation coefficient R is defined as the correlation between the predicted and observed Y:

$$\mathrm{R} = r_{Y\hat{Y}}.$$

As a prediction gets better, the correlation between the observed and predicted Y will also be higher. Therefore, R indeed reflects the quality of the prediction. In general, instead of R, its squared value R^2 is however used, and is also referred to as the *percentage of explained variance*. If R^2 is for instance .64, it is said that the regression model is able to explain 64% of the variance of Y. R^2 is regarded as a 'goodness of fit' measure. An 'adjusted' fit measure, that incorporates a penalty for the use of many predictor variables, is written as $\mathrm{R}^2_{\mathrm{adj}}$. We do not give its formula here. Most researchers find the adjusted fit measure the better indicator of model performance.

It is hard to say what acceptable values for R^2 are. Values around .80 are exceptional in social science. Depending on the research topic, some researchers are even content with values around .05. Much depends namely on the extent to which the phenomenon under investigation *is* predictable. Some processes are more accidental, others follow certain regular rules more. In the first case, we might be happy with an R^2 of around .10, in the second case we would expect higher values.

Regression models have obvious use for theory testing. If regression analysis would show that a variable has a regression coefficient of almost zero, then – in the absence of other explanations such as multicollinearity – we may conclude that clearly this variable does not play a role in generating Y, and remove the variable from our model. This makes our model more parsimonious. Adding and removing variables, and testing their contribution to the prediction of Y and model fit, is how models are built.

8.2.5 Tests

Just like we can test whether a mean in a sample is highly unlikely under a certain null hypothesis, so we can test whether finding a regression coefficient b or standardised coefficient β with a certain value is likely or unlikely under the null hypothesis:

$$H_0 : \beta = 0$$

with the alternative hypothesis:

$$H_1 : \beta \neq 0.$$

For testing whether a variable contributes significantly to the prediction of Y, it does not matter whether b or its standardised version is investigated: if b is significant, its standardised version is significant too. In fact it would be very strange if the particular scale in which a variable is measured would make a difference for how much that variable contributes to predicting a certain outcome.

If a regression weight differs significantly from 0, we state that the variable 'contributes – given the other variables in the model – significantly to the prediction of the dependent variable'. Just as in the case when we are testing means, regression coefficients will turn up significant sooner when samples are large, and will turn up significant less easily when samples are small.

And just like we can test whether the regression coefficients are significantly different from zero, can we test whether the R^2 from one model is significantly higher than the R^2 from another model. We can therefore test whether a model with a few extra variables leads to a significantly better prediction of Y. Such tests enable us to compare models with a statistical criterion.

We will now give an example of a regression analysis (Symons *et al.*, 2008). The analysis is part of a larger study into measures ('techno-prevention') to reduce burglary in Belgium. The regression analysis served to answer the question which aspects of 'techno-prevention' determined citizens' contentedness with it. Security officers had visited citizens in a number of neighbourhoods, and had given technical advice to decrease the risk of burglary, such as specialty locks, lights around the house, and the like. Variables were measured over three years: the researchers registered to what extent respondents were content (the dependent variable Y) with the techno-prevention intervention, and wanted to know to what extent this was predicted from whether a respondent had experienced a burglary the past year, the waiting time before the security officer paid his visit, the duration of the visit as well as whether a paper report of the visit had been sent to the respondent. As the year in which the visit had taken place might also play a role, that variable had also been added to the model. The results of the regression analysis are in Table 8.1.

Table 8.1: Example regression results

variable	b	standard error	β
constant a	4.363	.067	
victimisation	-.163	.030	-.175**
waiting time	-.086	.016	-.174**
duration visit	.147	.021	.226**
written report	.155	.032	.160**
year visit	.061	.030	.066*

$R^2 = .156$ * $p < .05$ ** $p < .001$

The model explains almost 16% of the variability of Y. The duration of the techno-preventive visit has the largest effect on citizens' contentedness, and a written report also improved the scores. Remarkably, citizens were more contented with the visit in the more recent years (as the coefficient of 'year visit' is positive, this means that a higher score on 'year visit' adds to the score on contentedness). Victimisation reduces contentedness, and so does a long waiting time.

8.2.6 Multiple regression as the workhorse of multivariate analysis

Multiple regression has been named the 'workhorse' of multivariate analysis. It is such an immensely powerful and handy technique because it can assess the effects of a large number of independent variables on a certain dependent variable that one aims to predict. In doing so – and this is likely its most attractive property – it gives back to the researcher the importance of each variable *given the other variables*. The importance of a variable therefore is a *conditional* importance, *net of* the other variables. This means that researchers obtain ground to make statements such as 'taking into account the impact of A, B and C, the factor D still significantly contributes to predicting Y. Or: 'the association between D and Y cannot be explained by third variables A, B or C'. This has made multiple regression a very important tool in theory building, in building models to explain the association between variables. It needs sample sizes of about 10 times the number of variables one would want to include.

The linear multiple regression model that we discussed is but one variety in a family of regression models. Depending on the type of variable that one wants to build a prediction model for, varieties of multiple regression exist. A very commonly used other type of regression model from that family is logistic regression, an adaptation of the multiple regression model where the dependent variable is not a continuous variable but a dichotomous variable (it has only two categories, such as 'yes' and 'no', or 'pass' and 'fail'). Other types exist, such as Poisson regression (for predicting very sparse events that follow a certain distribution, such as convictions), or Cox regression (for predicting variables that reflect the duration to a certain event, such as time to recidivism).

8.3 Analysis of variance model

In the analysis of variance model, we also attempt to predict the scores on a dependent variable Y from the scores on one or more independent variables X. Here, however, the X are not interval variables, but nominal. This means that for envisaging the model, the same conceptual representation as that for regression analysis (see Figure 8.3) can be used, but the X-variables are a different kind of variable.

Analysis of variance is in that sense a fairly straightforward analogue of regression analysis. Often, in addition to testing for significance of the independent variables, the impact of so-called interaction effects is assessed. Analysis of variance has numerous other attractive options too, like the possibility to analyse particular designs such as designs where respondents have been observed repeatedly, or designs where respondents have for instance been offered tasks to complete in a systematic manner.

The notation that we employ in analysis of variance is slightly different from the notation in regression analysis, independent variables are in many textbooks not written as 'X'

anymore, and the model specification appears different from what we were used, as does the format in which results are reported.

Analysis of variance is very widely used, particularly in evaluation research, such as for assessing the impact of a certain therapy. In research using so-called 'vignettes' it is the standard analysis technique: in vignette studies respondents are offered – usually in a revolving or randomised way – different alternative scenarios and asked for their assessment of a dependent variable embedded in that scenario. An example is where researchers artificially construct court files, in which certain aspects are randomised such as the sex of the offender, or the type of offence – all nominal variables. See also section 5.8. Analysis of variance detects what characteristics of these court cases and the respondents predict answers on the vignette dependent variable best.

8.3.1 When to choose analysis of variance

Analysis of variance – often abbreviated as AN(alysis)O(f)VA(riance) – is a suitable analysis technique whenever we are interested in finding out the impact of one or a number of independent variables on the scores on a dependent variable. The categories of the independent variables are treated as separate categories, so that they are indeed treated in the model as nominal variables. If we would have for instance an independent variable 'age', using it as an independent variable in an ANOVA would not be very efficient: each and every category (18, 19, 20, . . . , 65) would be treated as a separate category. In that case there are quite a lot of different categories, which may make inspection and interpretation quite cumbersome. In addition, as analysis of variance treats every category as a separate, qualitatively different category, just like the categories of, say, the nominal variable 'religion', the technique does not use all the information content of the independent variable: it does not take into account that the categories of 'age' are ordered. Where the regression model does do that, through the formula employed ($Y_i = a + bX_i$), in ANOVA that information is disregarded. That is so because the ANOVA model treats the categories '18' and '19' as qualitatively different as '18' and '43', or for that matter as 'Christian' and 'Buddhist'. So, when the independent variable is an interval-level variable, it is more efficient to employ a model (such as the regression model) that investigates the independent variable at the measurement level it was measured.

Notwithstanding the above, in some cases researchers do want to use the ANOVA model and have interval-level variables that they want to take along. If the independent variable has many categories, it is then often recoded into a smaller number of categories such as '18-22, '23-30', '31-40', and the recoded variable used as a nominal variable in the analysis. One important reason to do so is that one suspects that the impact of age on the dependent variable may not be linear. It may for instance be the case that one thinks that labour market orientation is pretty low when people are still studying, that it is higher as people need to find a job after graduating, between ages of 23 and 30, but declines somewhat as people are in the age group where they have settled in a job, are starting a family etc.

Analysis of variance is a technique that already gives good results with small sample sizes. Formally, it is assumed that the dependent variable Y is normally distributed. However, it has been shown that even with fairly substantive deviations from normality, the technique still performs well. It is, we say, *robust* against such deviations from normality. Analysis of variance is easy to interpret as well. For all these reasons, it is widely used. Some of the concepts it uses (like 'interaction') are standard fare in many other analysis techniques as well but are then less easily implemented.

8.3.2 Analysis of variance proper

In analysis of variance, we attempt to investigate whether the scores on an interval dependent variable Y can be predicted from one or more categorical variables. Usually, the independent variables that we have so far named X, appear under a different name in the model. Instead – and we will do the same here – variables are named 'A' and 'B' etc. – although they may be named 'Gender' or 'Type of Offence' too.

Starting with the simple example where there is just one independent variable A, its categories are named α. If A has 2 categories, there is α_1 and α_2 to denote the first and second category, if it has 3 categories there is α_1, α_2 and α_3. The analysis of variance model is now construed as follows:

$$Y_{ij} = \mu + \alpha_j + e_{ij},$$

in which Y_{ij} is the score on the variable Y for the i-th person in the j-th category of A, α_j is the 'effect' of the j-th category of the independent variable. The term μ is an overall average, a sort of starting point for the building of the model, just like the coefficient a in regression analysis. So, every respondent starts from the same μ. If a respondent has scored category 1 of the independent variable A, then for that respondent α_1 is added to μ, if a respondent has scored category 2, α_2 is added, etc. If the total number of respondents studied is N, then in each of the k categories of A we have n respondents (and, assuming equal cell sizes for simplicity: $N = n \times k$). In the model, α is computed such that the sum of all the α's over the respective k categories or so-called 'levels' of A is zero:

$$\sum_{j=1}^{k} \alpha_j = 0$$

Obviously, not all Y scores can be predicted perfectly in this way, so also here we need an error term to bridge the difference between the observed and the predicted Y-scores. The predicted Y is:

$$\hat{Y}_{ij} = \mu + \alpha_j,$$

and the error terms are again defined as:

$$e_{ij} = Y_{ij} - \hat{Y}_{ij}.$$

As in the regression model, and as for the α's, the error terms also add to zero, within each level of A and therefore by necessity also over all respondents:

$$\sum_{i=1}^{n} e_{ij} = 0.$$

But how are α and μ computed? Let us illustrate this with an example.

Suppose that I have measured the number of typing errors in 18 respondents, who were divided into three groups: one group consumed no alcohol, the next group consumed 1 glass of alcohol, the third group consumed 2 glasses of alcohol. See Table 8.2.

Table 8.2: Simple example of ANOVA

respondent i	no alcohol	1 glass alcohol	2 glasses alcohol
1	0	1	4
2	2	3	7
3	1	4	6
4	1	3	5
5	2	2	5
6	0	5	3
averages	1	3	5

As can be seen from the table, we have indeed a total of 18 respondents: 6 per category (often referred to as 'level') of A, so that we have 6 respondents 'per cell'. Those who consumed no alcohol make on average one mistake, those who consumed 1 glass make on average 3 mistakes, those who consume two glasses make on average 5 mistakes. We see a clear effect of alcohol: as alcohol consumption increases, the number of mistakes increases as well.

Next, the question we need to answer is whether this difference between the levels of A is significant: is the difference so high that we cannot attribute it to chance? More formally: are the differences so big that they would be very unlikely under the null hypothesis of 'no effect'? The null hypothesis is:

$$H_0 : \text{all } \alpha_j = 0$$

with the alternative hypothesis:

$$H_1 : \text{any } \alpha_j \neq 0.$$

First we compute the α's, and for that we first estimate the μ as the average $\bar{Y}$ of all scores. So, in this example μ would be estimated as 3. Next, the α are estimated as the deviations of the cell averages from that overall mean, so that:

$$\alpha_1 = \bar{A}_1 - \bar{Y} = -2$$

$$\alpha_2 = \bar{A}_2 - \bar{Y} = 0$$

$$\alpha_3 = \bar{A}_3 - \bar{Y} = +2$$

Note that indeed the α's sum to zero: -2 + 0 + 2 = 0. The error terms are the differences between the score for a respondent as predicted by the model (i.e. $\hat{Y}_{ij} = \mu + \alpha_j$) and the observed Y_{ij}. See Table 8.3 that gives the error terms for this example.

Table 8.3: Error terms in simple example of ANOVA

respondent i	no alcohol	1 glass alcohol	2 glasses alcohol
1	-1	-2	-1
2	1	0	2
3	0	1	1
4	0	0	0
5	1	-1	0
6	-1	2	-2

Figure 8.6: ANOVA example: improvement in calculus before and after course

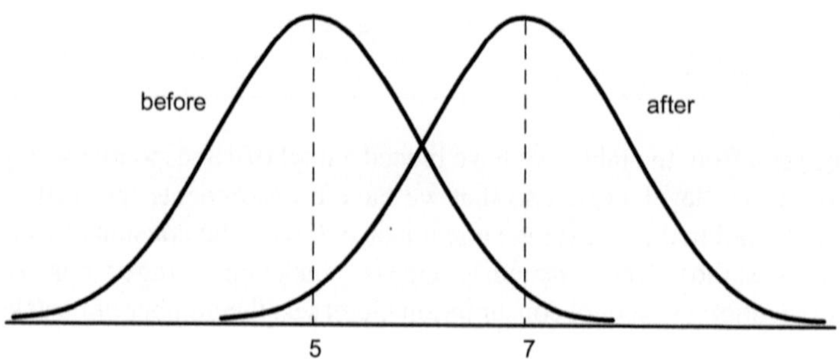

So, now that we have a value for μ, for the respective α_j's and for all the error terms e_{ij}, how can we determine whether the differences between the various α are significant? Before we give the computational specs, we will first explain conceptually the reasoning behind the computations. We do this with an example.

Suppose that I have developed a calculus course for those who become fearsome when presented with numbers. Before the course, the participants scored on average a '5' for calculus. After the course, they score on average a '7'. Not all had the same scores, there was some variability, but we can say that the average improvement was 2. This situation is depicted in Figure 8.6.

The figure shows how indeed the average scores improved, from an average 5 to an average 7. The figure also shows that there is quite some variability: some respondents still had – after finishing the course – low scores, some already had a '7' before the course started. Compare for that matter this figure with Figure 8.7. Here a situation with much less variability is depicted. Respondents here had scores that clung much more around the mean: almost all respondents had scores really close to 5 before the training, and almost all had scores around 7 after the course. The scores fluctuate much less.

Now if you would ask someone to tell you which result he or she would find more meaningful: the one in Figure 8.6 or the one in Figure 8.7, almost everyone would tell you

Figure 8.7: ANOVA example: calculus improvement with less variability

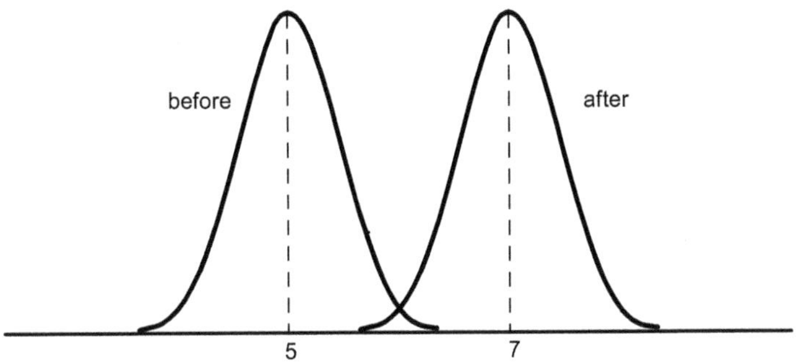

– without any formulas or complicated reasoning – that Figure 8.7 is the stronger result. This is remarkable, because the net difference is the same in both figures: in both figures people improved 2 points on average. However, the last figure is definitely the stronger one. And that is indeed the case exactly for the reasons we just enumerated: in the first figure already some people already had good marks before the training, and quite a few still had bad marks after the training. In the second figure, almost all respondents improved, the improvement was so to say 'en bloc'. Formulated more precisely, we find the second figure indicative of a stronger result because – even though the net average improvement is the same – it compares more favourably against the light of the smaller existing variability in the scores.

This is exactly what analysis of variance will tell you too. What analysis of variance does is nothing more than give you the same intuitively appealing conclusion – except for the fact that it uses formulas and gives you exact significance of results. What analysis of variance does to achieve that, is to evaluate the differences between a number of 'conditions' (before or after training, or between various categories of the independent variable A) against the random variability in the data. If the differences between the categories of the independent variable are much larger than the chance variation in the data, we find those differences 'significant'. If those differences are similar to the differences you might expect just by chance, or even smaller, analysis of variance will tell you that the result is not significant.

So, analysis of variance is exactly what its name says: analysis of the variance in the data, and more precisely an evaluation of the variability of the scores due to the independent variable against variation due to chance. For getting exact significance statements, ANOVA tests the ratio of these variations employing a statistical distribution, the F-distribution. The F-distribution differs from the normal distribution, but the principle for using it in testing is the same as the principle we have been discussing all the time. The null hypothesis is that there are no differences between the levels of the independent variable (hence: *all* α_j are equal to zero), and using the F-distribution it can be inferred what the chances are to find the sample results under this hypothesis. If that chance is very small, we reject the null hypothesis, and move to the alternative hypothesis, namely that there are categories of

A that have an effect on the dependent variable. We then say that A has a significant effect on the dependent variable. Again, we can test at a 1%, 2%, 5% level; as usual we are the ones as researchers to decide what chance to take the wrong decision if H_0 is true we find acceptable.

How then exactly is this ratio of variances computed? For this, first for each respondent the corresponding α_j is squared, and all squared terms next added. Each respondent's α_j is the part of his or her score that is attributable to him or her being in a particular category of the independent variable A. The result is called 'SS_A', meaning the sum of squares (SS) of all terms pertaining to the independent variable A:

$$n \sum_{j=1}^{k} \alpha_j^2 = \text{SS}_A.$$

Next, for each respondent his or her error term is squared and all terms again added. Each respondent's e_{ij} is the part of his score that is attributable to chance. The result of adding up the squared terms is called 'SS_{error}', meaning the sum of squares of all terms pertaining to random fluctuation, not attributable to any independent variable:

$$\sum_{j=1}^{k} \sum_{i=1}^{n} e_{ij}^2 = \text{SS}_{\text{error}}.$$

Next, both SS_A and SS_{error} are divided by the so-called 'degrees of freedom', terms that take into account the fact that SS_A can only become higher if we define more levels of A, and that SS_{error} can only be higher if we observe more respondents. It would be an unfair comparison if we did not correct for that in some way: we might then find that with exactly the same variability, and exactly the same mean difference, one test turns up significant while the other does not – only because of having more or fewer respondents. Correcting for such issues, we now arrive at mean sums of squares (MS) for both A:

$$\frac{\text{SS}_A}{k-1} = \text{MS}_A,$$

and for the error terms:

$$\frac{\text{SS}_{\text{error}}}{k(n-1)} = \text{MS}_{\text{error}}.$$

Once these terms MS_A and MS_{error} have been computed, we have arrived at the point where we can finally do the testing. This is done by computing their ratio, just like we intuitively did in the figures above:

$$\frac{\text{MS}_A}{\text{MS}_{\text{error}}} = F_A.$$

This F-value is the test statistic, just like the z-value was in the examples in chapter 7. How significant a certain F-value is, given the degrees of freedom for A and the error terms, can be looked up in a table, and statistical software packages do that for the user. In general, the larger the value of the F-statistic, the smaller the likelihood of this result under the null hypothesis. Table 8.4 gives the analysis of variance results for the typing errors example we discussed.

Table 8.4: Example ANOVA results

source of variation	SS	df	MS	F	*sign*
A	48	2	24.0	15	1%
error	24	15	1.6		
total	72	17			

In Table 8.4, the F-statistic is as we see highly significant. In practice, F-statistics of around 8 and higher are (almost) always significant. (Indeed, it would be highly counterintuitive if an effect due to the independent variable that is 8 times larger than chance would not be regarded significant.) This means that we conclude that there are significant differences in the value of Y between the categories of the independent variable A, meaning that A contributes significantly to the prediction of the dependent variable.

Note that we cannot state on the basis of the significance test that people who consume more alcohol make more typing mistakes. We do not know this – we only know that differences have been measured that are very unlikely to occur by chance if it were irrelevant whether someone consumes no alcohol, 1 glass or two glasses of alcohol. Inspecting the means, we see that indeed people who consume more alcohol are the ones who make more mistakes. Further tests, that we will not detail here, would be necessary to determine whether those who consume no and 1 glass of alcohol, and those who consume 1 and 2 glasses of alcohol, each time also differ significantly from each other. The ANOVA test tells us only that – overall – there are significant differences between the *levels* of the independent variable.

As said, analysis of variance or ANOVA is widely used in many areas of social research. Numerous extensions are possible to the simplest design we just discussed. However, in each design, the principle is always the same. We inspect the variability attributable to differences between categories of one (or a combination of) independent variables. We gauge that against the random fluctuation. If the fluctuation due to the independent variable is much higher than the fluctuation due to chance, we conclude that the independent variable has an impact on the dependent variable.

For ease of understanding, we have here always referred to the independent variable as 'A' and denoted its corresponding sums of squares as 'SS_A'. Often, the independent variable is labelled as 'Between', as it reflects the variation between categories of the independent variable. Correspondingly, the error variation is then referred to as 'Within' as this reflects the variability within the categories of A.

Figure 8.8: ANOVA: example of interaction effect

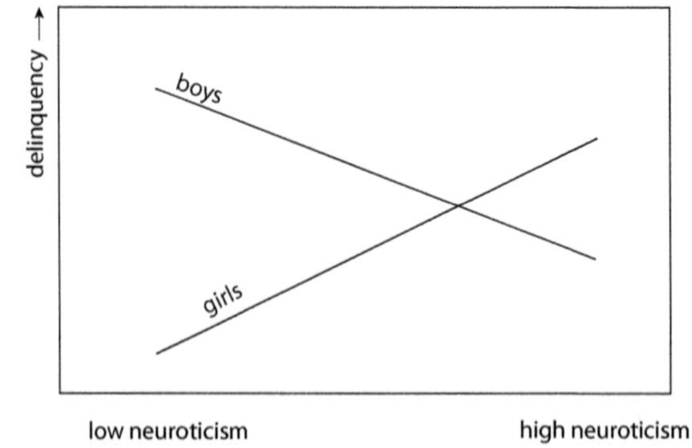

8.3.3 Factorial analysis of variance

Now the same can be said for analysis of variance that we said for regression analysis: a model with just one predictor is not likely to be a model to give very good results and is likely to be too simplistic for our purposes. So, just like in regression analysis, additional independent variables can be added and should sometimes be added. One example of such a model is

$$Y_{ijkl} = \mu + \alpha_j + \beta_k + \gamma_l + e_{ijkl},$$

for the situation where we have three independent variables. This is called a *factorial* analysis of variance. Now, ANOVA has the option to not only include additional predictors, but to make it possible that these variables are modelled to *interact*. What is meant by that? Again we illustrate this with an example.

In research on delinquency it has been found that the psychological trait ‘neuroticism’ does not predict delinquency. Those who are highly, average, or below average (all categorised into norm scores) neurotic, all have approximately equal delinquency levels. However, if we disaggregate these findings for boys and girls, we find that for boys neuroticism is a *protective* factor: boys who are above average neurotic have lower delinquency scores. For girls, on the other hand, we find the opposite: neurotic girls have increased delinquency scores. So, the overall result of ‘no difference’ was actually attributable to a leveling out of these opposite effects over boys and girls. There is heterogeneity. See Figure 8.8 that sketches the situation.

As can be inferred from this figure, there is only a slight difference between the delinquency levels of those who are highly neurotic and those who score low on neuroticism: if we would average the scores, we would find an almost horizontal line. There is a clear difference between delinquency levels of boys and girls: if we would average the scores for boys and those for girls, we would see that boys have on average higher neuroticism levels than girls. Because of the lines that cross, there is an interaction effect of gender and neuroticism: for boys neuroticism levels affect delinquency scores differently than for girls. Thus: one could say that gender *moderates* the effect of neuroticism. Gender changes the effect of the independent variable neuroticism on the dependent variable delinquency. If we would write the model for this situation it would be:

$$Y_{ijk} = \mu + \alpha_j + \beta_k + \alpha\beta_{jk} + e_{ijk},$$

with α and β now referred to as *main effects* and the term $\alpha\beta$ referred to as the interaction effect between A and B. Such interaction effects are often written as $A \times B$, or even 'Neuroticism × Gender'. A hypothetical example of a table with results for this analysis of variance is given in Table 8.5.

Table 8.5: ANOVA example with interaction terms

source of variation	SS	df	MS	F	sign
neuroticism	3	2	1,5	$F_A = 0{,}75$	< 1
gender	10	1	10	$F_B = 5$	5%
neuroticism × gender	36	2	18	$F_{AB} = 9$	1%
error	68	34	2		
total	107	39			

The table shows what we inferred already from the figure. There is a – significant it turns out – main effect of gender. The effect of neuroticism is non-significant (any F-value below 1 is always nonsignificant, as then the variation in scores of the dependent variable due to the categories of the predictor variable is actually less than chance variation). The interaction effect is pretty significant at the 1% level.

More complicated models are possible with interaction effects between more than two variables:

$$Y_{ijkl} = \mu + \alpha_j + \beta_k + \gamma_l + \alpha\beta_{jk} + \alpha\gamma_{jl} + \beta\gamma_{kl} + \alpha\beta\gamma_{jkl} + e_{ijkl},$$

where $\alpha\beta_{jk}, \alpha\gamma_{jl}$ and $\beta\gamma_{kl}$ would be labeled '1st order interaction effects', and $\alpha\beta\gamma_{jkl}$ would be labelled the '2nd order interaction effect'. Just as we had in the univariate case a test for F_A, now we have separate tests for F_A, F_B, F_C, F_{AB}, F_{AC}, etc.

Models and computations become increasingly complex with more independent variables. The principles, however, remain the same. Each time we test differences due to (combinations of) categories of variables against chance variation.

Also here, for the analysis of variance model, the same difficulties may arise that we sketched for the regression model, and for models in general. As models become more complicated, they become harder to interpret: how should we for instance interpret a 5th order interaction effect? In addition, as more independent variables and more interaction terms are added to the model, the cells along which the squared error terms are added become smaller and the error variance (the variability within the groups formed by the combination of categories of the variables) decreases too. This inflates the F-statistics. As such – to prevent opportunistic addition and spurious inflation of these F-statistics – it is the rule that independent variables and interaction terms be added to the model only when there are strong theoretical reasons to do so.

8.3.4 Tests

We discussed tests for the analysis of variance model. For each main and interaction effect, an F-test is carried out, that tells you what the likelihood is of finding the results if the data come from a population with no differences between the various categories of (the combinations of) the independent variables. As we said before, such tests tell you whether there are *any* differences between the (combination of the) categories of the independent variable(s). If you were interested in particular differences, say whether dosage p and dosage q of a drug differ significantly in migraine incidence, it is possible to carry out so-called specific contrast tests.

8.3.5 Model fit

When doing analysis of variance, it is not customary to present measures of model fit. Such measures are available, however. The most often used is ω^2, that is the analogue of R^2 in the regression situation. As such, ω^2 tells you how much of the variance of the dependent variable is explained by the entire ANOVA model. It is also possible to express the effects of the respective factors in a so-called η, with the η for each factor reflecting how much variance is explained by the respective factor.

8.4 The analogy between regression analysis and ANOVA

It may seem odd, after the fairly different formulas, to reiterate that regression and analysis of variance models are essentially the same. Nevertheless, that is the case. The analysis of variance model is a more general case of the regression model, or the regression model a special case of the analysis of variance model. We will not go into the mathematical details here, and simply note that it is important not to forget the similarities: in each case we are trying to predict a dependent variable from one or more independent variables. In each case the model is linear. While we introduced interaction terms for analysis of variance, interaction terms can be incorporated as well in regression analysis. The difference between the two techniques is in the manner in which the different measurement levels are accommodated.

8.5 Further reading

A classic (type 'Bible') on analysis of variance is Kirk (1968). For regression analysis, we recommend Cohen, Cohen, West *et al.* (2002).

Chapter 9

Qualitative data analysis

9.1 Introduction

In chapter 2 and chapter 4 we already discussed qualitative research and qualitative data collection methods. We presented qualitative research as juxtaposed to quantitative research: where quantitative studies describe a limited number of issues for a large number of people, qualitative research describes many issues in their interrelatedness generally, for a specific, not necessarily representative set of people. Where quantitative research isolates variables and studies the impact of these on other variables, in qualitative research pre-defined variables or factors are less often studied, let alone in isolation: working from the premise that all human behaviour is contextual, qualitative researchers study humans within their complex, natural setting.

Qualitative researchers work from the premise that behaviour cannot be understood in isolation or from the outside, but that we need to know the *meaning* that events and behaviour have, the perspective that people employ, the context in which their behaviour takes place, their frame of reference, to be able to understand why people behave as they do. Therefore, context and meaning are key concepts in any qualitative study.

This has important implications for the manner in which qualitative data are analysed. As qualitative researchers argue that behaviour must be understood within its particular context, it is not strange that qualitative researchers rarely use standardised, 'pre-fab' instruments. Given that each context is unique, standardised instruments to measure behaviour or people's characteristics are inherently useless: these instruments bear no reference to the context in which people move and behave. Therefore, more often than not, qualitative researchers actually start their analysis from the physical world and human behaviour as observed in it. Data themselves are often the starting point of analysis, and meaning and structure is derived from the data and not imposed upon it as a Fremdkörper. Some grounded theorists even go as far as to carry out a literature review only after fieldwork, after all the data have been collected.

This – 'topsy-turvy' – approach is given the epistemological stance of qualitative research not illogical. Phenomena can only be understood after the researcher has grasped the meaning of behaviour, of the symbolic or cultural or historical meaning of happenings, occurrences. Hence the strong emphasis of qualitative research on embeddedness, on immersing oneself as researcher in the world of those who are to be studied: in youth culture, in groups that may or may not join gangs, in other contexts, in order to *understand* in the research why the objects of study behave as they do, why they take certain decisions. For that matter, as we stated in chapter 2, qualitative research is also referred to as *interpretative* empirical, with quantitative research conversely labelled as *analytical* empirical; parallel labels are *inductive* for qualitative research and *deductive* for quantitative.

It therefore also follows that qualitative data collection procedures are generally much less prescribed and more open and adaptable. Researchers often start by interacting with the people they aim to study, and derive themes and draw up hypotheses as they go along, with the most prototypical of such qualitative research ethnographic research. Researchers ask as many questions as they need to understand the phenomenon they are studying, meet people, have short factual exchanges, observe, read. As they do not know beforehand what will cross their path, interviews cannot be pre-designed and it would be fairly unthinkable to administer web surveys: interviews must take place in preferably face-to-face settings, where researchers are able to note facial expression, inclinations and deflections of voice, see emotion in people's faces, are able to probe, able to respond to the new unexpected issues of topics that the respondents bring up. Researchers by definition do not yet know their object of study beforehand, and must get to know it through interacting with the research subjects or respondents, within their habitat, so that interviews and exchanges preferably also take place in day-to-day, naturalistic settings. Ideally, researchers would have to be able to regard the world from their research subjects' perspectives. They cannot know, really understand their respondents' predilections, motives, constraints, etc., unless they are able to – in a sense – lead their lives with them. Qualitative research is therefore *holistic*. Studies that have best achieved this, such as the famous study on gang life and the urban poor in Chicago by Venkatesh (2008), have been immensely important if not at times groundbreaking for theory formation.

We discussed at length in chapter 4 how qualitative data collection often occurs in ethnographic set-ups, open or topical interviews, and how the data that result from such fieldwork generally consist of transcriptions of interviews. Qualitative data can also consist of documents or video material (or even movies or advertisements, youtube uploads, instagram pictures). Other sources to be analysed are field notes. What all these data have in common is that they are generally (highly) unstructured. In order to make sense of them, to analyse them and arrive at conclusions, we must therefore re-order the material, re-combine and re-organise it so that structure can emerge.

In qualitative data analysis, that process is generally iterative. By that we mean that the researcher evolves, iterates over explanations of the data: in each step s/he visits the raw material, drafts an analysis or explanation, revisits the material and checks – looking at all the transcripts and notes whether that analysis is tenable or needs to be adjusted, then revisits to see whether the adjusted hypothesis really holds etc., until a conclusion is reached that is satisfactory and is in line with everything that is in the data.

We also said that the research cycle that was introduced for quantitative research in section 2.2 and that is travelled through in one 'loop' for a quantitative study, is in fact in qualitative research traversed in ever so many loops as are needed for answering the research question. This means that it is not only so that in qualitative research data may be collected in several small steps and analyses performed several small steps (consisting of as many iterations as needed), but that data collection and analysis are actually interwoven. Qualitative researchers collect data, analyse the data and arrive at a tentative conclusion (such as written down in analytic memos) but may then also return to the field, collect new data and test their tentative conclusion against new information that is gathered. Once such iterative loops do not lead to adjustment of the conclusions (no new insights are gathered from additional interviewing or observation, and the various interpretations that were put forward converge) it is said that *saturation* has been reached (see for a classic reference Glaser & Strauss, 1967). See for a short discussion also Wincup (2017, pp. 132-133).

This process, where one samples respondents up to the point where adding new sample members would not change the conclusions, is referred to as *theoretical sampling*. At the point where the researcher decides that data collection can be stopped and saturation has been reached, it is then also said that *theoretical validity* has been achieved.

It is generally advised to test this to the limit in the sense that researchers are encouraged, once their preliminary interpretation of the data has been formed, to actively seek out cases for inclusion in the sample that seem *not* to match the tentative conclusions. The practice of such a deviant or negative-case analysis, would be regarded as unthinkable if one would strive for randomness of research subjects. In qualitative data collection and analysis, it serves however to test the preliminary conclusion, to see whether this conclusion still holds in seemingly different cases, and as such to test the generality of the conclusion. It can, in addition, also be regarded as a kind of quota or stratified sampling (where one aims to have sufficient spread in the sample over possible subgroups of respondents) or as a robustness check. All in all, it is clear that sampling and analysis can be very much interwoven in qualitative research. Qualitative research unfolds all in all quite differently from the quantitative research mould.

Given that in qualitative research the data collection, the posing of questions, formulating hypotheses, are all so interwoven, an integral treatment of these might be better. In that sense, it may be considered a particularly bad choice in this book to discuss qualitative analysis methods in a separate chapter! However, treating the entire qualitative research process separately would again have entailed a separation of the qualitative process from the quantitative process, a separation that is also artificial and unhelpful as there are also many similarities between interviews and observation for qualitative and quantitative research questions. In addition, as we will see below, qualitative material can also be quantified and then analysed using quantitative methods (see section 9.3 below). Therefore, we choose to discuss qualitative data analysis separately in this chapter, and refer back to relevant text in earlier parts of the book on data collection or analytic issues.

Before we start our discussion of qualitative data analysis, it should be noted that there appears, just like with quantitative researchers, less than perfect agreement among qualitative researchers on what suitable or preferred methods are for specific analysis questions. As qualitative research may study idiosyncracies, also many qualitative researchers adhere to their own, or special analytic 'culture'. Textbooks on qualitative research are for that reason often an amalgam of various methodological approaches and 'schools', working from different epistemological stances. While there is fairly general agreement among quantitative researchers on how a regression analysis should be carried out (although, as we showed, at times there can be wide ranging differences too on the 'right' approach for answering a specific quantitative research question!), there may be less agreement among qualitative researchers on what suitable methodological approaches are. Given the scope of this book, it will be impossible to address all these different schools and traditions and nuances. What we will do, is discuss a number of analytic approaches and tools that are shared among most qualitative scholars.

As we discussed in previous chapters, qualitative data collection methods can consist of various types: ethnography, where the researcher in a sense immerses him/herself in the world of the objects of study and where a combination of approaches is generally used (interviews, observation, dialogue, documents), interviews, where generally open or in-depth modes of interviewing or narratives are used, and observation, where the researcher observes the study objects but does not take part in any social interaction with them (the researcher is in a sense a 'fly on the wall', not participating, unobtrusive and only registering behaviour). As we discussed briefly, the use of documents or secondary material, where essentially also the researcher 'observes', can be considered a separate source. Under such 'patient' sources, we also classify blogs, videos, films, advertising material, diaries and the like.

These modes can be thought of as on a continuum of 'participation' or 'immersion': the most participatory method is then ethnography, where the researcher may him or herself even 'become' the instrument as we said; interviews assuming a middle position, where the researcher plays a role in what is said as s/he poses the questions, decides on what to probe, registers emotions (or not) so that the researcher influences to a certain extent what behaviour and verbal utterances the respondents show; and observation (under which we also classify the study of documents) the most 'unparticipatory', where a researcher need not even have any exchanges with the respondents or objects of study.

On the other hand, these three modes of data collection can also be ordered differently, on a continuum of 'naturalness' with which study participants may be expected to behave. Interviews are then the mode in which respondents' behaviour would be least natural, ethnography would assume a middle position as the researcher will collect data such, that the study participants can go about their ways as normally as possible but the researcher remains a stranger in their midst, and observation (under which again the use of existing materials) would be the data collection mode (especially when unobtrusive methods are employed such as through CCTV cameras, the 'fly-on-the-wall' mode) where respondents could behave as naturally as possible. Figure 9.1 depicts this in schematic fashion.

All analysis of qualitative material, whether that was gathered using ethnographic methods, interviews, or observation, can be done employing a '*formal* mode' and an '*informal* mode'. By the formal mode, we mean methods to structure and analyse the material using tools and methods that are interchangeable between researchers. A researcher can employ for instance first level coding and second level coding using the tools that we outline below. However, during data collection, also informal methods may be used. By these we mean for instance that researchers may also pick up implicit information that is unique to one particular researcher, such as a specific response that fieldworkers encountered upon entering gang turf, or a response by an interviewee that may be tied to characteristics of the researcher.

Such information can definitely be used in analysis: in fact, some text parts or parts of interviews may even give you as a researcher a particular feeling, or even a sensory

Figure 9.1: Schematic representation of three modes of qualitative data collection

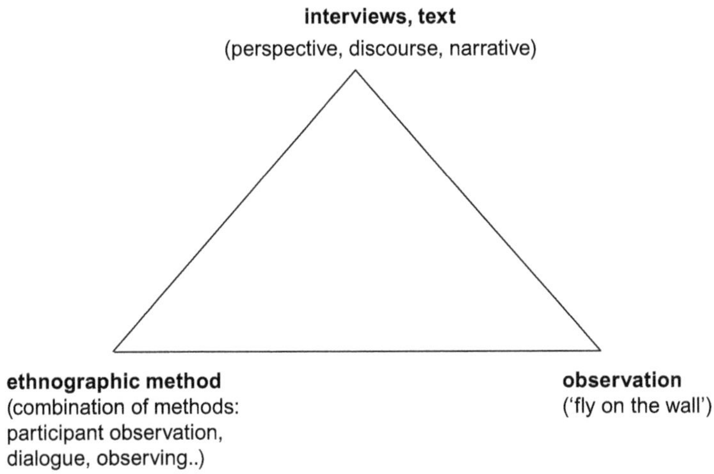

experience such as nausea or a shudder which may offer important clues for analysis. And such sensations should therefore definitely be employed in analysing the material; during coding (formal mode), researchers should then ask themselves: why does this particular sentence or expression affect me so much? Pondering such particularities that may be tied to yourself as data collector or researcher is important, and qualitative researchers should indeed in this sense be sufficiently 'reflective'.

Clearly, such information that is related uniquely to the researcher, is less easily exchanged with or found by other researchers. A particular response may be tied to a researcher's gender, so that a researcher with a different gender would not even receive the cue, or responses may be due to cultural differences or preconceptions. Last, researchers may use meta-information that they happened to pick up or gather during the fieldwork or in other phases. Using such informal modes of analysis is part and parcel of qualitative analysis. This all in all means that qualitative data analysis is partly determined by personal experiences and individual characteristics of the researcher.

Below we will discuss first- and second level coding, techniques that are common in qualitative analysis. They are formal modes of analysis, as it is possible to have a coding process replicated by a second, independent researcher (for instance to assess reliability).

Miller (2013), in a study that we referred to previously in section 4.6, showed how much the outcome of the analytic process can depend on the person of the researcher (and one could say, in methodological terms, how difficult it is to achieve interrater reliability). Using two cases (one a fictional description on what happened in a police station when a woman tried to report a crime, the other an actual description of gang violence at an American secondary school by a gang member) she asked 31 qualitative scholars working in criminology, to each – independently – retrieve the most important 'themes' (i.e. the topics that are meaningful elements of the text) from the transcript. Miller found that there was not a single theme retrieved from the raw material that was brought up by more than 50% of the scholars. While Miller acknowledges that analysis of qualitative material may differ across scholars and that such divergence is not worrisome per se, she states that when scholars diverge so much on what can be seen as the rough data – namely, the themes that are relevant – reliability may indeed be compromised (see also section 2.6). Some analysis techniques for qualitative content analysis are quite methodical, and it is then also easier to achieve reliability.

9.2 Qualitative data analysis of (written) material

Qualitative data can be interviews, transcripts, notes, uploaded videos, and in fact almost anything. Before it can be analysed, much material first needs to be transformed into such a format that it can be analysed. Very often, interviews are transcribed or data transferred into text format. Data are often first, as is said, 'textified'. After this, text is generally coded or subdivided into small meaningful units.

Techniques for coding are, as the reader will notice below, not very circumscribed and explicit – and definitely much less recipe-like than techniques for quantitative data analysis. A number of tools can be recommended, although none of these are again very exact and are more like guidelines. Just like qualitative data collection is embedded, so learning the tools of the qualitative data analysis trade is embedded: most researchers are taught the tools by example and through on-the-job training (and much less so from textbooks).

First, before any analysis can start, the researcher should familiarise him- or herself with the data. This means taking several good looks at the data, reading through texts, and noting what strikes you. Researchers generally look at four specific things. Firstly, they look at patterns that emerge: what issues recur at several points, what are the most 'blatant' messages? Are certain expressions or wordings repeated? Does a consistent message come across? Mostly, themes emerge from this inspection of the data, where the researcher scans for recurrent topics.

Second, researchers look for surprises. What is surprising or unexpected, in light of the literature or theory? Are some things illogical? Do results emerge that are very different as compared to other contexts? Third, researchers look for puzzles or contradictions. These need clarification or may be the key to important discoveries.

Fourth and last, it is also important to take notice of what is *not* being said. Silences and gaps are important, as are evasions, sudden changes of topic. These generally signal issues that are taboo or dangerous, or that evoke emotions people do not wish to feel or express, meaning – generally – that important clues are to be found here, or that additional probing or supplementary data collection is necessary. Good transcription of the data is immensely important here: if one does not code in the transcript that people are silent for a while, or look the other way, or appear to become emotional, one would fail to pick up such clues. Searching for such in a sense subliminal cues, changes in inflection or pitch, is particularly relevant for the analysis of (taped) in-depth interviews. Analytic memos may give important cues too. Ryan and Bernard (2003) give the example of interviewees who did not respond that they disapproved of government policy, but simply went silent if a question to this effect was asked. Interpretation becomes more slippery here however, because how can one interpret something that is not there? And how can one be sure that the interviewee is silent because s/he disagrees with government policy? Maybe the interviewee is simply fed up, or thought the question trivial.

9.2.1 First level coding

Analysis generally starts with first level coding, also referred to as open coding, first cycle or primary cycle coding. Here one essentially tries to give labels to the content of the data, tries to group sentences or pieces of text under meaningful headers. First level coding is fairly 'flat' and easy as it is descriptive, one only codes *what* is in the data. For that matter it is also sometimes referred to as 'emergent' coding.

How does one find such first level, descriptive codes? A number of tips and tricks can be given, but none of these are very explicit. First, one looks for repetition. Are certain elements, issues, phrasings repeated several times? Candidates for codes are topics or words that one encounters again and again; researchers lump these under one descriptive code. Second, one looks for particular expressions that have been used, so-called 'indigenous categories', literally the words that the respondents used. These may be phrasings particular for the group studied, jargon or marked expressions, or expressions that appear untranslatable. Third, one looks for metaphors. Quinn (1996), referred to in a recommended article on coding by Ryan and Bernard (2003), studied American marriages. She noted that respondents often used metaphors: interviewees would state that a marriage was like 'the rock of Gibraltar' or was 'nailed in cement'. Last, transitions are important, where people (suddenly) change topic, or where they pause. These generally indicate that a qualitatively different topic is now broached.

Figure 9.2 gives an example of a transcription of interviews with a non-random sample of Dutch citizens. They were asked about their parents and grandparents and the manner in which World War II had influenced their life and habits.

Researchers code in order to help them to identify 'themes' that represent the content of the data. Themes can be derived from the data and as voiced or expressed by the persons who are being studied (an inductive approach, also referred to as 'emic' or 'in vivo'), or the researcher can seek to identify explicit pre-given themes (for instance as provided by theory, also referred to as 'etic'). The advantage of the first approach is that it is possible to find things that are unexpected (serendipity); the advantage of the second approach is that it links directly to theory and is likely more efficient. The first is what one would typically do in a more grounded approach. If one uses the very words that the interviewees use, this is called *in vivo* coding or also *emic* coding.

Coding can be done very detailed, giving each part of a sentence its own label, and it can be done more coarsely. The first kind is also referred to as 'fractured' coding and the latter as 'lumped' coding. The advantage of fine-grained coding is that all nuances and little fragments are preserved and remain highlighted. Obviously, the downside is that the codings may become too fine-grained to be able to see much: there may then simply be too much detail. In practice, researchers who start out with very detailed coding later lump categories together; those who start out more coarsely will quickly disaggregate labels into different, more specific labels. The first level coding stage, essentially amounts to a sorting stage.

Figure 9.2: Transcriptions of parts of interviews on World War II

My mother never throws away anything. I remember my grandmother would also never throw away any food! God forbid!! So with my mum it is sort of the same, she is very frugal, she is not mean you know or stingy, but she is careful. You never throw away anything because maybe you can use it again.

I know that my father was really hungry in the war. He lived in Haarlem and they really had no food. At some point he was almost too weak to go to school and the children could not concentrate, he told me. My father eats a lot. He always finishes his plate too. As if he's afraid still there is no more food tomorrow.

My grandfather was 14 when the war started and he very quickly had to hide so that the Nazi's would not come and get him to work in Germany. I know that he spent all those years in hiding and he could not finish secondary school and my grandmother says, yeah he is dead now, she says this was stolen from him. Afterwards he became a businessman, but that was maybe what he had wanted, who can tell? All his children studied and got degrees.

My grandfather was held prisoner in Germany, he was rounded up in the Arbeitseinsatz. He did not have of a nice youth, no. My grandmother lived in Rotterdam, Rotterdam had been bombed. Her father was a carpenter, but there was no work anymore. I don't know how they got by. They would burn anything and they would all live around the stove in just one room. They were hungry too.

My father was 10 years old when the war broke out and my mother was 6 years old. They did not have a normal childhood, no not at all. My father lived in the area where the Hungerwinter struck and he was really, really hungry and skinny. He ate tulip bulbs, bah. My mom she lived in Rotterdam and she has never really wanted to talk about it. It was bad. I think she saw a lot.

My mother was interned by the Japanese in the Dutch East Indies, on Java, in a camp. She told us they would get only so little food, and very awful food like some slimy porridge and intestines, and she was so exhausted towards the end she couldn't lift a bucket of *kapok*, they had to work for the Japanese. My grandmother almost died, she weighed only 33 kilo's when they were liberated, and her teeth were coming loose. My mother sometimes has this really strange behaviour that she likes to look in bins for food that supermarkets have thrown away. I think she became like that.

I don't think my grandparents really suffered bad things [in the war] you know, like some of their family were killed or so? But the war has changed them or well, living in such a period made them who they are I think? They were very hungry, I know. They told me. And now like, well, ehm, like they are careful. With food, and things. They find it difficult to throw things away when they are still good. Because you never know? It's that kinda thing, like 'you never know' or 'it may happen again'. They are not really afraid of it, but 'you never know'.

Figure 9.3 gives an example of parts of interviews that have been coded, in a rough first sweep, using ATLAS.ti. The data are the same that were shown in Figure 9.2 above. The print-out of ATLAS.ti shows the various answers, with a small number of first level codings. As the codes show, a number of topics return regularly, such as 'hungry' and 'suffering'. Some codes are literal ('emic' or 'in vivo'), other codes are rough descriptions or already interpretations ('weird food habit') of the underlying text block. Coding was done inductively, no pre-set categories were employed.

Coding is seldom finished in one round. Researchers mostly go back to their original codes and change them slightly, and may go back again and make new choices again given new data that they encountered, or more recent interview material that has been added. They may also compare all chunks of text that received the same code, and check whether all those text parts are really well subsumed under the same heading. This constant scrutiny, and flexible and malleable use of codes is referred to as the *constant comparative method.*

The codes serve to help to reveal structure in the data. The codes that are given should be described and documented, and it should be explained what segments of text are given what label. Most researchers also maintain – just like during fieldwork – a certain diary-like record of all choices and alterations they made during coding and why. Software packages like ATLAS.ti are a very handy aid for doing so, as they store the codes, give an overview of them, enable regrouping of codes and the like.

It is hard to say how many final codes one should aim for. This firstly depends on the richness and breadth of the material. It is theoretically possible to employ a scheme with hundreds of different codes. Here the limit is not the technique, as software packages enable researchers to work with numerous different codes (see below). The issue is whether so many codes are conceptually feasible. It is generally, in order to be able to get a grasp of the material and to be able to get an overview, better not to work with so many codes that grouping of the material becomes unwieldy.

Figure 9.3 illustrates the coding process of the World War II interviews. One sees on the left hand side the various codes and their frequencies, generated by ATLAS.ti. Inspecting such software-generated overviews helps to refine the coding. For this small example, it is easy to see that the codings for 'stolen youth', 'stolen childhood' and 'stolen education' could possibly be combined into something labelled 'stolen youth'. The list in Figure 9.3 also shows how 'hunger' is a frequent topic and therewith a clear candidate for a theme. The same might go for 'suffering' and 'traumatic experiences'. After a first researcher has entered his or her first level codings, it is possible to have a second researcher enter his or her own codes on the same material; many software packages aid in determining interrater reliability.

After giving first level codes, researchers next need to extract structure from the data by identifying relations between the codes. For doing so, researchers generally quickly attempt to identify relations between the codes. There is not really a risk that such steps are taken too soon. As said, the analysis process is generally iterative, and researchers can flexibly return to previous codings and modify them if that is desirable. Relations between codes can be horizontal in the sense that codes co-occur often ('axial coding'), or hierarchical in the sense that certain codes can actually be subsumed under larger codes ('hierarchical coding'). We discuss this in the next section.

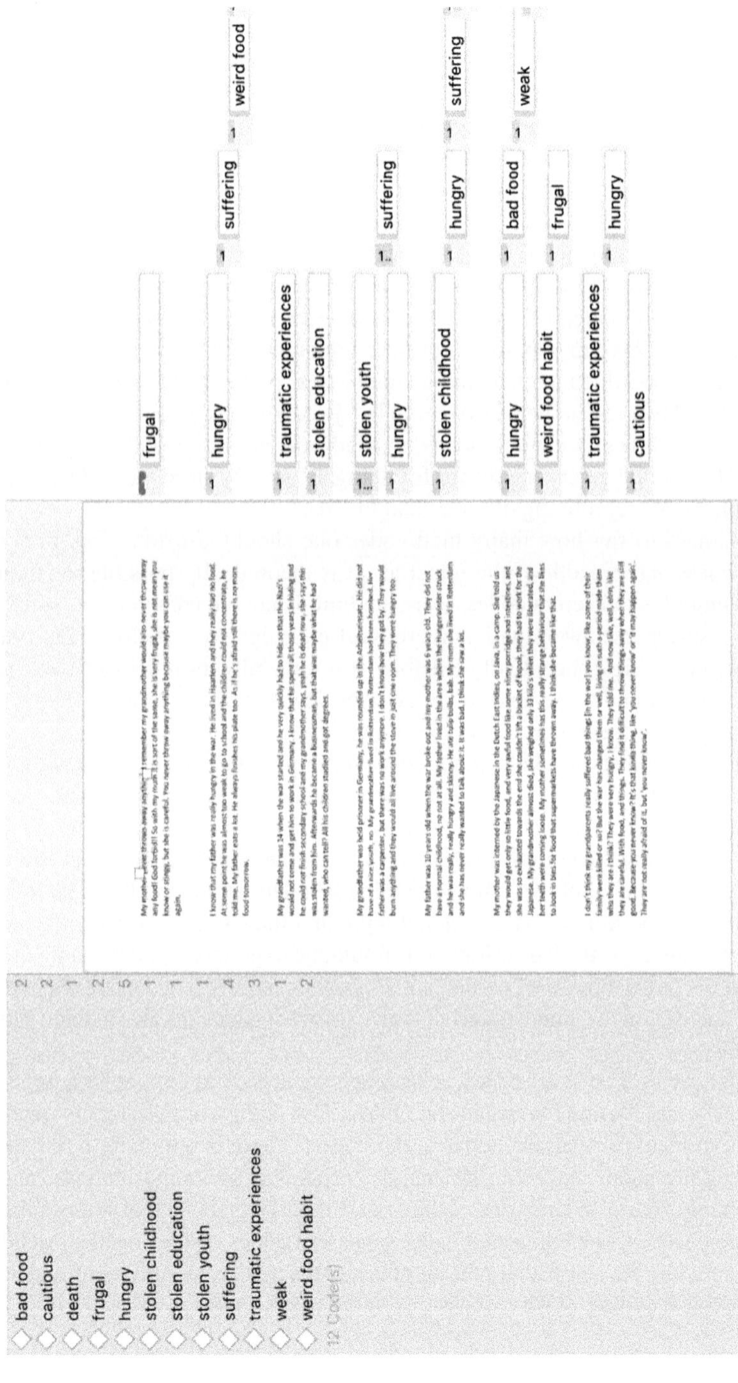

Figure 9.3: First level codings in interviews on World War II

9.2.2 Second level coding

After the raw material has been coded, at the stage of second level coding one starts analysing the data more thoroughly. Here researchers try to combine the codes to a different level, namely the level where the codes do not serve to summarise and describe the data, but to extract meaning. Second level coding, which is also referred to as 'secondary cycle coding', is therefore of a qualitatively different nature than first level coding.

To be able to move to this higher, interpretative level, one could first revisit the codes and attempt to label the chunks of text not by what is said literally but by the *meaning* or implication of the words. Here one delves deeper into the meaning that sentences and messages have, and attaches new labels accordingly. One way to do this, is by reorganising the text (and this where qualitative data analysis packages come in so handy) so that all text parts that have the same label, are regrouped to appear together. One can then re-read all (parts of) sentences and see whether better, conceptual 'umbrella'-concepts describe the various text blocks under different labels. For the World War II material discussed above, one such umbrella-label could be 'Food', where both 'hungry' and 'bad food' combines. But if that is considered too descriptive, an umbrella-label could also be 'Suffering', under which 'hungry' and 'traumatic experiences' are gathered. But 'suffering' upon second inspection contains three text bits that refer to physical exhaustion, and perhaps these should be relabeled?

An example of the manner in which software packages help in this process, is given in Figure 9.4, in which we see a screenshot of all segments of text subsumed under first level codings. Inspecting these text parts, the four text slivers under 'suffering' are grouped together and it is easy to see how they could be regrouped in two meaningful parts actually: one that refers to having very scarce resources (containing only the first text bit 1:6), and the second referring to 'physical exhaustion' (containing the text bits 1:9,1:14 and 1:23). This process of identifying co-occurring or reappearing codes, or patterns or sequences of codes is referred to as 'axial coding' or 'hierarchical coding'. As said, codings can be made and undone again, the process is iterative.

The study by Quinn (1996) that we referred to earlier had identified metaphors such as that a marriage was like 'the rock of Gibraltar' or was 'nailed in cement'. Quinn in a second level analysis interpreted these specific metaphors as indication that marriages were intended to last, and that apparently, this lastingness was a dominant issue. In the small bits of interview that we gave here, we see that respondents three times mentioned that the war 'stole' things from their ancestors: the chance for an education, a childhood. The metaphor can be interpreted in various ways: to say that what had happened was a crime, or to indicate that what was lost was irretrievable. Other interpretations are possible.

An illustrative example of such axial coding is the analysis by Lindegaard *et al.* that we described previously in section 4.5. Lindegaard and her co-authors (2016) had coded from CCTV fragments the behaviour of all persons present in a number of robberies (victims, bystanders and perpetrators). They had done this first in as neutral, descriptive and as neutral terms as possible, describing the movement of people's limbs, the direction they looked, whether they stood still or moved, moved back or moved forward. Codes that were given in this first phase were codes such as 'hands at waist', 'pushing victim', 'touching arms of bystander'. In a subsequent coding step, they *interpreted* these behavioural categories and

Figure 9.4: Screen shot of text blocks under labels

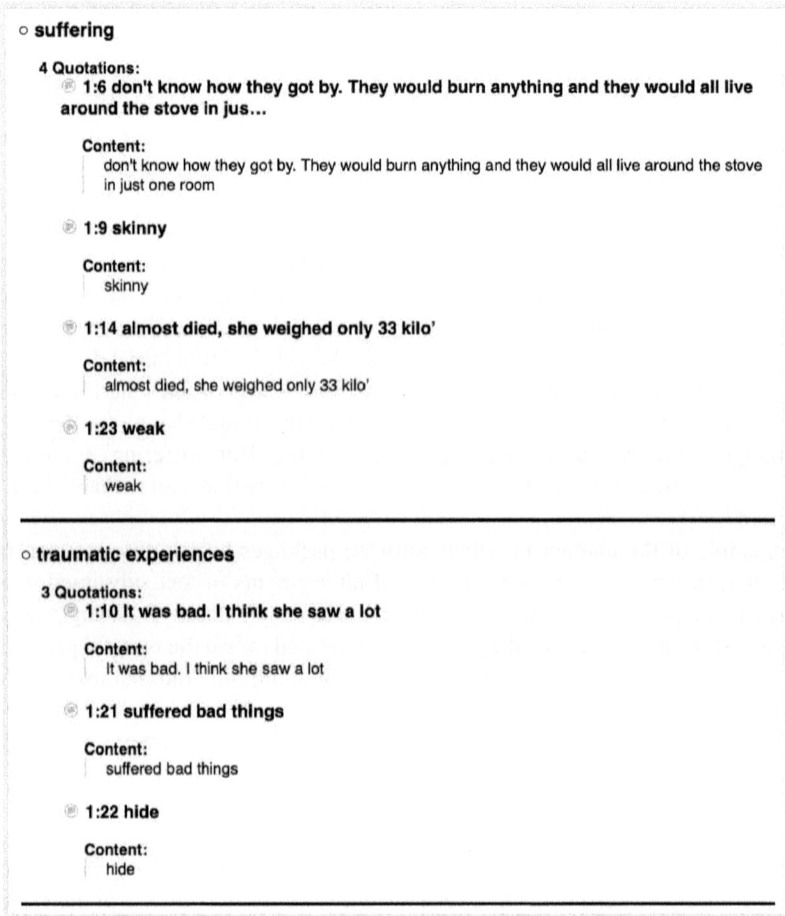

○ **suffering**

4 Quotations:

1:6 don't know how they got by. They would burn anything and they would all live around the stove in jus...

Content:
don't know how they got by. They would burn anything and they would all live around the stove in just one room

1:9 skinny

Content:
skinny

1:14 almost died, she weighed only 33 kilo'

Content:
almost died, she weighed only 33 kilo'

1:23 weak

Content:
weak

○ **traumatic experiences**

3 Quotations:

1:10 It was bad. I think she saw a lot

Content:
It was bad. I think she saw a lot

1:21 suffered bad things

Content:
suffered bad things

1:22 hide

Content:
hide

attached labels to them that were not descriptive anymore but captured what that behaviour *meant* in that particular situation. They coded for instance whether the behaviour constituted 'resistance by victim', or whether certain offender behaviour constituted a 'threat'.

In this axial coding stage, theoretical sampling may very well be employed. As codes and meanings emerge from the material, a search for empirical data that do not match the emerging interpretation can aid to strengthen the interpretation (when it turns out such 'negative cases' cannot be found) or broaden the scope or generalizability by extending the theoretical findings (by adding on to the interpretation from new, slightly different cases). Throughout second level coding, researchers often keep a diary-like record of the choices that were made, the interpretations that emerged, etc.

9.3 Content analysis

In content analysis one aims to assess the meaning or symbolic or covert intent of communications, whether these be written, oral, in images or even iconic representations. Qualitative content analysis can involve any source that sends or may send a message. Qualitative content analysis therefore also often involves the coding of text or other material. As described in section 9.2, written text or non-written materials can then similarly be first level coded descriptively, after which second level analysis can combine these codings and look at the co-occurrence of messages or patterns of occurrence to identify implicit or symbolic messages, leading to themes or sub-themes.

That said, content analysis is in fact a fairly wide class of analytic techniques that attempt to uncover the hidden or implicit meanings of communications. Both quantitative and qualitative approaches are viable to do so. Often, and especially when the material to analyse is voluminous, special software is used to carry out the analysis of qualitative material. When communication is written, one can use software such as discussed below in section 9.5. When communication does not exist of written or transcribed communication, researchers generally resort to coding the material in one way or another, entering these codes in some format and then analyzing the codes. The study by Lindegaard, Bernasco and De Vries (2016) of CCTV footage that we discussed just now is a textbook example: footage was coded second by second and the codes next analysed.

Once all material has been coded, that is, once descriptive, first level categories have been assigned, one starts, just like for the analysis of regular qualitative material, to search for meaning in the coded or raw material. What does the material say? What message is there? Analyzing transcriptions of boardroom meetings in law firms, one can analyse what is said, literally, in the first level coding. However, one is mostly after more, such as the meaning and impact of communication, or the symbols behind expressions, tones or gestures, the messages that people infer. In the literature, numerous labels are given to the methods to do so. Essentially what one does in content analysis is nothing different from ordinary qualitative analysis: to uncover themes in the qualitative material (and possibly sub-themes), selecting from all themes the ones that are relevant for answering the research question, connecting these themes in a meaningful way so as to answer the research question, and – lastly – linking the findings back to theory. It does not differ in a fundamental way from the coding and analysis of regular interviews or field notes.

Content analysis can however also be quantitative. By that we mean that the qualitative material is analysed and quantified, after which a regular quantitative analysis can be carried out. In a quantitative content analysis in its simplest form, one could, for instance count the frequency with which certain words appear (such as 'enemy' or 'danger'), or the context in which these words are used. Quantitative content analysis could then be carried out using all sorts of quantitative measurements of the material, such as word frequencies, time or space devoted to certain aspects. Quantitative analysis can be made more interesting by not only looking at such means or percentages ('univariate analysis'), but by combining occurrences of words. One would then look at relational patterns: do for instance parents use different adjectives for sons than for daughters? Or do fathers use different adjectives for their children than mothers? In a sense, one then carries out a bivariate analysis. In multivariate varieties one can look at numerous combinations of words or phrases and contexts. Summarising, content analysis can be quantitative as well as qualitative, or a combination of both.

Ryan and Bernard (2003) give a succinct overview of what they name observational and analytic techniques for content analysis. Some of the analytic techniques they describe require sophisticated quantitative skills to extract the themes from the qualitative material, such as multidimensional scaling or factor analysis. They also give useful examples of observational, more qualitative techniques.

Schmader, Whitehead and Wysocki (2007) carried out a quantitative analysis of qualitative material. They analysed letters of recommendation for male and female biochemists. Using special software for text analysis (Linguistic Inquiry Word Count (LIWC), Pennebaker, Francis, & Booth, 2001), they analysed how often particular words appeared in letters of recommendation, gauged against the total number of words in the recommendation letters. These words were: achievement words (e.g., goal), communication words (e.g., talk), positive emotions (e.g., happy), negative emotions (e.g., worthless), tentative words (e.g., perhaps), and certainty words (e.g., always). In addition, they studied the appearance of, amongst others, 'grindstone traits' (such as hard-working), ability traits, and standout adjectives (such as 'great' or 'brilliant'). The study showed that letters for male and female candidates were quite similar in terms of the various word counts, but that recommenders had used significantly more standout adjectives for male candidates as compared to female candidates, even though objective criteria showed no gender differences in qualifications.

Hsieh and Shannon (2005) give a more in-depth discussion of qualitative content analysis. The short, pragmatic and very readable overview of the analysis of themes in qualitative analysis by Ryan and Bernard (2003) is also recommended.

9.4 Analysing other material

Qualitative research can be conducted on, as said, a wide variety of materials. Materials can be primary (when the researcher has gathered them him/herself) or secondary. In the latter case, the material can be documents (such as discussed under content analysis), but news items can be analysed as well, as can be movies, memes, ads, song lyrics. While the analysis of some of these materials may be slightly different, in the end some 'textification' of the materials is generally done, after which the materials can be analysed by regular methods, using first level and second level coding. While there may therefore be slight differences with the steps as we discussed them before, the basic principles are the same.

This is less easily said when the materials have been gathered during participant observation. Here, it is likely that interviews and conversations, observations and text materials, video images and even music comprise the material on which analysis should take place, but much of the information that will be relevant for analysis is likely stored in the researcher's head. It is then much harder to describe how analysis should proceed, what the steps are, and: how one arrives at conclusions, as much of the material may be tied in with the researcher's experiences and perceptions. Because of the wealth of material collected, and the researcher's immersion in data collection, it is more likely to find the corkscrew-like types of empirical cycle here, with researchers formulating a string of intermediate conclusions as they proceed through fieldwork, that are constantly contrasted and challenged and modified until the interpretation converges.

Formulated differently, in such participant observation, the researcher him or herself has in a sense become the data collection instrument, or even: the data. While qualitative data analysis is already by nature contextualised, this is even more strongly so in the case of ethnographic research. It is then extremely difficult to outline steps for data analysis, let alone beforehand. Apart from generic principles and tools outlined here, not many specific procedures or guidelines can be prescribed.

9.5 Software

Many researchers these days use software to organise and analyse their qualitative data. CAQDAS (Computer-aided qualitative data analysis software) is the generic name for such software packages. They all have in common that they enable to structure and restructure the data, regroup fragments of text, attach codings and subcodings to text blocks. Such software is quickly necessary to get an overview if there is a massive amount of material – and as transcripts of interview can easily add up to hundreds of typed pages, this is indeed quickly the case. A veteran programme is ATLAS.ti (see `atlasti.com`). ATLAS.ti has been around for many years and the current version is already the 8th; it is available for many platforms (Mac, Windows, and there is even a smartphone version); we showed one example of coding using ATLAS.ti. Other packages are NVivo (`qsrinternational.com`) and MAXQDA (`maxqda.com`). In addition to tools for coding, most commercially available packages also aid in aggregation and visualisation of the data. Quite a number of free packages are available as well but these generally offer coding only; an exception is qdap (acronym for Quantitative Discourse Analysis Package), an R-based package that offers word extracting, statistical analysis and visualisation (see `cran.r-project.org/web/packages/qdap/index.html.`).

9.6 Description of findings

Qualitative analysis findings are described in articles and reports just like quantitative analysis findings are. In general, there are very few tabulations. Findings are generally more wordy, and not many researchers present all the steps in their analytic process, as that in general consumes too much space for standard journal articles.

Qualitative researchers often present *exemplars* or *vignettes* in their reports, that is, parts of interviews or delineated portions of text or other material, collected during fieldwork, that are exemplary for what the researcher believes has been found. In some cases, respondents formulate so succinctly and precisely, or a life-story of a respondent in a sense illustrates the themes so well, that these are *verbatim* reproduced. Artificial exemplars in the sense that the researcher has constructed them are also often used and are – perhaps confusingly – also called 'vignettes', just like vignettes in experimental quantitative research. If not immediately obvious from the context, we will in the remainder indicate them as 'qualitative vignettes'.

9.7 Further reading

We have in this chapter only touched upon qualitative data analysis. There are many different approaches, schools and types of analysis. We refer to textbooks on qualitative research for more examples than we gave in our cursory overview of qualitative data analysis. Classics are Stern (1995), and Glaser and Strauss (1967). Webley (2010) discusses qualitative methods specifically for empirical legal research. An often referenced textbook on qualitative research in general is Denzin and Lincoln (2011), and a fairly practical one on ethnography is Hammersley and Atkinson (2007). A concise and accessible general textbook on qualitative research is Tracy (2013), and one specifically on qualitative methods in criminology is Wincup (2017).

Part IV

STATISTICS AND RESEARCH METHODOLOGY IN CRIMINOLOGY

Chapter 10

Statistical and methodological issues in criminological research

In criminology, the *tesseras criminologica* is studied: prevalence (what and how many crimes have been committed, where, when?), etiology (what are the causes?), reaction (what (non-)judicial response followed?) and victims (what were the consequences for victims, what are their needs?). Roughly speaking, this translates into studies on numbers and nature of crimes, perpetrators and contexts, interventions and victims. Because we are studying crime – a particular kind of behaviour – we are faced with fairly severe measurement and statistical problems. We will outline a number of reasons for that below, and next detail these statistical and methodological particularities.

10.1 The particular setting of criminological research

Crime is punishable behaviour, behaviour that has been criminalised by the authorities. It may entail – if convicted and sometimes even when prosecuted – fines, community service, a rap sheet, or even imprisonment. This means that offenders may attempt to hide their behaviour. Firstly from the justice authorities, but likely also from outsiders. Confessing to people that you have committed a robbery generates a *risk* that is perhaps better avoided. This means that – because of the risk of detection – offenders will likely not report certain offending behaviour to us as researchers.

Tied in with this is the fact that offenders do not have a *common interest* with the researcher, they have nothing to gain from criminological research. To explain this, we give an example. Suppose that I am a medical doctor working at a university hospital. I treat patients for disease X. If I ask patients to participate in a study into the effectiveness of a certain new drug, many will consent. Better treatment of disease X may be in each patient's own interest. And if not in his or her own interest, then in the interest of fellow or future sufferers. Now suppose that a number of patients have consented to participate and that after administration of the drug, they are for a while free of symptoms. But for some, the disease will return. What would a patient do if there is a relapse? S/he would likely make an appointment with the physician to report the relapse as soon as possible and be prescribed different treatment, or the same again.

This situation is fundamentally different from that of an offender. Suppose that we ask a group of convicts whether they would like to participate in a study on efficacy (defined as the extent to which people do not recidivate) of community service versus a fine. Both are administered by the criminal justice authorities. To be able to measure efficacy, I would have to have good measures of recidivism. It is however quite unlikely that convicts report their new offence as soon as possible to the authorities, or even to me as a researcher. In fact, it is far more likely that they will try to stay out of the hands of the criminal justice authorities as long as possible!

Staying with this example, we illustrate a third particularity. The example shows that the criminological researcher will very often not be able to conduct experimental studies at levels 3 or higher of the Maryland Scientific Methods Scale: for most of the interventions handed out to offenders, the researcher does not administer the intervention him/herself. It is the judge, or the prosecutor who decides what sentence is just and proportional, taking into account all properties of the case as well as characteristics and personal situation of the offender. This situation – particularly as regards the characteristics of the offender – is even the opposite of what is desirable from the perspective of internal validity. In an experimental design we would prefer the intervention to be administered randomly: chance decides whether someone is administered intervention X or a control intervention. Judges do the opposite: they administer sanctions tailored to 'the person of the offender' as it is often phrased, i.e. as unrandomly as possible. This constitutes one important reason why it is so much harder in criminological as compared to other social science research to conduct true randomised experiments.

Criminal behaviour – in addition to it being punishable – is also behaviour that people may not be exactly proud of. While this differs per offence (burglars may boast of clever break-ins) in general we must assume that offenders might also for reasons of saving face rather not admit certain criminal behaviour. There is therefore in addition to risk, also *shame* involved. This may pertain to violent behaviour, or behaviour that involves vulnerable or defenceless victims. For that reason, it is for instance assumed by many researchers that self-report studies (see section 11.5.3) are only marginally useful to obtain data on sexual offending.

A number of offenders suffer from mental illness, or have led lives with serious drug abuse. This may have impaired their memory and perception of events. Some offenders may be fairly inaccessible living in marginalised sections of society. (Chronic) offending is not only associated with deviance, but often leads to poverty, making that offenders have no (registered) telephone, may be homeless. This makes them less easy to reach. Van der Geest, Bijleveld and Verbruggen (2013) reported that their study of high-risk men and women was much more expensive than regular surveys, because it was so much harder to contact sample members. Instead of the regular rule of three contact attempts, after which the sample member is registered as a 'non-contact', they approached sample members eight times before giving up. They employed special approach procedures for homeless respondents (as no address was available for these), for instance through local Salvation Army offices, through associations catering for drugs addicts, and the like. They also conducted a number of interviews in prisons and mental asylums.

Obviously, not all research needs to be channeled through offenders. As will be shown in chapter 11 below, citizens (victims as well as non-victims) are regularly interviewed to obtain estimates of crime prevalence too. However, victims may not wish to talk about some crimes they experienced, afraid to be re-traumatised, or simply not wanting to revisit that experience again, or may have forgotten the incident.

Most crimes, and especially serious crimes, are – fortunately – rare events. This means that only relatively few commit such crimes and that relatively few become its victims. And the more serious the crime the rarer generally its occurrence. However, these serious offences are generally the offences that we would be most interested to understand, more so than common and relatively 'innocuous' offences such as fare dodging. So we must draw huge samples to have enough 'signal'. If we would draw a flat random sample of the Dutch population of secondary school students of, say, 200 respondents, and ask them how many offences they have committed the past year, it is likely that 150 will have travelled on public transport without paying. It is however to be expected that no one, or perhaps only 1 or 2, will have committed an armed robbery. Thus, to be able to study armed robbery by secondary school students, very large samples would be needed to have enough of such events to reliably describe their properties, the characteristics of the offenders, etc.

This is one reason why criminological researchers often employ so-called 'high-risk' samples, samples of men and women who are at high risk to offend and where not such an enormous data collection effort has to be made to arrive at reliable estimates. The flip side of working with high-risk samples is generalizability: how can we be sure that the findings are generalisable to the high-risk population? Generally no sampling frame of 'high-risk' citizens is available, so this is hard to guarantee. A different but not unimportant issue is to what extent findings for high-risk samples are applicable to average citizens.

On the other hand, criminological researchers find themselves in a luxurious position in the sense that in most societies there are agencies trying to collect the kind of data criminologists are interested in. The police and the judiciary register data on crimes and criminals, and sometimes on its victims, and these databases can often – if permission has been secured – be used for academic research. As is to be expected, this easy availability comes at a price: we cannot expect those who enter the criminal justice system to be a random or representative sample of all offenders. Also, the data may not have been collected according to our own quality standards. We should therefore be fairly cautious in too easily drawing generalisable conclusions from such official data. These issues are further discussed in chapter 11.

All in all, research on crime, on victims, perpetrators and the (non-)judicial reaction to crime takes place in a setting that generates particular methodological issues. In criminological research, we are trying to obtain data on sensitive matters. Offenders may not want to speak with researchers about their offences (although for some offences some do). For offenders and victims we have no sampling frame. Some offenders may be fairly inaccessible living in marginalised sections of society, having no telephone, perhaps even homeless. Also, not all victims want or can speak about crimes that they underwent. Data from the criminal justice system are relatively easily and cheaply available, but are incomplete, must be assumed to be biased, and may not meet academic quality standards.

Below we will discuss the statistical and methodological consequences of this particular setting in some more detail.

10.2 Statistical issues

The particular setting in which data on crime, offenders, (judicial) interventions and victims is collected firstly generates statistical particularities. We focus on two of these.

10.2.1 Lack of sampling frame

To start with, in criminological research we generally lack a sampling frame. Sampling frames are hard to envisage for offenders or for victims. All known sufferers of a certain disease may be registered – also not leading to complete sampling frames as for some diseases symptoms may be so mild that patients never know they have the disease, or some patients may never visit a physician. All legal immigrants to a country are registered. But offenders generally do not volunteer to be registered on lists of any kind. The same goes for victims.

This means that it is hard to know whether samples are representative, and that, strictly speaking, we will therefore always be working with non-probability samples, or samples of which we are not sure whether they are probabilistic – and thus generalisable – or not.

10.2.2 Strangely distributed data

Given that crime is such a rare phenomenon, offending measures are bound to be quite skewed. Only a fraction of the population commit (serious) offences. Thus, if we would ask a sample out of the population whether they had ever stolen something, it is likely that about half or even more would if they answered truthfully, say 'yes'. If we ask how many have ever been convicted, numbers would go down, although not as much as most would expect: Van der Geest, Langendoen and Bijleveld (2006) showed that in a cross-section of the male population of the Netherlands aged 35, 26% had ever been prosecuted for or convicted of an offence. A variable measuring whether someone is convicted or not would thus be skewed in the sense that almost 75% would score 'no' and a little over a quarter 'yes'. For women, the data are even more skewed, with – as an example from the Netherlands – about 5% of adult women ever convicted and 95% never (Bijleveld, 2005).

In addition to this so called *prevalence* of offending being concentrated in a small segment of the population, it is known that also offending is not distributed uniformly over offenders. It is a consistent finding in life-course criminology that a small number of offenders are responsible for a large proportion of all offending (Farrington, 1995). Thus, if we would want to analyse data on frequency of offending, that data would be extremely skewed.

While most standard analysis technique can handle a little skewness, some techniques are affected by deviations from normality in the variables. Not many techniques can handle extreme skewness. This means that either non-parametric techniques must be used or that variables are dichotomised (and thus effectively turned from a continuous into a dichotomous variable), and the analysis run with methods for dichotomous data such as odds ratios. See Farrington and Loeber (2000).

10.3 Methodological issues

As briefly described above, the fact that we are interested in behaviour that is penalised, people may be ashamed of, people may not want to discuss experiencing, we have particular problems gathering data. The people we want to extract information from, may have an opposite interest to ours. Even if they are confident that we will not report their offending behaviour to the authorities, they do not gain by seeing their profile, or their modus operandi exposed.

Secondly, offenders may inhabit segments of society that are less well regulated than those of non-offending citizens. They may live in poor housing, neighbourhoods with little social control, may choose not to have name plates on their doors, not open the door to prevent encountering the bailiff, not have (registered) telephone numbers, be registered as living somewhere different from where they actually reside, etc. This makes approaching and contacting offenders much harder than would be the case for 'average' citizens.

10.3.1 Sensitive data and elusive populations

When doing criminological research, a researcher is after so-called 'sensitive data'. This means that special techniques may have to be employed to extract those data, or to obtain valid data, and that more effort than is usually will have to be made to trace the people on the list of sample members. Below, in chapter 11.7 we will discuss a number of special data collection strategies that have been developed or adapted especially to deal with this problem. Before that, also in chapter 11, issues to do with questionnaire structure, format of administering, and control questions are addressed.

10.3.2 Dark number

As said, many researchers in criminology resort to police or prosecution/court data to answer their research questions. This may be perfectly reasonable and a good solution (for instance if we want to know whether sentence lengths for domestic violence have changed over the years), but it may also be a second-best option.

Using, for instance, police data for answering questions about offenders or crimes, our data will always suffer from bias in the sense that it must be assumed that a select sample of offences and offenders end up in the police registration, from validity issues in that we cannot be sure that academic quality standards were met when the data were entered, and from underestimation as we are certain that not all crimes (nor all offenders) become known to the police.

The latter is commonly referred to as the *dark number*, or that part of offending that remains unknown to the police. We will never know how 'dark' that dark number is, because we have no external 'true' measure against which to gauge the police data. In chapter 11 we will discuss these matters further.

10.3.3 Non-experimental designs

Given that criminological research and intervention in criminal careers are not united in the same institution (as they are for instance in a lot of medical research), the criminological researcher is in a sense always a bystander, and his or her research non-experimental or observational (see section 5.5). This means that criminological researchers – when it comes to the assessment of the effectiveness of judicial interventions – are often in a methodological sense handicapped: they lack the possibility to hand down criminal justice interventions. This means that in practice they resort to either naturalistic, observational studies with poor internal validity and good external validity, or they resort to vignette studies with good internal validity but poor external validity.

That conducting true experimental studies on sentencing is not impossible was proven several times. In Switzerland, Killias, Gillieron, Villard *et al.* (2010) conducted a controlled experiment in which 123 convicts were randomly assigned to community service or custody (up to a maximum of 14 days). Re-convictions and social integration were studied over a period of over 11 years. Although statistically not significant, re-offending was tentatively more common among ex-prisoners in the long run. Eleven years later, ex-prisoners did better however, complied better with tax regulations, and did not fare worse regarding employment history or marital status. In line with recent systematic reviews, the results do not confirm the widespread assumption that short custodial sanctions are harmful when compared to community service.

Ten Boom, Ferwerda and Van Leiden (2007) evaluated 'HALT', an intervention for juvenile transgressors in the Netherlands, that had in previous non-experimental designs been found to be associated with lower recidivism rates than usual. These researchers discovered – in a controlled design with random assignment to either HALT or no intervention (the juvenile was sent home with no sanction) – hardly any difference: in the experimental group the one-year recidivism rate was 29.9%, in the control group it was 29.1%.

10.3.4 Policy and political relevance

Lastly, criminological research can take place in a highly politicised setting. Politicians may want to be tough on crime, want to show that their policies worked – and, not unimportantly, money is involved. While very few topics are studied in the splendid isolation of the ivory tower, this is particularly not so for studies on crime. This means on the one hand that research findings are eagerly reported upon by newspapers and other media, implying that as a researcher you may easily get 'exposure' and a chance to present your findings on radio or TV. It may also mean, however, that some people may not like your findings.

Studies on recidivism have caused turmoil, and have led to questions asked in parliament. Studies into sex offending – especially when against children – are particularly prone to end up being discussed in governmental bodies such as those in charge of sex offender registries. As criminological research may have such wide ranging practical and policy consequences, triangulation and replication are immensely important. We discuss one example extensively.

Sherman and Berk (1984) studied the effects of mandatory arrest for cases of domestic violence in the United States, using a randomised controlled trial (RCT). In the study, domestic violence suspects were either arrested, removed from the home, or admonished. The design was not entirely perfectly randomised as police officers had been given some leeway to arrest in cases they deemed very serious or life-threatening. Recidivism was 13% in the arrest cases and 26% in the group that had been removed from the home only. The study had massive implications. Mandatory arrest was introduced in 40 of the 52 states of the United States.

Afterwards, the study was replicated five times. In three studies, no effect of arrest was found. In a fourth study, it was found that arrest reduced recidivism in European Americans but *increased* it in African Americans. In the fifth study it was found that arrest reduced recidivism in employed arrestees but increased it in unemployed arrestees. Summarising, these *replication studies* showed either no effect, or a negative effect in socially weaker groups. Richard Lempert wrote as a reaction 'Humility is a virtue' (1989), that can be read as a warning against too hastily drawn conclusions and uncorroborated acceptance of findingsfrom a single study.

This saga of domestic violence studies shows that replication studies should perhaps be requested before research findings are implemented into policy or practice. In a replication study, one essentially re-does a study, collects new data according to the original design and instruments. A narrower definition of a replication study (also called reproduction study) is one where different researchers independently re-analyse the existing material. Replication is necessary as meta-studies have shown that interventions are generally found to have larger effects if the designer of the intervention is the one investigating their effect. The necessity of replication studies is increasingly recognised, even though it may be hard to get replication studies published in academic journals.

Chapter 11

Statistics and methodology for criminological research

As outlined in the previous chapter, research on crime, on victims, perpetrators and the (non-)judicial reaction to crime takes place in a setting that generates particular methodological and statistical problems. As we noted, offenders must be assumed to be in general unwilling to come forward with information on their offending behaviour, and this may be supposed to be especially so if that behaviour is not known to the authorities. For a number of phenomena, we have no sampling frame. The police may have lists of known offenders, but as we stated, these cannot be assumed to constitute a random sample of all offenders, and these lists must in fact be presumed to constitute biased samples: only a fraction of offences become known to the authorities, and arrested offenders are unlikely to be a random sample of all offenders.

Criminological researchers have developed a number of methods and techniques that are specifically geared towards overcoming or mitigating these and other issues. In the realm of statistics, adaptations pertain mainly to the use of particular statistical tests or transformations of the data such that standard testing is possible.

11.1 Statistics

11.1.1 Descriptive statistics

To deal with skewed data, criminologists represent central tendency often with the median. As described above in section 6.3.1, the arithmetic mean is sensitive to outliers, and to skewness. The median is insensitive to such distributional oddities. So, for instance if we want to describe the time from arrest to case clearance for homicide, we would not do right to compute the mean. As is well known, homicide clearance times are extremely skewed. Many suspects are identified upon discovery of the body, but some cases may take 20 years to clear. In the US, 50% of cases are cleared within one week, and another 38% in six months (Wellford & Cronin, 1999). A small number are solved after more than a year and some 'cold' cases may take decades. A number also remain unsolved. If we would want to give an indication of the average time that homicides take to be cleared, we firstly have a problem with the unsolved cases. Of course, we might simply throw them out and say that we discuss only the solved cases. But even if we compute the arithmetic mean for those cases, we may end up presenting an uninformative image. The median is not bothered by all these complications.

11.1.2 Rates

In criminological research it is common, particularly for macro-type statistics, to report rates per a certain time period rather than absolute numbers. This is so, because the populations from which measurements have been obtained may vary greatly, and also the relevant time period may vary quite a bit. So if we report homicides, we will give the number of homicides per 100,000 population per year for instance. If we report the number of prisoners, we generally also do so per 100,000 population. Another way to gauge this latter number, which is perhaps fairer, is to compute the rate per 100,000 persons who are 'eligible' to be incarcerated: in that case we would divide by the population between – for the Netherlands – 15 and 65 years of age. The lower limit of 15 is chosen because juveniles under 15 are by law preferably not, and in practice hardly ever incarcerated. The upper limit of 65 is chosen because older people can be incarcerated but this is an incredibly rare phenomenon in the Netherlands; particularly with an aging population including those over 65 might blur proper appreciation of the rate.

Similarly, recidivism rates are not informative if no period is specified. A recidivism rate of 40% in the first month after release from prison is, for the Netherlands, fairly high, but such a figure would be on the low side if it would refer to 10 years after release. It is therefore important to, also here, state the time period over which recidivism is measured, otherwise recidivism figures are uninformative.

11.2 Sampling

As explained in the previous chapter, we are when we study crime faced with the odd situation that for quite a number of situations, we do not have a sampling frame. Some populations are even entirely, as we say, hidden. This has two implications for criminological research practice.

The first is that we may need to apply special sampling techniques to be able to – within reasonable time and financial constraints – arrive at a sample. One such sampling method we detailed above in chapter 3: snowball sampling. When populations are hidden such as illegal residents or drug users, we may need to start from a few 'seeds' or starting respondents and snowball our way until we have reasonable coverage over the population.

The second implication is that it will be very hard to be certain that our samples are representative. Our samples may be representative for a population, but given that people who offend and people who are victimised or who are extremely afraid to be victimised differ from 'average citizens' in the extent to which they can be reached by conventional survey methods, it is likely that attrition and therefore our final research group will underrepresent certain groups. Thus, generalisation is in criminological research generally harder than with research into 'conventional' topics.

11.3 Testing and analysis

Criminological data may be (extremely) skewed. They may also in a different manner be oddly distributed. Standard statistical tests make distributional assumptions. For instance, for testing whether two groups of respondents differ significantly on some variable of interest, it is generally assumed that this variable follows a distribution that does not deviate too much from the normal distribution. Then, a z-test or t-test can be used. In order to be able to test whether a correlation coefficient differs significantly from zero, we assume that the two variables are bivariate normally distributed. When such distributions cannot be assumed, the tests are not valid, and one cannot trust the results.

In the latter case two approaches are available. The first is to resort to using tests that do not rely on distributional assumptions. Such tests are called non-parametric tests. Examples are the sign test, the runs test and the Mann-Whitney test. See Hinkle, Wiersma and Jurs (2003) or any other accessible statistics textbook for details. This is a straightforward and simple solution. A disadvantage is however that non-parametric tests have less statistical power than conventional distribution-based tests. One can then therefore less easily detect significant effects.

In most cases, if we want to carry out bivariate or even multivariate analyses such as multiple regression, distributional assumptions are generally made. If the data cannot reasonably be assumed to meet those assumptions, a first option is, as above, to simply transform the data such that they do meet these assumptions. An often used transformation is the logarithmic transformation. In such cases one does not anymore analyse the original variable, but its logged version, and interpretations refer to the logged variable as well.

For instance, Van der Geest and Bijleveld (2005) attempted to predict with regression analysis the volume of post-release offending in a cohort of juveniles who had been treated for severe conduct problems in a correctional treatment facility. They quickly found that their dependent variable (volume of post-release offending) was severely skewed. They therefore log-transformed the variable reflecting volume, and tested whether the transformed variable was distributed such that regression analysis would be feasible. This turned out to be the case. Their regression model then showed that (the logarithm of) post-release offending was best predicted by the number of serious offences before admission, drug use, bad relations with peers, and a negative evaluation of treatment. While transforming may seem an attractive option, it is obviously much harder to interpret variables that represent the 'natural logarithm of...' than the actual variables themselves.

Instead of transforming a skewed variable such that the variable is approximately normally distributed again, many researchers recommend to simply cut the variable in two, thereby turning it into a dichotomous variable. If the variable is interval but there are clear threshold values (such as a threshold for 'clinical depression') or a midpoint that cuts the variable in two, like the median, then methods for dichotomous variables such as the odds ratio can be used for the newly created dichotomous variable. Of course, this implies data loss.

Another option is to not transform the data, but to use models that are either robust against violation of the model assumptions, or that can accommodate variables with odd distributions. For instance, analysis of variance is known to be fairly robust against departures from normality. Analysis with simulated data has shown that the conclusions from analysis of variance generally hold, and are relatively unaffected when the data do not meet the assumptions put by the technique. It is therefore in many cases safe to run analysis of variance, even when the dependent variable is clearly not normally distributed. This is not to say that these models can deal with any extremely distributed data – some caution should always be exercised.

Lastly, techniques can be used that, just like non-parametric statistical tests, simply do not make any distributional assumptions. Such techniques are called distribution-free, or exploratory techniques. Various multivariate analysis techniques are available in software packages like SPSS, like exploratory cluster analysis, multiple correspondence analysis, exploratory principal components analysis, and exploratory multi-set analysis. These techniques were designed as non-linear versions of regular numerical multivariate techniques. On top of the fact that they are distribution-free and can deal with mixed measurement level variables, they are also very flexible interpretation tools. However, as 'soft' analysis tools, they do not produce statistical tests: they are more modest in their assumptions, and they produce in a sense more modest results. This is generally viewed as a disadvantage.

11.4 Official data

In most countries, statistics are collected on crimes, police activities, prosecution and sentencing. These are essentially statistics on the activities of the criminal justice system (CJS). For the Netherlands, for instance, Statistics Netherlands in collaboration with the WODC Research Center of the Ministry of Justice and Security produces a yearly booklet, that lists all data one could dream of containing data on the operations of the criminal justice system. We can see how many men, how many women were questioned by the police, tried, for what offences, what sentences were handed down, etc. The UN also publishes statistics, as do other organisations such as the consortium 'the European sourcebook' (Aebi *et al.*, 2010).

Such data are a luxury for the researcher. Often, surfing to the websites of the publishing organisation is sufficient; some organisations even have a tool through which you can compile tailored tables. In this manner, a lot of time and money is saved. In general such *secondary* data have several disadvantages too, however (as said, also in research methodology there's no such thing as a free lunch).

The first of these is that secondary CJS data generally only shed light on those offences and offenders that became known to the CJS. Depending on reporting behaviour and clearance rates, the dark number can be huge. For the Netherlands, previous estimates held that one in three offences (overall) becomes known to the police, and of these – depending on the year one is studying – one in seven to one in five is cleared. That means that – overall and roughly speaking – for approximately 5 - 7% of offences a suspect is registered by the police. This calculation is obviously slightly flawed as it does not take into account multiple offences by one offender. Nor does it take into account that both reporting and the clearance rate for more serious offences is better than for lesser offences (although sexual offences are believed an exception to this rule). Nevertheless, official data are generally believed to paint a biased picture of reality. Secondly, as said, in using such official data one employs data that have been gathered by others, generally not trained academicians, so that one cannot be sure that validity and reliability are as they should be. There is therefore – in addition to a representativeness issue – also a quality issue.

Nevertheless, official data are often used by criminologists. Even though the quality of the data may be suboptimal and the data may be less useful for assessing prevalence levels and the like, their easy availability makes that they are an attractive option. In addition, it is generally accepted that for investigating patterns in the data (such as: do women commit different crimes than men, do rapists have more violent criminal careers than sexual assaulters), and for making relative statements their unrepresentativeness may be less of an issue.

While in some countries such official information is public and offenders' names and criminal careers can be pulled from websites, in many countries this is not the case. Then, one needs to ask permission to use the data. Often, such permission is not granted by one overarching agency. It may even be the case that for each source of information, separate permissions need to be obtained.

Official data generally pertain to an entire population. If one has access to electronic police records, why not investigate *all* suspects? Time and financial constraints then do not play a role any more. Thus, the availability of official data may also mean that we have access to the entire population and that sampling and statistical inference become, strictly speaking, unnecessary.

11.4.1 Police data

Police data generally stretch to the level of the arrest. Depending on the country one is studying, data may also be available at the level of reports, i.e. statements by witnesses or victims of crimes. The type of data that is collected varies by country, and for some countries even by region. The quality of the data varies by the nature of the variable measured. It is generally believed that characteristics of offences and/or offenders that have little practical bearing to day-to-day police work are less precisely registered. For example, for the Netherlands, it is believed that information on weapons use (which makes an offender dangerous and may necessitate employing a special arrest unit) is better registered than information on victims. The same goes for hard drugs use, residence status and the like.

In some countries, arrest data are actually nothing more than that. They tell you who was arrested for what kind of offence. Heading up in the criminal justice chain, persons may be acquitted, or may be convicted of a different offence than the police charged them with, for instance: not for a serious assault but for a public order offence – the first categorised as a violent offence, and the second not. As such, police data do not tell you what kind of offence was *committed*, but how the arrest was registered – nothing more and nothing less. So looking at offender's crimes in police data actually tells you not something about criminal careers, but about arrest careers.

In many countries, police records are electronic. Files can be exported to formats that can be used for statistical software packages.

11.4.2 Prosecution and conviction data

Most prosecution services also register the cases they process, as do courts. These registrations may be electronic or, although less and less so, on paper. Paper archives are much more time-consuming to screen for information. In general, as we move up the criminal justice ladder, the information that can be obtained on offenders and cases becomes more detailed and rich. For court cases, files may contain psychological screenings, or information on the background of the offender, or the motivation for the offence, or the modus operandi or forensic traces, witness statements. Court files may contain literal transcripts of interrogations, or telephone taps.

Such sources have their complications too. For expediency reasons, offences are often combined in one case: the offender then needs to be 'processed' only once. If we would want to count numbers or kinds of crimes tried by the courts, we would get into trouble cases as cases with more than one offence are generally (although not always) registered under the offence that carries the heaviest penalty. This means that the lesser offences are 'hidden' behind the more serious ones.

Especially court data have some nice substantive advantages. If a judge finds a defendant guilty, we can assume that what has been written in the trial reports has been proven, and we can take it along as 'true' or 'valid'. This is however the case only in criminal justice systems where no plea bargaining system exists. Whenever the possibility for plea bargaining is present, an offender may plea 'down' the type of offence to a different one than he or she was charged with and committed. This is one of the reasons why for instance in the US – that has plea bargaining – researchers prefer to work with arrest data. In continental countries like the Netherlands, conviction data are considered a relatively valid source for investigating criminal behaviour.

11.4.3 Prison data

Lastly, prison data are an interesting source of data. Obviously, if one is interested in prison life, prison is the place to collect data. Apart from that, many criminologists like to collect data in prisons because offenders are relatively easily accessible, tend to be bored and therefore willing to talk, and in general present a more interesting segment of the offender population, namely those who were convicted of relatively serious crimes. Also, they are in some countries allowed to receive only a small or even no remuneration or incentive for their participation.

However, it will be clear that as one moves up the criminal justice chain, the type of offender and the type of offence one encounters becomes more and more particular. Also, the numbers one can study are in a sense funnelled: while relatively many will be arrested, fewer are prosecuted, fewer are led before a judge, and many fewer are sentenced to imprisonment. While the extent of such funnelling may vary by country – in some Scandinavian countries very few are sentenced to imprisonment, in the US relatively more are – the tendency is the same. Moving up the criminal justice chain one usually obtains better and particularly richer data, it is easier to get access to the people themselves, but the flip side is that numbers dwindle and that the offender group becomes more and more particular.

11.4.4 Comparing official data over countries

Suppose that we would want to compare the sentencing of violent offenders between France and the Netherlands. The data collection phase is relatively easy. Next, however, trouble starts. Official data are hard to compare across judicial systems. First, offence definitions may vary. The Netherlands penal code is already different from the French penal code and the material properties of the acts for which defendants are in practice convicted of violent offences may differ too. Secondly, the administrative systems may differ, meaning that offences and convictions are registered differently in official records. There are several other reasons for incongruities between countries. All in all, comparison of such data over countries is therefore always an endeavour to be extremely cautious in.

The European sourcebook (wp.unil.ch/europeansourcebook/) that we already briefly mentioned above is an attempt by a number of researchers, all from countries that are member to the Council of Europe, to synchronise statistics on the criminal justice system. Using uniform definitions, all these researchers have teased out from their own respective countries' official data a number of key statistics. Because of the uniform operationalisations employed over countries, these statistics are comparable over countries. So, if the European Sourcebook tells us that in the Netherlands in 2000 an average 24.6 persons were convicted of theft, and in Germany this figure was much lower at 13.1, we can be pretty confident that we are not comparing apples and oranges, and may start wondering what may be the cause for these differences. The 2007-2011 version appeared in 2014, see wp.unil.ch/europeansourcebook/ and heuni.fi/en/index/tiedotteet/2014/09/europeansourcebookofcrimeandcriminaljusticestatistics2014published.html.

The United Nations (un.org) also maintain numerous international statistics and databases, see for an example unstats.un.org/unsd/demographic/products/vitstats/. These statistics have generally been less scrupulously synchronised over countries, but are nevertheless better comparable than the statistics produced by the respective countries for national use – the flip side of this being that a statistic published by the UN and that same statistic published by the original country may sometimes differ! Within the UN, the ODCCP (Office on Drugs and Crime) has as its special task to collect statistical information on crime. All data is downloadable from their website (see unodc.org).

The World Health Organisation also compiles statistics on causes of death, amongst which deaths due to violence, such as homicide: who.int/violence_injury_prevention/violence/world_report/en/index.html.

11.5 Data from surveys

Official data are what we call *secondary* data. They have been collected by others, for various purposes, using sometimes different quality standards from ours or collection methods that they may not reveal. Sometimes such data employ classifications that bother us, such as the 'lumping' of characteristics that we might want to disaggregate. For instance, the police may report statistics on sexual offences, but we might be interested to investigate whether rapes have – as the newspapers say – increased. The police have not disaggregated sexual offences into rape, sexual assault, sexual acts against minors, etc., so the police data do not help to answer our question. So, if particular data are needed to answer the research question, or if data are needed at the offender level (i.e. on a micro level), researchers often (need to) resort to gathering those data themselves. Such data we call *primary* data. They are collected by the researchers themselves, often through surveys, relatively large scale investigations of a sample of the population. For criminology, two types of surveys are particularly important: victim surveys (surveys of possible victims) and self-report surveys (surveys of possible offenders). Before discussing those, we will first discuss some general issues of surveys.

11.5.1 Surveys

A survey is a generally fairly extensive study in which properties of a sample out of the population are collected. Surveys are mostly studies where the sample members are approached directly and observed or interviewed. Instead of interviewing, paper and pencil questionnaires may be used, and – increasingly – online questionnaires or questionnaires on laptops. For a discussion of their relative merits, we refer to section 4.2.

While much more costly, face-to-face interviewing has the advantage that the interviewer who is present can clarify questions if necessary, can put the respondent at ease, can refer the respondent to organisations at the end of the interview. For those respondents who refuse when the interviewer turns up at their doorstep, the interviewer can ask for the reason for refusal (see further on this topic section 3.6 and section 4.2), and can take down characteristics of the house of this respondent: does it look shabby, are the curtains drawn in the daytime, what kind of neighbourhood does the refusing respondent live in? Are there used needles in the street? Abandoned supermarket carts? Or does it look really neat?

While especially web interviews are efficient and cheap, for certain topics it might be better to conduct face-to-face interviews, such as interviews on sexual violence victimisation. If interviews are held on such emotional topics (sexual violence, domestic violence), interviewers usually have with them referral addresses, booklets and flyers from organisations that the victim can contact if he or she wants assistance in coming to terms with victimisation and its aftermath. It is said that especially in interviews after sexual violence, victims may suffer from secondary victimisation due to the interview: the interview itself makes victims relive their experiences, or brings back complaints, and in that sense the interview re-traumatises the victim. Caution, good preparation, good training of interviewers, good protocols, and of course REB permission (see section 2.9.1) are warranted.

11.5.2 Victim surveys

Victim surveys are generally regarded as a valid method to obtain information on the incidence of crime and the characteristics of victims. The idea is that while police data suffer from registration and reporting bias, culminating in a sizeable dark number, tailored surveys among the general population do not suffer from such distortions and biases.

Victim surveys are in fact nothing more than relatively standard questionnaires administered to a sample of the general population, in which particular questions are asked on victimisation. In general, respondents are asked whether they became a victim of offences, such as theft, assault, burglary etc. If they respond in the positive, further questions are asked, such as when the offence took place, who the perpetrator was, whether the victim was hurt, what the damages were, and whether the victim went to the police to report the offence and whether the victim actually signed a statement (so that the crime was recorded in the police statistics). Also, if the victim did not go to the police to report the crime, it is asked why he or she did not do so. These questions are very important for understanding the link between incidence levels of crime as recorded by the police and incidence as inferred from victim surveys. In principle, the latter two should – with some weighting for sample proportions, match.

Official statistics and victimisation estimates from victim surveys generally do not match, however. This is so for several reasons. To start with, a number of crimes are not captured by victim surveys. So-called 'victimless' crimes, such as drugs dealing or vandalism, cannot be reported by victims. Secondly, victims may forget certain incidents. Or, they may overreport – although this is believed to be much less prevalent. Some crimes are measured less well with victim surveys. It is for instance generally assumed that sexual offences are seriously underreported in victim surveys: Lisak and Miller (2002) mention that around 80% is not mentioned. For rape, reporting may be better, and it may be better for sexual crimes committed by strangers, but much depends on the social stigma that sexual crimes bear in a society. Also, the exact wording of surveys, and the purpose of the survey can have a wide impact on prevalence rates: Jewkes and Abrahams (2002) report a nationally representative 12-month rape prevalence from the 1999 South African National Survey of Victims at 390 per 100,000 women aged 17 and over. From a different study, by Jewkes, Penn-Kekana, Levin *et al.* (1999), that was non-representative as it was conducted in three provinces but did have much more tailored wording and a sensitive questionnaire environment conducive to reporting rape, a 12-month rape prevalence of 1,300 per 100,000 women aged 18-49 years was reported. In all likelihood, the geographical differences and different age range in both surveys cannot explain away the huge, more than threefold difference in prevalence, and part must be attributed to method differences – the most striking of which is the wording of the questions. Surveying sexual crimes is probably best done with tailored surveys.

Victim surveys are generally administered to respondents of 15 years and older. This is problematic as we know that many children are also victimised, often by their parents. This makes for an inherent discrepancy with police data. It is generally assumed that for questioning children, special questionnaires are needed; one example is the Juvenile Victimisation Questionnaire (JVQ) developed by Hamby and Finkelhor, see `unh.edu/ccrc/jvq/available_versions.html`, and see also Hamby and Finkelhor (2000). A second discrepancy may occur because a survey's definition of a crime need not be identical to the criminal law definition.

In general, victim surveys attempt to use wording that describes pretty factually the type of victimisation that is asked after. So one would not easily encounter questions such as: 'Were you assaulted during the past year?', but rather questions like 'Did someone push you, hit you, slap you during the past year?' The wording of the questions should be such, that the questions ask after as factual issues as possible and leave little room for interpretation by the respondent. For instance, the International Crime Victimisation Survey (ICVS, see below) asks after (attempted) robbery in the following manner: *'Over the past five years has anyone stolen something from you by using force or threatening you, or did anybody try to steal something from you by using force or threatening force?'* to which respondents can answer *'Yes'*, *'No'*, or *'Do not know'*. This question is what is called a *screener question*. Once a respondent indicates that he or she has undergone this particular crime, a bunch of follow-up questions are then asked such as when exactly this happened, where it happened, who the offender was, what the consequences of the offence were for the victim, whether the offence was reported to the police, whether it was recorded, how the victim felt about the way the police dealt with the offence, etc.

Most surveys ask back a certain period, the so-called reference period or *recall period*. If one would ask whether a certain incident had ever happened to the respondent, one would be asking after the *lifetime victimisation prevalence*. While this may be an interesting figure, it is not very useful for assessing current victimisation trends: much of the life-time prevalence may actually have been incurred in childhood. In the question we just showed, the respondent is asked after incidence five years back.

Researchers differ in what they consider a good reference period for assessing victimisation prevalence. While the ICVS employs five years, many other surveys do not ask back over periods longer than one year, or even 6 months. One reason to do so is that memory loss becomes a bigger issue – particularly it is assumed for less serious offences – with a longer recall period. A second reason to do so, is that respondents have better 'anchors' if one keeps the reference period relatively short. For secondary school pupils, the period is often 'this school year' as pupils will generally be able to anchor what happened to them using cues related to the school grade they are in.

In this latter case, the issue is not so much to prevent forgetting incidents, as preventing misplacement in time. This faulty time-framing of events is called *telescoping*. What is meant by that is the all too common phenomenon that when we remember something, and try to remember when exactly that happened, we often catch ourselves discovering that the incident happened actually much longer ago than we thought: 'Oh! is that already so long ago!' Like other people, respondents in surveys have the tendency to 'telescope' events, to perceive things as closer by in time than they actually are. A shorter recall period is believed to aid in minimising such telescoping effects.

Many countries administer their own yearly or biyearly victim surveys. Apart from such general surveys, also many tailored surveys are administered, for instance into domestic violence or, as illustrated above, sexual violence. With support from the UN as well as the European Union, an *International Crime Victim Survey* is held with some regularity. This *International Crime Victim Survey (ICVS)* was administered in 1989, 1992, 1996, 2000, 2004-2005 and 2010. The questionnaire is uniform over all collaborating countries, with minor adaptations in translation. This survey has the same advantage for international comparison of victimisation prevalence rates that the European Sourcebook has for official statistics: the questionnaire and sampling and data collection method are synchronised over countries so that the data suffer from minimal *method differences*, and prevalence rates are therefore comparable over countries. In each wave, approximately 50,000 respondents were contacted. For most participating industrialised countries, the interviews were carried out over the telephone. For non-industrialised countries, and countries with low telephone penetration, face-to-face interviewing was employed.

The sampling method is through *random digit dialing* (RDD): telephone numbers were generated randomly and the numbers called. For the Netherlands the response rate of the 2005 wave was 46% with approximately 1,200 respondents successfully interviewed. For less developed countries, mostly only major cities were surveyed with an additional rural sample. For findings for a number of African countries, see Naudé, Prinsloo and Ladikos (2006).

The ICVS has questions on victimisation for ten 'conventional crimes': vehicle related crimes, (attempted) burglary, theft of personal property, and robbery, sexual offences, assaults and threats. In most countries, questions have been added on street-level corruption, consumer fraud, including internet-based fraud and credit card theft, drug-related problems and hate crimes. Also, the questionnaire asks after fear of crime and reporting behaviour. For details see `unicri.it/services/library_documentation/publications/icvs/data/`. An informative website is `wp.unil.ch/icvs/`. An overview of the various ICVSs is given by Van Kesteren, Van Dijk and Mayhew (2014).

11.5.3 Self-report surveys

Instead of asking possible victims after experienced crimes, we could of course also ask possible offenders about committed offences. Such surveys are called self-report studies or self-report surveys. Self-report surveys are most often conducted with juveniles. A usual format is where pupils fill out questionnaires while in the classroom. Response rates are generally high, and respondents are generally – and sometimes amazingly – open about offences they committed. Self-report studies generally can be conducted from ages where juveniles have sufficient reading ability to fill out questionnaires. Mostly this is at age 12, although younger respondents have been included as well. With adult respondents, self-report studies are much less common.

It is known that some respondents answer less openly than others. Others overreport in the sense that they report each and every minor transgression. Some may even 'brag'. In that sense, there are definitely validity issues. Validation studies have shown that – depending on the type of offence and the type of respondent – between 10% and 60 – 70% of all offences is reported in such self-report surveys. It is believed that more serious offences, and especially sex offences, are underreported. More recently committed offences also appear to be somewhat underreported. See Van der Heijden, Van Gils, Bouts *et al.* (2000).

To enhance the quality of the data, some self-report studies have therefore built in an option, where the face-to-face interviewer for certain questions ('Did you hit, slap, push or punch someone in the past year in such a way that that person was injured?') reverses the laptop and lets the respondent him/herself type in the answer. After hitting the `ENTER` button, the laptop is reversed back again, and the interviewer cannot go back to the original answer to the question.

As a warning against possible undisclosed offending and other untrue answers, some surveys ask respondents as a last question how truthfully they replied to the questionnaire:

'Did you reply to the questions: a. honestly, b. mostly honestly, c. mostly dishonestly?' This question does not help the researchers in assessing the true level of offending. It does however signal invalidity of answers.

An International Self-reported Delinquency Study (ISRD) was started in 1990, at the initiative of the research center of the then Netherlands Ministry of Justice, the WODC. Together with researchers from other countries, a 'core'-questionnaire was designed, to which some countries added questions, or deleted questions from. A total of 11 countries participated when the first wave of the study was carried out in 1994: the Netherlands, Switzerland, Portugal, Spain, England and Wales, Finland, the USA, Germany, Italy, Northern Ireland and Belgium. Only the first five countries had succeeded in drawing a nationally representative sample for the survey; the other countries had interviewed only town dwellers. For the Netherlands 1,000 respondents in the age range 14-21 participated.

The ISRD asked after 'ever offending' (a sort of lifetime-measure) and offending in the past calendar year. A fourth of all respondents (25%) reported violent offending during the past year. Lifetime figures were higher, and varied quite a bit: 94% of Finnish respondents had ever committed an offence, for England and Wales this was 58%. See Junger-Tas, Haen Marshall and Ribeaud (2003).

A second wave was conducted in 2007 (He & Haen Marshall, 2010); a third wave is reportedly underway at the time of writing of this book. The ISRD has the same advantage for the international comparison of offending rates that the European Sourcebook has for official statistics, and the ICVS has for victimisation rates: the questionnaire and sampling and data collection method are as much as possible synchronised over countries. This means that the data suffer from minimal *method differences*, and that prevalence rates are therefore comparable over countries

11.6 On the differences between official and survey crime data

In their authoritative overview 'The self-report method for measuring delinquency and crime' (2000, accessible at `ncjrs.gov/App/Publications/abstract.aspx?ID=185538`), Thornberry and Krohn cite the renowned American criminologist Thorsten Sellin who wrote in 1931: *"the value of a crime rate decreases as the distance from the crime itself in terms of procedure increases"* (Sellin, 1931, p. 337). So, data from prisons are less useful than data from court records that are again less useful than prosecutor's office data etc. For statements on crime levels, data become less and less valid as they are collected from institutions higher up the criminal justice chain. The reason for this is that at every layer or level, new distorting mechanisms play a role: victim reporting behaviour, efforts of the police to clear offences, prosecutorial policy, etc. This implies that crime is best measured as closely to the source as possible.

One possibility for that is the victim survey. We can simply ask people whether they became the victim of an offence. The other possibility is to move even closer to the source of the criminal behaviour, and that is: the offender. We can ask samples of respondents whether they committed certain offences. For both types of surveys we can either ask after one-year prevalence or life-time prevalence, or five years back. In general, it appears that sexual offences assume a special position: both in victim as well as self-report surveys they tend to be underreported.

11.7 Special data collection strategies

11.7.1 Randomised response

As stated above, one problem with criminological research is that the data we wish to obtain are 'sensitive'. Those involved may not wish to share the information we researchers are after, because they are ashamed to talk about their deeds or their experiences, or because they fear or may not want to risk reprisals. If the researcher knows that person X has committed an offence, there is always a risk, so respondents may argue – in spite of promises of confidentiality and the like – that this gets exposed.

An elegant way to deal with this reluctance of respondents to talk about their offending behaviour is to actually *sever* the link between the identity of the respondent and the behaviour in question. This method is called randomised response and the procedure is as follows. After asking a number of factual questions in an interview situation, such as the respondent's age, education, family situation and the like, the interviewer moves on to questions about offending behaviour. As a simplified example, the interviewer may want to know whether the offender: a. stole something last year, b. assaulted someone last year c. vandalised something last year. Before posing these questions, the interviewer in each instance asks the interviewee to toss a coin. The interviewee inspects the result and does not tell the interviewer whether heads or tails is up. The interviewer then tells the respondent to respond 'yes' if heads are up, and to give a truthful answer if tails are up. This procedure is repeated for each sensitive question. So, whenever the respondent finds heads, s/he answers 'yes' (a forced answer) and whenever s/he finds tails, s/he answers the question (a real answer).

Now, the interviewer is left with virtually useless answers to each of the three questions for this particular respondent: if the respondent answered 'no', then we know for sure that s/he did not steal something last year. However, if s/he answered 'yes', we do not know whether that is because s/he actually did steal something or whether that is because heads were up. And we can never find out why the respondent answered 'yes' because that was visible to the respondent only. For each question, the respondent tossed the coin, and replied 'yes' for heads and only gave a truthful answer in 50% of the cases, namely when tails were up.

However, while the answers may not be useful at the individual level, at the aggregate level they are. Suppose that we conducted interviews in the above described manner for 100 respondents. And suppose that, for the stealing question, 60 respondents replied 'yes' and 40 replied 'no'. We know that, by chance, we would expect 50 respondents to reply 'yes' anyway, because we know that coins have a 50% chance that their heads side turns up when we toss them. So, this means that 50 of the 60 'yes'-answers are simply due to the result of the toss, and that 10 of the 60 can be assumed to be truthful answers to the stealing question. All in all, this means that out of 50 persons giving a truthful answer as the coin's tails was up, 10 said they did steal something and 40 said they did not steal something.

This means that we can estimate that 20% of our respondents stole something last year.

This data collection method is called 'randomised response'. Validation studies have shown that randomised response methods give notably better results (in terms of the prevalence of reported offending behaviour) than other interviewing methods. This applies not only to surveys on offending behaviour, but also to surveys on other sensitive issues such as sexual behaviour or alcohol use; see Van der Heijden, Van Gils, Bouts *et al.* (2000). Lensvelt-Mulders and Hox (2004) and Lensvelt-Mulders, Hox, Van der Heijden *et al.* (2005) showed that with increasing sensitiveness of the research questions, the gain of the use of randomised response methods increases.

Other designs for randomised response data collection are possible. In the example given above, respondents know that there is a 50% chance that any respondent answers 'yes' when responding to the question on stealing. Formulated differently, respondents in the example given above know that if they admit to committing an offence because they did commit an offence, their answer easily blends in the background of the many positive answers. However, randomised response is in that sense an expensive method: half of our respondents serve as 'cover' for the other half who are instructed to give truthful answers. Of course this cover is effective, but even so, if we could provide a seemingly as effective cover and be able to make use of a larger part of our data that would be better. Sikkel, Van der Heijden and Van Gils (2006) designed a more efficient set-up where respondents are asked to roll two dice, and instructed to respond 'yes' when the sum of the two dice is 2, 3 or 4 or when it is 11 or 12, and to respond truthfully to the question when the sum is 5, 6, 7, 8, 9 or 10. To the lay-eye, this may appear like an even division: it appears that the chance for a true answer or a forced 'yes' answer is about equal. However, the likelihood that a respondent is instructed to truthfully respond to the question is 27/36, or 75%. In this way, respondents may tend to believe that they have more cover than they actually have, and less data is collected for cover only.

A number of assumptions are made in a randomised response method. The first one is, that the respondent *understands* the procedure. Particularly for less highly educated respondents with limited intellectual capacities, one may wonder whether that is the case. Also, it can be doubted whether highly distrustful persons will not suspect some 'trick'. In the examples with the dice or the coin, tricks are hard to envisage. However, suppose that interviewing is Computer-Assisted (like CAPI) and dice are thrown or numbers generated randomly by the computer, some may suspect that the researcher will be able to match their identity with the numbers that determine the type of answer given.

All in all, respondents in the randomised response method who roll dice or flip coins do not need to trust the interviewer's promise of confidentiality, as they are *de facto* anonymous and protected as the link between the respondent's identity and the sensitive issues in question is cut. The answers have meaning only at the aggregate level.

One disadvantage of this would appear to be that we cannot link the respondents' background characteristics to the sensitive behaviour we are measuring. However, if we would compare, within our sample, male and female respondents, assuming that the prevalence of real and forced answers is the same in both groups, we can compare the proportion of 'yes' and 'no' answers between males and females, and in that manner see what effect gender has on the proportion of positive answers. This can be done for other variables too, also continuous variables, such as age. In that manner we are able to establish associations between background characteristics and the behaviour of interest.

Even though randomised response therefore has its limitations, it is an accepted and effective method for eliciting information on sensitive issues. Disadvantages are cost: as part of the respondents serve only for 'cover' we need much bigger sample sizes, although this is, some say, amply compensated by better answers. Also, it is not possible to pose follow-up questions such as on the circumstances of the sensitive behaviour, or any judicial reaction. So far, methods for asking with randomised response not only whether someone committed an offence, but to ask also how often that offence was committed are in their infancy only. Researchers should carefully test their randomised response designs, paying particular attention to whether respondents understand what is expected of them.

11.7.2 Capture-recapture

In criminology, we sometimes want to estimate the size of a population that we cannot measure. Mostly this is so, because the members of this population do not want to be measured. They are illegal residents, or they are criminals. In each case, we do not have a listing of these people we are interested in. This situation is often encountered in criminology. It is also encountered in other disciplines. Some populations are so elusive, or live in the margins of our society where they exist by virtue of remaining unknown, that they are unregistered.

While this situation is often encountered in criminology, it is not unique for criminology. Particularly biologists are also often faced with this complication. Suppose that I want to know how many baboons live in the Jebel Imatong area in southern Sudan, or how many fish lake Victoria holds? Biologists (and it appears a fisheries expert named Petersen; see for an historical overview of the invention of the capture-recapture technique Goudie and Goudie, 2007) have developed a conceptually simple method for estimating the size of a population when it is impossible to enumerate its members. The method works as follows.

Suppose indeed that we are standing in front of a lake and that we want to know how many fish are in that lake. What we can do to discover that is the following. We catch 10 fish, we tag them, and throw the poor animals back into the lake. We stir the lake with a very big wooden spoon. After a while, we re-catch 10 fish. Suppose that of that second catch, one fish has a tag, and is therefore one of the original catch. We then estimate that the lake contains 100 fish. An intuitive way to understand how this estimate is arrived at is by imagining that if we would want to recapture all original 10 tagged fish, we would need to do another nine catches to retrieve them all, in which case we would end up with a total of 100 fish.

The method works from a number of assumptions. Firstly, it is assumed that the population is closed: no members leave the population between the first and the second catch (fish do not leave the lake, nor do they die or are new fish born). Second, it is assumed that all fish are equally likely to be caught. Third, it is assumed that matching between the first and second list is perfect (fish do not lose their tag). Fourthly, it is assumed that capture the first time does not influence capture the second time: the catches are independent.

This method is called capture-recapture. Outside of biology and animal ecology and other areas, it has been applied in criminology to estimate the size of the population of illegal residents (Engbersen, Staring, Van der Leun *et al.*, 2002), to estimate the number of illegal weapon holders, and to estimate the number of drunk drivers (Van der Heijden, Cruyff & Van Houwelingen, 2003). In practice, the method works as follows. For instance, for estimating the size of the illegal population, two lists are compared: one that contains all apprehended illegal residents in say, January 2017, and one that contains all apprehended illegal residents in January 2018. The lists are compared, and the total number of people apprehended the first time is registered (A) and the total number of people apprehended the second time is registered (B), as well as the overlap between the two lists (M). The total number of people (i.e. the size of the population) from where the two lists were drawn is then estimated.

Figure 11.1 gives a simple example of the technique. Suppose that we have two lists of illegal residents who were registered during police patrols, in December and January: list 1 and list 2. The number of people on list 1 is 5, we call this number A. The number of people on list 2 is 6, we call this number B. The number of people who appear both on list 1 and list 2 equals 2, we call this number M. Assuming that appearing on list 1 and appearing on list 2 are independent events, the probability to appear on both lists is the product of these two probabilities:

$$\frac{A}{N} \times \frac{B}{N} = \frac{M}{N},$$

with N the unknown size of the population. This can be reworked into:

$$\frac{A \times B}{N^2} = \frac{M}{N},$$

so that:

$$\frac{A \times B}{M} = \frac{N^2}{N},$$

so that:

$$\frac{A \times B}{M} = N.$$

This shows that we can use A, the number of people on list 1, times B, the number of people on list 2, divided by M, the number of people on both lists, as an estimate for N. In formula:

$$\hat{N} = \frac{A \times B}{M}.$$

This means that if we have two lists with names of individuals, we can use the overlap between the two lists to estimate the size of the total population of individuals, under the assumptions given above. See Figure 11.1.

Of course, for applying this method and getting good results, we must firstly be sure that the individuals are well-matched. If we fail to match a person who is on list A with the same person on list B, for instance because the name is spelled differently, M becomes too small, the denominator too small, and we overestimate the size of the population. In biology, this is often referred to as 'tag loss'. If we over-match, the population size is underestimated. When the assumptions are violated, the methods do not estimate the size of the population accurately.

Figure 11.1: Example of capture-recapture situation

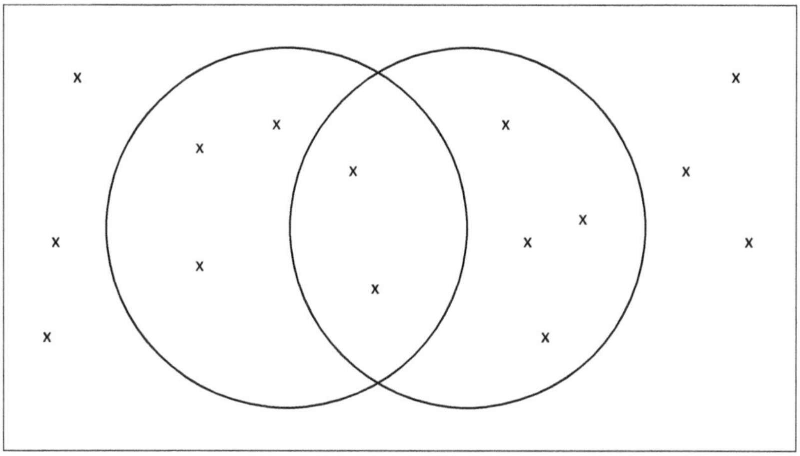

Obviously, in many practical instances of research, we can not be sure that the assumptions are met. Often, we are even pretty sure that they are violated. Does this mean that the method cannot be used at all? Not necessarily.

Some violations are worse than others. If the population is not closed, this means that we do know the A, B and M, but that $N_1 \neq N_2$. We are then left with an equation that has too many unknowns. As we said, under-matching (tag loss) and overmatching of people on lists seriously biases the estimates. For instance if we study illegal immigrants, who may have different or no ID cards, and who may work under one name and in reality have another name, one should be very careful to check whether this assumption can realistically be assumed to hold. If there is under-matching (which is in general more likely than overmatching) the results cannot be trusted anymore.

With the advent of computer technology, 'linkage' and 'deduplication' technology (that is, methods to identify people or units that are identical) has much improved. This includes the possibility to employ a probabilistic matching process in the sense that units are not just considered either 'match' or a 'non-match', but that probabilities for a match are given. Also, nice features are available such as software that matches people not on identical spelling of the name, but on the similarity of the pronunciation of the name (where 'Thornberry' and 'Thornbury' would be considered a probable match). It is also possible to attach more importance to some characteristics that are considered more stable and unchangeable (height) than to others (a beard). Extensive, sometimes technical, discussion of such and other techniques can be found in Herzog, Scheuren and Winkler (2007), and in Christen (2012).

Obviously, if the time between the first catch and the second catch is long, there will be some population loss (and maybe some replacement as well), and in general populations will never be entirely closed. But, in the case of the illegal residents example, if there had been massive repatriations of illegals between the first and second catch, this might seriously affect the estimates. Dependence between lists also biases the estimates. If there is positive dependence (those who appear on list 1 are more likely to appear on list 2 than those who don't), the estimates will be biased downward: estimates of N are too small. If there is negative dependence (those who appear on list 1 are less likely to appear on list 2), the estimates will be biased upward: estimates of N are too large. The last assumption, equal capture probability, may be unlikely too.

Capture-recapture methods can be extended to multiple lists. The advantage of this is that more data can be used and in principle better estimates obtained. Such methods are commonly referred to as either 'capture-recapture methods with multiple lists' or as 'multiple systems estimation'. We discuss these in section 13.3.5. Numerous examples of capture-recapture methods and multiple systems estimation for the social and medical sciences are given in Bohning, Van der Heijden and Bunge (2017), including their statistical foundations.

11.7.3 Indirect surveys

Researchers have devised a number of other inventive strategies to obtain data on crimes. We will not discuss these in detail, but mention the gist of such methods, namely to tap information on crimes from other sources. A first example is to check hospital records. Those who are brought in with gunshot wounds, with stab wounds, are generally victims of violent offences. In the Netherlands, researchers have attempted to assess the prevalence of violent victimisation through report forms, filled in by first-aid nurses. Nurses had to fill in what the injuries of the patient were, and what the causes were (fighting, accidents, etc).

A second way is through insurance data (assuming that companies would be willing to grant access). The number of burglary claim forms will give an approximation of the number of burglaries. Other creative strategies have been designed. The idea is all the time, that one does not search for the crime or the criminal behaviour itself, but for (almost) necessary sequels to the crime – that should ideally be registered with a certain completeness.

We will encounter an example of such indirect surveying in section 13.4.2, where satellite images of soil were used to estimate crime prevalence.

11.8 Triangulation

In criminology, because of uncertainty about the quality of the central variable – with police data suffering from a sizeable dark number, possibly overrepresenting less clever offenders and offences that the police targets and with victim surveys underrepresenting certain offences – increasing emphasis is on triangulation of findings. Triangulation is a term from land surveying. To determine the exact location of a point, it should be viewed from two angles. The two views towards that point constitute a triangle, hence triangulation.

In the context of research, triangulation indicates the use of multiple, different methods to study one and the same phenomenon. Such studies are therefore also referred to as a mixed methods study. If I would study whether violent offending by girls is on the rise in my home town, I could use police data. I might then see that indeed the number of arrests of girls in my home town for violent offences is going up. But does that tell me whether female crime is on the rise, or whether police policy is now focused on intervening early in the lives of these violent women? It might be wise, given the various degrees of freedom in the interpretation of the police data, to add some more information. It might be wise for instance to interview a number of youth workers from the neighbourhoods that these girls come from. Or to interview heads of secondary schools. These interviews might inform me that the rise is due to two gangs that have recently been formed. Or that there is in fact a decrease, and that the rising police registrations are due to a clamp down on a troubled neighbourhood where both boys and girls were involved in drugs dealing. Or that the number of arrests is indeed rising, and girls are more often involved in fights than they used to be, but that the incidents are minor.

Where we employ triangulation in this example, we use different methods, that each have their weaknesses and strengths. Using different methods for answering the same question, the aim is to have the methods each compensate for the weakness of the other: the quantitative method gives us the broad overview, the qualitative method gives us understanding of the dynamics generating the data.

Part V

STATISTICS AND RESEARCH METHODOLOGY IN SUPRANATIONAL CRIMINOLOGY

Chapter 12

Issues in the study of international crimes

The next four chapters will discuss statistical and methodological particularities in the study of conflicts and international crimes. Four chapters will follow as we adhere to the *tesseras criminologica*. We will therefore discuss methodological and statistical issues per pillar: for studying the prevalence, i.e. the number of crimes that have been committed (homicide or in a broader sense mortality, sexual offences, property offences and other offences; chapter 13), etiology (the risk factors and causes for offending; chapter 14), reactions to international crimes (prosecution, sentencing, truth commissions, amnesties; chapter 15), and victims (victims' needs and the long-term consequences of international crimes; chapter 16).

The statistical issues we will encounter are often not particular to the criminological pillar studied. As we will show in the following chapters, drawing a good (random) sample during or after post-conflict situations may be compromised. If we are unable to draw a representative sample this affects the generality of our statements whether we are attempting to arrive at prevalence estimates or whether we are studying perpetrators or victims. Such problems in drawing good samples also occur when studying non-conflict situations, such as when we are unable to sample drugs traders or victims of sexual violence.

However, the fact that we are studying people in situations of widespread conflict and population upheaval – in which in general two or more parties fight for their own aims, parties of which one is more often than not a government that may be attempting to hide or minimise the destruction from the eyes of the world, the 'international community' and aid organises, conflicts that occur frequently in less developed countries, in which in general massive mortality is incurred – does generate a number of particular problems over and above regular methodological issues. We will outline these below before we discuss particularities per criminological pillar in the ensuing chapters.

12.1 Thin, incomplete and biased data

To start with, in many conflict situations, the government of a country is itself party to the conflict. It may also be that a country or an area where international crimes are committed is effectively not ruled at all. Whichever of these is the case, this has implications for the availability and quality of data.

Conflicts do not erupt spontaneously. This means that before a conflict becomes manifest, tensions may have been smouldering. Certain ethnic groups may have feel repressed for a while, the ruling elite may have attempted to marginalize religious groups. In many instances, this has implications for the reliability of baseline data. For Rwanda before the 1994 genocide, it has been reported that many Tutsi preferred to label themselves as Hutu in population administration systems. Brunborg (2009), in attempting to assess the size and ethnic composition of Kosovo in the early 1990s, notes that it is hard to rely on the 1991 census as that census was boycotted by Albanians. In southern Sudan, in which civil wars raged from 1955 - 1972 and from 1983 - 2005, the last census over those years that can be judged reliable was conducted in the mid 1950s by the British colonial administrators. For many conflict areas, it appears we have suspect, unreliable, biased or simply no baseline statistics. As we will see in the following chapters, good baseline data are vital for some estimation methods.

However, even if good baseline data were available, such as from censuses, the conflicts during which international crimes occur often generate massive population upheaval. This means that people are dispersed, have moved to relatives or to IDP camps, or even across the border. This makes it very difficult to draw samples of the reference population in a traditional way, such as through an existing sampling frame. Those who have remained behind are often a select subset of the population, and we cannot generalize our findings from that subset to the entire population.

Secondly, in most peaceful countries of the world the government (i.e. the police and the criminal justice authorities) attempt to apprehend criminals and record the numbers of crimes committed. However, if the authorities themselves are involved in atrocities, this may mean that the police do not attempt to uncover crimes, but may in fact be actively attempting to hide crimes committed by the authorities. This we label as a *double dark number*.

In ordinary research settings, i.e. settings where we study crimes committed on a national scale so to say, the deficiencies of police data can be compensated by conducting so-called victim surveys (cf. section 11.5.2). We then ask a sample of the population whether they during a certain recall period became victims of a list of crimes. If we find that, say, 10% report that their bicycle was stolen the past year, we can – assuming the sample is representative of the population – extrapolate these findings to the population to conclude that 10% of all citizens had their bike stolen. However, for studying international crimes, victim surveys may be less straightforward to use. Firstly, as will be detailed below, mortality in international criminology is often assessed through so-called household studies: a 'main' family member is asked how many people lived in his or her household during a certain designated period, and how many died (and of what causes). However, in conflicts with extremely high mortality, or where entire villages have been wiped out, entire families may have died. In that case, it is impossible to find a respondent to report on that mortality. For sexual violence committed during conflicts, it is often found that victims of sexual violence are extremely reluctant to speak of their experiences. For such offences, researchers are faced with what we will refer to as a *triple dark number*: not only is only a fraction of offences reported to the police, and not only do the police not record these crimes well, also victims are unwilling to report them to us as researchers. The well-known dark number of crime is likely much darker when we study international crime.

12.2 Unique and complex events

Conflicts and international crimes are massive events that often defy imagination, but they are also rare. They occur in unique and complex constellations of risk factors. As conflicts and international crimes occur within such intricate multi-layered complex settings, there is in a methodological sense strong confounding. It is hard to isolate the impact of one 'causal agent' from the operation of other factors: generally these all operate simultaneously. We encounter this complication when we study etiology, responses and the aftermath of international criminality.

This implies that 'manipulation' of possible causal agents, a standard methodological tool for investigating the impact of presumed causal factors, is generally impossible. More often than not, for identifying what caused the atrocities to occur, why perpetrators committed these crimes, cannot be studied as we would for other phenomena. While this is not unique to criminological research (we also could not manipulate in the methodological sense child abuse victimisation), the rare and unique nature of international crimes makes it very difficult if not at times impossible to find matching periods, regions, non-perpetrators, non-victims etc.

12.3 Dangerous research conditions

Collecting data in post-conflict (and especially during conflict) situations can obviously be difficult. Data collection may be dangerous. Some areas may be too risky to venture into at all. This can imply that sampling is affected (not all regions or villages that were randomly selected can be approached), and so generalizability is at stake. It may also mean that certain questions cannot be asked, thus making that we do not achieve our research aims. In terse situations, the authorities may choose to have researchers 'monitored' by their staff. This can turn out to be not only annoying, but may lead to harassment for interviewees, problems for local interviewers, or to increased refusal rates by respondents for fear of harassment. In such conditions, it will be very difficult to ensure the principle of non maleficence ('Do No Harm'-principle).

Risky conditions may also make it impossible to do research for mundane reasons, such as that insurance companies do not cover our staff anymore. But even if conditions are still workable in some regions of an area in conflict, the fact that we do not venture into those areas that are considered too dangerous also affects the quality of our data: those areas are where we would expect more crime to have occurred, where victimise was highest. Generalising from the areas that are safe affects our estimates: we are likely to underestimate the severity of what happened.

12.4 Charged research environment

Then, research into international crimes takes place in a generally heavily 'politicised' or morally charged environment. Often, gross human rights violations are taking place or have taken place, on a large scale. This means that multitudes have suffered, and may be damaged for life. Mortality estimates have been produced that were heavily contested, often when low estimates of victimisation appeared to pay no justice to the scope of the atrocities, or to jeopardize the release of relief funds. This author had an article rejected for publication by a journal because its lower than until then accepted estimate of victimisation was according to one reviewer 'belittling the suffering of victims'. The opposite has occurred too, when estimates of mortality were so high that they elicited denial by responsible parties afraid of political fallout.

Non-governmental organises (NGOs) have generally flocked to the locations where internally displaced persons (IDPs) fled, and attempt to aid the destitute. Aid organises however are more often than not badly in need of money to be able to dispense aid as – at times – the United Nations and the international community may be slow and less than forthcoming with money to finance aid operations. This means that data provided by independent NGOs (often the only ones with access to the field) may not be always as completely independent as would be desirable. Conversely, some NGOs may not be willing to share any information, as they may want to preserve their neutrality.

12.5 A new and unshared methodology

Lastly, the relatively new field of supranational criminology does not have its own methodology (yet). Epidemiologists, lawyers, psychologists, development economists, anthropologists, sociologists and demographers all have flocked to this field. Researchers from these different disciplines all have their own methodological traditions, shared and agreed upon within each respective discipline. Psychologists tend to use quantitative methods, prefer large and representative samples, and focus strongly on measurement aspects, such as scale construction and reliability of their measures. Anthropologists on the other hand often use ethnographic methods, that are qualitative, generally study small samples that do not even strive to be representative.

International crimes are thus being studied by researchers from a wide array of disciplines. Each researcher brings his or her own methodological tradition to this field. But these traditions do not necessarily prescribe the same method for investigating one problem. Etiology can be studied using 'hard-core' quantitative regression-type methods or through in-depth qualitative interviews. Not surprisingly, studies conducted from such different disciplinary backgrounds need not generate the same answers (often they in fact ask different questions). This juxtaposition of methodological traditions we find in all domains of criminological interest: prevalence, etiology, reaction and victims.

Indeed, in the past years mortality estimates have been published that were generated through different methods – leading to widely diverging estimates. And even when researchers used essentially similar techniques, such as household surveys, also different estimates have been the result. This is partly due to the fact that the field of study is relatively new. The application of sophisticated survey methods in unsettled conditions, often unfamiliar to (western) researchers is a relatively new area of expertise.

Until a solid body of methodological knowledge has been generated on which – importantly – researchers agree, diverging estimates will continue to occur, and thus far researchers do not necessarily agree to disagree. In fact, scenes have been witnessed by this author at conferences where researchers got involved in vitriolic fights over methods and data quality. In some cases, external bodies have examined the widely ranging estimates from different studies conducted by researchers from different disciplines and passed judgment as to which study (and what estimate therefore) is likely the best, or the least problematic.

Chapter 13

Investigating prevalence

13.1 Introduction

As detailed above, a first question we generally pose in criminology is: 'what happened'? Before we can start explaining crimes, understanding the contexts in which they occurred, or test theories on why offenders committed their crimes, we first need to know what happened. This means assessing what crimes occurred, where, when, how, and how often.

Assessing prevalence is in national contexts already quite complicated (see chapter 11 above). Only a part of offences becomes known to the police, and interviewing victims does not always give us unambiguous data either. Assessing the prevalence of international crimes is much more difficult. As briefly touched upon in the previous chapter, we have to work in an immensely more difficult setting for data collection, we have little or no recourse to police or CJS data, we have in general hardly any baseline data to go upon. Where in a national setting when there has been a homicide, we generally (for the Netherlands in some 80% of cases) have one corpse and one suspect, a coroner's report, witness statements, and transcribed or taped questioning sessions of the alleged perpetrator, for international crimes we may be faced with estimates of thousands of victims whose bodies will mostly never be retrieved – let alone examined. Often it is hard to speak of one 'perpetrator'. Offences occur in confused and unclear circumstances, in which many are scared and very few have an overview. As detailed below, classical notions about perpetrators (men (mostly) with blood on their hands) also become less relevant, as the human toll of international crimes is accrued mostly not through direct killings but for a significant part indirectly.

This chapter will discuss methods to assess mortality as well as the prevalence of other crimes (notably sexual crimes). It devotes much space to methods for assessing mortality. This is firstly so, because mortality is the gravest consequence of international crimes. A second reason is that we will be discussing a variety of methods for assessing mortality, some of which are new to the set of established methods from social science methodology or even criminology, borrowed at times from epidemiology or from demography.

A readable recent book on some of the methods discussed in this chapter is Seybolt, Aronson and Fischhoff (2013). It also contains recommended reading on the politics of the measurement of casualties.

13.2 Definitional and conceptual issues

Before we discuss the available methodologies for measuring mortality, we first review a number of conceptual issues. This is necessary because we need to define what we exactly mean by for instance 'mortality': are we interested only in homicides, i.e. manslaughter and murder? This would be a fairly clear definition, but it has the disadvantage that it misses by a large margin the total human cost of international criminality, or of conflicts in which such crimes are committed. As many examples below will show, mortality due to 'direct' causes, i.e. violence, is but a (sometimes extremely small) fraction of total mortality: for the Democratic Republic of Congo (DRC), it was estimated by 2008 that of 2.1 million excess deaths since the formal end of the war in 2002, only 0.4% was 'direct', that is to say, attributable to violence (Coghlan, Ngoy, Mulumba *et al.*, 2008), so that the remainder was due to indirect causes. Wagner, Heft-Neal, Bhutta *et al.* (2018) demonstrated how conflicts, even geographically removed and even several years back, significantly and substantially impact child mortality, in all likelihood partially through indirect mechanisms. Focusing on direct violence only, therefore misses out on a large part of the picture (or does not altogether get the picture one could say).

But, if we are interested in total mortality and not just in direct deaths, how do we take into account that in peacetime some people would have died as well, i.e. not all deaths are due to the conflict? And what about soldiers? Do we count their deaths as well as being part and parcel of the total human toll? A demographer probably would, but would a prosecutor want to include them in his or her charge? And do we stop counting fatalities once a peace accord has been signed or do we take a broad view and also include elevated mortality after a conflict has formally ended? These issues will first be discussed below.

Second, we discuss a number of essentially epidemiological measures that we need if we want to determine excess mortality. These are the so-called crude mortality rate and under 5 mortality rate, widely employed in epidemiological research. We will briefly discuss each, and end with a few examples.

13.2.1 Direct and indirect mortality

If we want to know how many people died as a consequence of a conflict, we can disaggregate that overall human cost into five categories:

(1) *Military deaths*

During conflicts, soldiers fight and are killed in combat. From a demographic point of view, these military deaths constitute as we said 'part and parcel' of the consequences of that conflict. Whether their deaths constitute a crime is a different matter. Many would choose to exclude them. It should be noted that in some cases their deaths might constitute a crime too (for instance when they are killed after they have been taken as prisoner of war). That their deaths can have massive consequences has been shown in history: after World War I, an entire generation of British women suffered the consequences of the massive deaths in the trenches in northern France: in the 1921 census, for those aged between 25 and 29, there were 1,209 single women for every 1,000 men. When the next census was taken ten years later, 50 per cent of those women were still single. Long-term statistics showed that 35 per cent of them failed to marry during their reproductive years (Nicholson, 2007). Whether fallen soldiers are seen as victims of a crime or not, their deaths affect society as a whole, in various ways, and over an extended period of time, long after the conflict as such has ended.

(2) *Direct civilian deaths*

Next, direct civilian deaths constitute the most obvious manifestation of an (international) crime. Civilians not taking part in the fighting have then been killed, who may have been unarmed, and while they most often will be men, they may also be women and children or the elderly. Civilians are killed in targeted attacks, such as in Rwanda during the genocide, or in Darfur. In that case, these civilian deaths constitute a crime, and the number of civilian victims in conflicts is part and parcel of the death toll of that conflict.

Having said so, some part of direct civilian mortality may nevertheless be classified as 'collateral damage', unavoidable civilian deaths accrued in the pursuit of a legitimate military aim, such as during attacks, or during bombing raids. If such deaths were indeed unavoidable and – importantly – proportional to the aim to be achieved, they need not be labelled as crimes in legal proceedings. Once the extent of civilian casualties becomes 'excessive', such civilian deaths may however constitute crimes. For the Syrian conflict, many have argued that the civilian deaths in eastern Aleppo can be classified as 'excessive' and therewith as war crimes. Whether civilian deaths occur in intrastate or interstate conflicts does not make much of a difference for our evaluation of this type of mortality. See for more general issues also Tabeau (2009, Introduction), and Daponte (2008).

(3) *Indirect civilian deaths*

In conflicts where international crimes are committed, indirect civilian deaths generally greatly exceed direct civilian deaths. Most conflicts generate 'indirect' deaths due to deteriorated health systems, limited access to medical facilities, living in poor hygienic conditions, pollution, destruction of economic infrastructure and subsequent fewer resources for citizens, unemployment, reduced governmental spending on health, reduced social cohesion and traumatic stress in affected populations. All these factors are associated with decreased life expectancy and thus with increased mortality.

Obviously, some indirect civilian mortality can be expected as a consequence of conflict. It is likely unavoidable that civilians are affected by war, as not only military targets are hit, but neighbouring structures and areas where civilians live may be struck as well (although modern warfare may be getting better at preventing this). If hospitals and health facilities or sewage systems are hit, it is likely that civilians will also suffer. Again, for assessing the issue whether any such damage is proportional to the military aims, determining the scale of that indirect mortality is vital. That scale is also vital for establishing the human cost of war, and for assessing the 'justness' of interventions such as sanctions (such as sanctions against a dictatorial regime; viz. Daponte, 2008).

(4) *Post-conflict military deaths*

The formal end of a conflict is generally not the end of elevated mortality. People may have been wounded during the war, and may die later. People may have been affected in non-physical manners, which also lowers their life expectancy, for instance because they have been rendered incapable to work, or because they are unable to find a romantic partner. Any increased mortality due to such factors is labeled indirect post-conflict mortality. Also, the end of a conflict may not mean the end of hostilities. After a conflict, weapons are often still around in undesirable amounts, tensions may not have been resolved, scores may not have been settled. So, after the signing of peace agreements, former combatants remain at elevated risk of a violent and thus direct death. Both phenomena add up to post-conflict military mortality.

(5) *Post-conflict civilian deaths*

The same goes for civilian deaths. Civilians may have been wounded before the formal end of the conflict but succumb after it ends, civilians may have been traumatised which lowers their life expectancy, and it may take a while before civilians are back in their houses and on their land, and have re-achieved their old living standards. It may take quite a while before the infrastructure of a destroyed country has been rebuilt, and before the health system is back at its pre-conflict level, and before civilians again have access to the same level of care that they had before the war. So, also civilians remain at elevated risk to die after a conflict has ended. Not including such mortality in the statistics would underestimate the total cost. It might also paint a biased picture. As Li and Wen (2005) showed, there are sizeable 'lingering' effects of armed conflict. In their analysis of sex-specific adult mortality rates across 84 countries from 1961 to 1998 (with, unfortunately, data for African countries missing), they showed that intrastate conflicts generated larger immediate effects and stronger effects on mortality for men, but that the lingering effects of interstate conflicts were large and that women were as much affected by these as men.

Obviously, a problem is when to stop attributing elevated mortality to the conflict. Should one stop after 5 years, or would effects still linger after 50 years? Attribution becomes arguably increasingly harder as the time lag between mortality and a conflict increases.

The previous enumeration serves to structure our thinking, and our research questions. Items (1) and (2) combined comprise total direct mortality during a conflict. Items (1) and (4) add up to total military mortality. Items (2) and (3) comprise total civilian mortality during a conflict. From a demographic perspective, one would be interested to know the sum of (1) to (5). From a criminological perspective, one might add (2), (3) and (5) into the total prevalence, even though some might argue that only (2) and the direct part of (5) would count as such. From a more pragmatic prosecutorial perspective, one might only use (2), although in the ICC application for an arrest warrant against the president of Sudan, Omar el Bashir, an estimate of indirect mortality was used – a landmark occurrence (see `icc-cpi.int/NR/rdonlyres/64FA6B33-05C3-4E9C-A672-3FA2B58CB2C9/277758/ICCOTPSummary20081704ENG.pdf`, p. 7).

In many conflicts particular ethnic or political groups are targeted. Thus, one would ideally like to have a breakdown of the numbers by ethnicity, age, sex, religion or political affiliation, and by any other relevant characteristic. Such breakdowns are necessary not only to describe the conflict well, but also to be able to understand it. If mainly adult males were killed, this tells a different story than if equal numbers of adult females and young children were killed. Similarly, if particular ethnicities are overrepresented, this also 'tells a story'.

Incident-based databases for conflict: UCDP and PRIO

Two large databases have information on global numbers of battle deaths. The first of these is the database built by the Peace Research Institute in Oslo (PRIO database). It has data on conflict deaths from 1946 onwards. The second of these is the Uppsala Conflict Data Program (UCDP) that has data on conflict deaths from 1989 onwards. The PRIO database is updated at (ir)regular intervals, the last update carried out in 2009; the UCDP database is updated annually. While the two databases show very similar trends in yearly number of fatalities from conflict, the curve of the PRIO data is generally higher. This is because different methodologies are used by the two databases for arriving at yearly fatalities figures. PRIO uses summary estimates, that is, estimates made by experts on the total number of fatalities of conflicts. UCDP by contrast compiles yearly fatalities data as the sum of the number of fatalities in individual violent incidents, gathering data from NGOs, human rights organisations and the like. As not all deaths are recorded, this almost always leads to an underestimate of the true number of fatalities in the UCDP. On the plus side, UCDP data are quite detailed and have a lot of background information, with for instance geo-coded information on incidents, disaggregation into types of violence, etc. For more, see `pcr.uu.se/digitalAssets/666/c_666984-l_1-k_hsrp_est.battle_deaths_1.2.13.pdf`.

Both the PRIO and ACDP databases have been used extensively by researchers. Wagner, Heft-Neal, Bhutta *et al.* (2018) used the UCDP data to link geocoded information on violent deaths in Africa with information on child mortality from all Demographic and Health Surveys from 1995-2015 in and around the same areas where violent conflict had occurred. Next, they investigated per area whether during periods of conflict child mortality was higher than during periods without conflict. They found that this was indeed the case. They found that the risk for children to die was still elevated substantively and significantly if the conflict had taken place at a distance of up to 100 kms, and found that an effect of conflict on child mortality was still noticeable 8 years after the conflict had ended. In their study, they controlled for numerous micro-level confounders, such as mother's education and age, sex of the child, and meso-level confounders such as rainfall, temperature, and food prices.

Both databases have excellent websites that are worth a visit, with news, graphs and downloadable (replication) data files.

13.2.2 Excess and baseline mortality

In the previous paragraphs, we at times used the term *excess mortality* but did not explain what we meant by that. Excess mortality is a term frequently encountered in prevalence studies. Excess mortality is defined as mortality exceeding ordinary mortality levels. In peacetime, people die too. Most of this ordinary mortality is due to diseases such as (mainly) cardiovascular diseases and cancer. A small fraction of the population dies of unnatural causes, such as accidents, violence or suicide. All this is regarded as 'normal' mortality.

Excess mortality now is defined as those deaths exceeding ordinary levels. Say that in peacetime we would have expected 1,000 deaths to occur in a certain region during a certain time span. If for a similar population size during a similar period in which fighting took place in that region instead 8,500 deaths have occurred, we would say that there are 7,500 excess deaths. For all the types of mortality we distinguished above, we would likely attribute only the excess part of the mortality we observe to the conflict we are studying.

Now the question is of course, what is then 'normal mortality'? How can we measure and express it? That normal mortality, phrased also as *baseline mortality*, can be expressed using two epidemiological measures: in the crude mortality rate (CMR) and in the under 5 mortality rate (U5MR). They can be defined as follows:

(1) the crude mortality rate is defined as the total number of deaths that occurred in a population of a certain size during a certain period

(2) the under 5 mortality rate is defined as the total number of deaths of children under 5 years of age that occurred in a population of children under 5 years during a certain period

Note that both mortality measures are rated over a time period, that is to say, they are expressed as pertaining to a population of a certain size, during a certain period. So we can express for instance the CMR as per 10,000 population, or per 100,000 population. We can similarly compute the rate per month, per year, or per day.

Baseline mortality rates vary by country, depending on factors such as immunisation coverage, access to health care, the shape of the population pyramid, food security, and other factors. Figure 13.1 gives an overview of the CMR (here defined as the number of deaths per 1,000 population per year; this measure is more often used by demographers and is also referred to as the Crude Death rate) taken from a World Bank web publication in 2018 (`data.worldbank.org/indicator/sp.dyn.cdrt.in?view=map`). The graph clearly shows wide differences, with many countries with high death rates located in the central African region but also, remarkably, in Europe. The death rate depends on the age distribution of a population, and in countries with aging populations the death rate is likely higher than in countries with similar conditions but younger populations.

For assessing excess mortality, a country-specific baseline CMR is required. As we will see below, this figure may not always be available. In such cases, a next-best approximation can be used, such as from a population with similar composition and similar access to health facilities and physical surroundings, often a neighbouring country or adjacent region.

Figure 13.1: Crude Mortality Rate by country

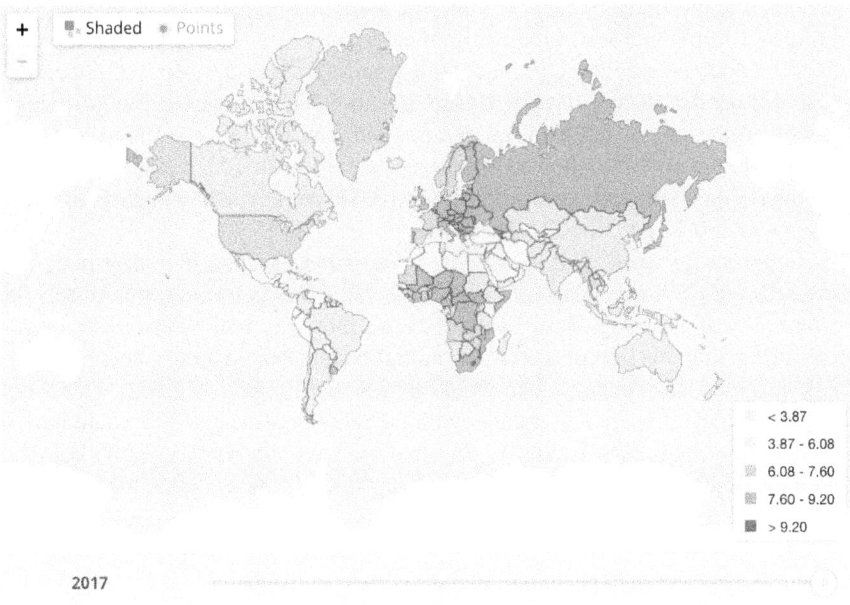

source: `data.worldbank.org/indicator/sp.dyn.cdrt.in?view=map`

In this book we will express both the CMR as well as U5MR as is common in epidemiological research and in studies into emergencies, namely per 10,000 population per day. Daily rates are eminently more useful as they are able to capture and describe fluctuations in mortality due to violence, outbreaks of disease or periods of food scarcity. Each mortality rate can be rewritten into a rate with a different period and/or reference population size. For instance, a CMR of 1 per 10,000 population per day can be written as follows:

1 death / 10,000 / day = 30.4 deaths / 10,000 / month =

364.8 deaths / 10,000 / year = 36.48 deaths / 1,000 / year.

If we compare this CMR with the CMRs depicted in Figure 13.1, we see that it is extremely high. It is indeed a number that would also for most African countries be regarded as indicative of an emergency situation. In the absence of more tailored data, many studies take as a standard baseline CMR for sub-Saharan Africa 0.44, 0.46 or 0.5 / 10,000 / day, which would translate to a CMR of 18.24 deaths / 1,000 / year. For the U5MR as a similar rule of thumb a value of 1.0 / 10,000 / day may be taken for sub-Saharan countries. As young children are more vulnerable, the U5MR is generally double that of CMR.

For each measure, CMR and U5MR, a doubling of the rate is generally labeled as an 'emergency' rate. So, if 0.5 is the baseline rate for total mortality, a rate of 1.0 would be seen as indicative of an emergency. Given that the U5MR is often double that of the CMR, if then a baseline mortality rate of 1.0 would be a reasonable baseline for young children, a doubling to 2 would be seen as indicative of emergency.

It is to be doubted whether current default values (such as 0.5 per 10,000 per day for CMR and 1.0 per 10,000 per day for U5MR in sub-Saharan Africa) are not too high, as these default values are at least several decades old, and mortality levels have decreased worldwide. Weissman (2018) showed for instance that in northern Nigeria in Maiduguri the CMR of the resident population was at 0.19 per 10,000 per day, while that of the displaced population was at 0.41 per 10,000 per day.

It is important to work with as specific as possible baseline mortality rates for the conflict under study: if one takes as a baseline a value that is too low, one overestimates excess mortality, if a too high value is used, excess mortality will be underestimated – all this notwithstanding that getting the 'right' mortality data can be quite a challenge.

Thus, in practical situations, one would assess the number of deaths over a certain conflict period, and compare that number with the number of deaths that would have been expected under normal circumstances. Say that we have interviewed 1,000 households, with an average household size of 4.9. And say that 100 households lost 1 household member each over the course of one year. This means that over the course of one year 5,000 people were at risk to die (4.9 alive household members × 1,000 households = 4,900 live persons + 100 deceased persons). This translates to a CMR of 100 per 5,000 per year, or 20 per 1,000 per year. If we assume that the baseline mortality is 0.5 per 10,000 per day, the baseline CMR per 1,000 per year is 18.24 deaths. This means that in the population we surveyed we would have expected that 18.24 × 5 = 91.2 deaths would have occurred over the year. However, 100 occurred. The excess mortality is therefore 100 (the conflict number) - 91.2 (the baseline number) = 8.8 deaths.

So, 8.8 is the excess number of deaths that occurred in the sample of households (100 households covering 5,000 respondents) we studied. Suppose now that these are a representative sample out of a larger population of 50,000 IDPs. The population out of which we drew our sample is then 10 times as large. This means that we can now estimate the excess mortality for this sample to be 10 × 8.8 = 88 deaths.

Two issues still need to be addressed. First, in the simple calculations we just made, we assumed that the population at risk was stable over the entire year. We assumed, when we interviewed our 1,000 families, that all family members who were there at the time of the interview had been at risk during the entire recall period of one year. In general, this is not the case. Especially in times of population upheaval and migration, some family members may flee first, move in with relatives, move out again, to for instance an IDP camp, where other family members may join them, of whom some may leave again.

So, suppose that in our example above, of the 4,900 residing family members, some 1,000 were recent arrivals who had only stayed in the household for a short while. This means that not all 5,000 people we have data on were at risk to die during the whole year. For 11 months of the past year, the 100 deaths were accrued over a smaller base population. This implies that we have underestimated mortality: the 100 deaths originate from a smaller 'reservoir' of people at risk to die than the final 4,900 we saw in their tents.

Suppose on the other hand that a much larger group of refugees stayed for almost the entire year in the households we surveyed and that these recently moved out. This means that our 5,000 population members in the denominator of the ratio are an undercount and that we overestimated mortality.

Without precise calculations, these examples hopefully make clear that it is important to take into account the population size over the entire recall period, and not just during the time of the interview. And what goes for 'emigration' and 'immigration' into the family applies as well to deaths and births. For that reason, many researchers use slightly modified formulas where they add one half of the people who leave the population for one reason or another during the recall period to the population at risk, and subtract one half of the people who enter the population during the recall period. This adaptation assumes that such 'emigration' from and 'immigration' into the population is uniformly distributed over the recall period, which need to always be the case. More refined measurement methods are possible, such as counting per person the number of days that he or she stayed in the household and thus added to the population at risk, but getting such data would require more interview time (see also section 13.3.2). Also, it is to be doubted whether respondents have accurate recall of all these movements.

Second, we must mention that the U5MR can be volatile. By that we mean that during flight, in unhygienic camp circumstances or when contagious disease breaks out, the U5MR can literally shoot up and become extremely high. Young children are the most vulnerable in such conditions, and children can be struck massively and mercilessly. For some sites in southern Sudan in the late 90s, U5MRs towards 30 have been reported. This implies also that, if disease strikes so fiercely, almost all very young children may succumb in a short period. If that happens, the strange phenomenon occurs that the U5MR may in fact go down to 'normal' levels: there are simply – cynically speaking – very few children still at risk to die.

The CMR and U5MR do not only aid us in estimating (excess) mortality, but they also tell us something about the causes of death. Given that the probability to die follows a J-shaped curve, the so-called Gompertz curve (Gompertz, 1825), it follows that death is relatively likely in (very) young children, but that very quickly the probability to die decreases and stays fairly low until about age 50, when it reaches postnatal levels. Because death is so rare in adults, an elevated CMR is therefore in first instance attributed to non-natural causes, i.e. violence, and thus regarded as more indicative of direct mortality. As we stated in the previous paragraph, young children are quite vulnerable in situations during flight, when infectious diseases may break out or when contaminated water and unhygienic conditions bring diarrhoea. Conversely, the U5MR is therefore considered more as a marker of indirect mortality. More specifically, Ratnayake, Degomme, Altare *et al.* (2008) proposed to interpret a situation where an increase in the U5MR outweighs the increase in the CMR as a situation where deaths are mainly due to indirect causes. If the increase in the CMR outweighs that in the U5MR, and the U5MR is itself not elevated, this would typically be a situation where the main causes of mortality are likely to be direct, i.e. violence. If the increase in the CMR outweighs that in the U5MR but the U5MR is itself elevated as well then both direct and indirect causes would likely contribute to mortality (Ratnayake, Degomme, Altare *et al.*, 2008, p. 25 – 26).

13.3 Methods for assessing mortality

In the following subsections we will discuss methods to assess mortality. These can be subdivided into two generic types. The first is *counting* methods or tallying, that will be briefly discussed in section 13.3.1. If we count or tally, we have a list of victims, so that we have in principle all the names of the deceased, we know their identities. We then often not only know who they are, but also where and when they died. We then also may know their age, sex, plus possible other relevant characteristics such as their religion or ethnicity, and the circumstances in which they died. This means that in a statistical sense, we attempt in these methods to arrive at an inventory or enumeration of the entire victim population.

The second type are methods to *estimate* mortality. These can be divided into four types: methods that use retrospective mortality surveys (discussed in section 13.3.2), methods that combine and integrate data from existing mortality and morbidity surveys with other data (detailed in section 13.3.3), counterfactual methods that use extrapolations (section 13.3.4) and, lastly, capture-recapture methods (discussed in section 13.3.5, and previously in a more general sense in section 11.7.2).

13.3.1 Counting

It can be envisaged that, in a country where fighting takes place for a certain period, and persons die due to that conflict, one could count the number of death certificates registered during the period of the fighting, deduct the number of people who would die ordinarily during a time span such as the conflict took, and one would have the total excess mortality, mortality above peacetime mortality levels, comprising both direct and indirect mortality.

Unfortunately, such an 'ideal' research setting is extremely rare in conflict settings. Usually, statistical organisations stop functioning – and some never functioned at all before the conflict started.

Another option would be to compare census lists before the conflict with census lists after the conflict. Also that option is extremely rarely practically doable. In many countries in which international crimes are committed, censuses have not been conducted for a long time, and if they have been conducted they are often not considered reliable. In countries with smouldering tensions and cleavages between political and/or ethnic/religious groups, census enumerations may be used for political purposes, or may be used to harass people. Two examples also mentioned in the previous chapter underscore the problems that such situations generate. In Kosovo, ethnic Albanians boycotted the census just before the war broke out, making that they were undercounted and that mortality in their ethnic group would also be undercounted if one relied solely on those lists. In Rwanda, it is reported that ethnic Tutsi reported for census purposes that they were Hutu for fear of being stigmatised and discriminated against. While such issues would not necessarily result in an undercount of total mortality, it would distort our view of the ethnic dimension of the genocide.

A big problem with the comparison of census lists is that people may go missing without having died. In the turmoil and confusion of refugee streams, people get lost and may not re-emerge until long after the conflict has ended. Some of the missing may in fact have emigrated abroad, and may even choose not to reveal where they are. To count all these missing and emigrated persons as deceased inflates mortality figures.

Lastly, the comparison of census lists may be too slow a procedure for practical purposes. While conflicts are ongoing, there may be a need for quick data on mortality and the size of the affected population. Censuses require a good deal of organisation and generally do not take place until well after the country has a modicum of normalcy again, order has been restored, many have returned to their original homes and there is money again in the government's coffers for such an expenditure.

All in all, the counting (or: tallying) of victims of international crimes from official population registration data is an endeavour that is seldom possible. Preconditions are the availability of relatively good population administration systems before the conflict erupted, and relatively good population administration systems during and after the conflict ended. Not many countries meet those criteria.

The former Yugoslavia is one of the exceptions. The so-called 'Bosnian Book of Dead' is the outcome of a project intended to establish a country-wide database covering the victims of the Bosnian war. The project started from a database that had been compiled by an NGO called 'Muslims against genocide', as well as several other existing computerised lists of victims. Further sources used for the Bosnian Book of the Dead include statements from eye witnesses, relatives, neighbours, and close friends, lists from books, reports, and press articles, names from grave tombs, newspaper memorials, other newspapers records (single or lists), government sources, microfilms etc. The Bosnian Book of the Dead (Ball, Tabeau & Verwimp, 2007), now held by the Research and Documentation Centre in Sarajevo, is essentially an excel-file with records of 96,985 unique individuals who were killed during the years 1992-1995 in Bosnia-Herzegovina during the war there. It must be said that the compilation of the lists of names was not finished until well after the war ended.

The Book contains their name, date of birth, place of birth, sex, father's name, ethnicity, religion, occupation, marital status, criminal record, educational level. All are individuals who were killed, died in war-related circumstances, or went missing. About 40% were civilians and about 60% military or police officers. Information on the latter had been validated against information on military cemeteries, from military sources, and the like. The authors note that, even so, some deceased classified as military may actually have been ranked such at the request of family members, as this might enable them to receive benefits and as some families may have found it honourable to have their relative buried in a military setting. While the database gives the cause of death, the database does not give information on how the victim died, that is, whether that was in a combat situation or not.

Ball, Tabeau and Verwimp, who reviewed the quality of the data, also note that the database, while an enumeration of all people killed, should be seen as an approximation, and more specifically as an approximation of a minimum number killed. They do note that recent additions have been marginal, meaning that the list is in all likelihood virtually complete. The list may still contain (by 2007 when the review was done) about 1% duplicates, variables are missing more often for civilians than for military victims. The authors recommend that the data be validated against new information, such as from exhumations. They specifically suggest that the database can be further validated against other high-quality databases such as the 1991 Population census or the so-called Federation of Bosnia and Herzegovina (FBH) 1992-1995, the Mortality database established in 2002 by the Federal Institute for Statistics in Sarajevo, or the Republika Srpska (RS) 1992-1995 Mortality Database compiled by the Statistical Office of Republika Srpska in Banja Luka.

Figure 13.2: Bosnian Book of the Dead: Absolute numbers of male victims by age in 5-year intervals

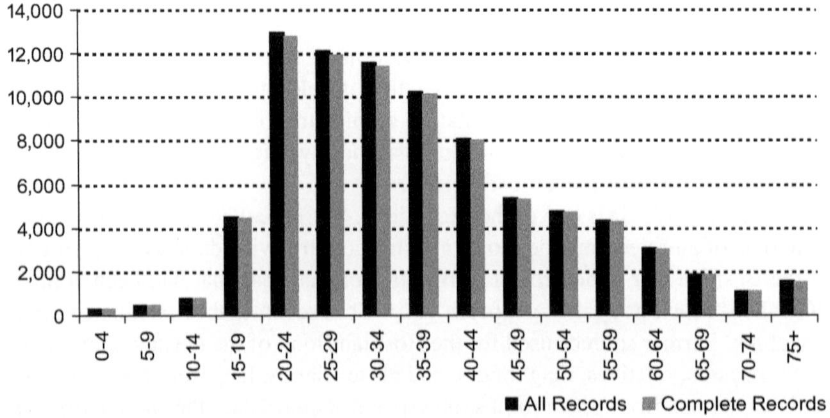

source: Ball, Tabeau and Verwimp (2007)

Figure 13.3: Bosnian Book of the Dead: Absolute numbers of female victims by age in 5-year intervals

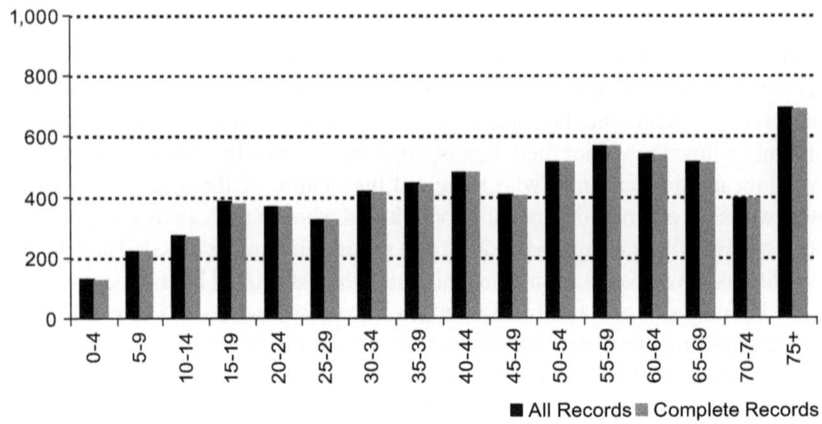

source: Ball, Tabeau and Verwimp (2007)

The need for validation of findings – however relatively 'hard' they may be (such as these Yugoslavian findings) – against other sources is a recurrent theme in this chapter. We should be aware that we are always working with incomplete and possibly tainted data. This led the reviewers of the Bosnian Book of the Dead to recommend to still be cautious and not present these data as a final result, but as an 'approximation of a minimum'.

Figures 13.2 and 13.3 from the Bosnian Book of the Dead show how the age distribution for men differs strongly from that for women: mortality is for men highly concentrated in the 20-24, 25-29, 30-34 and 35-39 age brackets. For women, it is much more uniformly distributed, with a peak for older, likely frailer women. This suggests a different mechanism of violence directly specifically against men. Note that the absolute numbers along the y-axes are much higher for men than for women. A combined graph for both sexes would only show the male pattern as the smaller numbers of female victims would be depressed against the much larger numbers for men.

Two more illustrations from the review of the Bosnian data are given in Figures 13.4 and 13.5. These illustrate how the birth dates of some victims may have been unknown: we see peaks at the 1st day of the month and on 1 January. Figure 13.5 further shows slight elevations around every 5th day: possibly these are the result of rounding off of dates of birth. Such rounding off regularly emerges (also in Western countries) if one asks people after their age: bar charts then show peaks around every 5- and 10-year interval.

In general, the conflict in the former Yugoslavia constitutes an exceptional case: before the war, relatively good population data was available, quite a bit of money was available for research after the conflict with the ICTY having its own research unit, a concerted effort has exhumed bodies from numerous mass graves, and the names of the victims are now almost all known. This is not the case in numerous other situations: most victims in Darfur, in southern Sudan, DRC, Cambodia, Armenia, Namibia, will remain, for various reasons, likely nameless to the outside world.

Since the advent of social media and much increased storage capacity on ordinary computers, many conflicts have been documented by organisations that aim to archive violent civilian deaths. Below, we discuss of these the Iraq Body Count project in more detail. The aim of these organisations is often to build an archive or a memory of civilian mortality by listing for each violent death that the organisation becomes aware of, the name of the victim, some demographic characteristics, as well as the situation in which the violent death took place. Often, a number of organisations attempt to do so simultaneously. Price, Klingner and Ball (2013) report how for the Syrian conflict between 2011 and 2012, at least nine organisations were collecting data on mortality: the Violation Documentation Centre (VDC), the Syrian Network for Human Rights (SNHR), the Syrian Revolution General Council (SRGC), the Syria Shuhada Website (SS), the March 15 Group (15Mar), the Syrian Observatory for Human Rights (SOHR), the Syrian government (GoSY), the Strategic Research and Communication Centre, and Syria Tracker. Many of these organisations have their own websites where they publish names and background characteristics of violence victims as well as characteristics of the lethal attacks. Such efforts where reported deaths are being recorded and collected from sources published by others, and where no particular effort is made to find unreported deaths, are labeled *passive surveillance*.

Guha-Sapir, Schlüter, Rodriguez-Llanes, *et al.* (2017) analysed data on Syria from one organisation, the Violation Documentation Center dataset. VDC is a non-profit non-

Figure 13.4: Bosnian Book of the Dead: Records by month of birth

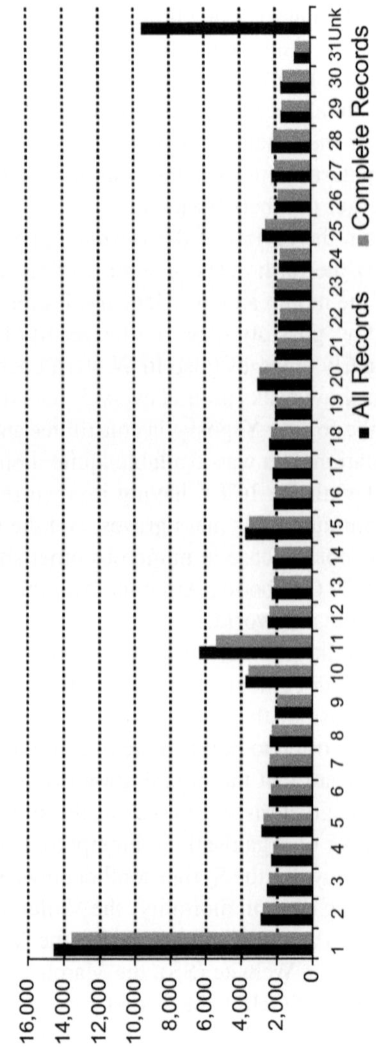

source: Ball, Tabeau and Verwimp (2007)

Figure 13.5: Bosnian Book of the Dead: Records by day of birth

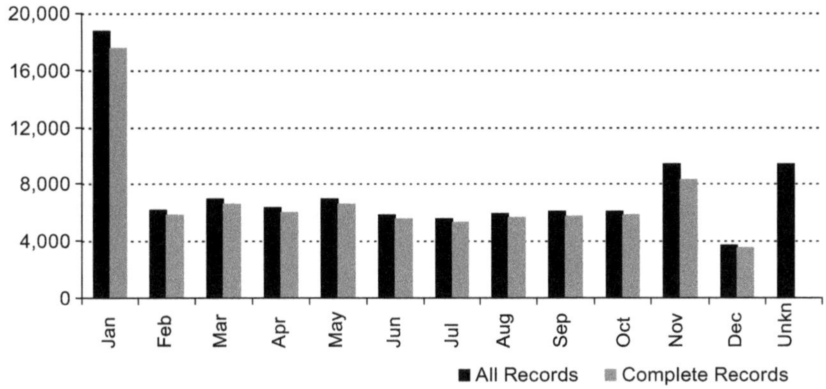

source: Ball, Tabeau and Verwimp (2007)

governmental organisation that tracks and documents human rights violations for the armed conflict in Syria, from 2011 onwards. It has staff on the ground as well as at its headquarters in Switzerland. The VDC applies international standards for documentation of human rights violations. VDC covers only non-government held territory, and the authors in fact chose not to include data from government-controlled areas because of uncertainties in such data. The authors use the VDC data to investigate trends in violence. Analysis of the VDC data revealed 145,849 recorded deaths from March 18, 2011 to Dec 31, 2016. After over 2,200 deaths were excluded because of partially missing data or errors, 143,630 deaths remained that had complete information on date and place of death, demographic group, civilian or combatant status, and cause of violent death. They reveal, amongst others, how increased and systematic use of air bombardments of populated areas caused increasing numbers of deaths of women and children, with deaths of children concentrated in Aleppo. The findings do not generalise to government-held territory.

The data from various sources can also be combined to arrive at one tally: it is likely that some datasets will have captured unique deaths, and if we combine these, we will likely gather a more comprehensive tally. What one would immediately run into, is that some victims will appear more than once as they would have been registered by more than one organisation. To prevent double counting, the dataset has to be *de-duplicated*: multiple entries that refer to the same death must be combined in one single entry. This process is not without complications. When the number of casualties is high, de-duplication cannot be done by hand, instead it has to be done automatically. But, without manual check, small spelling differences will record the same person as two persons, and therefore result in overcounting. Similarly, names that are not distinctive (such as in the Netherlands Jansen, or the UK Johnson) may label different persons as one death. The performance of such automated algorithms hinges on sufficiently detailed and unique names, personal characteristics and situational details. This means that it will probably be undoable in cultures where people do not have family names but refer to themselves by a sequence of ancestors' names (father and grandfather), such as Ali Ahmed Ali. When people do not know their date of birth, the certainty with which people can be identified further decreases (in some countries people know at best their year of birth and birthdays are routinely estimated at January 1). For some languages, very good de-duplication software exists, that matches also on the phonetic resemblance of names, and gives a probability that two entries refer to the same person. Probable matches are inspected manually ('clerical review'). De-duplication, also called *record linkage* is discussed by Fellegi and Sunter (1969), Christen (2012), and by Herzog, Scheuren and Winkler (2007).

The Iraq Body Count project

The Iraq Body Count (IBC) project was established in 2003 by volunteers who believed that records should be kept of civilian mortality in Iraq after the US invasion. IBC registers media-published violent incidents where civilians died, or bodies were found, supplemented by and cross-checked against hospital, morgue, and NGO records as well as official statistics. For each violent incident, further characteristics are recorded if possible, of the incident (likely weapons or perpetrators, such as US forces, coalition forces, rebel forces) as well as of the victim(s) (such as age, sex, occupation). While the numbers are the 'hardest' data in the IBC project, there is some doubt whether the civilian status of victims is always correctly recorded.

Given the IBC's reliance on (English language) media sources, it can be argued that deaths in safer areas, that are better accessible to reporters, in Baghdad and the other larger cities are overrepresented. Deaths in the safer areas may also be overrepresented as they are more remarkable and newsworthy there. Isolated deaths (with one or two casualties) that are likely to be underreported in the media are also likely underrepresented. Empirical evidence for the latter was found when the Wikileaks War Logs were released.

Carpenter, Fulkler and Roberts (2013) investigated to what extent these 'Wikileaks' deaths had also been captured in the IBC database. Working from a systematic random sample of violent deaths, the authors found that (23.8%) had (likely) matches in IBC records. However, they also found that events that had killed more people were substantially more likely to be present, with 94.1% of events in which 20 or more people had been killed found in the IBC records, against only 17.4% of events in which one individual had been killed. This phenomenon, that larger events are more likely to be picked up by passive surveillance systems, is referred to as *event size bias*.

Figure 13.6: Monthly numbers of victims in whole of Iraq against Baghdad

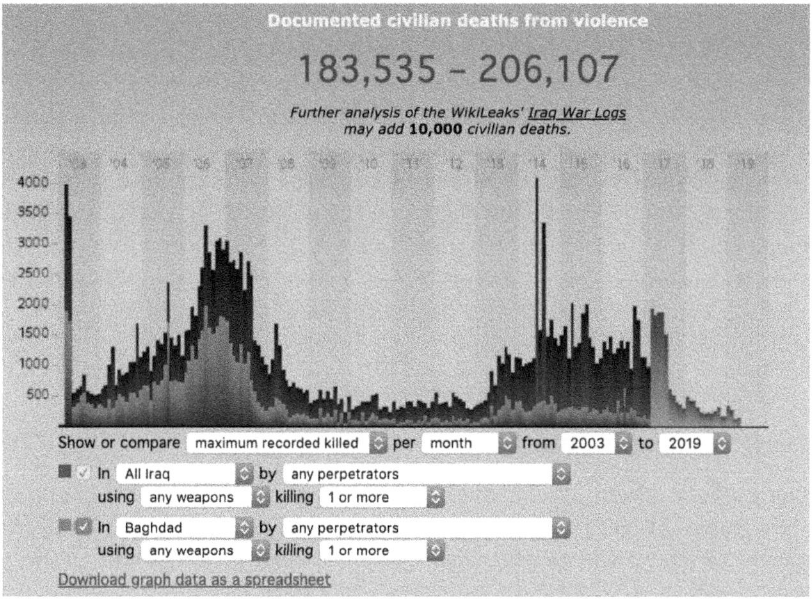

The IBC generates a lower limit to civilian violent mortality, as not all deaths are captured. How large the IBC undercount is, remains unsure. The study by Carpenter, Fulkler and Roberts (2013) estimated that a little under half (46.3%) of all deaths that were present in the Wikileaks War Logs were also included in the IBC records. But clearly, it is also unknown to what extent the Wikileaks War Logs capture all deaths. The IBC data should therefore be regarded as a lower limit on violent mortality among civilians in Iraq. Trends in IBC mortality correlate strongly with trends as assessed through other methods (Sloboda, Dardagan, Spagat *et al.*, 2013).

As said, the IBC data can – as a lower limit to total violent civilian mortality – be used to gauge other measurements. We will encounter the IBC again in our discussions below on other studies in Iraq. Also, the longitudinal data could be used as an indicator for trends in mortality. However, given that the data are also taken from press reports, one could argue that the trends in mortality are confounded with trends in reporting on mortality.

The IBC project has an interesting and well-maintained website that is worth a visit. The website gives an overview of types of analyses that have been done on the data, see `www.iraqbodycount.org/analysis/`, and it even features a FAQ section. Publications are downloadable and the data can be downloaded too, and interactive graphs can be compiled.

As an example, we include a graph compiled from the IBC website in which total deaths in Iraq since 2003 are compared against deaths in Baghdad (see Figure 13.6). The grey bars for more recent months are based on preliminary data. The figure shows that the monthly mortality patterns of Baghdad in the early years quite closely followed those of all of Iraq, until approximately spring 2014. Mortality from then onwards stayed low in Baghdad but rose sharply in the remainder of Iraq.

An excellent overview of the IBC, its inception, rationale and measurements strategies is given in Sloboda, Dardagan, Spagat *et al.* (2013).

13.3.2 Retrospective mortality surveys

The following four subsections will discuss methods not to measure, but to *estimate* mortality, This means that each of these methods will generate a finding that is uncertain, or more specifically, more uncertain than the counting or tallying methods just discussed.

The method that we will discuss in this section is essentially a victim survey (see section 11.5.2). As we are interested to assess mortality, we cannot however – strictly speaking – use a victim survey: the victims we want to know about are not alive anymore. Therefore the so-called *retrospective mortality surveys* generally interview family members of the deceased. This implies that the sampling units are not persons but households. These surveys are called household surveys. A household is defined in most studies as a group of people living under the same roof and eating together.

Household surveys that aim to measure mortality depart from the assumption that at least one household member has survived. If that is not the case, and all household members have perished, then the entire family cannot be not captured in the mortality data and mortality is *underestimated.* This bias is inherent to household surveys, it is commonly referred as *survivor bias* or mortality bias. Survivor bias is especially strong in populations with high maternal mortality, and in situations with high adult mortality or where mortality is strongly clustered. Such clustering may occur when mortality is largely due to violent attacks. In cases where survivor bias is suspected, supplementary methods should be used such as indirect estimation methods, for instance through the number of orphans, or by graveyard tallies.

Cluster sampling

For household surveys, cluster sampling is generally used. Cluster samples are often chosen for surveys on mortality as they are efficient, quick and easy to implement. As already explained in section 3.3.1, if we would want to draw a flat or simple random sample, we would need to have a list of all population members. In many countries such lists do not exist, and in situations of population displacement such lists are not valid anymore. Cluster sampling has the immense advantage over simple random sampling that lists of population members are not necessary: we only need an overview of the spread of the population members over the region that we are intending to survey.

Once we know the spread of the population, we can divide the population in clusters of different sizes such as villages, camps, towns or any other settlement, and randomly draw clusters proportionate to size (also referred to as PPS sampling). We can then interview every member in the cluster, or sample a number from the cluster.

If we do not interview every member of the selected clusters, but again only a sample out of the clusters, this is called a *multistage* or *two-stage cluster sample*. This type of sample is *self-weighting*: because clusters are drawn proportional to size and equal numbers selected per cluster, every member of the population has an equal chance of ending up in the sample.[1] These chances should be equal for the sample to be representative. Obviously, we can also achieve equal selection probabilities by not drawing clusters proportionate to size but sampling a fixed percentage of the population per cluster.

All in all, if we decide to draw a cluster sample, we have made our life much easier: we do not need to have a complete list of population members before we can draw a sample, we only need to know how many people reside in the various locations we plan to survey. Next we select our clusters, and then we need to enumerate only those in our cluster sample (a fraction of the population), and can proceed to interview them. This is definitely a much simpler task than having to enumerate all population members – which may in fact be impossible in many conflict settings. The cluster sample is therefore not only a huge saving in time and money but for many practical situations in fact the only option available.

---

[1] As an example, assume that we have 10 clusters, 5 of size 200 (clusters A to E) and 5 of size 100 (clusters F to J). There are therefore 1500 population members. We want to interview 150 respondents. And we want to draw 3 clusters and interview 50 from each cluster. We draw 3 clusters at random, but need to take into account their sizes. An easy way to do this is by having each large cluster appear twice, and each small cluster only once. This reflects exactly their size difference. We therefore arrange the clusters as follows: A - A - B - B - C - C - D - D - E - E - F - G - H - I - J, that we have a list of 15 clusters to draw from. Any random number generator can now be used to randomly pick the clusters, for instance: 6 - 7 - 4. This means that we pick cluster F and G and cluster D. We therefore end up with two small clusters and one large cluster. The outcome could have been different, as it is a random process.

Does every population member have an equal chance of ending up in the sample? The chance that a large cluster is selected is $\frac{2}{15}$. The chance that a small cluster is selected is $\frac{1}{15}$. Once a cluster is selected, we can also compute a cluster member's chance to end up in the final sample. For a large cluster this probability is $\frac{50}{200}$. For a small cluster this probability is $\frac{50}{100}$. For someone from a small cluster the chance to end up in the sample is therefore:

$$p\,(\text{ending up in sample})_{\text{small cluster member}} = p\,(\text{small cluster selected}) \times p\,(\text{selected} \mid \text{small cluster selected}) =$$

$$\frac{1}{15} \times \frac{50}{100} = \frac{1}{30}.$$

For someone from a large cluster the chance to end up in the sample is

$$p\,(\text{ending up in sample})_{\text{large cluster member}} = p\,(\text{large cluster selected}) \times p\,(\text{selected} \mid \text{large cluster selected}) =$$

$$= \frac{2}{15} \times \frac{50}{200} = \frac{1}{30}.$$

Even so, all this is perhaps easier said than done. A first issue is how to select the clusters, and more specifically: where to get information on cluster size? In many countries, census data are outdated, maps are old. When people are on the move, it is unclear where they are at all, and villages may have been emptied. However, once people have settled in refugee locations or IDP camps, these can be used as new clusters. In general, for such settlements at least a rough indication of the number of inhabitants is available. NGOs generally have a fairly accurate overview of recent population flows and resettlement, and so population distribution. Satellite images have also been used to estimate the number of settlements, compounds or even tents. A more innovative approach may be to use food distribution lists as an indication for the number of settlers in locations. Once we know the approximate size of settlements where the people live we want to survey, we can draw a cluster sample. However, as Shannon, Hutson, Kolbe *et al.* (2012) note, without precise information on population size, the method is perhaps better labeled as 'PPES' or 'proportionate to estimated size'.

Selection of respondents within clusters

Once we have selected our clusters, we must draw a sample of respondents in each cluster. By far the most often used method for this is the so-called 'EPI' method. This method was first used for studies on immunisation coverage under the World Health Organisation's Expanded Program on Immunisation (EPI). Studies had shown that cluster surveys of 30 clusters with seven households each per cluster gave estimates of vaccination coverage with a 95% confidence interval (CI) no more than 10% around the true value (see for this also section 3.7). Simulations have concluded that overall the method achieves those aims (Lemeshow, Tserkovnyi, Tulloch *et al.*, 1985; Lemeshow & Robinson, 1985; Shannon, Hutson, Kolbe *et al.*, 2012).

The idea is that once the clusters have been selected, field staff travel to the center of the clusters, where they position a pen on the ground, or a bottle tied to a rope, which they spin around (the method is therefore also called the 'spin-the-pen'-method or the 'spin-the-bottle'-method). Once the pen or bottle stops, it points in a certain direction. The interview staff then draws a (straight as far as possible) line in that direction to the periphery of the settlement, and enumerates the houses along that line. Next, they draw a random number from the list of numbers and start with that house, next interviewing all adjacent six houses, thus achieving a sample of seven households per cluster.

Figure 13.7 illustrates the EPI method. It is a stylised example of four villages, drawn as clusters proportionate to their size. In each cluster the field workers tied a bottle to a string and swung it round. Walking in the direction indicated when the bottle stopped, they enumerated the houses they encountered. Next they drew out of these numbers at random one number, started interviewing in the house with that number, and surveyed in total 7 households, all lumped around that first randomly selected household.

This method has been used for hundreds if not thousands of surveys in developing countries, on immunisation coverage but also victimisation, with or without adaptation. Its overwhelming advantage is that it is very simple to carry out. Specialised data are needed only to select the clusters, but from then on the field work can be done with locally trained staff, quickly, and also with relatively limited resources. No specialised sampling skills are

Figure 13.7: Visual representation of household selection in EPI method

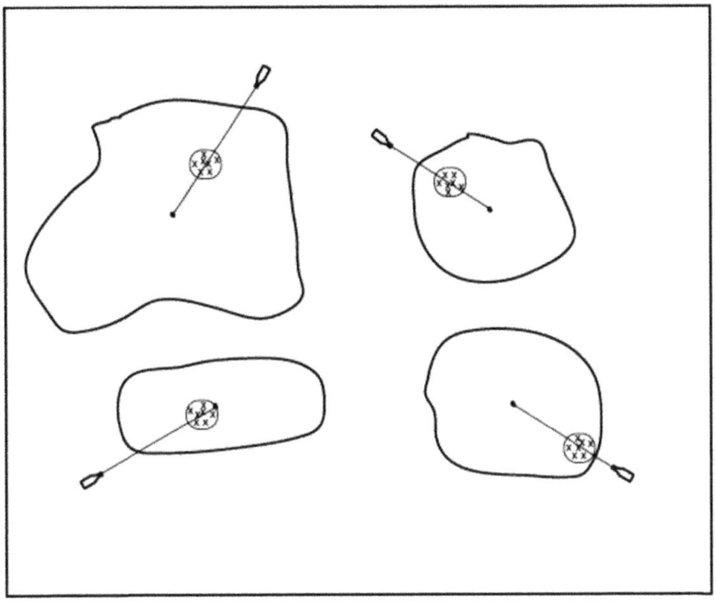

needed for the fieldwork, and no comprehensive and up-to-date sampling frame of people or households in the clusters is needed.

The method does have limitations. Firstly, communities are selected with probability proportional to size, but if the information on settlement size is outdated or wrong, the sample cannot become representative. Secondly, the spin-the-pen method is not truly random. It can easily be argued that if the method as outlined above is followed, inhabitants of the outer areas of settlements have a lower chance of ending up in the sample (the sampling method is 'center-biased'). Especially if towns are surveyed this is a real risk. Once people start moving way from conflict areas, many will move to the larger cities for safety, and often reside in squatter camps glued onto towns. These areas will have the poorest access to health care and resources and may have the highest mortality levels, either due to their inhabitants' poorer living conditions or (pre-)flight experiences. The method may then generate an underestimate.

The problems that Burnham, Lafta, Doocy *et al.* (2006) ran into illustrate the biases that such seemingly random strategies may incur. These authors selected 47 clusters for their study on mortality after the US invasion to Iraq; within each cluster (village or city) they identified the main streets, selected randomly a main street, then enumerated the cross streets of that main street and randomly selected a cross street. In the cross street they then numbered the houses and randomly selected a house, which was the start house and

Figure 13.8: Representation of main street, cross street and resulting unreached households

source: Johnson, Spagat, Gourley *et al.*, 2008

around which adjacent residences were surveyed until a total of 40 households had been interviewed.

Johnson, Spagat, Gourley *et al.* (2008) showed that this cross street sampling algorithm leads to so-called *main street bias*, resulting in an overestimation of mortality. Cross streets are as the authors write a natural habitat for police stations, road blocks, cafes, street markets, and therefore for car bombs, drive-by shootings, attacks on patrols, street market bombings, and abductions. The sampling method hardly ever reaches more backyard, remote houses that are away from such bustling, more violence-prone areas. See Figure 13.8 for an example. The inhabitants of households on cross streets, because they likely spend most of their time in their houses or in the immediate vicinity, are more likely to be exposed to violence than those living further away in the more remote residential areas.

The authors show that this main street bias (which can be seen as a special variety of the bias generated by the spin-the-pen-method given that the main congregational areas of settlements such as centers and main streets are oversampled) may likely have caused the mortality estimate to be a factor 3 too high.

Thirdly, methods like the EPI are sensitive to conscious or unconscious bias of the interviewer: the interview staff may prefer to pick certain houses, or avoid certain houses, and there is no control on that selection process being truly random. Fourthly and lastly, it is unclear to what extent nonresponse affects the results although in general very high response rates are achieved in this type of mortality survey: Spiegel and Salama (2004) incurred no refusals during their survey in Kosovo, Burnham, Lafta, Doocy *et al.* (2006)

had only 15 refusals (0.8%) in their survey of post-invasion mortality in Iraq. While some researchers revisited houses where everyone was absent at a later time of the day, or called in the aid of neighbours to track down absent inhabitants, most studies have simply skipped houses where people were absent and moved to the next adjacent house. This explains the very low rate of refusers, but will lead to bias if non-contacts differ systematically from those who do participate, although it is unclear in which direction.

Improvements over the EPI method have therefore been proposed by various authors. A simple improvement would be not to spin a pen but to draw a random walk through a village, for instance in a spiral, beginning in the center, and ending at the periphery, enumerate the (larger) number of houses encountered thus, and then select one randomly. This would eliminate the inherent center bias of the spin-the-pen-method. Another approach would be to superimpose a grid on a map of the cluster, randomly choose coordinates on the grid, and identify the closest compounds. This can be done with map sketches (see Grais, Rose, & Guthmann, 2007), or by randomly selecting GPS coordinates, then drawing a 20 m circle around selected spots, and subsequently randomly selecting houses within the selected circle – and if necessary randomly selecting households within larger houses (see Shannon, Hutson, Kolbe *et al.*, 2012). These alternative methods, however, lead to higher probabilities of choosing households in low density areas of the clusters. Other improvements have been suggested (see Grais, Rose & Guthmann, 2006).

While much is therefore to be said against the widely used EPI method, its great strength is its easy applicability. Once the field work is made more difficult, this will in practice mean that more supervision is needed and that therefore fieldwork will be slower, surveys more costly, so that sample size will have to be reduced, so the gain will come at a price. A nice overview of the history of the EPI method can be read at `ph.ucla.edu/epi/rapidsurvey.html`, where software can be found and even a full course, and a syllabus for the methodology downloaded (`ph.ucla.edu/epi/rapidsurveys/RScourse/RSsyllabus.html`).

Depoortere, Checchi, Broillet *et al.* (2004) conducted two-stage, household-based cluster surveys in four sites in West Darfur after estimating numbers of internally displaced people through a combination of community health worker censuses, shelter counts, and area mapping. For each of the four sites, the researchers defined a number of clusters within sites, proportional to the population size of the site. In the second stage, households were selected per cluster by walking in a random direction from the center to the periphery of the site of the site. As the field workers entered the selected cluster, the first household they encountered was selected, and all adjacent households interviewed until the desired number of households had been interviewed. At each site but one, 30 households were interviewed in each of 30 selected clusters, rendering approximately 900 surveyed households per site.

Questions and questionnaires

Once households to be surveyed have been selected, a next issue is to decide what questions to ask household members. As this paragraph is about mortality surveys, we would for sure want to ask head of households whether any household members died, and due to what causes. In most surveys, we also ask at least a number of background characteristics, such as ethnicity, occupation. We might also want to ask our respondents' experiences for instance during resettlement, their health needs and the like.

It is generally recommended that – as much as possible – standardised questionnaires are used for these surveys. A first reason for that is that such questionnaires have been pre-tested and will generally have good methodological properties. A second advantage is that if standardised questionnaires are used, their outcomes can be compared across studies. We will then be able to gauge our findings, and will be able to say whether mortality is higher in one area, or in one conflict or during a certain period. One laudable initiative is the so-called SMART (Standardised Monitoring and Assessment of Relief and Transitions) methodology, a set of tools and guidelines for conducting nutrition and mortality surveys (see `smartmethodology.org/`). SMART is an inter-agency initiative launched in 2002 by a network of organisations and humanitarian practitioners. It offers a survey method for the assessment of severity of a humanitarian crisis based on two vital public health indicators, namely the nutritional status of children less than five years old, and the mortality rate of the population. A manual for this method can be found on the web (`unhcr.org/45f6abc92.html`). The manual is extremely practical as it provides examples of calculations of various mortality rates, examples of questionnaires and event calendar forms, and the like. It has been written in a non-technical manner so that it is also comprehensible for those with a non-academic or non-epidemiological background.

We discuss three aspects in somewhat more detail. Firstly, for assessing mortality we want to know how many people belonged to a household, for how many months. While we are essentially interested in numbers only, it is advisable to not just ask for numbers, but to identify each household member and each person who lived in the household during the recall period by name. This may take slightly longer to ask, but greatly improves precision and therefore data quality. An example of a filled out checklist for this, taken from World Food Programme and Centers for Disease Control manual for studies on malnutrition and mortality (WFP, 2005) is given in Figure 13.9.

The list in this figure enumerates every household member (the household is fairly big). For each, the sex and age is given, plus whether the person was present at the start of the recall period and whether the person is present in the household now. With these data, a mortality rate can be computed, by adding one half of the people who left the population during the recall period, and subtracting one half of the people who entered the population during the recall period. Ideally, in order to be able to calculate the mortality rate more precisely, we could attempt to draw an event calendar per person who was ever a member of the household as given in Figure 13.10.

Using this event calendar, we will be able to exactly specify how many months how many persons were at risk to die. As already mentioned in section 13.2.2, this will however be done against the cost of longer interviews, plus that it is to be doubted whether recall is so accurate that family members' presences can be timed to the week or even day.

A second important issue is the recall period: over what period do we ask people the composition of their household and the deaths or disappearance of any family members? For most general victim surveys, recall periods longer than one year are advised against. Recall may become more hazy, events may be forgotten, memory affects the exact recollection of events. That said, recall periods of more than 10 years have been employed in the study of international crimes, reasoning that people will be able to recall traumatic events quite well even after long periods, and that if conflicts have stretched over several years, we want to know victimisation over that entire period.

Figure 13.9: Checklist for household members' presence, absence and death

Figure 2.3 Example of household mortality data collection form

Survey district: Ambo | Village: Limbo | Cluster number: 4

HH number: 23 | Date: 12- Aug - 04 | Team number: 2

1 ID	2 Sex	3 Current age (in years)	4 Present now	5 Present at beginning of recall period	6 Current status (1 – Alive; 2 – Dead; 3 – Unknown)
1	F	23	Yes	Yes	1
2	M	26	Yes	Yes	1
3	M	54	Yes	Yes	1
4	F	48	Yes	Yes	1
5	F	18	Yes	NO	1
6	F	12	Yes	Yes	1
7	M	8	Yes	Yes	1
8	M	2 mos	Yes	NO	1
9	F	4	Yes	Yes	1
10	M	1	Yes	Yes	1
11	M	3	Yes	NO	1
12	F	29	NO	Yes	2
13	M	33	NO	Yes	1
14	M	8	NO	Yes	1
15	M	31	NO	Yes	3

Tally (if data on household members will not entired into the computer)

	Number above	Data come from:
a. Number of HH members at end of recall period	11	Column 4
b. Number of children < 5 years at end of recall period	4	Columns 3 & 4
c. Number of HH members at beginning of recall period	12	Column 5
d. Number of children < 5 years at beginning of recall period	2	Columns 3 & 5
e. Total number of deaths	1	Column 6

source: World Food Programme (2005)

Figure 13.10: Event calendar for household members

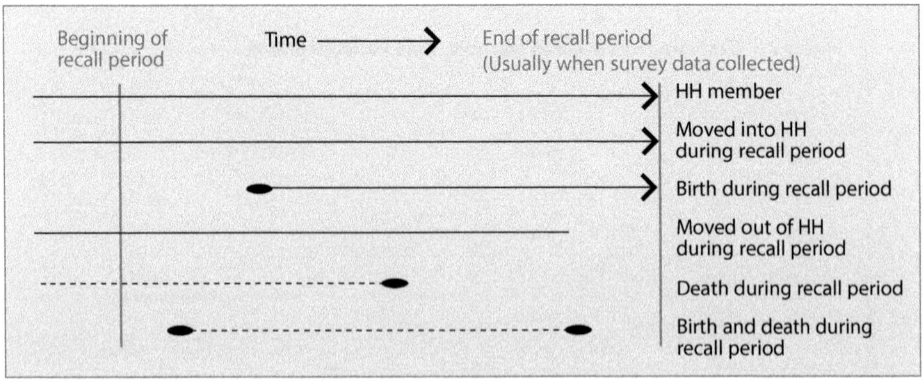

source: World Food Programme (2005)

If we want to know, for instance, mortality before flight, during flight and in the camps, we have to use a recall period that is able to capture all three 'types' of mortality, perhaps stretching more than a year back. If we are interested in mortality due to recent outbreaks of diseases, a short recall period would be more feasible. In each case, it is wise to demarcate the beginning of the recall period not with abstract notions such as '1 year ago' but with concrete events that people remember, such as 'since last year's Ramadan' or 'since you migrated to this camp'.

Shorter recall periods may be expected to generate less retrieval problems: people will more accurately remember events, such as cause of death, or symptoms of the deceased in the weeks before death. However, for statistical reasons a longer recall period might be preferable: if the recall period is longer, we will 'capture' more deaths and will thus with greater precision be able to say something about the mortality rate. Longer recall periods will however be more difficult to reconstruct and will take more interview time. And, as interviews take longer, data quality may affected negatively too. The recall period that is most suitable depends therefore first and foremost on the research question, with constraints in terms of interview time and likely respondent fatigue.

In mortality surveys, we are thirdly, especially when these are carried for studying international crimes, also interested to know the cause of death. A first distinction is whether family members died due to violence or due to other causes. Most respondents are able to correctly classify deaths as either violent or non-violent. We could ask respondents for instance whether a family member who died, died because of an injury, such as from an assault, an accident, or fire etc. If the answer is 'no', then we can classify the death as non-violent; if the answer is 'yes' we may attempt to further specify the cause of death, and attempt to find out whether the injury was caused by a gun, machete, bombardment or other weapons during a conflict situation.

More refined instruments are available, such as verbal autopsy forms. Using such instruments, a set of questions is administered asking after many symptoms before the person died. When these questions entered into a certain format, the cause of death can be classified into the ICD-10 (International Classification of Diseases) format. Such questionnaires however need very well-trained interviewers, who may more than not be unavailable in emergency settings. See World Health Organization (2012).

Questionnaires should be translated into all local languages, and subsequently 'back-translated' into the original language, which is often English. If discrepancies emerge, these should be settled before piloting and fieldwork starts. It is advisable to enlist the support of local health workers for translation. Many common diseases such as measles or neonatal tetanus, have local names, and it is wise to use those. The aim of such rigourous translation is to achieve not only *semantic equivalence*, namely translating words well literally, but also *functional equivalence*, that is, words or texts also evoking the same functions or meaning that they would in the original language.

Even so, during piloting and testing of the questionnaires, new issues often arise, and time should be reserved for solving any emergent issues. Functional equivalence may be compromised if there are large cultural or systemic differences between the countries of the original language of the instrument and the language in which it has to be worded. Some terms in one language may not even have a literal translation in another language. It may also be that the literal translation of a term has a broader or narrower meaning in another language. Clearly, if one does not translate such that the translated version is as close as possible to the original version, and at the same time captures the same meaning in translation that it had in the original language, one cannot be sure that the original and translated instrument measure the same thing. Whenever such cultural or systemic differences are likely (and they are especially likely when questionnaires enquire after sexual relations, domestic violence, death and family ties) extreme care and diligence is called for.

While much of the literature on mortality employs quantitative methods, Foster Lynch (2013), however, cautions against quantitative survey methodology to estimate casualties post-conflict. She argues that respondents who are forced into a 'survey mould' and have questionnaires administered, are more likely to either promote, protect or modify their self and that of others. This may occur for various reasons: embarrassment, guilt, desire to be seen in a positive light, suspicion that the interview is not really confidential and the interviewer does not speak the truth, desire to portray one's country well, inability to remember events for lack of cues, and other reasons. Qualitative methods would prevent many of such biases, she argues. An important first reason for that is the greater ability to build *rapport*. Second, interviewees are to a larger extent participants in qualitative research. Repeat interviewing improves the quality of the data, as does the option to adapt the signals that the interviewer gives about his or her local knowledge as the interview proceeds. For more, see Foster Lynch (2013).

The 2006 Burnham *et al.* Iraq mortality survey

In October 2006, an article was published in the Lancet, a respected medical journal, in which it was estimated that there had been 654,965 excess deaths due to the war in Iraq. The study quickly was attacked from various sides. Many believed that the death estimates were impossibly high. Guha-Sapir, director of the Center for Research on the Epidemiology of Disasters, translated the research findings in the sense that if the 650,000-plus deaths were true, this meant that Iraq should have witnessed 500 predominately violent deaths per day, which it by far did not. The IBC stated in a press release that 'Half a million death certificates were received by families which were never officially recorded as having been issued' (`iraqbodycount.org/analysis/beyond/reality-checks/`). Some journalists compared the estimate with morgue figures, and concluded that the estimate was 'way off their charts'. A number of researchers noted that the mortality estimates were much higher than other surveys had found, such as the Iraq Family Living Conditions survey which covered deaths until May 2004. Subsequently, the researchers were attacked for numerous other alleged wrongdoings.

How was the study conducted and what were its findings? Burnham, Lafta, Doocy *et al.* (2006) selected, as described, 47 clusters for their study on mortality after the US invasion to Iraq; within each cluster they surveyed 40 households. In total 1,849 households were visited, and data on 12,801 individuals was gathered; 1474 births were recorded and 629 deaths were reported. Information was gathered about deaths between 1 January 2002 to 18 March 2003, the date of the US invasion. Subsequent mortality data were gathered through to July 2006.

Interviewers were all medical doctors fluent in English and Arabic, who had been trained for 2 days. Per location a team consisted of 2 females and 2 males. Houses were approached and if a house was empty or a refusal was given, a next house was chosen. Households where all members had died or had left were excluded.

The survey enumerated all household members and coded births and deaths, in- and outflow of household members, to be able to determine the mortality rate. For security reasons, no distinction was made between combatant and non-combatant deaths. The interviewers always asked after cause of death, and asked to see a death certificate, and probed if any information thereon differed from the information provided.

The authors calculated the pre-invasion crude mortality rate as 5.5 per 1,000 people per year. For the overall post-invasion period they calculated it as 13.3 per 1,000 people per year. Extrapolating the survey findings to the total Iraqi population, the authors estimated that the total mortality in the post-invasion period had been 942,636, with the expected mortality estimated at 392,979, resulting in the figure of over 650,000 deaths. Of these deaths, the authors estimated that about 600,000 had been due to violence. The authors note that their pre-invasion mortality rate (the baseline mortality) is in accordance with other sources. They also note that their estimates for earlier years are in accordance with findings from an earlier study.

While the authors concede that their estimate is much higher than any thus far published, they remark that passive surveillance of deaths (such as in the Iraq Body Count project, see the text box devoted to the IBC in section 13.3.2) rarely accounts for more than 20% of total mortality, and that facility-based methods have also been known to underestimate mortality by a factor of 10. They also note that their trends in mortality, while at higher average levels, match those of the IBC.

Guha-Sapir and Degomme (2007) scrupulously reviewed the study. They firstly checked the data, and compared the findings against those from other sources, validating and triangulating the estimates. They started by removing some data: they removed 11 deaths from the data as household size was unknown for these cases, and removed 24 car bomb deaths that occurred after the recall period. Then, they noted that governorates with high mortality had been oversampled, and governorates with low mortality had been undersampled. They therefore applied weights to the estimates to correct for this. Corrections for these issues already led to a lowered estimate of 460,000 to 550,000 deaths.

Third, they calculated the design effect, and noted that it was extremely high (for violence-related deaths 5.4, and for some specific causes 9.6), making generalisation of the findings hazardous. Fourthly, they corrected a number of technical issues with the denominator of the mortality rate, and the fact that the authors had not corrected for in- and outmigration, which affects the denominator (number of person-months at risk to die), and therefore the mortality rate. The authors next combined the Burnham data with those from the Iraq Family Living Conditions survey (FLCS), and the IBC tally, essentially subtracting the overestimated fraction as determined by comparison with the FLCS from the Burnham estimates from the years not covered by the FLCS, and downscaled the estimate considerably, arriving at a likely mortality of around 125,000.

As mentioned, Johnson, Spagat, Gourley *et al.* (2008) had concluded that the Burnham estimates might have been a factor 3 too high, so would therefore be around 200,000.

While we will likely never know exactly how many people died due to the violence after the US invasion of Iraq, the controversies around the Burnham *et al.* study teach us a few lessons. Firstly, the heatedness of the debate and the nature of some of the attacks show how politically charged the context is in which these studies take place. The data were scrutinised by many and the study was negatively evaluated for minor aspects – all this in spite of the fact that it had appeared in one of the most acclaimed peer-reviewed journals. Secondly, as Guha-Sapir and Degomme (2007) also note, the publication of very precise estimates (654,965 instead of 650,00) gives an impression of precision that boomerangs back the moment flaws are discovered. Validation, corroboration and triangulation are always necessary, because data collection is so difficult and the topic so charged.

13.3.3 'Meta-analytic' methods

In this section we discuss methods to estimate mortality that collate and combine findings from different studies to arrive at one, integrated, estimate of mortality. The earliest and probably best example of this kind of estimation is a study conducted by the Center for Research on the Epidemiology of Disasters, that estimated mortality in Darfur from September 2003 to January 2005. We will use that study as an example, even though the authors later published an improved and extended version of their earlier analysis.

We label the methodology we discuss in this section as 'meta-analytic' even though there are quite a few differences between a meta-analysis proper and the methods illustrated here. In a meta-analysis, one analyses not data from one's own field work, but findings from studies published by others. For instance, suppose that I would want to know whether treatment prevents recidivism in fraudsters. Of course, I could design a study myself, go into the field, collect data on people convicted for fraud, whether they received treatment or not, wait for a number of years and then look up their recidivism data in a criminal records database, conduct the analysis and present my results. What I could also do, is collect all studies that have ever been conducted on treatment and recidivism in fraud offenders, and combine these findings. In general, I will be somewhat faster with the publication of my results, I will also be able to describe findings for a much larger sample, and I do not need to go into the field myself – saving money as well.

This is essentially what a 'meta-analysis' does. It combines findings from studies that have already been carried out. What distinguishes it from a so-called *narrative review* of studies is that it produces one final result: it combines all results in to one conclusive answer.[2] For more on meta-analysis as such, see Mullen (1989).

Now, the methods we will be discussing in this section are also meta-analytic in the sense that they attempt to extract findings from a collection of studies, and re-use these for a new analysis. They however do not weight these findings into one number, as in the

[2]Suppose that five studies into the effectiveness of some treatment are available, and that the test values for these studies are as follows: 1.83 (N = 40), -0.45 (N = 220), 2.43 (N = 20), 1.76 (N = 42), and 1.68 (N = 40), with high test values (z = 1.68 and higher) indicating that there was a significant effect for the treatment group. If we would simply summarise these findings, we would report that four out of five studies show that treated respondents do better. The evidence would thus overwhelmingly (80% of studies) point in favour of treatment. If we however look in more detail, we see that the only study that did not report a positive effect was a very large study: by itself it contained more respondents than the other four studies combined.

Here the meta-analytic principle kicks in. Meta-analysis combines these findings, but does so in a 'weighted' manner: more important studies have a louder voice. One obvious manner to weight these findings here is to do by sample size: we could give the 1.83 z-value a weight of 40, the -0.45 z-value a weight of 220, etc., to arrive at a combined weighted z-value:

$$z_{\text{combined}} = \frac{\sum_{j=1}^{k} N_j z_j}{\sqrt{\sum_{j=1}^{k} w_j^2}},$$

with j the index denoting the study number, numbered from 1 to k=5.
This weighted z-value equals:

$$\frac{73.2 + -99 + 48.6 + 73.92 + 67.2}{\sqrt{1600 + 48400 + 400 + 1764 + 1600}} = \frac{32.78}{\sqrt{53764}} = \frac{32.78}{231.87} = 0.14,$$

showing that overall, weighting each study result by its importance, the effect of treatment is not significantly different from zero (p = .5557).

example above, but combine the findings from previous studies to be better able to estimate mortality.

To elucidate, let us return to the retrospective mortality survey discussed in the previous section. In such a survey a sample out of a population is interviewed about the number of deaths over a certain recall period, as well as the number of people who were at risk to die during that period. If these data are available, it is possible to compute a mortality rate, Assuming a baseline mortality rate, excess mortality can be computed. However, if we do so, we assume that the mortality rate is constant, we average it over the population over the entire period. Such a so-called *blanket estimate* may be too coarse: most conflicts do not start full force from one day to the next, but smoulder and escalate, and stop after a peace accord is signed, or peter out beforehand. Also, it is generally so that not a whole region is affected from day 1: it takes a while for conflicts to spread. All in all, conflicts may wax and wane and start in one place and extend to the next.

This implies that we would actually want to have mortality rates that capture trends in mortality over time, separately for regions that were differentially affected, in magnitude and over time. If we had such data, we might be able to estimate mortality in a more refined manner, taking into account geographical as well as temporal variability in mortality. This is exactly where the methods discussed in this section improve upon the previously discussed techniques, and why they are superior.

In 2005, Guha-Sapir and Degomme (2005b) searched the Complex Emergencies Database (CE-dat, see `cred.be/cedat`) held in the Center for Research on the Epidemiology of Disasters (CRED) in Brussels, Belgium for surveys on nutritional status and mortality in Darfur. This database is a repository of studies (several thousand) on vaccination coverage, morbidity and mortality, for different periods in different countries by relief agencies and research institutes. Some of the indicators included in the database are crude, infant and under 5 mortality rates.

For this study into mortality in Darfur, the authors were able to locate 24 surveys that contained mortality data collected during the period April 2004 – January 2005 in Darfur; the recall periods in the various surveys covered the period September 2003 – January 2005. Figure 13.11 graphically represents the estimated CMRs and the recall periods for the surveys from West Darfur, Figure 13.12 those from North Darfur, and Figure 13.13 those from South Darfur. As the figures show, the levels of the CMRs differ, as well as the trends over time.

Now, these figures also show that the data are patchy, that is, they have gaps and for some periods different levels have been reported for the same region. Next, the authors therefore attempted to construct monthly mortality rates from interpolation of these data, to arrive at complete data: a mortality rate per month per region. While doing so, they were conservative as they removed outliers so that they would underestimate rather than overestimate mortality. From this interpolation (for which they used a variety of techniques amongst which a special kind of regression), they extracted CMRs. All in all, they had built in this manner a database with for each month during the conflict, for each of the three regions in Darfur, an estimated CMR.

Next, the authors used the affected population over time, see Figure 13.14, to arrive at an estimate of casualties. They did so because they argued that calculations with the elevated monthly CMRs should not be done on the entire population of Darfur, but only

Figure 13.11: CMRs and recall periods for surveys from West Darfur

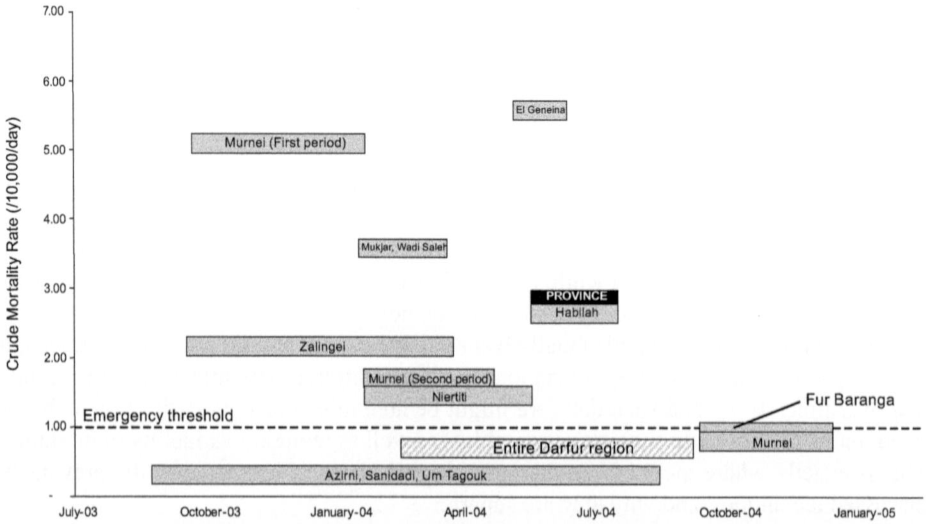

source: Guha-Sapir and Degomme (2005b)

Figure 13.12: CMRs and recall periods for surveys from North Darfur

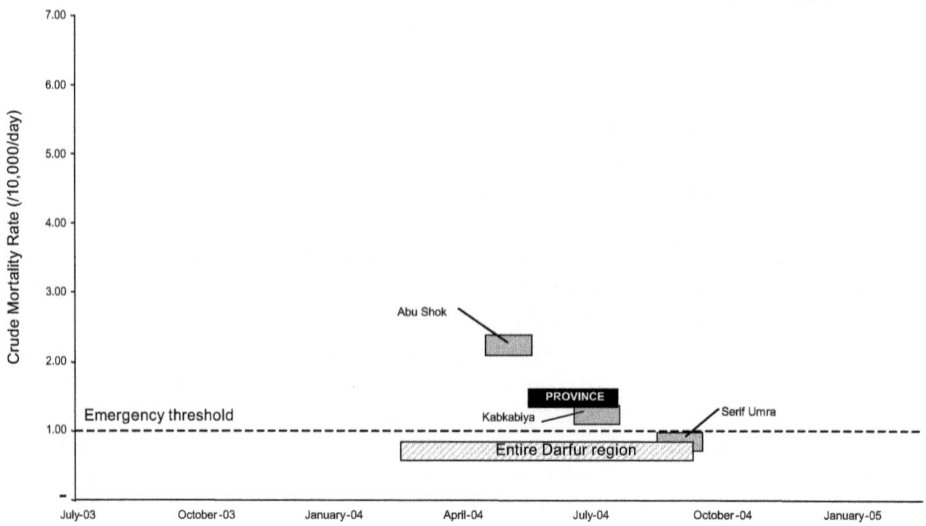

source: Guha-Sapir and Degomme (2005b)

Figure 13.13: CMRs and recall periods for surveys from South Darfur

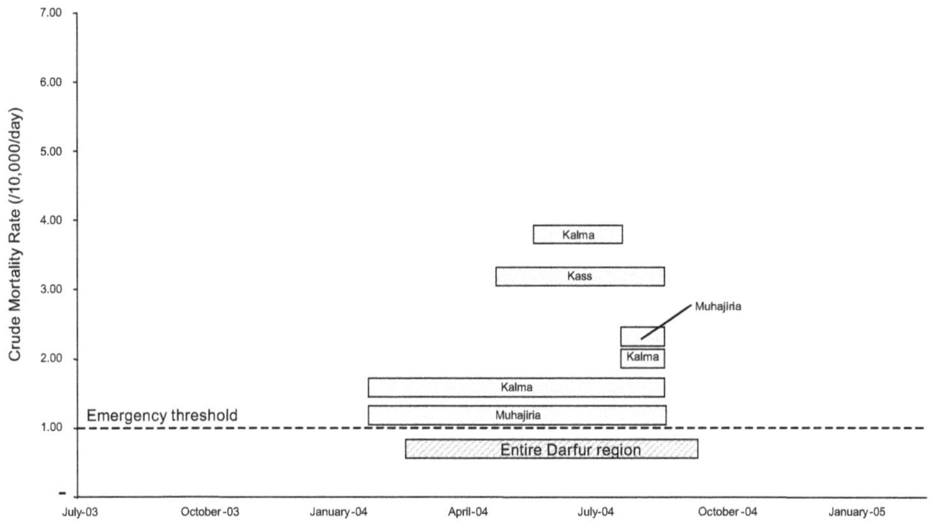

source: Guha-Sapir and Degomme (2005b)

Figure 13.14: Affected population in Darfur (Sept 2003-Jan 2005)

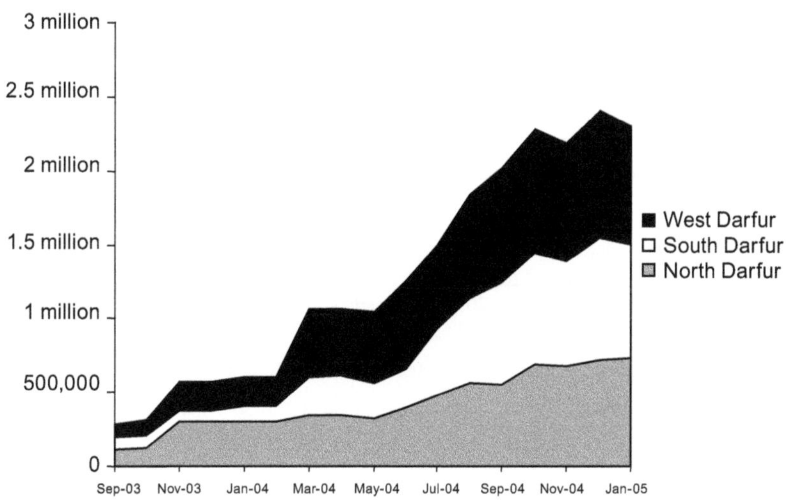

source: Guha-Sapir and Degomme (2005b)

on that part of the population that was actually affected by the conflict in that month. As Figure 13.14 shows, this part grew sizeably over time, for each region. [3]

Next, Figure 13.15 gives an overview of the results and the procedure in estimating mortality in Darfur, in the sense that it shows that while the Crude Mortality Rate (the line) decreased after a peak in December 2003, the estimated number of deaths (the bars) increased. This is due to the fact that the affected population increased steeply from early 2004 onwards, particularly in South Darfur.

The estimated total number of deaths was 121,582. To this, the authors added 10% for refugees in Chad for whom no surveys were available in the CE-DAT database, arriving at a total mortality estimate of 133,740.

Obviously, this 133,740 is an estimate for total, and not excess mortality. No CMR baseline data were available for Darfur, However, the U5MR for Darfur that was available was similar to the national U5MR. The authors assumed that the Darfur CMR also equalled the national CMR of 0.3 per 10,000 per day. After subtraction of expected mortality, excess mortality was estimated at 118,142.

The various surveys that had served as the building blocks for the meta-analytic study had listed what percentage of mortality was due to violence. Using these, the authors estimated that about 35,000 or almost 30% of deaths had been violence related, an unusually high fraction. In the ICC prosecutor's application for a warrant of arrest against Omar Hassan al Bashir, president of Sudan, it is stated on page 4: 'In Darfur 35,000 people have been killed outright in such attacks'. Interestingly, the prosecutor here uses an *estimate* of violent mortality in the legal process.

CRED published an update to this first estimate a few months later (Guha-Sapir & Degomme, 2005a), covering February to July 2005, and later published an estimate covering early 2004 to the end of 2008 (Degomme & Guha-Sapir, 2010). In this last article, they used a less refined method than previously, again disaggregating CMRs for South, West and North Darfur, but not anymore per month, but instead for six qualitatively different phases of the conflict. They estimated excess mortality from 2004 – 2008 at 298,271 (95% CI 178,258 – 461,520), or almost 300,000. They also concluded that although violence was the main cause of death during 2004, diseases were the cause of most deaths since 2005, with displaced populations being the most susceptible. A reduction in humanitarian assistance was associated with worsening mortality rates.

[3] As an example on how they went about doing so, suppose that for a certain month 1 the CMR is 1.2 per 10,000 per day, for month 2 it is 1.4 and for month 3 it equals 0.75; suppose further that the affected population for a certain region is 100,000 in month 1, 120,000 in month 2, and 200,000 in month 3. Total mortality could then be calculated for these three months (assuming they each span 30 days) for this region as:

month 1 = 1.2/10,000/day for 30 days $\rightarrow$ 12/100,000/day $\rightarrow$ $12 \times 30 = 360$

month 2 = 1.4/10,000/day for 30 days $\rightarrow$ 16.8/120,000/day $\rightarrow$ $16.8 \times 30 = 504$

month 3 = 0.75/10,000/day for 30 days $\rightarrow$ 15/200,000/day $\rightarrow$ $15 \times 30 = 450$.

The total amounts to $360 + 504 + 450 = 1{,}314$. Note that this number represents the total mortality, i.e. including peacetime expected 'normal' mortality. Baseline mortality still needs to be subtracted to arrive at an estimate for excess mortality.

Figure 13.15: Estimated number of deaths and CMR (Sept 2003-Jan 2005)

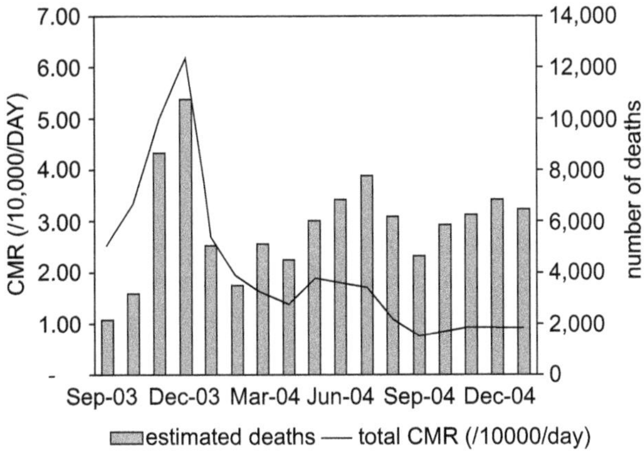

source: Guha-Sapir and Degomme (2005b)

The GAO assessment of Darfur mortality estimates

By mid 2006, various mortality estimates were around for the Darfur crisis that had by then been ongoing for over three years. The US Government Accountability Office (GAO) had the most important of these estimates, ranging from about 100,000 to almost 400,000, reviewed by a panel of experts. The panel assessed the relative accuracy, methodological strengths and shortcomings of the various studies, and identified general challenges to estimating the death toll in Darfur and similar crises.

The six estimates that were reviewed were the CRED estimate just discussed, and by the US Department of State (2005), Coebergh (2005), Hagan, Rymond-Richmond and Parker (2005), Reeves (posted on the now defunct `www.reeves.org`) and the WHO (2004). The Hagan *et al.* study had been published in the highest-ranking criminological journal 'Criminology'.

For each study, the panel scrutinised the manner in which estimates had been arrived at, and some authors were asked for clarifications. Interestingly, quite a number of studies had used similar sources to arrive at different estimates: CRED and the State Department had both used the mortality surveys held in the CE-dat database, Hagan, the WHO, Coebergh and Reeves all used (parts of) WHO, the Atrocities Documentation Team (ADT) and MSF surveys. Table 13.1 gives a (rough) overview of the methods used by the various studies; for more we refer to the interesting and readable GAO report (2006).

Figure 13.16 gives an overview of the various estimates generated by the six studies. The estimates obviously differ, as they span different periods. They are also bound to differ as they used different baseline mortality rates: those who use 0.5 are bound to find lower excess mortality – all else being equal – than those using 0.3, with, at the extreme, Hagan, Rymond-Richmond and Parker who assumed a baseline mortality of zero. Nevertheless, they differ widely in their monthly casualty results: the Hagan study is highest with about 17,300 casualties per month. The State Department estimate is at midpoint much lower at under 6,000 per month.

None of the studies was deemed flawless. The CRED study was generally ranked as relatively the strongest, with experts expressing in absolute terms moderate confidence in the estimates. The State Department estimate ended a close second. Experts had moderate to low confidence in the WHO estimate. Almost all experts had low confidence in the Coebergh, Hagan and Reeves estimates. Extrapolations were viewed as unrealistic, and based on too few data points, making the estimates highly unstable. Coebergh and Hagan used constant mortality rates for the period of the conflict (the so-called 'blanket estimate') and assumed fixed estimates of the affected population over time. Particularly the studies by Coebergh and Reeves were rated as less objective and more characteristic of advocacy or journalistic involvement, than of academic endeavour.

The GAO panel report is interesting as it illustrates how difficult it is to estimate mortality in a challenged research environment such as in Western Sudan. In resonance with the challenges outlined above, the report mentions problems with access to certain regions, security issues, language problems, definitional confusion, reluctance of respondents to talk about death, underreporting for fear of foregoing food rations, underreporting of infant deaths, survivor bias, the presence of government staff on the research team which can lead to over- as well as underreporting, recall problems and misplacement in time of the death of family members.

13.3.4 Counterfactual methods

The next estimation method we discuss is commonly referred to as the 'counterfactual' method. Here, one uses demographic methods to arrive at an estimate of mortality. Represented very rudimentarily, the method works with a so-called starting-population size at the beginning of conflict, an end-population size after the conflict has ended, and a hypothetical ('counterfactual') population size at the end of conflict. The counterfactual population size represents what the population size would have been had the conflict not taken place (of course, a conflict has taken place so this value can only be hypothetical). Under a number of assumptions and using a model for the peacetime development of population size, one estimates such a likely hypothetical value of population size. Subtracting the actual population size yields excess mortality. This may sound pretty abstract.

Let us assume that we are investigating a conflict and that, at the start of the conflict, population size was 2 million. At the end of the conflict, that lasted three years, population

Figure 13.16: Authors, (excess) mortality estimates and time frame covered

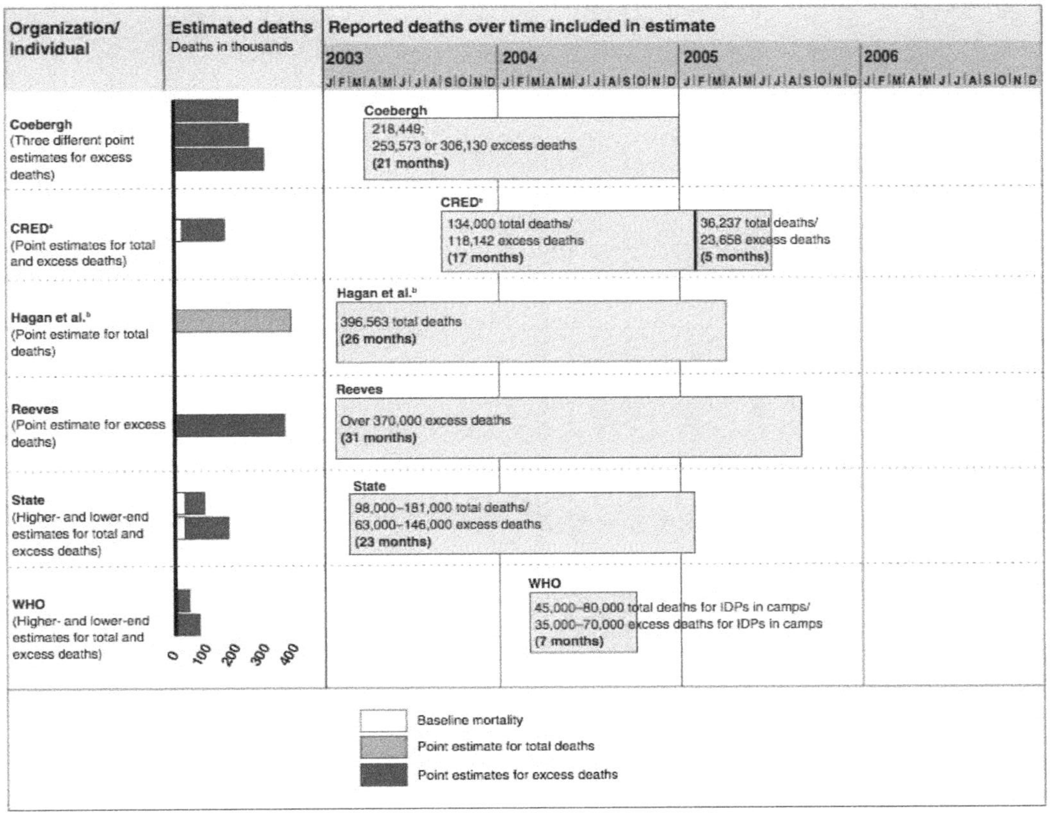

source: Government Accountability Office (2006)

Table 13.1: Overview of methodological aspects of Darfur studies

Author(s)	Data	Cause of death	Temp. MR	Geog. MR	Baseline MR	Affected pop.
Coebergh	ADT, WHO and MSF; estimates by officials	+	-	-	0.5	+
CRED	CE-dat surveys	+	+	+	0.3	+
Hagan *et al.*	ADT, WHO	+	-	-	0	+
Reeves	ADT WHO	+	+	-	0.3	+
State	CE-dat surveys	-	+	+	0.5	+
WHO	WHO	-	-	-	0.5	+

source: Government Accountability Office (2006)

size is 1.95 million. Population growth before the conflict was 2.2% per year. We can then apply the following reasoning. If the conflict had not erupted and the population had grown as it normally would have, then population size after three years would have been:

by year 1: 2,000,000 + (2.2% of 2,000,000 =) 44,000 = 2,044,000

by year 2: 2,044,000 + (2.2% of 2,044,000 =) 44,968 = 2,088,968

by year 3: 2,088,968 + (2.2% of 2,088,968 =) 45,957 = 2,134,925.[4]

For this example we would therefore arrive at a population deficit of 2,134,925 - 1,950,000 = 184,925, which we would attribute to the conflict. We would therefore conclude that this conflict generated an excess mortality of 184,925 or almost 185,000. Note that this number represents excess mortality, as the growth rate of 2.2% represents the net yearly growth of the population, i.e. the number of births minus the number of deaths (and taking into account in- and outmigration).

Figure 13.17 illustrates the calculations. The figure shows how the measured population size is lower after conflict than before, at 1.95 million. The decrease is likely a toll of the conflict. However, the death toll is larger than that absolute decrease: we know that during the conflict children have been born, so that more and more people were members of that population. Many more have therefore been killed or died – these would have been alive had the conflict not been there. Thus it is the difference between the hypothetical

[4]Which can be computed faster as $2{,}000{,}000 \times 1.022^3 = 2{,}000{,}000 \times 1.067462648 = 2{,}134{,}925$.

Figure 13.17: Representation of counterfactual computations

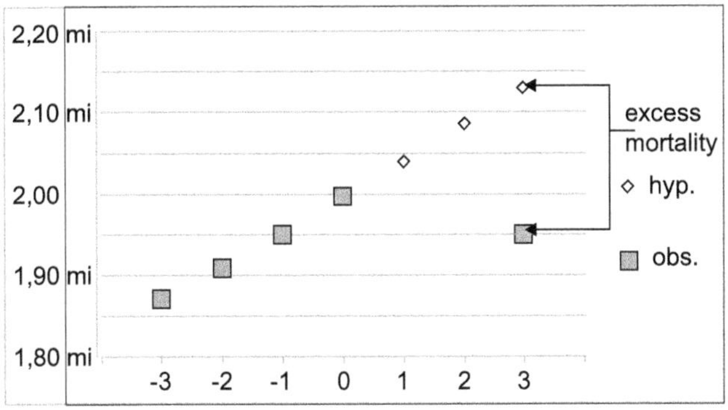

population size at year 3 (the last blue diamond) and the observed populated size at year 3 (the red square) that is the actual population loss.

Note that this simple calculation is carried out under a number of assumptions. Firstly, we assume that fertility during the conflict (the number of births) is stable and identical to pre-conflict fertility. We therefore assume that people continue having children at the peacetime rate. This may be unrealistic as women may conceive less easily during stressful situations, men may be be away from the home, and other factors may decrease fertility. It may also be that – all else being equal – pre-conflict fertility was in fact increasing: it may be that at year 0, right before the conflict started, population growth was 2.2%, but that at year -1 it was 2.1% and at year -2 it was 2.0%. In that case, we should perhaps linearly extrapolate fertility during conflict to equal 2.3% during year 1, 2.4% during year 2, and 2.5% during year 3. There is no way of knowing what is realistic, what would have happened had the conflict not erupted. Some researchers revert to taking as the counterfactual the growth rate in a comparison region with a similar population structure and physical geography – but no conflict. Clearly, all these choices influence the value of the final estimate: if we assume that the growth rate would have increased per year, we will find a larger counterfactual population size and therefore estimate that mortality was higher. If we use a more conservative growth rate, we will estimate mortality as lower.

We also pretend that we know exactly the population size at day 1 of the conflict and that we also have a complete enumeration of the population on the first day that the conflict ended. Both are unrealistic. In practice, both the end population and the starting population are not exactly determined, and may be estimates themselves. Lastly, the method assumes that all those who are not counted at the end of the conflict have died – they may as well have migrated as those who flee the country during conflict may not return immediately (or may even not return at all). We therefore need to have a reasonable assessment of that proportion of the population and account for those in our calculations, or we would overestimate mortality.

This description gives but the essential idea of the method. The method is coarse, as it assumes a constant rate of growth and assumes average mortality, fertility and migration for different ages and sexes. This is why this coarse variety is at times referred to as a 'naive' projection method (it is also encountered as the *balancing equation method* or *demographic balancing equation*). Demographers prefer more refined versions of this method, such as the so-called *cohort component method*. This method can give more tailored estimates, as it disaggregates the population at a certain time point into age intervals, determines fertility, mortality and (in- and out)migration per age interval per gender, and thus is better able to project population growth. In addition, it can also employ further disaggregation for instance for different ethnic groups, for which fertility and mortality (and migration) may follow a different pattern.

Figure 13.18 illustrates the cohort component method. The figure, that gives a schematic representation for one gender, shows how per age category separate arrows are defined for in-migration, outmigration, fertility and mortality. The method is generally used per five years. The figure clearly shows how the method is more refined in that for each new projection (projections are generally made per 5 year-interval), mortality, in- and outmigration are incorporated. Suppose that many young women of a certain ethnic group would have perished in a conflict, then this affects the fertility for the entire population, which can be accounted for in projections for the years to come. An extension to the cohort component model is the so-called multistate cohort component model, which incorporates various other determinants of fertility. One such determinant is education. Fertility varies with education, with the higher educated generally having fewer children. If victims had been made mainly within the well-educated strata of society, such differential impact can also be incorporated in these models, and improve the estimates.

While the cohort component method is therefore superior to the 'naive' method that we outlined at the beginning, its big drawback for studying international crimes is obviously that high quality data are required, while in many cases such detailed data on mortality, fertility and migration will be unavailable – let alone disaggregated by sex and age. This means that for many practical situations, we may simply not have the data required, and will for that reason have to resort to the cruder 'naive' method, that averages over age intervals and gender. For more on demographic population projections, see O'Neill, Balk, Brickman *et al.* (2001).

While the 'naive' method is cruder, it does have its advantages. Firstly, it is simpler to use and therefore less prone to errors. Secondly, the simplicity of the 'naive' method may be a virtue in the estimation of conflict mortality: it does not have the disadvantage of the cohort component method that is, perhaps deceptively, veiled in exactness.

Depending on which assumption is employed, estimates can vary (substantially). It is therefore advisable to assess the variability of one's estimates against these assumptions. In our example of the 'naive' method, we assumed that the population growth rate was 2.2% for all three years. There is however uncertainty. The population growth rate in the years before the conflict may have been 2.2%, but in two neighbouring countries it may actually have been 2.0 and 2.3% respectively. It could thus very well be that the growth rate was actually 2.0% – or 2.3%, or anything in between. To investigate the impact of such different assumptions on our results we can compute several estimates: under the low and high growth rate scenario. The high growth rate scenario would amount to an estimated hypothetical end of conflict population equalling $2{,}000{,}000 \times 1.023^3 = 2{,}141{,}198$. The low growth rate scenario would amount to an estimated hypothetical end of conflict population equalling $2{,}000{,}000 \times 1.020^3 = 2{,}122{,}416$. Thus, we can conclude that excess

Figure 13.18: Representation of cohort component method

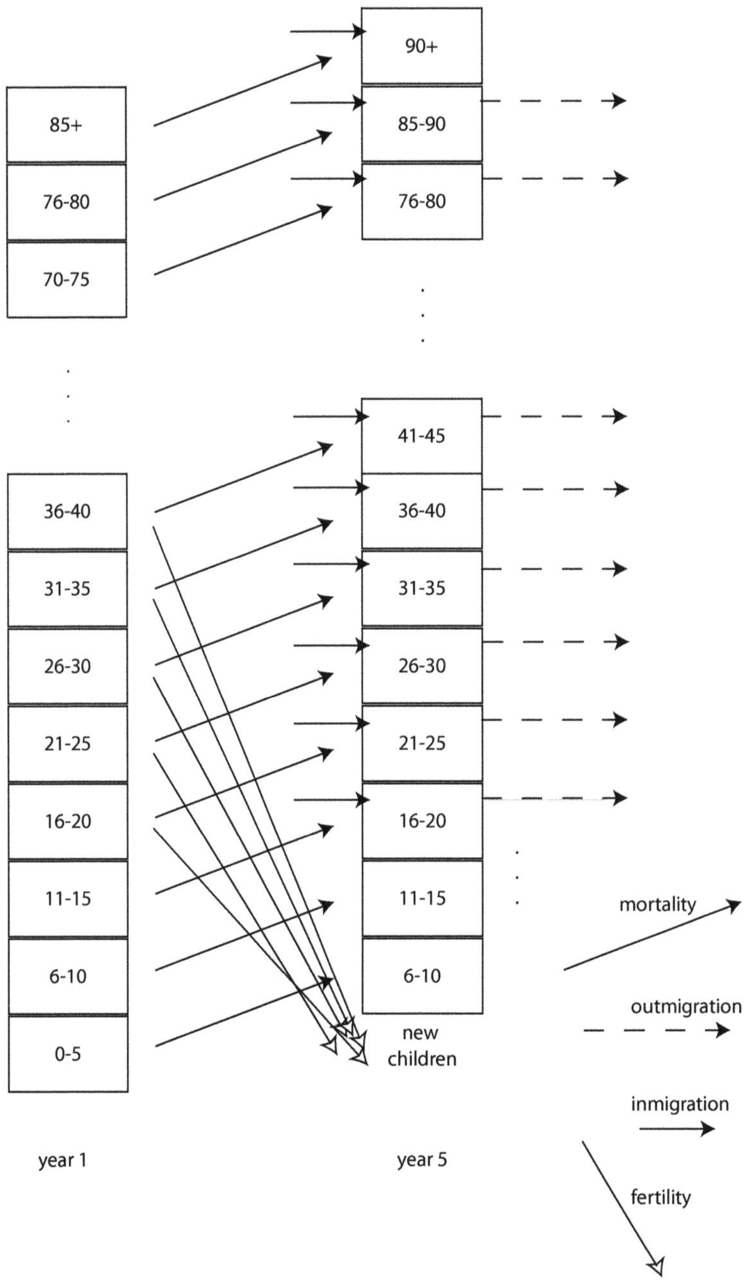

mortality would lie in a likely range of 172,416 – 191,198. Such an analysis of the extent to which estimates vary by different hypothetical values (or are 'robust' against different assumptions for such values) is called a *sensitivity analysis.*

The counterfactual method should perhaps be viewed as a method of last resort if no better survey data on mortality are available. It can be used for conflicts of relatively short duration, as the uncertainty of forecasts increases exponentially as the length of the forecasting period increases. Another issue is that if it were used for a long time, say 25 years, it would assume that a number of children were born, who again conceived children within that long period. The method might then estimate that people perished who were in fact never born.

The cohort component method and its coarser variety were used to determine mortality for various conflicts. Bijleveld and Hoex (2008) estimated mortality in the context of the civil war in Sierra Leone between 1991 to 2002. Different estimates of civilian mortality as an immediate consequence of these gross human rights violations do exist, ranging from 35,000 to 200,000 deaths, that are however barely substantiated. For estimating total excess mortality, the authors estimated a hypothetical population size in 2002, had the population grown uninterruptedly in a non-conflict situation. For that, they extrapolated the population size in Sierra Leone in 1990, which they set at 4,087,000, using a conservative growth rate of 1.96. Correcting for migration they arrived at a hypothetical population size by 2002 of $4{,}022{,}000 \times 1.0196^{10.5} = 4{,}979{,}321$. For 2002, no census data were available. However, a census had been held in 2004. Backcalculating from this census, and again correcting for migration, they estimated the Sierra Leonean population size by early 2002 at approximately 4,517,330. This means that total excess mortality, estimated as the difference between the hypothesized and the actual population, is approximately 4,979,321 - 4,517,330 = 461,990. It should be stressed that this is a conservative estimate. The authors carried out the same computations for a growth rate that is higher at 2.17%, but deemed by some to be more realistic. Employing that growth rate, total excess mortality is estimated at 521,593. The authors therefore conclude that between 460,000 and 520,000 Sierra Leoneans lost their lives due to the 1991-2002 civil war.

For the civil war and ensuing Khmer Rouge period in Cambodia, Heuveline (2001) used the cohort component method to estimate mortality for the years 1970 – 1980. Heuveline analysed the sizes of various population groups, by age and sex, before 1970 and after 1980. He projected forward from old censuses to arrive at a likely starting population in 1970, which he estimated at 7.7 million. Projecting backward from a later voting register, he also arrived at a likely population for 1980. Investigating the trends in mortality and fertility, and accounting for migration, he arrived at a likely total excess mortality for the Khmer Rouge period of around 2 million. His models used several parameters of which the values are unsure. By setting each at its minimum as well as maximum value, he calculated a range for excess mortality between 1.17 to 3.42 million deaths.

For the Extraordinary Chambers in the Courts of Cambodia, the hybrid court established to try a number of former Khmer Rouge leaders, Tabeau and Kheam reviewed all existing mortality estimates for the Khmer Rouge period (2009). Comparing estimates by Heuveline and others, they narrowed down excess mortality to a most likely 1.747 to 2.2 million, out of a range of 1.6 to 2.2 million.

13.3.5 Multiple systems estimation

In section 11.7.2 we discussed the so-called capture-recapture methods. Capture-recapture methods estimate the size of an unknown population from at least two so-called captures. Under fairly stringent assumptions, namely that of a closed population, i.e. a population that no members leave or enter, no tag loss, equal capture probabilities and of independence of captures, it is possible to estimate the size of the entire population.

This fairly simple method has been extended to use in the estimation of mortality in conflicts. Extensions to the method are necessary for two reasons. Firstly, in the context in which this method is used, often more than two lists are available. Conflict fatalities may be marked on IDP camp lists, or on graves, on lists compiled by NGOs, or may have been reported dead by families on other lists. Secondly, the assumption of independence of captures must be considered untenable for many conflict situations. If a victim has been marked as deceased on a camp list, it is likely that he or she is buried in a marked grave. If someone perished in flight, it is unlikely that his or her death is registered or that there is a marked grave. This means that the – strong – assumption of independence is violated, in which case we cannot anymore use the straightforward multiplication of chances as outlined in section 11.7.2.

Ball and his colleagues (the example we will discuss is in Ball, Betts, Scheuren *et al.*, 2002) applied an extension to this method that was developed by Zaslavsky and Wolfgang (1993) called *multiple systems estimation*. The 'multiple' refers to the fact that it entails the estimation of the size of a population from three or more lists. In addition, the method accommodates list dependence, i.e. dependence of capture probabilities. We will discuss the method using Ball, Betts, Scheuren *et al.*'s (2002) estimation of mortality in Kosovo from March – June 1999. Their report was presented in the trial against Milosevic. The method was used as well for estimation of mortality in Timor Leste, in Peru and for several other conflicts; a fairly non-technical overview with examples is given by Lum, Price and Banks (2013).

First we describe the data. The authors had four sources that listed killings. A first had been compiled from interviews by the American Bar Association Central and East European Law Initiative (ABA/CEELI, further abbreviated as ABA). A second had been compiled from interviews by Human Rights Watch (HRW). Then, a third from interviews conducted by the Organisation for Security and Cooperation in Europe (OSCE), and a last had been formed from records of exhumations conducted by international teams on behalf of the International Tribunal for the former Yugoslavia (to which we refer as EXH). All lists had names and particulars of the deceased, and added up to 10,000 entries. These entries were first compared to remove duplicates. After this deduplication process, a total of 4,400 unique individual victims remained. This process was a scrupulous and important one. Undermatching (i.e. if one fails to register that one person occurs on two or more lists) would inflate the estimate of the total population. Overmatching would spuriously decrease it.

Some of the uniquely identified victims appeared on one list only, some on two list, some on three and some even on four. Table 13.2 gives an overview of the data and the overlap across lists. Obviously, what we are interested in, is finding the people who appear on none of the lists (the 'n.a.' in the right column and bottom row).

Table 13.2: Number of individual victims of killing by list

	ABA	yes	yes	no	no	
	EXH	yes	no	yes	no	
HRW	OSCE					total
yes	yes	27	32	42	123	
yes	no	18	31	106	306	
no	yes	181	217	228	936	
no	no	177	845	1,131	n.a.	
	total					4,400

Now, if we were to simply employ the two-list capture-recapture approach we would go about as follows. We could inspect the overlap between EXH and ABA, and estimate the size of the total population. And do the same for OSCE and HRW. We could do the same for all six possible combinations of lists. If the assumptions underlying the method are met, and if each list is an equally relevant sample out of the total population of victims, we would expect to find exactly the same result for each comparison.

This is exactly what the authors check. And what they find not to be the case. First, they note that the lists cover different regions of the relevant area, indicating heterogeneity. Second, they note that the two-list estimations of total mortality differ considerably: from 5,461 for OSCE and HRW to 9,689 for the combination of HRW and ABA. At the time of writing of their report, the lowest available tally for documented killings was 7,155 – four out of the six estimates were below that number. Thus, the estimates generated by the two-list comparisons give unrealistically low estimates. According to the authors, this shows that there is positive dependence between some of the lists. Their reasoning is as follows. In case of positive dependence, the overlap between two lists becomes higher than it would be in case of no dependence. The estimated size of the population then becomes too small. Given that we have in these comparisons a number of estimates that appear unrealistically low, it is therefore likely that there is positive list dependence. For more on their preliminary analysis, see the original report by Ball and his colleagues (2002).

The authors now proceed to estimate the total number of victims as follows. They first formulate an ANOVA-type of model to predict the logarithm of the cell frequencies m_{ijkl}:

$$\log(\mathrm{m}_{ijkl}) = \mathrm{u} + \mathrm{u}_{1(i)} + \mathrm{u}_{2(j)} + \mathrm{u}_{3(k)} + \mathrm{u}_{4(l)} +$$
$$\mathrm{u}_{12(ij)} + \mathrm{u}_{13(ik)} + \mathrm{u}_{14(il)} + \mathrm{u}_{23(jk)} + \mathrm{u}_{24(jl)} + \mathrm{u}_{34(kl)} +$$
$$\mathrm{u}_{123(ijk)} + \mathrm{u}_{124(ijl)} + \mathrm{u}_{134(ikl)} + \mathrm{u}_{234(jkl)} + \mathrm{u}_{1234(ijkl)},$$

with ‘u’ comparable to the overall mean μ in ANOVA, the term $u_{1(i)}$ – comparable to a main effect as in ANOVA – the main effect for being on list 1 (with the terms $u_{2(j)}$, $u_{3(k)}$ and $u_{4(l)}$ defined correspondingly), the terms $\mathrm{u}_{12(ij)}$ to $\mathrm{u}_{12(kl)}$ representing the 1st order interaction effects of being on list 1 *and* list 2, on list 1 *and* list 3 ... etc., $\mathrm{u}_{123(ijk)}$ to

$u_{234(jkl)}$ representing the 2nd order interaction effects, and lastly $u_{1234(ijkl)}$ the 3rd order interaction effect.

The niceties of this model are firstly that if we have parameter terms for all the main and interaction effects, we will be able to estimate the logarithm of the frequency of the cell for which we have no data, that is, the 'n.a.' cell in the table. For this, we estimate the (log of the) frequency for the situation where all effects are zero. Secondly, the model is able to capture list dependence: this is exactly what the interaction terms are for. So, instead of list dependence wrecking the model that was discussed in section 11.7.2, in this model list dependence is explicitly incorporated.

We cannot discuss all the details of this loglinear model here, but will limit ourselves to the essentials for the thrust of the story. For that, we first mention that various models may be fitted on the data. We could for instance fit a model in which we assume that only main effects explain the data, i.e. no list dependence is modelled:

$$\log(m_{ijkl}) = u + u_{1(i)} + u_{2(j)} + u_{3(k)} + u_{4(k)}.$$

However, we could also choose to explicitly model list dependence between each pair of two lists, in which case the model would become:

$$\log(m_{ijkl}) = u + u_{1(i)} + u_{2(j)} + u_{3(k)} + u_{4(k)} +$$
$$u_{12(ij)} + u_{13(ik)} + u_{14(il)} + u_{23(jk)} + u_{24(jl)} + u_{34(kl)}.$$

Other specifications are possible, incorporating higher-order list dependence. It is also possible to model all effects, but in that case, the model is as we say 'saturated': it is not really a model anymore as all possible factors are used to predict cell frequencies. This will generate a perfect fit – the model is then not a simplification of reality anymore. As stated in section 8.1.2, we want our models to be as simple as possible against, as we said in section 8.1.3, as high possible a fit. Such a saturated model we therefore do not regard as meeting the requirement of parsimony.

After estimation of a model, a so-called model fit can be computed, comparable to what we discussed for the regression model in section 11.7.2. The measure for that model fit tells us – roughly speaking – how much the observed data differ from the data as predicted by the model. The model fit measure is the so-called X^2, i.e. the sample value for the χ^2:

$$X^2 = \sum \frac{(\text{Observed - Expected})^2}{\text{Expected}},$$

with 'Observed' the data as observed, and 'Expected' the data as expected under the specific model, viz section 6.4.3. Here, if a model fits the data, we expect the observed frequencies to closely match the frequencies as expected if the model had generated the data. This means that for deciding that a model fits the data we would want the statistic to be *not* significantly different from 0.

If we choose a model with only main effects then we would expect that model to fit less well than a model that also specifies interaction effects. If a model fits really badly, the statistic generated by this technique will tell us that it is highly unlikely to find these data if the specified model were the model generating the data. We then reject the model.

If the chance to find the data under the specified model is higher than p =.05, we accept the model. However, we also want a model that is as parsimonious as possible. This means that we will be searching for the simplest model with relatively the best fit.

Using these 'playing rules', the authors next proceeded to estimate a set of models, that use various specifications of main effects and (2nd and 3rd order) interaction terms. From the solutions, they discarded those with an inadequate fit ($p < .05$). Next, they also discarded those models that gave a fairly high fit (they selected $p > .30$ as a cutoff). This may seem counterintuitive, but such models generally have a large number of parameters and are therefore not parsimonious. From the remaining set of solutions, they then selected that model that had relatively the best fit given the number parameters used.

The model they finally selected had main effects for all lists, first order interaction effects for ABA and OSCE, ABA and EXH, and for OSCE and EXH, for HRW and OSCE and for HRW and EXH (meaning that one interaction effect was left out) as well as one second-order interaction effect (between ABA, OSCE and EXH). The model generated a total estimated mortality of 10,356 (with a 95% confidence interval 9,002 – 12,122), meaning that 5,956 killed individuals had been uncaptured by any list.

Multiple systems estimation is a technically challenging technique. The statistically feeble-hearted should perhaps not embark upon it. While it appears highly sophisticated, a number of decisions have to be made that may be considered subjective. For instance, Ball and his co-authors decided to reject models with a p-value exceeding .30. This .30 is however an arbitrary cutoff value. Only two of the models had fairly high p-values (p=.796 and p=.603, respectively). If only those two, as a distinct category, had been omitted, the criterion to select that model that had the best possible fit against the lowest number of parameters would have led the authors to pick a model that had a higher estimated N (13,760) with a much wider confidence interval (95% confidence interval 9,695 – 20,752). A second best would have been a model with an estimated N of 22,923. This shows that – even though the method is statistically sophisticated – there is some individual leeway left, with marked impact on the numerical outcomes. In spite of the perhaps ad hoc reasoning, the estimate that Balland his co-authors chose is, however, the estimate for the simplest model with the fewest number of parameters.

As the number of lists from which mortality data have been captured becomes larger, the number of possible models to fit can become too large to handle. In that case, instead of choosing one model as a 'best' model, it may be better to derive an average solution from all these models. The procedure with which this is done is called Bayesian model averaging. It also solves for the fairly arbitrary cutoff chosen above, where models with p-values exceeding .30 were excluded: now, all models are incorporated. Lum, Price, Guberek *et al.* (2010) describe a procedure for averaging over models for the estimation of killings and disappearances in Casanare, Colombia. Using data from 15 lists, that had been carefully cleaned and deduplicated, they specified a total of over 3,000 different models for all possible combinations of three datasets (had they also included models combining four and more lists the analysis would have been unwieldy). The averaging method resulted in total numbers of 5,832 killings (95% confidence interval: 3,822 – 9,332) and 2,345 disappearances (95% confidence interval: 1,221 – 4,901) between 1998 and 2007. Note that the confidence intervals are quite wide.

The data requirements for multiple systems estimation are quite low. All that is needed is a number of lists on which people (or units) appear. The lists need to be linked to identify who appears only on one list, and who appears on multiple lists. The data requirements are therefore fairly low, which makes it suitable for application in conflict settings. However, one of the assumptions on which the technique hinges is correct matching. The technique for that reason requires scrupulous checking of names to avoid over- and undermatching. When lists with names are large or there are many lists, the process of visual or matching maybe become almost impossible to carry out. In such instances, researchers generally resort to automated matching, in which software categorises names or units into 'matches', 'non-matches' and 'possible matches'. The possible matches are then reviewed by hand (so-called 'clerical review'); an overview of such techniques for matching (linkage and de-duplication) can be found in Christen (2012). Even so, capture-recapture techniques and multiple systems estimation are suitable only in situations where we can be certain that we can match people. This means that in societies where no unique family names are employed, it may be unfeasible.

Some statisticians believe that the numbers generated by the MSE estimation methods should be regarded as indicative or exploratory, rather than definitive. Regardless, capture recapture and multiple systems estimation methods have assumed a clear place in social research. A recent – fairly technical – overview of capture-recapture models, multiple systems estimation and varieties thereof, including numerous applications, is Bohning, Van der Heijden and Bunge (2017).

13.4 Assessing the prevalence of sexual and other crimes

While much of the attention in research into prevalence of international crimes is devoted to the measurement or estimation of killings and more broadly excess mortality, many other crimes are committed in the course of conflicts. These constitute international crimes as well insofar as they fall under the scope of legal definitions. As Agirre (2010) argues, empirical evidence and analysis have been used successfully mainly in the investigation of large-scale killings, destruction, and displacement, and the use of empirical methods for the prosecution of sexual violence remained markedly limited. Agirre argues that there is a need to overcome this gap.

In the following, we will discuss methods for measuring the incidence of sexual violence (section 13.4.1) and methods for studying other crimes, such as property crimes and destruction.

13.4.1 Sexual violence

Sexual violence is more often than not part and parcel of conflicts. During the wars that raged in Bosnia, Rwanda, Sierra Leone, DRC and Darfur, numerous women, children and also men were sexually victimised. Sexual violence victimisation is notoriously difficult to study. It may be excruciatingly difficult for victims to speak of their sexual victimisation experiences. Perpetrators are generally especially unforthcoming when questions pertain to sexual crimes.

Many studies that have been carried out on sexual violence are qualitative studies on the nature of rape, victims, and the motives perpetrators may have had (Wood, 2006). Studies of violent mass conflicts and investigations have shown that rape may be extremely widespread (see for Sierra Leone: Physicians for Human Rights, 2002; for Congo: Human Rights Watch, 2005; for South Sudan, see `hrw.org/news/2018/12/18/south-sudan-spate-sexual-violence`. Studies on rape victimisation are generally difficult to carry out (Lisak & Miller, 2002) and carrying out research on rape and other forms of sexual violence in a country in conflict is incrementally more difficult. The extent to which rape is widespread in a period of collective violence, or its quantitative impact, remains therefore unclear. That it occurs regularly and frequently seems clear: it has been estimated that 20,000 to 50,000 women were raped during the war in Bosnia in the early 1990s, in Sierra Leone, between 50,000 and 64,000 internally displaced women suffered sexual assault at the hands of combatants; Bijleveld, Morssinkhof and Smeulers (2009) estimated that a lower limit of 250,000 women were raped during the 100 days of the Rwandan genocide.

Sexual violence is important to study. In a sense it stands apart, because of its particularly destructive nature. Rape may serve to break the resistance of victims, to humiliate victims, as the spoils of war, as revenge, and ultimately to destroy also those who survived rape itself and break up their societies, by bestowing them with these victims and their mostly unwanted offspring, and often also with HIV infections. As such, reliable estimates of rape prevalence are necessary to evaluate comprehensively the qualitative and quantitative impact of the international crimes. Population-based surveys of its occurrence can aid in establishing to what extent it was systematic.

For studying sexual violence, victim surveys are generally used. The design of such surveys requires particular care, however. Bijleveld, Morssinkhof and Smeulers (2009) enumerate a number of reasons for this. The first reason is that victims may be extremely reluctant to speak about rape victimisation. Rape carries an immense social stigma in many societies, and women are reported not be willing to declare that they have been raped for fear of not being able to ever find a husband: in a number of societies, women are rejected by their families if they have been raped. Also, women may have been raped by men they know, or by men who may even still be living in their vicinity. They may be apprehensive of speaking out about the rape as they fear reprisals. Next, survivors may be unwilling to speak about their experiences as they suffer from survivor's guilt. Lastly, many victims or witnesses are afraid to speak out because they fear being called to testify. Also, some women report that speaking out about their victimisation is not worth the trouble and the risk. They feel let down by the legal system.

A second reason that such studies require special care, is that sexuality is not an easy topic to talk about. Words for sexual victimisation are also not always unambiguous. In one culture, forced intercourse during marriage may be viewed as rape, in other cultures this may not be the case. For that reason, the same rules apply that were enumerated in section 11.5.2 for victim surveys in general: questions should be worded as factually, as behaviourally specific as possible. Even so, misunderstanding about wording may not elicit the required information. As an example: in some countries sexual enslavement is commonly referred to as 'being forced to cook for someone'; Swiss, Jennings, Aryee *et al.* (1998) therefore recommend to always enlist the aid of local specialists to correctly phrase questions such that they are understood as they are intended. If one uses standardised questionnaires, translation and backtranslation are of even greater importance than in 'ordinary' surveys.

A third reason is not particular to the study of international crimes, but related to the well established fact within criminology that a large proportion of sexual victimisation remains unreported, also in victim surveys. Lisak and Miller (2002) estimated that around 80% of all sexual offences remains not reported. For rape this figure may be lower, but considering the strong social stigma on rape in many societies it may be realistic to suppose strong underreporting for rape as well. Victim surveys that have more questions, that are presented as studies into sexual victimisation, and that have behaviouraly specific and tailored questions, generally elicit higher prevalence rates. It is assumed that such tailored surveys give better estimates of sexual abuse victimisation than general surveys, as studies into sexual victimisation that use behaviourally specific questions generally find higher levels of sexual victimisation (cf. Tjaden & Thoennes 1998).

As we already discussed briefly in section 11.5.2), Jewkes and Abrahams (2002) reported the nationally representative 12 month rape prevalence for South Africa from the 1999 National Victims of Crime Survey as 390 per 100,000 women aged 17 and over. From a different study (Jewkes, Penn-Kekana, Levin *et al.* 1999), that was non-representative as it was conducted in three provinces but did have much more tailored wording and a sensitive questionnaire environment conducive to reporting rape, a 12 month rape prevalence of 1,300 per 100,000 women aged 18 – 49 years was generated. For the US, the National College Women Sexual Victimisation Study (NCWSV) elicited a tenfold higher victimisation rate for completed rape than the National Violence Against Women Study (Fisher, 2009). Analysis of these differences showed that the incongruity is likely attributable to the fact that the NCWSV employed behaviourally specific so-called screener questions.

Physicians for Human Rights (2002) conducted a survey in Sierra Leone in 2000 and 2001 to investigate the prevalence of war-related sexual violence among IDPs. Four sample locations from three different districts were selected as well as from a western part of Sierra Leone, representing 91% of the registered IDP population in Sierra Leone; 9% of estimated IDPs were inaccessible due to insecurity. At the various locations, systematic and cluster sampling were used to sample per location. The response rate was 95%. The questionnaire contained 49 questions, asking after a variety of experiences, amongst which also the life time prevalence of non-war related sexual violence, as well as looting and destruction of their houses, and forced labour. The referral period for war-related experiences was 10 years, a quite lengthy period for a victim survey (cf. section 11.5.2).

The questionnaire had been designed in English, and was translated into Krio, the lingua franca of Sierra Leone, and backtranslated into English. The questions on sexual violence and sexuality had been designed by Sierra Leonean female professionals, either researchers into the topic or women who provided services to survivors of sexual violence. The Krio questionnaire was next translated into Mende and Temne, two other main languages in Sierra Leone, which were checked for accuracy. Regional human rights and sexual violence experts reviewed the questionnaire for content validity. The questionnaire was piloted on 12 women, upon which clarifications and further improvements were added.

The interviewers were all professionals regarding the topic. They were all trained for eight to nine days, and subsequently supervised during the first days of interviewing. Interviews lasted between 25 – 60 minutes. A most private setting was sought for each interview. Permission for the study had been granted by UN officials, camp administrators as well as by local community leaders. Respondents offered verbal informed consent, and did not receive remuneration or presents. For those under 18, verbal consent was obtained from (a) parent(s).

A total of 94 (9%) of respondents reported war-related sexual victimisation. Rape was reported by 84 out of these 94 victims; more than one in three had been gang-raped. Over half of victims had sustained injuries, 6 (6%) reported they had become pregnant. Over half of the abuse had taken place in their own village. Most of the abuse had taken place within a fairly narrow time frame, i.e. between 1997 and 1999. The prevalence of war-related sexual victimisation was equal to the life time prevalence of non-war related sexual violence. The authors extrapolate their findings to the entire IDP population in Sierra Leone, concluding that 50,000 to 64,000 Sierra Leonean IDP women may have suffered sexual violence during the war. For more, see the extensive but readable report (Physicians for Human Rights, 2002).

Studies on other conflicts have generated other prevalence rates. While some of the variability in prevalence may be due to differences in study methodology (design, questionnaire, approach, etc.), some of the variability probably reflects true variation in victimisation. In some conflicts, as Wood argued (2006), sexual violence is more common than in other conflicts. Also the nature of the sexual violence differs. Using a population based survey for eastern DRC, Johnson, Scott, Rughita *et al.* (2010) reported that almost 40% of women and almost a quarter of men had been victimised sexually, with only 1.3% of rapes among women gang rapes. A survey in Liberia conducted in 1994 yielded a prevalence rate of 15%. This study employed a tailored questionnaire that had been developed by local women and pretested for content validity, and in which great care was taken not to violate cultural taboos. For instance, in Liberia it is considered inappropriate that an older women be asked about sex by a younger woman – even if she herself is already 50; for that reason all older women were addressed with special respectful phrases. Sampling was a mixture of convenience sampling (at markets) and systematic sampling using food relief lists as a sampling frame. Differences in prevalence (Liberia is adjacent to Sierra Leone and the two conflicts were related) may be due to the different questionnaires, different designs, different response styles – or reflect a different victimisation prevalence.

Recent studies have increasingly pointed to the fact that sexual violence is not only perpetrated against women, and not only by men. See Johnson, Scott, Rughita *et al.* (2010). It is assumed that male victims may underreport even more strongly than female victims (see Wijkman, Bijleveld & Hendriks, 2012).

13.4.2 Violence, property and other crimes

As said above, many other crimes than sexual crimes are committed as part of international criminality. These are perhaps even more 'neglected' in empirical research and prosecution than sexual crimes. One reason for that is because they may be regarded as less serious crimes. A second may be because they are harder to measure and to quantify. However, if people's livelihoods are destroyed (their homes burnt, their cattle killed or looted, their wells poisoned, their crops and seeds destroyed), these may constitute international crimes as well. Studying the prevalence of such non-violent crimes is also important from the perspective of the etiology of these crimes (viz. chapter 14). The destruction of villages may also signal, or serve as a 'marker' for, the physical destruction of ethnic groups. The geographical or ethnic patterning of such destruction is important from the perspective of etiology as well.

These other crimes can be quite prevalent. From the Physicians for Human Rights study on sexual violence in Sierra Leone (2002), it was reported that 9.3% of household members had been abducted; 20% of respondents reported that their homes had been burned or their possessions looted. Among Liberian female respondents (Swiss, Jennings, Aryee *et al.* 1998), 17% reported having been beaten, tied up, or detained under an armed guard. It is known that the property of most Jews who were deported under the Nazi rule in WW II was stolen – reportedly on a 'Napoleonic' scale. The cultural artefacts that were stolen and never returned have been labeled as 'the last prisoners of war' (cf. O'Donnell, 2011). The property of the Armenians was looted before the Armenian genocide. For Darfur, it is reported that Janjaweed and government forces would attack villages at the crack of dawn, chase out the population, after which trucks would enter villages, load all possessions on to these trucks and quickly speed off so that they could still make the morning market in the larger villages and sell the spoils on that same day (El Khatir, 2009) – after which the village would be torched. Looting and destruction therefore likely occur regularly in the context of international crimes, and property crimes are likely quite prevalent, if only as a by-product of international crimes.

Obviously, such crimes can be measured using victim surveys. Just as respondents can be asked after mortality, after sexual victimisation, we can also ask them whether they have been beaten, tortured, or subjected to other types of violence. We can also ask them after destruction of their property, and after looting. If violent crimes are addressed through interviewing respondents, the same issues are important for questions and questionnaire design, study design and sample selection that we described in the previous chapters. The same goes if we want to find out about property crimes, or crimes of destruction, and we refer to those chapters for general guidelines on how to design and carry out such surveys.

However, not many studies report population-based estimates of the prevalence of these crimes, as only a number of surveys include questions on such robbery and looting. Also, it is to be doubted whether victims are always aware of the destruction and looting of their property, especially if they have been displaced.

The destruction of villages has also been studied with innovative, indirect methods such as using satellite images. Prins (2008) mapped the burning of villages in Darfur using satellite imagery of Darfur. The study had been commissioned by Amnesty International to verify reports by eye witnesses of large-scale attacks and destruction. As the area was then still extremely dangerous and inaccessible to researchers, it was impossible to conduct a study 'on the ground'. Prins used low resolution satellite so-called 'Lansat' imagery for a 32,000 square kilometer area in West Darfur, and compared the identification of recently burnt villages (as indicated by decreased so-called *albedo* or reflectivity) with high resolution satellite images by the USAID Humanitarian Information Unit, Google Earth and Amnesty International. Also, various ground reports of burnt villages were available on the internet and used in the analysis (e.g. Human Rights Watch, 2004) to verify the location of other burnt sites; using the geo-coded reports of incidents, these could be directly con-

Figure 13.19: Landsat ETM+ image scenario of a village before (top) shortly after (middle) burning with *albedo* change (bottom)

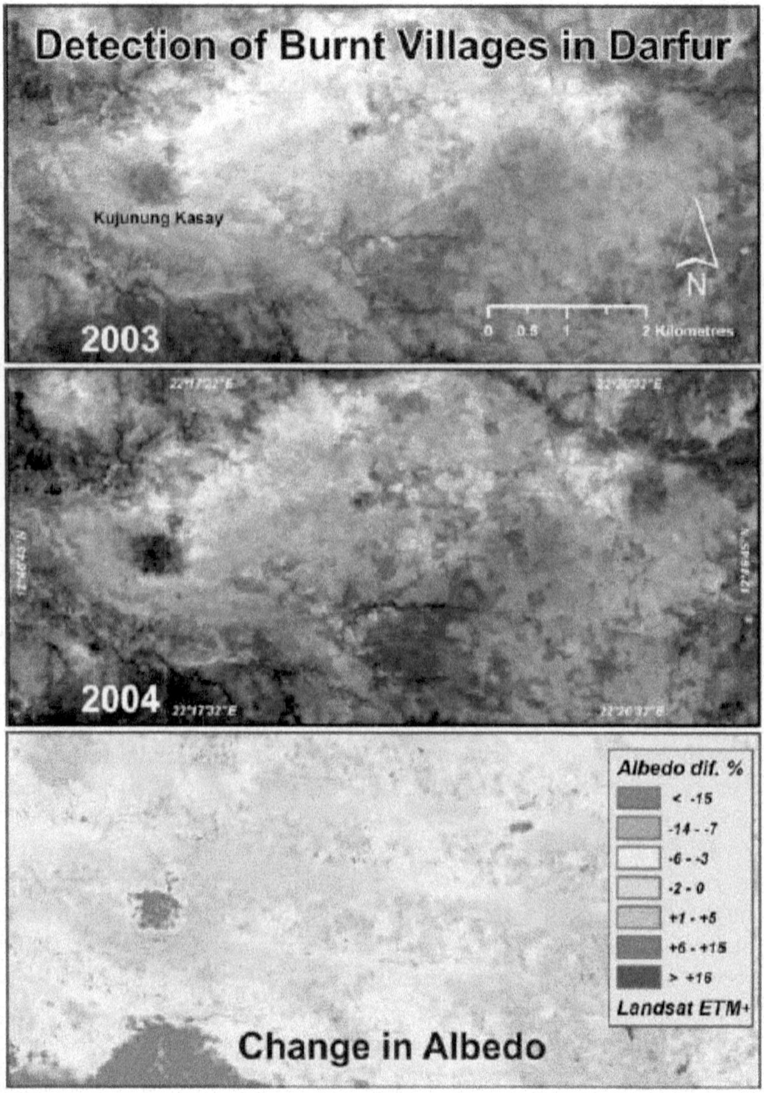

source: Prins (2008)

nected to the satellite maps for verification. About half of the studied 352 villages showed decreased *albedo*, a finding 90% consistent with Google Earth images: the low resolution images missed some smaller, more dispersed villages and may not distinguish bushfires from burnt infrastructure.

Figure 13.19 gives an example of the analysis for one village. The top image is a Landsat+ image before burning, the middle gives the image shortly after burning. The bottom picture indicates the change in reflection (*albedo*): the red blob in the left side of the picture is the burnt village. The red patch at the bottom left side is due to a bush fire.

The method is relatively cheap and provides a fast way to identify and monitor large-scale destruction during conflicts. It is to be doubted whether it can be used in areas with thick forest cover or with wet climates.

In principle it would be possible to carry out self-report surveys to estimate the incidence of violent and property crimes. This author is unaware of any studies to estimate incidence using population-based perpetrator or self-report surveys. One complicating factor – over and above the issues discussed section 11.5.3 – is that perpetrators may be less easily accessible than victims (many of whom may be living in relatively safe IDP camps).

13.5 On the need for corroboration and triangulation

As we saw in the preceding section, measuring the prevalence of international crime is no easy task. We discussed several case studies in which a number of estimates was around, that varied widely and where it was no easy feat to determine the 'best' estimate – perhaps better phrased as the 'least problematic' estimate. As we saw, publication in a top-notch scientific journal is no guarantee that an estimate is correct.

As things go, usually the first estimate to get published, lingers. Also, that first victimisation estimate is generally the least sound. As author upon author cites the same figure, quoting each other, these first estimates tend to lead lives of their own ('everybody says it is 50,000'), and to become internalised and 'reality'. Estimates that are compiled later – generally using better data – tend to be lower than previous estimates (with some exceptions, it must be noted).

As Tabeau and Bijak (2005) show, the early estimates of war-related deaths from Bosnia and Herzegovina ranged from 25,000 to 329,000 deaths. Carefully reviewing each of the estimates published, they show how most of the locally produced estimates relied on only one source, extrapolating to the entire population. Often, it was unclear what methods exactly for this were being used, and authors using the same sources even arrived at different estimates. Definitions were often unclear too. There were duplicates in lists (so that victims were double counted, aggravated by researchers taking estimates from various lists and simply adding them up without checking whether there was overlap). Many studies never distinguished between conflict related and regular deaths. Apart from 'sloppy work' the authors attribute another part of the difficulties to the fact that statistical institutions did not function during the conflict, that in places there was wanton destruction of vital records, and that data on out-migration were often lacking or vague.

Basing themselves on ten different sources (i.e. (1) military records for Bosnia Herzegovina, (2) military records from the Republika Srpska, (3) Military records from the Croatian Defence Council, (4) ICRC PHR lists of missing persons, (5) the FIS database (death records), (6) the HSS Mortality database (survey), (7) the MAG mortality database (NGO), (8) death records from funeral homes, (9) exhumation records from Krajina, and (10) the Prijedor Missing persons book), they compiled a new estimate. Their sources were selected on the basis of several criteria: they had to be deemed reliable and complete ('prosecutable evidence'), they had to give information on whether the person was a civilian or military person, and on cause of death. Crossvalidating these sources, they arrive at an estimate of 107,395 deaths, of which 67,530 were war-related. Even though they note that their estimate is much better than any previous estimate, the authors remark that it is still incomplete and should be seen as work in progress. An account of similar estimations for Cambodia is given by Tabeau and Zwierzchowski (2013).

Palermo and Peterman (2011) discuss similar processes with regard to rape victimisation in conflicts. They state that flawed estimates of sexual victimisation prevalence are often perpetuated out of desire to illustrate the magnitude of the violence. They note that two kinds of data are generally available: monitoring data (giving tallies) that typically undercount, and survey data, that often have been collected with insufficient rigour. Flawed estimates may go two ways, being too low or too high. For instance, as the authors write, it has been repeatedly claimed by the media that more than three quarters (75%) of Liberian women were raped during the country's civil war, the three-quarters estimate however originating from a study conducted on a sample of survivors of different types of sexual violence, of whom 77% had experienced rape. This estimate became cited as if it were generalisable to all women in Liberia. For Rwanda, Bijleveld, Morssinkhof and Smeulers (2009) illustrate how an estimate of 250,000 women raped during the genocide was commonly quoted. This estimate had a very weak basis as it has been extrapolated from the number of recorded pregnancies resulting from rape (approximately 2,000 – 5,000). It was estimated that one pregnancy would result from every 100 rapes, which is arguably a fairly low rate, leading to an inflated estimate (often a pregnancy rate per single rape of 5% is used). As both Bijleveld and her co-authors (2009) and Palermo and Peterman (2011) show, the estimate is untenable: only women reporting rape and subsequent pregnancy were included, post-menopausal women, men and children were excluded. It is likely that many pregnancies were never reported, were aborted or children abandoned. These factors all again deflate the estimate. All in all, the estimate is much too unreliable.

Scientific rigour is needed when studying prevalence. Estimates should always be corroborated against different sources – if available. Different methods should be employed – if possible – to triangulate the findings. Specialists should always be consulted to check the validity of key assumptions. A sensitivity analysis should be done to generate an interval within which the estimate likely falls. Very precise estimates mislead naive readers to expect exactness.

There are many 'ifs' with these 'shoulds' as in many situations there is simply only poor data. This illustrates that there is still quite a road to travel. This road to travel is not only in the collection of good quality data, but also in agreeing on an acceptable methodology for certain questions, for particular conflicts, with their own particular data situations, even if researchers generally bring their own methodological standards.

Chapter 14

Studying etiology

When we study etiology, we want to know the causes of crime. What made offenders commit crimes? What contexts are more conducive to the occurrence of crime than others? Are there structural factors in some population groups or organisations that make it more likely that crime is committed there? Do factors at the societal level predispose some societies more to crime than others? These are the type of questions that are posed when we want to investigate what brought about crime. In the following, we will first structure the methods that will be discussed in this chapter along two dimensions: qualitative versus quantitative, and along the level of aggregation at which explanations are sought.

14.1 Types of studies into etiology

The methods that can be used for answering etiological questions are quite diverse. In the preceding chapter there was also quite a bit of variation in the methods used, as they stemmed from different disciplines, such as epidemiology and demography. They were however predominantly quantitative. Most methods were designed such that they could answer the question 'how much?' The questions that are posed in the study of the etiology of crime may of themselves be different, however. We may be interested to know whether offenders have more of a certain property than non-offenders. In that case a quantitative method would be suitable. We may however also pose the 'why'-question. Why is it that offenders commit these crimes? Is it out of greed, out of sadism, because they are afraid that they and their families will get killed themselves if they do not participate? If questions are formulated such, we need not quantitative but qualitative research. We need research that enables us to delve deeply. We need context, and we need to be able to portray the complicated setting in which crimes occur. We must design our studies such that we can unravel the mechanisms. For that reason, for answering questions on etiology often qualitative research is used.

In qualitative research, we generally do not administer questionnaires with closed-end questions on laptops. Usually we do not send questionnaires by e-mail but have face-to-face contact. We talk to people, lengthily, usually in much freer format. We use interviews, structured or topical interviews, or even in-depth interviews. We may also observe people, or study documents. If we talk about sensitive subjects, we may need to get acquainted with our subjects so that they trust us, understand why we are interested.

Peters carried out fieldwork for a study into child soldiers' motives to join the ranks of combatant groups in Sierra Leone. He studied former child soldiers who were transitioning back into society. Peters and Richards (1998) describe the setting for this research:

"*Most of the ex-child combatants stayed in so-called 'Interim Care Centres' which helped them in their transition process from combatant to civilian, while family tracing was going on. While there was still fighting going on in the hinterland, these centres were located closely to the coastal capital of Freetown. I started visiting the centres several times each week. For the first weeks I was just 'hanging out' with the children, playing football or drafts, joining in their classes or having casual conversations – which included me telling about my life and country of birth as much as they did about their lives. This allowed me to build up rapport which later proved essential when I started to conduct (and tape-record) the more structured interviews. Spending time with them and participating in their daily life activities – normally referred to as 'participant observation' in anthropology – also allowed me to put together a context, which then helped me to reflect on issues raised during the interviews. For example, the few incidents the ex-child combatants had with staff and the nearby community did say something about the way these young people perceived non-military authority, despite the often made claim that they were now civilians themselves and respected civilian authority.*

I also built up contacts with some of the ex-child combatants who had left the Interim Care Centre – they would normally stay there for 6 to 9 months – and who were living with family or foster-parents. This allowed me to observe these young people away from the rather artificial environment of a transit centre, and in particular their interaction with civilians."

While all studies strive to be generalisable, qualitative research often cannot meet that criterion. Even so, many qualitative researchers do try to ensure that their samples have good spread over relevant subgroups in the population, to make findings as generalisable as possible. Peters describes (2008) this – in a follow-up study to the one referred to above – as follows:

"*My interviews (about 75 in all) were conducted in both urban and rural settings, geographically spread over the country. The three major factions, the RUF, the CDF and the SLA/AFRC are represented, but the focus was on the hitherto neglected combatants of the RUF. Furthermore, both male and female ex-fighters were interviewed. Careful attention was paid to the inclusion of ordinary rank-and-file as well as commanders, and those who were forcibly conscripted as well as those who joined voluntarily.*

Informants were located in different ways. Agencies facilitating the reintegration process of ex-combatants were sometimes willing to bring me into contact with former RUF combatants who participated in their programmes. Others were introduced to me by ex-RUF combatants with whom I had already built up rapport. Moreover, after some months I started to notice the little signs indicating that someone might have had a RUF past, for in-

stance in terms of the language he or she used. This enabled me to identify some informants in public places, among the taxi-motorbike riders or in palm wine bars, for instance."

It is clear from Peters' description that he did not attempt to study a representative sample. And randomly selected respondents would not necessarily all make equally good respondents: respondents must be able to voice what they feel, to explain, to remember. Peters did try to achieve good spread over relevant factions, gender and rank. In that sense, his sample has characteristics of a quota sample.

In qualitative studies, statistical tests are generally not carried out. Even if quantitative measures are collected, there is often simply not enough time to interview sufficient numbers. In addition, statistical criteria are not as forcefully present in qualitative research. As stated in chapter 2, the aim is not to produce generalisable quantitative statements, but to unravel a number of mechanisms, to *understand* what happened. We used a picture to illustrate this (see Figure 2.2), where qualitative research was depicted as of limited generalizability, but delving deep, and quantitative research essentially as a broad, shallow pancake. We said that a qualitative study may even study just one respondent (a so-called N=1 study).

All in all, for answering questions about etiology we can – depending on the exact research question – use quantitative or qualitative methods. This is a first dimension along which the methods that we will discuss in this chapter can be ordered.

A second distinction can be made. That second distinction has to do with the fact that causality can be sought – and found – at different levels or layers. As there is general human agency in behaviour and so in the commission of international crimes, a first level at which we can seek for causes is the individual perpetrator. Here, questions are posed such as: what distinguishes perpetrators from non-perpetrators? What motives do perpetrators give for their criminal activities? Note, that the first question could be addressed using a quantitative design, the second one would perhaps be better suited to analyse using a qualitative design. This level is called the *micro-level* of explanation.

However, there may also be factors at play at higher levels of aggregation. For instance, it may be that one faction of rebel fighters relatively often commits rape, while another does not. In that case, it is apparently not so much the particular characteristics of the individual players, but factors at this so-called *meso-level* that play a role. It could be the case that there is a certain ideology that this one faction holds, or it may be that the leader of this band has installed measures that forbid sexual pillage, or on the other hand that sexual violence is a tool for armed factions that struggle with cohesion: sexual violence asserts norms of virility and masculinity, breaks down social taboos and increases mutual esteem (Cohen, 2016). The level of explanation is then this higher level of aggregation, these structural or group-level factors. We now look for structural factors that explain the prevalence of sexual violence at the meso-level.

Then, there is an even higher level of aggregation to explain the etiology of conflict. At this level, it is not the individuals or the meso-structures within which they operate, but factors at an even higher level. That level could be the occurrence of natural disasters, political decisions made at the supranational level, country-level strife going back to colonial times or economic downturns. This we call the *macro-level*. Studies here can again be either quantitative or qualitative.

Finkel and Straus (2012) report that in the study of genocide, particularly meso-studies are underdeveloped. They state that meso-level studies are uniquely suited to investigate the causal chains and mechanisms in genocide. Given that country-level factors are constant, meso-level studies can focus on variation in local outcomes and unravel what local factors made genocide occur in one area of a country but not, or less so, in another. Explaining variation in outcomes across different regions and communities may offer important causal clues. Micro-level research, the authors state, does a poor job in focusing on strategies that actors have in conflict situations (participate, refuse, aid victims). In addition, they state that much of the scholarship has been dominated by studies on the Holocaust and Rwanda (the former much more than the latter) and that very little use is made of systematic comparisons or experimental designs.

It must be said that the distinction between micro-, meso- or macro-level studies can not always be very clearly made. Some studies combine data from different levels. Such mixed methods studies are important as they may be able to model the complexity of interaction between personal factors and community level conditions.

Below we will give a number of examples of studies on the etiology of international crimes at the micro-, meso- and macro-level. In doing so, we will discuss their design, measurement instruments and analysis. Issues of sampling, instrument design and data analysis do not differ from what we discussed in the chapters before. As said, studies can be qualitative or quantitative. A few notable warnings are to be made in case we would want to interview perpetrators.

14.2 Micro-level studies

Perhaps the most famous study into the etiology of mass atrocities is Hannah Arendt's (1963) study on Eichmann, a high-level Nazi. Arendt studied Eichmann at his trial, and from all that was said and not said, drew several conclusions. Her study therefore can be classified as a qualitative study, based on documents and observations, and careful analysis of the information in these. She argued how Eichmann was not a monster but a fact a quite adapted and normal man, who had simply been doing his job, perhaps overeager to please his superiors, weak on independent thinking, and overeager to belong. One of her conclusions was that – as the Nazis had subdivided the extermination of the Jews into ever so many little acts – the evil that was committed became banal for every cog in the wheel, like Eichmann was. Her study is not uncontested. Cesarani (2004) stated that she sat in on only part of the trial, and that she herself was prejudiced; see also Haslam and Reicher (2008).

Arendt's work was important in that it compellingly argued for a theory of 'normalcy' of perpetrators of the most heinous offences. Browning (1992) gave essentially the same analysis, again carrying out a case study, now of one battalion of men in WW II ('Reserve Police Battalion 101', a Nazi killing unit that murdered around 40,000 Polish Jews), arguing that they were not demons or Nazi fanatics but ordinary middle-aged men of working-class background who killed out of a basic obedience to authority and peer pressure, not bloodlust or primal hatred. Like Hannah Arendt's, also Browning's work is not uncontested.

The theoretical reasoning as proposed by Arendt and Browning's qualitative work is supported by the famous Milgram (1974) and Zimbardo (2007) quantitative experiments, that showed how many ordinary people could virtually electrocute innocent co-respondents or become a de-facto torturer in fairly artificial prison conditions (being a 'guard'). Zimbardo's study was experimental in that the researchers randomly assigned respondents to one group or the other. While the latter two researchers ventured slightly different explanations for their findings, they underscore Hannah Arendt's interpretation.

Bjørkhaug (2010) attempted to address the issue of whether child soldiers must be regarded as being victimised to become soldiers or whether they should be regarded as children with agency who had voluntarily chosen to join the ranks of the rebel groups. These contrasting paradigmata were studied by interviewing 11 former child soldiers in Colombia. The author does not specify exactly what kind of interviews were held, but as they were lengthy and some involved repeated sessions, it must be assumed that they were topical interviews, and the research therefore classified as predominantly qualitative.

The former child soldiers were contacted through the International Organization for Migration (IOM): all had participated in a disarmament, demobilisation and reintegration (DDR) program. The author does not state how exactly the children were chosen and whether she attempted to guarantee some kind of representativeness. She does note that the manner in which these children were selected (after they had been through a DDR programme) may have affected the kind of answers and interpretations they gave, as organisations that aim to aid child soldiers usually work from the conviction that – whether or not these children chose to join the ranks of armies – they lack social and political agency, which turns them into victims by definition. Also, the reasons children give to an interviewer for joining may have legal consequences, so it is possible that they might not have reported the 'true' reasons for joining. Lastly, the selection interviewed must be considered biased because it excludes child soldiers who might be expected to differ, such as children who did not survive, children who chose not to leave the ranks and children who did not complete the DDR programme. This means that the validity and generalizability of the findings are likely limited.

Taking in mind these limitations, the author concludes that the children generally joined the armed groups voluntarily. The author clearly problematises and nuances this by stating that the division between voluntary and forced suggests a dichotomy that may not exist in reality. Obviously, she argues, the war was not chosen by these children, so in that sense these children were victimised by a situation that was forced upon them. From that context, children mostly joined to escape a dreary life, to escape a marginalised position at home, or out of dreams to become a heroic soldier. The qualitative analysis clearly highlights the context within which children 'chose' to join an armed group. Rather, the author states, there are degrees of force and voluntariness, and a gray zone between voluntariness and forced recruitment, in which each child with his own particular experiences and circumstances – as shown in the interviews – makes his own choices.

Verwimp (2003) studied perpetration using a quantitative design. He studied Rwandan households that had participated in a rural household survey, conducted in 1989-1992 – that is, before the Rwandan genocide in 1994. The anonymised data from this survey had been preserved electronically, but the addresses and names had been stored before the genocide at an unknown location with the Rwandan Ministries of Agriculture and Economic Planning and their respective statistics departments. Since the former regime and its allies had had to evacuate Kigali in a hurry and had not had the time to destroy their archives (they only destroyed or stole the computers), the author believed to have a (small) chance of finding the old survey forms, and indeed, under a layer of dust in one of the archives, he did find the original questionnaires with the location and the names of the heads of households mentioned on the first page.

This meant that data collected before the genocide could be linked with household members' perpetration and victimisation during the genocide that had occurred a few years later. In that manner, a *prospective* study design was built, in which information on the pre-genocide situation of household members was available, as it had been collected before the behaviour of household members during the genocide became known. Given the prospective design, the study is not compromised by selection on the dependent variable: Verwimp was able to study the 'positives' (those who participated) as well as the 'negatives' (those who did not participate), and compare their characteristics that were undistorted by any hindsight- or other bias.

Of the available 1,248 households, for budgetary reasons 352 were selected for further study from three préfectures (Gitarama, Kibuye and Gikongoro). These were selected firstly because for these there were complete records so that households could be traced. Secondly, these areas were relatively safe. Thirdly, *imidugudu* policy (villagesation) was implemented to a lesser degree in these préfectures compared to other préfectures, making it more likely that households would still be in the same location as before the genocide. Fourthly, the préfectures had a mix of a very complete genocide (Gikongoro and Kibuye) and a less complete genocide (Gitarama). Fifthly, the préfectures had a sizeable Tutsi population before the war. Sixthly, the préfectures were a mixture of both very poor and not so poor communes. All in all, these préfectures were chosen because there was good spread over the independent and dependent variables, households could be traced well, and they were safe to work in. Verwimp discusses how representativeness is likely somewhat compromised.

When the fieldwork started, research assistants were told to approach the households in a prudent manner, taking time to explain that the research was only done for scientific purposes and that they neither belonged to the Rwandan judiciary, nor to the International Tribunal or to the government. In fact, if research assistants thought that households were not approachable, they could gather the information for this stage of the project by talking to neighbours or to government authorities. Since tracing of households requires extensive knowledge of the area of residence, highly-educated research assistants were selected, from the same *commune* as the field work – although not from the same sector – from both major ethnicities. Assistants were trained to cross-check all information they obtained. A total of a little over 1,800 of the 1,900 people in the original sample were traced.

Next, each household member was classified as either: (1) victim/survivor; (2) perpetrator; (3) thief; (4) innocent; (5) protector; (6) type unknown. If necessary, research assistants could fill in two types for the same person, starting with the most appropriate. This happened when, for example, a person had both killed as well as hidden Tutsi in their own house or when a person both protected Tutsi in his or her house and looted property in someone else's house. In this way, the researchers tried to capture the ambiguity and complexity of people's behaviour. Of 1,838 household members 1,657 were Hutu, 155 Tutsi

Table 14.1: Socio-economic differentiation of Hutu peasants in rural Rwanda

	quasi-landless peasants, employees	middle-sized farmers	landlords, employers landlords
land owned (hectares)	<.05	.05 – 1	>1
% land rented	>10%	< 10%	0
off-farm income	1,000 – 10,000	<1,000	> 10,000
# in the sample	91	151	39
# hh with at least 1 perpetrator	21	20	11
% hh with at least 1 perpetrator	23.0%	13.2%	28.2%

$\chi^2 = 6.465$ (df=2, $p = .039$)
$N = 281$

source: Verwimp (2003)

and 26 Twa. Among the 461 Hutu adult males (age > 12), there were 59 perpetrators, 44 thieves, 334 innocent and 22 protectors.

Next, using quantitative methods, mainly regression and crosstabulations, Verwimp investigated the hypothesis that perpetrators are over-represented among farmers experiencing low productivity. In a series of regression analyses he showed that, amongst others, age, sex, the size of rented land, personal off-farm income and gross household income significantly predicted the probability of a household member to become a perpetrator of genocide. Next, he classified the Hutu households into three groups: quasi-landless peasants/employees, middle-sized peasants, and landlords/employers. Table 14.1 shows how the number of households with at least one perpetrator is overrepresented in both the first and the third group.

Verwimp interprets these results as follows. Both employees (off-farm workers who are land-poor) and employers (off-farm workers who are land-rich) have in common that they had before the genocide lost their peasant identity. The landlords or employers had their privileged position in Rwandan society to defend, and gained in that way from participating in the genocide. The poor, landless group on the other hand were very vulnerable. They likely participated to gain: it has been widely documented that a large number of low-level participants were interested in the property of the murdered Tutsi, whose land especially was much desired.

A recurrent issue in studies on etiology is how to avoid selection on the dependent variable (see section 5.6). Also for this chapter this is an important topic: how can we design studies such that we can identify for perpetrators and non-perpetrators those properties and situational characteristics that distinguish the two groups and that may thus validly serve as explanation for participation in such crimes? A good example of a study that was designed for just that is the study by Humphreys and Weinstein (2008), who tested three rivalling theories to explain participation in the Sierra Leonean civil war. Very briefly summarised these are: a theory that emphasises social class as the differentiating factor between combatants and non-combatants, a theory that focuses on ethnic and political grievances, and a third that focuses on citizens' alienation from society (resembling 'anomie'). The basis for their study was a survey administered among over 1,000 former combatants. Combatants had been sampled in an ingenious manner, sampling from former combatants lists compiled by the National Commission on Demobilization, Disarmament and Reintegration, from 45 randomly selected chiefdoms in a 63×17 cluster design, such that samples were proportional to the estimated ex-combatants population in each locality. A control group of noncombatants was sampled by the 'spin-the-pen' method in the same localities that the ex-combatants had been sampled from. The authors argue that this has the advantage that the two groups are better comparable on background characteristics. The disadvantage is, that while the ex-combatants sample was designed to be representative of all ex-combatants, this cannot be said of the noncombatants, they are likely not representative of all noncombatants in Sierra Leone. Apart from finding that the grievances model has little empirical support, Humphreys and Weinstein's study is recommended reading for its thoughtful discussion of methodological choices and conceptual analysis.

In the search for etiology, many researchers have interviewed prisoners. Hatzfeld (2005) interviewed convicted *génocidaires* in Rwandan prisons. His often cited book contains the transcripts of a number of interviews with perpetrators. While the book makes for fascinating and bewildering reading, it does not present a study as such: the book is basically raw transcripted interview material and does not provide a qualitative or quantitative analysis. Several other studies have been conducted on persons sentenced or remanded to prison for perpetration of international crimes. A first reason for this popularity of prisoners as research subjects is that prisoners are easy to find. Assuming no false convictions, incarceration the dominant sanction and a small dark number, visiting prisons is an efficient search algorithm if one wants to interview perpetrators. Secondly, one may assume that once people have been convicted they will have little reason to lie about their acts (although they might not come forward with acts they were not convicted for). Also, prisoners have so much free time and are generally bored, and will therefore likely agree to participate. Lastly, they come 'cheap': as they are not employed and most prisons forbid handing out gifts, they can be interviewed (almost) for free.

Obviously, there are flip sides to this coin. Especially in large-scale conflicts, not every perpetrator will be apprehended. Prisoners therefore constitute a select group. Maybe they were the conspicuous ones, the ones that the newly empowered wanted out of the way, or maybe they hail predominantly from the executioners rather than the master minds. Also, it is unclear whether prisoners can really speak freely: prisons are not always extremely private places. Then, it is to be doubted whether prison staff will let researchers speak freely to any prisoner they would want to, or whether only particular prisoners (in favour of the regime?, well behaved?) are accessible. If prison wardens or directors decide who may be interviewed and who not, there is little control over sample selection. There are ethical issues as well. Are prisoners free to refuse? Can they give informed consent? Are the researchers sure that the interviewed will not suffer any repercussions? Such issues should be well thought out before permission for a study is asked and fieldwork in prison starts.

Summarising, qualitative and quantitative studies are both feasible options for micro-level explanations of international crimes. We can interview and survey perpetrators and preferably investigate to what extent their characteristics differ from those of non-perpetrators. If one is interested in motives as such, or group processes in the commission of such crimes, one could interview perpetrators, or even do more ethnographic research. As we stated in the introduction, such fieldwork needs careful preparation, getting acquainted with the situation and context of the violence, as well as cultural sensitivity. Mkandawire (2002, p.186), however, warns against retrospectively interviewing perpetrators if one is interested in motive:

"*In a situation where individuals commit terrible crimes, the need for rationalisation is enormous, so that one cannot take the ex post explanations of individuals as evidence of the preferences for the sequence of their reasoning. A retrospective account of what drove them to commit the crimes is likely to be self-serving. And the motives and opportunities for concealing what one did and why are virtually unlimited.*"

The idea that one would get valid data by flying in to a country recently in conflict, carrying out a few interviews of one hour with warden-picked prisoners – as some studies do – is far-flung. Good data cannot be had on the cheap. Qualitative fieldwork for the study of international crimes is all in all a time-consuming, intensive affair. (Peters, 2008) lists the following issues to attend to:

(1) building up good rapport, often over a lengthy period

(2) minimising the investigation of more sensitive topics, such as asking about killings or rape cases the informant might be involved in, to reduce incentives to fabrication

(3) using internal triangulation, by interviewing different kinds of perpetrators

(4) judging the frankness of an informant by his/her willingness to accept objective facts about the conflict

(5) not interviewing informants with realistic reasons to fear prosecution

(6) offering the assurance of complete anonymity

(7) covering given topics in multiple ways, including repeated interviewing, and visiting locations to verify or revisit accounts

(8) cross-referencing of findings to other qualitative or quantitative data, collected by different researchers

These points of attention once more underscore to the need to be critical, and to even question at times what interviewees report. This may be very difficult when they report being victimised or when they have been traumatised. Fujii (2010) reports how a woman she was interviewing in Rwanda told harrowing tales of traumatisation and survival with a small child strapped to her back. This woman, Angélique, became however less and precise as the researcher probed in successive interviews. Her story went on to become fantastical, and by the fourth interview the researcher realised that Angélique had made up the story. The author however does not regard the story that Angélique made up as useless: she regards it as meta-data. Fujii distinguishes five kinds of such meta-data: rumors, inventions, denials, evasions, and silences. As the author states (2010):

"*In the aftermath of war, mass killing, and sexual violence, public accusations and private confessions can lead to reprisals from neighbors, rejection from family members, or repression by the state. In settings of high suspicion, where words can be a matter of life and death, attention to meta-data can help the researcher minimize risks to informants and maximize her chances of finding what she seeks.*"

Qualitative studies as well as quantitative studies are, as we saw, feasible to study etiology at the micro-level. Quantitative studies, whether they gather data in the field or use existing or archival data, have the immense advantage that the data thus gathered are objective, 'hard', quantifiable and generalisable. Obviously, explanations will generally be more 'superficial' in the sense that they can describe only a number of outward characteristics from which explanations at the level of theory can then be deduced. Qualitative studies are generally better able to make us understand what happened, to view the complexity of the context in which offending occurred and the motives that people may have had for perpetrating international crimes, or abstaining. The recommended option is to integrate whenever possible: to incorporate quantitative as well as qualitative data and analysis in each study.

14.3 Meso-level studies

When we study meso-level explanations for international crimes, we are looking for patterns, the coming together of variables at the group or organisation level. Such patterns in crime – which we classify under meso-analysis – are important for getting a grip on the motives behind crimes. Obviously, interviewing perpetrators might tell you what perpetrators believe were their motives: they may tell you that they were scared or that they were unaware what was happening. They may also leave out certain aspects: less heroic aspects or aspects that are still unknown to the authorities. However, while each perpetrator can in principle shed some light on his or her particular motives, international crimes are often crimes of scale, in which in addition to particular motives of each individual perpetrator, a 'master-plan' may be in operation. That is exactly the reason why we would want to perform analyses not only at the micro-level but at higher levels of aggregation too. 'Motive' – insofar as we can speak of motive at meso-level – might differ from micro-motives. While the particular motive of many low-level perpetrators may have been greed, the policy through which they targeted certain villages or areas may have effectuated ethnic cleansing, from which we can conclude that a different aim was actually behind the attacks. This may have been the motive of the higher-level perpetrators, the organisers or master-minds of the atrocities. Qualitative studies are exceptionally well positioned to be able to tackle the various levels operating in the unfolding of conflicts and international crimes.

Not all researchers are comfortable with the conceptualisation of a meso-level. As Goldhagen states "(...) *the vast literature on the Holocaust contains little on the people that were its executioners. (...) It is not sufficient to treat the institutions of killing collectively or singly as internally uncomplicated instruments of the Nazi leadership's will, as well-lubricated machines that the regime activated, as if by the flick of a switch* (...). *The study of the men and women who collectively gave life to the inert institutional forms, who peopled the institutions of genocidal killing must be set at the focus of scholarship on the Holocaust and become as central to investigations of the genocide as they were to its commission*" (1996, pp. 5 – 6).

Despite this inherent truth, a number of studies have convincingly shown that it is the existence of structures at the meso-level that has been decisive for certain outcomes, even if that meso-characteristic could be seen as the sum of micro-characteristics. Then, it is at the meso-level that outcomes are effectuated, and these outcomes cannot be explained from micro-level variation. The clearest example of this was given by Croes and Tammes (2004), who analysed the survival chances of Jews in the Netherlands during WW II. Their impressive and thoughtful study is a mixture of qualitative and quantitative methods.

Croes and Tammes had collected data (on the characteristics of Jews who survived and who did not survive) from documents and historical archives, all over the Netherlands, at micro-level as well as at the level of municipalities: for each municipality they collected numerous variables, amongst which whether the mayor collaborated with the Nazi occupier, the proportion of full-blooded Jews, as well as half- or quarter-blood Jews, the number of Christian Jews, the percentage of marriages with both partners from the same religious denomination, the percentage of police officers who collaborated with the Nazis, voluntary police, and the border police ('Marechaussee'), the percentage voters for the political party NSB (Nationaal-Socialistische Beweging, a political party that collaborated with the Nazis), and the first date when Jews had died due to persecution. At a somewhat higher level (which can be defined as meso or macro) they had information on the German *Sicherheitsdienst* (SD) and *Sicherheitspolizei* (Sipo), security apparatus departments that displayed different degrees of vigour in hunting down Jews, and were bureaucratically organised in seven regions over the Netherlands.

They conducted regression analyses per 'layer' of variables, that is, they first attempted to predict survival chances of Jews from the characteristics of the Jews themselves, and next from the characteristics of the municipality where Jews had resided. The first micro-analyses showed that older Jews and Jews with another nationality than Dutch or German had higher survival chances. The meso-analyses next showed that the higher the percentage of collaborating police officers, the lower survival chances were. Against expectation, survival chances of Jews in municipalities with relatively many Catholics were higher. In municipalities where more marriages were uni-denominational, survival chances were lower. In municipalities with relatively many Christian Jews survival chances were higher.

One might expect this latter effect to be the result of Christian Jews having higher survival chances, but this is not so. In the micro-analyses Christianity had not predicted survival chances. Only at the meso-level did the municipal percentage of Christian Jews play a role. The authors explain this quantitative finding through qualitative analysis of the information they had extracted from the various national and municipal archives they had studied. They postulated that these relatively large Christian Jewish populations functioned in each municipality as a 'bridge' between the Jewish and non-Jewish community. In municipalities with many Christian Jews, Jews had had more contact with non-Jews, and had been better able to find addresses for hiding, more successful in obtaining false identity cards and other means to be able to escape deportation. Thus, it was in fact the presence of a large Christian-Jewish group within a municipality that increased the survival chances of all Jews, rather than whether a Jew him- or herself was Christian or not.

Wood (2006) studied why rape does occur in some conflicts but not in others. In her seminal study, she first conducted essentially a systematic review of the literature on wartime rape. In the analysis of this literature, she described wartime rape in WW II by the Soviet army and in Nanjing, in Bosnia Herzegovina, Sri Lanka, Israel/Palestine, Sierra Leone, Vietnam, El Salvador and Peru. In doing so, she scrutinised authoritative research reports per conflict. She concluded first that the prevalence of sexual violence varies considerably across conflicts, in form, in perpetrators, motive, location, and by other characteristics. Second, she concluded that the type of conflict cannot explain this variation, noting however that part of the variation may be due to methodological differences rather than true differences in prevalence. In addition, peacetime levels of sexual violence may vary as well, so to what extent, she asks, is the observed variation during conflicts not merely a reflection of those pre-existing differences?

Before continuing to explain differences in wartime rape prevalence, she next states that rape may be higher during war than during peace because of opportunity, incentive (increased testosterone levels due to combat and stress) or instrumentality. She also reviews a rationale for its decreased prevalence during war, namely command structure and sanctions. Wood accedes that not one reason may serve to explain all kinds of wartime rape. She ventures a number of hypotheses. She states, amongst others, that it is likely that given an effective command structure, sexual violence is less likely to occur if insurgent groups depend on the civilian population for food and intelligence. Also, she argues that combatant groups with relatively many female combatants engage less in sexual violence.

Wood conducted a qualitative study. She selected a number of conflicts without arguing that they were representative. Wood however states that her study is not about prevalence estimates, but exploits variation in sexual violence to explain prevalence: while it is unsure whether her selection of cases is able to give a good prevalence estimate, it is not likely that the *patterns* she finds are unrepresentative. Thus, while an unrepresentative sample must be distrusted for describing the absolute levels of variables, it may still be useful for investigating the associations between variables.

Next, she noted for each conflict how often sexual violence occurred and what its characteristics were. Subsequently, she tested each explanation for sexual violence against the data she had obtained for each conflict and the nature of the sexual violence. The patterns she identified are tentative, Wood writes, and need further scrutiny, using more cases, and particularly also 'negative' cases, i.e. cases where sexual violence does *not* occur. Within-case analyses (comparing periods with and without sexual violence within the same conflict) should be employed to control for selection effects.

Agirre (2010) discusses the findings of the internationalised Commission of Inquiry into Post-Election Violence (CIPEV), established to investigate the post-election violence in Kenya in 2007 – 2008. While the commission did not conduct a scientific enquiry as such, their work resembles most – if one would want to categorise it – a mixed methods qualitative study. The commission used background material and reports from governmental, nongovernmental, and community-based organisations (NGOs and CBOs) and individuals. It also analysed data from recorded statements of victims taken by investigators and sworn testimony, statements and exhibits of witnesses who came before it.

The commission gave an overview of the magnitude and nature of the post-election violence. It not only describes but also analyses the data it had gathered: it searched for patterns in the violence and patterns in the factors that brought it about through careful scrutiny and interpretation of the material (CIPEV, 2008; pp. 246 ff.), similar most to a second level-analysis of qualitative material. After outlining the 'breeding ground' that Kenya had become in the years preceding the election violence, the commission firstly finds that in contrast to the pre-election violence, which was mainly between candidates and their supporters, the post-election violence had a distinct ethnic dimension. Secondly, initially this violence was spontaneous and was in part a reaction to the perceived rigging of elections. Subsequently, however, the pattern of violence showed planning and organisation by politicians, businessmen and others who enlisted criminal gangs to execute the violence, gangs that the police had ineffectively dealt with in previous years. The commission deduces this from analysis of the co-occurrence of characteristics of the attacks at different stages of the post-election violence. It finds that firstly, warnings were issued to the victims before some attacks; secondly, the violence involved large numbers of attackers, often mobilised from areas outside the location of the violence, which requires planning; thirdly, petrol and weapons were used in various places to carry out the attacks, which requires planning as well as these need to be bought, concealed and transported. Also, the commission infers planning from the fact that sometimes the attacks specifically targeted only members of given ethnic groups to the exclusion of others. The commission finds that the violence could become organised and widespread because of the enlisting of 'regular' criminal gangs for the execution of this violence.

Apart from the ethnic dimension, the commission's findings therefore lead to a theoretically relevant meta-conclusion. The results namely show that there is not one 'static' explanation for the violence, but that its etiology changed over time. The violence that started out as relatively spontaneous and unorganised, later turned organised.

The commission studied sexual violence explicitly and separately, and had enlisted special staff to do so, amongst which female investigators to examine sexual violence and a psychologist counsellor. A total of 31 women were willing to testify or give statements, no male adult or child victims were willing to do so. While statements are not interview data, they were analysed for content and meaning (see chapter 9) as interviews or other material could have been.

Twenty four out of 30 women who gave statements had been gang-raped. This is a large percentage but as the Commission itself notes, it is to be doubted whether those who came forward and were willing to speak are representative for all victims. The commission retrieved different 'typologies' of rapes, that reflected different motives on the part of the perpetrators. In some areas, sexual violence was a means used to pressure people to leave their homes, to retaliate against them for having voted for the wrong candidate in tandem with motives like domination, humiliation and degradation, in line with the overall 'aims'

Figure 14.1: Number of households of different ethnicities before and after conflict

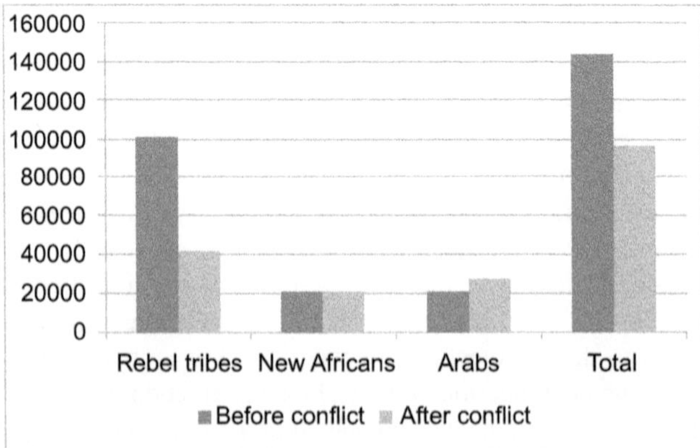

source: Olsson and Siba (2012)

of the post-electoral violence. In other cases, sexual violence was rather an opportunistic act that could be committed against a background of lawlessness and a vacuum of power. In other cases again, sexual violence was used to coerce and control helpless IDPs who traded sex unwillingly for basic needs, the perpetrators being inhabitants of the camp or the region, security personnel, or even humanitarian workers in the camps. These findings are theoretically relevant as they show that there are different motives at play behind sexual violence – part strategic (the first type), part opportunistic (the second and third types).

As a last example, we discuss a quantitative study by Olsson and Siba (2012) into patterns of destruction in Darfur. After the conflict in Darfur had erupted in 2003, a number of organisations pointed out that 'African' villages (villages with inhabitants from predominantly non-Arab tribes from whom the rebel groups originated) were more likely to be targeted for destruction than 'Arab' villages in the same vicinity. If it were the case that 'African' villages were being targeted and 'Arab' villages left undisturbed, this would point to a pattern and therefore likely policy in the destruction. See Figure 14.1, that shows a fairly convincing pattern in which the number of Arab households increased since the conflict and the number of 'rebel tribes' households strongly decreased.

The issue is of course how to determine whether the African tribes are actually being *targeted.* It could be that the observed pattern is a chance occurrence (that is, the pattern is not extremely unlikely under a hypothesis of randomness). It could also be that the destruction was not a chance occurrence, but confounded with properties of African villages (such as closeness to rebel strongholds) - in this case it was not the 'Africanness' of the villages that led to their destruction, but a third factor. In that case the association between destruction and dominant ethnicity is not causal but spurious. This one can investigate by trying to predict the chances for villages to be attacked from their ethnic composition as well as from a set of other potential explanatory variables. If a regression analysis shows an effect of ethnicity on the chance to be attacked over and above all other possible explanatory factors, one has shown that the effect is not spurious (as an effect of ethnicity remains even after taking into account the other possible explanations for the pattern).

Olsson and Siba indeed investigated this using (various kinds of) regression models. They had to use special regression models, amongst others because the dependent variables could assume only the values (0) or (1), they are dichotomous variables (see section 8.2.1). The specific model used in each case is an adaptation of the multiple regression model, adapted because the dependent variable does not meet the requirements of a regular regression model. The models that were used do not attempt to predict a numerical value (such as total number of victims or extent of the damage), but whether (1) or not (0) a village was attacked, and whether (1) or not (0) a village was abandoned. The fact that the dependent variable has only two categories changes the model as well as the computation and gives slightly different output, but the basic idea is the same.

Using a data set on 530 villages in Southwestern Darfur collected by an international organisation working in the area, they studied attacks and abandonment in 2003. We focus on their analyses of abandonment. A total of 329 villages were completely abandoned during the observation period, in which almost 800,000 people had lived. The data set contains information about the ethnic composition of the population in villages before and after the onset of the conflict and comprises all known rural villages in the area. The authors test two hypotheses: (1) the probability of abandonment of villages increases with the proportion of rebel tribes in the village population, and (2) the probability of abandonment of villages increases with the level of appropriable natural resources. Table 14.2 gives the final model with the predictor variables that were used.

On the basis of GIS data, the authors had first created a number of so-called *proxy variables*, i.e. variables representing but not measuring a relevant variable. An often used proxy variable for a country's standards of living is for instance GDP. The authors constructed proxy variables for appropriable natural resources: the density of vegetation, access to *wadis* (river beds) and alluvials soils (that offer good pasture and fertile fields), and distance to surface water. Villages with dense vegetation, access to *wadis* and alluvial soils may be considered fairly well-off. The authors included additional measures such as distance to roads (that offer quicker access to markets but also an easier access for militias) and administrative centers, and control for various other factors. The authors take into account so-called *spatial* dependence: one village may be more likely to be attacked because the attackers have already attacked a neighbouring village. Note also how the authors include logged versions of some variables (see section 11.3) to accommodate likely very skewed distributions of variables or a distorting impact of outliers.

In a regression analysis, one investigates the impact of several independent variables on the outcome variable. The regression weights for the variables express what each independent variable adds to the prediction of the outcome *given the other variables in the model*; see section 8.2.3. If we want to predict whether a village had been abandoned, and if we would enter as independent variables all properties of the villages that may be confounded with being attacked as well as ethnicity of the population, resgression analysis would return to us the regression weight of ethnicity *net of* all the other variables. The regression weight for ethnicity would tell us how important ethnicity is for predicting abandonment once factors such as natural resources, distance to main towns, distance to a wadi etc. have

Table 14.2: Probit regression predicting village abandonment

Variable	b	p-value
Inhabitants ethnicity rebel tribes	1.3320	.01
Vegetation	.0283	n.s.
Log Distance to wadi	.0049	.n.s.
Log Distance to alluvial soil	-.0320	.05
Log Distance to road	-.0716	.05
Log Distance to administrative center	.0528	.01
Distance to Nyala	-.0450	.10
Distance to El Geneina	.0140	n.s.
Distance to El Fasher	.0072	n.s.

source: Olsson and Siba (2012)

already been taken into account. In that manner we would see the importance of ethnicity in explaining village abandonment with any confounding with other explanatory variables in a sense removed.

Estimating models with various specifications to control for such spatial dependence, the authors find a consistent effect of the ethnic composition of a village on its probability to be abandoned (and in accompanying analyses also on a village's probability to be destroyed). Table 14.2 shows the coefficients and their significances for the final model in which village abandonment was predicted.

The table gives all predictors, with their regression coefficients b and significances. Probabilities above $p > .10$ have been indicated as 'n.s.' (not significant). Positive b-coefficients indicate a positive effect: high values of the independent variable predict a higher likelihood of abandonment and low values a lower likelihood of abandonment. Negative b-coefficients indicate a reverse impact: high values predict a lower likelihood of abandonment, and low values a higher likelihood.

The results indicate, as hypothesised, that villages that are relatively rich in resources were more prone to be abandoned: if the distance to alluvial soil was smaller, the chance that the village was abandoned was greater. If the village was closer to a major center (that generally has a market) or to Nyala (a major town) the chances for abandonment were also greater. Given that this is a regression model, the regression coefficients give us the effect of each independent variable for predicting village abandonment, net of the other independent variables. By far the strongest predictor (and this is consistently so), and one that holds therefore over and above the effect of resources and geographical location, was whether the village houses inhabitants from the same tribes as the rebels. Ethnic composition contributes significantly to abandonment. The hypothesis that this was a chance phenomenon or a spurious effect has therefore been rejected by this analysis.

14.4 Macro-level studies

At the macro level, researchers investigate global or country-level causes of conflict. Some of these studies are qualitative. Such studies use documents, interviews, inspect trends in weapons imports, political developments, peace treaties and thus combine all other possibly relevant factors to answer the macro-research question. Weitz (2003), an historian, discusses a number of causes for the genocides in the Soviet Union under Stalin, Nazi Germany, Cambodia under the Khmer Rouge, and the former Yugoslavia. Weitz explains the occurrences of these genocides from two major factors: race and nation. In each case, he argues, a strong state promoted extreme ideologies. Certain ethnic and national groups were next targeted, as their annihilation was regarded as the cure for the country's woes, and for the subsequent betterment of their co-citizens who had often been enlisted in the killings. For studies such as Weitz's, it is at times hard to define to what extent they are data-driven, and to what extent theory-driven. Some studies such as Weitz's emerge more as a theory illustrated with empirical examples, than a theory or explanation actually derived from empirical research.

Harff (1987) argued that three structural factors explain genocide and politicide, which can be briefly described as: national upheaval, sharp internal cleavages within a country and a lack of external constraints on, or foreign support for, a murderous regime. She illustrates this with examples from various countries such as Cambodia, Uganda and Namibia. In later work, Harff found support for these theorised mechanisms using quantitative models. In a study commissioned by the CIA, she used a case-control design to investigate the effect of structural factors on genocide and politicide. To each episode of genocide/politicide in each of a number of countries, she coupled ('matched') three countries that were otherwise comparable – apart from the fact that those countries had not experienced genocidal episodes. A total of 35 genocidal episodes were in this fashion matched to 91 non-genocidal countries.

Next, regression models were estimated that incorporated varying combinations of predictor variables, to find a best-fitting model. As predictor variables, Harff chose indicator variables reflecting political upheaval, whether a genocide had occurred previously, whether regimes used exclusionary ideologies and autocratic rule, whether there were ethnic and religious cleavages, whether the country was characterised by low economic development, as well as a measure of political interdependence of the country, i.e. a country's membership in regional and intercontinental organisations. As Harff selected all conflicts meeting the criteria over the research period (1955 – 1998), she did not in a statistical sense study a sample but the entire population of relevant conflicts.

A logistic regression model was chosen to predict from these variables whether a country in a certain year witnessed a genocide/politicide (that she combined into one variable) or not. A logistic regression model is an adaptation of the multiple regression model, adapted because the dependent variable is not a continuous variable but a dichotomous variable (see also section 8.2.1 or section 8.2.6). Therefore the model does not attempt to predict a numerical value (such as GDP or total number of victims), but whether (1) or not (0) a country experienced a genocide/politicide. The fact that the dependent variable has only two categories changes the model as well as the computation and the output, but the basic idea is the same: we try to predict from a number of independent variables (political up-

Table 14.3: Logistic regression predicting genocide/politicide

Variable	OR	*p*-value
Political upheaval	1.70	.05
Prior genocide	3.39	.09
Exclusionary ideology	2.55	.07
Autocratic regime	3.50	.03
Regime ethnic minority	2.56	.09
Lower trade openness	2.58	<.01
% genocides correctly classified	74%	
% non-genocides correctly classified	73%	

source: Harff (2003)

heaval, ethnic cleavages, etc) the score on a dependent variable, namely whether a country experienced an episode of genocide/politicide (1) or not (0).

The results of Harff's analysis are given in Table 14.3. Instead of regression coefficients, the table now contains odds ratios (ORs, see section 6.4.3) that show how much a certain variable increased the risk of genocide/politicide. If the odds ratio is higher than 1, the risk increases with higher values of the independent variable, if the odds ratio is below 1, the risk decreases with higher values of the independent variable.

As the table shows, six factors contribute significantly (at $p < .10$) to the prediction of the occurrence of a genocidal/politicidal episode. These are political upheaval (with an odds ratio of 1.70 the lowest risk increase), prior genocide, whether the regime used an exclusionary ideology, whether the regime was autocratic or an ethnic minority, and whether there was an absence of trade openness. Clearly, the model did not generate a perfect fit: roughly speaking about three quarters of genocides were predicted correctly, and about three quarters of non-genocides. Political upheaval, a central element in Harff's earlier theory gives – although significant – the lowest risk increase as indicated by the odds ratio, an autocratic regime and prior episodes of genocide are stronger predictors. Harff concludes by saying that better data would be needed to model the effects of other theoretically relevant factors such as the presence and expansion of private militias, paramilitary units, and state security agencies that operate with few restraints. Harff's work met some critique, notably for collapsing genocide and politicide into one variable.

Economists have contributed importantly to the study of macro-causes of genocide and civil war. Collier and Hoeffler (2004) analysed the effect of various explanatory variables on the outbreak of civil wars. They disaggregated data on 98 countries into 750 five year time slots over the period 1960-1999. While the authors therefore in a sense selected on the dependent variable (they selected countries on whether they had experienced conflict), they had for each country periods with conflict that they could contrast with periods without conflict. As they combined all these periods in one analysis, they altogether used a design that resembles a within-case analysis.

Civil war was defined as an internal conflict with at least 1,000 combat-related deaths per year, where both government and rebel forces suffered at least 5% of fatalities. The authors tested two models: an opportunity model where the rebellion is predicted from essentially opportunities to make a profit, and a grievances model that sees rebellions as violent protest to (political) grievances. For both explanations they gathered country-level time-varying variables that serve as proxy variables in either of the models. For instance, for the opportunity models, they incorporated variables reflecting GDP per capita, exports per GDP, whether there was a large diaspora (as a source of rebel finance), levels of male schooling (as an indicator of foregone profits by participating in a war), and whether the country had mountainous terrain (that would make it easier for rebel groups to hide), and social fractionalisation as an indicator for social cohesion. For the grievances model, they used explanatory variables such as political exclusion, political repression, and economic inequality. The authors also used logistic regressions, predicting whether civil war broke out (1) or not (0) in a country in a certain five-year period, separately for the opportunity and the grievances models. The authors fitted various models, incorporating different sets of independent variables to predict the outbreak of civil war.

Overall, the authors note that the grievances models fitted less well than the opportunity models. This means that the outbreak of civil wars is less well predicted by grievances than by opportunity indicators. Next, they combined the variables that contributed significantly to the prediction of civil war outbreaks in either models into one overarching model. Those predictors that had too little predictive value were removed. The results from this model are shown in Table 14.3. A total of eight predictors remained for the opportunity model, four for the grievances model, and three predictors were shared by both models. Note also how the authors included transformed versions of some variables (see section 11.3): they took the logarithm of the variable 'population' possibly to accommodate a skewed distribution, and incorporated also a squared version of 'primary commodity exports/GDP', possibly to model a nonlinear impact on the dependent variable.

As Table 14.4 shows, only one of the grievances predictors had been retained in the model. Of the predictors for the opportunity model, five had been retained. Of the shared predictors, three had been retained. The final model reveals that the effect of primary commodity exports is very prominent. Additional analyses had shown that, freely translated, countries where the main primary export product is oil were particularly vulnerable to civil war outbreaks. High levels of male secondary schooling 'protect' against the outbreak of civil war, as indicated by the negative coefficient (if schooling levels are high, the value of the dependent variable is low – and the lowest value '0' means no outbreak). GDP growth in the previous year (indicated by the subscript 't-1') also protects against civil war, as does social fractionalisation, a measure that reflects lack of social cohesion. This means that in countries with strong social cohesion, the risk is increased. Next we interpret the shared variables. From these we conclude that the longer countries have experienced peace, the lower the risk for new outbreaks; the greater the geographic dispersion, the lower the risk; the larger the population, the larger the risk. Of the grievances model, very few predictors

Table 14.4: Logistic regression combined opportunity and grievances models

	b	p-value
Predictors opportunities model		
Primary commodity exports/GDP	18.937	$p < .01$
(Primary commodity exports/GDP)^2	-29.443	$p < .01$
Male secondary schooling	-.031	$p < .01$
GDP growth$_{t-1}$	-.115	$p < .01$
Social fractionalisation	-.00002	$p < .05$
Shared predictors		
Peace duration	-.004	$p < .01$
Geographic dispersion	-2.487	$p < .05$
Ln(population)	0.786	$p < .01$
Predictors grievances model		
Ethnic dominance	1.592	$p < .10$

source: Collier and Hoeffler (2004)

'survived' in the final model so to say. Only ethnic dominance remained as a predictor: countries where one ethnic group was dominant had a (much) higher risk of civil war.

The contribution of this analysis is firstly, that it attempted to find 'control'-years for the 'experimental' years in which a country had an outbreak of genocide/politicide. Obviously, if the authors had only studied the cases in which genocide broke out and elaborated on the characteristics of those episodes, we would have had no way of knowing whether those characteristics are distinctive for outbreaks of genocides, or better said: discriminating between the episodes with and without genocide. By designing their study as a case-control study, they were able to uncover factors that differentiate between peacetime and genocidal episodes.

Its second contribution is that it, through the use of (logistic) multiple regression analysis, let two competing models – the grievances and the opportunities model – indeed 'compete' which one predicted the dependent variable best. In the regression model, the variables that played a role in these two models were all entered simultaneously. With all of them added to the model, the technique determined which of all these variables – given the other variables present – showed the strongest contribution to predicting outbreaks of genocide.

The analysis firstly showed that the models were actually not as competing as one might think: they actually shared a number of variables. Apparently, therefore, there is some overlap in the factors that play a role in both models. Next, the regression analysis showed that the opportunities model had the best cards for predicting genocide outbreaks. Had the authors run two models, one for the grievances model and one for the opportunities model, they might have concluded that both in fact predicted genocide outbreaks reasonably well (with perhaps not even significantly different fits). The strength of this overall analysis is the combination of all the predictors in one model: now we are able to see that the factors from one model actually outperform those from the other model.

Blattman and Miguel (2010) gave a thorough and informative narrative review of the recent economic literature on the causes of war. Amongst others, they draw three conclusions that are important for our methodological explorations. First, they show how at times authors have drawn remarkably different conclusions, when using the same data or even the same variables. For instance, Fearon and Laitin (2003) – whose model specifications have become somewhat of a standard for subsequent work – concur with part of Collier and Hoeffler's conclusions, but in addition find that weak central governments and environmental conditions favouring insurgents are also strong predictors of war. The different explanations of Fearon and Laitin as compared to Collier and Hoeffler are attributable to different methodological choices, amongst which attaching different interpretation to key variables, and different coding of wars (the same variables coded by different authors at times had correlation coefficients as low as 0.42). Second, Blattman and Miguel argue that not all conflicts are equal and that explanations that work for small conflicts or conflicts of short duration may not explain large-scale or smouldering conflicts. Third, the authors argue that micro-level evidence should be integrated with macro-studies.

Blattman and Miguel's analysis underscores how important it is to employ uniform operationalisations: without standardised or standardisable data, results do not accumulate but confuse. When findings diverge, this may be because mechanisms are actually different in different countries or periods, a finding that is theoretically highly relevant. But it may also be that the differences are actually *method differences*, differences simply due to the fact that different operationalisations were used. Hence the recurring emphasis in this book on using, where appropriate, standardised instruments, and building from the work of others.

Dumitru and Johnson (2007) investigated the impact of governmental policies on international crimes. They studied the behaviour of the local populations in Bessarabia (now Moldova) and Transnistria (part of Romania in southern Ukraine) towards the Jews persecuted in these two regions in World War II. The authors argue that this provided a *natural experiment*. The two regions had been part of Russia under the tsar, during which period the state actively sponsored anti-Semitism. However, after 1917 Transnistria became part of Romania, and Bessarabia became part of the Soviet Union. The authors argue, using historical documents, that the Soviet state attempted to implement inclusive policies and conducted re-education campaigns, which should have effected to better integrate Jews, amongst others by intermarriage and increased communication between Jews and non-Jews. The fact that one part of this territory fell to the Soviet Union and the other part not, can be argued to be a 'chance occurrence': it is unlikely that specific properties of the population or community characteristics had an influence on one part acceding and the other part remaining with Romania. Rather, it was a geographical gamble that made one region come under the influence of the Soviet regime and the other remain under Romanian policies that remained actively anti-Jewish. Therefore the differential exposure to inclusionary policies of the Transnistria and the Bessarabia region can be regarded as 'randomly' imposed.

In 1940, after the outbreak of World War II, the two regions came to be governed by the Romanian regime and persecution of Jews started. Using a mixed methods approach, the authors sent out several hundred questionnaires, studied archives, used quotes from testimonies and memoirs from the US Holocaust museum as well as the Yad Vashem, conducted interviews with 100 non-Jews who had witnessed the Holocaust in Romania, and used historical documents. They also conducted a quantitative analysis, where they rank ordered the severity of incidents described in a random sample of testimonies.

Even though in both regions, approximately 90% of Jews were killed, the authors argue that the local population acted differently towards the Jews, drawing upon their records. The authors show that the civilian population in the area that had been part of the Soviet Union was less likely to harm and more likely to aid Jews as compared with the region that had been part of Romania. They argue that this different treatment of Jews by the local population in Transnistria is due to the Soviet policies of promoted interethnic relationships that had been 'internalised' by the inhabitants. The authors' findings are not uncontested.

14.5 Summary of methodological issues

The examples discussed in this chapter revealed a number of methodological issues that are prominent when we study the etiology of international crimes. A first generic remark is that in searching for explanations for international crimes, we must be aware that mechanisms may evolve. In the beginning of conflict one explanation may be more emergent, but as the conflict dynamics shift so may reasons why, manners in which people commit atrocities, as well as the meso-constellation that is conducive to violence. A related issue is that different explanations may also concurrently explain the commission of international crimes. Not all conflicts are equal: different factors may explain different conflicts. All in all, a quest for 'the' explanation for why international crimes are committed is likely futile: numerous etiologies tend to co-exist and may evolve over time.

In studying etiology, an in essence unsurmountable problem is the retrospectiveness of much research. Those who attempt to answer the question why people commit atrocities often have no recourse but to ask perpetrators why, in hindsight, they committed their crimes. Such retrospective research is already in general regarded as suboptimal, but has massive risks when asking people why they participated in acts that may feel as if they are beyond human comprehension. We inserted a quote as a general warning against 'quick and dirty' studies that ask perpetrators, after the fact, for motives for such acts. If possible, studies should be prospective or have at least some data that are objective or undistorted by the events that unfolded during conflict. Prospective studies may be a matter of serendipity mostly, however. Retrospective studies that we will likely often resort to should therefore be cautious and allow for repeat interviewing, corroboration and checks. If they are qualitative they should allow for free format data as well in order to capture as naturalistically as possible people's motives, stressors, constraints and other relevant factors, and be able to relate motive and agency to context. Much time should be spent on building rapport and ethnographic observation. We gave a special warning against the interviewing of prisoners.

In order to arrive at explanations for human behaviour at the micro-level, at the meso- or macro-level, controls are crucial. Studies need controls or 'negative cases' to be able to identify causal factors. Only if we have both 'positive cases' (that committed atrocities/where atrocities occurred) as well as 'negative cases' (no atrocities) can we start to unravel what the factors are that distinguish these. Both qualitative and quantitative research can incorporate such controls: qualitative research by actively searching for such negative cases and incorporating them, quantitative research by solid designs with 'experimental' and 'control' groups. Some studies have employed natural experiments for this. Others have investigated variation: comparing conflicts where sexual violence was more prominent with where it was less prominent, or comparing municipalities where Jews had larger survival chances with those where survival chances were lower. In design-speak, more stringent quantitative case-control designs have compared countries with and without genocidal violence, and within-case designs have exploited variation over time within the same country, comparing genocidal episodes with peaceful ones and extracting discriminating factors.

The search for explanations for the occurrence of international crimes has shown that many of the potential causal factors are interrelated. There is therefore in general much confounding, which makes bivariate analysis inconclusive. This means that regression-type models that are able to reveal the effect of causal factors net of such confounders are particularly important. Regression models are also able to combine 'competing' explanatory schemes in one regression model, and thus investigate which scheme outperforms the others. Qualitative studies are uniquely well-suited to unravel the complex layers of contributing factors, and have employed varying degrees of rigour in doing so: from explaining variation to designs where positive and negative cases were systematically compared.

Itt appears from numerous studies that the etiology of international crimes cannot be understood solely at micro-, meso- or macro-level. Models that combine these levels and investigate specifically their interrelation are warranted, a standpoint underwritten by both micro- and macro-researchers. Combining different sources (archives, interviews, sentinel data) gives different perspectives, and different sources add depth: conclusions drawn from different sources are generally stronger. Similarly, the combination of quantitative and qualitative methods, and triangulation through such different methods also strengthens conclusions.

It is paramount that researchers strive for corroboration of findings from other research. For that, shared instruments are necessary. We saw how a narrative review quickly bumped into the complication that many studies employ their own idiosyncratic definitions, making for the blind alley of method differences, away from scientific progress. Comparability of results, and at the basis of that standardised operationalisation, is key if we want to understand the drivers of this seemingly highly inexplicable human behaviour. Medical and social science have benefitted greatly from meta-analyses. For international criminality there is probably still quite some way to go before a sufficient evidence base is built for such reviews.

We saw several examples of studies that in the confused long-lingering aftermath of conflict – though unable to draw probabilistic samples in the statistical sense – strived towards and were able to achieve spread over relevant factions, gender, ages etc. We encountered naturalistic experiments and randomised controlled trials. While standard procedures are definitely more difficult to roll out, much is possible.

Chapter 15

Studying (legal) responses

15.1 Introduction

In this chapter we will discuss methods used for the study of the legal and 'semi-legal' or special responses to international crimes. By the latter we mean responses that do not emanate from strictly judicial institutions such as courts or prosecutor's offices, but that nevertheless may give rights and have legal implications, such as amnesties and certain truth commissions.

The responses that we study in this chapter comprise firstly prosecution by domestic courts, international courts and tribunals. But also, in the aftermath of widespread atrocities and destruction, many countries have chosen, or saw no other option given vast numbers of perpetrators and a decimated judiciary, but to distribute justice by trying perpetrators through ad hoc courts, such as through the special *gacaca* courts in Rwanda. Next, some countries have chosen to establish truth commissions, at times complementary to the trying of a small number of high-level perpetrators (such as in Sierra Leone and in Cambodia). Lastly, a number of conflicts have not dealt with the aftermath of conflict through legal or ad hoc responses, but have simply unconditionally amnestied all.

These types of responses raise different types of questions. The first sort of questions is descriptive. How many perpetrators have been prosecuted, acquitted, convicted, sentenced, what crimes were they convicted for? What were the sentences handed down? How many perpetrators were dealt with through popular courts? How many people confessed and thus were granted amnesty? For what crimes? We will discuss such research briefly – most of the methods featured in chapters above and do not require detailed further discussion.

A second batch of questions relates to the legal process. Many of the institutions that deal with perpetrators of international crimes are relatively new (or have been established with the purpose to deal with only those crimes committed within a particular period or conflict). Most of them therefore do not have much jurisprudence to fall back on, they do not have a legal tradition, specific guidelines or even quantified sentencing guidelines. This raises a number of issues that relate back to fundamental principles of justice. One important such issue is consistency: similar cases should be treated similarly. As Hola (2012) argues, consistency of sentencing should be evident at two levels: the level of the 'approach' to sentence determination (i.e. reasoning) and the level of the outcome of sentencing. As 'approach' Hola defines the manner in which sentences are determined, decisions being based on common standards or general underlying principles, uniformly applied to the facts of each case. At the second level, of consistency in outcome, Hola states that comparable cases should receive comparable sentences. The first issue calls for research that investigates the manner in which standards are being referred to and actually used. This would be socio-legal research in a sense, research that scrutinises legal decisions, in which texts are scanned for active or passive referral to principles, and comparison of the application of such principles across cases and jurisdictions or tribunals. Such research would almost always be qualitative. The second issue calls for – as we will show below – fairly technical, quantitative analytic methods that are able to assess to what extent sentences are actually consistently determined, and therefore predictable.

Thirdly, we need to investigate ad hoc responses. Of the ad hoc semi-legal institutions the best known and perhaps best investigated example is the *gacaca* courts in Rwanda. How many perpetrators were tried? How did these generally function? How are they perceived? By perpetrators as well as victims, family members of the perished, as well as those called to testify? Truth commissions have often been established after conflicts as well. How many were established? What was their structure? Can they be perceived as effective in the sense that they prevented further conflicts from erupting, that they restored the moral order, that they gave closure? While similar questions could be asked for standard responses such as prosecution, for such relatively novel ad hoc responses these questions are relatively more prominent.

An inherent problem here is that the effectiveness of these responses cannot be easily assessed using designs to establish causality (see section 5.3 ff.), namely with an experimental and a control group. Also, case-control studies are hard to implement, as measures such as amnesties are generally universal or confounded with properties of the perpetrators. This means that for assessing effectiveness (whichever way out of a multitude of ways 'effectiveness' is operationalised) we often rely on in-depth qualitative studies or on cleverly designed surveys, such as those that through vignettes attempt to tap the 'active ingredients' of responses. Such particular, ad hoc or special responses can similarly be studied through surveys among the general population, through surveys amongst participants, and through vignette studies. Descriptive studies constitute an important part: firstly to describe and tabulate, for instance, how many people reported to, say, a truth commission, what their backgrounds were: were they victims, relatives of victims, or bystanders, or even perpetrators? Secondly, to describe how the public perceive the functioning of the truth commission, whether there are differences between members of the groups that were in conflict, and so forth. For that, population-based surveys can be used, or tailored surveys among participants.

Amnesties can be studied using a variety of studies. Firstly, descriptive studies are necessary and useful. Population-based surveys can be used to assess public perception and contentedness with these processes. A dominant question regarding amnesties is whether they can be perceived as effective in the sense that they actually heal and enable societies to continue after large-scale atrocities. After all, they go straight against the prevailing *mantra* that without justice there cannot be peace. However, for studying the effectiveness of amnesties again there is generally no statistically equivalent control group, and conflicts where amnesties have been applied and have not been applied generally differ on so many other relevant factors that it is hard to quantitatively determine the causal effect of the amnesty as such. Obviously, if a country remains peaceful, one may conclude that apparently conflict did not continue, but whether that can be *attributed* to the amnesty cannot be determined. That means that for this type of questions there is heavy reliance on qualitative, mostly macro-level studies that attempt to arrive at causal or effectiveness statements through the scrutiny of various types of documents, surveys, indicators, and interviews with specialists, triangulating and corroborating evidence from various sources.

In the following, we will describe studies and study methods along this categorisation. That is, we will first discuss methods to study prosecution and sentencing, and next methods to study ad hoc or special responses and amnesties. A large literature on transitional justice exists. As the methodological issues relevant for such studies do not differ much from those for sentencing and ad hoc responses, we end by briefly discussing a systematic review of this literature.

15.2 (Inter)national prosecution and sentencing

As stated in the introduction, (inter)national prosecution and sentencing can be studied firstly in a descriptive way. Means, medians and cross-tabulations give us an overview of the numbers prosecuted and sentenced, sentences distributed, and of differences between perpetrators of different offences, or even of differences between tribunals, special courts and hybrid institutions. Smeulers, Hola and Van den Berg (2013) give a detailed overview of international criminal justice since World War II. They describe numbers of cases prosecuted at nine international criminal courts and tribunals: the two tribunals established after WW II: the International Military Tribunal at Nuremberg (IMT), and the International Military Tribunal for the Far East (IMFGTE), the ICTY, ICTR, ICC, the Special Court for Sierra Leone (SCSL), the Extraordinary Chambers in the Courts of Cambodia (ECCC), the Special Tribunal for Libanon (STL), and the internationalised court in East Timor, referred to as the Special Panels of Dili (SPD).

The statistics that Smeulers, Hola and Van den Berg (2013) present give some interesting insights. For instance, they record that a total of 23 chief prosecutors were employed by these institutions, and 256 judges, for 745 people indicted and 356 who actually went on trial. Trials took longest at the ICTR at an average 3.9 years (with SCSL second at 3.6 years), and shortest at the Special Tribunal for Libanon at 4 months, Nuremberg coming second with 10 months. The authors explain this through the fact that ICTR and SCSL had a high percentage of high-level perpetrators so that cases were complicated, and that there were relatively few guilty pleas. The study is mainly descriptive and does not use testing or attempts to fit explanatory models.

Hola studied the process of international sentencing. She studied both consistency in approach (2012, chapter 2) and consistency in outcome (Hola, Bijleveld, & Smeulers, 2009) at the two international tribunals that have generated the largest number of sentences in recent history: the ICTR and the ICTY.

For consistency in approach (2012, chapter 2), Hola studied the sentencing case law produced by the ICTY and ICTR judges up to April 2011. Hola argues that it is defensible to combine these two tribunals because, firstly, the positive law framework is almost identical for both tribunals, and secondly the tribunals share a common Appeals Chambers which contributes to the development of a common jurisprudence. Her 'sample' of cases was composed of all verdicts in first instance and appeal issued by ICTY and ICTR, i.e. the entire population of decisions in which a verdict had been reached for the two tribunals up to a certain time point. She retrieved all the material from the respective websites of the two tribunals.

After discussing the positive law framework that regulates sentencing decision making at the tribunals, Hola analyses the case law. From what was said in each case, she first registers how the general principles of sentence determination are operationalised in practice: how do judges in their verdicts describe and operationalise these abstract principles? For instance, she notes that as regards the gravity of crimes *in abstracto* the judges, particularly in the more recent case law, do not wish to rank order genocide, crimes against humanity and war crimes – while in the more distant jurisprudence judges have noted that there is an inherent ordering in terms of gravity. She cites examples of this more recent stance such as from the judgment in Mrksič and Šljivančanin (IT-95-13/1) Appeals Chamber (5 May 2009, para. 375), and quotes the Appeals Chamber in the Tadič case where a majority ruled that: "*there is in law no distinction between the seriousness of a crime against humanity and that of a war crime. The Appeals Chamber finds no basis for such a distinction in the Statute or the Rules of the International Tribunal construed in accordance with customary international law; the authorised penalties are also the same, the level in any particular case being fixed by reference to the circumstances of the case.*" With this statement, the Chamber expresses that it is the particular circumstances of the case that determine the gravity of the crime, and not the type of crime.

Given that it is the gravity in *concreto* that determines the severity of crimes, next, Hola analyses how gravity in concreto has been assessed in individual cases. She notes that factors relevant to the concrete gravity assessment differ across cases. One reason for that is that neither positive law nor jurisprudence prescribe what factors should be relevant for the gravity assessment (or to aggravate or mitigate it). She describes how in the latest case law, the concept of gravity has been interpreted as encompassing (1) the particular circumstances of the case, i.e. the magnitude of harm caused by the offender and represented by, for example, the scale of the crime, the number of victims, the extent of victims' suffering, or the impact of the criminal conduct on victims and their relatives; and (2) the form and degree of the accused's participation in the crime – the offender's culpability. She subsequently notes that similar aspects of crimes have in some cases been judged to constitute part of the gravity of the offence, and in other cases as aggravating factors – indicating therewith inconsistency in approach.

The method used by Hola for the case law analysis is essentially a descriptive analysis, also referred to as 'case law analysis'; as she mainly analysed patterns and did not quantify the relations she found. It is an empirical legal study (Bijleveld, 2019), in this case perhaps best classified as a special kind of content analysis (see section 9.3).

Hola next studied aggravating and mitigating factors, i.e. factors that could make a sentence heavier, or reduce it. While aggravating factors need to be proven beyond all reasonable doubt for them to be accepted, for mitigating factors this does not apply. Hola found that there was inconsistency as well in the labeling of aspects as aggravating or

Table 15.1: Sentence length in years, by offence, offender rank and guilty plea

	trial			appeal		
	average sentence (SD)	median sentence	*N*	average sentence (SD)	median sentence	*N*
Average	15.3 (10.0)	14.0	60	14.6 (8.7)	14.0	56
Crimes against humanity	17.2 (10.2)	17.0	47	16.2 (8.9)	15.0	43
War crimes	8.4 (5.4)	7.0	13	9.1 (4.5)	9.0	13
High ranking	17.2 (10.2)	17.0	47	16.2 (8.9)	15.0	43
Middle ranking	13.5 (9.6)	10.0	25	13.3 (8.5)	10.0	24
Low ranking offenders	13.9 (6.5)	15.0	23	14.1 (6.1)	15.0	20
No guilty plea	15.9 (10.6)	15.0	40	15.1 (8.9)	15.0	36
Guilty plea	14.1 (8.9)	12.5	20	13.6 (8.3)	12.5	20

source: Hola, Bijleveld and Smeulers, 2009

mitigating: the same factor could be accepted as mitigating in one case but as aggravating in another. Hola however notes that whether a certain factor constitutes a mitigating or aggravating circumstance depended largely on particular circumstances of each case, and therefore does not label this as inconsistency. This shows once more how her analysis has most of the hallmarks of a qualitative analysis: she did not study facts in isolation but assessed their impact within the context of the particular legal case.

Hola concludes that sentencing principles are consistently discussed and emphasised by the ICTY and ICTR, and that judges from one tribunal often refer to the case law of the other in their general sentencing considerations, thus developing a common ICTY-ICTR narrative. She states that, in spite of some disparities, the analysis has not identified any major differences in the sentencing reasoning of judges at the ICTY and ICTR. There is confusion according to Hola in the ICTY and ICTR case law regarding the objectives of punishment: aims are unclear as are the exact meaning of sentencing objectives or their role in sentence determination. However, these, as Hola argues, do not affect the structure of sentencing argumentation nor the factors emphasised in meting out individual sentences.

In a second publication (2009), Hola, Bijleveld and Smeulers studied consistency in outcome. They investigated the impact of a number of legally relevant factors, such as mode of individual responsibility, mitigating and aggravating factors, guilty plea, and the like, on sentencing outcome. They wanted to know for instance whether a guilty plea had a significant impact on sentence length. They studied all 63 cases that had by the time the analysis was conducted been handed down, whether by the trial chamber if the case had been dealt with only in first instance, or by the Appeals Chamber if it had been decided upon in appeal. While these 63 cases comprised at that point in time the entire population

Table 15.2: Sentence length, by mode of individual responsibility

	trial			appeal		
	average sentence (SD)	median sentence	*N*	average sentence (SD)	median sentence	*N*
Superiors	11.8 (10.6)	7.8	18	10.7 (6.3)	9.0	15
Perpetrators	17.5 (8.0)	17.5	20	17.3 (7.7)	18.0	18
JCE	16.3 (9.8)	15.0	22	14.6 (8.4)	13.0	19
Planners	18.5 (9.2)	18.5	2	18.5 (9.2)	18.5	2
Instigators	19.8 (15.4)	25.0	3	20.7 (12.1)	25.0	3
Orderers	21.8 (12.8)	20.0	8	16.8 (7.8)	18.0	9
Aiders	14.1 (8.4)	13.0	17	16.2 (8.5)	15.0	18

source: Hola, Bijleveld and Smeulers, 2009

of cases in a statistical sense, for practical purposes it is a small sample (see section 3.1). This limits possibilities for analysis, as we will see below.

Hola and her co-authors first gave descriptives of these cases. The average number of counts for which a person was convicted was 4.6 (the number in first instance only was higher at 5.1). Defendants are most often convicted for persecution (35 in total). Next, they described sentence length in relation to a number of legally relevant factors. Table 15.1 lists average sentence length (in years), as well as sentence length broken down by a number of categories of offenders, and by whether or not the offender had pleaded guilty. The table gives not only means, but also median values as the distribution of sentence length was skewed (see section 6.3.1). The table shows that sentences in appeal were on average somewhat shorter. Crimes against humanity were sentenced more harshly, those who did not plead guilty received longer sentences as well. These findings are not surprising.

There were some unexpected findings too, however. While high-ranking offenders in general received the longest sentences, the sentences for middle-ranking offenders were surprisingly low, and those of the low-ranking offenders higher again – and in fact (if looking at the median in appeal) just as high as those of the high-ranking offenders. This finding is surprising as one would expect that those with greatest responsibility for the crimes would receive the longest sentences, and those with the least responsibility, lowest in the hierarchy of culpability, correspondingly the lowest sentences.

Hola and her co-authors next investigated this issue by looking at the different modes of individual responsibility underlying an offender's conviction. See Table 15.2.

Again, there was a similar surprising finding, namely that those with superior responsibility received the lowest sentences on average, lower even than the aiders. Hola *et al.* (2009) explain this by suggesting that superior responsibility entails passive behaviour, such as a failure to punish or prevent subordinates from committing crimes. The omissions of superiors are perhaps perceived to be less serious than active participation in criminal

Table 15.3: Regression analysis of ICTY sentence lengths in years

	b	β	*p*-value,
High rank	10.9	0.5	<.001
Middle rank	2.2	0.1	<.231
# Guilty counts	0.7	0.4	<.001
Conviction for crimes against humanity	6.1	0.3	<.001
# Mitigating factors	-0.6	-0.2	<.025
Instigation	7.7	0.2	<.032
Perpetration	3.4	0.2	<.079
Superior responsibility	-3.5	-0.2	<.058

$R^2 = .653$
$R^2_{adj} = .602$
$N = 63$

source: Hola, Bijleveld and Smeulers, 2009

activities, less serious than the activities of the executioners, those with 'blood on their hands'. On a bivariate level, Hola and her co-authors identified several other counterintuitive patterns in the ICTY sentencing, for instance aiders and abettors (that is, facilitators of crime with arguably a very limited role in the crimes) received on appeal sentences almost as high as orderers (who are arguably more culpable due to their decisive influence on hands-on perpetrators). Thus, sentence length is likely not only a function of a perpetrator's role, but of his or her role in conjunction with other aspects of the crime, such as cruelty, or the number of counts.

This implies that it does not make sense to investigate the effect of individual responsibility bivariately. As individual responsibility may be *confounded* with hands-on cruelty, one may end up with hard to interpret findings like those just discussed. Individual responsibility may even be confounded with additional factors, for instance, it may also be that aiders often are sentenced for less serious crimes. If aiders receive on average a shorter sentence, is that because they were aiders – or because they were responsible for less serious crimes? Or, do aiders receive shorter sentences not because they were aiders but because they often confessed to their crimes? To disentangle all such confounding, the authors chose to carry out a multivariate regression analysis.

In a multivariate regression analysis, one investigates the effect of each independent variable on an outcome variable, and the regression weights express the impact of the respective variables *given the other variables in the model.* See section 8.2.3. Thus, one would be able in a regression analysis to investigate the effect of being an aider *over and above* the effect of other variables present in the model. The model would give the net effect of being an aider, net of whether someone had shown excessive cruelty, had confessed to his crimes, had committed war crimes, etc. The regression coefficient reflects what a variable (being an aider) adds to the prediction of the dependent variable (sentence length) given all other factors (type of crime, mitigating factors, guilty plea, etc.) in the model. This is the reason why regression analysis is a suitable technique for the question at hand, namely what the impact is of one variable on another one, controlling for the distorting effects of other factors.

Table 15.3 gives the results of the regression analysis. In first instance, 14 predictors had been added to the model. One variable was added as a 'dummy variable': the variable 'perpetrator rank' had three categories and was not interval level (at most it may be considered ordinal level; see chapter 6.2.1). This variable was therefore included as two dichotomous variables, one indicating whether a perpetrator had high rank (1) or not (0), and a second one indicating whether a perpetrator had middle rank (1) or not (0). Even though the authors had wanted to include more predictors, the small sample size did not allow this (and 14 predictors was already stretching it given the 63 cases); recall that in general, it is advised that the sample size be at least 10 times the number of predictors (see section 8.2.6). Of the predictors, a number turned up not significant, and these were removed from the model to make it more parsimonious.

Next, the authors had to solve for the fact that in two instances (Stakič and Galič), life sentences had been handed down. In that case, there is no sentence length one can predict ('life' being indeterminate), so that the value for the dependent variable is technically speaking missing. For this analysis, they recoded life sentences to the expected duration of imprisonment given the convicted's age; for Stakič this led to a value of 30 years, for Galič 20 years. One could argue that these values are in a sense arbitrary and do not reflect that life imprisonment is intended to express a qualitatively differently sentence – much heavier – than determinate sentences. In that sense, the imputed value of 20 years for Galič may be seen as too low given that for instance the average sentence of orderers at trial was already 21.8 years. The authors ran several other models (thereby conducting a 'sensitivity' or 'robustness' analysis), in which different values for these life sentences were used. The interpretation however remained substantively the same. Given these results, the authors conclude that the findings are robust against different imputations of values for the life sentences. Obviously, as there were just two life sentences for which values had to be imputed against 61 determinate sentences, the results were not likely to be affected much.

The variables in Table 15.3 in the final model were all significant at the $p < 0.10$ level, and therefore retained. The fit of the model is quite reasonable; the drop from an R^2 of .653 to an R^2_{adj} of .602 (a penalty for the inclusion of many variables in the model given its N, see section 8.2.3) shows that the model, with 63 cases and more than six variables, may indeed have been slightly overloaded.

All in all, the multiple regression analysis leads to a number of conclusions. Firstly, the analysis shows that the fit values of this model are adequate; they are in fact comparable to fit values of 'national' analyses on sentencing consistency. International sentencing at the ICTY and ICTR therefore does not appear less consistent than regular national sentencing. Second, the analysis showed that higher-ranking offenders did indeed receive longer sentences: in the model, being a high-ranking offender adds 10.9 years to sentence length. As Table 15.3 reports unstandardised regression coefficients (see section 8.2.2), the regression weights translate directly into the impact they have on the dependent variable sentence length. The results show for instance how every additional guilty count adds 0.7 years or approximately 8 months to sentence length; conversely each mitigating factor deducts 0.6 years or approximately 7 months. The analysis also shows that the remarkable finding that those with superior responsibility received lower sentences was not due to any confounding with the variables in the model: perpetrators with superior responsibility on average received a 3.5 years lower sentence, also in the multivariate model.

A natural experiment could be employed by David (2014) to study public perceptions of domestic and international criminal prosecutions. David had developed an experimental vignette that was to be presented to a representative sample of Croatians, in which the case of a person with an ethnically neutral name ('Petrović') was described. In the vignette, Petrović was introduced as a member of either the Serbian or the Croatian army, and he had wilfully killed either a Croatian or a Serbian civilian. Described as a middle-ranking soldier, he could have received a punishment, but no punishment (a suspended sentence) would also not have been unrealistic. Last, the vignettes varied in that Petrović was tried at the ICTY or domestically. The design was therefore a $2 \times 2 \times 2$ design with 8 versions of the vignette. Respondents were asked to indicate on four dimensions to what extent they judged the outcome of the trial as just. David aimed to investigate not only what the effects were of the experimentally manipulated characteristics of the vignette (ethnicity, punishment and legal institution), but also whether respondents of Croatian descent would judge punishments of Croatians differently from punishments of Serbs.

During the administration of the vignettes, however, Karadzić was arrested, and was to be tried at the ICTY. This gave the author a unique opportunity to compare answers given by sample members before and answers given after Karadzić's arrest. David found a strong and significant effect, signalling enhanced approval of international criminal tribunals after Karadzić's apprehension.

Chlevickaite, Hola and Bijleveld (2019) studied insider witnesses at the ICTY, ICTR and ICC. They were interested to uncover factors influencing the numbers of witnesses called in international trials. By the end of 2018, the ICC and the two tribunals had handed down 111 trial judgments, within which judges had assessed 8,653 viva voce testimonies. The authors studied the trial judgments and other case-related documents, all publicly available, coding witness participation and other relevant aspects of the trials. As they surveyed all trials, they employed an, in a statistical sense, entire population.

Chlevickaite and her co-authors report that the ICTY had called the most witnesses in total (N = 5491). The authors next note that witness participation fluctuated over time, likely as a function of historical period and the type of cases, political context and changes in institutional practices. They also note that there was much variation in numbers of witnesses called, in fact more within than between legal institution. They attempted to explain the variability of numbers of witnesses from factors associated with case complexity and efficiency. They chose three indicator variables for the first factor: rank of the defendant, liability, mode, severity of the crime, and two indicators for the second factor: the number of non-viva voce witnesses and the number of adjudicated facts.

While they had aimed to combine ICTY, ICTR and ICC in one analysis, there was heterogeneity: the associations between variables were distinctly different at ICTR than at ICTY. With their dataset already containing a small number of cases, disaggregation of the dataset into separate samples per institution aggravated this issue more. Using crosstabulations and comparing means for ICTY and ICTR separately, certain case complexity characteristics turned out to be indeed associated with the number of trial witnesses. At the ICTR, high numbers of witnesses were associated with high authority levels of a defendant, more counts, longer periods of charges, and more categories of crimes charged. At the ICTY, very few results were significant, possibly due to the fact that the standard deviations of the variables were very high, caused by outliers of very large trials; as discussed in section 7.1.2 and section 3.4 it is hard to reach statistical significance if the data are very noisy. A moderate negative relationship did emerge between war crimes-only charges and the number of witnesses.

Doughty (2017) studied language and translation issues at the ICTR. The research is based on participant observation comprising three field visits to the ICTR during which the author attended case sessions in Arusha, lived with ICTR staff for a number of weeks and had access to the UN compound, library and courtrooms. She also conducted 40 interviews with judges, legal officers, defence counsellors, members of the Office of the Prosecutor, interns, public relations officials and interpreters. She made detailed notes during these interviews, that she transcribed. She was interested to investigate interpretation and translation at the tribunal, knowing that this was an understudied area.

Doughty's work is qualitative, and her approach likely best qualified as grounded. Doughty's transcribed quotes illustrate many situations of confusion over translation, leading in turn to confusion over reliability and credibility of witnesses, and even accusations of lying. The following exemplar illustrates this well:

"*Sometimes people get upset at the witness instead of realizing that it's an issue of translation. The witness says something, the translator may mistranslate it, then the questioner asks something that suggests the witness is stupid or lying or deliberately being confusing, and then the witness gets defensive. It can go downhill and people think he is a liar.*"

Repairing misunderstanding and wrong translations was extremely cumbersome in the absence of Kinyarwanda transcripts, which illuminates the marginalisation of the Africans who were being tried, and the Africans participating as witnesses, victims and translators. But the author also, from her conversations with translators, perceives a class distance between witnesses on the one hand and interpreters and prosecutors alike, as emanates from the following exemplar from an interview with a Rwandan prosecutor:

"*The people who come testify before the Tribunal, with their level of education, they are not distinguishing between what they saw, assumed, imagined, heard or thought. They jump to conclusions based on their imagination, and make decisions based on prior knowledge*"

Translators expressed frustration and described their symbolic and economic marginalisation at the Tribunal. The exasperation of Rwandans working at the court is voiced in the following parts of an exemplar:

"*(...) How do you get involved in a process in which you think all people are liars? (...) If you are an officer of the court, and you have the idea that all Rwandans are liars, how ill you do your job?*"

Doughty states that the relationship between interpretation errors, cross-examination and moral judgments warrants further examination in light of procedural justice of Rwandans brought before the court.

An overview of the empirical body of research on international sentencing was given by Hola (2018), in which she concludes that empirical scholarship on international criminal justice is still in its infancy. Hola identifies a number of reasons for this, of which we highlight three that are particularly relevant for us. First, she states that much research is scattered over different disciplines, which makes it hard to bring findings together and integrate them. Second she states that it is hard to generalise findings as much is unique to the setting of each particular conflict. Third, she mentions the difficulties in collecting data, at the international and post-conflict setting, exacerbated by dark numbers, missing data, language and cultural barriers, and scant resources.

15.3 Ad hoc responses

Next to courts and tribunals, offenders have been prosecuted also through ad hoc institutions, such as the *gacaca* courts and truth commissions. The research methods to study them vary from qualitative interviews to mixed methods, to naturalistic experiments in field settings, to experimental studies using vignettes. In the following, we will give a number of examples of such studies, discussing the rationale for the methods that were employed.

15.3.1 Ad hoc legal institutions

The Rwandan *gacaca* courts were established in 2001 to deal with the aftermath of the genocide, in which 90% of the entire judiciary had been killed. The country was faced with massive numbers of alleged perpetrators. It was clear that there would be no possibility to try these people in regular legal proceedings. Instead, *gacaca* courts, from which lawyers were banned and in which ordinary Rwandans functioned as judges, were to achieve this. The courts had not only the aim to try perpetrators, but also to establish the truth about what happened during the genocide, contribute to the unity and reconciliation of Rwandan society, and to fight against a culture of impunity. According to the Africa Research Institute, by 2012, around 400,000 defendants had been prosecuted (Africa Research Institute, 2012). However, according to the Rwandan National Service of Gacaca Courts (2012) by that same year over 900,000 people had been tried. By 2018, Hola (2018) states that over a million have been tried.

Various studies have been published that discuss the extent to which the *gacaca* courts met their aims. Some studies focused on the legal foundations of the courts (Oomen, 2009), others on the political situation in Rwanda (Le Mon, 2007) and on how that affected the functioning and eventual effectiveness of the courts. A fairly comprehensive one is the final study by Penal Reform International (PRI), published in 2010 after a long period in which this organisation regularly published monitoring reports on the courts (Penal Reform International, 2010).

The research carried out by PRI was mainly qualitative and participatory. Over the years, researchers employed by PRI employed a variety of techniques, such as observation techniques and in-depth and semi-structured interviews as well as focus group discussions. More than 2,500 individual interviews were undertaken. The focus of PRI's studies was not so much on the collection of facts but rather on tapping the 'meaning' that *gacaca* had for Rwandans. It that sense, qualitative methods were clearly warranted to study this question. Research was undertaken across rural and urban areas, as well as at cell, commune and préfecture levels in an attempt to make the findings as representative as possible. The researchers note that given the 'action' dimension of their research, that is, the explicit aim of PRI to contribute to the processes aimed at through *gacaca*, bias is possible. They also note that even though an explicit choice had been made for qualitative interviews to capture perception and behavioural issues, the disadvantage of such interviews is that answers are less consistent, and harder to compare over respondents.

PRI are mixed in their conclusions on the *gacaca* courts. On the one hand they state that *gacaca* has succeeded like no other institution could have, in involving a whole adult population in establishing the truth of what happened, and in so doing, in breaking the cycle of impunity. *Gacaca* has also been fast, and processed an enormous amount of cases. Laws were changed to further speed up the process of trying also the most serious cases. On the minus side, however, this put judges under strain and affected the quality of the legal process. Rulings were hastily handed down and defendants were not always given time to defend themselves, or even aware what charges had been brought against them. Witnesses were sometimes absent when they had been called at two courts at the same time,

While confessions have played according to PRI a positive role in encouraging the truth to emerge, the *gacaca* jurisdictions did not manage to uncover the whole truth. Even so, accused individuals and their families appreciated the confessions procedure as the interviews showed, and the process has contributed to relieving the enormous tensions created in the genocide's aftermath. The Rwandan state's involvement in the *gacaca* process was too intense, PRI judged, and led at times to manipulation of the process, and not giving judges sufficient leeway. PRI also quotes instances of corruption.

Overall, the authors conclude, the context of the atrocities renders reconciliation inherently difficult. The harsh social and economic realities faced by most of Rwanda's population make forgiveness harder. Convicted offenders are often simply unable to compensate victims, and both may be in equally desperate financial straits.

15.3.2 Truth commissions, amnesties and transitional justice

A number of countries have established truth commissions to deal with the aftermath of widespread conflict. Several researchers have studied individual truth commissions, amnesty and other post-conflict responses. Some have compared them. Most of this literature employs qualitative methods.

Dancy, Kim and Brahm (2010) compiled a database of truth commissions, including those commissions that functioned as temporary responses, sanctioned by the state, with investigative powers for patterns of abuses of personal integrity over time – some of which perpetrated by state actors. The authors note that several countries have had truth commissions operating in consecutive instances. They also note that several countries have seen unofficial truth projects springing up, at the initiative of civil society organisations. Also, truth commissions have often been operational in tandem with or prior to trials or reparations. This in a methodological sense confounding of truth commission with other interventions makes it harder to tease out any effects of the truth commissions per se, as it is hard to assess where changes can be attributed to the truth commission or to the other legal processes. They also note that there are wide differences between truth commissions, making it hard to establish an effect of 'truth commissions' as such.

Ranft and Freudenreich (2008) compared 20 different truth commissions. They used descriptive quantitative measures to uncover patterns in the manner in which these truth commissions were established and how they operated: they for instance computed the correlation between variables indicating whether amnesties had been granted and the naming of perpetrators, whether the hearings were public, whether reparations were made, and whether a report was written and published. Not many measures of association came up significant, however. The authors conclude that this may be due to heterogeneity: the effect of many characteristics of these commissions depended heavily on the national context. The authors did find that commissions that covered longer periods of conflict were larger and had a longer period in which they were functional. Commissions were more likely to be accompanied by reparations programs when they worked in the context of amnesty laws. When commissions held public hearings and when they had investigative powers, they were more likely to name the perpetrators of the violence. It is possible that the authors failed to identify more patterns as their sample size was so small. Correlation coefficients of 0.5, and higher even, did not turn up significant.

Qualitatively analyzing the empirical evidence from a number of post-conflict countries, Snyder and Vinjamuri (2003) investigated the short-term impact of trials, amnesties and truth commissions. Examining 32 civil wars (not necessarily implying that international crimes were committed) between 1989 and 2003, they investigated how trends in indicators of democracy, the rule of law and human rights standards correlated with the strategy of justice in each country. Obviously, as correlations do not imply causality, causal inferences cannot be made from this analysis. Only associations and patterns therein can be observed. As the authors note, this approach secondly does not capture short-term successes of amnesties in stopping the fighting (such as in Macedonia, Angola and the Chittagong Hills conflict in India). Through a more in-depth analysis of a number of civil wars, the authors attempt to unravel cause and effect in each unique context. Their analysis resembles best a narrative review.

The authors draw three conclusions. First, they conclude that trials contribute to the ending of abuses only if potential perpetrators of abuses do not constitute a powerful group, and a well-established infrastructure of justice is already in place before trials start. As the authors somewhat cynically note, 'trials work best when they are needed least'. Second, the authors conclude that the capacity of truth commissions to promote reconciliation is far more limited than advocates suggest. Truth commissions can contribute to democratic consolidation only, the authors state, if a pro-democracy coalition is in power in a fairly well institutionalised state – and truth commissions can even have negative effects. Third, the authors are (much more) positive about the impact that amnesties can have. Pre-conditions for such an effect are, summarised very briefly, that there is effective political backing and strong institutions to enforce their terms.

Backer (2009), in a recommended for reading chapter, outlines the properties and background of a large number of truth commissions, as well as of prosecutions post-conflict.

Backer states that countries exhibit marked differences in the selection and implementation of transitional justice strategies, but that the different truth commissions are not incomparable. Instead, sets of cases can be identified that share features and thus form 'types'. The main question to be addressed by research is whether they have been effective. Backer suggests that one way to do so, is by comparing population-based surveys longitudinally and to assess how the public's perception and approval of the truth commission evolved over time. Backer identifies three problems in the study of truth commissions – in methodological terms: in the study of very complicated processes of which one only has a few cases. This study is also an example of a narrative review.

A first problem is that cases may differ too much to be comparable. It is however exactly here that Backer recommends to situate research, and to in a sense exploit this variability. Firstly, for each commission a 'best match' (i.e. a case-control) could be sought within the set of other truth commissions, and causes for differences in outcomes between these two commissions sought in those characteristics on which they differ most. Conversely, one could search for countries where apparently quite different truth commissions have had comparable outcomes and then search for key variables that they share. This is however easier said than done, as most post-conflict societies have had not one, but several initiatives at reconciliation and other parallel processes. Cases therefore do remain fairly idiosyncratic within their specific context, and comparability is not easily achieved.

Secondly, the workings of each truth commission can be understood only if one truly knows the country, the conflict and actors, has in-depth local knowledge, also of unpublished, material, developments before, during and after the conflict. If one needs to compare numerous truth commissions, it may be impossible for one researcher to have so much in-depth knowledge on so many conflicts.

Thirdly, if one wants to assess the effects of a truth commission (and this we mentioned before), the existence of that truth commission is generally not the only independent variable operating on outcomes. After truth commissions have completed their task, other developments may take place: oil may be discovered, a conflict in a neighbouring country may propel new animosities, refugee flows may strain a post-conflict country's meagre resources. In such cases it is hard to separate out the effect of that single, distal factor of the existence of the truth commission from the effects of these concurrent developments. There is all in all, a lot of confounding.

Gibson (2004) attempted to overcome such methodological quandaries by using a so-called vignette study (see section 5.8) for investigating the impact of the truth commission (TRC) in South Africa. More specifically, Gibson wanted to know what aspects of justice meted out by the truth commission contributed to the TRC being perceived as fair by South Africans. The study was carried out on a random sample of South Africans, so that the findings are generalisable to the South African population.

Gibson went about the vignette study as follows. First, he identified from the literature four kinds of justice that the TRC could provide that could compensate for the fact that amnesty for serious offenders may be perceived as inherently unfair. He identified four kinds: firstly, distributive justice, which implies that victims get (financial) compensation for the losses they suffered. Second, restorative justice, that implies restoration of relations between victims and offenders (summarised in the term *ubuntu*), entailing an apology by offenders. Thirdly, retributive justice – which was formally ruled out by the amnesty law

Table 15.4: Judgment of fairness by experimental condition

		punishment		no punishment	
		voice	no voice	voice	no voice
apology	compensation	5.19	4.15	5.11	4.70
apology	no compensation	3.14	2.60	3.29	2.58
no apology	compensation	4.52	4.03	4.21	3.84
no apology	no compensation	2.97	2.45	2.65	2.24

source: Gibson (2004)

– and is perhaps best captured by offenders publicly admitting their crimes, or suffering other negative consequences. Lastly, procedural justice refers mostly to whether victims are given a 'voice' in the process or not.

Gibson next designed 16 different vignettes, in which each of these types of justice was present or not. The reason why vignettes were designed is that in real cases that came before the truth commission, different kinds of justice were often confounded. If it is for instance the case that procedural justice is present, then restorative justice was always present as well; it is then impossible to disentangle the effects of the two and to isolate the effect of a single factor. However, by constructing these hypothetical vignettes, it is possible to compare cases where only one kind of justice was present (e.g. procedural justice) to those where only one other kind of justice was present (e.g. restorative justice).

Then, Gibson gave each respondent a description of a situation in which a perpetrator of a political group that was probably disliked by the respondent figured. Each respondent was randomly given a story about a certain 'Philip', a perpetrator, for which s/he was asked to judge how fair the outcome was to the families of the victims.

An example of a vignette follows here, in which only the 'punishment' kind of justice is present.

Philip was a member of (the respondent's least liked group). Philip sought amnesty for setting off a bomb that killed several innocent people. At his amnesty hearing, the families of the victims were denied a chance to tell how the bombing had affected their lives, even though they had insisted that they wanted to tell their story [no procedural justice]. *Philip then told his version of the bombing. In reaction to Philips disclosures, Philip's family said that they were deeply ashamed of what he had done, and his wife subsequently divorced him* [retributive justice]. *Philip apologised for his actions, but his apology was rejected as insincere by the families and the victims* [no restorative justice]. *Philip was granted amnesty. Afterward, the families of the victims were not given any financial compensation, because the government said it had no funding for compensating victims. The government did, however, express its sympathy for the victims* [no distributive justice].

Table 15.4 gives the tabulation of the various combinations of the four kinds of justice. A first conclusion from this table is that none of the outcomes is judged as very fair. Across all vignettes, as Gibson notes, only 24.3% is judged as fair. When all types of justice are present, the outcome is judged as relatively fairest. However, in absolute terms, even then still only 45.7% of respondents judge the outcome as fair, and 52.7% believe it is unfair. Gibson concludes that amnesty is, even under the best of circumstances, judged as unfair.

All 'manipulations', i.e. all kinds of justice entered as present or not in the vignettes had a significant effect on perceptions of fairness, with significance assessed using analysis of variance (cf. section 8.3). Compensation, i.e. distributive justice, predicted best whether respondents viewed the response as fair. The effects of the various kinds of justice are expressed by Gibson in a so-called η, that reflects how much variance is explained by the factor. The distributive justice factor had an η of .30, for restorative justice it was $\eta = .09$, for retributive justice η equalled .01, for procedural justice η equalled .10. See section 8.3.5.

Does this mean that the most important aspect to pay attention to in truth commissions is distributive justice? The author stresses that the other kinds of justice (perhaps as they are also easier to administer – in South Africa compensation was reportedly slow and much less than aimed for) should not be neglected: for instance the effects of procedural and restorative justice together are roughly two-thirds the size of the effect of distributive justice in the South African study.

The Gibson study is an example of an elegant, thoroughly-designed study. Given the experimental set-up, there was internal validity, and given the fact that a representative sample of the South African population was studied, also external validity. One downside of the study may be that it can be regarded as slightly 'artificial' in that respondents were asked to rate the fairness of outcomes in hypothetical cases, in that regard its ecological validity may be compromised.

An experimental and naturalistic design was used for assessing the effectiveness of truth and reconciliation forums in Sierra Leone. Cilliers, Dube and Siddiqi (2016) describe how an NGO called Fambul Tok in 2007 started community-level reconciliation forums in Sierra Leonean villages. These forums took on average 2 days, victims and perpetrators described their experiences, and the latter asked for forgiveness. After a forum, a peace tree would be planted. In 2011, when Fambul Tok was ready to expand to new districts, random assignment was used so that some sections would be assigned the intervention, and others not. The districts to which this pertained were similar to other districts in Sierra Leone with regard to exposure to wartime atrocities and socioeconomic indicators, so that the findings are likely generalisable to Sierra Leone. For each village in which a ceremony took place, a random control village close by was sought, meaning the authors employed a case-control design. For a first wave of 40 villages, measurements were made after 9 and 31 months so that long- and short-term effects could be measured. In each cluster (experimental village and control village) 10-12 adults were interviewed. Attrition at wave 2 was low at 13%. Because of its emphasis on long-term effects, it can also be classified as a longitudinal study.

Surveys measured trust, forgiveness, social network indicators as well as a community group participation index. Psychological health as well as PTSD was measured with translated standardised instruments that had been extensively tested for construct validity after translation and back-translation. Reliability indices of the measures had been found to be sufficient.

Using regression analyses, the authors established that all factors capturing 'societal healing' improved due to the Fambul Tok forums. However, psychological health was significantly lower in the experimental villages: for instance clinical PTSD was 36% higher in experimental villages. Across time, these effects held. The authors, in additional analyses, show that also non-victims were in terms of psychological health negatively affected by the forums. At the same time, the authors note a clear effect on forgiveness of war perpetrators and on trust of former rebel combatants.

The Sierra Leone experimental study is exceptionally strong in that it employed an experimental design in a natural setting, so that the findings not only have internal validity but likely also ecological validity. The study used standardised (so that measures are internationally comparable), locally adapted instruments (so that they are relevant for the local context) for measuring a broad range of measures, and had intricate analyses to control for rivaling explanations. For more, we refer to the extensive descriptions in Cilliers, Dube and Siddiqi (2016) and supplementary materials mentioned therein.

15.3.3 Transitional justice studies: a review

Thoms, Ron and Paris (2008) carried out an, as it appears, fairly systematic (but in the end narrative) review of existing studies on transitional justice, as the authors list: 'trials and other judicial proceedings against individuals alleged to have committed gross violations of human rights; truth commissions designed to establish a factual historical record of past wrongdoing; reparations to victims of past abuses; and vetting of individuals to determine if their past activities or affiliations render them ineligible for public office, law enforcement or other key roles'. The authors do not make explicit how they selected their studies to review: it appears that they selected both case studies (single-country or single-intervention studies), as well as studies with small to moderate N, as well as large N studies. These comprise some studies that we discussed above, such as the Gibson study (2004). The very readable review contains numerous methodological lessons.

The authors discuss case studies from a wide variety of countries (amongst others Uganda, Afghanistan, el Salvador, Eastern Europe), conflicts, and across different categories of traditional justice. A first conclusion the authors draw is that most studies have focused on one situation, and that rigourous cross-national analyses are particularly absent. Most studies are analytically weak, as they are 'relying largely on impressionistic descriptions of a small number of well-known cases, rather than systematically comparing impacts across a broad range of cases, including societies in which transitional justice has not been pursued'. In terms of research design (see chapter 5) this translates to the authors saying that only experimental groups were employed, without control groups or case-controls, for opportunity samples. Second, the overall evidence on the impact of transitional justice is weakly positive to null. Findings are highly inconsistent, and this is partly due, the authors state, to different methodologies employed in different evaluations, among which differing operationalisations. The latter causes what we have labeled method differences: seemingly different substantive findings that are however attributable to diverging operationalisations. Third, inherent to the evaluation of the impact of any transitional justice category is the fact, as the authors note, that theoretically plausible causal agents will always be confounded with factors outside of the control of the researchers. Thus, observed associations between assumed causal factors and outcomes will never exceed the level of correlations. Formulated differently: they will never exceed level 1 or 2 of the Maryland Scientific Methods Scale (see section 5.5).

Thoms, Ron and Paris (2008) make a number of recommendations for future transitional justice research. They state that, firstly, key variables (causes, effects and controls) need to be better defined. They pronounce next that no single method is likely uniquely suited for analyzing transitional justice mechanisms and outcomes. Rather, they advocate a mixed methods approach in which qualitative, quantitative and process indicators are combined, at the individual and group level, where they may corroborate each other. The analysis of micro-processes should be complemented with macro-studies. Quasi-experimental or experimental studies would be especially warranted, given the current lack of such studies with relatively 'hard' causal indicators. A shorter version of the report can be found in Thoms, Ron and Paris (2010).

15.4 Summary of methodological issues

From the examples that we discussed in this chapter, a number of generic methodological issues arise that are common for the study of the reaction to international crimes. A first one is that if we want to study legal responses to international crimes such as delivered by tribunals and the ICC, we will often end up with small samples even though we may be able to study an – in a statistical sense – entire population. Tribunals such as ICTY, ICTR, SCSL, let alone the ICC, have dispositioned relatively small numbers of cases. For regular quantitative research this may limit the number of factors that can be investigated and the complexity of explanatory models. Effect sizes or the absolute magnitude of effects, may then be more relevant than statistical significance. Ad hoc or special courts may have been able to deal with larger numbers of cases. The gacaca courts appear an outlier given the massive number of cases that were 'tried'. Also, if we would study witnesses, we would have access to far larger numbers of respondents. Trial documentation is generally publicly available (although parts have been redacted). On the plus side, this makes for readily and freely available data.

Second, we saw how it may be difficult to assess and explain the effects of legal responses and interventions such as amnesties and truth commissions for lack of adequate 'controls'. By this we mean that in many situations, no control cases are available against which we can gauge the impact of post-conflict interventions: post-conflict measures are generally imposed on the entire region where atrocities were committed. Employing as controls other regions or countries, or periods within the same country, is problematic as every conflict in which international crimes were committed has its own unique context, that is, constellation of pre- and post-conflict factors that shape and influence the impact of interventions. It is therefore in general quite hard to assess the impact of such interventions using traditional, quantitative methods. Qualitative methods therefore appear specifically apt here, as they do not rely on statistical power, but are geared towards the explanation of phenomena within their unique context, equipping us as well as possible to understand why this particular intervention had these specific effects for this unique conflict in this historical period.

Third, this does not mean that 'experiments' in the methodological sense of the word are impossible. The design of the study to assess the impact of truth and reconciliation forums in Sierra Leone could be employed because these forums were for capacity reasons being gradually rolled out in Sierra Leone, so that some villages were already exposed and others not yet. Exploiting this, it was possible to investigate the impact of the intervention in a design that was both naturalistic and strong. The reception of transitional justice has also been studied using vignettes. Coupled with representative sampling, vignette studies have strong internal and external validity and advance our knowledge of the reception of transitional justice.

A fourth issue, that ties in with the second one, is that responses to international crimes are almost always confounded with numerous other interventions: food aid, the lifting of sanctions, the return of refugees, a return to democracy, etc. Disentangling the impacts of these changes from the responses to atrocities is a methodologists' nightmare, especially given the lack of adequate controls. This again necessitates qualitative and historical methods, that are able to investigate the workings of a multitude of interrelated factors in specific historical and geopolitical contexts. Some authors used tailored methodologies (regression models) to deal with such confounding, others employed stylised vignettes where the impact of different factors was simply isolated.

We presented a number of studies that had attempted to conduct a systematic review of responses to international criminality. All were hampered by heterogeneity of intervention and heterogeneity of settings. A number mentioned how comparisons were compromised by method differences. The narrative reviews of transitional justice studies that we did discuss identified these and other weaknesses, and urged for more comparative research, i.e. where findings across several conflicts are systematically compared, using mixed methods, representative samples, better (and preferably more consistent or standardised) definitions of key concepts, and more studies that employ stronger, experimental designs.

Chapter 16

Studying victims and post-conflict societies

16.1 Introduction

The last domain in our *tesseras criminologica* concerns the victims, and more broadly speaking, post-conflict societies. As we will see in a number of illustrations below, the effects of conflict can be pervasive: extremely long-reaching and long-lasting.

The methods employed to assess this are varied. Surveys among the general population are widely used, as are surveys among specific populations such as victims. Some authors have used macro-level data to assess economic consequences. Econometric regression-type models have been applied, as well as statistical tests comparing groups, simple descriptives and qualitative analysis of interview material. For assessing wider impact, on schooling, existing surveys have been used, such as those organised at regular intervals by the UN (DHS surveys and MICS, see below). We see how in this area of study, many non-criminologists and non-lawyers are manifest: social psychologists are prominent in the study of collective shame and guilt, economists study economic consequences of conflicts, clinical psychologists and psychiatrists study trauma, and demographers study the impact of conflicts on marriage and fertility. All these disciplines bring with them their own, at times varying methods.

16.2 Studies of victims

A fairly wide body of literature has studied victims of international crimes. Many studies investigate the aftermath of victimisation in terms of trauma and associated conditions such as psychosomatic disease and general ill health. Some studies focus on the impact that criminal justice and other interventions have had on victims and might for that matter just as well be classified as studies into judicial responses.

Brounéus (2008) studied the impact that truth telling in post-conflict Rwanda has on victims. Brounéus conducted a small qualitative study on a convenience sample. She conducted semi-structured interviews (with the help of a translator) with 16 victims at a widows' association that provides medical, psycho-social and economic assistance. The first four women arriving each morning were asked by the association staff whether they would be willing to participate. Four interviews per day were conducted. Respondents received compensation for their travel costs, which was announced after the interview had been completed. Interviews were tape-recorded and lasted on average a little under three quarters of an hour. The author states that the sample is likely of a peculiar kind, but whether the women were better off than most victimised women (as they could still make it to the association's premises), or worse off (as they needed assistance) is hard to tell. Thus the generalizability of the findings may be compromised.

Brounéus asked the interviewees at some point during the interview to tell her what they had experienced during the genocide. The researcher did not prompt, as these experiences were not the main focus of the study and as it was difficult for women to speak of their experiences.

Analysis of this taped material revealed the following about the women's experiences. Many women had lost loved ones: only one had survived with all her children. Almost all had been widowed. One woman was not raped. Many had genital and other health problems. Seven spoke explicitly of the sexual violence they had suffered, and eight did so implicitly. Almost all women were extremely worried about continuing hostile attitudes towards Tutsi.

The researcher extracted two main themes from the interviews: security problems and ill-health. For all women, insecurity in the form of harassment and threats started *after* they had given testimony in a *gacaca* court: women had been physically attacked, had had stones thrown against their house during the night and reported feeling ostracised. Complaints to security officials (often implicated in the genocide) were not responded to, and some women had felt intimidated by jeering and insulting *gacaca* audiences. A number of exemplars illustrate how the women's security and even physical survival was threatened (Brounéus, 2008, p.67):

"*There is no security because they bring their cows to graze whatever has grown on my land plot ... Since I gave testimony, I am threatened*"

Another woman related the following (Brounéus, 2008, p.68):

"*I am not safe because the people who hurt me have been released from prison. They often pass by my house. I think they have bad intentions... I was afraid when I gave testimony in the gacaca because the people were yelling... Afterwards, they came; they broke my windows, I was afraid. I thought I would be killed... I do not go to gacaca any longer. I am scared to be attacked or killed. My sister was killed in February after she had given testimony*"

Ill-health often started before gacaca. Many women feared the testifying, being confronted with their attackers. Some reportedly could not continue during the testimony. Several women said they had suffered a '*traumatisme*', that is: reliving the experience, accompanied by shaking, crying or fainting. Women reported that these gave them shame, to relive the horror in front of the gacaca audience. The second hurtful aspect was that they were not checked upon afterwards, whether they were doing well again. The author shows how these two aspects, ill-health and insecurity, are in fact related. The loneliness that women experienced (apart from being shunned by neighbours, many had lost almost all of their family) made the women feel extremely vulnerable. Being alone was not only painful and threatening in the here and now, but also meant that no one would care for a woman when she grows old.

The author concludes that unless *gacaca* courts and similar truth-telling initiatives are buffered by security and assistance to witnesses before, during and after proceedings, such efforts to deal with the aftermath of conflict may even prove counterproductive. This finding resonates with findings for Sierra Leone in which an experimental design was used to evaluate a reconciliation programme (Cilliers, Dube and Siddiqi, 2016; see section 15.3.2).

In a second study, Brounéus (2010) carried out a quantitative survey on the same topic. Now, she drew a multistage cluster sample for each of the four provinces in Rwanda that ensured regional variation as well as spread over urban and rural settings. All provinces had been severely struck by the genocide. In the provinces, cells were contacted, that is, the lowest level of administration after the district and sector level, each cell consisting of one or more *nyumbakumis* (blocks of 10 houses). Heads of households were systematically selected in each selected cell, such that 300 people per province were interviewed with equal numbers of survivors, neighbours and *inyangamugayo* (judges in the *gacaca* courts). The International Rescue Committee (IRC) in Kigali conducted the survey; ethical consent as well as permission had been obtained from the researcher's own (New Zealand) university, the National Unity and Reconciliation Commission, the National Institute for Statistics at the Ministry of Finance, and *Ibuka* (the National Association for Genocide Survivors). Questionnaires were administered in on average 45 minutes, consisting of 112 questions, containing a number of international symptom checklists (for post-traumatic stress symptoms, amongst which depression), that had been translated and backtranslated into Kinyarwanda.

The author concludes that witnesses in the *gacaca* proceedings reported higher levels of post-traumatic stress symptoms than non-witnesses, also when controlling for possible confounders such as sex and violence exposure. This applied both to victims as well as to judges and neighbours, with the effects even much stronger in the latter group. Secondly, the longer *gacaca* proceedings had been conducted in a certain region, the higher the prevalence of these complaints. Lastly, the author shows that, comparing her findings with those in an earlier study, overall levels of depression and PTSD had not decreased. Therefore, she concludes, it must be severely doubted whether the *gacaca* courts and the processes of witnessing and testifying heal Rwandan society. In the discussion to her study she reiterates her earlier findings (Brounéus, 2008) that testifying may even generate insecurity and counteract any beneficial effects. The second study by Brounéus (2010) does a nice job of describing fieldwork preparations and the various steps in designing a quantitative survey, and is recommended for reading.

Vollhardt and Bilewicz (2013) edited a special issue dedicated to the aftermath of genocide. Their overview of studies focuses not only on victims but also on perpetrators and bystanders. As the authors note, conceptually disjunct categories of victims and perpetrators (and bystanders for that matter) are in empirical reality often much more fuzzy. Some people are perpetrator and victim, some fulfill all roles as they are bystander in some situations, victimised in other and may even commit atrocities themselves. While conceptually attractive categories, in real life people may therefore assume a multiplicity of roles, and these roles may assumed concurrently or consecutively. As Vollhardt and Bilewicz state, much research on the aftermath of genocide has been on victims' psychological adaptation. Studies have focused on negative outcomes such as PTSD or feelings of revenge, but also on positive outcomes such as resilience, coping and altruism.

Much research has been conducted on Holocaust survivors. A meta-analysis of studies on Holocaust survivors (Barel, Van IJzendoorn, Sagi-Schwartz *et al.*, 2010) investigated long-term psychiatric, psychosocial, and physical outcomes. Combining data from 71 studies with almost 13,000 Holocaust survivors, they found substantially more post-traumatic stress symptoms in survivors than in a control group that had not experienced the Holocaust. Perhaps surprisingly, survivors had only slightly lower scores in several other domains of functioning (such as physical health, stress-related physical measures, and cognitive functioning). The authors conclude that many Holocaust survivors had remarkable resilience.

To be able to conduct such a meta-analysis, one needs a large number of studies with comparable outcome measures. Evidence on victims from other conflicts than the Holocaust is much sparser, which may be the reason that for these conflicts we did not come across any meta-analyses. Using a sample of 40 survivors of the Armenian genocide now residing in the US, Kalayjian, Shahinian and Gergerian (1996) administered semi-structured interviews that focused on stressors and coping methods. Respondents reported that destruction of life, physical harm, deportation, pillaging, and loss of status were the main stressors they had experienced. Coping methods and sources of survival were mentioned to be religion, family, work, denial, and resignation. Remarkably, only few respondents had shared their traumatic experiences with others.

Bolton, Michalopoulos, Mohammed Amin Ahmed *et al.* (2013) conducted a qualitative study among survivors of torture and genocide in Kurdistan. From 1986 to 1989 the Kurdish population was subjected to the so-called 'Anfal', a campaign of amongst others military incursions, detentions, torture, and chemical warfare. The authors first interviewed a mixed convenience/purposive sample of 42 survivors from the Suleimaniyah governorate. They used a so-called 'free list interview' where interviewees were asked to list the problems of torture survivors.

For data analysis, the authors next retrieved those problems that had been mentioned at least twice. In a 'cleaning step', they then combined problems, even if worded differently, under one heading if they referred to one underlying problem. See section 9.2.2. Although the authors do not specify how they achieved this, the team next in all likelihood through axial coding retrieved three major psychosocial themes: problems directly related to the torture and other violence experienced during the Anfal (such as recurrent nightmares, rage, forgetfulness), problems related to people's current situation (such as distress about their current family and economic problems, regret about supporting the Peshmerga, substance abuse) and problems related to the way they were treated by others in society (notably here were feelings of abandonment, being looked down upon).

Next, 21 key informants were interviewed and presented with these themes and asked to supply problems they witnessed in survivors with regard to the main themes. Key informants were sampled from the network of the researchers, and some key informants stemmed from the pool of previous interviewees if they had been judged to be particularly knowledgeable. Key informants were asked to report not about their own problems but about problems of survivors as they saw them. This was done to prioritise the reporting of widely held knowledge rather than key informants' personal opinion and feelings, and to facilitate the reporting of sensitive or stigmatising issues. It also shows how the approach was clearly grounded. All key informants were interviewed repeatedly. Repeat interviews were not held if the key informant turned out to be less than knowledgeable or if he or she refused. None of the key informants were mental health workers as the authors wanted to extract problems unstructured by moulds imposed by any previous education. Most interviewees and key informants were male.

Further analysis showed how interwoven causes and consequences were. For instance, substance abuse was mentioned both as a consequence of torture experiences, a coping mechanism, and as a cause for current problems such as lack of employment. Insomnia and depression were both found to be consequence of violent experiences and cause for new problems.

The authors note how many of the findings resemble findings from earlier studies on torture survivors. They note how an existing explanatory framework may well describe their findings, a framework that postulates that ongoing stressors (both before and after torture) disrupt five adaptive systems: safety, attachment, justice, existential meaning and identity. Disruption in each of these systems leads to different problems. Even though the sample was small and unrepresentative, the authors believe the findings create ground for adaptation of existing instruments to measure trauma and anxiety and depression checklists, by including also stressors related to current circumstances.

16.3 Methods for assessing wider societal sequelae of international crimes

16.3.1 Intergenerational effects

A sizeable number of studies, qualitative and quantitative, have investigated intergenerational effects of international crimes. Some looked at the intergenerational transmission of trauma and resilience. Lorens Braga, Feijó Mello and Paulo Fiks (2012) conducted a qualitative study among second generation survivors of the Holocaust. The authors note that the evidence on intergenerational transmission of trauma from international crimes is inconclusive: on the one hand there is ample clinical evidence of such transmission, on the other hand meta-analytic studies have failed to find evidence for such a transmission to second and third generation descendants. To shed light on the existence, nature and mechanisms behind such intergenerational transmission, the authors interviewed 15 children of Holocaust survivors in Brazil. Using a grounded theory approach, they analysed in-depth individual interviews to uncover experiences, meanings and subjective processes of the participants.

Interviews were semi-structured and open-ended. The interviews lasted one to three hours, and were taped and transcribed verbatim. The sample size may appear small, but after 15 interviews, the researchers had reached what they refer to as 'theme saturation'.

The authors describe how the analysis of the transcribed interviews proceeded in five steps. For reference, see section 9.2. First, the researchers read all the transcribed material. Next, they analysed all interviews, both per interview (a within-case analysis) as well as across cases (cross-case analysis). In this second step some similarities, differences and negative cases emerged. As a third step, the researchers attached codes to text blocks. Categories and subcategories were defined, inductively (or 'emic') derived from the content of the interviews. Coding proceeded first through descriptive, first level coding, and next through second level, axial coding, where they arrived at conceptual categories. Table 16.1 gives a number of examples of both the descriptive and conceptual categories that were derived in this manner. Interrater scoring (by three independent raters) ensured interrater reliability.

The conceptual categories and the data was next analysed again using the constant comparative method, which led to new conceptual categories specifically related to the intergenerational transmission of trauma or resilience. These were firstly communication style: subcategories that were identified were, amongst others, open, loving everyday communication (which contributed to resilient outcomes in offspring), communication through formal records and documents, indirect communication, secrets, silences and unsaid things (that made it harder for the second generation to arrive at biographical and psychological integration of these events). Second, the experience of trauma was subdivided in subcategories, such as a terrifying world view inherited from their parents which made offspring feel they had to be ready always for imminent catastrophes, as exemplified by the following exemplars (Lorens Braga, Feijó Mello and Paulo Fiks, 2012, p. 9):

"*You have to be successful, have power, clout, [to] be able to get by in a disaster situation [...] To this day, I bear a trace of this Holocaust survival handbook [...]: if I'm at a meeting with human beings, I'll never be among the last to leave. Why? Because, in a way, I was told, you have to recognize the signs of a disaster before others do.*"

"*Expired passport: not an option. It doesn't matter if you're not going to travel for the next twenty years []: you have to renew it, you always have to have, let's say, a pair of underwear and a pair of socks at hand so you can take off. Always ready.*"

Third, mechanisms of psychological working over and resilience were identified, with subcategories such as search for a radical singularity from parental history (for instance by imagining the parent Holocaust survivor was a hero, or special), or the defense of universal, humanist values, as illustrated by the following exemplar (Lorens Braga, Feijó Mello and Paulo Fiks, 2012, p. 12):

"*It really pisses me off when someone says something discriminatory. Even when a Jew says: "because we, the Jews, the chosen people"... Who aren't a chosen people? Blacks aren't? [...] When we go out into the street, we see everyone's Holocaust. [The homeless] are just as imprisoned as if in a [concentration] camp; society looks, but doesn't see.*"

While the article is interesting, also as it gives a quite detailed outline of the qualitative analysis steps, the authors do not solve the quandary that they started their article with: why intergenerational transmission is regularly found in clinical settings, but not retrieved in large-scale studies. An important finding is that trauma as well as resilience can be

Table 16.1: Construction of first level and second level codes

original transcription	descriptive category	conceptual category
'This secret I carried, I found out that it was their secret (c1) ... between us, there are no relations of love, there are survival relations (c2) ... It's this whole strategy for infusing their children with a manual for surviving a collective disaster. To this day, I bear a trace of this Holocaust survival handbook (c3)... in a way, I was told, you have to recognize the signs of a disaster before others do (c4)'	c1: transmission of family secrets c2: impaired parental function c3: transmission of fear & terrifying world view c4 transmission of mistrust and anticipation of disasters	c2: parenting style c1, c3, c4: transgenerational transmission of trauma
'Each day I tell the story of my father, in this play I am performing in the theatre, it seems I understand a little more (c5)... To tell this story in an artistic way – using music, dance, the theatre, painting – is also a way of showing the world what happened' (c6)	c5: symbolic dimension of art c6: art as a possibility of representing	c5, c6 pathways of psychical work over by offspring
'My father shows me the story of a man who lived through all those things and is here, right now, moving forward (c7)... this attitude reaches me in a certain way. I think I grew up with very few fears' (c8)	c7: resilient expressions in parents' lives c8: pathways of resilience in offspring	c7, c8: intergenerational transmission of resilience

source: Lorens Braga, Feijó Mello and Paulo Fiks (2012)

transmitted, through communication, through the repercussions of trauma in survivors' lives and through survivors' processing ('working over') of trauma.

Tames (2009), using a mixture of qualitative and quantitative survey methods, historical and document analysis, studied the children of Dutch collaborators with the Nazi occupiers in the Netherlands. Tames used published and unpublished accounts and documents, newspaper articles and was able to analyse archival material. In addition, she conducted interviews with 18 children themselves. In the Netherlands, immediately after the conclusion of World War II, children of collaborator parents (when both parents had been arrested) were generally placed in foster homes or institutions; those who could stay with their mother, saw their father arrested and taken away. All in all, the end of the war was for many of these children the beginning of a traumatic period, the 'real' war as some phrased it. Those who were raised in care, were raised along the prevailing pedagogical ideals of the period, that is, that discipline and order should prevail, and that children should break with their old identity and the morals of their national-socialist parents. Children were confronted with gruesome pictures from the concentration camps, and their parents linked directly to the Holocaust.

For many children this was hard to believe. Some simply refused to believe that such things had truly happened. Others started to mistrust their parents. Also children who were born after the war to parents who had collaborated with the occupiers, often felt that 'something was wrong'. In that era, silence was judged best in times of trouble, children were not told what had gone on, and this in fact led to some children making gross deductions, and mistrusting everything for lack of information. Many ended up in grave conflicts of loyalty towards their parents. Conversely, some copied the reasoning of their parents and stated that their parents had done nothing wrong during the war, and were simply victims of a vengeful society. Being a child from a collaborator family carried for many a life-long stigma. Tames concludes that the families themselves were key in how children coped with their intergenerational 'stigma'. Where families did not speak or did not find some modus vivendi with the past, children did not know how to respond to hateful remarks, bullying, or shunning. This meant that children did not have anchors, neither at home nor in the outside world. An English-language article appeared as Tames (2015).

Collective guilt has been studied extensively by social psychologists. Here, as social psychologists often do, randomly composed groups are given different tasks or vignettes, and it is investigated whether those with certain stimuli respond differently than those with only control stimuli. Zebel, Doosje and Spears (2009) studied feelings of guilt for historical in-group atrocities against out-groups. The authors postulated that out-group perspective taking promotes group-based guilt among those who identify weakly with perpetrator group members, but that perspective taking actually hinders it among those who identify more strongly with the perpetrator group. To study this, they conducted two experiments, of which we will describe the first here. In this experiment, 153 secondary school pupils with ethnic Dutch backgrounds participated. They were asked to score to what extent they identified as Dutch.

Two factors were next manipulated. First students were presented with a scenario describing either how the Dutch harmed African slaves or a scenario that described how the Dutch harmed Dutch Jews. Crossed with this was the second factor, that entailed whether students were asked (in the perspective taking condition) to imagine themselves as being

Figure 16.1: The effect of out-group perspective taking on group-based guilt as a function of national identification

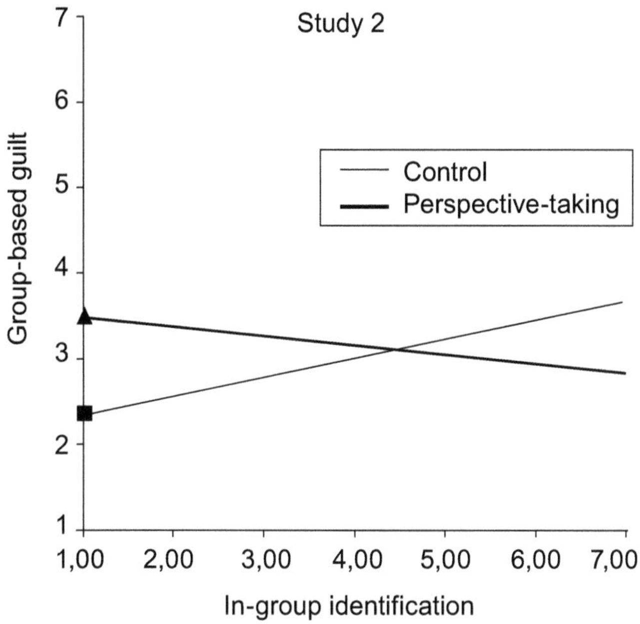

source: Zebel, Doosje and Spears (2009)

a slave during the Dutch slave trade respectively as being a Jew in WW II by writing a short story about this, or where no such thing was asked. The experiment in this manner had four conditions: slave + perspective taking, slave + no perspective taking, Jew + perspective taking, Jew + no perspective taking. The dependent variables were measures of group-based guilt and regret.

Analysis of variance (see section 8.3) showed that, firstly, there were no main effects of any of the predictor variables (national identification, harmed out-group, or perspective taking). This can be translated by saying that neither national identification nor whether one was asked to take the perspective of a slave or a Jew, or whether one was given the scenario of the Dutch harming the Jews or the Dutch harming the slaves, impacted guilt or regret. The interaction effect between the extent to which pupils identified as Dutch and perspective taking was however, as predicted, significant: $F(1{,}145) = 6.29$, $p = .013$. Figure 16.1 aids in interpreting the interaction effect (see section 8.3.3).

We see in this figure how for those who were not asked to take the perspective of a harmed out-group (slaves or Jews), that is, the controls, with increasing in-group identification, group-based guilt increases. Thus, generalising, the stronger one's identification with the perpetrator in-group, the more pronounced group-based guilt is. For the experimental pupils we see, however, the reverse effect. These pupils, who were asked to take the perspective of the harmed out-group, express in fact *less* group-based guilt the higher their in-group identification. The authors explain this phenomenon by stating that the perspective taking task evoked identity-protective strategies among those who identified (in a sense derived their identity) more from the in-group. Higher-identifiers, as the authors state,"*avoided self-critical guilt feelings when they were instructed to focus on the plight of the victim*".

Within social psychology, numerous smaller and larger experiments have been undertaken to investigate in-group and out-group behaviour, guilt and emotion, and bystander behaviour. Many such experiments are conducted 'in the lab', often employing students or secondary school pupils, or through members of panels. This puts the external validity of these experiments in question, that is, to what extent findings would generalise to family members of real perpetrators, or to descendants of perpetrators, or to people in actual conflict situations. More naturalistic research would be needed to answer that question.

16.3.2 Economic damage

Lindgren (2006) studied the economic damage of conflict. Costs of conflicts can be either direct (i.e. destroyed infrastructure such as buildings, hospitals, damage to roads, and the like) or indirect (such as capital flight, or missed educational opportunity costs for combatants). Direct costs can be observed and counted. Indirect costs cannot always be counted that easily, and some assumptions may have to be built in to estimate them. As an example of the size of such effects, Lindgren relates that it has been calculated that in a group of less developed countries 8.6% of private wealth was held abroad before conflict erupted, but that at the end of the war this had risen to 19.7%.

Lindgren next distinguishes two types of methods to assess damage: *accounting* methods and *counterfactual* methods. In the accounting methods, also referred as 'bookkeeping' methods, one incorporates only damages suffered. In that sense, these methods entail a tally and/or estimate of damages. They use few assumptions, and that makes them robust and dependable. However, their downside is that they might miss a major part of the costs, such as opportunity costs (capital flight that we already mentioned, but also decreased tourist streams and unrealised foreign direct investment). Lindgren states that accounting methods for that reason generally do not produce reasonable estimates: accounting methods tend to generate estimates that capture but a fraction of the entirety of the damage suffered.

Counterfactual methods do exactly what they are called. They build a model that predicts how economic performance would have been had the conflict not erupted. In that sense they resemble the counterfactual models discussed in section 13.3.4 for estimating mortality. Counterfactual models can firstly *extrapolate* pre-conflict growth levels, to arrive at a likely – hypothetical – economic development at the end of conflict had peacetime conditions prevailed. Of course, it is problematic to simply use pre-conflict figures for this, and extrapolate them uncritically or simply linearly over the conflict years. It is already better to look at trends in pre-conflict indicators of economic performance, but even so the questions remains whether we can safely assume that the country would have continued to perform economically as predicted from pre-conflict data and trends.

A second way to go about assessing the economic cost of conflict, is by identifying a *control region* as a counterfactual. A control region is a region that resembles the conflict zone, but for one difference: it did not experience conflict. It is in that sense a *control group* for the *'experimental'* conflict country or zone. One then assumes that the economy of the country that underwent conflict would have developed just like the economy in this control region developed: would have witnessed the same downturns in tourist streams due to natural disasters, would have flourished similarly from increasing popularity of sun-drenched holidays, etc. For instance, for Sri Lanka, Southern India might be a suitable control region, for Myanmar that might be Thailand, etc. As said, in design terms we have a quasi-experimental set-up (see section 5.4), with one region that did not experience conflict and the other that did.

While the use of control regions seems fairly straightforward, it is not without it drawbacks. One of the most important of these is that it is unlikely that regions that are good comparison regions (in which case they will mostly be neighbouring the conflict zone, have similar geographic layout, terrain, resources, agriculture, tourism development) are unaffected by the conflict. In fact, it is likely that such neighbouring regions are affected. This may go two ways: first, it may be so that the comparison region is itself also negatively affected by the conflict: refugees may flood in, rebel groups may seek refuge in border areas and make these insecure. In that case, there is spillover and – in a design sense – insufficient separation between groups (see section 5.4.1): the control regions also suffer some – be it diluted – impact of the conflict. The impact of the conflict on the neighbouring region may also go the other direction: for instance, as tourists are unable to visit their holiday destination while a conflict is ongoing, they may instead opt for the neighbouring country with similar palm-fringed beaches, calming ocean breezes and the like. In that case, we are faced with – in a design sense – *perceived differences between groups* (see again section 5.4.1). In the first case we will underestimate the impact of the conflict, in the second case we will overestimate the impact of the conflict.

A more sophisticated approach is the third method we will discuss. Here, models are estimated that use a so-called *synthetic region* as a counterfactual. A synthetic region is a region that does not exist, but that is constructed by the researcher as a weighted sum of a number of comparison regions. This may sound fairly obscure so we will explain the rationale behind this method and the manner in which it – roughly – works in separate steps. We refer to Abadie and Gardeazabal (2003) and Abadie, Diamond and Hainmueller (2015) for relatively nontechnical explanations of these methods.

As we stated above, the use of extrapolation is rough and shaky in the sense that assumptions have to be made (for instance about growth rates and trends in other variables in the model) that are essentially untestable ('GDP growth in the conflict period would have continued to develop as it did before the conflict erupted'). If we could use a control region as a counterfactual, that would be a large improvement. We would then have a comparable region or country without conflict and could simply gauge observed trends in our experimental region against trends in the control region. Any differences between the two we attribute to the conflict. Such a conclusion can however only be drawn if the control region does not differ systematically from the experimental, conflict region on other aspects too. If it does, we cannot be sure anymore whether we may attribute all differences to the conflict or whether they would for some part be attributable to these factors on which the two regions are dissimilar. Setting aside issues of incomparability, even if we were able to find a good comparison region, we are still faced with the fact that the data will constitute a 'small sample' in a statistical sense (we will have observations over a small number of years or time periods) and that we are unable to argue that sampling was random (which, as reader may recall, constitutes the basis for statistical testing). We are therefore compromised in carrying out regular statistical testing. Also, as we discussed above, a control region may itself be impacted (positively or negatively) by the conflict. The synthetic region method enables us to deal with such objections to a large extent.

A synthetic region is a control region that, as said, does not exist but is *constructed* by the researcher from a number of comparable regions. How this is done we will illustrate with the study by Abadie, Diamond and Hainmueller (2015), who wanted to estimate the costs of German reunification for West Germany. The dependent variable was West German GDP per capita.

The authors in a first step selected a so-called *donor pool* of countries who were candidates to contribute to the synthetic region the authors wanted to build: Australia, Austria, Belgium, Denmark, France, Greece, Italy, Japan, the Netherlands, New Zealand, Norway, Portugal, Spain, Switzerland, the United Kingdom, and the United States. Next, the authors took the years before reunification (1960-1990) to predict GDP/capita in West Germany from GDP measured for those same years in the *donor* countries. Using a multiple regression model, they were able to construct a weighted sum from five of these countries that very closely resembled West-German GDP. Different from a usual regression set-up, the units ('respondents') were not people or villages, but they were years: the authors attempted to predict West-German yearly GDP (the dependent variable) from the yearly GDP of the donor countries (these were the predictor variables). The formula they arrived at was:

$$\hat{\text{GDP}}_{\text{West Germany}(t)} = 0.42 \times \text{GDP}_{\text{Austria}(t)} + 0.16 \times \text{GDP}_{\text{Japan}(t)} + 0.09 \times \text{GDP}_{\text{Netherlands}(t)}$$
$$+0.11 \times \text{GDP}_{\text{Switzerland}(t)} + 0.22 \times \text{GDP}_{\text{United States}(t)}$$

The 'synthetic' GDP ($\hat{\text{GDP}}$) that was computed in this way, matched the real GDP of West Germany very closely for the years 1960 – 1990 as can be seen in Figure 16.2. Next, using the same formula, the authors computed synthetic GDP-values for the years 1990 – 2003 for West Germany. These estimated GDP values now are the counterfactual; they are indicated by the dashed line in Figure 16.2. The dashed line represents how West Germany would have performed economically, had reunification not taken place.

Figure 16.2 at a glance reveals the impact of reunification: we see how without the reunification intervention from 1990, GDP would have grown virtually unchanged. The figure also reveals how a dip in GDP did not arrive until after a few years, in all likelihood when investment in the East seriously began. The differences between the two lines can be written as a percentage of lost GDP, an 'effect size'.

In such a synthetic region model, it is recommended to conduct several kinds of sensitivity analyses. A first type of additional analysis has two components. The first comprises rerunning the analysis, but placing the intervention (in the example above: reunification) not in the year it actually took place, but in any other year. If we would now find a similarly large effect for this non-existing 'intervention', this would greatly undermine our

Figure 16.2: GDP of West Germany and synthetic West Germany

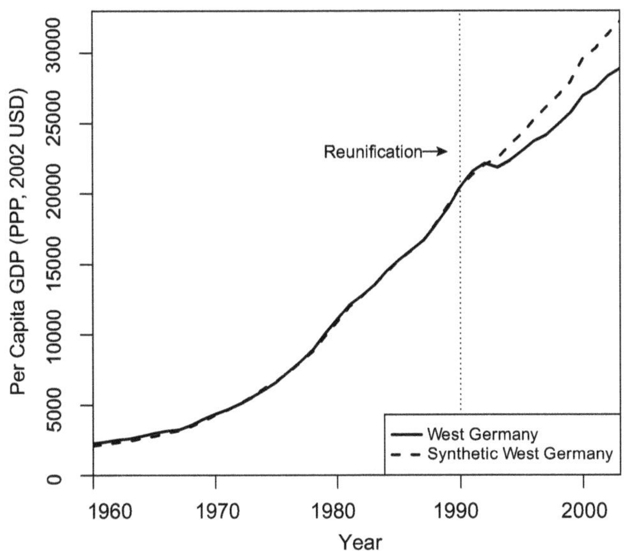

source: Abadie, Diamond and Hainmueller (2015)

confidence in our analysis results: our effect would then be just as large as the effect of a non-existing intervention. Of course, we expect that the effect of such a nonexisting intervention would be small. This re-analysis can be done for a large number of years: each time one would expect the impact of the imaginary but non-existing intervention to be small to non-existent. Such an analysis is called an *in-time placebo analysis.*

Similarly, one could reassign the intervention not to the country where the intervention took place, but rerun the model pretending the intervention took place in one of the countries in the donor pool. Also here, our confidence in our findings would be undermined if we would find a large effect for a non-existing intervention in one of our donor countries. Such an analysis is called an *in-space placebo analysis.*

Running such placebo analyses is highly recommended. In fact, if one does so systematically, across all possible time points and for all possible other donor regions, one gets a distribution of placebo effect sizes against which one can gauge the effect found in the real analysis. In this manner, one does not only get a feel for how large the observed effect is, but one overcomes both the 'small sample' and 'non-random sample' problem that we discussed above. We can now gauge our effect as found in the real analysis against our collection of effects in our placebo analyses – across years and across regions – and see how exceptional it is, to what extent it stands out as different from numerous placebo analyses.

Robustness checks are recommended. Such checks assess whether the substantive conclusions stand if the model were built differently. Formulated conversely, robustness analy-

Figure 16.3: GDP of West Germany, synthetic West Germany and various leave-one-out versions of synthetic West Germany

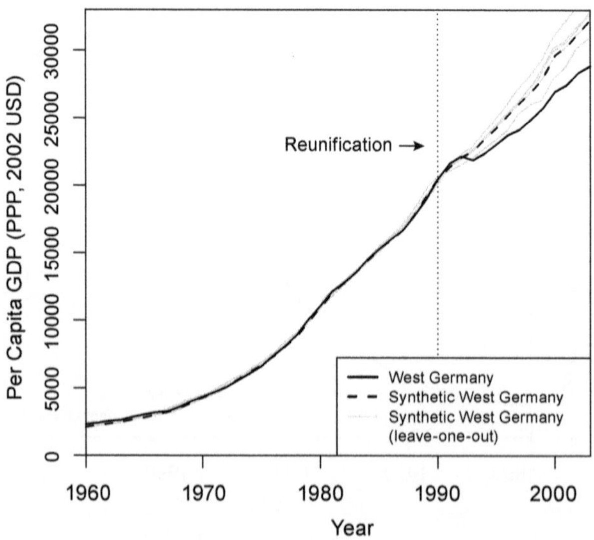

source: Abadie, Diamond and Hainmueller (2015)

sis checks whether the finding does not depend on one particular specification of the model. Robustness checks can be carried out here by rerunning the analyses, but now each time omitting one of the donor countries from the pool. This 'leave-one-out'-procedure is also known in research methodology as *jackknifing*. For the example here, we would rerun the analysis five times: without Austria, without Japan, etc. This would give us five new 'synthetic' curves. Eyeballing these different curves gives us an interval or 'bandwidth' for our conclusion. For the analysis on German reunification, robustness analysis showed that even if the United States (that had the largest weight in the construction of the synthetic region) were left out, real GDP in West Germany would still be on average 3% lower than the estimated synthetic GDP. See Figure 16.3.

The synthetic region method also has its drawbacks, as things go. One concern is that the control countries in the donor pool may themselves have been influenced by the intervention ('spillover effects'), in design terms: insufficient separation between groups or *perceived differences between groups* (see section 5.4.1). It could for instance be the case that the Dutch or Austrian economies were boosted by reunification as there was great demand for builders. In that case we would overestimate the cost of reunification. Second, it may be impossible to accurately reconstruct the dependent variable for the pre-interventions years from the donor region variables. As an example, Abadie and Gardeazabal (2003) tried to use the synthetic region method to estimate the economic impact of the ETA attacks in the Basque region of Spain. In this analysis however, they were unable to reproduce GDP growth accurately enough in the Basque region before the years when terrorist attacks occurred. As an alternative, they employed a period when a truce had been announced as a natural experiment, investigating whether in that period economic indicators differed from the preceding period and the period after the truce had ended. The disadvantage to the latter design is obviously that it can be doubted whether the truce was truly exogenous (that is, truly unconfounded: one side may have declared it because they had to recuperate financially) and whether business and the public actually believed the truce was going to hold (ETA had broken promises of truces previously).

Summarising, the synthetic region method is the most elegant way to construct a counterfactual for investigating the impact on societies of conflict. It can also be applied to estimate the impact of conflict on other macro-level indicators. It is not guaranteed that a synthetic region can be constructed that matches the pre-conflict trend in the dependent variable satisfactorily. Also, causal attribution to the conflict and to the conflict only of differences in trends between the synthetic region and the region under conflict is not watertight. Systematic differences may still exist or may have emerged once the conflict started, that are partly responsible for diverging trends. Such alternative explanations (viz section 5.3) are less likely the longer the number of pre-intervention time points that are employed in the model. Software for constructing a synthetic region is available in Stata, a statistical software package, see `stata.com`.

16.3.3 Effects on schooling

UNESCO (2010) studied the effect of conflicts on schooling levels. Information on conflicts was taken from the UCDP-PRIO database, which lists armed conflicts that took place since World War II; for more information, see the box on UCDP and PRIO in section 13.2.1. Data on schooling were taken from the Demographic and Health Surveys (DHS) and the Multiple Indicator Cluster Surveys (MICS).

In the UNESCO study (2010), the DHS surveys for Zimbabwe for 2005 – 2008 were used. The authors employed an essentially exploratory method, in which they compared trends in education before, during and after conflicts. Figure 16.4 (UNESCO Institute for Statistics, 2010, p.105) gives an illustration of the data the study used. The graph shows that the proportion of men without formal education was steadily decreasing from 1950 onwards. Men from richer families already almost all had education in 1950: only a little over 10% did not have formal education yet, and this percentage was down to around 5% by 1970. The dots in the graphs are the values as obtained from the surveys employed: it can be seen that these fluctuate some, likely due to sampling error. The solid line drawn in between is constructed from the values for young men aged 13-17, being the 5-year moving average for men aged 15. The line for the moving average is smoother and easier to interpret than the dots.

Figure 16.4: Share of the male Zimbabwean population without formal education, by wealth quintile

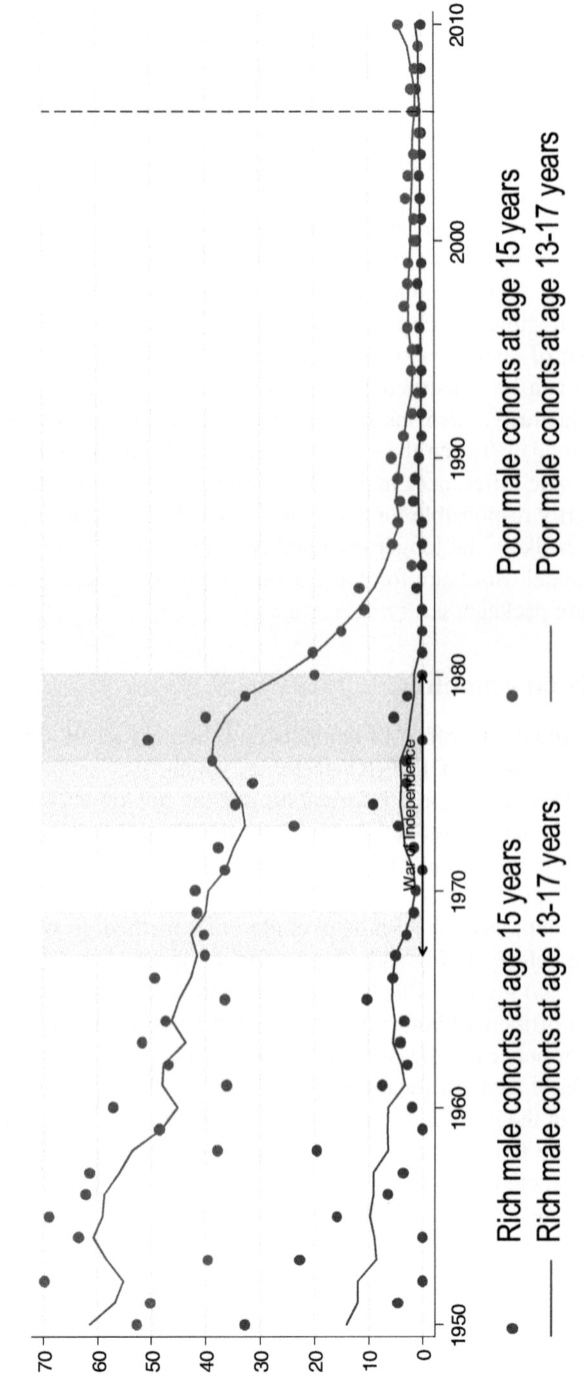

source: UNESCO, 2010

Demographic and Health Survey (DHS) and Multiple Indicator Cluster Survey (MICS)

The Demographic and Health Surveys were launched in 1984 by the United States Agency for International Development (USAID) to provide data on population and health trends in developing countries (Rutstein & Rojas, 2006). DHS surveys take place every year, for a varying list of countries, and the goal is to cover every participating country every three to five years. DHS data can be obtained from the website `measuredhs.com`.

The Multiple Indicator Cluster Surveys were developed in the 1990s by the United Nations Childrens Fund (UNICEF) in collaboration with the World Health Organisation, UNESCO, the UN Statistics Division, USAID, the London School of Hygiene and Tropical Medicine, and the United States Centers for Disease Control and Prevention. The original purpose of the MICS was to collect data for the monitoring of progress toward the goals of the World Summit for Children that took place at the United Nations in New York in 1990. The MICS also provide data for the monitoring of the Millennium Development Goals (MDGs) – that were not reached at the millennium but whose progress is still being monitored (UNICEF, 2006). DHS and MICS surveys are closely coordinated to avoid overlapping data collection in one country. MICS data are available at the site `childinfo.org/mics4_tools.html`.

The DHS and the MICS are an important data resource and have been a backbone for research into international crimes. They have been used extensively by researchers to study the impact on schooling, health, mortality and the like. Their rich, standardised and uniform measures across countries and years enable researchers to make comparisons and gauge findings.

The data can be analysed by comparing years with conflict against years without conflict, inspecting how the trend in education is perturbed by periods of conflict, essentially a within-case analysis. The graph shows that there is a small increase in the percentage of men without formal education from wealthy families from 1973-1976 during the war of independence, but after this levels remain basically at 0. Thus, it appears as if the trend in basic education for men from rich families has continued virtually unperturbed from 1950 to the end of the observation period. For men from poor families, however, the picture is quite different. Here we see that firstly these men in 1950 much more often lacked formal education: the percentage is about 60%. From 1950 the trend is strongly downward, reaching a little over 40% at the start of the independence war in the late 1960s and 1970s. The trend however continues virtually uninterrupted until 1973, when the percentage of men without formal schooling sharply increases. This was a period in the war with particularly intense fighting.

Towards the end of the 1970s this negative development is reversed and levels of schooling pick up quickly again, and by 1983 levels are back to where they would have

Figure 16.5: Years of schooling by Rwandan children's age for two cohorts

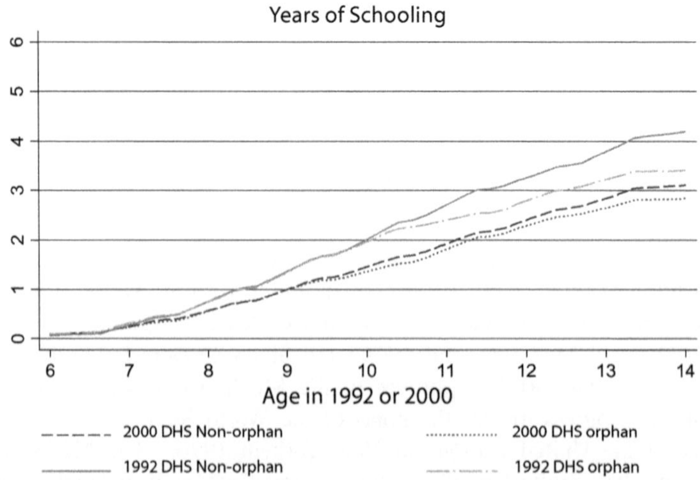

source: Akresh and DeWalque (2008)

been, had the trend continued uninterrupted, While, all in all, 15-year old cohorts in 1983 were positioned in terms of schooling where they would have been had the war of independence not occurred, the men who were 15 in the intervening years from 1973 to 1983 suffered in terms of schooling. By 1993, the percentages without formal schooling for the poor and rich cohorts are almost equal, with the poorer segments only a little behind. The graph thus clearly demonstrates how the war affected educational levels of boys from poor families mainly.

Akresh and De Walque (2008) investigated the effect of the Rwandan genocide on schooling levels. Using the the 1992 and 2000 Demographic and Health Surveys (DHS) for Rwanda to measure educational attainment and grade completion rates, they investigated schooling for two cohorts: children of different ages surveyed before the genocide, and children of different ages surveyed 6 years after the genocide. Using a fairly complicated regression analysis that we will not delve into here, the authors produce graphs that can be interpreted as trends in educational achievement for the two different measurement cohorts. Figure 16.5 presents the results.

The figure shows that among the respondents investigated before the genocide (the red solid line), the younger respondents (ages 20 – 22) had had more years of schooling than older respondents. This is logical, as educational levels generally improved over the years in Rwanda so that one would expect younger cohorts to have had more education. Among the respondents investigated after the genocide (the blue dashed line), we see the same pattern: as respondents age, their schooling improves (logical because when people are older they can have experienced more years of schooling), but the line tips and declines

Figure 16.6: Years of schooling by Rwandan children's age by cohorts and orphan status

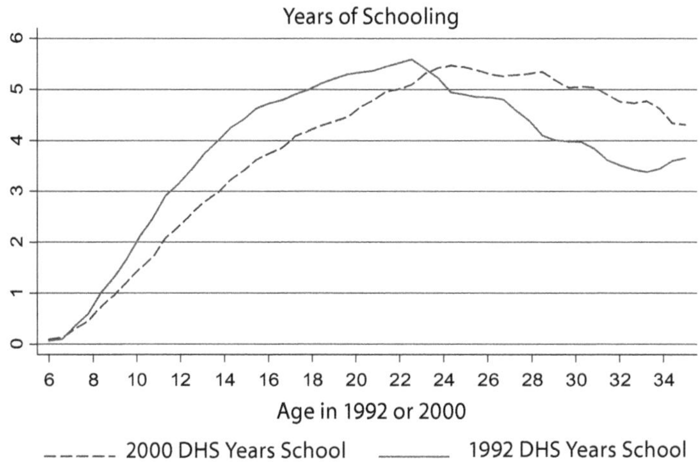

source: Akresh and DeWalque (2008)

when people become so old that they were born in the years when schooling was not as widely available. However, it is the position of this line as compared to the red solid line that is of interest. That comparison shows namely that after the genocide, schooling levels dropped. In fact, if we compare for instance the schooling levels of children aged 14, we see that those who were 14 in 1992, before the genocide, had had on average a little over 4 years of schooling. In 2000, after the 1994 genocide, children 14 years of age had had on average around 3 years of schooling.

Next, the authors investigated one explanation for this. As approximately 10% of the Rwandan population died in 1994 and those deaths were concentrated among adults, it might be that orphanhood was one of the main driving forces of decreased schooling levels. Figure 16.6 displays the years of education disaggregated for orphans and non-orphans in 1992 and 2000, for children aged 6 to 14 inclusive. The figure illustrates that years of schooling is consistently higher in 1992 than in 2000, both for orphans and non-orphans. What is most remarkable is, however, that orphans in 1992 were even better off, in terms of educational achievement, than non-orphans in 2000. Also, the differences between orphans and non-orphans in 2000 are much smaller than they are for the 1992 DHS. This makes it unlikely according to the authors that the decline in educational attainment for the young cohort exposed to the genocide is mainly due to orphanhood caused by genocide.

16.3.4 Demographic consequences

Verwimp and Van Bavel (2005) showed that refugee status was associated with demographic differences. The authors analysed data from a national survey conducted between

1999 and 2001 in Rwanda that covered 6,420 former refugee and non-refugee households. The findings showed that refugee women had had more children, likely to compensate for children lost, and at shorter intervals. Also, newborn girls were at greater risk to die than boys. This finding is surprising as it reverses the well-known sex differential in child survival, namely that newborn boys are at greater risk to die than newborn girls. The authors suggest that in times of food scarcity, parents may have chosen to allocate scarce resources to their sons rather than to their daughters. An underlying explanation for this may be Rwandan paternal inheritance rights, particularly for land, that were in force until 1994.

In most conflicts, young adult men are disproportionately often killed. This may in turn affect marital chances for women (who have a smaller pool of potential husbands to choose from) as well as those of surviving men (who have a larger pool of potential spouses to choose from). In section 13.2.1 we already discussed how after World War I, an entire generation of British women suffered the consequences of massive male mortality in the trenches: more than one in three of women aged between 25 and 29 in 1921 failed to marry during their reproductive years (Nicholson, 2007).

Employing a variety of simple descriptive methods, regression models as well as more refined econometric modeling, Abramitzky, Delavande and Vasconcelos (2010) analysed regional data in France after WW I. In France during WW I, soldiers' mortality varied between approximately 10 to 20%. The authors compared regions with higher male mortality (to be regarded as experimental regions) to regions with lower mortality (that can be regarded as control regions). Essentially conducting a case-control analysis, the authors show how in regions with higher male mortality women's chances in the marriage market worsened and those of men improved. The proportion of men who married in those regions increased, and – importantly – they married women of higher social class than their own. They thus achieved social ascension in that they 'married up'. Women were, conversely, less likely to marry and married at later ages. The age gap between partners increased. Men's relative scarcity in experimental regions, made them more attractive on the marriage market. In regions with higher military mortality, there were also more out-of-wedlock births and fewer divorces.

16.3.5 Health consequences

Akresh, Verwimp and Bundervoet (2007) show that so-called 'economic shocks' experienced at or around birth can have lasting consequences. Using data on the health status of young children, from a survey conducted by UNICEF in January 1992, they showed that boys and girls in Rwanda who were born in regions experiencing civil conflict had lower height for age scores (z-scores -0.30 and -0.72 lower respectively). As the authors argue, it is known from the literature that a child that at age 5 has shorter than normal height for age, will not be able to catch up later in life. Likely, these effects are therefore life-lasting, and will translate into negative outcomes in adult life in terms of health, education and socio-economic status.

In the Netherlands, researchers from the TNO Netherlands Organisation for Applied Scientific Research and the Leiden University Medical Center (LUMC) studied people born or conceived in the Dutch 'Hunger winter', the winter from 1944 – 1945 that was extremely cold and in which particularly the west of the Netherlands under the Nazi occupation suffered severe food shortages. In the winter and spring of 1944 after a railway strike, the Nazi German occupiers limited rations such that people received as little as 400 – 800 calories per day. It was known that babies born during or right after this period had lower birthweight. The TNO and LUMC study was designed to study long-term consequences of this famine.

The researchers studied three groups of people. Firstly they studied children born during the Hunger winter or right after (and thus conceived during that period), who could be called the 'experimental' group; these children had been found through the registries of the Midwifery schools in Amsterdam and Rotterdam, and the delivery ward in the Leiden University Academic Hospital. These were therefore children born in the west of the country where the famine was worst. A second group consisted of children born in the same clinics, but in 1943 or in 1947, so before or after the Hunger winter; this group served as a control group of children born in the same location, but not exposed to the famine. A third group consisted of relatives of the children in the first group, sisters for the females and brothers for the males. This group served as controls in the sense that they stemmed from the same gene pool and control for congenital diseases was thus possible. A total of 1,075 people participated. The design of the study is prospective, and the researchers exploit the natural variation in exposure of children born or conceived just before, during and after the Hunger winter. By adding the siblings of the babies, they have a second kind of control group who are different in the sense that they did not experience the famine in utero, but are genetically and socio-economically similar.

As Rooseboom, De Rooij and Painter (2006) show, women exposed to the famine during mid- to late gestation had babies with significantly reduced birth weights. Babies whose mothers were exposed only during early gestation had normal birth weights; however, they grew up to have higher rates of obesity than those born before and after the war and higher rates than those exposed during mid- to late gestation. The increased weight was on average almost 5 kgs. At age 56 to 59, men as well as women exposed to famine during the early stage of gestation performed worse on a selective attention task (De Rooij, Wouters, Yonke *et al.*, 2010). The studies have all in all identified both physical and mental long-term health consequences.

This shows how pervading and far-reaching the consequences of conflict can be, even for those not yet born when hostilities take place. The consequences might extend even further: a next group of researchers is now studying the children of the daughters of the Hunger winter-mothers. The idea is that, as a woman's eggs are formed in utero, effects of a reduced diet might be visible in a next generation too.

16.4 Summary of methodological issues

In this chapter we discussed examples of studies on victims. Most of these studies aimed to find out how victims were doing, psychologically, socially, physically. Qualitative studies in general exploited the strength of qualitative free-format interviewing modes in that they were able to delve into the manner in which victims felt traumatised, or how resilience manifested itself, sometimes in unexpected ways. Qualitative and quantitative studies sometimes generated different conclusions, with quantitative studies overall reporting fewer effects in victims and their descendants and qualitative studies reporting stronger effects. Part of this difference may be due to the fact that qualitative studies, because of the fact that they do not aim to conduct representative studies, may be more prone to select on the dependent variable, investigating so-called *clinical samples*, i.e. samples of persons who have been referred for psychological or other problems, who may have joined survivors' associations and the like. Respondents sampled in such a way – in general because they are relatively accessible – has the risk of overrepresenting persons burdened more by their experiences than those who do not seek assistance or the company of like-minded co-survivors (hence: 'clinical' samples). While some studies laid bare explanations for diverging qualitative and quantitative results (namely, that intergenerational transmission of trauma may even out intergenerational transmission of resilience), few studies had the combination of mixed qualitative and quantitative methods to be able to do this.

Having said so, the need for qualitative studies appears particularly prominent for victimological research. Understanding victims' experiences and resilience is culture- and context-bound, as several studies have shown (for a particularly well-developed example, see Zraly & Nyirazinyoye, 2010). If models and checklists and interventions do not incorporate constructs in the manner that corresponds with victims' own perceptions, in a manner that makes sense and resonates in victims' daily lives, it is hard to imagine interventions being effective. All in all, while qualitative research appears of particular importance for victimological research, its often unrepresentativeness hampers its value, both for theory and practice. Mixed methods research might be able to overcome this.

Some authors have warned against overly simplistic categorisations of victims, perpetrators, helpers and bystanders, stressing that rules that people assume during conflict may be fluid and overlapping or transforming in time. Qualitative studies have pointed out to a similar interwovenness of conceptually different variables: consequences of one post-conflict outcome (such as depression) were shown to be new causes for other outcomes (unemployment). All this shows that models to understand the impact of conflicts, for victims and post-conflict societies, should by necessity be complex, layered, must have numerous contextual variables. Again, qualitative research that is able to capture the fluidity and fuzziness of roles is much called for.

Both for trauma and economic consequences, we saw that damage can be direct and indirect, as evidenced from the difference between accounting and counterfactual models and as evidenced by intergenerational patterns in victimisation.

Researchers have attempted to find 'controls' in various ways. For the economic studies that attempt to assess economic damage, we saw how control regions were 'constructed' or amalgamated using an elegant procedure that also solves issues with statistical inference. Some studies have, within one nation at war, contrasted regions where the independent variable (conflict, or mortality) was higher, with regions where it was lower. Many studies have exploited variation in long-term patterns over time, scrutinising trends for sudden dips or jumps that co-occur with the onset of conflict, with periods where fighting was particularly fierce or there was a lull. Periods where a truce was announced have been similarly used as a 'control' period, against which outcomes in the experimental conflict period can be gauged. Many of these studies (on the economy, mortality and marriage patterns, schooling) have relied on using secondary, macro-data, such as the data from revolving surveys like the DHS en the MICS surveys, or on data such as collected by national statistics agencies on GDP and the like. Nevertheless, we saw how the use of prospective studies adds particular strength to conclusions on long term effects, as here we are able to assess effects within persons over time.

Studies were extremely mixed methodologically, partly due to their different disciplinary background. We find econometric models, social psychology experiments, medical studies, demographic, anthropological and in general social research.

All in all, methodological issues that were particularly prominent here were firstly how to design studies such that they are sensitive enough to understand victimisation with its specific cultural and geo-political context, how to ensure that findings on victims are generalisable and do not overrepresent those who do particularly badly, and how to find adequate controls: regions, people, periods and countries.

Part VI

CONCLUSIONS

Chapter 17

Concluding remarks

In the various chapters of this book, we first discussed the basics of research design: research design proper, design of measurement instruments (interviews, observation and other instruments), and sampling. We also discussed testing and analysis techniques: simple descriptive statistics, measures of association and much more complicated multivariate models.

After this fairly general introductory part, we discussed issues particular to criminological research, mainly to do with the fact that we want to analyse behaviour that is deviant, unacceptable or even punishable. We discussed the various methods criminologists have employed to circumvent or solve such measurement problems.

Once we arrived at international crimes, we divided our text into four blocks, each to do with the 'pillars' of interest in criminology: prevalence, etiology, reaction and victims. We discussed for each pillar a number of studies that gave an impression of measurement and analysis methods. While methods were a fairly motley crew in our chapter on prevalence, stemming from epidemiology, biology, demographics and regular social science methodologies, and we outlined new and particular methodologies mainly in chapter 13 and chapter 16, the examples we gave in chapter 14 and chapter 15 were not hugely novel from a methodological point of view: they comprised regular qualitative interviews, surveys, regression analysis, experiments, observations and tabulations.

However, we did indicate here and there where things might be different because of our particular topic of study: extremely serious crimes, generally conducted on a large scale, with complicit state authorities. Crimes that are often preceded by political tension or oppression, that likely generate large population upheaval, displacement and downright extremely dangerous conditions, in which it is also extremely hard to conduct research according to regular 'peacetime' standards. Moreover, much research on these gravest crimes codified is met with intense scrutiny and emotion – not surprising the often in a sense immeasurable scale of suffering. In terse political post-conflict climates, findings may be confronted with outright hostility or may be 'hijacked' for propaganda purposes. Explanations intertwined at micro-, meso- and macro-level, in highly particular and unique constellations. Crimes that people cannot report because mortality may be so high that entire families have been wiped out, or that are so traumatic that victims do not wish to report about them. All in all, it appears the dark number of crime is particularly dark for international crimes.

At the end of each of the chapters dealing with prevalence, etiology, reaction and victims, we outlined the most prominent methodological and statistical issues, and some solutions. We will not reiterate these here, but highlight some particularities.

One group of issues had to do with security, with inaccessibility, and with the politics of conflict. This in turn generated often small samples and often unrepresentative samples. Small samples were also often encountered when studies focused on the international reaction to crime as so few trials have yet been completed. Sparse data is also a theme in the sense that ordinary population statistics were often flawed or non-existing, limiting the possibilities to assess trends in mortality. The fact that governments may be complicit in the criminality has generated in places what we phrased as a 'double dark number'; the fact that victims of particularly sexual violence are hesitant to speak 'triples' it. The all-pervasive, destructive and incomprehensible forces of conflict make the criminological researcher's standard tools such as police and prosecution data, victim surveys and self-report surveys less useful – to useless.

A next group of issues had to, firstly, do with the fact that much research can only be conducted (unless researchers have serendipitous luck) retrospectively. This creates particular issues with causal inference. Conflicts and international crimes cannot be imposed randomly. Many researchers have employed inventive strategies to find, or even build controls to be able to compare cases who experienced international crimes or conflict with cases that didn't, exploiting regional variation, temporal variation, genetic variation or natural experiments. Controlled experiments are seen increasingly, both more stylised experiments that survey samples with vignettes as well as more naturalistic ones.

The multi-disciplinary group of researchers that study these crimes have – at least in part – contributed to existing definitional confusion, confusion that leads to idiosyncratic operationalisations and incomparability of findings across disciplines, but also across conflicts, regions and even within these. The fact that conflicts occur in highly particular constellations of risk and disadvantage has generated much qualitative research that is uniquely suited to lay bare and extricate tangled mechanisms, but often leads to generally unique and ungeneralisable explanations. Standardisation is sorely needed, in terms of instruments but also in terms of methodology in a generic sense.

With the advance of the internet and increased technological possibilities with simple hand-held devices such as smartphones, the story of the international crimes as they unfold is increasingly captured on images. The immense amount of information on the geography of the world that is accessible from researchers' desks has made it possible to identify the exact location of crimes, and much about the identity of the perpetrators. Such digital forensic evidence will likely become increasingly important in the prosecution of international crimes. Similarly, satellite imagery now routinely supports witness statements in reports by organisations such as Human Rights Watch. The use of such data for scientific purposes is a novel avenue that needs exploring.

Civil society and private initiative have had a marked impact on the data landscape for the study of conflict and international crimes. Human rights groups and affected relatives in various parts of the world have since long documented the names of the disappeared (and killed), and campaigned for information, justice and redress. These organisations have been crucial not only in the push for justice, but also for writing history. Extending from De las Casas who described in words what he witnessed, current witnesses to atrocities still document, publish and archive micro-information on the events and the individuals involved, as victims or perpetrators. Numerous organisations, with the Iraq Body Count project an extensively discussed example, have sprung up in recent conflicts, that document the names of civilian victims of conflict, data that are increasingly made public on the internet. These data sources have proven invaluable for rising above estimates, for counting the countless and naming the nameless.

17.1 Recommendations

We conclude with a number of recommendations.

17.1.1 Know the conflict setting

As a first rule, it is important to be extremely well read about the conflict and the international crimes conducted during its course. It is an illusion to think that valid research can be conducted without intricate, hands-on specialised knowledge of the region where the atrocities were committed. This includes knowing the population composition, culture, manner in which local administrations are run, how families cohabit, what seasonal movements any nomadic groups make, and of course: knowing in detail how the conflict unfolded and where, when and how atrocities were committed.

While this may not be doable in all cases, it is highly recommended that if fieldwork needs to be conducted that researchers speak – at least at a basic level – one of the local languages, or the lingua franca. Very good interpreters must be hired, who must also be screened at times by independent other translators. Similarly, if fieldwork is to be conducted, researchers must acquaint themselves with local customs, do's and don'ts, in terms of behaviour and dress. This is already vital if fairly 'superficial' quantitative fieldwork is conducted. It is therefore not surprising that for the more qualitative types of research, where participant observation is employed, or in-depth interviews, much deeper knowledge and awareness is required. Respondents and researchers should reserve time to build up rapport, and the researcher should in fact be immersed in local life and customs, well before fieldwork proper can begin.

Not adhering to these principles will generate flimsy data and flimsy conclusions that probably – unsurprisingly – confirm all hypotheses the researcher had beforehand.

17.1.2 Know your sources

In the highly charged and often still politicised research environment during or after conflict, it is vital that researchers are critical towards their sources. They should be willing to question what respondents tell them, cross-checking information, and acquainting themselves well with respondents' backgrounds. This may be difficult and may be experienced as 'heartless' given the stomach and heart-churning experiences that respondents relate.

However, as Fujii (2010) reported, respondents may have various motives for relating other experiences than what really happened to them.

Similarly, secondary data should also be checked for biases and trustworthiness. As we stated previously, researchers should ideally use only data from independent sources, but, as we discussed, 'independence' may be a difficult criterion in conflict situations where NGOs – put bluntly – make a living from caring for the sick, the destitute and the wounded. So checks and counterchecks, and a constant awareness for the pitfalls of the use of such 'second-hand' data are mandatory.

If possible, data from multiple sources should be used and cross-compared. This applies to interviews with victims or bystanders, but also to data that one uses from agencies.

17.1.3 Triangulate and corroborate

As the setting in which international crimes are studied is so much more fraught with risks for biases and distortions – for various methodological or political reasons – it is therefore also much more important than in ordinary non-conflict situations to employ differing, complementary methodologies to investigate the research questions. Such triangulation protects researchers from weak designs or faulty data in one method: each of the different methods buffers against the weaknesses of the other methods. As the risk of conclusions that are wrong are arguably larger when studying international crimes than when doing research in standard settings, triangulation is also much more important. Triangulation offers a methodological check on the conclusions to be drawn from the study, just as screenings on the respondents serve as a check on the validity of their reports. Corroboration is vital, as we saw from a number of examples where studies in spite of apparent sound design got it horribly wrong. Employing mixed methods, if only by adding regular focus groups of experts to the study, may prevent wasted effort and confusion.

17.1.4 Standardise

Whenever possible, researchers should standardise their instruments and definitions. While especially in medical and social sciences meta-analyses have propelled forward our knowledge, this is still far away for the field of international crimes. We discussed a number of studies that had attempted to synthesise findings; almost all recommended that definitions and operationalisations be made more uniform and therefore comparable.

The web provides an array of standardised methodologies for sampling and interviewing populations. Researchers do not only save time and money if they use them, but also pay the field a service.

17.1.5 Fieldwork: ensure ethics and safety

Then, ethics and safety are much larger issues when we do fieldwork for international crimes. Victims as well perpetrators, neighbours and bystanders all suffer in the aftermath of conflict. And all may run risks. Ethics approval is therefore important and when doing fieldwork, researchers, just like in ordinary settings, must ensure respondents confidentiality. It may however be harder to be able to ensure this, given instabilities and political tension. Respondents may be threatened simply for giving an interview, or for being in contact with a conspicuous foreign researcher. If one is not a local researcher, it may also be hard to know whether the promise of confidentiality constitutes a guarantee: how can one be sure that interpreters do not gossip? Is one aware of power relations between the destitute and the better-off researchers and research assistants? Is it safe to leave field notes in one's office or hotel room? The Do No Harm-principle is an even more prominent beacon in the study of international crimes.

One should also ponder whether IDPs or refugees are actually always able to give full informed consent, given how precarious their situation is. If one hands out rewards or small gifts, they may be so destitute that they see no other option but to consent.

Silva and Marwaha (2006) mention security issues in studying counterinsurgency mortality in Amritsar, India. They related how they worked with an advocacy organisation and how that organisation had wanted to use the data gathered during fieldwork for their own campaigns. The researchers had however decided against this. The researchers relate how they were afraid of potential violations of confidentiality, and of undermining of validity and reliability as respondents might 'embellish' reports in the hope of later benefits through the advocacy organisation.

Silva and Marwaha also discuss security issues. They relate how a former researcher, who had discovered 6,000 illegal cremations in just one district had been arbitrarily arrested, detained, tortured and killed. They next report that staff that they themselves employed as surveyors, had to report twice a day to their field supervisor, as well as every day at 630 pm. The researchers forbade personal errands during fieldwork and any non-scheduled stops. Field staff were instructed that work was to be immediately terminated when staff noticed they were being followed. In addition, all staff received specific training related to security issues. The researchers also, as a preventive measure, prepared and set up a legal team in case incidents would occur. See Silva and Marwaha (2006).

All in all, the risks for staff and respondents of such research should not be underestimated, and one should be street-wise, and critical and attentive rather than relaxed and easy-going.

17.1.6 Acknowledge uncertainty of estimates

We saw, especially in chapter 13, several examples of estimates that eventually turned out to be way off the mark. The Burnham study on Iraq that we discussed extensively in section 13.3.2 is one such example, and the controversies over the Darfur estimates (see section 13.3.3) illustrate the point as well.

Given the difficulties in sampling and data collection, and given – often – lack of good baseline demographic data, it is not surprising that estimates of mortality or victimisation of international crimes may have broad margins of uncertainty. Reporting such margins is necessary to express the uncertainty, but may also in a sense 'backfire': given wide margins, readers may infer that there is too much uncertainty to say anything about the conflict. In such cases, one could resort to reporting the lower limit of the estimates, the number one is pretty certain that is the minimum mortality that occurred: while the true value is bound to be higher, it is not very likely to be lower. This argument was used by Alison des Forges (1999) for estimating that approximately 500,000 people were killed in the Rwandan genocide: these were the numbers she was certain of. Obviously other estimates have been made for mortality in Rwanda during the genocide: around 800,000 by Prunier (1995) and even around 1.1 million victims from a survey by the government of Rwanda (see Reyntjes, 1997). Such a wide margin is problematic for various reasons, but will remain all there is for some conflicts.

As the case study of the Yugoslavian wars by Tabeau and Bijak illustrated (2005), early estimates of mortality tend to be generally on the high side, and tend to be downscaled by later estimates once better data become available, or more concurrent data to gauge estimates against (viz. the Iraq controversy). As Bijleveld, Morssinkhof and Smeulers (2009) stated, early estimates tend to lead lives of their own, with authors citing each other in long uncontested strings, until better estimates can be made.

Admitting uncertainty, and not pretending to be exact by listing very precise estimates but rather giving rounded numbers that reflect the coarseness of the estimates is better practice.

17.1.7 Get specialist advice before and after

Last, it is recommended that conclusions from research be subjected to expert scrutiny before they are published. While specialists who know the conflict, have worked there during upheavals, or who have otherwise specialised knowledge of the conflict region often do not have intricate quantitative knowledge of the prevalence of victimisation, they are generally able to judge whether assumptions are realistic, whether the conclusions hold against other evidence. They will be able to protect the research from the severest mistakes.

Obviously, getting such specialist advice is best done before one embarks upon the research. It should be part of preparation: reading up on the conflict, official literature, grey literature, websites and unpublished materials. Much knowledge is in the heads of people who were (independent) witnesses to the atrocities. And much of that knowledge is not written down. That knowledge should not be missed, and is part and parcel of writing the story of the international crimes that were committed, their etiology, societal responses and their aftermath.

References

Abadie, A., Diamond, A., & Hainmueller, J. (2015). Comparative politics and the synthetic control method. *American Journal of Political Science, 59*, 495–510. Retrieved from economics.mit.edu/files/11858 doi: 10.1111/ajps.12116

Abadie, A., & Gardeazabal, J. (2003). The economic costs of conflict: A case study of the Basque country. *The American Economic Review, 93*, 113–132. Retrieved from nyu.edu/gsas/dept/politics/faculty/beck/abadie_aer.pdf

Abramitzky, R., Delavande, A., & Vasconcelos, L. (2010). *Marrying up: The role of sex ratio in assortative matching* (Tech. Rep. No. 36). MICROCON. Retrieved from www2.econ.iastate.edu/classes/econ321/Orazem/Abramitzky_marriage_france_wwII.pdf

Aebi, M. et al. (2010). *European sourcebook of crime and criminal justice statistics - 2010* (4th ed.; Tech. Rep.). Université de Lausanne. Retrieved from wp.unil.ch/europeansourcebook/printed-editions-2/5th-edition/

Africa Research Institute (2012). *How Rwanda judged its genocide* (Tech. Rep.). Africa Research Institute. Retrieved from africaresearchinstitute.org/newsite/?s=How+Rwanda+judged+its+genocide

Agirre Aranburu, X. (2010). Sexual violence beyond reasonable doubt: Using pattern evidence and analysis for international cases. *Leiden Journal of International Law, 23*, 609–627.

Akresh, R., & De Walque, D. (2008). *Armed conflict and schooling: Evidence from the 1994 Rwandan genocide* (Tech. Rep. No. 4606). World Bank. Retrieved from papers.ssrn.com/sol3/papers.cfm?abstract_id=1149109#\%23

Akresh, R., Verwimp, P., & Bundervoet, T. (2007). *Civil war, crop failure, and child stunting in Rwanda* (Tech. Rep. No. 4208). World Bank. Retrieved from ssrn.com/abstract=980826

Arendt, H. (1963). *Eichmann in Jerusalem: A Report on the Banality of Evil.* New York: Penguin.

Asher, J., Banks, D., & Scheuren, F. J. (2008). *Statistics for Human Rights.* New York: Springer.

Bachman, R., & Schutt, R. K. (2017). *The Practice of Research in Criminology and Criminal Justice* (6th ed.). Thousand Oaks, CA: Sage.

Backer, D. (2009). Cross-national comparative analysis. In H. Van der Merwe, V. Baxter, & A. R. Chapman (Eds.), *Assessing the Impact of Transitional Justice. Challenges for Empirical Research* (pp. 23–89). Washington: United States Institute of Peace.

Baier, D. (2017). Computer-assisted versus paper-and-pencil self-report delinquency surveys: Results of an experimental study. *European Journal of Criminology*, *15*, 385–402.

Ball, P., Betts, W., Scheuren, F., Dudukovich, J., & Asher, J. (2002). *Killings and refugee flow in Kosovo March–June 1999* (Tech. Rep.). American Association for the Advancement of Science. Retrieved from shr.aaas.org/kosovo/icty_report.pdf

Ball, P., Tabeau, E., & Verwimp, P. (2007). *The Bosnian Book of the Dead: Assessment of the database* (Tech. Rep. No. 5). Households in Conflict Network. Retrieved from hicn.org/research_design/rdn5.pdf

Barel, E., Van IJzendoorn, M. H., Sagi-Schwartz, A., & Bakermans-Kranenburg, M. J. (2010). Surviving the Holocaust: A meta-analysis of the long-term sequelae of a genocide. *Psychological Bulletin*, *136*, 677–698. doi: 10.1037/a0020339

Bernard, T., Snipes, J., Vold, G., & Gerould, A. (2015). *Vold's Theoretical Criminology* (7th ed.). Oxford: Oxford University Press.

Bijleveld, C. C. J. H. (2003). *Mens, durf te meten! Over Methoden en Technieken van Criminologisch Oonderzoek [hey! Measure up! On Research Methods for Criminological Research]*. Den Haag: Boom Juridische uitgevers.

Bijleveld, C. C. J. H. (2005). *Delinquency over five generations.* (Paper presented 20 October 2005 at the Institute of Criminology Cambridge Lecture Series)

Bijleveld, C. C. J. H. (2018). *Methoden en Technieken van Onderzoek in de Criminologie [Research Methods in Criminology]* (7th ed.). Den Haag: Boom Criminologie.

Bijleveld, C. C. J. H. (2019). *Research Methods for Empirical Legal Studies: an Introduction.* Den Haag: Eleven international publishing.

Bijleveld, C. C. J. H., & Hoex, L. (2008). Direct and indirect mortality in Sierra Leone, 1991–2002. In R. Ratnayake, O. Degomme, C. Altare, & D. Guha-Sapir (Eds.), *Methods and tools to evaluate mortality in conflicts: Critical review, case studies and applications* (pp. 18–19). CRED. Retrieved from humansecuritygateway.com/documents/CRED_MethodsToolsToEvaluateMortalityInConflicts.pdf

Bijleveld, C. C. J. H., Hola, B., & Poelhekke, A. (2014). *Social science evidence and the Special Court for Sierra Leone.* (Paper presented at 9th International Conference on Forensic Inference and Statistics, Leiden, 21 August 2014)

Bijleveld, C. C. J. H., Morssinkhof, A., & Smeulers, A. L. (2009). Counting the countless. Rape victimisation during the Rwandan genocide. *International Criminal Justice Review*, *19*, 208–224.

Bijleveld, C. C. J. H., Van de Weijer, S. G. A., Ruiter, S., & Van der Geest, V. R. (2018). *Analysis techniques for non-experimental data: An introduction.* Den Haag: Eleven international publishing.

Bjørkhaug, I. (2010). *Child soldiers in Colombia: The recruitment of children into non-state violent armed groups* (Tech. Rep. No. 27). MICROCON. Retrieved from core.ac.uk/download/pdf/6406917.pdf

Blattman, C., & Miguel, E. (2010). Civil war. *Journal of Economic Literature*, *48*, 3–57. Retrieved from aeaweb.org/articles?id=10.1257/jel.48.1.3 doi: 10.1257/jel.48.1.3

Bohning, D., Van der Heijden, P. G. M., & Bunge, J. (2017). *Capture-recapture methods for the social and medical sciences.* Boca Raton, FL: Chapman and Hall.

Bolhuis, M. P., & Van Wijk, J. (2015). Alleged war criminal in the Netherlands: Excluded from refugee protection, wanted by the prosecutor. *European Journal of Criminology, 12*, 151–168. doi: doi.org/10.1177/1477370814554721

Bolton, P., Michalopoulos, L., Mohammed Amin, A., Murray, L. K., & Bass, J. (2013). The mental health and psychosocial problems of survivors of torture and genocide in Kurdistan, Northern Iraq: A brief qualitative study. *Torture, 43*, 1–14. Retrieved from mhpss.net/?get=250/5.MH-and-psychosocial-problems-ofsurvivorsoftorture_PaulBoltonetal.pdf

Bøås, M., & Bjørkhaug, I. (2010). *DDRed in Liberia: Youth remarginalisation or reintegration?* (Tech. Rep. No. 28). MICROCON. Retrieved from ssrn.com/abstract=1650589

Brounéus, K. (2008). Truth-telling as talking cure? Insecurity and retraumatization in the Rwandan gacaca courts. *Security Dialogue, 39*, 55–76. Retrieved from journals.sagepub.com/doi/pdf/10.1177/0967010607086823 doi: 10.1177/0967010607086823

Brounéus, K. (2010). The trauma of truth-telling: Effects of witnessing in the Rwandan gacaca courts on psychological health. *Journal of Conflict Resolution, 54*, 408–437.

Browning, C. (1992). *Ordinary Men: Reserve Police Battalion 101 and the Final Solution in Poland.* New York: Harper Collins.

Bruinsma, G. J. N., & Luykx, F. (2003). De vuurwerkramp en de gevolgen daarvan op de criminaliteit in Enschede [The fireworks disaster and its consequences for crime in Enschede]. *Tijdschrift voor Veiligheid en Veiligheidszorg, 2*, 3–24.

Brunborg, H. (2009). Report on the size and ethnic composition of the population of Kosovo; 14 August 2002. In E. Tabeau (Ed.), *Conflict in Numbers. Casualties of the 1990s wars in the former Yugoslavia (1991–1999)* (pp. 977–996). Helsinki Committee for Human Rights in Serbia. Retrieved from helsinki.org.rs/doc/testimonies33.pdf

Burnham, G., Lafta, R., Doocy, S., & Roberts, L. (2006). Mortality after the 2003 invasion of Iraq: A cross-sectional cluster sample survey. *The Lancet, 368*, 1421–1428. Retrieved from download.thelancet.com/pdfs/journals/lancet/PIIS0140673606694919.pdf?id=40bade4753939e7f:2e5f8cf2:13a92896c36:6f931351085264835 doi: 10.1016/S0140-6736(06)69491-9

Canter, D., & Youngs, D. (2015). The LAAF procedure for exploring offenders' narratives. *The Howard Journal of Crime and Justice, 54*, 219–236. doi: 10.1111/hojo.12124

Carpenter, D., Fulkler, T., & Roberts, L. (2013). Wikileaks and Iraq Body Count: the sum of parts may not add up to the whole – A comparison of two tallies of Iraqi civilian deaths. *Prehospital and Disaster Medicine, 28*, 1–7. doi: 10.1017/S1049023X13000113

Cesarani, D. (2004). *Eichmann: His Life and Crimes.* London: Heinemann.

Chlevickaite, G., Hola, B., & Bijleveld, C. C. J. H. (2019). Thousands on the stand: Exploring trends and patterns of international witnesses. *Leiden Journal of International Law, 32*. doi: doi:10.1017/S0922156519000396

Christen, P. (2012). *Data matching. Concepts and techniques for record linkage, entity resolution, and duplicate detection.* Berlin Heidelberg: Springer. doi: 10.1007/978-3-642-31164-2

Cilliers, J., Dube, O., & Siddiqi, B. (2016). Reconciling after civil conflict increases social capital but decreases individual well-being. *Science*, *352*, 787–794.

CIPEV (2008). *Report of the Commission of Inquiry into Post-Election Violence* (Tech. Rep.).

Coebergh, J. (2005). Sudan: Genocide has killed more than the tsunami. *Parliamentary Brief*, *9*, 5–6.

Coghlan, B., Ngoy, P., Mulumba, F., Hardy, C., Nkamgang Berno, V., Stewart, T., ... Brennan, R. (2008). *Mortality in the Democratic Republic of Congo: An ongoing crisis* (Tech. Rep.). International Rescue Committee. Retrieved from `rescue.org/sites/default/files/document/661/2006-7congomortalitysurvey.pdf`

Cohen, D. (2016). *Rape during Civil War*. Ithaca & London: Cornell University Press.

Cohen, J., Cohen, P., West, S. G., & Aiken, L. S. (2002). *Applied Multiple Rregression/Correlation Analysis for the Social Sciences*. Hillsdale, NJ: Lawrence Erlbaum.

Collier, P., & Hoeffler, A. (2004). Greed and grievance in civil war. *Oxford Economic Papers*, *56*, 563–595. Retrieved from `econ.nyu.edu/user/debraj/Courses/Readings/CollierHoeffler.pdf`

Cook, T. D., & Campbell, D. T. (1979). *Quasi–experimentation: Design and Analysis Issues for Field Settings*. Boston, MA: Houghton Mifflin.

Croes, M., & Tammes, P. (2004). *'Gif laten wij niet voortbestaan'['Poison we shall not allow to live on']*. Amsterdam: Aksant.

Crowne, D. P., & Marlowe, D. (1960). A new scale of social desirability independent of psychopathology. *Journal of Consulting Psychology*, *24*, 349–354.

Dancy, G., Kim, H., & Brahm, E. (2010). The turn to truth: Trends in truth commission experimentation. *Journal of Human Rights*, *9*, 45–64.

Daponte, B. (2008). Why estimate direct and indirect casualties from war? The rule of proportionality and casualty estimates. In J. Asher, D. Banks, & F. J. Scheuren (Eds.), *Statistics for Human Rights* (pp. 51–63). New York: Springer.

David, R. (2014). International criminal tribunals and the perception of justice: The effect of the ICTY in Croatia. *The International Journal of Transitional Justice*, *8*, 476–495. doi: //doi.org/10.1093/ijtj/iju012

Degomme, O., & Guha-Sapir, D. (2010). Patterns of mortality rates in Darfur conflict. *The Lancet*, *375*, 294–300. Retrieved from `download.thelancet.com/pdfs/journals/lancet/PIIS014067360961967X.pdf?id=4d037fefcb72946c:cc129d8:13b18964eb1:42f71353331356358`

De Jong, J. D. (2007). *Kapot moeilijk. [Fuckin' cool]* (Unpublished doctoral dissertation). University of Groningen.

De Keijser, J. W., & Van Koppen, P. J. (2004). Compensatoir straffen: Over de relatie tussen bewijs, overtuiging en straf [Compensatory punishment: On the association between proof, conviction and punishment]. In J. W. De Keijser & H. Elffers (Eds.), *Het Maatschappelijk Oordeel van de Strafrechter: De Wisselwerking tussen Rechter en Samenleving [Societal Judgments of Judges: Interaction between Judges and Society]* (pp. 133–183). Den Haag: Boom Juridische uitgevers.

De las Casas, B. (1552, reprinted in translation 1992). *A Short Account of the Destruction of the Indies*. London: Penguin Books.

Denzin, N. K., & Lincoln, Y. S. (Eds.). (2011). *Handbook of Qualitative Research* (4th ed.). Thousand Oaks, CA: Sage.

Depoortere, E., Checchi, F., Broillet, F., Gerstl, G., Minetti, A., Gayraud, O., ... Brown, V. (2004). Violence and mortality in west Darfur, Sudan (2003-04): Epidemiological evidence from four surveys. *The Lancet, 364*, 1315–1320. doi: 10.1016/S0140-6736(04)17187-0

De Rooij, S. R., Wouters, H., Yonker, J. E., Painter, R., & Roseboom, T. J. (2010). Prenatal undernutrition and cognitive function in late adulthood. *Proceedings of the National Academy of Sciences, 107*, 16881–16886. doi: 10.1073/pnas.1009459107

Des Forges, A. (1999). *Leave none to tell the story: Genocide in Rwanda* (Tech. Rep.). Human Rights Watch. Retrieved from `hrw.org/reports/1999/rwanda/`

Dixon, J. C., Singleton, R. A., & Straits, B. C. (2016). *The Process of Social Research*. Oxford: Oxford University Press.

Doughty, K. (2017). Language and international criminal justice at the ICTR. *International Journal of Transitional Justice, 11*, 239–256.

Dumitru, D., & Johnson, C. (2007). Constructing interethnic conflict and cooperation: Why some people harmed Jews and others helped them during the Holocaust in Romania. *World Politics, 63*, 1–42.

Ellis, L., Hartley, R. D., & Walsh, A. (2010). *Research Methods in Criminal Justice and Criminology*. Lanham, MD: Rowman & Littlefield.

Engbersen, G. R., Staring, R., Van der Leun, J., De Boom, J., Van der Heijden, P. G. M., & Cruyff, M. (2002). *Illegale vreemdelingen in Nederland. Omvang, overkomst, verblijf en uitzetting* (Tech. Rep.). Rotterdam: Erasmus University Rotterdam: RISBO.

Farrington, D. P. (1995). The development of offending and antisocial behaviour from childhood: Key findings from the Cambridge Study in Delinquent Development. *Journal of Child Psychology and Psychiatry, 36*, 929–964.

Farrington, D. P. (2003). Methodological standards for evaluation research. *The Annals of the American Academy of Political and Social Sciences, 587*, 49–68.

Farrington, D. P., Gallagher, B., Morley, L., StLedger, R. J., & West, D. J. (1990). Minimizing attrition in longitudinal research: Methods of tracing and securing cooperation in a 24–year follow–up study. In D. Magnusson & L. R. Bergman (Eds.), *Data Quality in Longitudinal Research* (pp. 122–147). Cambridge: Cambridge University Press.

Farrington, D. P., & Loeber, R. (2000). Some benefits of dichotomization in psychiatric and criminological research. *Criminal Behavior and Mental Health, 10*, 100–122.

Fearon, J. D., & Laitin, D. D. (2003). Ethnicity, insurgency, and civil war. *American Political Science Review, 97*, 715–735.

Fellegi, I. P., & Sunter, A. B. (1969). A theory for record linkage. *Journal of the American Statistical Association, 64*, 1183–1210.

Finkel, E., & Straus, S. (2012). Macro, meso, and micro research on genocide: Gains, shortcomings, and future areas of inquiry. *Genocide Studies and Prevention: An International Journal, 7, 1, 7*. Retrieved from `scholarcommons.usf.edu/cgi/viewcontent.cgi?article=1048&context=gsp`

Fisher, B. S. (2009). The effects of survey question wording on rape estimates: Evidence from a quasi-experimental design. *Violence Against Women, 15*, 133–147.

Foster Lynch, M. (2013). Collecting data on civilian casualties. In T. B. Seybolt, J. B. Aronson, & B. Fischhoff (Eds.), *Counting Civilian Casualties* (pp. 123–143). Oxford: Oxford University Press.

Frerichs, R. R., & Shaheen, M. A. (2001). Small community-based surveys. *Annual Review of Public Health, 22*, 231–247.

Freudenreich, J., & Ranft, F. (2008). Learning from the past. An empirical study on the existence of a pattern of truth commissions. *MenschenRechtsMagazin, 1*, 22–44.

Fujii, L. A. (2010). Shades of truth and lies: Interpreting testimonies of war and violence. *Journal of Peace Research, 47*, 231-241. doi: 10.1177/0022343309353097

Gibson, J. L. (2004). *Overcoming Apartheid. Can Truth Reconcile a Divided Nation?* New York: Russell Sage.

Glaser, B., & Strauss, A. (1967). *The Discovery of Grounded Theory: Strategies for Qualitative Research.* Chicago: Aldine De Gruyter.

Goldhagen, D. J. (1996). *Hitler's Willing Executioners. Ordinary Germans and the Holocaust.* New York: Alfred A. Knopf.

Gompertz, B. (1825). On the nature of the function expressive of the law of human mortality, and on a new mode of determining the value of life contingencies. *Philosophical Transactions of the Royal Society of London, 115*, 513–585. doi: 10.1098/rstl.1825.0026

Gottfredson, M. R., & Hirschi, T. (1990). *A General Theory of Crime.* Stanford: Stanford University Press.

Goudie, I. B. J., & Goudie, M. (2007). Who captures the marks for the Petersen estimator. *Journal of the Royal Statistical Society. Series A (Statistics in Society), 170*, 825–839.

Government Accountability Office (2006). *Death estimates demonstrate severity of crisis, but their accuracy and credibility could be enhanced* (Tech. Rep. No. GAO-07-24). GAO. Retrieved from gao.gov/assets/260/253101.pdf

Grais, R. F., Coulombier, D., Ampuero, J., Lucas, M. E. S., Barretto, A. T., Jacquier, G., ... Brown, V. (2006). Are rapid population estimates accurate? A field trial of two different assessment methods. *Disasters, 30*, 364–376. Retrieved from fieldresearch.msf.org/msf/bitstream/10144/16895/1/grais.pdf

Grais, R. F., Rose, A. M. C., & Guthmann, J. P. (2007). Don't spin the pen: Two alternative methods for second-stage sampling in urban cluster surveys. *Emerging Themes in Epidemiology, 4.* Retrieved from ete-online.com/content/4/1/8 doi: 10.1186/1742-7622-4-8

Guha-Sapir, D., & Degomme, O. (2005a). *Darfur: Counting the deaths (2). What are the trends?* (Tech. Rep.). Brussels: CRED, University of Louvain.

Guha-Sapir, D., & Degomme, O. (2005b). *Darfur: Counting the deaths. Mortality estimates from multiple survey data* (Tech. Rep.). Brussels: CRED, University of Louvain. Retrieved from cred.be/sites/default/files/DarfurCountingtheDeaths.pdf

Guha-Sapir, D., & Degomme, O. (2007). *Estimating mortality in civil conflicts: Lessons from Iraq. Triangulating different types of mortality in Iraq.* (Tech. Rep.). CRED, University of Louvain. Retrieved from reliefweb.int/sites/reliefweb.int/files/resources/20A03C0F8F4BC3ABC125743500318AF6-cred_jun2007.pdf

Guha-Sapir, D., Schlter, B., Rodriguez-Llanes, J. M., Lillywhite, L., & Hsiao-Rei Hicks, M. (2017). Patterns of civilian and child deaths due to war-related violence in Syria: A comparative analysis from the Violation Documentation Center dataset, 2011-16. *The Lancet Global Health*, *6*, 103–110. Retrieved from thelancet.com/journals/langlo/article/PIIS2214-109X(17)30469-2/fulltext doi: doi.org/10.1016/S2214-109X(17)30469-2

Hagan, J., Rymond-Richmond, W., & Parker, P. (2005). The criminology of genocide: The death and rape of Darfur. *Criminology*, *43*, 525–561.

Hamby, S. L., & Finkelhor, D. (2000). The victimization of children: Recommendations for assessment and instrument development. *Journal of the American Academy of Child and Adolescent Psychiatry*, *39*, 829-840.

Hammersley, M., & Atkinson, P. (2007). *Ethnography: Principles in Practice*. Oxon: Routledge.

Harff, B. (1987). The etiology of genocides. In M. N. Dobkowski & I. Wallimann (Eds.), *The Age of Genocide* (pp. 41–59). Westport, CT: Greenwood Press.

Harff, B. (2003). No lessons learned from the Holocaust? Assessing risks of genocide and political mass murder since 1955. *American Political Science Review*, *97*, 57–73. Retrieved from http://migs.concordia.ca/documents/HarffAPSRarticle.pdf

Haslam, S. A., & Reicher, S. D. (2008). Questioning the banality of evil. *The Psychologist*, *21*, 16–19. Retrieved from thepsychologist.org.uk/archive/archive_home.cfm/volumeID_21-editionID_155-ArticleID_1291-getfile_getPDF/thepsychologist/0108hasl.pdf

Hatzfeld, J. (2005). *Machete Season: The Killers in Rwanda Speak*. New York: Farrar, Straus and Giroux.

He, N., & Haen-Marshall, I. (2010). *The International Self-Report Delinquency (ISRD) study* (Tech. Rep.). College of Criminal Justice, Northeastern University, Boston, USA.

Heckatorn, D. D. (1997). Respondent-driven sampling: A new approach to the study of hidden populations. *Social Problems*, *44*, 174–199.

Hensman Kettrey, H., Marx, R. A., & Tanner-Smith, E. E. (2019). *Effects of bystander programs on the prevention of sexual assault among adolescents and college students* (Tech. Rep.). Campbell Collaboration. Retrieved from campbellcollaboration.org/library/bystander-programs-sexual-assault-adolescents-college-students.html

Herzog, T. N., Scheuren, F. J., & Winkler, W. E. (2007). *Data quality and record linkage techniques*. New York: Spinger.

Heuveline, P. (2001). The demographic analysis of mortality crises: The case of Cambodia. In H. Reed & C. Kelley (Eds.), *Forced Migration and Mortality* (pp. 102–129). Washington: National Academy Press.

Hinkle, D. E., Wiersma, W., & Jurs, S. E. (2003). *Applied Statistics for the Behavioural Sciences* (5th ed.). Boston: Houghton Mifflin.

Hissel, S., Bijleveld, C. C. J. H., & Kruttschnitt, C. (2011). The well-being of children of incarcerated mothers. An exploratory study for the Netherlands. *European Journal of Criminology*, *8*, 346-360.

Hola, B. (2012). *International sentencing – A game of Russian roulette or consistent practice?* (Unpublished doctoral dissertation). VU University.

Hola, B. (2018). *International criminal justice at the crossroads: Aspirations, promises and realities.* (Keynote address European Society of Criminology)

Hola, B., Bijleveld, C. C. J. H., & Smeulers, A. L. (2009). Is ICTY sentencing predictable? An empirical analysis of ICTY sentencing practice. *Leiden Journal of International Law*, *22*, 79–97.

Hsieh, H. F., & Shannon, S. E. (2005). Three approaches to qualitative content analysis. *Qualitative Health Research*, *15*, 1277–1288.

Human Rights Watch (2004). *Darfur destroyed* (Tech. Rep.). Retrieved from hrw.org/sites/default/files/reports/sudan0504full.pdf

Human Rights Watch (2005). *Seeking justice. The prosecution of sexual violence in the Congo war* (Tech. Rep.). Human Rights Watch. Retrieved from hrw.org/reports/2005/drc0305

Humphreys, M., & Weinstein, J. M. (2008). Who fights? The determinants of participation in civil war. *American Journal of Political Science*, *52*, 436–455.

Jewkes, R., & Abrahams, N. (2002). The epidemiology of rape and sexual coercion in South Africa: An overview. *Social Science and Medicine*, *55*, 1231–1224.

Jewkes, R., Penn-Kekana, L., Levin, J., Ratsaka, M., & Schrieber, M. (1999). *"He must give me money, he mustn't beat me". Violence against women in three South African Provinces* (Tech. Rep.). Medical Research Council. Retrieved from 196.21.144.194/gender/violence.pdf

Johnson, K., Scott, J., Rughita, B., Kisielewski, M., Asher, J., Ong, R., & Lawry, L. (2010). Association of sexial violence and human rights violations with physical and mental health in territories of the Eastern Democratic Republic of the Congo. *Journal of the American Medical Association*, *304*, 553–562. Retrieved from ncbi.nlm.nih.gov/pubmed/20682935

Johnson, N. F., Spagat, M., Gourley, S., Onnela, J.-P., & Reinert, G. (2008). Bias in epidemiological studies of conflict mortality. *Journal of Peace Research*, *45*, 653–663.

Junger-Tas, J., Haen Marshall, I., & Ribeaud, D. (2003). *Delinquency in an international perspective. The international self-reported delinquency study (ISRD).* Den Haag: Kugler.

Kalayjian, A. S., Shahinian, S. P., Gergerian, E. L., & Saraydarian, L. (1996). Coping with Ottoman Turkish genocide: An exploration of the experience of Armenian survivors. *Journal of Trauma and Stress*, *9*, 87–97.

Khatir, M. S. (2009). *Personal communication* (Tech. Rep.).

Killias, M., Gilliéron, G., Villard, F., & Poglia, C. (2010). How damaging is imprisonment in the long-term? A controlled experiment comparing long-term effects of community service and short custodial sentences on re-offending and social integration. *Journal of Experimental Criminology*, *6*, 115–130.

Kirk, R. E. (1968). *Experimental design: Procedures for Behavioral Sciences*. Belmont, CA: Wadsworth.

LaFree, G. (2012). *Modeling situational dynamics of maritime piracy.* (Paper presented 14 September 2012 at the European Society of Criminology Annual Meeting in Bilbao)

Lemeshow, S., & Robinson, D. (1985). Surveys to measure programme coverage and impact: A review of the methodology used by the Expanded Programme on Immunization. *World Health Statistics Quarterly*, *38*, 65–75.

Lemeshow, S., Tserkovnyi, A. G., Tulloch, J. L., Dowd, J. E., Lwanga, S. K., & Keja, J. (1985). A computer simulation of the EPI survey strategy. *International Journal of Epidemiology*, *14*, 473–481.

LeMon, C. (2007). Rwanda's troubled Gacaca courts. *Human Rights Brief*, *14*, 16–20.

Lempert, R. (1989). Humility is a virtue: On the publicization of policy-relevant research. *Law and Society Review*, *23*, 146–161.

Lensvelt-Mulders, G. J. L. M., & Hox, J. J. (2004). *Meta-analysis of randomized response research: 35 years of validation studies* (Tech. Rep.). Universiteit Utrecht. Retrieved from `joophox.net/papers/p021502.pdf`

Lensvelt-Mulders, G. J. L. M., Hox, J. J., Van der Heijden, P. G. M., & Maas, C. J. M. (2005). Meta-analysis of randomized response research: 35 years of validation. *Sociological Methods and Research*, *33*, 319–348.

Li, Q., & Wen, M. (2005). The immediate and lingering effects of armed conflict on adult mortality: A time-series cross-national analysis. *Journal of Peace Research*, *42*, 471-492. doi: 10.1177/0022343305054092

Lindegaard, M., Bernasco, W., & De Vries, T. (2016). *Overvallen in beeld.* [Robbery images] (Tech. Rep.). Apeldoorn/Amsterdam: Politie & Wetenschap/NSCR.

Lindgren, G. (2006). *Studies in conflict economics and economic growth.* (Unpublished doctoral dissertation). Uppsala University.

Lisak, D., & Miller, P. M. (2002). Repeat rape and multiple offending among undetected rapists. *Violence and Victims*, *17*, 73–84.

Lorens Braga, L., Mello, F., & Paulo Fiks, J. (2012). Transgenerational transmission of trauma and resilience: A qualitative study with Brazilian offspring of Holocaust survivors. *BMC Psychiatry*, *12*, 134. Retrieved from `bmcpsychiatry.biomedcentral.com/articles/10.1186/1471-244X-12-134` doi: 10.1186/1471-244X-12-134

Lucia, S., Hermann, L., & Killias, M. (2007). How important are interview methods and questionnaire designs in research on self- reported juvenile delinquency? An experimental comparison of internet vs paper-and-pencil questionnaires and different definitions of the reference period. *Journal of Experimental Criminology*, *3*, 39–64.

Lum, K., Price, M., & Banks, D. (2013). Applications of multiple systems estimation in human rights research. *The American Statistician*, *67*. doi: 10.1080/00031305.2013.821093

Lum, K., Price, M., Guberek, T., & Ball, P. (2010). Measuring elusive populations with Bayesian model averaging for Multiple Systems Estimation: A case study on lethal violations in Casanare, 1998-2007. *Statistics, Politics, and Policy*, *1*. doi: doi.org/10.2202/2151-7509.1005

Mahoney, J., & Goertz, G. (2004). The possibility principle: Choosing negative cases in comparative research. *American Political Science Review*, *98*, 653–669. doi: doi.org/10.1017/S0003055404041401

Mahoney, J., & Goertz, G. (2006). A tale of two cultures: Contrasting quantitative and qualitative research. *Political Analysis*, *14*, 227–249. doi: doi:10.1093/pan/mpj017

Martindale, D. (1960). *The Nature and Types of Sociological Theory*. Boston: Houghton Mifflin Co.

Maxfield, M. G., & Babbie, E. (2005). *Research Methods for Criminal Justice and Criminology* (7th ed.). Stamford, CT: Cengage Learning.

McLoughlin, S., & Weerdesteijn, M. (2016). Eliminating rivals, managing rivalries: A comparison of Robert Mugabe and Kenneth Kaunda. *Genocide Studies and Prevention: An International Journal, 9*, 116–136. doi: dx.doi.org/10.5038/1911-9933.9.3.1318

Milgram, S. (1974). *Obedience to Authority.* New York: Harper & Row.

Miller, J. (2013). Epistemology and rigor in criminological research: An exploratory journey. In S. Ruiter, W. Bernasco, W. Huisman, & G. Bruinsma (Eds.), *Eenvoud en Verscheidenheid. Liber amicorum voor Henk Elffers [Frugality and Diversity. Liber amicorum for Henk Elffers* (pp. 491–502). Amsterdam: NSCR & Afdeling Strafrecht en Criminologie, Vrije Universiteit Amsterdam.

Mkandawire, T. (2002). The terrible toll of post-colonial 'rebel movements' in Africa: Towards an explanation of the violence against the peasantry. *Journal of Modern African Studies, 40*, 181–215.

Mullen, B. (1989). *Advanced BASIC meta-analysis.* Hillsdale, NJ: Erlbaum.

Nabarro, D. (2004). *Mortality projections for Darfur* (Tech. Rep.). World Health Organization. Retrieved from who.int/mediacentre/news/briefings/2004/mb5/en/index.html

Naing, L., Winn, T., & Rusli, B. N. (2006). Practical issues in calculating the sample size for prevalence studies. *Archives of Orofacial Sciences, 1*, 9–14.

National Service of Gacaca Courts (2012). *Summary of the report presented at the closing of* gacaca *courts activities.* (Tech. Rep.). Kigali: National Service of Gacaca Courts.

Naudé, C. M. B., Prinsloo, J. H., & Ladikos, A. (2006). *Experiences of crime in thirteen African countries: Results from the International Crime Victim Survey.* UNICRI-UNODC. Retrieved from wp.unil.ch/icvs/files/2012/11/ICVS-13-African-countries.pdf

Nicholson, V. (2007). *Singled Out: How Two Million Women Survived without Men after the First World War.* New York: Viking.

O'Donnell, T. (2011). The restitution of Holocaust looted art and transitional justice: The perfect storm or the raft of the Medusa? *European Journal of the International Law, 22*, 49–80. doi: 10.1093/ejil/chr004

Olsson, O., & Siba, E. (2012). *Ethnic cleansing or resource struggle in Darfur? An empirical analysis.* (Tech. Rep.). University of Gothenburg. Retrieved from economics.handels.gu.se/digitalAssets/1369/1369622_darfur6.pdf

O'Neill, B., Balk, D., Brickman, M., & Ezra, M. (2001). A guide to global population projections. *Demographic Research, 4*, 203–288. Retrieved from demographic-research.org/volumes/vol4/8/4-8.pdf doi: 10.4054/DemRes.2001.4.8

Oomen, B. (2009). Rwanda's gacaca: Objectives, merits and their relation to supranational criminal law. In R. Haveman & O. Olusanya (Eds.), *Sentencing in Supranational Criminal Law.* Antwerpen: Intersentia.

Pager, D. (2003). The mark of a criminal record. *American Journal of Sociology, 108*, 937-975. Retrieved from scholar.harvard.edu/files/pager/files/pager_ajs.pdf

Palermo, T., & Peterman, A. (2011). Undercounting, overcounting and the longevity of flawed estimates: Statistics on sexual violence in conflict. *Bulletin of the World Health Organization, 89*, 924–925. Retrieved from `who.int/bulletin/volumes/89/12/11-089888/en/index.html` doi: 10.2471/BLT.11.089888

Penal Reform International (2010). *Eight years on A record of* gacaca *monitoring in Rwanda.* (Tech. Rep.). Penal Reform International. Retrieved from `https://violenceagainstchildren.un.org/sites/violenceagainstchildren.un.org/files/expert_consultations/restorative_justice/nikhil_roy_gacaca.pdf`

Pennebaker, J. W., Francis, M. E., & Booth, R. J. (2001). *Linguistic Inquiry and Word Count: LIWC2001*. Mahwah, NJ: Lawrence Erlbaum.

Peters, K. (2008). *Methodological issues in the contextualisation of- and unravelling of motives for young and under-age people involved in armed combat* (Tech. Rep.).

Peters, K., & Richards, P. (1998). 'Why we fight': Voices of youth combatants in Sierra Leone. *Africa, 68*, 183–210.

Physicians for Human Rights (2002). *War-related sexual violence in Sierra Leone. A population-based assessment* (Tech. Rep.). PHR. Retrieved from `s3.amazonaws.com/PHR_Reports/sierra-leone-sexual-violence-2002.pdf`

Portelli, A. (2013). *A dialogical relationship. An approach to oral history* (Tech. Rep.). The People's Institute for Rethinking Development and Education. Retrieved from `swaraj.org/shikshantar/expressions_portelli.pdf`

Price, P., Klingner, J., & Ball, P. (2013). *Preliminary statistical analysis of documentation of killings in the Syrian Arab Republic* (Tech. Rep.). The Benetech Human Rights Program. Retrieved from `hrdag.org/wp-content/uploads/2015/07/Benetech-final-SY-report.pdf`

Prins, E. (2008). Use of low cost Landsat ETM+ to spot burnt villages in Darfur, Sudan. *International Journal of Remote Sensing, 29*, 1207–1214. doi: 10.1080/01431160701730110

Prunier, G. (1995). *The Rwanda Crisis, 1959-1994: History of a Genocide,*. London: C. Hurst & Co.

Quinn, N. (1996). Culture and contradiction: The case of Americans reasoning about marriage. *ETHOS, 24*, 391–425.

Ratnayake, R., Degomme, O., Altare, C., & Guha-Sapir, D. (2008). *Methods and tools to evaluate mortality in conflicts: Critical review, case studies and applications* (No. 237). Retrieved from `humansecuritygateway.com/documents/CRED_MethodsToolsToEvaluateMortalityInConflicts.pdf`

Reyntjes, F. (1997). Estimation du nombre de personnes tuées au Rwanda en 1994. In S. Marysse & F. Reyntjens (Eds.), *L'Afrique des grands lacs. Annuaire 1996–1997* (pp. 179–186). Paris: L'Harmattan.

Roberts, B., Morgan, O. W., & Sultani, M. G. e. a. (2010). A new method to estimate mortality in crisis affected and resource-poor settings: A validation study. *International Journal of Epidemiology, 39*, 1584–1596.

Roberts, J., & Horney, J. (2010). The Life Event Calendar method in criminological research. In A. Piquero & D. Weisburd (Eds.), *Handbook of Quantitative Criminology* (pp. 289–312). New York: Springer.

Roseboom, T., De Rooij, S., & Painter, R. (2006). The Dutch famine and its long-term consequences for adult health. *Early Human Development*, *82*, 485–491.

Rubin, H. J., & Rubin, I. S. (1995). *Qualitative Interviewing: The Art of Hearing Data*. Thousand Oaks, CA: Sage.

Rutstein, S. O., & Rojas, G. (2006). *Guide to DHS statistics* (Tech. Rep.). Calverton, MD: ORC Macro.

Ryan, G. W., & Bernard, H. R. (2003). Techniques to identify themes. *Field Methods*, *15*, 85–109. doi: 10.1177/1525822X02239569

Scagliola, S. (2011). The Dutch Veterans Interview Project: Recognition and attention in exchange for valuable information. In *Interuniversitary Seminar on Armed Forces and Society, Chicago, 21-23 October 2011*. Retrieved from `eur.nl/sites/corporate/files/IPNVen_pres_04b_Pdf.pdf`

Schmader, T., Whitehead, J., & Wysocki, V. H. (2007). A linguistic comparison of letters of recommendation for male and female chemistry and biochemistry job applicants. *Sex Roles*, *57*, 509–514.

Sellin, T. (1931). The basis of a crime index. *Journal of Criminal Law and Criminology*, *22*, 335–356.

Seybolt, T. B., Aronson, J. B., & Fischhoff, B. (2013). *Counting Civilian Casualties*. Oxford: Oxford University Press.

Shadish, W. R., Cook, T. D., & Campbell, D. (2002). *Experimental and Quasi-Experimental Designs for Generalized Causal Inference*. Boston: Houghton-Mifflin.

Shannon, H. S., Hutson, R., Kolbe, A., Stringer, B., & Haines, T. (2012). Surveys to measure programme coverage and impact: a review of the methodology used by the expanded programme on immunization. *Emerging Themes in Epidemiology*, *9*. Retrieved from `ete-online.com/content/pdf/1742-7622-9-5.pdf` doi: 10.1186/1742-7622-9-5

Sherman, L. W., & Berk, R. A. (1984). The specific deterrent effects of arrest for domestic assault. *American Sociological Review*, *49*, 261–272.

Sherman, L. W., Gottfredson, D. C., MacKenzie, D. L., Eck, J., Reuter, P., & Bushway, S. (1998). *Preventing crime: What works, what doesn't, what's promising.* (Tech. Rep.). National institute of Justice. Retrieved from `ncjrs.gov/pdffiles/171676.PDF`

Sikkel, D., Van der Heijden, P. G. M., & Van Gils, G. (2006). *Methoden voor omvangsschattingen van verborgen populaties, met name illegalen [Methods for estimating the size of hidden populations, particularly illegal residents]* (No. 243). Den Haag: WODC/BJU.

Silberzahn, R., & Uhlmann, E. L. (2015). Crowdsourced research: Many hands make tight work. *Nature*, *526*, 189–191. doi: 10.1038/526189a

Silva, R., & Marwaha, J. (2006). *Collecting sensitive human rights data in the field: A case study from Amritsar, India.* (Tech. Rep.). HRDAG. Retrieved from `hrdag.org/wp-content/uploads/2013/02/silva-marwaha-JSM-2011.pdf`

Silva, R., & Price, M. (2011). Trade-offs in using indirect sampling to measure conflict violence. *Journal of the American Medical Association*, *306*, 547–548.

Sloboda, J., Dardagan, H., Spagat, M., & Hsiao-Rei Hicks, M. (2013). A case-study in the uses of incident-based conflict casualty data. In T. B. Seybolt, J. B. Aronson, & B. Fischhoff (Eds.), *Counting Civilian Casualties* (pp. 53–75). Oxford: Oxford University Press.

Smeulers, A. L., Hola, B., & Van den Berg, T. (2013). 65 Years of international criminal justice. *International Criminal Law Review, 13*, 7–41. Retrieved from pure.uvt.nl/portal/files/1523643/Sixty_five_years.pdf

Snyder, J., & Vinjamuri, L. (2003). Trials and errors. Principle and pragmatism in strategies of international justice. *International Security, 28*, 5–44.

Spiegel, P. B., & Salama, P. (2004). War and mortality in Kosovo, 1998-99: an epidemiological testimony. *The Lancet, 355*, 2204–2209. Retrieved from conflict.lshtm.ac.uk/media/Kosovo_Mortality_in_Kosovo_Spiegel_Salama_Lancet_2001.pdf

Stark, L., Roberts, L., Wheaton, W., Acham, A., Boothby, N., & Ager, A. (2010). Measuring violence against women amongst war and displacement in northern Uganda using the 'neighbourhood method'. *Journal of Epidemiology and Community Health, 64*, 1056–1061.

State Department (2005). *Sudan: Death toll in Darfur* (Tech. Rep.). State Department. Retrieved from 2001-2009.state.gov/s/inr/rls/fs/2005/45105.htm

Stern, P. N. (1995). Grounded theory methodology: Its uses and processes. In B. G. Glaser (Ed.), *Grounded Theory 1984-1994, vol. 1* (pp. 29–39). Mill Valley, CA: Sociology Press.

Stouthamer-Loeber, M., Loeber, R., Wei, E., Farrington, D. P., & Wikstrom, P.-O. H. (2002). Risk and promotive effects in the explanation of persistent serious delinquency in boys. *Journal of Consulting and Clinical Psychology, 70*, 111–133.

Strauss, A., & Corbin, J. (1990). *Basics of Qualitative Research: Grounded Theory Procedures and Techniques*. Newbury Park, CA: Sage.

Strauss, A. L., & Corbin, J. (Eds.). (1998). *Basics of Qualitative Research: Techniques and Procedures for Developing Grounded Theory* (2nd ed.). London: Sage.

Swiss, S., Jennings, P. J., & Aryee, G. V. e. a. (1998). Violence against women during the Liberian civil conflict. *Journal of the American Medical Association, 279*, 625–629. doi: 10.1001/jama.279.8.625

Symons, L. et al. (2008). *Onderzoeksrapport tevredenheid en effectiviteit van technopreventief advies [Research report contentedness and technopreventive advice]* (Tech. Rep.). Katholieke Universiteit Leuven. Retrieved from http://besafe.jdbi.eu/sites/besafe.localhost/files/kcp/projecten/Janec/EindrapportTPAonderzoek\%20\%283\%29.pdf

Tabeau, E. (2009). *Conflict in Numbers. Casualties of the 1990s wars in the former Yugoslavia (1991–1999)* (No. 33). Helsinki Committee for Human Rights in Serbia. Retrieved from helsinki.org.rs/doc/testimonies33.pdf

Tabeau, E., & Bijak, J. (2005). War-related deaths in the 1992-1995 armed conflicts in Bosnia and Herzegovina: A critique of previous estimates and recent results. *European Journal of Population, 21*, 187–215. Retrieved from link.springer.com/article/10.1007\%2Fs10680-005-6852-5

Tabeau, E., & Kheam, T. (2009). *Khmer Rouge victims in Cambodia, April 1975-January 1979. A critical assessment of major estimates* (Tech. Rep.). Extraordinary Chambers in the Courts of Cambodia. Retrieved from eccc.gov.kh/sites/default/files/documents/courtdoc/D140_1_1_Public_Redacted_EN.PDF

Tabeau, E., & Zwierzchowski, J. (2013). A review of estimation methods for victims of the Bosnian war and the Khmer Rouge regime. In T. B. Seybolt, J. B. Aronson, & B. Fischhoff (Eds.), *Counting Civilian Casualties* (pp. 213–243). Oxford: Oxford University Press.

Tames, I. (2009). *Besmette Jeugd. Kinderen van NSBers na de Oorlog [Contaminated Youth. Children of Collaborators after the War].* Amsterdam: Balans.

Tames, I. (2015). Children of Dutch Nazi collaborators. *European Review of History, 22,* 221–241.

Ten Boom, A., Ferwerda, H., & Van Leiden, I. (2007). Een pioniersstudie in justitieland: De evaluatie van Halt in een experimentele setting [A pioneer study in justice country: The evaluation of Halt in an experimental setting. *Tijdschrift voor Criminologie, 49,* 33–44.

Thoms, O. N. T., Ron, J., & Paris, R. (2008). *The effects of transitional justice mechanisms. A summary of empirical research findings and implications for analysts and practitioners* (Tech. Rep. No. 46). University of Ottawa. Retrieved from aix1.uottawa.ca/~rparis/CIPS_Transitional_Justice_April2008.pdf

Thoms, O. N. T., Ron, J., & Paris, R. (2010). State-level effects of transitional justice: What do we know? *The International Journal of Transitional Justice,* 1–26. Retrieved from gsdrc.org/wp-content/uploads/2015/11/Thoms-Ron-Paris-effects-of-TJ.pdf doi: 10.1093/ijtj/ijq012

Thornberry, T. P., & Krohn, M. D. (2000). The self-report method for measuring delinquency and crime. In D. Duffee (Ed.), *Measurement and Analysis of Crime and Justice. Criminal Justice 2000* (Vol. 4, pp. 33–84). Washington: National Institute of Justice.

Tjaden, P., & Thoennes, N. (1998). *Prevalence, incidence, and consequences of violence against women: Findings from the national violence against women survey* (Tech. Rep.). National Institute of Justice, Centers for Disease Control and Prevention. Retrieved from ncjrs.gov/pdffiles/172837.pdf

Tracy, S. (2013). *Qualitative Research Methods.* Chichester: Wiley.

UNESCO Institute for Statistics (2010). *Think piece commissioned for the EFA Global Monitoring Report 2011, The hidden crisis: Armed conflict and education* (Tech. Rep. No. 2011/ED/EFA/MRT/PI/50). UNESCO. Retrieved from www.protectingeducation.org/sites/default/files/documents/unesco_-_the_quantitative_impact_of_conflict_on_education.pdf

UNICEF (2006). *Multiple Indicator Cluster Survey manual 2005: Monitoring the situation of women and children* (Tech. Rep.). UNICEF. Retrieved from unesdoc.unesco.org/images/0019/001913/191304e.pdf

Van den Berg, C., Blommaert, L., Bijleveld, C., & Ruiter, S. (2017). Veroordeeld tot (g)een baan: hoe delict- en persoonskenmerken arbeidsmarktkansen beïnvloeden [Condemned to (un)employment: how crime and personal characteristics impact labour market chances]. *Tijdschrift voor Criminologie, 59,* 113–135.

Van der Geest, V. R., Bijleveld, C. C. J. H., & Verbruggen, J. (2013). *Vallen en opstaan. Mannen en vrouwen 17 jaar na vertrek uit een justitiële jeugdinrichting [Stumble and rise. Men and women 17 years after leaving judicial youth care]* (Tech. Rep.). Amsterdam: NSCR/VU.

Van der Geest, V. R., Bijleveld, C. C. J. H., & Wijkman, M. (2005). *Recidive na behandeling [Recidivism after treatment]* (Tech. Rep. No. NSCR-2005-4). Leiden: NSCR.

Van der Geest, V. R., Langendoen, M., & Bijleveld, C. C. J. H. (2006). Brave burgers? IJkingsonderzoek naar justitiecontacten van Nederlandse mannen [Good citizens? Gauging criminal justice system contacts of Dutch men]. *Secondant, 20*, 31–35.

Van der Heijden, P. G. M., Cruyff, M., & Van Houwelingen, H. C. (2003). Estimating the size of a criminal population from police records using the truncated Poisson regression model. *Statistica Neerlandica, 57*, 289–304.

Van der Heijden, P. G. M., Van Gils, G., Bouts, J., & Hox, J. J. (2000). A comparison of randomized reponse, CASAQ, and direct questioning; Eliciting sensitive information in the context of social security fraud. *Sociological Methods and Research, 28*, 505–537.

Van de Weijer, S. G. A., & Bijleveld, C. C. J. H. (2016). *Military service as a turning point in the intergenerational transmission of criminal behaviour.* (Paper presented 2 April 2016 at the ESSHC conference, Valencia)

Van Kesteren, J., Van Dijk, J., & Mayhew, P. (2014). The International Crime Victims Surveys. A retrospective. *International Review of Victimology, 20*, 49–69.

Van Wijk, J., & Smeulers, A. (2017). Criminologie van internationale misdrijven: Kroniek [Criminology of international crimes: Chronicle]. *Tijdschrift voor Criminologie, 59*, 194–205.

Venkatesh, S. (2008). *Gang Leader for a Day: A Rogue Sociologist Takes to the Streets.* Londen: Penguin.

Verwimp, P. (2003). *An economic profile of peasant perpetrators of genocide. Micro-level evidence from Rwanda* (Tech. Rep.). Catholic University of Leuven. Retrieved from `econpapers.repec.org/article/eeedeveco/v_3a77_3ay_3a2005_3ai_3a2_3ap_3a297-323.htm`

Verwimp, P., & Van Bavel, J. (2005). Child survival and fertility of refugees in Rwanda. *European Journal of Population, 21*, 271–290. doi: 10.1007/s10680-005-6856-1

Vogt, F., Heudtlass, P., & Guha-Sapir, D. (2011). *Health data in civil conflicts: South Sudan under scrutiny* (Tech. Rep. No. 282). Center for Research on the Epidemiology of Disasters. Retrieved from `cred.be/sites/default/files/WP_282.pdf@article`

Vollhardt, J. R., & Bilewicz, M. (2013). After the genocide: Psychological perspectives on victim, bystander and perpetrator groups. *Journal of Social Issues, 69*, 1–15.

Wagner, Z., Heft-Neal, S., Bhutta, A. A., Black, R., Burke, M., & Bendavid, E. (2018). Armed conflict and child mortality in Africa: a geospatial analysis. *The Lancet, 392*. Retrieved from `thelancet.com/journals/lancet/article/PIIS0140-6736(18)31437-5/fulltext` doi: doi.org/10.1016/S0140-6736(18)31437-5

Wald, P. (2001). To 'establish incredible events by credible evidence': The use of affidavit testimony in Yugoslavia war crimes tribunal proceedings. *Harvard International Journal, 42*, 535–553.

Webley, L. (2010). Qualitative approaches to empirical legal research. In P. Cane & H. M. Kritzer (Eds.), *The Oxford Handbook of Empirical Legal Research* (pp. 927–950). Oxford: Oxford University Press.

Weissman, F. (2018). *Mortality emergency threshold: A case for revision* (Tech. Rep.). ReliefWeb. Retrieved from reliefweb.int/report/world/mortality-emergency-threshold-case-revision

Weitz, E. (2003). *A Century of Genocide: Utopias of Race and Nation*. Princeton, NJ: Princeton University Press.

Wellford, C., & Cronin, J. (1999). *An analysis of variables affecting the clearance of homicides: A multistate study* (Tech. Rep.). Justice Research and Statistics Association. Retrieved from jrsa.org/pubs/reports/Clearance_of_Homicide.html

Wijkman, M. D. S., Bijleveld, C. C. J. H., & Hendriks, J. (2012). 'Women don't do such things!' Characteristics of female sex offenders and offender types. *Sexual Abuse, a Journal of Research and Treatment*, *22*, 135–156.

Wijkman, M. D. S., Bijleveld, C. C. J. H., & Hendriks, J. (2014). Juvenile female sex offenders: Offender and offense characteristics. *European Journal of Criminology*, *11*, 23–38. doi: 10.1177/1477370813479077

Wincup, E. (2017). *Criminological Research: Understanding Qualitative Methods*. London: Sage.

Wood, E. (2006). Variation in sexual violence during war. *Politics & Society*, *34*, 307–342.

World Food Programme (2005). *A manual: Measuring and interpreting manutrition and mortality* (Tech. Rep.). World Food Programme, Center for Disease Control. Retrieved from unhcr.org/45f6abc92.html

World Health Organization (2012). *Verbal autopsy standards: The 2012 WHO verbal autopsy instrument. Release Candidate 1.* (Tech. Rep.). World Health Organization. Retrieved from who.int/healthinfo/statistics/WHO_VA_2012_RC1_Instrument.pdf

Wright, R., Decker, S. H., Redfern, A. K., & Smith, D. L. (2001). A snowball's chance in hell: Doing fieldwork with active residential burglars. In J. M. Miller & R. Tewksbury (Eds.), *Extreme Methods. Innovative Approaches to Social Science Research* (pp. 94–102). Boston: Allyn and Bacon.

Yansaneh, I. (2005). Overview of sample design issues for household surveys in developing and transition countries. In United Nations (Ed.), *Household Sample Surveys in Developing and Transition Countries* (pp. 11–34). UN Department of Economic and Social Affairs Statistics Division. Retrieved from unstats.un.org/unsd/hhsurveys/pdf/Household_surveys.pdf

Zaitch, D. (2003). Colombianen betrokken in de cocainehandel in Nederland [Colombians involved in the cocaine trade in the Netherlands]. In F. Ester et al. (Eds.), *Jaarboek Kwalon. Tijdschrift voor Kwalitatief Onderzoek in Nederland* (Vol. 8, pp. 25–44).

Zaslavsky, A. M., & Wolfgang, G. S. (1993). Triple system modeling of census, post-enumeration survey, and administrative list data. *Journal of Business and Economic Statistics*, *11*, 279–288. Retrieved from jstor.org/stable/1391952 doi: 10.2307/1391952

Zebel, S., Doosje, B., & Spears, R. (2009). How perspective-taking helps and hinders group-based guilt as a function of group identification. *Group Processes & Intergroup Relations*, *12*, 61–78. doi: journals.sagepub.com/doi/pdf/10.1177/1368430208098777

Zimbardo, P. (2007). *The Lucifer effect*. New York: Random House.

Zraly, M., & Nyirazinyoye, L. (2010). Don't let the suffering make you fade away: An ethnographic study of resilience among survivors of genocide-rape in southern Rwanda. *Social Science & Medicine*, *70*, 1656–1664. doi: 10.1016/j.socscimed.2010.01.017

Subject index

Author index